WITHDRAWN

PHILO

III

247

PHILO

IN TEN VOLUMES
(AND TWO SUPPLEMENTARY VOLUMES)

III

WITH AN ENGLISH TRANSLATION BY

F. H. COLSON, M.A.

LATE FELLOW OF ST. JOHN'S COLLEGE, CAMBRIDGE

AND

THE REV. G. H. WHITAKER, M.A.

LATE FELLOW OF ST. JOHN'S COLLEGE, CAMBRIDGE

CAMBRIDGE, MASSACHUSETTS
HARVARD UNIVERSITY PRESS
LONDON
WILLIAM HEINEMANN LTD
MCMLXXXVIII

American
ISBN 0-674-99272-5

British
ISBN 0 434 99247 X

First printed 1930
Reprinted 1954, 1960, 1968, 1988

Printed in Great Britain by
Thomson Litho Ltd, East Kilbride, Scotland

CONTENTS OF VOLUME III

CONTENTS

PREFACE TO VOLUME III

THE death of Mr. Whitaker in May does not prevent his name from appearing as joint translator in this volume. Both the treatises for which he was primarily responsible, viz. *De Agricultura* and *De Plantatione,* were in print at the time, and had been examined and criticized by myself, as the other three, which fell to my share, had been by him. It has remained for me to carry out the final revision, and to draw up the Appendix and most of the footnotes.[a] It should be added that his name will not disappear from Vols. IV. and V. The whole of Vol. IV., both his share and mine, was in typescript at the date of his death, and had been the subject of a certain amount of correspondence between us. His share of Vol. V. is in MS., though it has not been in any way revised.

The translators have to acknowledge, as in Vols. I. and II., the assistance they have received from the German translation still in progress. But Mr. Whitaker, like myself, felt that a special tribute was due to the admirable work of Dr. M. Adler on the treatises *De Ebrietate* and *De Sobrietate*, and his corrections of Wendland's text. If our text of these treatises is, as we both have hoped, superior in places to that of Wendland, it is mainly due to him.

[a] In a few cases, where I felt doubtful whether Mr. Whitaker would have accepted them, I have appended my initials.

PREFACE

The second and larger volume of Leisegang's index to Philo, which had previously only reached to Zeta, appeared almost simultaneously with Mr. Whitaker's death. Though neither volume deals with more than a selection of Philo's words, the first volume was much valued by both translators, and the complete work, which has already been of considerable use to the survivor in his final revision, should greatly promote the accuracy of the translation.

F. H. C.

Oct. 1930.

LIST OF PHILO'S WORKS

SHOWING THEIR DIVISION INTO VOLUMES
IN THIS EDITION

LIST OF PHILO'S WORKS

[1] Only two fragments extant.
[2] Extant only in an Armenian version.

x

ON THE UNCHANGEABLENESS
OF GOD
(QUOD DEUS IMMUTABILIS SIT)

ANALYTICAL INTRODUCTION

THIS treatise,[a] which is really a continuation of the *De Gigantibus*, discusses the following verses, Gen. vi. 4-12.

I. (1-19) And after this when the angels of God went in unto the daughters of men, and begat for themselves . . . (v. 4).

II. (20-73) But the Lord God seeing that the wickednesses of men were multiplied upon the earth and that every man is purposing in his heart carefully evil things every day, God had it in His mind that He had made man upon the earth and He bethought Him. And God said, I will blot out man whom I have made from the face of the earth . . . because I was wroth that [b] I had made him (vv. 5-7).

III. (74-121) But Noah found grace before God. Now these are the generations of Noah. Noah was a just man, being perfect in his generation, and Noah was well pleasing to God (vv. 8-9).

IV. (122-139) And the earth was " corrupted " (or destroyed) before God, and the earth was filled with iniquity (v. 11).

V. (140-end) And the Lord God saw the earth, and it was corrupted, because all flesh destroyed His way upon the earth (v. 12).

---

[a] The title is not very appropriate and applies only to §§ 20-32.   [b] Or " in that.

3

PHILO

I. Having suggested (1-3) that " after this " means " after the Spirit of God had departed," Philo goes on to discuss what is meant by saying that these " angels," which in the previous treatise he had taken to mean " evil angels " or " evil souls," beget " for themselves." This is shewn, first by contrast with Abraham (4) and (5-6) with Hannah, who gave her child as a thank-offering to God. This leads to a short meditation on the purifying power of thankfulness, and our need of such purification (7-9), and this is followed by a digression on the words of Hannah's psalm : " The barren hath borne seven, but she that had many children has languished," which are treated as contrasting the sacred number " seven " with selfish plurality (10-15). This brings back the thought of " begetting for themselves," as mere selfishness which, as in the case of Onan, brings destruction (16-19).

II. The idea that the words " God had it in His mind," etc. suggest that God had repented of making man is rejected as impious (20-22). God is unchangeable. Even among men the sage may live a life of constancy and harmony (23-25), and while most of us are the victims of fickleness and inconstancy, partly because we are unable to gauge the future, it is not so with God, for time is His creation and His life is eternity (27-32).

What then is the meaning of " God had in His mind that He had made man " ? To explain this, Philo reproduces the Stoic theory of the four classes of things which we find in nature. First there is ἕξις (coherence), *i.e.* inorganic objects such as stones and dead wood. This ἕξις is conceived of as a " breath " (πνεῦμα) continually passing up and down,

4

and thus binding them together (33-36). Secondly there is φύσις (growth), as seen in plants, and here Philo takes the opportunity to dilate on the wonders of the annual resurrection (37-40). Third comes animal life (ψυχή) with its threefold phenomena (again Stoic) of " sense," " presentation " and " impulse " (41-44). All these have been mentioned to lead up to the fourth stage, that of the rational mind of man, which alone has free-will and is therefore alone liable to praise or blame, and it was this misused freedom of man which God " had in mind " (45-50).

We have still to do with the concluding words, " I was wroth that I made man." Here Philo, who evidently had the variant ἐθυμώθην for ἐνεθυμήθην, is in great difficulty. He cannot allow anger to God and he repeats the explanation of such anthropomorphic phrases (which he gave in De Sac. 94 f.), namely that they are accommodated to our weaker natures, which require the discipline of fear (51-69). But this alone does not satisfy him. His further explanation is hardly intelligible, but seems to mean that as it is anger and similar passions which produce human wickedness, God's judgement on the wicked may be spoken of as caused by God's anger (70-73).

III. But we must observe that this phrase, " I was wroth," etc., is followed at once by the words, " Noah found grace," and this contrast brings us to the thought that God in His dealings mingles mercy with judgement, as our weak nature requires (74-76). This " mingling " in fact is a necessary condition before we can understand the divine at all (77-81), and the contrast of the mixed and the unmixed, which is the same as that of the One and the Many, is illustrated

5

by the words " God spake once and these two things have I heard " (for God's speech is single, while our hearing is produced by different factors) (82-84), and also by the way in which Moses shews us the one just man side by side with the many unjust (85).

We can now consider more fully the phrase " Noah found grace with the Lord God." The word " found " leads to reflections first on the differences between finding (εὕρεσις) and " refinding " or " recovering " (ἀνεύρεσις) (86), and this difference is illustrated by an allegorical interpretation of the rules laid down for the " Great Vow " in Num. vi. (86-90), and then by the way in which the gifted by nature absorb knowledge without difficulty, while the efforts of the inapt come to disaster (91-93). This distinction extends to questions of conduct also, for those who with no good motive force themselves to right actions, against which their nature rebels, merely cause misery to themselves (94-103). Again the phrase " found *grace* " (χάρις) may be best interpreted as meaning that the just man " finds " that what we have is God's free *gift* (also χάρις) (104-108). Yet Philo seems at once to ignore this forced interpretation and to identify the meaning of the words " found grace " with the subsequent " was well pleasing " (εὐαρεστῆσαι) and after pointing out, as usual, that the double phrase " Lord God " represents God's two aspects of " sovereignty " and " goodness " (109-110), proceeds to contrast Noah with Joseph, " who found grace with the ruler of the prison " into which he was thrown. This story of Joseph teaches us the lesson that if we are the prisoners of passion, we should at least avoid the friendship of our gaoler and not become his satellites (111-116). This contrast between Noah and Joseph brings us to the consideration of the words " these are the generations (γενέσεις) of Noah." Philo takes γένεσις to mean " becoming " or " development," and explains it in this case by the words that follow, " just," " perfect " " well pleasing to God " (117-118), and illustrates it from the text, " Joseph was keeping sheep with his brothers, being young, with the sons of Bilhah and Zilpah," where the γένεσις is from the higher nature of Jacob to that of the " young " Joseph and the bastard sons (119-121).

IV. Philo now turns to the words " the whole earth was corrupted or destroyed [a] " (122). The first view put forward is that Goodness (*i.e.* Noah) necessarily works the destruction of the Bad (123). But this passes at once into a really different thought [a] that Goodness shews up the Bad in its true light. This is illustrated from three points or rules in the law of leprosy ; first, that the appearance of " healthy colour " makes the leper unclean (123-126) ; secondly, that complete leprosy is clean, while the partial is unclean, shewing that the completely and therefore involuntarily immoral condition is innocence compared with the partial enlightenment, by which the soul knows that it is sinful but does not amend (127-130) ; thirdly, that the infected house is pronounced unclean by the priest who visits it, shewing again that the entrance of divine reason will reveal the impurity of the soul (131-135). The same moral is found in the words of the widow of Zarephath to

---

[a] On the first interpretation ἐφθάρη means " was destroyed "; on the second " was corrupted," *i.e.* made to appear in its real badness.

7

Elijah, " O man of God, thou hast entered to remind me of my sin " (136-139).

V. The important point here is that " destroyed his way " means " destroyed God's way " (140-143), and this reminds us of the passage in which Israel asked for leave to pass through Edom's territory, and said " we will go by the king's way " (144) But Philo cannot endure to be confined to these two words, but deals with the whole content of Num. xx. 17-20 in a way which, perverse as it is, shews much richness of thought as well as ingenuity. (α) When Israel says " I will pass through thy land " we have the resolve of the Wise both to test the life of the pleasure-lover, so as to reject it through experience and not mere ignorance, and also not to stay in it (145-153). (β) On the other hand, " we will not go through the fields and vineyards " means " we will abide in the fields of heavenly fruits and the vineyards of virtue and true joy " (154). (γ) " We will not drink of thy well " means that " we on whom God rains his mercies have no need of the scanty water of the wells of earthly pleasures " (155-158). (δ) " We will go by the king's way " is " we will tread the road of wisdom " (159-161). (ε) " We will turn neither to the right nor to the left " shews that this way of wisdom is in the mean, as e.g. courage is the mean between rashness on the right and cowardice on the left (162-165). (ζ) When in reply to Edom's refusal and threat of war Israel replies, " we will pass along the mountain," Philo by a strange play on ὄρος (the mountain) and ὅρος (definition) extracts the idea that the wise man's course is on lofty thoughts based on scientific analysis (166-167). (η) " If I drink of thy water, I will give thee its value "

($\tau\iota\mu\dot{\eta}$) is turned into " If I truckle to you, I shall be giving to the worthless an honour which will lead the weak to honour it also " (167-171). (θ) The words " the matter is nothing " (see note on 145) are taken to mean the vanity of earthly things. And this leads to a meditation on the witness of history to the instability of national prosperity and indeed of all human aims (172-180). Thus we arrive at the conclusion that while Edom would bar the king's way, the divine reason will bar that of Edom and its associates (180).

This last word leads to some concluding thoughts about Balaam as one of these " associates." The sections (181-end), which otherwise have little connexion with the preceding matter, go back to the thought of 122-139, and describe Balaam as the type of those who reject the warning of divine reason as the inward judge and thus are past all cure.

ΟΤΙ ΑΤΡΕΠΤΟΝ ΤΟ ΘΕΙΟΝ

1 I. " Καὶ μετ᾿ ἐκεῖνο " φησίν " ὡς ἂν εἰσ-
επορεύοντο οἱ ἄγγελοι τοῦ θεοῦ πρὸς τὰς θυγατέρας
τῶν ἀνθρώπων, καὶ ἐγέννων αὐτοῖς.[1] " οὐκοῦν ἄξιον
σκέψασθαι, τίνα ἔχει λόγον τὸ " μετ᾿ ἐκεῖνο."
ἔστι τοίνυν ἀναφορὰ δεικνύουσά τι τῶν προ-
2 ειρημένων ἐναργέστερον. προείρηται δὲ περὶ θείου
πνεύματος, ὃ καταμεῖναι μέχρι τοῦ παντὸς αἰῶνος
ἐν πολυσχιδεῖ καὶ πολυμόρφῳ ψυχῇ σαρκῶν ὄχλον
βαρύτατον ἄχθος ἀνημμένη δυσεργότατον εἶπεν
[273] εἶναι. μετ᾿ ἐκεῖνο δὴ | τὸ πνεῦμα οἱ ἄγγελοι πρὸς
3 τὰς θυγατέρας τῶν ἀνθρώπων εἰσίασιν. ἕως μὲν
γὰρ ἐλλάμπουσι τῇ ψυχῇ καθαραὶ φρονήσεως αὐγαί,
δι᾿ ὧν τὸν θεὸν καὶ τὰς αὐτοῦ δυνάμεις ὁρᾷ
ὁ σοφός, οὐδεὶς τῶν ψευδαγγελούντων ἐπεισ-
έρχεται τῷ λογισμῷ, ἀλλ᾿ ἔξω περιρραντηρίων
ἅπαντες εἴργονται· ὅταν δὲ ἀμυδρωθὲν ἐπισκιασθῇ
τὸ διανοίας φῶς, οἱ τοῦ σκότους ἑταῖροι παρ-
ευημερήσαντες πάθεσι τοῖς κατεαγόσι καὶ τεθη-
λυμμένοις, ἃς θυγατέρας εἴρηκεν ἀνθρώπων, συν-

---

[1] Most MSS. αὐτοῖς, but Philo's argument shows that in
accordance with the generally received text of the LXX he
wrote ἑαυτοῖς or αὑτοῖς.

---

[a] E.V. " and they bare children to them."
[b] or " horde." ὄχλος carries with it the idea both of a

10

ON THE UNCHANGEABLENESS
OF GOD

I. " And after that," says Moses, " when the angels 1
of God went in unto the daughters of men and begat
for themselves " [a] (Gen. vi. 4). It is worth our while
to consider what is meant by the word " after that."
The answer is that it is a reference back, bringing
out more clearly something of what has been already
stated. That something is his words about the divine 2
spirit, that nothing is harder than that it should abide
for ever in the soul with its manifold forms and
divisions—the soul which has fastened on it the
grievous burden of this fleshly coil.[b] It is after that
spirit [c] that the angels or messengers go in to the
daughters of men. For while the soul is illumined 3
by the bright and pure rays of wisdom, through which
the sage sees God and His potencies, none of the
messengers of falsehood has access to the reason, but
all are barred from passing the bounds which the
lustral water has consecrated.[d] But when the light
of the understanding is dimmed and clouded, they
who are of the fellowship of darkness win the day,
and mating with the nerveless and emasculated
passions, which he has called the daughters of men,

mob and the trouble and confusion caused by it. The flesh
(plural) is here and elsewhere conceived of as manifold.

   [c] *i.e.* after the spirit has gone.
   [d] See App. p. 483.

4 ἔρχονται καὶ γεννῶσιν ἑαυτοῖς, οὐ τῷ θεῷ. τὰ
μὲν γὰρ οἰκεῖα τοῦ θεοῦ γεννήματα αἱ ὁλόκληροι
ἀρεταί, τὰ δὲ συγγενῆ φαύλων αἱ ἀνάρμοστοι
κακίαι.   μάθε δ', εἰ θέλεις, ὦ διάνοια,
τὸ μὴ ἑαυτῇ γεννᾶν οἷόν ἐστι παρὰ 'Αβραὰμ τοῦ
τελείου, ὃς τὸ ἀγαπητὸν καὶ μόνον τῆς ψυχῆς
ἔγγονον γνήσιον, τῆς αὐτομαθοῦς σοφίας εἰκόνα
ἐναργεστάτην, ἐπίκλησιν 'Ισαάκ, ἀνάγει θεῷ καὶ
ἀποδίδωσι μετὰ πάσης εὐθυμίας ἀναγκαῖον καὶ
ἁρμόττον χαριστήριον συμποδίσας, ὥς φησιν ὁ
νόμος, τὸ καινουργηθὲν ἱερεῖον, ἤτοι παρόσον ἐπ'
οὐδενὸς θνητοῦ βαίνειν ἅπαξ ἐπιθειάσας ἠξίου,
ἢ παρόσον ἀνίδρυτον καὶ ἄστατον κατεῖδε τὴν
γένεσιν, ὅτε τὴν περὶ τὸ ὂν ἀνενδοίαστον ἔγνω
βεβαιότητα, ᾗ λέγεται πεπιστευκέναι.

5 ΙΙ. τούτου γίνεται μαθητρὶς καὶ διάδοχος 'Άννα,
τῆς τοῦ θεοῦ δώρημα σοφίας· ἑρμηνεύεται γὰρ
χάρις αὐτῆς. ἐπειδὴ γὰρ ἐγκύμων ἐγένετο παρα-
δεξαμένη θείας γονὰς καὶ τελεσφόροις ἐχρήσατο
ὠδῖσι, τὸν τεταγμένον ἐν τῇ τοῦ θεοῦ τάξει τρόπον
ἀποκυήσασα, ὃν ‹ἐπ›εφήμισε Σαμουήλ—καλεῖται
δ' ἑρμηνευθεὶς τεταγμένος θεῷ—, λαβοῦσα ἀνταπο-
δίδωσι τῷ δόντι μηδὲν ἴδιον ἑαυτῆς κρίνουσα ἀγαθόν,

6 ὃ μὴ χάρις ἐστὶ θεία. λέγει γὰρ ἐν τῇ πρώτῃ
τῶν βασιλειῶν αὕτη τὸν τρόπον τοῦτον· "δίδωμί σοι
αὐτὸν δοτόν," ἐν ἴσῳ τῷ δοτὸν ὄντα, ὥστ' εἶναι
"τὸν δεδομένον δίδωμι."   κατὰ τὸ ἱερώτα-

_____
ᵃ See App. p. 483.

beget offspring for themselves and not for God.
For the offspring of God's parentage are the perfect 4
virtues, but the family of evil are the vices, whose
note is discord.   If thou wilt know, my
mind, what it is to beget not for thyself, learn the
lesson from the perfect Abraham. He brings to God
the dearly loved, the only trueborn offspring of the
soul, that clearest image of self-learned wisdom,
named Isaac, and without a murmur renders, as in
duty bound, this fitting thank-offering. But first he
bound, as the law tells us, the feet of the new strange
victim (Gen. xxii. 9), either because having once received God's inspiration he judged it right to tread
no more on aught that was mortal, or it may be
that he was taught to see how changeable and in-
constant was creation, through his knowledge of the
unwavering stedfastness that belongs to the Existent ; for in this we are told he had put his trust
(Gen. xv. 6).   II. He finds a disciple and 5
successor in Hannah, the gift of the wisdom of God,
for the name Hannah interpreted is " her grace." She
received the divine seed and became pregnant. And
when she had reached the consummation of her
travail, and had brought forth the type of character
which has its appointed place in God's order, which
she named Samuel, a name which being interpreted
means " appointed to God," she took him and rendered him in due payment to the Giver, judging
that no good thing was her own peculiar property,
nothing, which was not a grace and bounty from God.
For she speaks in the first book of Kings in this wise, 6
" I give to Thee him, a gift ^{a} " (1 Sam. i. 28), that is
" who is a gift," and so " I give him who has been
given."   This agrees with the most sacred

τον Μωυσέως γράμμα τοῦτο· "τὰ δῶρά μου,
δόματά μου, καρπώματά μου διατηρήσετε προσ-
7 φέρειν ἐμοί." τίνι γὰρ εὐχαριστητέον ἄλλῳ
πλὴν θεῷ; διὰ τίνων δὲ ὅτι μὴ διὰ τῶν
ὑπ᾽ αὐτοῦ δοθέντων; οὐδὲ γὰρ ἄλλων εὐπορῆσαι
δυνατόν. χρεῖος δ᾽ οὐδενὸς ὢν κελεύει προσφέρειν
αὐτῷ τὰ ἑαυτοῦ δι᾽ ὑπερβολὴν τῆς πρὸς τὸ
γένος ἡμῶν εὐεργεσίας· μελετήσαντες γὰρ εὐ-
χαριστητικῶς ἔχειν καὶ τιμητικῶς αὐτοῦ καθ-
αρεύσομεν ἀδικημάτων ἐκνιψάμενοι τὰ καταρρυ-
παίνοντα τὸν βίον ἔν τε λόγοις καὶ νοήσεσι[1] καὶ
[274] 8 ἔργοις. καὶ γὰρ εὔηθες εἰς μὲν τὰ ἱερὰ | μὴ
ἐξεῖναι βαδίζειν, ὃς ἂν μὴ πρότερον λουσάμενος
φαιδρύνηται τὸ σῶμα, εὔχεσθαι δὲ καὶ θύειν
ἐπιχειρεῖν ἔτι κεκηλιδωμένῃ καὶ πεφυρμένῃ διανοίᾳ.
καίτοι τὰ μὲν ἱερὰ λίθων καὶ ξύλων ἀψύχου τῆς
ὕλης πεποίηται, καθ᾽ αὑτὸ δὲ καὶ τὸ σῶμα ἄψυχον·
ἀλλ᾽ ὅμως ὂν ἄψυχον ἀψύχων οὐ προσάψεται μὴ
περιρραντηρίοις καὶ καθαρσίοις ἁγνευτικοῖς χρησάμενον, ὑπομενεῖ δέ τις τῷ θεῷ προσελθεῖν ἀκάθαρτος ὢν ψυχὴν τὴν ἑαυτοῦ τῷ καθαρωτάτῳ, καὶ
9 ταῦτα μὴ μέλλων μετανοήσειν; ὁ μὲν γὰρ πρὸς
τῷ μηδὲν ἐπεξεργάσασθαι κακὸν καὶ τὰ παλαιὰ
ἐκνίψασθαι δικαιώσας γεγηθὼς προσίτω, ὁ δ᾽ ἄνευ
τούτων δυσκάθαρτος ὢν ἀφιστάσθω· λήσεται γὰρ
οὐδέποτε τὸν τὰ ἐν μυχοῖς τῆς διανοίας ὁρῶντα
καὶ τοῖς ἀδύτοις αὐτῆς ἐμπεριπατοῦντα.
10 III. τῆς μέντοι θεοφιλοῦς ψυχῆς δεῖγμα ἐν-
αργέστατόν ἐστι καὶ τὸ ᾆσμα, ἐν ᾧ περιέχεται τὸ
" στεῖρα ἔτεκεν ἑπτά, ἡ δὲ πολλὴ ἐν τέκνοις
11 ἠσθένησε." καίτοι γε ἑνός ἐστι μήτηρ τοῦ

---

[1] Conj. Cohn for ms. ὀνείδεσι or εἴδεσι: Wend. ἐννοίαις.

ordinance of Moses, " My gifts, My offerings, My fruits
ye shall observe to bring to Me " (Num. xxviii. 2).
For to whom should we make thank-offering save to 7
God ? and wherewithal save by what He has given
us ? for there is nothing else whereof we can have
sufficiency. God needs nothing, yet in the exceeding
greatness of His beneficence to our race He bids us
bring what is His own. For if we cultivate the spirit
of rendering thanks and honour to Him, we shall be
pure from wrongdoing and wash away the filthiness
which defiles our lives in thought and word and deed.
For it is absurd that a man should be forbidden to 8
enter the temples save after bathing and cleansing
his body, and yet should attempt to pray and sacrifice
with a heart still soiled and spotted. The temples
are made of stones and timber, that is of soulless
matter, and soulless too is the body in itself. And
can it be that while it is forbidden to this soulless
body to touch the soulless stones, except it have
first been subjected to lustral and purificatory con-
secration, a man will not shrink from approaching
with his soul impure the absolute purity of God and
that too when there is no thought of repentance in
his heart ? He who is resolved not only to commit 9
no further sin, but also to wash away the past, may
approach with gladness : let him who lacks this resolve keep far away, since hardly shall he be purified.
For he shall never escape the eye of Him who sees
into the recesses of the mind and treads its inmost
shrine.   III. Indeed of the nature of the soul 10
beloved of God no clearer evidence can we have than
that psalm of Hannah which contains the words " the
barren hath borne seven, but she that had many
children hath languished " (1 Sam. ii. 5).   And yet it 11

15

Σαμουὴλ ἡ λέγουσα. πῶς οὖν ἑπτὰ τετοκέναι
φησίν, εἰ μή τι μονάδα ἑβδομάδι τὴν αὐτὴν
φυσικώτατα νομίζει, οὐ μόνον ἐν ἀριθμοῖς, ἀλλὰ
καὶ ἐν τῇ τοῦ παντὸς ἁρμονίᾳ καὶ ἐν τοῖς τῆς
ἐναρέτου λόγοις ψυχῆς; ὁ γὰρ τεταγμένος μόνῳ
θεῷ Σαμουήλ, ἄλλῳ δὲ τὸ παράπαν συνιὼν μηδενί,
κατὰ τὸ ἓν καὶ τὴν μονάδα, τὸ ὄντως ὄν, κεκό-
12 σμηται. αὕτη δ᾽ ἡ κατάστασίς ἐστιν ἑβδομάδος,
ἀναπαυομένης ἐν θεῷ ψυχῆς καὶ περὶ μηδὲν τῶν
θνητῶν ἔργων ἔτι πονουμένης, κατὰ ἀπόλειψιν
ἑξάδος, ἣν ἀπένειμε τοῖς τὰ πρωτεῖα λαβεῖν μὴ
δυνηθεῖσι, δευτερείων δ᾽ ἐξ ἀνάγκης μεταποιου-
13 μένοις. τὴν μὲν οὖν στεῖραν, οὐ τὴν ἄγονον, ἀλλὰ
τὴν στερρὰν καὶ ἔτι σφριγῶσαν, τοὺς διὰ καρτερίας
καὶ ἀνδρείας καὶ ὑπομονῆς ἐπὶ κτήσει τοῦ ἀρίστου
διαθλοῦσαν ἄθλους, ἑβδομάδι τὴν ἰσότιμον μονάδα
τίκτειν εἰκὸς ἦν· εὔτοκος γὰρ καὶ εὔπαις ἡ φύσις.
14 τὴν δὲ πολλὴν ἀσθενεῖν ἐν τέκνοις εἶπεν ἀψευδῶς
καὶ σφόδρα ἐναργῶς· ὅταν γὰρ μία οὖσα ψυχὴ
πολλὰ ὠδίνῃ τοῦ ἑνὸς ἀποστᾶσα, μυρία κατὰ τὸ
εἰκὸς γίνεται, κἄπειτα πλήθει τέκνων ἐξηρτημένων
βαρυνομένη καὶ πιεζομένη—ἔστι δὲ ἡλιτόμηνα καὶ
15 ἀμβλωθρίδια τὰ πλεῖστα αὐτῶν—ἐξασθενεῖ. τίκτει
μὲν γὰρ τὰς πρὸς σχήματα καὶ χρώματα δι᾽
ὀφθαλμῶν ἐπιθυμίας, τίκτει δὲ τὰς πρὸς φωνὰς δι᾽

---

a Cf. De Post. 64.　　b Or " since his soul rests."
c For Philo's ideas about Six and Seven cf. Leg. All.
i. 2-16.
d In identifying στεῖραν, " barren," with στερράν, " firm,"
Philo is not so far out as in most of his philological vagaries.
The two words may be the same in origin, " hard ground "
being " barren ground."

is the mother of one child—Samuel—who is speaking.
How then can she say that she has borne seven? It
can only be that in full accordance with the truth of
things, she holds the One to be the same as the
Seven,[a] not only in the lore of numbers, but also in
the harmony of the universe and in the thoughts of
the virtuous soul. For Samuel who is appointed to
God alone and holds no company with any other has
his being ordered in accordance with the One and
the Monad, the truly existent. But this condition 12
of his implies the Seven, that is a soul which rests [b]
in God and toils no more at any mortal task, and has
thus left behind the Six, which God has assigned to
those who could not win the first place, but must needs
limit their claims to the second.[c] We might well 13
expect, then, that the barren woman, not meaning the
childless, but the " firm " or solid [d] who still abounds
in power, who with endurance and courage perseveres
to the finish in the contest, where the prize is the
acquisition of the Best, should bring forth the Monad
which is of equal value with the Seven; for her
nature is that of a happy and goodly motherhood.
And when she says that she who had many children 14
languishes, her words are as clear as they are true.
For when the soul that is one departs from the one
and is in travail with many, she naturally is multiplied
a thousand-fold,[e] and then weighed down and sore
pressed by the multitude of children that cling to
her—most of them abortions born out of due time—
she languishes utterly. She brings forth the desires 15
of which the eyes and the ears are the channels,
these for shapes and colours, those for sounds; she

[e] Or " vast is the number of children born to her." See
App. p. 483.

17

PHILO

ὤτων, ἐγκύμων δ' ἐστὶ καὶ τῶν γαστρὸς καὶ τῶν
ὑπ' αὐτήν, ὥστε πολλῶν ἐκκρεμαμένων ἐγγόνων
βαρύτατον ἄχθος φέρουσα παρίεται καὶ χεῖρας ὑπ'
ἀσθενείας καθεῖσα ἀπολέγεται. τοῦτον μὲν δὴ τὸν
τρόπον ἡττῆσθαι συμβαίνει πᾶσιν, ὅσοι φθαρτοῖς
ἑαυτοῖς φθαρτὰ γεννῶσιν.

[275]

16   IV. Ἔνιοι δ' | οὐχ ἧτταν μόνον ἀλλὰ καὶ θάνα-
τον ὑπὸ φιλαυτίας ἀνεδέξαντο. ὁ γοῦν Αὐνάν, "αἰσθό-
μενος ὅτι οὐκ αὐτῷ ἔσται τὸ σπέρμα," οὐ πρότερον ἐπαύσατο τὸ λογικόν, ὅπερ ἄριστον τῶν ὄντων γένος ἐστί, διαφθείρων ἢ καὶ αὐτὸς ἀνεδέξατο
φθορὰν παντελῆ, σφόδρα ὀρθῶς καὶ προσηκόντως·

17 εἰ γὰρ ἅπαντα πράξουσί τινες αὑτῶν ἕνεκα, μὴ
γονέων τιμῆς, μὴ παίδων εὐκοσμίας, μὴ σωτηρίας
πατρίδος, μὴ νόμων φυλακῆς, μὴ ἐθῶν βεβαιότητος,
μὴ ἰδίων μὴ κοινῶν ἐπανορθώσεως, μὴ ἱερῶν ἁγιστείας, μὴ τῆς πρὸς θεὸν εὐσεβείας ἐπιστρεφόμενοι,

18 κακοδαιμονήσουσιν. ἑνὸς γὰρ ὧν εἶπον χάριν ἀντι-
καταλλάξασθαι καὶ αὐτὸ τὸ ζῆν εὐκλεές, οἱ δ' ἄρα
καὶ ἀθρόων τῶν οὕτω περιμαχήτων φασίν, εἰ μή
τινα ἡδονὴν μέλλοι περιποιεῖν, κατολιγωρήσειν.
τοιγάρτοι πονηρὰν εἰσήγησιν ὁ ἀδέκαστος θεὸς
ἐκφύλου δόγματος, ἐπίκλησιν Αὐνάν, ἐκποδὼν ἀν-

19 ελεῖ.   παραιτητέοι δὴ πάντες οἱ γεν-
νῶντες αὑτοῖς, τὸ δ' ἐστὶν ὅσοι τὸ ἴδιον λυσιτελὲς
μόνον θηρώμενοι τῶν ἄλλων ὑπερορῶσιν, ὥσπερ
αὑτοῖς μόνοις φύντες, οὐχὶ δὲ μυρίοις ἄλλοις, πατρί,

---

^a Or " gives up the fight."
^b The sections 16-19 largely repeat *De Post.* 180, 181.
^c See App. p. 483.

18

is pregnant with the lusts of the belly and those which have their seat below it, and thus, under the crushing load of the many children that hang upon her, she grows faint and dropping her hands in weakness sinks in prostration.[a] This manner of defeat is the lot of all who engender things corruptible for their corruptible selves.

IV. Some[b] there are who through self-love have 16 brought upon themselves not only defeat but death. Thus Onan " perceiving that the seed will not be his " (Gen. xxxviii. 9), ceased not to destroy the reasoning principle, which in kind is the best of all existing things, till he himself underwent utter destruction. And right just and fitting was his fate. For if there 17 shall be any whose every deed is self-seeking, who have no regard for the honouring of their parents, for the ordering of their children aright, for the safety of their country, for the maintenance of the laws, for the security of good customs, for the better conduct of things private and public, for the sanctity of temples, for piety towards God, miserable shall be their fate. To sacrifice life itself for any single one 18 of these that I have named is honour and glory. But these self-lovers—they say that if these blessings, desirable as they are, were all put together, they would utterly despise them, if they should not procure them some future pleasure.[c] And therefore God in His impartial justice will cast out to destruction that evil suggestion of an unnatural creed, called Onan.   We must indeed reject all those 19 who " beget for themselves," that is all those who pursue only their own profit and think not of others. For they think themselves born for themselves only and not for the innumerable others, for father, for

PHILO

μητρί, γυναικί, τέκνοις, πατρίδι, ἀνθρώπων γένει, εἰ
δὲ δεῖ προελθόντας τι περαιτέρω φάναι, οὐρανῷ, γῇ,
τῷ παντὶ κόσμῳ, ἐπιστήμαις, ἀρεταῖς, τῷ πατρὶ καὶ
ἡγεμόνι τῶν συμπάντων· ὧν ἑκάστῳ κατὰ δύναμιν
ἀπονεμητέον τὸ ἁρμόττον μὴ τὰ πάντα προσθήκην
ἑαυτοῦ, ἑαυτὸν δὲ τῶν πάντων νομίζοντα.

20 V. Τούτων μὲν δὴ ἅλις, τὰ δ' ἀκόλουθα τῷ
λόγῳ συνυφήνωμεν. "ἰδὼν" οὖν φησι "κύριος ὁ
θεὸς ὅτι ἐπληθύνθησαν αἱ κακίαι τῶν ἀνθρώπων
ἐπὶ τῆς γῆς, καὶ πᾶς τις διανοεῖται ἐν τῇ καρδίᾳ
ἐπιμελῶς τὰ πονηρὰ πάσας τὰς ἡμέρας, ἐνεθυμήθη
ὁ θεός, ὅτι ἐποίησε τὸν ἄνθρωπον ἐπὶ τῆς γῆς,
καὶ διενοήθη. καὶ εἶπεν ὁ θεός· ἀπαλείψω τὸν ἄνθρωπον ὃν ἐποίησα ἀπὸ προσώπου τῆς γῆς."

21   ἴσως τινὲς τῶν ἀνεξετάστων
ὑποτοπήσουσι τὸν νομοθέτην αἰνίττεσθαι, ὅτι ἐπὶ
τῇ γενέσει τῶν ἀνθρώπων ὁ δημιουργὸς μετέγνω
κατιδὼν τὴν ἀσέβειαν αὐτῶν, ἧς χάριν αἰτίας
ἐβουλήθη σύμπαν διαφθεῖραι τὸ γένος. ἀλλ' ἴστω-
σαν ὅτι ταῦτα δοξάζοντες ἐπελαφρίζουσι καὶ ἐπι-
κουφίζουσι τὰ τῶν παλαιῶν ἐκείνων ἁμαρτήματα
22 δι' ὑπερβολὴν τῆς περὶ αὐτοὺς ἀθεότητος. τί γὰρ
ἂν ἀσέβημα μεῖζον γένοιτο τοῦ ὑπολαμβάνειν τὸν
[276] ἄτρεπτον τρέπεσθαι; καίτοι | τινῶν ἀξιούντων
μηδὲ πάντας ἀνθρώπους ταῖς γνώμαις ἐπαμφοτερί-
ζειν· τοὺς γὰρ ἀδόλως καὶ καθαρῶς φιλοσοφήσαντας
μέγιστον ἐκ τῆς ἐπιστήμης ἀγαθὸν εὕρασθαι τὸ μὴ
τοῖς πράγμασι συμμεταβάλλειν, ἀλλὰ μετὰ στερ-
ρότητος ἀκλινοῦς καὶ παγίου βεβαιότητος ἅπασι
23 τοῖς ἁρμόττουσιν ἐγχειρεῖν.   VI. ἀρέσκει

ᵃ Lit. "unexamined," *i.e.* by themselves.
ᵇ See App. p. 483.

mother, for wife, for children, for country, for the human race, and if we must extend the list, for heaven, for earth, for the universe, for knowledge, for virtues, for the Father and Captain of all; to each of whom we are bound according to our powers to render what is due, not holding all things to be an adjunct of ourselves, but rather ourselves an adjunct of all.

V. Enough on this point. Let us extend our dis- 20 cussion to embrace the words that follow. " The Lord God," says Moses, " seeing that the wickednesses of men were multiplied upon the earth and that every man intended evil in his heart diligently all his days, God had it in His mind that He had made man upon the earth, and He bethought Him. And God said, I will blot out man, whom I made, from the face of the earth " (Gen. vi. 5-7).   Perhaps some 21 of those who are careless inquirers [a] will suppose that the Lawgiver is hinting that the Creator repented of the creation of men when He beheld their impiety, and that this was the reason why He wished to destroy the whole race. Those who think thus may be sure that they make the sins of these men of old time seem light and trivial through the vastness of their own godlessness. For what greater impiety 22 could there be than to suppose that the Unchangeable changes? Indeed some maintain [b] that even among men vacillation of mind and judgement is not universal; for those who study philosophy in guilelessness and purity, it is held, gain from their knowledge this as their chief reward, that they do not change with changing circumstances, but with unbending stedfastness and firm constancy take in hand all that it behoves them to do.   VI. It is a tenet 23 of the lawgiver also that the perfect man seeks for

δὲ καὶ τῷ νομοθέτῃ τὸν τέλειον ἠρεμίας ἐφίεσθαι·
τὸ γὰρ εἰρημένον τῷ σοφῷ ἐκ προσώπου τοῦ
θεοῦ " σὺ δὲ αὐτοῦ στῆθι μετ᾽ ἐμοῦ " τὸ
ἀκλινὲς καὶ ἀρρεπὲς τῆς γνώμης καὶ ἱδρυμένον
24 πάντῃ σαφέστατα παρίστησι. τῷ γὰρ ὄντι θαυ-
μάσιον, ὥσπερ τινὰ λύραν τὴν ψυχὴν μουσικῶς
ἁρμοσάμενον οὐκ ὀξέσι καὶ βαρέσι τοῖς φθόγγοις,
ἀλλ᾽ ἐπιστήμῃ μὲν τῶν ἐναντίων,[1] χρήσει δὲ τῶν
ἀμεινόνων, μήτε ἐπιτεῖναι προσυπερβάλλοντα μήτε
ἀνεῖναι μαλθάξαντα τὴν ἀρετῶν καὶ τῶν φύσει
καλῶν ἁρμονίαν, δι᾽ ἴσου δ᾽ αὐτὴν φυλάξαντα
25 κροτεῖν καὶ ἐπιψάλλειν ἐμμελῶς. ὄργανον γὰρ
τελεώτατον ὑπὸ φύσεως δημιουργηθὲν ἀρχέτυπον
τῶν χειροκμήτων τοῦτό γε· ὅπερ εἰ καλῶς ἁρμο-
σθείη, τὴν πασῶν ἀρίστην συμφωνίαν ἀπεργάσεται,
ἥτις οὐκ ἐν κλάσει καὶ τόνοις ἐμμελοῦς φωνῆς,
ἀλλ᾽ ἐν ὁμολογίᾳ τῶν κατὰ τὸν βίον πράξεων ἔχει
26 τὸ τέλος. ὅπου γοῦν ἀνθρώπων ψυχὴ τὸν πολὺν
κλύδωνα καὶ σάλον, ὃν καταρραγὲν σφοδρὸν πνεῦμα
τὸ κακίας αἰφνίδιον ἤγειρεν, ἐπιστήμης καὶ σοφίας
αὔραις ἀποτίθεται καὶ τὸ κυμαῖνον καὶ παρῳδηκὸς
ὑφεῖσα νηνέμῳ εὐδίᾳ χρωμένη γαληνιάζει, εἶτ᾽
ἐνδοιάζεις, ὅτι ὁ ἄφθαρτος καὶ μακάριος καὶ τῶν
ἀρετῶν καὶ αὐτῆς τελειότητος καὶ εὐδαιμονίας
ἀνημμένος τὸ κράτος οὐ χρῆται γνώμης μεταβολῇ,
μένει δὲ ἐφ᾽ ὧν ἐξ ἀρχῆς ἐβουλεύσατο οὐδὲν αὐτῶν
27 μετατιθείς;   ἀνθρώποις μὲν οὖν τὸ εὐ-
μετάβολον ἢ διὰ τὴν ἐν αὐτοῖς ἢ διὰ τὴν ἐκτὸς
ἀβεβαιότητα συμβαίνειν ἀνάγκη· οἷον οὕτως φίλους
ἑλόμενοι πολλάκις καὶ βραχύν τινα αὐτοῖς συν-

[1] Wend. approves of Mangey's τῶν ⟨ἀγαθῶν καὶ τῶν⟩
ἐναντίων (cf. 49).   But see App. p. 483.

quietude. For the words addressed to the Sage with God as the speaker, " stand thou here with Me " (Deut. v. 31), shew most plainly how unbending, unwavering and broad-based is his will. Wonderful 24 indeed is the soul of the Sage, how he sets it, like a lyre,[a] to harmony not with a scale of notes low and high, but with the knowledge of moral opposites, and the practice of such of them as are better ; how he does not strain it to excessive heights, nor yet relax it and weaken the concord of virtues and things naturally beautiful, but keeps it ever at an equal tension and plays it with hand or bow in melody. Such a soul is the most perfect instrument fashioned 25 by nature, the pattern of those which are the work of our hands. And if it be well adjusted, it will produce a symphony the most beautiful in the world, one which has its consummation not in the cadences and tones of melodious sound, but in the consistencies of our life's actions. Oh ! if the soul of man, when 26 it feels the soft breeze of wisdom and knowledge, can dismiss the stormy surge which the fierce burst of the gale of wickedness has suddenly stirred, and levelling the billowy swell can rest in unruffled calm under a bright clear sky, can you doubt that He, the Imperishable Blessed One, who has taken as His own the sovereignty of the virtues, of perfection itself and beatitude, knows no change of will, but ever holds fast to what He purposed from the first without any alteration ? With men then 27 it must needs be that they are ready to change, through instability whether it be in themselves or outside them. So for example [b] often when we have chosen our friends and been familiar with them for

[a] See App. p. 483. [b] See App. p. 484.

διατρίψαντες χρόνον, οὐδὲν ἐγκαλεῖν ἔχοντες ἀπ-
εστράφημεν, ὡς εἰς ἐχθρῶν ἢ ἀγνοουμένων γοῦν
28 τάξιν ἐμβιβάσαι. τοῦτο τὸ ἔργον κούφην εὐχέρειαν
ἡμῶν αὐτῶν ἐλέγχει τὰς ἐξ ἀρχῆς ὑποθέσεις ἀδυ-
νατούντων κραταιῶς διαφυλάττειν· ὁ δὲ θεὸς οὐχ
ἁψίκορος. καὶ μὴν ἔστιν ὅτε διανοούμεθα μὲν
ἐπιμένειν κριτηρίοις τοῖς αὐτοῖς, οἱ δὲ προσελθόντες
οὐκ ἔμειναν ἐν ὁμοίῳ, ὥστ' ἐξ ἀνάγκης καὶ αἱ
29 ἡμέτεραι γνῶμαι συμμετέβαλον. προϊδέσθαι γὰρ
ἢ μελλόντων πραγμάτων συντυχίας ἢ γνώμας
ἑτέρων ἄνθρωπον ὄντα ἀμήχανον, τῷ δὲ θεῷ ὡς
ἐν αὐγῇ καθαρᾷ πάντα ἀρίδηλα. καὶ γὰρ ἄχρι
[277] τῶν ψυχῆς μυχῶν | φθάσας, ἃ τοῖς ἄλλοις ἐστὶν
ἀόρατα τηλαυγῶς πέφυκε καθορᾶν, καὶ προμηθείᾳ
καὶ προνοίᾳ χρώμενος, οἰκείαις ἀρεταῖς, οὐδὲν
ἀπελευθεριάζειν καὶ ἔξω τῆς ἑαυτοῦ καταλήψεως
βαίνειν ἐᾷ· ἐπειδήπερ οὐδ' ἡ τῶν μελλόντων ἀδη-
λότης αὐτῷ συμβατή· οὔτε γὰρ ἄδηλον οὔτε
30 μέλλον οὐδὲν θεῷ. δῆλον μὲν οὖν, ὅτι καὶ τῶν
γεννηθέντων τὸν φυτεύσαντα καὶ τῶν δημιουργηθέντων τὸν τεχνίτην καὶ τὸν ἐπίτροπον τῶν
ἐπιτροπευομένων ἐπιστήμονα [ἀναγκαῖον] εἶναι δεῖ.
ὁ δὲ θεὸς πατὴρ καὶ τεχνίτης καὶ ἐπίτροπος τῶν
ἐν οὐρανῷ τε καὶ κόσμῳ πρὸς ἀλήθειάν ἐστι. καὶ
μὴν τά γε μέλλοντα συσκιάζεται ὑπὸ τοῦ αὖθις
χρόνου, τοτὲ μὲν βραχεῖ, τοτὲ δὲ μακρῷ δια-
31 στήματι. δημιουργὸς δὲ καὶ χρόνου
θεός· καὶ γὰρ τοῦ πατρὸς αὐτοῦ πατήρ—πατὴρ
δὲ χρόνου κόσμος—τὴν κίνησιν αὐτοῦ γένεσιν
ἀποφήνας ἐκείνου· ὥστε υἱωνοῦ τάξιν ἔχειν πρὸς
θεὸν τὸν χρόνον. ὁ μὲν γὰρ κόσμος οὗτος νεώτερος

---

^a See App. p. 484.

a short time, we turn from them, though we have no charge to bring against them, and count them amongst our enemies, or at best as strangers. Such action proves the facile levity of ourselves, how little capacity we have for stoutly holding to our original judgements. But God has no such fickleness. Or again, sometimes we are minded to hold to the standards we have taken but we find ourselves with others who have not remained constant, and thus our judgements perforce change with theirs. For a mere man cannot foresee the course of future events, or the judgements of others, but to God as in pure sunlight all things are manifest. For already He has pierced into the recesses of our soul, and what is invisible to others is clear as daylight to His eyes. He employs the forethought and foreknowledge which are virtues peculiarly His own, and suffers nothing to escape His control or pass outside His comprehension. For not even about the future can uncertainty be found with Him, since nothing is uncertain or future to God. No one doubts that the parent must have knowledge of his offspring, the craftsman of his handiwork, the steward of things entrusted to his stewardship. But God is in very truth the father and craftsman and steward of the heaven and the universe and all that is therein. Future events lie shrouded in the darkness of the time that is yet to be at different distances, some near, some far. But God is the maker of time *a* also, for He is the father of time's father, that is of the universe, and has caused the movements of the one to be the source of the generation of the other. Thus time stands to God in the relation of a grandson. For this universe, since we perceive it by our senses,

25

PHILO

υἱὸς θεοῦ, ἅτε αἰσθητὸς ὤν· τὸν γὰρ πρεσβύτερον
[οὐδένα εἶπε]¹—νοητὸς δ' ἐκεῖνος—πρεσβείων ἀξιώ-
32 σας παρ' ἑαυτῷ καταμένειν διενοήθη. οὗτος οὖν
ὁ νεώτερος υἱὸς ὁ αἰσθητὸς κινηθεὶς τὴν χρόνου
φύσιν ἀναλάμψαι καὶ ἀνασχεῖν ἐποίησεν. ὥστε
οὐδὲν παρὰ θεῷ μέλλον τῷ καὶ τὰ τῶν χρόνων
ὑπηγμένῳ πέρατα· καὶ γὰρ οὐ χρόνος, ἀλλὰ τὸ
ἀρχέτυπον τοῦ χρόνου καὶ παράδειγμα αἰὼν² ὁ
βίος ἐστὶν αὐτοῦ³· ἐν αἰῶνι δὲ οὔτε παρελήλυθεν
οὐδὲν οὔτε μέλλει, ἀλλὰ μόνον ὑφέστηκεν.

33 VII. Ἱκανῶς οὖν διειλεγμένοι περὶ τοῦ μὴ
χρῆσθαι μετανοίᾳ τὸ ὂν ἀκολούθως ἀποδώσομεν,
τί ἐστι τὸ " ἐνεθυμήθη ὁ θεὸς ὅτι ἐποίησε τὸν
34 ἄνθρωπον ἐπὶ τῆς γῆς καὶ διενοήθη." ἔννοιαν
καὶ διανόησιν, τὴν μὲν ἐναποκειμένην οὖσαν
νόησιν, τὴν δὲ νοήσεως διέξοδον, βεβαιοτάτας
δυνάμεις ὁ ποιητὴς τῶν ὅλων κληρωσάμενος καὶ
χρώμενος ἀεὶ ταύταις τὰ ἔργα ἑαυτοῦ καταθεᾶται.
τὰ μὲν δὴ μὴ λείποντα τὴν τάξιν τῆς πειθαρχίας
ἕνεκα ἐπαινεῖ, τὰ δὲ μεθιστάμενα τῇ κατὰ λιπο-
τακτῶν ὡρισμένῃ μετέρχεται δίκῃ.

35 τῶν γὰρ σωμάτων τὰ μὲν ἐνεδήσατο ἕξει, τὰ δὲ
φύσει, τὰ δὲ ψυχῇ, τὰ δὲ λογικῇ ψυχῇ. λίθων μὲν
οὖν καὶ ξύλων, ἃ δὴ τῆς συμφυΐας ἀπέσπασται,
[278] δεσμὸν κραταιότατον ἕξιν | εἰργάζετο· ἡ δέ ἐστι
πνεῦμα ἀναστρέφον ἐφ' ἑαυτό· ἄρχεται μὲν γὰρ

---

¹ Wend. regards οὐδένα εἶπε as a Christian interpolation.
The Translator suggests ὃν γὰρ πρεσβύτερον τοῦδ' ἕνα εἶχε, which
with the transference of τ and the substitution of χ for π is
the same as the ms.   ² mss. δι' ὧν.   ³ mss. αὐτῶν.

ᵃ See App. p. 484.
ᵇ The fourfold classification which follows has been
already given shortly in *Leg. All.* ii. 22-23.

is the younger son of God. To the elder son, I mean the intelligible universe, He assigned the place of firstborn, and purposed that it should remain in His own keeping. So this younger son, the world of our 32 senses, when set in motion, brought that entity we call time to the brightness of its rising. And thus with God there is no future, since He has made the boundaries of the ages subject to Himself. For God's life is not a time, but eternity, which is the archetype and pattern of time [a]; and in eternity there is no past nor future, but only present existence.

VII. Having now discoursed sufficiently on the 33 theme that the Existent does not experience repentance, we will explain in due sequence the words " God had it in His mind that He had made men upon the earth and He bethought Him " (Gen. vi. 6). "Having 34 in one's mind " and " bethinking," the former being the thought quiescent in the mind,[a] the latter the thought brought to an issue, are two most constant powers, which the Maker of all things has taken as His own and ever employs them when He contemplates His own works. Those of His creatures who do not leave their appointed places, He praises for their obedience. Those who depart from it He visits with the punishment which is the doom of deserters.

This is explained by consideration of the 35 different conditions, which He has made inseparable from the various bodies.[b] These are in some cases cohesion, in others growth, in others life, in others a reasoning soul. Thus, in stones and bits of wood which have been severed from their organism, He wrought cohesion, which acts as the most rigid of bonds. Cohesion [c] is a breath or current ever re-

[a] See note in App. on *Leg. All.* ii. 22.

ἀπὸ τῶν μέσων ἐπὶ τὰ πέρατα τείνεσθαι, ψαῦσαν
δὲ ἄκρας ἐπιφανείας ἀνακάμπτει πάλιν, ἄχρις ἂν
ἐπὶ τὸν αὐτὸν ἀφίκηται τόπον, ἀφ' οὗ τὸ πρῶτον
36 ὡρμήθη· ἕξεως ὁ συνεχὴς οὗτος δίαυλος ἄφθαρτος,
ὃν οἱ δρομεῖς ἀπομιμούμενοι ταῖς τριετηρίσιν ἐν
τοῖς ἀνθρώπων ἁπάντων κοινοῖς θεάτροις ὡς
μέγα δὴ καὶ λαμπρὸν καὶ περιμάχητον ἔργον ἐπιδείκνυνται.

37 VIII. Τὴν δὲ φύσιν ἀπένειμε τοῖς φυτοῖς κερασάμενος αὐτὴν ἐκ πλείστων δυνάμεων, θρεπτικῆς
τε καὶ μεταβλητικῆς καὶ αὐξητικῆς. καὶ γὰρ
τρέφεται τροφῆς ὄντα χρεῖα, τεκμήριον δέ· τὰ μὴ
ἀρδόμενα φθίνει καὶ ἀφαυαίνεται, ὥσπερ αὖ τὰ
ποτιζόμενα ἐμφανῶς αὔξεται· τὰ γὰρ τέως διὰ
βραχύτητα χαμαίζηλα ἐξαίφνης ἀναδραμόντα ἔρνη
γίνεται περιμηκέστατα. τί χρὴ λέγειν περὶ μετα-
38 βολῆς αὐτῶν; ταῖς μὲν γὰρ χειμεριναῖς τροπαῖς
τὰ πέταλα μαρανθέντα εἰς τοὔδαφος χεῖται, οἵ τε
ἐν ταῖς κληματίσι λεγόμενοι πρὸς τῶν γεωπόνων
ὀφθαλμοὶ καθάπερ ἐν τοῖς ζῴοις καταμύουσι, τά
τε πρὸς τὰς ἐκφύσεις στόμια πάντα ἔσφιγκται τῆς
φύσεως εἴσω τότε συνειλημμένης καὶ ἡσυχαζούσης,
ἵνα διαπνεύσασα οἷά τις ἀθλητὴς προηγωνισμένος
καὶ συλλεξαμένη τὴν ἰδίαν ἰσχὺν πρὸς τοὺς ἐθάδας
ἄθλους ἐξ ὑπαρχῆς ἀπαντᾷ. γίνεται δὲ τοῦτο ταῖς
39 ἐαριναῖς καὶ κατὰ θέρος ὥραις· ὥσπερ γὰρ ἐκ
βαθέος ὕπνου περιαναστᾶσα τούς τε ὀφθαλμοὺς
διοίγνυσι τά τε μεμυκότα τῶν στομίων ἀναστείλασα
εὐρύνει, ὧν δ' ἐστὶν ἐγκύμων πάντα ἀποτίκτει,
πέταλα καὶ κληματίδας, ἕλικας, οἴναρα,[1] καρπὸν
ἐπὶ πᾶσιν· εἶθ' ὅταν τελεσθῇ, παρέχεται τὰς τροφὰς

---

[1] MSS. οἷον ἄρα.

turning to itself. It begins to extend itself from the centre of the body in question to its extremes, and when it has reached the outermost surface it reverses its course, till it arrives at the place from which it first set out. This regular double course of cohesion 36 is indestructible ; and it is this which the runners imitate at the triennial festivals in the places of spectacle universal among men, and exhibit as a great and splendid feat, well worthy of their efforts.

VIII. Growth God assigned to plants. It is a compound of many capacities, that of taking nourishment, 37 that of undergoing change and that of increasing. Nourishment plants receive as they need it, as the following proof shews. When they are not watered they decay and wither, just as their increase when watered is plain to see, for sprouts heretofore too tiny to rise above the ground suddenly shoot up and become quite tall. It is hardly necessary to speak of their function of change. When the winter solstice arrives, 38 the leaves wither and shed themselves to the ground, and the " eyes," as the husbandmen call them, on the twigs close like eyes in animals, and all the outlets which serve to put forth life are bound tight, for Nature [a] within them compresses herself and hibernates, to get a breathing-space, like an athlete after his first contest, and thus having regained her fund of strength, comes forth to resume the familiar conflict. And this comes to pass in the spring and summer seasons. For she arises as though from a 39 deep sleep and unseals the eyes, opens wide the closed outlets, and brings forth all that is in her womb, shoots, twigs, tendrils, leaves and, to crown all, fruit. Then when the fruit is fully formed, she

[a] Or "power of growth."

PHILO

οἷα μήτηρ τῷ γενομένῳ διά τινων ἀφανῶν πόρων,
οἳ τοῖς ἐν γυναιξὶ μαστοῖς ἀναλογοῦσι, καὶ οὐ
πρότερον παύεται τρέφουσα ἢ τὸν καρπὸν τελε-
40 σφορηθῆναι· τελεσφορεῖται δὲ ὁ πεπανθεὶς ἄκρως,
ἡνίκα, κἂν μηδεὶς δρέπηται, τῆς συμφυΐας αὐτὸς
ἐπείγεται διαζεύγνυσθαι ἅτε μηκέτι τροφῶν τῶν
ἀπὸ τῆς τεκούσης δεόμενος, ἱκανὸς δ' ὤν, εἰ χώρας
ἀγαθῆς ἐπιλάχοι, σπείρειν καὶ γεννᾶν ὅμοια τοῖς
φυτεύσασι.
41 IX. Ψυχὴν δὲ φύσεως τρισὶ διαλλάττουσαν ὁ
ποιῶν ἐποίει, αἰσθήσει, φαντασίᾳ, ὁρμῇ· τὰ μὲν
γὰρ φυτὰ ἀόρμητα, ἀφάνταστα, αἰσθήσεως ἀμέτοχα,
τῶν δὲ ζῴων ἕκαστον ἀθρόων μετέχει τῶν εἰρη-
42 μένων. αἴσθησις μὲν οὖν, ὡς αὐτό που δηλοῖ
τοὔνομα, εἴσθεσίς τις οὖσα τὰ φανέντα ἐπεισφέρει
τῷ νῷ· τούτῳ γάρ, ἐπειδὴ μέγιστόν ἐστι ταμεῖον
καὶ πανδεχές, πάνθ' ὅσα δι' ὁράσεως καὶ ἀκοῆς
καὶ τῶν ἄλλων αἰσθητικῶν ὀργάνων ἐντίθεται καὶ
43 ἐναποθησαυρίζεται. φαντασία δέ ἐστι τύπωσις |
[279] ἐν ψυχῇ. ὦν[1] γὰρ εἰσήγαγεν ἑκάστη τῶν αἰσθήσεων,
ὥσπερ δακτύλιός τις ἢ σφραγὶς ἐναπεμάξατο τὸν
οἰκεῖον χαρακτῆρα· κηρῷ δὲ ἐοικὼς ὁ νοῦς τὸ
ἐκμαγεῖον δεξάμενος ἄκρως παρ' ἑαυτῷ φυλάττει,
μέχρις ἂν ἡ ἀντίπαλος μνήμης τὸν τύπον λεάνασα
44 λήθῃ ἀμυδρὸν ἐργάσηται ἢ παντελῶς ἀφανίσῃ. τὸ
δὲ φανὲν καὶ τυπῶσαν τοτὲ μὲν οἰκείως τοτὲ δὲ
ὡς ἑτέρως διέθηκε τὴν ψυχήν. τοῦτο δὲ αὐτῆς τὸ

---

[1] mss. ἦν or ἐν or ἁ.

---

[a] " The word φαντασία, 'appearance' or 'appearing,' is
a technical term in Stoic logic for which no one English
equivalent is as yet unanimously adopted. It denotes the
immediate datum of consciousness or experience, whether
presented to the sense or in certain cases to the mind. Hence

30

provides nourishment, like the mother to the infant, through some hidden channels, which correspond to the breasts in women, and she ceases not to minister this nourishment till the fruit is brought to its consummation. That consummation comes to the fully 40 ripened fruit, when, if none pluck it, it automatically seeks to disengage itself from its organism, since it needs no longer the nurture which its parent supplies, and is capable, if it chance to drop on good soil, of sowing and producing other plants similar to those which gave it its existence.

IX. Life was made by its creator different from 41 growth in three ways. It has sensation, " presentation,[a] " impulse. For plants have no impulse, no " presentation," no gift of sense-perception, while each living creature participates in all three combined. Sensation or sense, as the name itself shews, 42 is " a putting in," and introduces what has appeared to it to the mind. For mind is a vast and receptive storehouse in which all that comes through sight or hearing and the other organs of sense is placed and treasured.   " Presentation " is an imprint 43 made on the soul. For, like a ring or seal, it stamps [b] on the soul the image corresponding to everything which each of the senses has introduced. And the mind like wax receives the impress and retains it vividly, until forgetfulness the opponent of memory levels out the imprint, and makes it indistinct, or entirely effaces it. But the object which has pre- 44 sented itself and made the impression has an effect upon the soul sometimes of an appropriate kind,[b] sometimes the reverse. And this condition or state

' presentation ' is nearer than ' perception ' or ' impression ' (Hicks on Diog. Laert. vii. 43 ; Loeb translation, vol. ii. p. 152).   [b] See App. p. 484.

πάθος ὁρμὴ καλεῖται, ἣν ὁριζόμενοι πρώτην ἔφασαν
εἶναι ψυχῆς κίνησιν.

45 Τοσούτοις μὲν δὴ ζῷα προὔχει φυτῶν· ἴδωμεν
δὲ τίνι τῶν ἄλλων ζῴων ὑπερβέβληκεν ἄνθρωπος.
X. ἐξαίρετον οὗτος τοίνυν γέρας ἔλαχε διάνοιαν,
ἣ τὰς ἁπάντων φύσεις σωμάτων τε ὁμοῦ καὶ
πραγμάτων εἴωθε καταλαμβάνειν. καθάπερ γὰρ
ἐν μὲν τῷ σώματι τὸ ἡγεμονικὸν ὄψις ἐστίν, ἐν δὲ
τῷ παντὶ ἡ τοῦ φωτὸς φύσις, τὸν αὐτὸν τρόπον
46 καὶ τῶν ἐν ἡμῖν τὸ κρατιστεῦον ὁ νοῦς· ψυχῆς γὰρ
ὄψις οὗτος οἰκείαις περιλαμπόμενος αὐγαῖς, δι᾽
ὧν ὁ πολὺς καὶ βαθὺς ζόφος, ὃν κατέχεεν ἄγνοια
τῶν πραγμάτων, ἀνασκίδναται. τοῦτο τῆς ψυχῆς
τὸ εἶδος οὐκ ἐκ τῶν αὐτῶν στοιχείων, ἐξ ὧν τὰ
ἄλλα ἀπετελεῖτο, διεπλάσθη, καθαρωτέρας δὲ καὶ
ἀμείνονος ἔλαχε τῆς οὐσίας, ἐξ ἧς αἱ θεῖαι φύσεις
ἐδημιουργοῦντο· παρὸ καὶ μόνον τῶν ἐν ἡμῖν εἰ-
47 κότως ἄφθαρτον ἔδοξεν εἶναι διάνοια. μόνην γὰρ
αὐτὴν ὁ γεννήσας πατὴρ ἐλευθερίας ἠξίωσε, καὶ τὰ
τῆς ἀνάγκης ἀνεὶς δεσμὰ ἄφετον εἴασε, δωρησά-
μενος αὐτῇ τοῦ πρεπωδεστάτου καὶ οἰκείου κτήματος αὐτῷ, τοῦ ἑκουσίου, μοῖραν, ἣν ἠδύνατο
δέξασθαι· τὰ μὲν γὰρ ἄλλα ζῷα, ὧν ἐν ταῖς ψυχαῖς
τὸ ἐξαιρούμενον εἰς ἐλευθερίαν, νοῦς, οὐκ ἔστι,
καταζευχθέντα καὶ ἐγχαλινωθέντα πρὸς ὑπηρεσίαν
ἀνθρώποις παραδέδοται ὥσπερ οἰκέται δεσπόταις,
ὁ δὲ ἄνθρωπος ἐθελουργοῦ καὶ αὐτοκελεύστου
γνώμης λαχὼν καὶ προαιρετικαῖς χρώμενος τὰ
πολλὰ ταῖς ἐνεργείαις εἰκότως ψόγον μὲν ἔσχεν
ἐφ᾽ οἷς ἐκ προνοίας ἀδικεῖ, ἔπαινον δὲ ἐφ᾽ οἷς ἑκὼν

---

of the soul is called impulse or appetite, which has been defined as the first movement of the soul.[a]

In all these ways living creatures excel plants. 45 Let us now see where man has been made superior to other animals. X. We find that the special prerogative he has received is mind, habituated to apprehend the natures both of all material objects and of things in general. For as sight holds the leading place in the body, and the quality of light holds the leading place in the universe, so too in us the dominant element is the mind. For mind is the sight of the 46 soul,[a] illuminated by rays peculiar to itself, whereby the vast and profound darkness, poured upon it by ignorance of things, is dispersed. This branch of the soul was not formed of the same elements, out of which the other branches were brought to completion, but it was allotted something better and purer,[b] the substance in fact out of which[c] divine natures were wrought. And therefore it is reasonably held that the mind alone in all that makes us what we are is indestructible. For it is mind alone which the 47 Father who begat it judged worthy of freedom, and loosening the fetters of necessity, suffered it to range as it listed, and of that free-will which is His most peculiar possession and most worthy of His majesty gave it such portion as it was capable of receiving. For the other living creatures in whose souls the mind, the element set apart for liberty, has no place, have been committed under yoke and bridle to the service of men, as slaves to a master. But man, possessed of a spontaneous and self-determined will, whose activities for the most part rest on deliberate choice, is with reason blamed for what he does wrong with intent, praised when he acts rightly of

48 κατορθοῖ. τῶν μὲν γὰρ ἄλλων φυτῶν τε καὶ
ζῴων οὔτε αἱ εὐφορίαι ἐπαινεταὶ οὔθ' αἱ κακο-
πραγίαι ψεκταί—τὰς γὰρ ἐφ' ἑκάτερα κινήσεις καὶ
μεταβολὰς ἀπροαιρέτους καὶ ἀκουσίους ἔλαβον—,
μόνη δὲ ἡ ἀνθρώπου ψυχὴ δεξαμένη παρὰ θεοῦ τὴν
ἑκούσιον κίνησιν καὶ κατὰ τοῦτο μάλιστα ὁμοιω-
θεῖσα αὐτῷ, χαλεπῆς καὶ ἀργαλεωτάτης δεσποίνης,
[280] τῆς ἀνάγκης, ὡς οἷόν τε ἦν ἐλευθερωθεῖσα | κατη-
γορίας ἂν δεόντως τυγχάνοι, ὅτι τὸν ἐλευθερώ-
σαντα οὐ περιέπει· τοιγάρτοι τὴν κατ' ἀπελευθέρων
ἀχαρίστων ἀπαραίτητον δίκην ὀρθότατα τίσει.

49   Ὥστε " ἐνεθυμήθη καὶ διενοήθη ὁ θεὸς " οὐχὶ
νῦν πρῶτον, ἀλλ' ἐξέτι πάλαι παγίως καὶ βεβαίως,
" ὅτι ἐποίησε τὸν ἄνθρωπον," τουτέστιν ὁποῖον
αὐτὸν εἰργάσατο· εἰργάσατο γὰρ αὐτὸν ἄφετον καὶ
ἐλεύθερον, ἑκουσίως καὶ προαιρετικαῖς χρησόμενον
ταῖς ἐνεργείαις πρὸς τήνδε τὴν χρείαν, ἵνα ἐπιστάμενος ἀγαθά τε αὖ καὶ κακὰ καὶ καλῶν καὶ
αἰσχρῶν λαμβάνων ἔννοιαν καὶ δικαίοις καὶ ἀδίκοις
καὶ ὅλως τοῖς ἀπ' ἀρετῆς καὶ κακίας καθαρῶς ἐπι-
βάλλων αἱρέσει μὲν τῶν ἀμεινόνων, φυγῇ δὲ τῶν
50 ἐναντίων χρῆται.   παρὸ καὶ λόγιόν ἐστι
τοιοῦτον ἀναγεγραμμένον ἐν Δευτερονομίῳ· " ἰδοὺ
δέδωκα πρὸ προσώπου σου τὴν ζωὴν καὶ τὸν
θάνατον, τὸ ἀγαθὸν καὶ τὸ κακόν, ἔκλεξαι τὴν
ζωήν." οὐκοῦν ἀμφότερα διὰ τούτου παρίσταται,
ὅτι καὶ ἐπιστήμονες τῶν ἀγαθῶν καὶ τῶν ἐναντίων γεγόνασιν ἄνθρωποι καὶ ὀφείλουσι πρὸ τῶν
χειρόνων αἱρεῖσθαι τὰ κρείττω λογισμὸν ἔχοντες ἐν
ἑαυτοῖς ὥσπερ τινὰ δικαστὴν ἀδωροδόκητον, οἷς ἂν

34

his own will. In the others, the plants and animals, 48
no praise is due if they bear well, nor blame if they
fare ill : for their movements and changes in either
direction come to them from no deliberate choice or
volition of their own. But the soul of man alone has
received from God the faculty of voluntary movement, and in this way especially is made like to Him,
and thus being liberated, as far as might be, from
that hard and ruthless mistress, necessity, may justly
be charged with guilt, in that it does not honour its
Liberator. And therefore it will rightly pay the inexorable penalty which is meted to ungrateful freed-
men.

Thus God " had it in His mind and bethought 49
Him " not now for the first time, but ever from of
old—a thought that was fixed and stedfast—" that
He had made man," that is He thought of what
nature He had made him. He had made him free
and unfettered, to employ his powers of action with
voluntary and deliberate choice for this purpose,
that, knowing good and ill and receiving the conception of the noble and the base, and setting himself in sincerity to apprehend just and unjust and in
general what belongs to virtue and what to vice, he
might practise to choose the better and eschew the
opposite.   And therefore we have an 50
oracle of this kind recorded in Deuteronomy. " Behold, I have set before thy face life and death, good
and evil ; choose life " (Deut. xxx. 15, 19). So then
in this way He puts before us both truths ; first that
men have been made with a knowledge both of good
and evil, its opposite ; secondly, that it is their duty
to choose the better rather than the worse, because
they have, as it were, within them an incorruptible

35

ὁ ὀρθὸς ὑποβάλλῃ λόγος πεισθησόμενον, οἷς δ᾽ ἂν
ὁ ἐναντίος ἀπειθήσοντα.

51 XI. Δεδηλωκότες οὖν ἀποχρώντως περὶ τούτων
τὰ ἑξῆς ἴδωμεν. ἔστι δὲ ταῦτα· " ἀπαλείψω τὸν
ἄνθρωπον ὃν ἐποίησα ἀπὸ προσώπου τῆς γῆς, ἀπὸ
ἀνθρώπου ἕως κτήνους, ἀπὸ ἑρπετῶν ἕως πετεινῶν
τοῦ οὐρανοῦ, ὅτι ἐθυμώθην, ὅτι ἐποίησα αὐτόν."

52 πάλιν τινὲς τῶν εἰρημένων ἀκούσαντες ὑπολαμβάνουσι θυμοῖς καὶ ὀργαῖς χρῆσθαι τὸ ὄν. ἔστι δ᾽ οὐδενὶ ληπτὸν πάθει τὸ παράπαν· ἀσθενείας γὰρ ἀνθρωπίνης τὸ κηραίνειν ἴδιον, θεῷ δὲ οὔτε τὰ ψυχῆς
ἄλογα πάθη οὔτε τὰ σώματος μέρη καὶ μέλη συν-
όλως ἐστὶν οἰκεῖα.   λέγεται δὲ
οὐδὲν ἧττον παρὰ τῷ νομοθέτῃ μέχρι τινὸς εἰς-
αγωγῆς τὰ τοιαῦτα, τοῦ νουθετῆσαι χάριν τοὺς
53 ἑτέρως μὴ δυναμένους σωφρονίζεσθαι. τῶν γὰρ
ἐν ταῖς προστάξεσι καὶ ἀπαγορεύσεσι νόμων, οἳ
δὴ κυρίως εἰσὶ νόμοι, δύο τὰ ἀνωτάτω πρόκειται
κεφάλαια περὶ τοῦ αἰτίου, ἓν μὲν ὅτι " οὐχ ὡς
ἄνθρωπος ὁ θεός," ἕτερον δὲ ὅτι ὡς ἄνθρωπος.
54 ἀλλὰ τὸ μὲν πρότερον ἀληθείᾳ βεβαιοτάτῃ πεπίστωται, τὸ δ᾽ ὕστερον πρὸς τὴν τῶν πολλῶν διδασκα-
[281] λίαν εἰσάγεται· παρὸ καὶ | λέγεται ἐπ᾽ αὐτοῦ· " ὡς
ἄνθρωπος παιδεύσει τὸν υἱὸν αὐτοῦ"· ὥστε παιδείας
ἕνεκα καὶ νουθεσίας, ἀλλ᾽ οὐχὶ τῷ πεφυκέναι τοι-
55 οῦτον εἶναι λέλεκται. τῶν γὰρ ἀνθρώπων οἱ μὲν
ψυχῆς, οἱ δὲ σώματος γεγόνασι φίλοι· οἱ μὲν οὖν
ψυχῆς ἑταῖροι νοηταῖς καὶ ἀσωμάτοις φύσεσιν ἐνομιλεῖν δυνάμενοι οὐδεμιᾷ τῶν γεγονότων ἰδέᾳ
παραβάλλουσι τὸ ὄν, ἀλλ᾽ ἐκβιβάσαντες αὐτὸ πάσης

ᵃ See App. p. 485.

judge in the reasoning faculty, which will accept all that right reason suggests and reject the promptings of its opposite.

XI. Having made this point sufficiently clear let 51 us consider the next words, which are as follows, " I will blot out man whom I made from the face of the earth, from man to beast, from creeping things to fowls of heaven, because I was wroth in that I made him " (Gen. vi. 7). Again, some on hearing these 52 words suppose that the Existent feels wrath and anger, whereas He is not susceptible to any passion at all. For disquiet is peculiar to human weakness, but neither the unreasoning passions of the soul, nor the parts and members of the body in general, have any relation to God.   All the same the Lawgiver uses such expressions, just so far as they serve for a kind of elementary lesson, to admonish those who could not otherwise be brought to their senses. Thus, in the laws which deal with commands and 53 prohibitions (laws, that is, in the proper sense of the word),[a] there stand forth above others two leading statements[a] about the Cause, one that " God is not as a man " (Num. xxiii. 19) ; the other that He is as a man. But while the former is warranted by grounds 54 of surest truth, the latter is introduced for the instruction of the many. And therefore also it is said of Him " like a man He shall train His son " (Deut. viii. 5). And thus it is for training and admonition, not because God's nature is such, that these words are used. Among men some are soul lovers, some 55 body lovers. The comrades of the soul, who can hold converse with intelligible incorporeal natures, do not compare the Existent to any form of created things. They have dissociated Him from every cate-

ποιότητος—ἐν γάρ τι τῶν εἰς τὴν μακαριότητα
αὐτοῦ καὶ τὴν ἄκραν εὐδαιμονίαν ἦν τὸ ψιλὴν ἄνευ
χαρακτῆρος τὴν ὕπαρξιν καταλαμβάνεσθαι—τὴν
κατὰ τὸ εἶναι φαντασίαν μόνην ἐνεδέξαντο μὴ μορ-
56 φώσαντες αὐτό. οἱ δὲ συμβάσεις καὶ σπονδὰς
πρὸς σῶμα θέμενοι, ἀδυνατοῦντες ἀπαμφιάσασθαι
τὸ σαρκῶν περίβλημα καὶ μόνην καὶ καθ᾽ ἑαυτὴν
ἀπροσδεᾶ καὶ ἁπλῆν φύσιν ἰδεῖν ἀμιγῆ καὶ ἀσύγ-
κριτον, οἷα περὶ ἑαυτῶν τοιαῦτα καὶ περὶ τοῦ
πάντων αἰτίου διενοήθησαν, οὐ λογισάμενοι ὅτι
τῷ μὲν ἐκ πλειόνων συνόδου δυνάμεων γενομένῳ
πλειόνων ἔδει μερῶν πρὸς τὴν τῶν καθ᾽ ἕκαστον
χρειῶν ὑπηρεσίαν, XII. ὁ δὲ θεὸς ἅτε ἀγένητος
ὢν καὶ τὰ ἄλλα ἀγαγὼν εἰς γένεσιν οὐδενὸς ἐδεήθη
57 τῶν τοῖς γεννήμασι προσόντων·   ἐπεὶ καὶ
τί φῶμεν; εἰ κέχρηται τοῖς ὀργανικοῖς μέρεσι,
βάσεις μὲν ἔχει τοῦ προέρχεσθαι χάριν—βαδιεῖται
δὲ ποῖ πεπληρωκὼς τὰ πάντα; καὶ πρὸς τίνα
μηδενὸς ὄντος ἰσοτίμου; καὶ ἕνεκα τοῦ; οὐ γὰρ
ὑγείας φροντίζων ὥσπερ καὶ ἡμεῖς—καὶ χεῖρας
μέντοι πρὸς τὸ λαβεῖν τε καὶ δοῦναι· λαμβάνει μὲν
δὴ παρ᾽ οὐδενὸς οὐδέν—πρὸς γὰρ τῷ ἀνεπιδεεῖ καὶ
τὰ σύμπαντα ἔχει κτήματα—, δίδωσι δὲ λόγῳ
χρώμενος ὑπηρέτῃ δωρεῶν, ᾧ καὶ τὸν κόσμον
58 εἰργάζετο. ὀφθαλμῶν γε μὴν οὐκ ἐδεῖτο, οἷς ἄνευ
φωτὸς αἰσθητοῦ κατάληψις οὐ γίνεται· τὸ δὲ αἰσθητὸν φῶς γενητόν, ἑώρα δὲ ὁ θεὸς καὶ πρὸ γενέ-
59 σεως φωτὶ χρώμενος ἑαυτῷ. τί δὲ δεῖ λέγειν περὶ

ᵃ See App. p. 485.

gory or quality, for it is one of the facts which go
to make His blessedness and supreme felicity that
His being is apprehended as simple being, without
other definite characteristic ; and thus they do not
picture it with form, but admit to their minds the
conception of existence only. But those who have 56
made a compact and a truce with the body are unable
to cast off from them the garment of flesh, and to
descry existence needing nothing in its unique soli-
tariness, and free from all admixture and composition in its absolute simplicity. And therefore they
think of the Cause of all in the same terms as of
themselves, and do not reflect that while a being
which is formed through the union of several faculties
needs several parts to minister to the need of each,
XII. God being uncreated and the Author of the
creation of the others needs none of the properties
which belong to the creatures which He has brought
into being.   For consider, if He uses our 57
bodily parts or organs He has feet to move from one
place to another. But whither will He go or walk
since His presence fills everything ? To whom will
He go, when none is His equal ? And for what
purpose will He walk ? For it cannot be out of care
for health as it is with us.[a] Hands He must have to
receive and give. Yet He receives nothing from
anyone, for, besides that He has no needs, all things
are His possessions, and when He gives, He employs
as minister of His gifts the Reason wherewith also
He made the world. Nor did He need eyes, which 58
have no power of perception without the light which
meets our sense. But that light is created, whereas
God saw before creation, being Himself His own
light. Why need we speak of the organs of nourish- 59

39

τῶν τῆς τροφῆς ὀργάνων; εἰ γὰρ ταῦτ' ἔχει, καὶ
τρέφεται καὶ πληρωθεὶς μὲν ἀποπαύεται,[1] παυ-
σάμενος δὲ δεῖται πάλιν, καὶ τἄλλα ὅσα τούτοις
ἀκόλουθα οὐκ ἂν εἴποιμι· ἀσεβῶν αὗται μυθοποιίαι
λόγῳ μὲν ἀνθρωπόμορφον ἔργῳ δὲ ἀνθρωποπαθὲς
60 εἰσαγόντων τὸ θεῖον.   XIII. τίνος οὖν
[282] ἕνεκα Μωυσῆς βάσεις, χεῖρας, εἰσόδους, | ἐξόδους
φησὶν εἶναι περὶ τὸ ἀγένητον, τίνος δὲ χάριν
ὅπλισιν τὴν πρὸς ἐχθρῶν ἄμυναν; ξιφηφοροῦντα
γὰρ ⟨εἰσάγει⟩ καὶ βέλεσι χρώμενον καὶ πνεύμασι
καὶ φθοροποιῷ πυρί—καταιγίδα καὶ κεραυνὸν
ἑτέροις ὀνόμασι ταῦτα ποιηταὶ προσαγορεύοντες
ὅπλα τοῦ αἰτίου φασὶν εἶναι—, πρὸς δὲ ἔτι ζῆλον,
θυμόν, ὀργάς, ὅσα τούτοις ὅμοια ἀνθρωπολογῶν
διεξέρχεται; ἀλλὰ τοῖς πυνθανομένοις ἀποκρίνεται·
61 ὦ οὗτοι, τῷ ἄριστα νομοθετήσοντι τέλος ἓν δεῖ
προκεῖσθαι, πάντας ὠφελῆσαι τοὺς ἐντυγχάνοντας.
οἱ μὲν οὖν εὐμοίρου φύσεως λαχόντες καὶ ἀγωγῆς
ἐν πᾶσιν ἀνυπαιτίου, τὴν μετὰ ταῦθ' ὁδὸν τοῦ βίου
λεωφόρον καὶ εὐθεῖαν εὑρίσκοντες, ἀληθείᾳ συν-
οδοιπόρῳ χρῶνται, παρ' ἧς μυηθέντες τὰ περὶ τοῦ
ὄντος ἀψευδῆ μυστήρια τῶν γενέσεως οὐδὲν προσ-
62 αναπλάττουσιν αὐτῷ.   τούτοις οἰκειότατον πρόκειται κεφάλαιον ἐν τοῖς ἱεροφαντηθεῖσι χρησμοῖς,
ὅτι "οὐχ ὡς ἄνθρωπος ὁ θεός," ἀλλ' οὐδ' ὡς
οὐρανὸς οὐδ' ὡς κόσμος· ποιὰ γὰρ εἴδη ταῦτά γε
καὶ εἰς αἴσθησιν ἐρχόμενα, ὁ δ' ἄρα οὐδὲ τῷ νῷ
καταληπτὸς ὅτι μὴ κατὰ τὸ εἶναι μόνον· ὕπαρξις

---

[1] Wend. with some MSS. ἀποπατεῖ, but see App. p. 485.

[a] See App. p. 485.

ment ? If He has them, He eats and is filled, rests awhile and after the rest has need again, and the accompaniments of this I will not dwell upon. These are the mythical fictions of the impious, who, professing to represent the deity as of human form, in reality represent Him as having human passions.

XIII. Why then does Moses speak of feet and hands, 60 goings in and goings out in connexion with the Uncreated, or of His arming to defend Himself against His enemies ? For he describes Him as bearing a sword, and using as His weapons winds and death-dealing fire (thunderbolt and storm blast the poets call them, using different words, and say they are the weapons of the Cause). Why again does he speak of His jealousy, His wrath, His moods of anger, and the other emotions similar to them, which he describes in terms of human nature ? But to those who ask these questions Moses answers thus : " Sirs, 61 the lawgiver who aims at the best must have one end only before him—to benefit all whom his work reaches. Those to whose lot has fallen a generously gifted nature and a training blameless throughout, and who thus find that their later course through life lies in a straight and even highway, have truth for their fellow-traveller, and being admitted by her into the infallible mysteries of the Existent do not overlay the conception of God with any of the attributes of created being. These find 62 a moral most pertinent in the oracles of revelation, that " God is not as a man " nor yet is He as the heaven or the universe.[a] These last are forms of a particular kind which present themselves to our senses. But He is not apprehensible even by the mind, save in the fact that He is. For it is His

γὰρ ἔσθ' ἦν καταλαμβάνομεν αὐτοῦ, τῶν δέ γε
63 χωρὶς ὑπάρξεως οὐδέν.   XIV. οἱ δέ γε
νωθεστέρᾳ μὲν καὶ ἀμβλείᾳ κεχρημένοι τῇ φύσει,
περὶ δὲ τὰς ἐν παισὶ τροφὰς πλημμεληθέντες, ὀξὺ
καθορᾶν ἀδυνατοῦντες ἰατρῶν δέονται νουθετη-
τῶν,[1] οἳ πρὸς τὸ παρὸν πάθος τὴν οἰκείαν ἐπι-
64 νοήσουσι θεραπείαν· ἐπεὶ καὶ ἀναγώγοις καὶ
ἄφροσιν οἰκέταις φοβερὸς δεσπότης ὠφέλιμος, τὰς
γὰρ ἐπανατάσεις καὶ ἀπειλὰς αὐτοῦ δεδιότες
ἄκοντες φόβῳ νουθετοῦνται. μανθανέτωσαν οὖν
πάντες οἱ τοιοῦτοι τὰ ψευδῆ, δι' ὧν ὠφεληθήσον-
ται, εἰ μὴ δύνανται δι' ἀληθείας σωφρονίζεσθαι.
65   καὶ γὰρ τοῖς τὰ σώματα κάμνουσιν
ἐπισφαλῶς οἱ δοκιμώτατοι[2] τῶν ἰατρῶν τἀληθῆ
λαλεῖν οὐχ ὑπομένουσιν εἰδότες ἀθυμοτέρους μὲν
ἐκ τούτου γενησομένους καὶ οὐ ῥωσθησομένην[3]
τὴν νόσον, ἐκ δὲ τῆς τῶν ἐναντίων παρηγορίας
πραότερον τὰ ἐν χερσὶν οἴσοντας καὶ τὸ ἀρρώστημα
66 λωφῆσον. τίς γὰρ ἂν τῶν εὖ φρονούντων εἴποι
τῷ θεραπευομένῳ· ὦ οὗτος, τετμήσῃ, κεκαύσῃ,
ἀκρωτηριασθήσῃ, κἂν εἰ μέλλοι ταῦτ' ἐξ ἀνάγκης
ὑπομένειν; οὐδεὶς ἐρεῖ. προαναπεσὼν γὰρ τὴν
γνώμην ἐκεῖνος καὶ νόσον ἑτέραν τῆς ψυχῆς ἀργαλεωτέραν τῆς προϋπούσης τοῦ σώματος προσ-
[283] λαβὼν ἀπερεῖ πρὸς τὴν θεραπείαν, ἄσμενος | δὲ
ἐκ[4] τοῦ τὰ ἐναντία ἀπάτῃ τοῦ θεραπεύοντος προσ-
δοκῆσαι τλητικῶς πάνθ' ὑποστήσεται, κἂν ἀλ-
67 γεινότατα ᾖ τὰ σῴζοντα. γενόμενος οὖν τῶν τῆς

---

[1] mss. νομοθετῶν, which Adler would retain.
[2] mss. νομιμώτατοι.
[3] Perhaps, as Cohn suggests, omit οὐ—" the disease will
gain strength."

42

existence which we apprehend, and of what lies outside that existence nothing.   XIV. But 63
they whose natural wit is more dense and dull, or
whose early training has been mishandled, since they
have no power of clear vision, need physicians in the
shape of admonishers, who will devise the treatment
proper to their present condition. Thus ill-disciplined 64
and foolish slaves receive profit from a master who
frightens them, for they fear his threats and menaces
and thus involuntarily are schooled by fear. All
such may well learn the untruth, which will benefit
them, if they cannot be brought to wisdom by truth.
        Thus too in dealing with dangerous 65
sicknesses of the body,[a] the most approved physicians
do not allow themselves to tell the truth to their
patients, since they know that this will but increase
their disheartenment, and bring no recovery from
the malady, whereas under the encouragement, which
the opposite course of treatment gives, they will bear
more contentedly their present trouble, and at the
same time the disease will be relieved.
For what sensible physician would say to his patient, 66
" Sir, you will be subjected to the knife, the cautery
or amputation " even if it will be necessary that he
should submit to such operations. No one. For the
patient will lose heart beforehand, and àdd to the
existing malady of the body a still more painful
malady of the soul and break down when faced with
the treatment. Whereas if through the physician's
deceit he expects the opposite, he will gladly endure [b]
everything with patience, however painful the
methods of saving him may be. So then the lawgiver, 67

---

[a] See App. p. 485.   [b] See App. p. 486.

---

[c] Conj. Tr.: MSS. ἄσμενος ἐκ δὲ. See App. p. 486.

ψυχῆς παθῶν καὶ νοσημάτων ἄριστος ἰατρὸς ὁ
νομοθέτης ἓν ἔργον καὶ τέλος προύθετο, αὐταῖς
ῥίζαις τὰς τῆς διανοίας νόσους ἐκτεμεῖν, ἵνα μή τις
ὑπολειφθεῖσα βλάστην ἀρρωστήματος ἐνέγκῃ δυσ-
68 ιάτου. τοῦτον δὴ τὸν τρόπον ἤλπισεν ἐκκόψαι
δυνήσεσθαι, εἰ χρώμενον ἀπειλαῖς καὶ ἀγανακτήσεσι
καὶ ἀπαραιτήτοις ὀργαῖς, ἔτι δὲ ἀμυντηρίοις ὅπλοις
πρὸς τὰς κατὰ τῶν ἀδικούντων ἐπεξόδους εἰσαγάγοι
τὸ αἴτιον· μόνως γὰρ οὕτως ὁ ἄφρων νουθετεῖται.
69 παρό μοι δοκεῖ τοῖς προειρημένοις δυσὶ κεφαλαίοις,
τῷ τε " ὡς ἄνθρωπος " καὶ τῷ " οὐχ ὡς ἄνθρωπος
ὁ θεὸς " ἕτερα δύο συνυφῆναι ἀκόλουθα καὶ συγγενῆ,
φόβον τε καὶ ἀγάπην· τὰς γὰρ διὰ τῶν νόμων εἰς εὐσέβειαν ὁρῶ παρακελεύσεις ἁπάσας ἀναφερομένας
ἢ πρὸς τὸ ἀγαπᾶν ἢ πρὸς τὸ φοβεῖσθαι τὸν ὄντα.
τοῖς μὲν οὖν μήτε μέρος μήτε πάθος ἀνθρώπου
περὶ τὸ ὂν νομίζουσιν, ἀλλὰ θεοπρεπῶς αὐτὸ δι᾽
αὐτὸ μόνον τιμῶσι τὸ ἀγαπᾶν οἰκειότατον, φοβεῖσθαι
δὲ τοῖς ἑτέροις.
70   XV. Ἃ μὲν οὖν προκαταστήσασθαι τῆς ζητήσεως ἁρμόττον ἦν, τοιαῦτά ἐστιν. ἐπανιτέον δὲ
ἐπὶ τὴν ἐξ ἀρχῆς σκέψιν, καθ᾽ ἣν ἠπορoῦμεν,
τίνα ὑπογράφει νοῦν τὸ " ἐθυμώθην ὅτι ἐποίησα
αὐτούς." ἴσως οὖν τοιοῦτόν τι βούλεται παραστῆσαι, ὅτι οἱ μὲν φαῦλοι θυμῷ γεγόνασι θεοῦ, οἱ
δ᾽ ἀγαθοὶ χάριτι. καὶ γὰρ ἑξῆς φησι· " Νῶε δὲ
71 εὗρε χάριν." τὸ δὲ κυριολογούμενον ἐπ᾽ ἀνθρώπων
πάθος ὁ θυμὸς εὐθυβόλως[1] εἴρηται τροπικώτερον

---

[1] εὐθυβόλως is omitted in some mss. It may be merely an
addition to explain κυριολογούμενον.

---

[a] See App. p. 486.

thereby being now approved as the best of physicians for the distempers and maladies of the soul, set before himself one task and purpose, to make a radical excision of the diseases of the mind and leave no root to sprout again into sickness which defies cure. In this way he hoped to be able to eradicate the 68 evil, namely by representing the supreme Cause as dealing in threats and oftentimes shewing indignation and implacable anger, or again as using weapons of war for His onslaughts on the unrighteous. For this is the only way in which the fool can be admonished. And therefore it seems to me that with the two aforesaid maxims, " God is as a man," and " God is not as a man," he has linked two other principles closely connected and consequent on them, namely fear and love. For I observe that all the exhortations to piety in the law refer either to our loving or our fearing the Existent. And thus to love Him is the most suitable for those into whose conception of the Existent no thought of human parts or passions enters, who pay Him the honour meet for God for His own sake only. To fear is most suitable to the others.

XV. Such are the points which needed to be 70 established as preliminaries to our inquiry. We must return to the original question which caused us difficulty, namely, what thought is suggested by the words " I was wroth in that I made them." [a] Perhaps then he wishes to shew us that the bad have become what they are through the wrath of God and the good through His grace. For the next words are " but Noah found grace with Him " (Gen. vi. 8). Now the passion of wrath, which is properly speaking 71 an attribute of men, is here used in a more meta-

ἐπὶ τοῦ ὄντος εἰς τὴν ἀναγκαιοτάτου[1] πράγματος
δήλωσιν, ὅτι πάνθ' ὅσα δι' ὀργὴν ἢ φόβον ἢ λύπην
ἢ ἡδονὴν ἤ τι τῶν ἄλλων παθῶν πράττομεν,
ὑπαίτια καὶ ἐπίληπτα ὁμολογουμένως ἐστίν, ὅσα
δὲ μετ' ὀρθότητος λόγου καὶ ἐπιστήμης, ἐπαινετά.
72 ὁρᾶς ὅσῃ καὶ περὶ τὴν προφορὰν κέχρηται προ-
φυλακῇ, ὅτι " ἐθυμώθην, ὅτι ἐποίησα αὐτούς "
εἰπών, ἀλλ' οὐ κατ' ἀναστροφήν· διότι ἐποίησα
αὐτούς, ἐθυμώθην. τοῦτο μὲν γὰρ μετανοοῦντος
ἦν, ὅπερ ἡ τὰ πάντα προμηθουμένη θεοῦ φύσις
οὐκ ἀνέχεται, ἐκεῖνο δὲ δόγμα συνεκτικώτατον
εἰσηγουμένου, ὅτι πηγὴ μὲν ἁμαρτημάτων θυμός,
73 λογισμὸς δὲ κατορθωμάτων. μεμνημένος δὲ τῆς
περὶ πάντα τελείας ἀγαθότητος ἑαυτοῦ ὁ θεός, κἂν
τὸ σύμπαν ἀνθρώπων πλῆθος ἐξ ἑαυτοῦ δι' ὑπερβολὰς ἁμαρτημάτων περιπίπτῃ,[2] τὴν δεξιὰν καὶ
[284] σωτήριον χεῖρα ὀρέγων ὑπολαμβάνει | καὶ ἐξαν-
ίστησιν οὐκ ἐῶν εἰσάπαν φθαρῆναι καὶ ἀφανισθῆναι
74 τὸ γένος.   XVI. διὸ νῦν φησι τὸν Νῶε
χάριν εὑρεῖν παρ' αὐτῷ, ὅτε οἱ ἄλλοι φανέντες
ἀχάριστοι τίνειν μέλλουσι δίκας, ἵνα τὸν σωτήριον
ἔλεον ἀνακεράσηται τῇ κατὰ ἁμαρτανόντων κρίσει·
καθάπερ καὶ ὁ ὑμνῳδὸς εἶπέ που· " ἔλεον καὶ
75 κρίσιν ᾄσομαί σοι "· εἰ γὰρ βουληθείη ὁ θεὸς
δικάσαι τῷ θνητῷ γένει χωρὶς ἐλέου, τὴν κατα-
δικάζουσαν ψῆφον οἴσει μηδενὸς ἀνθρώπων τὸν
ἀπὸ γενέσεως ἄχρι τελευτῆς βίον ἄπταιστον ἐξ
ἑαυτοῦ δραμόντος, ἀλλὰ τὸ μὲν ἑκουσίοις, τὸ δὲ

---

[1] mss. ἀναγκαιοτάτην τοῦ.
[2] περιπίπτῃ suspectum: fortasse πίπτῃ (Wend.), but cf.
Thuc. ii. 65 αὐτοὶ ἐν σφίσι . . . περιπεσόντες ἐσφάλησαν.

---

[a] Or " (I will destroy him) because I was wroth in that I

46

phorical sense, yet still correctly, of the Existent, to bring out a vital truth, that all our actions by general consent are worthy of blame and censure, if done through fear or anger, or grief or pleasure, or any other passion, but worthy of praise if done with rectitude of reason and knowledge. Mark what 72 caution he shows in his form of statement. He says " I was wroth in that I made them," [a] not in the reverse order, " because I made them, I was wroth." The latter would show change of mind or repentance, a thing impossible to the all-foreseeing nature of God. In the former he brings before us a doctrine of great importance that wrath is the source of misdeeds, but the reasoning faculty of right actions. But God, 73 remembering His perfect and universal goodness, even though the whole vast body of mankind should through its exceeding sinfulness accomplish its own ruin, stretches forth the right hand of salvation, takes them under His protection and raises them up, and suffers not the race to be brought to utter destruction and annihilation. XVI. And therefore 74 it now says that when the others who had proved ungrateful were doomed to pay the penalty, Noah found grace with Him, that so He might mingle His saving mercy with the judgement pronounced on sinners. And so the Psalmist said somewhere (Ps. c. [ci.] 1), " I will sing to thee of mercy and judgement." For if God should will to judge the 75 race of mortals without mercy, His sentence will be one of condemnation, since there is no man who self-sustained has run the course of life from birth to death without stumbling, but in every case his foot-

made him," *i.e.* the first ὅτι may (1) introduce the quotation, or (2) be part of the quotation.

ἀκουσίοις χρησαμένου τοῖς ἐν ποσὶν ὀλισθήμασιν.
76 ἵν᾽ οὖν ὑπάρχῃ τὸ γένος, κἂν πολλὰ τῶν εἰδικῶν
βύθια χωρῇ, τὸν ἔλεον ἀνακίρνησιν, ᾧ πρὸς εὐεργεσίας καὶ τῶν ἀναξίων χρῆται, καὶ οὐ μόνον
δικάσας ἐλεεῖ, ἀλλὰ καὶ ἐλεήσας δικάζει· πρεσβύτερος γὰρ δίκης ὁ ἔλεος παρ᾽ αὐτῷ ἐστιν ἅτε
τὸν κολάσεως ἄξιον οὐ μετὰ τὴν δίκην, ἀλλὰ πρὸ
77 δίκης εἰδότι.   XVII. διὰ τοῦτο ἐν
ἑτέροις εἴρηται· " ποτήριον ἐν χειρὶ κυρίου, οἴνου
ἀκράτου πλῆρες κεράσματος· " καίτοι τό γε κεκραμένον οὐκ ἄκρατον. ἀλλ᾽ ἔχει λόγον ταῦτα φυσι-
κώτατον καὶ τοῖς προειρημένοις ἀκόλουθον· ὁ γὰρ
θεὸς ταῖς δυνάμεσι πρὸς μὲν ἑαυτὸν ἀκράτοις
χρῆται, κεκραμέναις δὲ πρὸς γένεσιν· τὰς γὰρ
ἀμιγεῖς θνητὴν ἀμήχανον φύσιν χωρῆσαι. ἢ νομί-
78 ζεις ἄκρατον μὲν τὴν ἡλίου φλόγα μὴ δύνασθαι
θεαθῆναι—σβεσθήσεται γὰρ πρότερον ἡ ὄψις μαρ-
μαρυγαῖς τῶν ἀκτίνων ἀμυδρωθεῖσα ἢ προσβάλ-
λουσα καταλήψεται· καίτοι καὶ ἥλιος ἕν ἦν ἔργον
θεοῦ, μοῖρα οὐρανοῦ, πίλημα αἰθέριον—, τὰς δὲ
ἀγενήτους ἄρα δυνάμεις ἐκείνας, αἳ περὶ αὐτὸν
οὖσαι λαμπρότατον φῶς ἀπαστράπτουσιν, ἀκράτους
79 περινοῆσαι δύνασθαι; ὥσπερ οὖν τὰς ἡλιακὰς
ἀκτῖνας ἔτεινε μὲν ἀπ᾽ οὐρανοῦ μέχρι τερμάτων
γῆς τὸ σφοδρὸν τῆς ἐν αὐταῖς θερμότητος ἀνεὶς
καὶ χαλάσας ἀέρι ψυχρῷ—τοῦτο γὰρ αὐταῖς
ἀνεκεράσατο, ὅπως τὸ αὐγοειδὲς ἀπὸ τοῦ φλογώ-
δους πυρὸς ἀνασταλέν, τὴν μὲν τοῦ καίειν μεθ-

ᵃ See App. p. 486.

steps have slipped through errors, some voluntary, some involuntary. So then that the race may sub- 76 sist, though many of those which go to form it are swallowed up by the deep, He tempers His judgement with the mercy which He shews in doing kindness even to the unworthy. And not only does this mercy follow His judgement but it also precedes it. For mercy with Him is older than justice, since He knows who is worthy of punishment, not only after judgement is given, but before it. XVII. And 77 therefore it is said in another place, " there is a cup in the hand of the Lord of unmixed wine, full of mixture " (Ps. lxxiv. [lxxv.] 8). But surely the mixed is not unmixed, and yet there is a meaning in these words most true to nature, and in agreement with what I have said before. For the powers which God employs are unmixed in respect of Himself, but mixed to created beings. For it cannot be that mortal nature should have room for the unmixed. We cannot look even upon the sun's flame un- 78 tempered, or unmixed, for our sight will be quenched and blasted by the bright flashing of its rays, ere it reach and apprehend them, though the sun is but one of God's works in the past, a portion of heaven, a condensed mass of ether.[a] And can you think it possible that your understanding should be able to grasp in their unmixed purity those uncreated potencies, which stand around Him and flash forth light of surpassing splendour ? When God extended the 79 sun's rays from heaven to the boundaries of earth, He mitigated and abated with cool air the fierceness of their heat. He tempered them in this way, that the radiance drawn off from the blazing flame, surrendering its power of burning but retaining that

49

ειμένον δύναμιν, τὴν δὲ τοῦ φωτίζειν περιέχον τῷ
ταμιευομένῳ ἐν ταῖς ὄψεσι συγγενεῖ αὐτοῦ καὶ
φίλῳ ὑπαντιάσαν ἀσπάσηται· ἡ γὰρ τούτων ἐξ
ἐναντίας εἰς ταὐτὸ σύνοδός τε καὶ δεξίωσις τὴν δι᾽
ὁράσεως ἀντίληψιν ἐργάζεται—, οὕτως ἐπιστήμην
θεοῦ καὶ σοφίαν καὶ φρόνησιν καὶ δικαιοσύνην
καὶ τῶν ἄλλων ἑκάστην ἀρετῶν τίς ἂν ἀκραιφνῆ
δέξασθαι δύναιτο θνητὸς ὤν; ἀλλ᾽ οὐδ᾽ ὁ σύμπας
80 οὐρανός τε καὶ κόσμος. εἰδὼς τοίνυν ὁ δημιουργὸς
τὰς περὶ αὐτὸν ἐν ἅπασι τοῖς ἀρίστοις ὑπερβολὰς
καὶ τὴν τῶν γεγονότων, εἰ καὶ σφόδρα μεγαλ-
[285] αυχοῖεν, φυσικὴν ἀσθένειαν οὔτε | εὐεργετεῖν οὔτε
κολάζειν ὡς δύναται βούλεται, ἀλλ᾽ ὡς ἔχοντας
81 ὁρᾷ δυνάμεως τοὺς ἑκατέρου μεθέξοντας. εἰ δὴ
τοῦ ἀνειμένου καὶ μεσότητας ἔχοντος τῶν δυνάμεων
αὐτοῦ κράματος ἐμπιεῖν καὶ ἀπολαῦσαι δυνηθεί-
μεν, ἀποχρῶσαν ἂν εὐφροσύνην καρπωσαίμεθα, ἧς
τελειοτέραν μὴ ζητείτω λαβεῖν τὸ ἀνθρώπων γένος·
ἐδείχθησαν γὰρ αἱ ἀμιγεῖς καὶ ἄκρατοι καὶ τῷ
ὄντι ἀκρότητες περὶ τὸ ὂν μόνον ὑπάρχουσαι.
82   XVIII. τοῖς δ᾽ εἰρημένοις ὅμοιόν ἐστι
καὶ τὸ ἑτέρωθι λεχθὲν '' ἅπαξ κύριος ἐλάλησε, δύο
ταῦτα ἤκουσα.'' τὸ μὲν γὰρ ἅπαξ ἔοικε τῷ ἀκράτῳ
—καὶ γὰρ τὸ ἄκρατον μονὰς καὶ ἡ μονὰς ἄκρατον—,
τὸ δὲ δὶς τῷ κεκραμένῳ· τὸ γὰρ κεκραμένον[1] οὐχ
ἁπλοῦν ἅτε καὶ σύγκρισιν καὶ διάκρισιν ἐπιδεχόμε-
83 νον. μονάδας μὲν οὖν ἀκράτους ὁ θεὸς λαλεῖ· οὐ
γάρ ἐστιν ὁ λόγος αὐτῷ γεγωνὸς[2] ἀέρος πλῆξις ἀνα-
μιγνύμενος ἄλλῳ τὸ παράπαν οὐδενί, ἀλλὰ ἀσώματός

---

[1] mss. ἑκάτερον γὰρ.   [2] mss. γεγονώς.

---

[a] See App. p. 486.
[b] E.V. '' God hath spoken once, twice have I heard this,''
50

of giving light, might meet and hail its friend and kinsman,[a] the light which is stored in the treasury of our eyes ; for it is when these converge to meet and greet each other that the apprehension through vision is produced. Just in the same way if God's knowledge and wisdom and prudence and justice and each of His other excellences were not tempered, no mortal could receive them, nay not even the whole heaven and universe. The Creator then, 80 knowing His own surpassing excellence in all that is best and the natural weakness of His creatures, however loud they boast, wills not to dispense benefit or punishment according to His power, but according to the measure of capacity which He sees in those who are to participate in either of those dispensations. If indeed we could drink and enjoy this diluted 81 draught, wherein is a moderate measure of His powers, we should reap sufficient gladness, and let not the human race seek a more perfect joy. For we have shewn that these powers at their full height unmixed and untempered subsist only in the Existent.

XVIII. We have something similar to 82 the above-mentioned words in another passage, " The Lord spake once, I have heard these two things " [b] (Ps. lxi. [lxii.] 11). For " once " is like the unmixed, for the unmixed is a monad and the monad is unmixed, whereas twice is like the mixed, for the mixed is not single, since it admits both combination and separation. God then speaks in unmixed 83 monads or unities. For His word is not a sonant impact of voice upon air, or mixed with anything else at all, but it is unbodied and unclothed and in

where " once, twice "=repeatedly. The LXX probably meant the same.

τε καὶ γυμνός, ἀδιαφορῶν μονάδος. ἀκούομεν δ'
84 ἡμεῖς δυάδι· τὸ γὰρ ἀφ' ἡγεμονικοῦ πνεῦμα διὰ τρα-
χείας ἀναπεμπόμενον ἀρτηρίας τυποῦται μὲν ἐν στό-
ματι ὥσπερ ὑπὸ δημιουργοῦ τινος γλώττης, φερόμενον δ' ἔξω καὶ ἀναμιχθὲν ἀέρι συγγενεῖ καὶ πλῆξαν
αὐτὸν τὴν δυάδος κρᾶσιν ἁρμονίως ἀποτελεῖ· τὸ γὰρ
συνηχοῦν ἐκ φθόγγων διαφερόντων δυάδι μεριστῇ τὸ
πρῶτον ἁρμόζεται ὀξὺν καὶ βαρὺν τόνον ἐχούσῃ.
85 παγκάλως οὖν τῷ πλήθει τῶν ἀδίκων
λογισμῶν ἀντέθηκεν ἕνα τὸν δίκαιον, ἀριθμῷ μὲν
ἐλάττονα δυνάμει δὲ πλείονα, ἵνα μὴ ταλαντεῦσαν
ὥσπερ ἐπὶ πλάστιγγος βρίσῃ τὸ χεῖρον, ἀλλὰ κράτει
τῆς ἐναντίας πρὸς τὸ βέλτιον ῥοπῆς ἀνακουφισθὲν
ἀσθενήσῃ.
86 XIX. Τί δέ ἐστι τὸ " Νῶε εὗρε χάριν ἐναντίον
κυρίου τοῦ θεοῦ," συνεπισκεψώμεθα· τῶν εὑρι-
σκόντων οἱ μὲν ἃ πρότερον ἔχοντες ἀπέβαλον
αὖθις εὑρίσκουσιν, οἱ δὲ ἃ μὴ πάλαι νῦν δὲ πρῶτον
περιεποιήσαντο. τουτὶ μὲν οὖν τὸ ἔργον εὕρεσιν,
ἐκεῖνο δὲ ἀνεύρεσιν οἱ ζητητικοὶ τῶν κυρίων
87 ὀνομάτων καλεῖν εἰώθασι. τοῦ μὲν οὖν
προτέρου παράδειγμα ἐναργέστατον τὰ περὶ τῆς
μεγάλης εὐχῆς διατεταγμένα. ἔστι δὲ εὐχὴ μὲν
αἴτησις ἀγαθῶν παρὰ θεοῦ, μεγάλη δὲ εὐχὴ
τὸν θεὸν αἴτιον ἀγαθῶν αὐτὸν ἀφ' ἑαυτοῦ
νομίζειν μηδενὸς ἑτέρου [τῶν] εἰς τὸ δοκεῖν
ὠφελεῖν συνεργοῦντος, μὴ γῆς ὡς καρποτόκου, μὴ
ὑετῶν ὡς σπέρματα καὶ φυτὰ συναυξόντων, μὴ

---

no way different from unity. But our hearing is the product of two factors, of a dyad. For the breath 84 from the seat of the master-principle driven up through the windpipe is shaped in the mouth by the workmanship, as it were, of the tongue, and rushing out it mixes with its congener the air, and impinging on it produces in a harmonious union the mixture which constitutes the dyad.[a] For the consonance[a] caused by different sounds is harmonized in a dyad originally divided which contains a high and a low pitch. Right well then did the lawgiver 85 act when he opposed to the multitude of unjust thoughts the just man as one—numerically less, but greater in value. His purpose is that the worse should not prove the weightier when tested as in the scales, but by the victorious force of the opposite tendency to the better cause should kick the beam and prove powerless.

XIX. Now let us consider what is meant by " Noah 86 found grace before the Lord God " (Gen. vi. 8). Finders sometimes find again what they possessed and have lost, sometimes what they did not own in the past and now gain for the first time. People who seek exactitude in the use of words are wont to call the process in the second case " finding " or " discovery " and in the first " refinding " or " recovery." We have a very clear example 87 of the former in the commandment of the Great Vow (Num. vi. 2). Now a vow is a request for good things from God, while a " great vow " is to hold that God Himself and by Himself is the cause of good things, that though the earth may seem to be the mother of fruits, rain to give increase to seeds and plants, air to have the power of fostering them,

PHILO

ἀέρος ὡς τρέφειν ἱκανοῦ, μὴ γεωργίας ὡς φορᾶς
αἰτίας, μὴ ἰατρικῆς ὡς ὑγείας, μὴ γάμου ὡς γε-
88 νέσεως παίδων. πάντα γὰρ ταῦτα δυνάμει θεοῦ
[286] μεταβολὰς | δέχεται καὶ τροπάς, ὡς τἀναντία πολ-
λάκις τοῖς ἐξ ἔθους ἀποτελεῖν. τοῦτον οὖν φησι
Μωυσῆς " ἅγιον " εἶναι, " τρέφοντα κόμην τρίχ-
κεφαλῆς," ὅπερ ἦν τὰς ἐν τῷ ἡγεμονικῷ τῶν ἀρετῆς
δογμάτων κεφαλαιώδεις ἀνατολὰς συναύξοντα καὶ
τρόπον τινὰ κομῶντα καὶ σεμνυνόμενον ἐπ' αὐ-
89 ταῖς. ἀλλ' ἔστιν ὅτε ἀπέβαλεν αὐτὰς αἰφνίδιον
κατασκήψαντος οἷά τινος τυφῶνος εἰς τὴν ψυχὴν
καὶ τὰ καλὰ πάντα αὐτῆς ἐξαρπάσαντος· ὁ δὲ
τυφὼν οὗτος τροπή τίς ἐστιν ἀκούσιος παραχρῆμα
90 τὸν νοῦν μιαίνουσα, ἣν καλεῖ θάνατον. ἀλλ' ὅμως
ἀποβαλὼν αὖθις καὶ καθαρθεὶς ἀναλαμβάνει καὶ ἀνα-
μιμνήσκεται ὧν τέως ἐπελέληστο, καὶ ἅπερ ἀπέβαλεν εὑρίσκει, ὡς τὰς προτέρας τῆς τροπῆς ἡμέρας ἀλόγους ἐξετάζεσθαι, ἢ διότι παράλογον ἡ
τροπὴ πρᾶγμα, ἀπᾷδον ὀρθοῦ λόγου καὶ φρονήσεως
ἀμέτοχον, ἢ παρόσον οὐκ ἔστιν ἀξία καταριθμεῖ-
σθαι· " τῶν γὰρ τοιούτων " ἔφη τις " οὐ λόγος οὐδ'
91 ἀριθμός."   XX. πολλάκις δὲ ἐνετύχομεν

---

^a The translation follows Mangey in omitting τῶν before
εἰς τὸ δοκεῖν ὠφελεῖν. This, however, is not quite satisfactory,
as εἰς τὸ δοκεῖν would naturally mean " as regards semblance."
Perhaps retain τῶν and for ὠφελεῖν substitute ὠφελίμων.

^b Literally "fostering the head's hair as long locks."
In the allegory the " head's hair " becomes the " growths of
truths," which are of the nature of heads or leading principles, and since κομᾶν, " to wear long hair," also means " to
be proud," κόμη is interpreted as the pride which we should
feel in virtue.   For further elucidation see App. p. 487.

^c In the original no doubt this means that as contact with

54

husbandry to be the cause of the harvest, medicine the cause of health, marriage of childbirth, yet nothing else is His fellow-worker that we may think of them as bringing us benefit.[a] For all these things, 88 through the power of God, admit of change and transition, so as often to produce effects quite the reverse of the ordinary. He who makes this vow then, says Moses, must be " holy, suffering the hair of his head to grow [b] " (Num. vi. 5). This means that he must foster the young growths of virtue's truths in the mind which rules his being ; these growths must be to him as it were heads, and he must take pride in them as in the glory of the hair. But sometimes he 89 loses these early growths, when as it were a whirlwind swoops suddenly down upon the soul and tears from it all that was beautiful in it. This whirlwind is a kind of involuntary defection straightway defiling the soul, and this he calls death (Num. vi. 9). He 90 has lost, yet in time, when purified, he makes good the loss, remembers what he had forgotten for a while, and finds what he has lost, so that the " former days," the days of defection, are regarded as not to be counted [c] (Num. vi. 12), either because defection is a thing beyond all calculation, discordant with right reason and having no partnership with prudence, or because they are not worthy to be counted. For of such as these there is, as has been said,[d] no count or number.   XX. On the other hand, it 91

the corpse cancels the vow, the days before the defilement must not be reckoned as part of the necessary period, and indeed Philo's Greek might be translated as " the days before the defection "; but the argument requires that the words should be taken as in the translation.

[d] A proverbial expression. *Cf.* Theocritus, *Id.* xiv. 48
ἄμμες δ' οὔτε λόγω τινὸς ἄξιοι οὔτ' ἀριθματοί.

τούτοις, ἃ μηδ᾽ ὄναρ πρότερον εἴδομεν· ὥσπερ
γεωπόνον φασί τινες ὑπὲρ τοῦ τι τῶν ἡμέρων
δένδρων φυτεῦσαι σκάπτοντα χωρίον θησαυρῷ
92 περιτυχεῖν ἀνελπίστῳ χρησάμενον εὐτυχίᾳ. ὁ γοῦν
ἀσκητὴς πυθομένου τοῦ πατρὸς αὐτοῦ τῆς ἐπιστήμης τὸν τρόπον τοῦτον· "τί τοῦτο ὃ ταχὺ εὗρες,
τέκνον;" ἀποκρίνεται καὶ φησιν· "ὃ παρέδωκε
κύριος ὁ θεὸς ἐναντίον μου." ὅταν γὰρ ὁ θεὸς
παραδιδῷ τὰ τῆς ἀιδίου¹ σοφίας θεωρήματα καμά-
του χωρὶς καὶ πόνου, ταῦτα ἐξαίφνης οὐ προσδοκή-
σαντες θησαυρὸν εὐδαιμονίας τελείας εὑρίσκομεν.
93 συμβαίνει δὲ πολλάκις τοῖς μὲν ἐπιπόνως ζητοῦσιν
ἀποτυγχάνειν τοῦ ζητουμένου, τοῖς δ᾽ ἄνευ φρον-
τίδος ῥᾷστα καὶ ἃ μὴ διενοήθησαν εὑρίσκειν· οἱ
μὲν γὰρ νωθέστεροι καὶ βραδεῖς τὰς ψυχὰς ὥσπερ
οἱ τὰ ὄμματα πεπηρωμένοι τὸν εἰς τὸ θεωρῆσαί
τι τῶν κατ᾽ ἐπιστήμην πόνον ἴσχουσιν ἀτελῆ, οἱ
δὲ φύσεως εὐμοιρίᾳ δίχα ζητήσεως μυρίοις ἐν-
έτυχον εὐθυβόλῳ καὶ εὐθίκτῳ χρησάμενοι προσβολῇ, ὡς δοκεῖν αὐτοὺς μὲν μὴ σπουδάσαι τοῖς
πράγμασιν ἐντυχεῖν, ἐκεῖνα δὲ μεθ᾽ ὁρμῆς προ-
απαντήσαντα εἰς ὄψιν ἐλθεῖν ἐπειχθῆναι καὶ τὴν
ἀπ᾽ αὐτῶν ἀκριβεστάτην ἐμποιῆσαι κατάληψιν.
94   XXI. τούτοις ὁ νομοθέτης
φησὶ δίδοσθαι "πόλεις μεγάλας καὶ καλάς, ἃς οὐκ
ᾠκοδόμησαν, οἰκίας πλήρεις τῶν ἀγαθῶν, ἃς
[287] οὐκ ἐνέπλησαν, λάκκους λελατομημένους, | οὓς οὐκ
ἐξελατόμησαν, ἀμπελῶνας καὶ ἐλαιῶνας, οὓς οὐκ
95 ἐφύτευσαν." πόλεις μὲν οὖν καὶ οἰκίας συμβολικῶς
τάς τε γενικὰς καὶ τὰς εἰδικὰς ἀρετὰς ὑπογράφει·

¹ mss. ἰδίου.

56

is a common experience that things befall us of which we have not even dreamt, like the story of the husbandman who, digging his orchard to plant some fruit-trees, lighted on a treasure, and thus met with prosperity beyond his hopes. Thus the Practiser, 92 when his father asked him in this manner of the source of his knowledge,[a] " What is this that thou hast found so quickly, my son ? " answered and said, " It is what the Lord God delivered before me " (Gen. xxvii. 20). For when God delivers to us the lore of His eternal wisdom without our toil or labour we find in it suddenly and unexpectedly a treasure of perfect happiness. It often happens that those 93 who seek with toil fail to find the object of their search, while others without thought and with the utmost ease find what had never crossed their minds. The slow-souled dullards, like men who have lost their eyesight, labour fruitlessly in the study of any branch of knowledge, while to others richly blessed by nature it comes unsought in myriad forms ; theirs is a ready and unfailing grasp ; it seems as though they trouble not to come in contact with the objects of their study, rather that these are impelled to take the lead and hurry to present themselves before the student's vision, and create in him the unerring apprehension which they have to give.

XXI. It is to these men that are given, in the law- 94 giver's words, " cities great and beautiful which they built not, houses full of good things which they did not fill, pits hewn out which they did not hew, vine-yards and olive-gardens which they did not plant " (Deut. vi. 10, 11). Under the symbol of cities and 95 houses he speaks of the generic and specific virtues.

* Or " the father of his knowledge." See App. p. 487.

πόλει μὲν γὰρ ἔοικε τὸ γένος, ὅτι κἂν μείζοσιν ἐξ-
ετάζεται περιγραφαῖς καὶ πλειόνων κοινόν ἐστιν, εἶδος
δὲ οἰκίᾳ τῷ συνῆχθαί τε μᾶλλον καὶ πεφευγέναι τὴν
96 κοινότητα. προητοιμασμένοι δὲ λάκκοι τὰ χωρὶς[1]
τῶν πόνων τούτοις πρόχειρα ἆθλα, οὐρανίων καὶ
ποτίμων δεξαμεναὶ ναμάτων, πρὸς φυλακὴν τῶν
προειρημένων ἀρετῶν εὐτρεπεῖς θησαυροί, ἐξ ὧν
εὐφροσύνη περιγίνεται ψυχῇ τελείᾳ φῶς τὸ ἀληθείας
ἀπαστράπτουσα. τοὺς μὲν οὖν ἀμπελῶνας εὐφροσύνης, τοὺς δ᾽ ἐλαιῶνας φωτὸς πεποίηται σύμβολον.
97   εὐδαίμονες μὲν οὖν οὗτοι, παραπλήσιόν
τι πάσχοντες τοῖς ἐκ βαθέος ὕπνου διανισταμένοις
καὶ τὸν κόσμον ἐξαίφνης ἀπόνως καὶ χωρὶς πραγ-
ματείας ὁρῶσιν, ἄθλιοι δὲ οἷς πρὸς ἃ μὴ πεφύκασιν
ἀντιφιλονεικεῖν συμβαίνει, ἔριδι, ἀργαλεωτάτῃ νόσῳ,
98 ἐπαιρόμενοι. πρὸς γὰρ τῷ τοῦ τέλους ἀποτυγχάνειν
ἔτι μετ᾽ οὐ μικρᾶς βλάβης μεγάλην αἰσχύνην
ὑπομένουσιν, ὥσπερ αἱ πρὸς ἐναντία πνεύματα
νῆες ἐνθαλαττεύουσαι· πρὸς γὰρ τῷ μὴ τυγχάνειν
ὑποδρόμων ἐφ᾽ οὓς ἐπείγονται, πολλάκις αὐτοῖς
πλωτῆρσι καὶ φορτίοις ἀνατραπεῖσαι λύπην μὲν
φίλοις, ἡδονὴν δὲ ἐχθροῖς ἐμπαρέσχον.
99 XXII. λέγει οὖν ὁ νόμος, ὅτι "παραβιασάμενοί
τινες ἀνέβησαν ἐπὶ τὸ ὄρος, καὶ ἐξῆλθεν ὁ Ἀμορ-
ραῖος ὁ κατοικῶν ἐν τῷ ὄρει ἐκείνῳ, καὶ ἐτίτρω-
σκεν αὐτούς, ὡς ἂν ποιήσειαν αἱ μέλισσαι, καὶ
100 ἐδίωξεν αὐτοὺς ἀπὸ Σηεὶρ ἕως Ἑρμᾶ," ἀνάγκη
γὰρ καὶ τοὺς ἀφυῶς ἔχοντας πρὸς τὰς τῶν

---

[1] MSS. ἑτέροις.

[a] For the symbolism of oil = light cf. Quod Det. 118.
[b] See App. p. 487.
[c] E.V. " were presumptuous." The LXX may have in-

For the genus resembles the city, because its limits
are marked out by wider circuits and it embraces a
larger number. The species on the other hand resembles the house, because it is more concentrated
and avoids the idea of community. The pits which 96
they find provided are the prizes ready to be won
without toil, cisterns of waters heavenly and sweet
to drink, treasure-cells fitly prepared to guard the
afore-mentioned virtues, from which is secured to
the soul perfect gladness shedding with its beams the
light of truth. And for that gladness and light he
gives us a symbol in the vineyards for the former, in 97
the olive-gardens *a* for the latter.   Happy
then are these, and their case is as the state of those
who waken from deep sleep, and suddenly without
toil or active effort open their eyes upon the world.
Miserable are those *b* whose lot it is to compete
earnestly for ends for which they were not born,
urged on by the grievous poison of contentiousness. 98
Not only do they fail to gain their end, but they
incur great shame and no small damage to boot.
They are like ships ploughing the seas in the face of
contrary winds ; for not only do they fail to reach
the roadsteads to which they press, but often they
capsize, vessel, crew and cargo, and are a source of
grief to their friends and joy to their foes.   99
XXII. So the law says that " some went up with
violence *c* into the mountain, and the Amorite who
dwelt in that mountain came out and wounded them,
as bees might do, and chased them from Seir to
Hormah " (Deut. i. 43, 44). For it must needs be that 100
if those, who have no aptness for the acquisition of

tended the same by παρα-. But Philo's argument turns entirely on " force " or " violence."

PHILO

τεχνῶν ἀναλήψεις, εἴ τι βιαζόμενοι πονοῖντο περὶ
αὐτάς, μὴ μόνον σφάλλεσθαι τοῦ τέλους, ἀλλὰ καὶ
αἰσχύνην ὀφλεῖν, καὶ τοὺς ἄλλο τι τῶν δεόντων
ἀσυγκαταθέτῳ γνώμῃ πράττοντας ⟨μὴ⟩ ἐθελουσίως
βιαζομένους δὲ τὸ παρ᾽ αὐτοῖς ἑκούσιον μὴ κατορθοῦν, ἀλλὰ πρὸς τοῦ συνειδότος τιτρώσκεσθαί
101 τε καὶ διώκεσθαι. καὶ τοὺς τὰς ὀλιγοχρημάτους
παρακαταθήκας ἀποδιδόντας ἐπὶ θήρᾳ στερήσεως
μειζόνων εἴποις ἂν πίστει διαφέρειν ⟨τῶν⟩¹ οἳ
καὶ ὅτε ἀπέδοσαν πολλὰ τὴν ἔμφυτον ἀπιστίαν
ἐβιάσαντο, ὑφ᾽ ἧς μήποτε παύσαιντο² κατακεν-
102 τούμενοι; θεραπείαν δὲ ὅσοι τοῦ μόνου σοφοῦ
νόθον ἐπετήδευσαν, ὥσπερ ἐπὶ σκηνῆς ἱερο-
πρεπεστάτην³ ἄχρι τοῦ μόνον ἐπιδείξασθαι τοῖς
συνεληλυθόσι θεαταῖς προαίρεσιν ἐνδύντες βίου,
βωμολοχίαν πρὸ εὐσεβείας ἐν τῇ ψυχῇ φέροντες,
οὐχ αὑτοὺς ὥσπερ ἐπὶ τροχοῦ κατατείνουσι καὶ
[288] βασανίζουσι | ἀναγκάζοντες ⟨μὴ⟩ ἐπιμορφάζειν ψευδῶς,
103 ἃ πρὸς ἀλήθειαν ⟨μὴ⟩ πεπόνθασι; τοιγάρτοι
βραχὺν χρόνον ἐπισκιασθέντες διὰ τῶν δεισιδαιμονίας συμβόλων, ἣ κώλυσις⁴ μέν ἐστιν ὁσιότητος,
μεγάλη δὲ καὶ τοῖς ἔχουσι καὶ τοῖς συνιοῦσι ζημία,
εἶτ᾽ αὖθις ἀπαμφιασάμενοι τὰ περίαπτα γυμνὴν
ἐπιδείκνυνται τὴν ὑπόκρισιν καὶ τότε ὥσπερ οἱ
ξενίας ἁλόντες νοθεύονται τῇ μεγίστῃ πόλεων
ἀρετῇ μηδὲν προσήκοντας ἑαυτοὺς παρεγγράψαντες.

¹ τῶν ins. Tr. See App. p. 488.
² Some mss. παύσοιντο. The opt. in either tense may be
explained as oratio obliqua dependent on εἴποις. But
παύσονται which Wend. conjectures would be more usual.
³ So Mangey: mss. and Wend. ἱεροπρεπεστάτης.
⁴ mss. κόλασις: conj. Cohn and Wend. κόλουσις, *i.e.*
mutilation.
60

the arts, use force or compel themselves to labour at them, they not only fail in their purpose, but also incur disgrace. Those, too, who perform any other right action without the assent of their judgement or will, but by doing violence to their inclination, do not achieve righteousness,[a] but are wounded and chased by their inward feelings. Would you say 101 there was any difference in the matter of honesty between those who repay an insignificant deposit in the hope of securing an opportunity to defraud on a larger scale, and those who actually make a large repayment but in doing so have to do violence to their natural inclination to dishonesty, which never ceases to prick them with the stings of regret? What of those who render an insincere worship to 102 the only wise God, those who as on a stage assume a highly sanctified creed and profession of life, which does no more than make an exhibition to the assembled spectators? Are not these men, whose souls are filled with ribaldry rather than piety, racking and torturing themselves as on the wheel, compelling themselves to counterfeit what they have never felt? And therefore, though for a short time 103 they are disguised by the insignia of superstition, which is a hindrance to holiness, and a source of much harm both to those who are under its sway and those who find themselves in such company, yet in course of time the wrappings are cast aside and their hypocrisy is seen in its nakedness. And then, like convicted aliens, they are marked as bastard citizens, having falsely inscribed their names in the burgess-roll of that greatest of commonwealths, virtue, to which they had no claim. For

[a] See App. p. 487.

τὸ γὰρ βίαιον ὀλιγοχρόνιον, ὡς καὶ αὐτό που δηλοῖ
τοὔνομα παρὰ τὸ βαιὸν εἰρημένον· βαιὸν δὲ τὸ
ὀλιγοχρόνιον ἐκάλουν οἱ παλαιοί.

104 XXIII. Τί δέ ἐστι τὸ " Νῶε εὗρε χάριν παρὰ
κυρίῳ τῷ θεῷ," διαπορητέον. ἆρ᾽ οὖν τοιοῦτόν
ἐστι τὸ δηλούμενον, ὅτι χάριτος ἔτυχεν, ἢ ὅτι
χάριτος ἄξιος ἐνομίσθη; ἀλλὰ τὸ μὲν πρότερον
οὐκ εἰκὸς ὑπονοεῖν· τί γὰρ αὐτῷ πλέον δεδώρηται
πάντων, ὡς ἔπος εἰπεῖν, ὅσα οὐ συγκέκριται μόνον,
ἀλλὰ καὶ στοιχειώδεις ἁπλαῖ φύσεις εἰσί, χάριτος
105 ἠξιωμένων θείας;   τὸ δ᾽ ὕστερον ἔχει
μέν τινα οὐκ ἀνάρμοστον λόγον, κρίνοντος τοῦ
αἰτίου δωρεῶν ἀξίους τοὺς τὸ θεῖον ἐν ἑαυτοῖς
νόμισμα, τὸν ἱερώτατον νοῦν, αἰσχροῖς ἐπι-
τηδεύμασι μὴ διαφθείροντας, ἴσως δὲ οὐκ ἀληθῆ.
106 πηλίκον γάρ τινα εἰκὸς γενέσθαι τὸν ἄξιον χάριτος
κριθησόμενον παρὰ θεῷ; ἐγὼ μὲν γὰρ ἡγοῦμαι
μόλις ἂν καὶ σύμπαντα τὸν κόσμον τούτου λαχεῖν·
καίτοι τό γε πρῶτον καὶ μέγιστον καὶ τελεώτατον
107 τῶν θείων ἔργων ἐστὶν οὗτος.   μήποτ᾽
οὖν ἄμεινον ἂν εἴη ἐκδέχεσθαι τοῦτο, ὅτι ζητητικὸς
καὶ πολυμαθὴς γενόμενος ὁ ἀστεῖος ἐν οἷς ἅπασιν
ἐζήτησε τοῦθ᾽ εὗρεν ἀληθέστατον, χάριν ὄντα θεοῦ
τὰ πάντα, γῆν, ὕδωρ, ἀέρα, πῦρ, ἥλιον, ἀστέρας,
οὐρανόν, ζῷα καὶ φυτὰ σύμπαντα. κεχάρισται
δὲ ὁ θεὸς αὐτῷ μὲν οὐδέν—οὐδὲ γὰρ δεῖται—,
κόσμον δὲ κόσμῳ καὶ τὰ μέρη ἑαυτοῖς τε καὶ
108 ἀλλήλοις, ἔτι δὲ τῷ παντί. οὐδὲν δὲ κρίνας ἄξιον
χάριτος ἄφθονα καὶ τῷ ὅλῳ καὶ τοῖς μέρεσι δεδώρηται τὰ ἀγαθά, ἀλλ᾽ ἀπιδὼν εἰς τὴν ἀίδιον

violence is short-lived, as the very name (βίαιον) seems to shew, since it is derived from βαιός; for that was the word used in old times for short-lived.

XXIII. But we must deal fully with the difficulty 104 in the words " Noah found grace with the Lord God." Is the meaning that he obtained grace or that he was thought worthy of grace ? The former is not a reasonable supposition. For in that case what more was given to him than to practically all creatures, not only those who are compounded of body and soul, but also simple elementary natures, all accepted as recipients of divine grace ?

The second explanation is founded on a not unreason- 105 able idea, that the Cause judges those worthy of His gifts, who do not deface with base practices the coin within them which bears the stamp of God, even the sacred mind. And yet perhaps that explanation is not the true one. For how great must we suppose 106 him to be, who shall be judged worthy of grace with God ? Hardly, I think, could the whole world attain to this, and yet the world is the first and the greatest and the most perfect of God's works.

Perhaps then it would be better to accept this ex- 107 planation, that the man of worth, being zealous in inquiring and eager to learn, in all his inquiries found this to be the highest truth, that all things are the grace or gift of God—earth, water, air, fire, sun, stars, heaven, all plants and animals. But God has bestowed no gift of grace on Himself, for He does not need it, but He has given the world to the world, and its parts to themselves and to each other, aye and to the All. But He has given His good things 108 in abundance to the All and its parts, not because He judged anything worthy of grace, but looking to

63

ἀγαθότητα καὶ νομίσας ἐπιβάλλον τῇ μακαρίᾳ
καὶ εὐδαίμονι φύσει ἑαυτοῦ τὸ εὐεργετεῖν. ὥστε
εἴ τίς μ' ἔροιτο, τίς αἰτία γενέσεως κόσμου, μαθὼν
παρὰ Μωυσέως ἀποκρινοῦμαι, ὅτι ἡ τοῦ ὄντος
[289] ἀγαθότης, ἥτις ἐστὶ | πρεσβυτάτη τῶν * * * χαρί-
109 των οὖσα ἑαυτῇ.¹ XXIV. παρατηρητέον
δ' ὅτι τὸν μὲν Νῶέ φησιν εὐαρεστῆσαι ταῖς τοῦ
ὄντος δυνάμεσι, κυρίῳ τε καὶ θεῷ, Μωυσῆν δὲ τῷ
δορυφορουμένῳ πρὸς τῶν δυνάμεων καὶ δίχα αὐτῶν
κατὰ τὸ εἶναι μόνον νοουμένῳ· λέγεται γὰρ ἐκ προσώπου τοῦ θεοῦ ὅτι '' εὕρηκας χάριν παρ' ἐμοί,''
δεικνύντος² ἑαυτὸν τὸν ἄνευ παντὸς ἑτέρου.
110 οὕτως ἄρα τὴν μὲν κατὰ Μωυσῆν ἄκραν σοφίαν
ἀξιοῖ χάριτος ὁ ὢν αὐτὸς δι' ἑαυτοῦ μόνου, τὴν
δὲ ἀπεικονισθεῖσαν ἐκ ταύτης δευτέραν καὶ εἰδι-
κωτέραν οὖσαν διὰ τῶν ὑπηκόων δυνάμεων, καθ'
ἃς καὶ κύριος καὶ θεός, ἄρχων τε καὶ εὐεργέτης
111 ἐστίν. ἕτερος δέ τις φιλοσώματος καὶ
φιλοπαθὴς νοῦς πραθεὶς τῇ ἀρχιμαγείρῳ τοῦ
συγκρίματος ἡμῶν ἡδονῇ καὶ ἐξευνουχισθεὶς
τὰ ἄρρενα καὶ γεννητικὰ τῆς ψυχῆς μέρη πάντα,
σπάνει κεχρημένος καλῶν ἐπιτηδευμάτων, ἀκοὴν
παραδέξασθαι θείαν ἀδυνατῶν, ἐκκλησίας τῆς ἱερᾶς
ἀπεσχοινισμένος ἐν ᾗ [σύλλογοι καὶ]³ λόγοι περὶ
ἀρετῆς ἀεὶ μελετῶνται, εἰς μὲν τὸ δεσμωτήριον τῶν

¹ Wend. suggests for the correction of this passage
πρεσβυτάτη τῶν ⟨θεοῦ δυναμέων, τῶν⟩ χαρίτων οὖσα πηγή. The
translator suggests and has rendered πρεσβυτάτη τῶν ⟨χαρίτων,
πηγή⟩ χαρίτων οὖσα αὐτή. See App. p. 488.
² mss. δεικνύς, which Cohn would retain, and correct λέγεται
to λέγει and ἑαυτὸν to αὐτόν.

His eternal goodness, and thinking that to be beneficent was incumbent on His blessed and happy nature. So that if anyone should ask me what was the motive for the creation of the world, I will answer what Moses has taught, that it was the goodness of the Existent, that goodness which is the oldest of His bounties and itself the source of others.

XXIV. But we must observe that he says that Noah 109 was well pleasing to the Potencies of the Existent, to the Lord and to God (Gen. vi. 8), but Moses to Him who is attended by the Potencies, and without them is only conceived of as pure being. For it is said with God as speaker, " thou hast found grace with Me " (Exod. xxxiii. 17), in which words He shews Himself as Him who has none other with Him. Thus, then, through His own agency alone does He 110 who IS judge the supreme wisdom shewn in Moses to be worthy of grace, but the wisdom which was but a copy of that, the wisdom which is secondary and of the nature of species, He judges as worthy through His subject Potencies, which present Him to us as Lord and God, Ruler and Benefactor.

But there is a different mind [a] which loves the body 111 and the passions and has been sold in slavery to that chief cateress (Gen. xxxix. 1) of our compound nature, Pleasure. Eunuch-like it has been deprived of all the male and productive organs of the soul, and lives in indigence of noble practices, unable to receive the divine message, debarred from the holy congregation (Deut. xxiii. 1) in which the talk and study is always of virtue. When this mind is cast

[a] See App. p. 488.

[b] See App. p. 488.

παθῶν εἰσάγεται, χάριν δὲ εὑρίσκει τὴν ἀτιμίας
112 ἀδοξοτέραν παρὰ τῷ ἀρχιδεσμοφύλακι. δεσμῶται
μὲν γὰρ κυρίως εἰσὶν οὐχ οὓς ἐν δικαστηρίῳ
καταδικασθέντας ὑπὸ κλήρῳ ἀρχόντων ἢ καὶ χειρο-
τονηθέντων δικαστῶν ἀπάγουσί τινες εἰς ἀποδεδειγ-
μένον χῶρον κακούργων, ἀλλ' ὧν ἡ φύσις κατ-
εδίκασε ψυχῆς τρόπων, οἵτινες ἀφροσύνης ⟨καὶ⟩
ἀκολασίας καὶ δειλίας καὶ ἀδικίας καὶ ἀσεβείας
113 καὶ ἄλλων ἀμυθήτων κηρῶν γέμουσιν. ὁ δὲ ἐπίτροπος καὶ φύλαξ καὶ ταμίας τούτων, ὁ ἡγεμὼν
τοῦ δεσμωτηρίου, σύστημα καὶ συμφόρημα κακιῶν
ἀθρόων καὶ ποικίλων εἰς ἓν εἶδος συνυφασμένων
ἐστίν, ᾧ τὸ εὐαρεστῆσαι μεγίστη ζημία· ἣν οὐχ
ὁρῶντες ἔνιοι, ἀπατώμενοι δὲ περὶ τὸ βλάπτον ὡς
ὠφελοῦν, προσίασί τε αὐτῷ μάλα γεγηθότες καὶ
δορυφοροῦσιν, ἵν' ὕπαρχοι καὶ διάδοχοι φυλακῆς
ἁμαρτημάτων ἀκουσίων τε καὶ ἑκουσίων πιστοὶ
114 κριθέντες γένωνται. ἀλλὰ σύ γε, ὦ ψυχή, τὴν
δεσποτείαν καὶ ἡγεμονίαν ταύτην ἀργαλεωτέραν
τῆς ἐπαχθοῦς δουλείας νομίσασα, μάλιστα μὲν
ἀδέσμῳ καὶ λελυμένῃ καὶ ἐλευθέρᾳ χρῆσαι προ-
115 αιρέσει τοῦ βίου· ἂν δ' ἄρα ἀγκιστρευθῇς ὑπὸ
πάθους, δεσμῶτις μᾶλλον ἢ εἰρκτοφύλαξ ὑπό-
μεινον γενέσθαι· κακωθεῖσα μὲν γὰρ καὶ στενάξασα
[290] ἔλεον εὑρήσεις, | σπουδαρχίαις δὲ καὶ λιμοδοξίαις
ὑποβαλοῦσα σαυτὴν ἡδὺ κακὸν τὸ εἰρκτοφυλακεῖν
καὶ μέγιστον ἀναδέξῃ, ὑφ' οὗ γενήσῃ πάντα
116 ἀγώγιμος τὸν αἰῶνα. XXV. τὰς μὲν οὖν παρὰ

into the prison of the passions, it finds in the eyes of the chief jailer a favour and grace, which is more inglorious than dishonour. For, in the true sense of 112 the word, prisoners are not those who after condemnation by magistrates chosen by lot, or it may be elected jurymen, are haled to the appointed place of malefactors, but those whose character of soul is condemned by nature, as full to the brim of folly and incontinence and cowardice, and injustice and impiety and other innumerable plagues. Now the over- 113 seer and warder and manager of them, the governor of the prison, is the concentration and congeries of all vices multitudinous and manifold, woven together into a single form, and to be pleasing to him is to suffer the greatest of penalties. But some do not see the nature of this penalty, but, being deluded into counting the harmful as beneficial, become right joyfully his courtiers and satellites, in the hope that having judged them to be faithful he may make them his subalterns and lieutenants to keep guard over the sins which are committed with the will or without it. My soul, hold such a mastery and cap- 114 taincy to be a lot more cruel than that slavery, heavy though it be. Follow indeed, if thou canst, a life-purpose which is unchained and liberated and free. But, if it be that thou art snared by the hook 115 of passion, endure rather to become a prisoner than a prison-keeper. For through suffering and groaning thou shalt find mercy ; but if thou put thyself in subjection to the craving for office or the greed of glory, thou shalt receive the charge of the prison, a pleasant task indeed, but an ill one and the greatest of ills, and its thraldom shall be over thee for ever. XXV. Put away then with all thy might what may 116

67

τοῖς ἀρχιδεσμοφύλαξιν εὐαρεστήσεις ἀνὰ κράτος
ἀπόθου, τῶν δὲ παρὰ τῷ αἰτίῳ διαφερόντως μετὰ
σπουδῆς τῆς ἁπάσης ἐφίεσο. ἐὰν δ᾽ ἄρα ἀδυνατῆς
—ὑπερβάλλον γὰρ τὸ τοῦ ἀξιώματος μέγεθος—,
ἴθι ἀμεταστρεπτὶ πρὸς τὰς δυνάμεις αὐτοῦ καὶ
τούτων ἱκέτις γενοῦ, μέχρις ἂν ἀποδεξάμεναι τὸ
συνεχὲς καὶ γνήσιον τῆς θεραπείας ἐν τῇ τῶν
εὐαρεστησάντων αὐταῖς κατατάξωσι χώρᾳ, καθάπερ
καὶ τὸν Νῶε, οὗ τῶν ἐγγόνων θαυμαστότατον καὶ
καινότατον πεποίηται τὸν κατάλογον·
117 φησὶ γάρ· '' αὗται αἱ γενέσεις Νῶε· Νῶε ἄνθρωπος
δίκαιος, τέλειος ὢν ἐν τῇ γενεᾷ αὐτοῦ· τῷ θεῷ
εὐηρέστησε Νῶε.'' τὰ μὲν γὰρ τοῦ συγκρίματος
γεννήματα πέφυκεν εἶναι καὶ αὐτὰ συγκρίματα·
ἵπποι γὰρ ἵππους καὶ λέοντες λέοντας καὶ βόες
ταύρους, ὁμοίως δὲ καὶ ἄνθρωποι ἀνθρώπους
118 ἐξ ἀνάγκης γεννῶσι· διανοίας δὲ ἀγαθῆς οὐ τὰ
τοιαῦτα οἰκεῖα ἔγγονα, ἀλλ᾽ αἱ προειρημέναι
ἀρεταί, τὸ ἄνθρωπον εἶναι, τὸ δίκαιον εἶναι, τὸ
τέλειον εἶναι, τὸ θεῷ εὐαρεστῆσαι· ὅπερ ἐπειδὴ
καὶ τελεώτατον ἦν καὶ ὅρος τῆς ἄκρας εὐδαιμονίας,
119 ἐφ᾽ ἅπασιν εἴρηται. γένεσις δὲ ἡ μὲν
ἀγωγὴ καὶ ὁδός τίς ἐστιν ἐκ τοῦ μὴ ὄντος εἰς τὸ
εἶναι—ταύτῃ φυτά τε καὶ ζῷα ἐξ ἀνάγκης ἀεὶ
χρῆσθαι πέφυκεν—ἑτέρα δ᾽ ἐστὶν ἡ ἐκ βελτίονος
γένους εἰς ἔλαττον εἶδος μεταβολή, ἧς μέμνηται
ὅταν φῇ· '' αὗται δὲ αἱ γενέσεις Ἰακώβ· Ἰωσὴφ
δέκα ἑπτὰ ἐτῶν ἦν ποιμαίνων μετὰ τῶν ἀδελφῶν
τὰ πρόβατα, ὢν νέος, μετὰ τῶν υἱῶν Βαλλᾶς καὶ

ᵃ Or (1) the honour which you seek ; (2) such a purpose
or ambition.

make thee well pleasing to the rulers of the prison, but desire exceedingly and with all zeal what may make thee pleasing to the Cause. But if so be that this is beyond thy powers—so vast is the greatness of His dignity [a]—set thy face and betake thee to His Potencies and make thyself their suppliant, till they accept the constancy and fidelity of thy service, and appoint thee to take thy place amongst those in whom they are well pleased, even as they appointed Noah; of whose descendants Moses has given a genealogy of a truly strange and novel sort.

For he says, "these are the generations of Noah. 117 Noah was a just man, perfect in his generation, Noah was well pleasing to God" (Gen. vi. 9). The offspring indeed of creatures compounded of soul and body, must also themselves be compound; horses necessarily beget horses, lions beget lions, bulls beget bulls, and so too with men. Not such are the offspring 118 proper to a good mind; but they are the virtues mentioned in the text, the fact that he was a man, that he was just, that he was perfect, that he was well pleasing to God. And this last as being the consummation of these virtues, and the definition of supreme happiness, is put at the end of them all.

Now one form of generation is the pro- 119 cess by which things are drawn and journey so to speak from non-existence to existence, and this process is that which is always necessarily followed by plants and animals. But there is also another which consists in the change from the higher genus to the lower species, and this it is which Moses had in mind when he says, "But these are the generations of Jacob. Joseph was seventeen years old, keeping sheep with his brethren, being still young, with the

μετὰ τῶν υἱῶν Ζελφᾶς τῶν γυναικῶν πατρὸς
120 αὐτοῦ·'' ὅταν γὰρ ὁ
ἀσκητικὸς καὶ φιλομαθὴς οὗτος λόγος ἀπὸ τῶν
θειοτέρων ἐννοημάτων εἰς ἀνθρωπίνας καὶ θνητὰς
δόξας καταβιβασθῇ, ὁ τοῦ σώματος καὶ τῶν περὶ
αὐτὸ χορευτὴς Ἰωσὴφ εὐθὺς ἀπογεννᾶται, νέος
ὢν ἔτι, κἂν μήκει χρόνου πολιὸς γένηται, πρεσβυτέρας οὔτε γνώμης οὔτε ἀκοῆς εἰσάπαν ἐπ-
ηρθημένος, ἣν οἱ Μωυσέως θιασῶται κατασταθέντες
κτῆμα καὶ ἀπόλαυσμα ὠφελιμώτατον ἑαυτοῖς τε
121 καὶ τοῖς ἐντυγχάνουσιν εὕραντο. διὰ τοῦτό μοι
δοκεῖ τὸν τύπον αὐτοῦ καὶ τὴν ἀκριβεστάτην τοῦ
χαρακτῆρος ἰδέαν βουλόμενος ἐκδηλοτέραν ἐγγράψαι
ποιμαίνοντα εἰσάγειν μετὰ γνησίου μὲν οὐδενός,
μετὰ δὲ τῶν νόθων ἀδελφῶν, οἳ παλλακίδων ὄντες
ἀπὸ τοῦ χείρονος γένους, τοῦ πρὸς γυναικῶν, ἀλλ'
οὐκ ἀπὸ τοῦ κρείττονος, τοῦ πρὸς ἀνδρῶν, χρη-
ματίζουσιν· υἱοὶ γὰρ τῶν γυναικῶν Βαλλᾶς καὶ
Ζελφᾶς, ἀλλ' οὐκ Ἰσραὴλ τοῦ πατρὸς νυνὶ καλοῦν-
ται.

122
[291] XXVI. Ζητήσαι δ' ἄν τις προσηκόντως, τίνος
ἕνεκα μετὰ τὴν ἐν ταῖς ἀρεταῖς τοῦ Νῶε τελείωσιν
εὐθὺς εἴρηται, ὅτι '' ἐφθάρη ἡ γῆ ἐναντίον τοῦ
θεοῦ καὶ ἐπλήσθη ἀδικίας.'' ἀλλ' ἴσως οὐ χαλεπὸν λύσεως εὐπορῆσαι τῷ μὴ σφόδρα παιδείας
123 ἀπείρῳ. λεκτέον οὖν ὅτι, ἐπειδὰν ἐν ψυχῇ τὸ
ἄφθαρτον εἶδος ἀνατείλῃ, τὸ θνητὸν εὐθέως φθεί-
ρεται· γένεσις γὰρ τῶν καλῶν θάνατος αἰσχρῶν
ἐπιτηδευμάτων ἐστίν, ἐπεὶ καὶ φωτὸς ἐπιλάμψαντος

sons of Bilhah and with the sons of Zelpah, his father's wives " (Gen. xxxvii. 2). For when this 120 reason, once so diligent of practice and filled with love of learning, is brought down from diviner concepts to human and mortal opinions, then at once Joseph is born, Joseph who follows in the train of the body and bodily things. He is still young, even though length of years may have made him greyheaded ; for never have there come to his knowledge the thoughts or lessons of riper age, which those who are ranked as members of the company of Moses have learnt, and found in them a treasure and a joy most profitable to themselves and to those who hold converse with them. It is for this reason, I think, 121 because he wished to portray Joseph's image and the exact form of his character in a clearer way, that Moses represents him as keeping sheep, not with any true-born brother, but with the base-born, the sons of the concubines, who are designated by the lower parentage, which is traced to the women, and not by the higher, which is traced to the men. For they are in this instance called the sons of the women Bilhah and Zilpah but not the sons of their father Israel.

XXVI. We may properly ask, why directly after 122 the recital of Noah's perfection in virtues, we are told that " the earth was corrupt before the Lord and filled with iniquity " (Gen. vi. 11). And yet perhaps save for one who is especially uninstructed it is not difficult to obtain a solution. We should 123 say then that when the incorruptible element takes its rise in the soul, the mortal is forthwith corrupted. For the birth of noble practices is the death of the base, for when the light shines, the darkness dis-

ἀφανίζεται τὸ σκότος.   διὰ τοῦτο
ἐν τῷ νόμῳ τῆς λέπρας ἀκριβέστατα διείρηται,
ὅτι "ἐὰν ἀνατείλῃ χρὼς ζῶν ἐν τῷ λεπρῷ, μιαν-
124 θήσεται." καὶ προσεπισφίγγων αὐτὸ τοῦτο καὶ
ὥσπερ ἐναποσημαινόμενος ἐπιφέρει "καὶ μιανεῖ
ὁ χρὼς ὁ ὑγιής," ἀντιτατόμενος τῷ εἰκότι καὶ
συνήθει· πάντες γὰρ οἱ ἄνθρωποι τὰ νοσοῦντα
φθορὰς τῶν ὑγιαινόντων καὶ τὰ νεκρὰ τῶν
ζώντων, οὐκ ἔμπαλιν τὰ ὑγιαίνοντα καὶ ζῶντα
125 τῶν ἐναντίων, ἀλλὰ σωτήρια νομίζουσι. καινό-
τατος δ' ἐν ἅπασι τὴν σοφίαν ὁ νομοθέτης ὢν καὶ
τοῦτο ἴδιον εἰσηγήσατο, διδάσκων ὅτι τὰ ὑγιαίνοντα καὶ ζῶντα τοῦ μὴ καθαρεύειν μιασμάτων
αἴτια γίνεται· τὸ γὰρ ὑγιαῖνον καὶ ζῶν ἐν ψυχῇ
χρῶμα ὡς ἀληθῶς φαινόμενον ἐπ' αὐτῆς ἔλεγχός
126 ἐστιν. οὗτος ὅταν ἀνάσχῃ, κατάλογον ποιεῖται
τῶν ἁμαρτημάτων αὐτῆς ἁπάντων, καὶ ὀνειδίζων
καὶ δυσωπῶν καὶ ἐπιπλήττων μόλις παύεται· ἡ
δ' ἐλεγχομένη γνωρίζει τὰ καθ' ἕκαστα, ὧν παρὰ
τὸν ὀρθὸν λόγον ἐπετήδευε, καὶ τότε ἄφρονα καὶ
ἀκόλαστον καὶ ἄδικον καὶ πλήρη μιασμάτων ἑαυτὴν
127 καταλαμβάνει.   XXVII. διὸ καὶ παραδοξότατον νόμον ἀναγράφει, ἐν ᾧ τὸν μὲν ἐκ
μέρους ὄντα λεπρὸν ἀκάθαρτον, τὸν δὲ ὅλον δι'
ὅλων ἀπὸ ἄκρων ποδῶν ἄχρι κεφαλῆς ἐσχάτης
κατεσχημένον τῇ λέπρᾳ καθαρόν φησιν εἶναι,

---

a E.V. "raw flesh"; χρώς can mean either "flesh" or
"colour." The lxx no doubt meant the former. Philo,
who in § 125 equates it with χρῶμα, took it as the latter.
b Variously translated as "Convictor," "Testing Power,"
"Challenger." It is almost equivalent to "Conscience";
compare the description in *Quod Det.* 23. Compare also

appears.   And therefore in the law of leprosy it is most carefully laid down, that if a living colour ^{a} arise in the leper, he shall be defiled (Lev. xiii. 14, 15). And by way of clinching this and so to 124 speak setting a seal upon it, he adds " and the healthy colour will defile him." This is quite opposed to the natural and ordinary view. For all men hold that things healthy are corrupted by things diseased, and living things by dead things, but they do not hold the converse, that the healthy and living corrupt their opposites, but rather that they save and pre-serve them. But the lawgiver, original as ever in his 125 wisdom, has here laid down something distinctly his own. He teaches us that it is the healthy and living which produce the condition which is tainted with pollution. For the healthy and living colour in the soul, when it makes a genuine appearance upon it, is Conviction.^{b} When this Conviction comes to the 126 surface it makes a record of all the soul's transgres-sions, and rebukes and reproaches and calls shame upon it almost without ceasing. And the soul thus convicted sees in their true light its practices each and all, which were contrary to right reason, and then perceives that it is foolish and intemperate and unjust and infected with pollution.

XXVII. For the same reason Moses enacts a law, 127 which is indeed a paradox, whereby he declares that the leper who is partially a leper is unclean, but that when the leprosy has taken hold of him through-out, from the sole of his foot to the crown of his head, he is clean (Lev. xiii. 11-13). One would

the functions of the Paraclete in John xvi. 8, where the R.V. gives for ἐλέγχει " convict," in the place of the " reprove " of the A.V.

τάχα ἄν τινος τὸ ἐναντίον, ὅπερ εὔλογον ἦν ὑπολαβεῖν, εἰκάσαντος, τὴν μὲν ἐσταλμένην καὶ περί τι
βραχὺ τοῦ σώματος λέπραν ἧττον ἀκάθαρτον, τὴν
δὲ κεχυμένην, ὡς ἅπαν περιλαβεῖν αὐτό, μᾶλλον.
128 δηλοῖ δ', ὡς ἔμοιγε φαίνεται, διὰ συμβόλων τούτων ἀληθέστατον ἐκεῖνο, ὅτι τὰ μὲν ἀκούσια τῶν
ἀδικημάτων κἂν ἐπιμήκιστα ὄντα ἀνυπαίτια καὶ
καθαρά, τὸ συνειδὸς βαρὺν κατήγορον οὐκ ἔχοντα,
τὰ δὲ ἑκούσια, κἂν μὴ ἐπὶ πλεῖστον ἀναχέηται
πρὸς τοῦ κατὰ ψυχὴν ἐλεγχόμενα δικαστοῦ, ἀνίερα
[292] καὶ μιαρὰ καὶ ἀκάθαρτα | δοκιμάζεται.
129 ἡ μὲν οὖν διφυὴς καὶ δύο ἐξανθοῦσα χρώματα
λέπρα τὴν ἑκούσιον ἐμφαίνει κακίαν· ἔχουσα γὰρ
ἡ ψυχὴ τὸν ὑγιαίνοντα καὶ ζωτικὸν καὶ ὀρθὸν ἐν
ἑαυτῇ λόγον τῷ μὲν οὐ χρῆται ὡς κυβερνήτῃ πρὸς
τὴν τῶν καλῶν σωτηρίαν, ἐκδοῦσα δ' αὑτὴν τοῖς
ναυτιλίας ἀπείροις ὅλον τὸ τοῦ βίου δὴ σκάφος ἐν
εὐδίᾳ καὶ γαλήνῃ δυνάμενον σῴζεσθαι περιέτρεψεν.
130 ἡ δ' εἰς ἓν εἶδος λευκὸν μεταβαλοῦσα τὴν ἀκούσιον διασυνίστησι τροπήν, ἐπειδὰν τὸ λογίζεσθαι ὁ
νοῦς ἐκμηθεὶς ὅλον δι' ὅλων, μηδενὸς τῶν εἰς τὸ
συνιέναι σπέρματος ὑπολειφθέντος, ὥσπερ οἱ ἐν
ἀχλύι καὶ σκότῳ βαθεῖ μηδὲν ὁρᾷ τῶν πρακτέων,
ἀλλ' οἷα τυφλὸς ἀπροοράτως πᾶσιν ἐμπίπτων
συνεχεῖς ὀλίσθους καὶ πτώματα ἐπάλληλα καὶ
131 ἀκούσια ὑπομένῃ.   XXVIII. τούτῳ
⟨δ'⟩ ὅμοιόν ἐστι καὶ τὸ περὶ τῆς οἰκίας διάταγμα,
ἐν ᾗ γίνεσθαι συμβαίνει λέπραν πολλάκις· φησὶ γὰρ
ὅτι " ἐὰν γένηται ἀφὴ λέπρας ἐν οἰκίᾳ, ἀφίξεται
ὁ κεκτημένος καὶ ἀναγγελεῖ τῷ ἱερεῖ λέγων· ὥσ-

ᵃ See App. p. 489.   ᵇ Or " symptom."

probably have conjectured the opposite, as indeed it would be reasonable to suppose that leprosy, if limited and confined to a small part of the body, is less unclean, but if diffused, so as to embrace all the body, is more unclean. But he is shewing, I think, 128 through these symbols (and a very true lesson it is), that such wrongdoings as are involuntary, however wide their extent, are pure and devoid of guilt, for they have no stern accuser in conscience, but voluntary sins, even though the space they cover be not large, are convicted by the judge within the soul and thus are proved to be unholy and foul and impure. Thus then the leprosy, which is 129 twy-natured and flowers into two colours, shews voluntary wickedness. For the soul has within it the healthy, lively upright reason, and yet it does not use it as its pilot [a] to guide it to the safety which things noble give, but abandons itself to those who have no skill of seamanship, and thus swamps utterly the bark of life which might have reached its bourn safely in calm and fair weather. But the leprosy 130 which changes into a single white appearance, represents involuntary error, when the mind is throughout reft of reasoning power, and not a germ is left of what might grow into understanding, and thus, as men in a mist and profound darkness, it sees nothing of what it should do, but, like a blind man tripping over every obstacle since he cannot see before him, it is subject to constant slips and repeated falls in which the will has no part. XXVIII. Similar 131 again is the enactment about the house in which leprosy is a frequent occurrence. For the law says that "if there is an infection [b] of leprosy in a house, the owner shall come and report it to the priest

75

περ ἀφὴ λέπρας ἑώραταί μοι ἐν τῇ οἰκίᾳ"· εἶτα
ἐπιφέρει· " καὶ προστάξει ὁ ἱερεὺς ἀποσκευάσαι
τὴν οἰκίαν πρὸ τοῦ εἰσελθόντα τὸν ἱερέα εἰς τὴν
οἰκίαν ἰδεῖν, καὶ οὐ γενήσεται ἀκάθαρτα ὅσα ἐν
τῇ οἰκίᾳ. καὶ μετὰ ταῦτα εἰσελεύσεται ὁ ἱερεὺς
132 καταμαθεῖν." οὐκοῦν πρὶν μὲν εἰσελθεῖν τὸν
ἱερέα, καθαρὰ τὰ ἐν τῇ οἰκίᾳ, ἀφ' οὗ δ' ἂν εἰσέλθῃ, πάντα ἀκάθαρτα· καίτοι τοὐναντίον εἰκὸς ἦν,
ἀνδρὸς κεκαθαρμένου καὶ τελείου, ὃς τὰς ὑπὲρ
ἁπάντων εὐχὰς ἀγιστείας ἱερουργίας εἴωθε ποιεῖσθαι, παρελθόντος εἴσω βελτιοῦσθαι τὰ ἔνδον[1] καὶ
ἐξ ἀκαθάρτων καθαρὰ γίνεσθαι· νυνὶ δὲ οὐδὲ ἐπὶ
τῆς αὐτῆς μένει χώρας, τρέπεται δὲ πρὸς μερίδα
τὴν χείρω κατὰ τὴν εἴσοδον τὴν τοῦ ἱερέως.

133   ἀλλὰ ταῦτα μὲν εἰ συνᾴδει τῇ ῥητῇ καὶ
προχείρῳ διατάξει, σκέψονται οἷς ἔθος καὶ φίλον·
ἡμῖν δὲ ἄντικρυς λεκτέον, ὅτι συνῳδὸν οὕτως οὐδὲν
ἄλλο ἄλλῳ, ὡς τὸ εἰσελθόντος τοῦ ἱερέως τὰ κατὰ
134 τὴν οἰκίαν μιαίνεσθαι. ἕως μὲν γὰρ ὁ θεῖος λόγος
εἰς τὴν ψυχὴν ἡμῶν καθάπερ τινὰ ἑστίαν οὐκ
ἀφῖκται, πάντα αὐτῆς τὰ ἔργα ἀνυπαίτια· ὁ γὰρ
ἐπίτροπος ἢ πατὴρ ἢ διδάσκαλος ἢ ὅ τι ποτὲ χρὴ
καλεῖν τὸν ἱερέα, ὑφ' οὗ νουθετηθῆναι καὶ σωφρο-
νισθῆναι μόνου δυνατόν, μακρὰν ἀφέστηκε. συγ-
γνώμη δὲ τοῖς δι' ἀμαθίαν ἀπειρίᾳ τῶν πρακτέων
ἁμαρτάνουσιν· οὐδὲ γὰρ ὡς ἁμαρτημάτων αὐτῶν
ποιοῦνται κατάληψιν, ἔστι δ' ὅτε κατορθοῦν ἐν

[1] MSS. ὄντα.

76

with the words ' what seems an infection of leprosy has appeared in my house,' " and then it adds " and the priest shall command that they empty the house, before the priest enters the house and sees it, and whatsoever is in the house shall not become unclean, and after that the priest shall go in to observe it " (Lev. xiv. 34-36). So then before the priest goes in, 132 the things in the house are clean, but after he has gone in they are all unclean. And yet we should have expected just the opposite, that when a man who has been purified and fully consecrated, who is wont to offer prayers and litanies and sacrifices for all men, has come within the house, its contents should thereby be bettered and pass from impurity into purity. But here we find that they do not even remain in the same position as before, but actually shift into the inferior region at the entrance of the priest.   Now whether in the plain and 133 literal sense of the ordinance these things are consistent with each other is a matter for those who are used to such questions and find pleasure in them. But *we* must say positively that no two things can be more consistent with each other than that, when the priest has entered, the belongings of the house are defiled. For so long as the divine reason has not 134 come into our soul, as to some dwelling-place, all its works are free from guilt, since the priest who is its guardian or father or teacher—or whatever name is fitting for him—the priest, who alone can admonish and bring it to wisdom, is far away. There is pardon for those whose sin is due to ignorance, because they have no experience to tell them what they should do. For they do not even conceive of their deeds as sins, nay often they think that their most grievous

77

135 οἷς πταίουσι μεγάλα νομίζουσιν. ὅταν δὲ εἰσέλθῃ
ὁ ἱερεὺς ὄντως ἔλεγχος εἰς ἡμᾶς ὥσπερ φωτός
[293] τις αὐγὴ | καθαρωτάτη, τηνικαῦτα γνωρίζομεν τὰ
ἐναποκείμενα ἡμῶν οὐκ εὐαγῆ τῇ ψυχῇ βουλεύματα
καὶ τὰς ἐπιλήπτους καὶ ὑπαιτίους πράξεις, αἷς
ἀγνοίᾳ τῶν συμφερόντων ἐνεχειροῦμεν. ταῦτ' οὖν
ἅπαντα ὁ ἱερωμένος ἔλεγχος μιάνας, ἀποσκευα-
σθῆναι καὶ ἀποσυληθῆναι κελεύει, ὅπως αὐτὴν
καθαρὰν ἴδῃ τὴν τῆς ψυχῆς οἰκίαν καί, εἴ τινες
ἐν αὐτῇ νόσοι γεγόνασιν, ἰάσηται.

136 XXIX. μεμίμηται δὲ τοῦτο καὶ ἡ ἐν ταῖς βασι-
λείαις ἐντυγχάνουσα τῷ προφήτῃ γυνὴ ⟨χήρα⟩·
χήρα δ' ἐστίν, οὐχ ἣν φαμεν ἡμεῖς, ὅταν
ἀνδρὸς ἐρήμη γένηται, ἀλλὰ τῷ χηρεύειν τῶν
φθειρόντων καὶ λυμαινομένων παθῶν τὴν διάνοιαν,

137 ὥσπερ καὶ ἡ παρὰ Μωυσῇ Θάμαρ· καὶ γὰρ ταύτῃ
προστέτακται χηρευούσῃ καθέζεσθαι ἐν τῷ τοῦ
μόνου καὶ σωτῆρος οἴκῳ πατρός, δι' ὃν ⟨εἰς⟩
ἀεὶ καταλιποῦσα τὰς τῶν θνητῶν συνουσίας καὶ
ὁμιλίας ἠρήμωται μὲν καὶ κεχήρευκεν ἀνθρωπίνων
ἡδονῶν, παραδέχεται δὲ θείαν γονὴν καὶ πληρουμένη
τῶν ἀρετῆς σπερμάτων κυοφορεῖ καὶ ὠδίνει καλὰς
πράξεις· ἃς ὅταν ἀποτέκῃ, τὰ κατὰ τῶν ἀντιπάλων αἴρεται βραβεῖα καὶ νικηφόρος ἀναγράφεται
σύμβολον ἐπιφερομένη φοίνικα τῆς νίκης· Θάμαρ
γὰρ ἑρμηνεύεται φοῖνιξ.

138 λέγει δὲ πρὸς τὸν προφήτην πᾶσα διάνοια χήρα
καὶ ἐρήμη κακῶν μέλλουσα γίνεσθαι· '' ἄνθρωπε
τοῦ θεοῦ, εἰσῆλθες πρὸς μὲ ἀναμνῆσαι τὸ ἀδίκημά
μου καὶ τὸ ἁμάρτημά μου.'' εἰσελθὼν γὰρ εἰς τὴν
ψυχὴν ὁ ἔνθους οὗτος καὶ κατεσχημένος ἐξ ἔρωτος

_____
[a] See App. p. 489.

78

stumblings are righteous actions. But when the true 135
priest, Conviction, enters us, like a pure ray of light,
we see in their real value the unholy thoughts that
were stored within our soul, and the guilty and
blameworthy actions to which we laid our hands in
ignorance of our true interests. So Conviction, discharging his priest-like task, defiles all these *a* and bids
them all be cleared out and carried away, that he
may see the soul's house in its natural bare condition,
and heal whatever sicknesses have arisen in it.

XXIX. We have a parallel to this in the widow in 136
the Book of Kings who discourses with the prophet
(1 Kings xvii. 10). She is a widow, not in our sense
of the word, when the wife has lost her husband,
but because she is widowed of the passions which
corrupt and maltreat the mind, like Tamar in the
books of Moses. Tamar was bidden to remain a 137
widow in the house of her father, her one and only
saviour (Gen. xxxviii. 11), for whose sake she has left
for ever the intercourse and society of mortals, and
remained desolate and widowed of human pleasures.
Thus she receives the divine impregnation, and, being
filled with the seeds of virtue, bears them in her
womb and is in travail with noble actions. And when
she has brought them to the birth, she wins the
meed of conquest over her adversaries, and is enrolled as victor with the palm as the symbol of her
victory. For Tamar is by interpretation a palm.

To return to the Book of Kings. Every 138
mind that is on the way to be widowed and empty
of evil says to the prophet, " O man of God, thou
hast come in to remind me of my iniquity and my
sin " (1 Kings xvii. 18). For when he, the God-
inspired, has entered the soul—he who is mastered

ὀλυμπίου καὶ διηρεθισμένος τοῖς τῆς θεοφορήτου
μανίας ἀκατασχέτοις οἴστροις μνήμην ἀδικημάτων
καὶ ἁμαρτημάτων ἀρχαίων ἐργάζεται, οὐχ ἵνα πάλιν
αὐτοῖς χρήσηται, ἀλλ᾽ ἵνα μέγα στενάξασα καὶ μέγα
κλαύσασα τὴν παλαιὰν τροπὴν τὰ μὲν ἐκείνης
ἔγγονα μισήσασα ἀποστραφῇ, οἷς δ᾽ ὑφηγεῖται ὁ
ἑρμηνεὺς τοῦ θεοῦ λόγος καὶ προφήτης ἔπηται·
139 τοὺς γὰρ προφήτας ἐκάλουν οἱ πρότερον τοτὲ μὲν
ἀνθρώπους θεοῦ, τοτὲ δὲ ὁρῶντας, κύρια ὀνόματα
καὶ ἐμπρεπῆ τῷ ἐπιθειασμῷ καὶ τῇ περιαθρήσει τῶν
πραγμάτων ᾗ ἐκέχρηντο τιθέμενοι.

140 XXX. Προσηκόντως οὖν ὁ ἱερώτατος Μωυσῆς
τότε φθείρεσθαι τὴν γῆν εἶπεν, ὅτε αἱ τοῦ δικαίου
Νῶε ἀρεταὶ διεφάνησαν· "ἦν δὲ" φησί "κατεφθαρ-
μένη, ὅτι κατέφθειρε πᾶσα σὰρξ τὴν ὁδὸν αὐτοῦ
141 ἐπὶ τῆς γῆς." δόξει μέν τισιν ἡ λέξις ἡμαρτῆσθαι
καὶ τὸ ἀκόλουθον τοῦ λόγου καὶ τὸ ἄπταιστον
οὕτως ἔχειν· ὅτι κατέφθειρε πᾶσα σὰρξ τὴν |
[294] ὁδὸν αὐτῆς· ἀνοίκειον γάρ ἐστι θηλυκῷ ὀνόματι,
τῇ σαρκί, ἀρρενικὴν ἐπιφέρεσθαι πτῶσιν, τὴν
142 αὐτοῦ. μήποτε δὲ οὐ περὶ μόνης σαρκός ἐστιν ὁ
λόγος τὴν αὐτῆς φθειρούσης ὁδόν, ἵνα εἰκότως
ἡμαρτῆσθαι τὰ περὶ τὴν λέξιν δοκῇ, ἀλλὰ περὶ
δυεῖν, σαρκός τε τῆς φθειρομένης καὶ ἑτέρου, οὗ
τὴν ὁδὸν λυμαίνεσθαί τε καὶ φθείρειν ἐπιχειρεῖ.
ὥσθ᾽ οὕτως ἀποδοτέον· κατέφθειρε πᾶσα σὰρξ τὴν
τοῦ αἰωνίου καὶ ἀφθάρτου τελείαν ὁδὸν τὴν πρὸς
143 θεὸν ἄγουσαν. ταύτην ἴσθι σοφίαν· διὰ γὰρ ταύτης
ὁ νοῦς ποδηγετούμενος εὐθείας καὶ λεωφόρου

by celestial yearning, stirred to his very depth by the irresistible goads of god-sent frenzy, he creates a memory of past iniquities and sins, and this not to the end that the soul should return to them, but that, with deep groaning and many tears for its old error, it should turn therefrom with loathing for all that it has engendered, and follow instead the guidance of that reason which is the interpreter and prophet of God. For the men of old days called the 139 prophets sometimes " men of God " and sometimes " seers " (1 Sam. ix. 9). And the names they gave were names of literal truth and well suited, the former to their inspiration, the latter to the wide vision of reality which they possessed.

XXX. Thus apt indeed are these words of Moses, 140 the holiest of men, when he tells us, that the earth was being corrupted at the time when the virtues of just Noah shone forth. But he goes on, " it was destroyed because all flesh destroyed his way upon the earth " (Gen. vi. 12). Some will think that we 141 have here a mistake in diction and that the correct phrase in grammatical sequence is as follows, " all flesh destroyed its way." For a masculine form like " his " (αὐτοῦ) cannot be properly used with reference to the feminine noun " flesh " (σάρξ). But perhaps 142 the writer is not speaking merely of the flesh which corrupts its own way, thus giving reasonable grounds for the idea of a grammatical error, but of two things, the flesh which is being corrupted, and Another, whose way that flesh seeks to mar and corrupt. And so the passage must be explained thus, " all flesh destroyed the perfect way of the Eternal and Indestructible, the way which leads to God." This way, 143 you must know, is wisdom. For wisdom is a straight

ὑπαρχούσης ἄχρι τῶν τερμάτων ἀφικνεῖται· τὸ δὲ
τέρμα τῆς ὁδοῦ γνῶσίς ἐστι καὶ ἐπιστήμη θεοῦ.
ταύτην τὴν ἀτραπὸν μισεῖ καὶ προβέβληται καὶ
φθείρειν ἐπιχειρεῖ πᾶς ὁ σαρκῶν ἑταῖρος· οὐδενὶ
γὰρ οὕτως οὐδὲν ἀντίπαλον ὡς ἐπιστήμῃ σαρκὸς
144 ἡδονή.¹ βουλομένοις γοῦν ταύτην πορεύεσθαι τὴν
ὁδὸν βασιλικὴν οὖσαν τοῖς τοῦ ὁρατικοῦ γένους
μετέχουσιν, ὅπερ Ἰσραὴλ κέκληται, διαμάχεται ὁ
γήινος Ἐδώμ—τοῦτο γὰρ διερμηνευθεὶς ὀνομάζεται
—μετὰ σπουδῆς καὶ παρασκευῆς τῆς πάσης εἴρξειν
ἀπειλῶν τῆς ὁδοῦ καὶ ἀτριβῆ καὶ ἀπόρευτιν
145 αὐτὴν κατασκευάσειν εἰσάπαν.   XXXI.
οἱ μὲν οὖν πεμφθέντες πρέσβεις λέγουσι ταῦτα·
" παρελευσόμεθα διὰ τῆς γῆς σου· οὐ διελευσόμεθα
δι' ἀγρῶν, οὐ δι' ἀμπελώνων, οὐ πιόμεθα ὕδωρ
λάκκου σου. ὁδῷ βασιλικῇ πορευσόμεθα· οὐκ
ἐκκλινοῦμεν δεξιὰ οὐδὲ εὐώνυμα, ἕως ἂν παρέλθω-
μέν σου τὰ ὅρια." ὁ δὲ Ἐδὼμ ἀποκρίνεται φάσκων·
" οὐ διελεύσῃ² δι' ἐμοῦ· εἰ δὲ μή, ἐν πολέμῳ ἐξελεύσομαί σοι εἰς συνάντησιν." καὶ λέγουσιν αὐτῷ οἱ
υἱοὶ Ἰσραήλ· " παρὰ τὸ ὄρος παρελευσόμεθα.³ ἐὰν
δὲ τοῦ ὕδατός σου πίω ἐγώ τε καὶ τὰ κτήνη, δώσω
σοι τιμήν· ἀλλὰ τὸ πρᾶγμα οὐδέν ἐστι, παρὰ τὸ
ὄρος παρελευσόμεθα." ὁ δὲ εἶπεν· " οὐ διελεύσῃ δι'
146 ἐμοῦ."   τῶν παλαιῶν τινα λόγος ἔχει
θεασάμενον ἐσταλμένην πολυτελῆ πομπὴν πρός

¹ Conj. Mangey : mss. and Wend. ἐπιστήμῃ . . . ἡδονῇ.
² mss. παρελεύσῃ.   ³ mss. διελευσόμεθα.

ᵃ E.V. " Let me, *without doing anything else*, pass through

high road, and it is when the mind's course is guided along that road that it reaches the goal which is the recognition and knowledge of God. Every comrade of the flesh hates and rejects this path and seeks to corrupt it. For there are no two things so utterly opposed as knowledge and pleasure of the flesh. Thus those who are members of that race endowed 144 with vision, which is called Israel, when they wish to journey along that royal road, find their way contested by Edom the earthly one—for such is the interpretation of his name—who, all alert and prepared at every point, threatens to bar them from the road and to render it such that none at all shall tread or travel on it. XXXI. The envoys 145 then who are dispatched to him speak thus, " We will pass by through thy land. We will not go through the cornfields nor through the vineyards. We will not drink water of any well of thine. We will journey by the king's way. We will not turn aside to the right or the left, till we have passed thy boundaries." But Edom answers, saying, " Thou shalt not pass through me, else I will come out in war to meet thee." And the sons of Israel say to him, " We will pass along the mountain country. But if I and my cattle drink of thy water, I will give thee value. But the matter is nothing, we will pass along the mountain country " (Num. xx. 17-20).[a] But he said, " Thou shalt not go through me." There is 146 a story that one [b] of the ancients beholding a gaily decked and costly pageant turned to some of his

on my feet." The LXX presumably meant " the thing which I ask is a trifle." Philo's interpretation of the words is given in § 171.

[b] Socrates. The story is told with some variations by Cic. *Tusc.* v. 91, and Diog. Laert. ii. 25.

τινας τῶν γνωρίμων ἀπιδόντα εἰπεῖν· "ὦ ἑταῖροι,
ἴδετε ὅσων χρείαν οὐκ ἔχω," διὰ βραχείας φωνῆς
μέγιστον καὶ οὐράνιον ὡς ἀληθῶς ἐπάγγελμα αὐχή-
147 σαντα. τί λέγεις; τὸν Ὀλυμπιακὸν ἀγῶνα κατὰ
τοῦ πλούτου παντὸς ἐστεφάνωσαι καὶ τῶν ἐν αὐτῷ
κεκράτηκας οὕτως, ὡς μηδὲν εἰς ἀπόλαυσίν τε καὶ
χρῆσιν τῶν ἀπ' αὐτοῦ παραδέχεσθαι; θαυμάσιος μὲν
ὁ λόγος, πολὺ δ' ἡ γνώμη θαυμασιωτέρα τοσοῦτον
πρὸς ἰσχὺν ἐπιδεδωκυῖα, ὡς ἤδη καὶ ἀκονιτὶ δύνα-
148 σθαι νικᾶν ἀνὰ κράτος.   XXXII. ἀλλ' οὐχ ἑνὶ
ἀνδρὶ ἔξεστι μόνον αὐχῆσαι παρὰ Μωυσῇ τὰ προ-
[295] τέλεια τῆς σοφίας ἀναδιδαχθέντι, ἀλλὰ | καὶ ὅλῳ
ἔθνει πολυανθρωποτάτῳ. τεκμήριον δέ· τεθάρρηκε
καὶ ἐπιτετόλμηκεν ἡ ἑκάστου ψυχὴ τῶν γνωρίμων
αὐτοῦ πρὸς τὸν βασιλέα τῶν φαινομένων ἁπάντων
ἀγαθῶν τὸν γήινον Ἐδὼμ—ὄντως γὰρ τὰ τῷ δοκεῖν
ἀγαθὰ πάντα γήινα—λέγειν· "ἤδη παρελεύσομαι διὰ
149 τῆς γῆς σου." ὦ ὑπερφυεστάτης καὶ μεγαλοπρεποῦς
ὑποσχέσεως. πάντα, εἴπατέ μοι, ὑπερβῆναι παρελθεῖν παραδραμεῖν τὰ φαινόμενα καὶ νομιζόμενα
γῆς [ὄντα] ἀγαθὰ δυνήσεσθε; καὶ οὐδὲν ἄρα τὴν
εἰς τὸ πρόσω ὑμῶν ὁρμὴν ἀντιβιασάμενον ἐφέξει
150 καὶ στήσει; ἀλλὰ τοὺς μὲν τοῦ πλούτου θησαυροὺς
ἅπαντας ἑξῆς πλήρεις ἰδόντες ἀποστραφήσεσθε καὶ
ἀποκλινεῖτε τὰς ὄψεις, τὰ δὲ τῶν προγόνων ἀξιώ-
ματα τῶν πρὸς πατρὸς καὶ μητρὸς καὶ τὰς ᾀδομένας
παρὰ τοῖς πολλοῖς εὐγενείας ὑπερκύψετε; δόξαν
δέ, ἧς ἀντικαταλλάττονται πάντα ἄνθρωποι, κατόπιν ὥσπερ τι τῶν ἀτιμοτάτων ἀπολείψετε; τί

disciples and said to them, " My friends, observe how many things there are I do not need." And the vaunt conveyed in this short utterance is a great and truly heaven-sent profession. " What is it you say ? " we ask him. " Have you won the Olympic crown 147 of victory over all wealth, and so risen superior to all that wealth involves, that you accept nothing of what it brings for your use and enjoyment ? " A wonderful saying ! And yet far more wonderful is the resolution which has grown so strong, that now it need exert no effort to win its complete victory. XXXII. But in the school of Moses it is not one 148 man only who may boast that he has learnt the first elements of wisdom, but a whole nation, a mighty people. And we have a proof thereof in these words of the envoys. The soul of every one of his disciples has taken heart and courage to say to the king of all that is good in outward appearance, the earthly Edom (for indeed all things whose goodness lies in mere seeming are of earth), " I will now pass by through thy land " (or " earth "). What a stupendous, 149 what a magnificent promise ! Will you indeed be able, tell me, to step, to travel, to speed past and over those things of earth which appear and are reckoned good? And will nothing, then, that opposes your onward march stay or arrest its course ? Will 150 you see all the treasuries of wealth, one after the other, full to the brim, yet turn aside from them and avert your eyes ? Will you take no heed of the honours of high ancestry on either side, or the pride of noble birth, which the multitude so extol ? Will you leave glory behind you, glory, for which men barter their all, and treat it as though it were a worthless trifle ? Will you pass unregarded the

δέ; ὑγείαν σώματος καὶ αἰσθήσεων ἀκρίβειαν καὶ κάλλος περιμάχητον καὶ ῥώμην ἀνανταγώνιστον καὶ τἆλλα ὅσοις ὁ τῆς ψυχῆς οἶκος ἢ τύμβος ἢ ὁτιοῦν χρὴ καλεῖν κεκόσμηται παραδραμεῖσθε, ὡς μηδὲν αὐτῶν κατατάξαι ἐν τῇ τῶν ἀγαθῶν μερίδι,

151 ὀλυμπίου καὶ οὐρανίου ταῦτα ψυχῆς τὰ μεγάλα τολμήματα τὸν μὲν περίγειον χῶρον ἀπολελοιπυίας, ἀνειλκυσμένης δὲ καὶ μετὰ τῶν θείων φύσεων διαιτωμένης· θέας γὰρ ἐμπιπλαμένη τῶν γνησίων καὶ ἀφθάρτων ἀγαθῶν εἰκότως τοῖς ἐφημέροις καὶ

152 νόθοις ἀποτάττεται.   XXXIII. τί οὖν ὄφελος παρελθεῖν πάντα τὰ θνητῶν θνητὰ ἀγαθά, παρελθεῖν δὲ μὴ σὺν ὀρθῷ λόγῳ, ἀλλ' ὡς ἔνιοι δι' ὄκνον ἢ ῥᾳθυμίαν ἢ ἀπειρίαν ἐκείνων; οὐ γὰρ πανταχοῦ πάντα, ἄλλα δὲ παρ' ἄλλοις τετίμηται.

153 τούτου χάριν βουλόμενος τὸ μετ' ὀρθότητος λόγου καταφρονητικοὺς τῶν εἰρημένων γενέσθαι παραστῆσαι τῷ " παρελεύσομαι " προστίθησι τὸ " διὰ τῆς γῆς σου "· τοῦτο γὰρ τὸ ἀναγκαιότατον ἦν, γενομένους ἐν ἀφθόνοις τῶν φαινομένων ἀγαθῶν ὕλαις ἁπάσαις ὑπὸ μηδενὸς τῶν προβληθέντων ὑφ' ἑκάστης δικτύων ἁλῶναι, πυρὸς μέντοι τὸν τρόπον ἰσχῦσαι ῥύμῃ μιᾷ τὰς ἐπαλλήλους καὶ

154 συνεχεῖς φορὰς διακλάσαι.   διὰ μὲν δὴ τούτων φασὶ " παρελεύσεσθαι," διὰ δὲ " ἀγρῶν καὶ ἀμπελώνων " οὐκέτι· τὰ γὰρ ἥμερα ἐν ψυχῇ φυτὰ ἡμέρους ἀποτίκτοντα καρπούς, ἀστείους μὲν

ᵃ i.e. they use διελευσόμεθα, which Philo takes to mean " to travel through " (at leisure) in contrast to παρελευσόμεθα " to pass through " (without stopping).

health of the body, the keenness of the senses, the coveted gift of beauty, the strength which defies opponents, and whatever else serves to adorn our soul's house, or tomb, or what other name it may be given, and rank none of them as belonging to the province of the good ? Great ventures such 151 as these betoken a celestial and heavenly soul, which has left the region of the earth, has been drawn upwards, and dwells with divine natures. For when it takes its fill of the vision of good incorruptible and genuine, it bids farewell to the good which is transient and spurious. XXXIII. Now 152 what can it profit us to pass by all the good things which are mortal as their possessors are mortal, if we pass them by not under the guidance of right reason, but as some do through faint-heartedness or indolence or inexperience of them ? For they are not all held in honour everywhere, but some value these, others those. And therefore to bring home to 153 us that it is under the guidance of right reason that we should grow to despise these things which I have named, he adds to the words " I will pass by " these others " through thy land." For this he knew was the most vital thing of all, that we should see our-selves surrounded by a rich abundance of all that goes to provide these seeming forms of good, and yet be caught by none of the snares which each flings before us, but be nerved to break like fire with a single rush through their successive and ceaseless onslaughts. Through these then, 154 they say, they will pass by. But they do not use the phrase " pass by " *a* of the fields and vineyards. For it would be monstrous folly to pass by the plants within the soul, whose fruit is kindly as themselves,

λόγους, ἐπαινετὰς δὲ πράξεις, ὠγύγιος[1] εὐήθεια
παρέρχεσθαι· μένειν γὰρ ἔδει καὶ δρέπεσθαι καὶ
ἀπλήστως ἐμφορεῖσθαι· κάλλιστον γὰρ ἡ ἐν
ἀρεταῖς τελείαις ἀκόρεστος εὐφροσύνη, ἧς οἱ
λεχθέντες ἀμπελῶνες σύμβολα.

155 | Οἷς δ' ὁ θεὸς ἐπινίφει καὶ ἐπομβρεῖ τὰς ἀγαθῶν
[296] πηγὰς ἄνωθεν, ἐκ λάκκου πίνομεν καὶ βραχείας
[καὶ] κατὰ γῆς λιβάδας ἀναζητοῦμεν, ὕοντος ἡμῖν
ἀνεπισχέτως οὐρανοῦ τὴν νέκταρος καὶ ἀμβροσίας
156 τῶν μεμυθευμένων ἀμείνω τροφήν; XXXIV.
ἔτι δὲ ποτὸν τεθησαυρισμένον ἐξ ἐπιτεχνήσεως
ἀνθρώπων ἐξανιμῶντες ὑπόδρομον καὶ καταφυγὴν
δυσελπιστίας ἔργον προσιέμεθα, οἷς τὸν ὀλύμπιον
θησαυρὸν εἰς χρῆσιν καὶ ἀπόλαυσιν ὁ σωτὴρ τοῦ
παντὸς ἤνοιξεν· εὔχεται γὰρ Μωυσῆς ὁ ἱερο-
φάντης, ἵνα " ἀνοίξῃ κύριος ἡμῖν τὸν θησαυρὸν
αὑτοῦ τὸν ἀγαθόν, τὸν οὐρανόν, δοῦναι ὑετόν·"
157 ἐπήκοοι δὲ αἱ τοῦ θεοφιλοῦς εὐχαί. τί δ'; ὁ
μηδ' οὐρανὸν ἢ ὑετὸν ἢ λάκκον[2] ἢ συνόλως τι τῶν
ἐν γενέσει νομίσας ἱκανὸν εἶναι τρέφειν ἑαυτόν,
ὑπερβὰς δὲ ταῦτα πάντα καὶ ὃ ἔπαθεν εἰπὼν " ὁ
θεὸς ὁ τρέφων με ἐκ νεότητος " ἆρα οὐ δοκεῖ σοι
πάντα ὅσα κατὰ γῆς ὕδατος συστήματα μηδ' ἂν
158 ἀξιῶσαι προσιδεῖν; οὐκ ἂν οὖν ἐκ λάκκου πίοι,
ᾧ δίδωσιν ὁ θεὸς τὰς ἀκράτους μεθύσματος πόσεις,
τοτὲ μὲν διά τινος ὑπηρετοῦντος τῶν ἀγγέλων, ὃν
οἰνοχοεῖν ἠξίωσε, τοτὲ δὲ καὶ δι' ἑαυτοῦ, μηδένα
τοῦ διδόντος καὶ τοῦ λαμβάνοντος μεταξὺ τιθείς.

---

[1] The transference of the meaning of ὠγύγιος from " prim-
eval " or " venerable " to " vast " (also found in *De Post.* 168)
is difficult. Mangey suggested in both διωλύγιος, *cf.* διωλύγιος
φλυαρία, Plato, *Theaet.* 161 D.
[2] mss. λόγον.

even worthy sayings and laudable actions. Rather it were well to stay and pluck them and feast upon them with the hunger that is never filled. For truly beautiful is that insatiable joy which the perfect virtues give, and of this the vineyards here mentioned are symbolic.

Again, shall we on whom God pours as in snow or rain-shower the fountains of His blessings from above, 155 drink of a well and seek for the scanty springs that lie beneath the earth, when heaven rains upon us ceaselessly the nourishment which is better than the nectar and ambrosia of the myths ? XXXIV. Or shall we draw up with ropes the drink which has 156 been stored by the devices of men and accept as our haven and refuge a task which argues our lack of true hope ; we to whom the Saviour of all has opened His celestial treasure for our use and enjoyment ? [a] For Moses the revealer prays that the Lord may open to us His good treasure, the heaven, to give us rain (Deut. xxviii. 12), and the prayers of him whom God loves are always heard. Or again, what of that Israel who thought that neither heaven 157 nor rainfall or well, or any created thing at all, was able to nourish him, but passed over all these and told his experience in the words " God who doth nourish me from my youth up " ? (Gen. xlviii. 15). Think you that all the waters which are gathered beneath the earth would seem to him worthy even of a glance ? Nay, he will not drink of a well on whom God bestows the undiluted rapture-giving draughts, 158 sometimes through the ministry of some angel whom He has held worthy to act as cupbearer, sometimes by His own agency, setting none to intervene between Him who gives and him who takes.

[a] See App. p. 489.

159 Ἀνυπερθέτως οὖν τῇ βασιλικῇ πειρώμεθα βαδίζειν ὁδῷ, οἱ τὰ γήινα παρέρχεσθαι δικαιοῦντες· βασιλικὴ δ' ἐστὶν ὁδός, ἧς δεσπότης ἰδιώτης μὲν οὐδὲ εἷς, μόνος δὲ ὁ καὶ μόνος βασιλεὺς ἀληθείᾳ.

160 αὕτη δ' ἐστί, καθὰ καὶ μικρῷ πρότερον εἶπον, σοφία, δι' ἧς μόνης ἱκέτισι ψυχαῖς ἡ ἐπὶ τὸν ἀγένητον καταφυγὴ γίνεται· εἰκὸς γὰρ τὸν δι' ὁδοῦ τῆς βασιλικῆς ἀκωλύτως ἰόντα μὴ πρότερον

161 καμεῖν ἢ ἐντυχεῖν τῷ βασιλεῖ. τότε δὲ τήν τε ἐκείνου μακαριότητα καὶ τὴν ἰδίαν εὐτέλειαν γνωρίζουσιν οἱ προσελθόντες· καὶ γὰρ Ἀβραὰμ ἐγγίσας τῷ θεῷ ἑαυτὸν εὐθὺς ἔγνω γῆν καὶ τέφραν

162 ὄντα.   μήτε δὲ ἐπὶ δεξιὰ μήτε ἐπὶ θάτερα τῆς βασιλικῆς ἀποκλινέτωσαν ὁδοῦ, ἀλλ' αὐτῇ τῇ μέσῃ προΐτωσαν. αἱ γὰρ ἐφ' ἑκάτερα ἐκτροπαὶ τῇ μὲν ὑπερβολὰς εἰς ἐπίτασιν τῇ δὲ ἐλλείψεις πρὸς ἄνεσιν ἔχουσαι ὑπαίτιοι· οὐ γὰρ ἧττον τοῦ εὐωνύμου τὸ δεξιὸν ψεκτὸν ἐνταῦθα·

163 παρὰ μέν γε τοῖς προπετῶς ζῶσι τὸ μὲν θράσος δεξιόν, ἀριστερὸν δὲ ἡ δειλία, παρὰ δὲ τοῖς ἀν-

[297] ελευθέροις περὶ χρημάτων | διοίκησιν δεξιὸν μὲν ἡ φειδωλία, εὐώνυμον δὲ αἱ ἀνειμέναι δαπάναι· καὶ ὅσοι μέντοι ἐν τῷ λογίζεσθαι περιττοί, κρίνουσι τὸ μὲν πανοῦργον αἱρετόν, τὸ δὲ εὐηθικὸν φευκτόν· καὶ δεισιδαιμονίαν μὲν ὡς δεξιὸν ἄλλοι μεταδιώκουσιν, ἀποδιδράσκουσι δ' ὡς φευκτὸν ἀσέβειαν.

164 XXXV. ἵνα οὖν μὴ ταῖς μαχομέναις κακίαις ἀναγκασθῶμεν ἐκτρεπόμενοι χρῆσθαι, τὴν μέσην ὁδὸν εὐθύνειν βουλώμεθά τε καὶ εὐχώμεθα· μέση δὲ θράσους μὲν καὶ δειλίας ἀνδρεία, ῥαθυμίας δὲ

---

[a] See App. p. 489.

So then brooking no delay should we essay to march by the king's high road, we who hold it our duty to pass by earthly things. And that is the king's road of which the lordship rests with no common citizen, but with Him alone who alone is king in real truth. This road is, as I said but now, wisdom, by which alone suppliant souls can make their escape to the Uncreated. For we may well believe that he who walks unimpeded along the king's way will never flag or faint, till he comes into the presence of the king. And then they that have come to Him recognize His blessedness and their own meanness ; for Abraham when he drew nigh to God straightway knew himself to be earth and ashes (Gen. xviii. 27).

And let them not turn aside to the right or to the left of the king's way, but advance along the midmost line. For deviations in either direction whether of excess or of deficiency, whether they tend to strain or to laxity, are in fault, for in this matter the right is no less blameworthy than the left. In the case of those who lead a reckless life, rashness is the right and cowardice the left. To those who are churlish in money matters, parsimony is the right and extravagance the left. And all who are oversharp and calculating in business count the knave's qualities worthy of their choice, but the simpleton's of their avoidance. And others pursue superstition as their right-hand path, but flee from impiety as a thing to be shunned. XXXV. Therefore, that we may not be forced to turn aside and have dealings with the vices that war against us, let us wish and pray that we may walk straightly along the middle path or mean.[a] Courage is the mean between rashness and cowardice, economy between

159

160

161

162

163

164

ἐκκεχυμένης καὶ φειδωλίας ἀνελευθέρου σωφροσύνη,
πανουργίας τε αὖ καὶ μωρίας φρόνησις, καὶ μὴν
165 δεισιδαιμονίας καὶ ἀσεβείας εὐσέβεια. αὗται μέσαι
τῶν παρ' ἑκάτερα ἐκτροπῶν εἰσι, βάσιμοι καὶ
λεωφόροι ὁδοὶ πᾶσαι, αἷς οὐ θέμις ὀργάνοις σω-
ματικοῖς ἀλλὰ ψυχῆς κινήσεσιν ἐφιεμένης τοῦ
ἀρίστου συνεχῶς ἐμπεριπατεῖν.
166 Ἐπὶ τούτῳ μάλιστα δυσχεράνας ὁ γήινος Ἐδὼμ
—δέδιε γὰρ περὶ τῆς τῶν ἑαυτοῦ δογμάτων ἀνα-
τροπῆς τε καὶ συγχύσεως—ἀπειλήσει πόλεμον
ἀκήρυκτον, εἰ βιαζοίμεθα διέρχεσθαι τέμνοντες καὶ
κείροντες ἀεὶ τὸν τῆς ψυχῆς αὐτοῦ καρπόν, ὃν ἐπ'
ὀλέθρῳ φρονήσεως σπείρας οὐκ ἐθέρισε· φησὶ γάρ·
" οὐ διελεύσῃ δι' ἐμοῦ· εἰ δὲ μή γε, ἐν πολέμῳ
167 ἐξελεύσομαί σοι εἰς ἀπάντησιν." ἀλλὰ μηδὲν
αὐτοῦ τῶν ἐπανατάσεων φροντίσαντες ἀποκρινώ-
μεθα, ὅτι " παρὰ τὸ ὄρος πορευσόμεθα," τουτέστιν
ὑψηλαῖς καὶ μετεώροις ἔθος ἔχοντες ἐνομιλεῖν
δυνάμεσι καὶ ὁρικῶς ἕκαστα σκοπεῖν, τὸν παντὸς
οὑτινοσοῦν λόγον ἐρευνῶντες, δι' οὗ τὸ τί ἦν εἶναι
γνωρίζεται, καταφρονητικῶς ἔχομεν πάντων ὅσα
ἐκτός τε καὶ περὶ σῶμα· ταπεινὰ γὰρ ταυτά γε καὶ
λίαν χαμαίζηλα, σοὶ μὲν φίλα, ἐχθρὰ δὲ ἡμῖν
αὐτοῖς, οὗ χάριν οὐδενὸς αὐτῶν προσαψόμεθα.
168 εἰ γὰρ ἄκρῳ δακτύλῳ τὸ τοῦ λόγου δὴ
τοῦτο μόνον ψαύσομεν, γέρας καὶ τιμήν σοι παρ-
έξομεν· φρυαττόμενος γὰρ αὐχήσεις, ὡς καὶ ἡμῶν
τῶν φιλαρέτων δελέασιν ἡδονῆς ὑπαχθέντων.
169 XXXVI. " ἐὰν γὰρ τοῦ ὕδατός σου " φησί " πίω

ᵃ We should expect θέμις οὐκ. Perhaps, however, θέμις is
reduced in meaning, " in which we *may* walk with soul
though not with body."
92

careless extravagance and illiberal parsimony, prudence between knavery and folly, and finally piety between superstition and impiety. These lie in the 165 middle between the deviations to either side, all of them high roads meet for the traveller's use, wherein we are bound in duty [a] to walk continually, not with the mechanism of the body, but with the motions of the soul which seeks the best.

Angered greatly at this, Edom, the earthly one, 166 since he fears lest the principles of his creed be confounded and overthrown, will threaten to wage war to the bitter end, if we should force our way through his land, tearing and ravaging ever, as we go, the fruits of his soul which he has sown for the destruction of wisdom, though he has not reaped them. For he says, "Thou shalt not go through me, else I will come out in war to meet thee." But let 167 us take no heed of his menaces, but make answer, "We will go along the mountain country." That is, "It is our wont to hold converse with powers that are lofty and sublime, and to examine each point by analysis and definition, and to search out in everything whatsoever its rationale, by which its essential nature [b] is known. Thus we feel contempt for all that is external or of the body ; for these are low-lying and grovelling exceedingly. You love them, but we hate them, and therefore we will handle none of them. For if we do but touch them 168 with our finger-tips, as the saying is, we shall provide honour and 'value' to you. You will plume yourself and boast that we too, the virtue-lovers, have yielded to the snares of pleasure." XXXVI. "For 169 if I or my cattle drink of your water," it runs, "I

[b] See App. p. 489.

ἐγώ τε καὶ τὰ κτήνη μου, δώσω τιμήν σοι," οὐ τὸν
λεγόμενον ὦνον παρὰ ποιηταῖς, ἀργύριον ἢ χρυσίον
ἢ ἄλλα ὅσα πρὸς τοὺς πιπράσκοντας ἔθος τοῖς
ὠνουμένοις ἀντικαταλλάττεσθαι, ἀλλὰ τιμὴν τὸ
170 γέρας νυνὶ παραλαμβάνει. τῷ γὰρ ὄντι πᾶς
ἀκόλαστος ἢ ἄδικος ἢ δειλός, ὅταν ἴδῃ τινὰ τῶν
αὐστηροτέρων ἢ πόνον φεύγοντα ἢ λήμματος
ἡττώμενον ἢ πρός τι τῶν ἡδονῆς φίλτρων ἐκνενευ-
[298] κότα, χαίρει καὶ γέγηθε καὶ τετιμῆσθαι | δοκεῖ,
καὶ πρὸς τοὺς πολλοὺς ἐπινεανιευόμενος[1] καὶ ἐπι-
χειρονομῶν ἄρχεται περὶ τῶν ἰδίων κακῶν ὡς
σφόδρα ἀναγκαίων καὶ χρησίμων φιλοσοφεῖν, οὐκ
ἄν, εἰ μὴ τοιαῦτα ἦν, φάσκων ὑπομεῖναι ἂν τὸν
171 δεῖνα εὐδόκιμον ἄνδρα χρῆσθαι. λέγωμεν οὖν
παντὶ μοχθηρῷ· ἐὰν τοῦ ὕδατός σου πίωμεν, ἐάν
τινός σου τῶν κατὰ τὴν ἄκριτον φορὰν ψαύσωμεν,
τιμὴν καὶ ἀποδοχὴν ἀντὶ δυσκλείας καὶ ἀτιμίας
—τούτων γὰρ ἄξιος ὢν τυγχάνεις—παρεξόμεθα·
172 καὶ γὰρ ἀμέλει τὸ πρᾶγμα περὶ ὃ
ἐσπούδακας συνόλως οὐδέν ἐστιν. ἢ νομίζεις τι
τῶν θνητῶν πραγμάτων ὄντως πρὸς ἀλήθειαν εἶναι
καὶ ὑφεστάναι, ἀλλ' οὐχ ὥσπερ ἐπ' αἰώρας τινὸς
ψευδοῦς καὶ ἀβεβαίου δόξης φορεῖσθαι κατὰ κενοῦ
βαίνοντα, μηδὲν ψευδῶν ὀνειράτων διαφέροντα;
173 εἰ δὲ μὴ θέλεις τὰς τῶν κατὰ μέρος
ἀνθρώπων ἐξετάζειν τύχας, τὰς χωρῶν ὅλων καὶ
ἐθνῶν πρός τε τὸ εὖ καὶ τὸ χεῖρον μεταβολάς·
ἤκμασέ ποτε ἡ Ἑλλάς, ἀλλὰ Μακεδόνες αὐτῆς τὴν

[1] MSS. ἔτι νεανιευόμενος.

---

[a] *i.e.* the ambiguous word τιμή is here used in the sense

shall give you value." The writer does not mean the pelf, to use the poet's word, silver or gold or aught else which the purchaser is wont to give in exchange to the vendor, but by " value " he here means honour.[a] For in very truth everyone that is 170 profligate or cowardly or unjust, when he sees any of the stricter folk shrinking from toil or mastered by gain or swerving aside to any of the love-lures of pleasure, rejoices and is glad and thinks that he has received honour. And then with swaggering airs and gestures of pride he begins to hold forth sagely to the multitude about his own vices, how necessary and profitable they are, " for," says he, " were they not so, would So-and-so, that much respected gentleman, be willing to indulge in them ? " Let us say, 171 then, to everyone of this sorry sort, " If we drink of thy water, if we touch aught that thy confused and turbid current carries, we shall provide thee with honour and acceptance, instead of the ill-repute and dishonour that are thy true deserts."
For in very truth " the matter " which has so en- 172 gaged thy zeal is absolutely " nothing." Or dost thou think that aught of mortal matters has real being or subsistence, and that they do not rather swing suspended as it were on fallacious and unstable opinion, treading the void and differing not a whit from false dreams ? If thou carest 173 not to test the fortunes of individual men, scan the vicissitudes, for better and worse, of whole regions and nations. Greece was once at its zenith, but the

of an honour conferred ($\gamma\acute{\epsilon}\rho\alpha s$). The position of the $\tau\acute{o}$, however, in the predicate is strange. Perhaps read $\tau\grave{o}$ " $\tau\iota\mu\acute{\eta}\nu$ " $\gamma\acute{\epsilon}\rho\alpha s$. A scribe failing to understand this use of $\tau\acute{o}$ before a quoted word or phrase might easily transfer it to before the neuter noun $\gamma\acute{\epsilon}\rho\alpha s$.

ἰσχὺν ἀφείλοντο. Μακεδονία πάλιν ἤνθησεν, ἀλλὰ διαιρεθεῖσα κατὰ μοίρας ἠσθένησεν, ἕως εἰς τὸ
174 παντελὲς ἀπεσβέσθη. πρὸ Μακεδόνων τὰ Περσῶν ἐν εὐτυχίᾳ ἦν, ἀλλὰ μία ἡμέρα τὴν πολλὴν καὶ μεγάλην βασιλείαν αὐτῶν καθεῖλε, καὶ νῦν Παρθυηνοὶ Περσῶν τῶν πρὸ μικροῦ ἡγεμόνων ἐπικρατοῦσιν οἱ τότε ὑπήκοοι. ἔπνευσέ ποτε λαμπρὸν καὶ ἐπὶ μήκιστον Αἴγυπτος, ἀλλ' ὡς νέφος αὐτῆς ἡ μεγάλη παρῆλθεν εὐπραγία. τί δὲ Αἰθίοπες, τί δὲ καὶ Καρχηδὼν καὶ τὰ πρὸς Λιβύην; τί δ' οἱ
175 Πόντου βασιλεῖς; τί δ' Εὐρώπη καὶ 'Ασία καὶ συνελόντι φράσαι πᾶσα ἡ οἰκουμένη; οὐκ ἄνω καὶ κάτω κλονουμένη καὶ τινασσομένη ὥσπερ ναῦς θαλαττεύουσα τοτὲ μὲν δεξιοῖς τοτὲ δὲ καὶ ἐναν-
176 τίοις πνεύμασι χρῆται;   χορεύει γὰρ ἐν κύκλῳ λόγος ὁ θεῖος, ὃν οἱ πολλοὶ τῶν ἀνθρώπων ὀνομάζουσι τύχην· εἶτα ἀεὶ ῥέων κατὰ πόλεις καὶ ἔθνη καὶ χώρας τὰ ἄλλων ἄλλοις καὶ πᾶσι τὰ πάντων ἐπινέμει, χρόνοις αὐτὸ μόνον ἀλλάττων τὰ παρ' ἑκάστοις, ἵνα ὡς μία πόλις ἡ οἰκουμένη πᾶσα τὴν ἀρίστην πολιτειῶν ἄγῃ δημοκρατίαν.
177 XXXVII. Οὐδὲν οὖν ἔστι τῶν ἀνθρωπίνων σπουδασμάτων ἔργον καὶ πρᾶγμα οὐδέν, ἀλλὰ σκιά τις ἢ αὔρα πρὶν ὑποστῆναι παρατρέχουσα. ἔρχεται γὰρ καὶ πάλιν ἄπεισιν ὥσπερ ἐν ταῖς παλιρροίαις· τὰ γὰρ ἀμπωτίζοντα πελάγη ποτὲ μὲν μετὰ συρμοῦ καὶ πατάγου βίᾳ φέρεται καὶ ἀναχεόμενα λιμνάζει τὴν τέως χέρσον, ποτὲ δὲ ἐξαναχωροῦντα
178 πολλὴν τῆς θαλάττης μοῖραν ἠπειροῖ· οὕτως

Macedonians took away its power. Macedonia flourished in its turn, but when it was divided into portions it weakened till it was utterly extinguished. Before the Macedonians fortune smiled on the 174 Persians, but a single day destroyed their vast and mighty empire, and now Parthians rule over Persians, the former subjects over their masters of yesterday. The breath that blew from Egypt of old was clear and strong for many a long year, yet like a cloud its great prosperity passed away. What of the Ethiopians, what of Carthage, and the parts towards Libya ? What of the kings of Pontus ? 175 What of Europe and Asia, and in a word the whole civilized world ? Is it not tossed up and down and kept in turmoil like ships at sea, subject now to prosperous, now to adverse winds ? For 176 circlewise moves the revolution of that divine plan which most call fortune. Presently in its ceaseless flux it makes distribution city by city, nation by nation, country by country. What these had once, those have now. What all had, all have. Only from time to time is the ownership changed by its agency, to the end that the whole of our world should be as a single state, enjoying that best of constitutions, democracy.[a]

XXXVII. So then in all wherewith men concern 177 themselves there is no solid work, no " matter," only a shadow or a breath which flits past, before it has real existence. It comes and goes as in the ebb and flow of the sea. For the tides sometimes race violently, roaring as they sweep along, and in their wide-spread rush make a lake of what till now was dry land, and then again they retreat and turn into land what was a great tract of sea. Even so the good 178

[a] See App. p. 489.

97

PHILO

[299] οὖν ἔστιν ὅτε | μέγα καὶ πολυάνθρωπον ἔθνος ἐπικλύσασα εὐπραγία ἑτέρωσε τὴν φορὰν τοῦ ῥεύματος παρατρέψασα οὐδὲ βραχεῖαν εἴασε λιβάδα, ἵνα μηδ᾽ ἴχνος ὑπολειφθῇ πιότητος ἀρχαίας.

179 τούτων δ᾽ οὐχ ἅπαντες ἀρτίους καὶ πλήρεις λαμβάνουσι λογισμούς, ἀλλ᾽ οἷς ἔθος συνομαρτεῖν ὀρθῷ καὶ πεπηγότι ὅρῳ καὶ λόγῳ. οἱ γὰρ αὐτοὶ ἄμφω ταῦτα λέγουσι, καὶ τὸ γενέσεως πρᾶγμα ὅλον οὐδέν ἐστι, καὶ παρὰ τὸ ὅρος πορευ-

180 σόμεθα· ἀδύνατον γὰρ τὸν μὴ ταῖς ὑψηλαῖς καὶ ὁρικαῖς χρώμενον ὁδοῖς ἀπογνῶναι μὲν τὰ θνητά, μετακλῖναι δὲ καὶ μεταναστῆναι πρὸς τὰ ἄφθαρτα.

Ὁ μὲν οὖν γήινος Ἐδὼμ τὴν οὐράνιον καὶ βασιλικὴν ἀρετῆς ὁδὸν ἐπιφράττειν ἀξιοῖ, ὁ δὲ θεῖος λόγος ἔμπαλιν[1] τὴν ἐκείνου καὶ τῶν ὁμοζήλων·

181 ὧν ἕνα καὶ τὸν Βαλαὰμ ἀναγραπτέον· γῆς γὰρ θρέμμα καὶ οὗτος, οὐκ οὐρανοῦ βλάστημα. τεκμήριον δέ· οἰωνοῖς καὶ ψευδέσι μαντείαις ἑπόμενος οὐδ᾽ ὅτε τὸ τῆς ψυχῆς μεμυκὸς ὄμμα ἀναβλέψαι[2] " εἶδε τὸν ἄγγελον τοῦ θεοῦ ἀνθεστῶτα," μετατραπόμενος ἐπέσχε τὸ ἀδικεῖν, ἀλλὰ πολλῷ τῷ τῆς ἀφροσύνης χρησάμενος ῥεύματι ἐπικλυσθεὶς

182 κατεπόθη. τότε γὰρ ὡς ἀληθῶς οὐ δυσθεράπευτα μόνον ἀλλὰ καὶ παντελῶς ἀνίατα γίνεται τὰ τῆς ψυχῆς ἀρρωστήματα, ὅταν ἐπιστάντος ἐλέγχου— λόγος δ᾽ ἐστὶ θεῖος, ἄγγελος ποδηγετῶν καὶ τὰ ἐν ποσὶν ἀναστέλλων, ἵνα ἄπταιστοι διὰ λεωφόρου

---

[1] mss. ἐν πᾶσι.
[2] So Mangey and old editions: mss. and Wend. ἀναβλέψας, presumably taking ὄμμα as acc. of respect. If so, it is of a type unusual in prose.

fortune which has flooded a great and populous nation sometimes turns the stream of its current elsewhere and leaves not even a tiny trickle behind it, that no trace of the old richness may remain.

But it is not all who can estimate these 179 truths justly and fully. Only they can do so who are wont to follow the rule of definition and reason which is straight and constant. The two sayings, " the matter of creation is all of it nothing " and " we will journey along the mountain country," come from the mouths of the same speakers. For it cannot be 180 that he who does not walk in the upland paths of definition should renounce mortal things and turn aside therefrom and make his new home with things indestructible.

So then the earthly Edom purposes to bar the heavenly and royal road of virtue, but the divine reason on the other hand would bar the road of Edom and his associates.   In the list of 181 these associates we must write the name of Balaam. For he too is no heavenly growth, but a creature of earth. And here we have the proof. He followed omens and false soothsayings, and not even when the closed eye of his soul received its sight and " beheld the angel of God standing in his way " (Num. xxii. 31) did he turn aside and refrain from evil-doing, but let the stream of his folly run full course and was overwhelmed by it and swallowed up. For it is then that the ailments of the soul become 182 not only hard to tend, but even utterly beyond healing, when though Conviction fronts us, Conviction, the divine reason, the angel who guides our feet and removes the obstacles before them, that we may walk without stumbling along the high road

βαίνωμεν τῆς ὁδοῦ—τὰς ἀκρίτους ἑαυτῶν γνώμας πρὸ τῶν ὑφηγήσεων τάττωμεν τῶν ἐκείνου,
183 ἃς ἐπὶ νουθεσίᾳ καὶ σωφρονισμῷ καὶ τῇ τοῦ παντὸς ἐπανορθώσει βίου συνεχῶς εἴωθε ποιεῖσθαι. διὰ τοῦθ' ὁ μὴ πεισθείς, μὴ μετατρεπόμενος τῷ ἀντιβαίνοντι ἐλέγχῳ φθορὰν τὴν "μετὰ τῶν τραυματιῶν" αὖθις ἐνδέξεται, οὓς κατεκέντησε καὶ κατέτρωσε τὰ πάθη. γενήσεται δ' ἡ τούτου συμφορὰ τοῖς μὴ τελέως δυσκαθάρτοις δίδαγμα αὐταρκέστατον τοῦ πειρᾶσθαι τὸν ἔνδον δικαστὴν ἔχειν εὐμενῆ· σχήσουσι δέ, εἰ μηδὲν τῶν ὀρθῶς ὑπ' αὐτοῦ γνωσθέντων ἀναδικάζοιεν.

(Psalm xc. [xci.] 11, 12), we yet set our ill-judged purposes before those counsels of his which he is wont to give without ceasing for our admonishing and chastening and the reformation of our whole life. Therefore he who listens not, who is not turned from 183 his course by the Conviction which stands in his path, will in time receive destruction " with the wounded " (Num. xxxi. 8) whom their passions stabbed and wounded with a fatal stroke. His fate will be to those who are not hopelessly impure a lesson which heeds no confirmation, that they should seek to have the favour of the inward judge. And have it they shall, if they do not remove or repeal aught of the righteous judgements which he has given.

ON HUSBANDRY
(DE AGRICULTURA)

ANALYTICAL INTRODUCTION

GEN. ix. 20 f. quoted at the beginning of *De Agricultura* is the text of this and the two following treatises. The part of it dealt with in the one before us is the words, " And Noah began to be a husband-man " or " gardener."

Having pointed out that this connotes scientific gardening, Philo describes scientific gardening in the literal sense (1-7), and then goes on to soul-gardening. This ministers to the Mind. Its aim is the fruit of virtue, and it is only for the sake of this that it occupies itself first with rudimentary subjects. What is harmful it prunes away. What is not fruit-bearing it uses for fencing. It deals in this way with mere theorizing, forensic speech, dialectics, and geometry, which all sharpen the intellect without improving the character (8-16). Soul-gardening sets out its programme (17 ff.). As such a soul-gardener righteous Noah is contrasted with Cain, who is a mere " worker of the earth " in the service of Pleasure (21-25).

There must surely be other pairs of opposites similar to this of the scientific tiller and the mere worker of the soil. Yes ; there is the shepherd and the rearer of cattle. The organs of the body are the cattle of each one of us. A careless Mind is unfit to guard them ; it will not check excess, or exercise needful discipline. These things a shepherd will do. So honourable is his calling that poets call kings " shepherds," and Moses gives this title to the wise,

104

the real kings. Jacob was a shepherd. So was Moses ; and he prays God not to leave Israel unshepherded, *i.e.* to save it from mob-rule, despotism and licence. Well may each of us make his prayer our own on behalf of our inner flock. God, the Shepherd and King of the Universe, with His Word and Firstborn Son as viceroy, is extolled in the Psalm " The Lord shepherds me." Only by the One Shepherd can the flock be kept together. This is our sure hope, and our sole need. So all who were taught by God made the shepherd's science their study, and their pride ; like Joseph's brethren who, though bidden by him to tell Pharaoh that they were " rearers of cattle," answered that they were " shepherds," shepherding, *i.e.* the faculties of the soul ; for Pharaoh, with royal and Egyptian arrogance, would have looked down on keepers of literal goats and sheep. The fatherland of these soul-shepherds is Heaven, and (as they told the King) they were but " sojourners " in Egypt, the land of the body and the passions (26-66).

We find in the Law a third pair of opposites. A sharp distinction is to be drawn between a " horseman " and a " rider." The mere " rider " is at the horse's mercy ; the horseman is in control like the man at the helm. The horses of the soul are high spirit and desire, and their rider the Mind that hates virtue and loves the passions. Israel's " Song by the Sea " celebrates the disaster that befalls the " fourfooted throng of passions and vices." It is clear that Moses' words about horses are symbolic, for so great a soldier as he must have known the value of cavalry. Again, though literal racehorse breeding is a poor business, those who ply it have the excuse that the spectators of a race catch the fine spirit of the horses ; whereas the figurative trainer, who sets an unqualified jockey on the back of vice and passion, is without excuse (67-92).

A glance at the prayer of Moses in Gen. xlix. 17 f. will shew how different the " horseman " is from the " rider." To understand that prayer we must note that " Dan " means " judgement," and that the " dragon," which he *is* or *has*, is Moses' serpent of brass. (Of course neither Moses' serpent nor Eve's can be literal. Serpents do not talk, tempt, or heal.) So Moses prays that Dan (or his serpent) may be on the road ready to assail Pleasure, and " bite the horse's heel," *i.e.* attack and overturn the supports which hold up Passion (94-106).

Here we come upon a piece of interpretation very characteristic of Philo. The biting of Passion's heel brings about the *horseman's fall.* So far from being daunted by this, our author positively revels in it. It is a fall which implies victory, not defeat. For, should Mind ever find itself mounted on Passion, the only course is to jump or fall off. Yes, if you cannot escape from fighting in a bad cause, court defeat. Nay, do not stop there. Press forward to crown the victor. The crown at which you are aiming is not won in contests of pitiless savagery, or for fleetness of foot, in which puny animals surpass men, but in the holy contest, the only true " Olympic " games, the entrants for which, though weaker in body, are strongest in soul (108-119).

Having noted the difference between the members of each of these three pairs of opposites, suggested to him by the word γεωργός in his text, Philo turns to the word ἤρξατο, " began " (124).

ON HUSBANDRY

" Beginning is half the whole." Yes, if we go on
to the end. But good beginnings are often marred
by failure to make proper distinctions. For instance,
one says that " God is the Author of all things,"
whereas he should say " of good things only."
Again, we are very scrupulous about rejecting priests
or victims on the ground of physical blemish. We
ought to be equally scrupulous to separate the profane from the sacred in our thoughts of God. And
again Memory, of which the ruminating camel is a
figure, is a fine thing, but the camel's undivided
hoof makes him unclean, and that reminds us
that Memory must reject the bad and retain the
good ; for practical purposes, not for sophistical
hair-splitting. Sophists are swine ; they divide *ad
nauseam*, but for perfection we must con over and
take in (125-146).

Sections 147 to 156 shew that the conditions of
exemption from military service laid down in Deut.
xx. 5 and 7 cannot be literally meant. In 157 ff.
the acquired possessions which exempt a man are
interpreted as faculties which must be enjoyed and
fully realized, before he who has acquired them is
trained and fit for the warfare with the sophists.

Right ending must crown good beginning. We
miss perfection unless we own that that to which we
have attained is due to the loving wisdom of God.
And wilful refusal to acknowledge God as the Giver
of success is far worse than involuntary failure.

" All this about start and goal has been suggested," Philo tells us, " by the statement that Noah
began to be a husbandman or gardener."

ΠΕΡΙ ΓΕΩΡΓΙΑΣ

1 **I.** " Καὶ ἤρξατο Νῶε ἄνθρωπος γεωργὸς γῆς
[300] εἶναι, καὶ ἐφύτευσεν ἀμπελῶνα, καὶ ἔπιε | τοῦ
οἴνου, καὶ ἐμεθύσθη ἐν τῷ οἴκῳ αὐτοῦ." [a]

Οἱ μὲν πολλοὶ τῶν ἀνθρώπων τὰς φύσεις τῶν
πραγμάτων οὐκ εἰδότες καὶ περὶ τὴν τῶν ὀνομάτων
θέσιν ἐξ ἀνάγκης ἁμαρτάνουσι· τοῖς μὲν γὰρ ὥσπερ
ἐξ ἀνατομῆς περινοηθεῖσι κύριαι προσρήσεις
ἕπονται, τοῖς δ' ὑποσυγκεχυμένοις οὐ σφόδρα
2 ἠκριβωμέναι. Μωυσῆς δὲ κατὰ πολλὴν περιουσίαν
τῆς ἐν τοῖς πράγμασιν ἐπιστήμης ὀνόμασιν εὐθυ-
βολωτάτοις καὶ ἐμφαντικωτάτοις εἴωθε χρῆσθαι.
πολλαχοῦ μὲν οὖν τῆς νομοθεσίας τὴν ὑπόσχεσιν
ἐπαληθεύουσαν εὑρήσομεν, οὐχ ἥκιστα δὲ κἂν τῷ
προτεθέντι κεφαλαίῳ, καθ' ὃ γεωργὸς ὁ δίκαιος
3 Νῶε εἰσάγεται. τίνι γὰρ τῶν προχειροτέρων οὐκ
ἂν δόξειε τὰ αὐτὰ εἶναι γεωργία τε καὶ γῆς ἐργασία,
καίτοι πρὸς ἀλήθειαν οὐ μόνον οὐκ ὄντα τὰ αὐτά,
ἀλλὰ καὶ λίαν ἀπηρτημένα, ὡς ἀντιστατεῖν καὶ
4 διαμάχεσθαι; δύναται μὲν γάρ τις καὶ ἄνευ ἐπιστήμης περὶ τὴν γῆς ἐπιμέλειαν πονεῖσθαι, γεωργὸς
δὲ τὸ μὴ ἰδιώτης ἀλλ' ἔμπειρος εἶναι καὶ τῷ ὀνόματι
πεπίστωται, ὅπερ ἐκ τῆς γεωργικῆς τέχνης, ἧς
5 φερώνυμός ἐστιν, εὕρηται. πρὸς δὲ τούτῳ κἀκεῖνο

---

[a] The lxx has ἐμεθύσθη καὶ ἐγυμνώθη ἐν τῷ οἴκῳ αὐτοῦ.

108

ON HUSBANDRY

I. " And Noah began to be a husbandman, and he 1
planted a vineyard, and drank of the wine, and became
drunken within his house ª " (Gen. ix. 20 f.).

Most men, not knowing the nature of things,
necessarily go wrong also in giving them names. For
things which are well considered and subjected as
it were to dissection have appropriate designations
attached to them in consequence; while others having
been presented in a confused state receive names
that are not thoroughly accurate. Moses, being abun- 2
dantly equipped with the knowledge that has to do
with things, is in the habit of using names that are
perfectly apt and expressive. We shall find the
assurance just given made good in many parts of the
Lawgiving, and not least in the section before us in
which the righteous Noah is introduced as a husbandman. Would not anyone who answers questions off- 3
hand think that husbandry and working on the soil
were the same things, although in reality they not
only are not the same things, but are ideas utterly
at variance with each other and mutually repugnant?
For a man is able even without knowledge to labour 4
at the care of the soil, but a husbandman is guaranteed
to be no unprofessional, but a skilled worker by his
very name, which he has gained from the science
of husbandry, the science whose title he bears. In 5

[301] λογιστέον, ὅτι ὁ μὲν γῆς | ἐργάτης πρὸς ἓν τέλος,
τὸν μισθόν, ἀφορῶν—ἔμμισθος γὰρ ὡς ἐπίπαν οὗτος
—οὐδεμίαν ἔχει φροντίδα τοῦ καλῶς ἐργάσασθαι,
ὁ μέντοι γεωργὸς πολλὰ ἂν ἐθελήσαι καὶ τῶν ἰδίων
εἰσφέρειν καὶ προσαναλίσκειν οἴκοθέν τι ὑπὲρ[1] τοῦ
καὶ τὸ χωρίον ὀνῆσαι καὶ πρὸς μηδενὸς τῶν ἰδόντων
μεμφθῆναι· βούλεται γὰρ οὐχ ἑτέρωθέν ποθεν, ἀλλ᾽
ἐκ τῶν γεωργηθέντων εὐτοκίᾳ χρωμένων ἀνὰ πᾶν
6 ἔτος τοὺς καρποὺς ἀναλαμβάνειν. οὗτος τὰ μὲν
ἄγρια τῶν δένδρων ἡμεροῦν, τὰ δ᾽ ἥμερα ἐπιμελείαις συναύξειν, τὰ δ᾽ ὑπὸ πλεοναζούσης τροφῆς
κεχυμένα τομαῖς στέλλειν, τὰ δ᾽ ἐσταλμένα καὶ
πεπιλημένα ἐπιφύσεων ἐκτάσεσι μηκύνειν, καὶ ὅσα
μὲν εὐγενῆ πολυκληματοῦντα κατὰ γῆς τείνειν ἐν
οὐ πάνυ βαθείαις τάφροις, ὅσα δὲ μὴ εὔκαρπα
ἑτέρων εἰς τὸν πρὸς ταῖς ῥίζαις κορμὸν ἐνθέσει
καὶ συμφυεστάτῃ ἑνώσει βελτιοῦν ἐθελήσει—καὶ
γὰρ ἐπ᾽ ἀνθρώπων τυγχάνει ταὐτόν, ὡς τοὺς θετοὺς
παῖδας γένεσιν ἀλλοτρίοις διὰ τὰς σφετέρας οἰκειου-
7 μένους ἀρετὰς παγίως ἐναρμόζεσθαι—· μυρία τοίνυν
καὶ αὐτόπρεμνα ῥίζαις αὐταῖς ἀνασπάσας κατέβαλε
τὰς εἰς εὐκαρπίαν ⟨ἐκ⟩φύσεις[2] ἐστειρωμένα καὶ
τοῖς φέρουσι μεγάλην ζημίαν ἐκ τοῦ παραπεφυ-
τεῦσθαι πλησίον ἐνεγκόντα. τοιαύτη μέν τίς ἐστιν

---

[1] mss. περί.   [2] Cf. Quod Deus 38.

addition to this there is the further point to be considered, that the worker on the soil is as a rule a wage-earner, and as such has but one end in view, his wages, and cares nothing at all about doing his work well ; whereas the husbandman would be willing not only to put into the undertaking much of his private property, but to spend a further amount drawn from his domestic budget, to do the farm good and to escape being blamed by those who have seen it. For, regardless of gain from any other source, he desires only to see the crops which he has grown yielding plentifully year by year and to take up their produce. Such a man will be anxious to bring under 6 cultivation the trees that were before wild, to improve by careful treatment those already under cultivation, to check by pruning those that are over-luxuriant owing to excess of nourishment, to give more scope to those which have been curtailed and kept back, splicing on new growths to stem or branch ; when trees of good kinds throw out abundant tendrils, he will like to train them under ground in shallow trenches ; and to improve such as yield poor crops by inserting grafts into the stem near the roots and joining them with it so that they grow together as one. The same thing happens, I may remark, in the case of men, when adopted sons become by reason of their native good qualities congenial to those who by birth are aliens from them, and so become firmly fitted into the family. To return to our subject. The 7 husbandman will pull up by the roots and throw away quantities of trees on which the shoots that should bear fruit have lost their fertility, and so, because they have been planted near them, have done great harm to those that are bearing fruit. The science,

PHILO

ἡ περὶ τὰ βλαστάνοντα ἐκ γῆς φυτὰ τέχνη, τὴν δὲ
ψυχῆς γεωργικὴν ἐν μέρει πάλιν ἐπισκεψώμεθα.
8 II. Πρῶτον μὲν τοίνυν σπείρειν ἢ φυτεύειν ἄγονον
οὐδὲν ἐπιτηδεύει, πάντα δ' ἥμερα καὶ καρποτόκα
φόρους ἐτησίους οἴσοντα τῷ ἡγεμόνι ἀνθρώπῳ·
τοῦτον γὰρ ἄρχοντα ἡ φύσις δένδρων τε καὶ ζῴων
τῶν ἄλλων ὅσα θνητὰ ἅπαξ ἁπάντων ἀνέδειξεν.
9 ἄνθρωπος δὲ ὁ ἐν ἑκάστῳ ἡμῶν τίς ἂν εἴη πλὴν ὁ
νοῦς, ὃς τὰς ἀπὸ τῶν σπαρέντων καὶ φυτευθέντων
ὠφελείας εἴωθε καρποῦσθαι; ἐπεὶ δὲ νηπίοις μέν
ἐστι γάλα τροφή, τελείοις δὲ τὰ ἐκ πυρῶν πέμματα,
καὶ ψυχῆς γαλακτώδεις μὲν ἂν εἶεν τροφαὶ κατὰ
τὴν παιδικὴν ἡλικίαν τὰ τῆς ἐγκυκλίου μουσικῆς
προπαιδεύματα, τέλειαι δὲ καὶ ἀνδράσιν ἐμπρεπεῖς
αἱ διὰ φρονήσεως καὶ σωφροσύνης καὶ ἁπάσης
ἀρετῆς ὑφηγήσεις· ταῦτα γὰρ σπαρέντα καὶ φυτευ-
θέντα ἐν διανοίᾳ καρποὺς ὠφελιμωτάτους οἴσει,
10 καλὰς καὶ ἐπαινετὰς πράξεις. διὰ ταύτης τῆς
γεωργικῆς καὶ ὅσα παθῶν ἢ κακιῶν δένδρα ἀνα-
βλαστόντα εἰς ὕψος ἐξήρθη φθοροποιοὺς φέροντα
[302] καρπούς, ὑποτεμνόμενα καθαίρεται, | ὡς μηδὲ
βραχύ τι λείψανον ἐαθῆναι, ἀφ' οὗ νέαι βλάσται
11 πάλιν ἁμαρτημάτων ἀναδραμοῦνται. κἂν εἴ τινα
μέντοι δένδρα εἴη μήτ' ὠφελίμων μήτ' αὖ βλαβερῶν
καρπῶν οἰστικά, ταῦτα ἐκκόψει μέν, οὐ μὴν ἐάσει
γε ἀφανισθῆναι, κατατάξει δ' αὐτὰ εἰς ἐναρμόνιον
χρῆσιν ἢ βαλλομένη χάρακας καὶ σταυροὺς ἐν
κύκλῳ στρατοπέδου ἢ φραγμὸν πόλεως, ἵνα ἀντὶ
12 τείχους ᾖ. III. λέγει γάρ· "πᾶν ὃ οὐ καρπό-
βρωτόν ἐστιν, ἐκκόψεις καὶ ποιήσεις χαράκωσιν

112

then, that has to do with growths that spring out of the earth is of the kind I have described. Let us consider in its turn soul-husbandry.

II. First, then, it makes it its aim to sow or plant 8 nothing that has no produce, but all that is fitted for cultivation and fruit-bearing, and likely to yield yearly tributes to man, its prince; for him did nature appoint to be ruler of all trees as well as of the living creatures besides himself that are mortal. But who else could the man that is in each of us be 9 save the mind, whose place it is to reap the benefits derived from all that has been sown or planted? But seeing that for babes milk is food, but for grown men wheaten bread, there must also be soul-nourishment, such as is milk-like suited to the time of childhood, in the shape of the preliminary stages of school-learning, and such as is adapted to grown men in the shape of instructions leading the way through wisdom and temperance and all virtue. For these when sown and planted in the mind will produce most beneficial fruits, namely fair and praiseworthy conduct. By means of this husbandry whatever trees 10 of passions or vices have sprung up and grown tall, bearing mischief-dealing fruits, are cut down and cleared away, no minute portion even being allowed to survive, as the germ of new growths of sins to spring up later on. And should there be any trees 11 capable of bearing neither wholesome nor harmful fruits, these it will cut down indeed, but not allow them to be made away with, but assign them to a use for which they are suited, setting them as pales and stakes to surround an encampment or to fence in a city in place of a wall. III. For he says, " Every 12 tree whose fruit is not edible thou shalt cut down and

ἐπὶ τὴν πόλιν, ἥτις ποιήσει πρὸς σὲ τὸν πόλεμον."
ταῦτα δ' εἰκάζεται τὰ δένδρα ταῖς περὶ λόγους
13 δυνάμεσι θεωρίαν ψιλὴν ἐχούσαις· ἐν αἷς θετέον
ἰατρολογίαν ἀπεζευγμένην ἔργων, δι' ὧν τοὺς κάμ-
νοντας εἰκός ἐστι σῴζεσθαι, καὶ ῥητορικῆς τὸ
συνηγορικὸν καὶ ἔμμισθον εἶδος οὐ περὶ τὴν εὕρεσιν
τοῦ δικαίου πραγματευόμενον, ἀλλὰ περὶ τὴν δι'
ἀπάτης πειθὼ τῶν ἀκουόντων, ἔτι μέντοι καὶ
διαλεκτικῆς καὶ γεωμετρίας ὅσα εἰς μὲν ἐπανόρθωσιν ἤθους οὐδὲν συνεργεῖ, παραθήγει δὲ τὸν
νοῦν οὐκ ἐῶντα ἀμβλείᾳ χρῆσθαι τῇ πρὸς ἕκαστα
τῶν ἀπορουμένων προσβολῇ, τομαῖς δὲ ἀεὶ καὶ
διαστολαῖς χρῆσθαι, ὡς τὴν ἑκάστου πράγματος
14 ἰδιότητα κοινῶν διαζευγνύναι ποιοτήτων. τὸν γοῦν
κατὰ φιλοσοφίαν λόγον τρίδυμον ὄντα τοὺς παλαιοὺς
ἀγρῷ φασιν ἀπεικάσαι, τὸ μὲν φυσικὸν αὐτοῦ
δένδροις καὶ φυτοῖς παραβάλλοντας, τὸ δ' ἠθικὸν
καρποῖς, ὧν ἕνεκα καὶ τὰ φυτά, τὸ δ' αὖ λογικὸν
15 φραγμῷ καὶ περιβόλῳ· καθάπερ γὰρ τὸ περι-
κείμενον τεῖχος ὀπώρας καὶ φυτῶν τῶν κατὰ τὸν
ἀγρόν ἐστι φυλακτήριον τοὺς ἐπὶ τῷ σίνεσθαι
παρεισφθείρεσθαι βουλομένους ἀνεῖργον, τὸν αὐτὸν
τρόπον τὸ λογικὸν μέρος φιλοσοφίας φρουρά τίς
ἐστιν ὀχυρωτάτη τῶν δυεῖν ἐκείνων, ἠθικοῦ τε καὶ
16 φυσικοῦ· τὰς γὰρ διπλᾶς καὶ ἀμφιβόλους ὅταν
ἐξαπλοῖ λέξεις καὶ τὰς διὰ τῶν σοφισμάτων
πιθανότητας ἐπιλύῃ καὶ τὴν εὐπαράγωγον ἀπάτην,

ᵃ "The modes . . . processes," lit. "dialectic and geometry" (or "logic and mathematics").
ᵇ See App. p. 490.

shalt make into a palisade to resist the city, which shall make war against thee " (Deut. xx. 20). The Scripture uses these trees to represent the purely intellectual activities which deal with theory alone. Among these we must place medical science dis- 13 sociated from practical measures such as lead to the recovery of the sick ; the kind of oratory practised by the hired advocate, that is concerned not to find out the rights of the case, but to influence the hearers by falsehood ; and over and above these we must include all the modes of reaching conclusions by argumentative and rigidly deductive processes,[a] that contribute nothing to the improvement of character,[b] but whet the mind, compelling it to pay keen attention to each problem as it presents itself ; and enabling it to draw clear distinctions, and to make the special character of the matter in hand stand out in bold relief against the background of the features which it has in common with others. Accordingly, they tell 14 us that the men of old likened philosophic discussion with its threefold division [b] to a field, comparing that part which deals with nature to trees and plants ; that which deals with morality to fruits and crops, for the sake of which the plants exist ; that part which has to do with logic to a fence enclosing it. For even as the wall built round it serves to protect 1£ the fruit and the plants that grow in the field, keeping off those who would like mischievously to make their way in with a view to plunder ; in the same way the logical part of philosophy is, so to speak, a strong barrier guarding those other two parts, the ethical and the physical. For when it disentangles ambiguous 16 expressions capable of two meanings, and exposes the fallacies created by tricks of argument, and using

μέγιστον ψυχῆς δέλεαρ καὶ ἐπιζήμιον, ἀναιρῇ διὰ
λόγων ἐμφαντικωτάτων καὶ ἀποδείξεων ἀνενδοιά-
στων, ὥσπερ κηρὸν λελειασμένον τὸν νοῦν ἀπ-
εργάζεται ἕτοιμον δέχεσθαι τούς τε φυσιολογίας
καὶ τοὺς ἠθοποιίας ἀσινεῖς καὶ πάνυ δοκίμους
χαρακτῆρας.

17   IV. Ταῦτ' οὖν ἡ ψυχῆς ἐπαγγελλομένη γεωργικὴ
προκηρύττει· τὰ ἀφροσύνης δένδρα καὶ ἀκολασίας
ἀδικίας τε καὶ δειλίας πάντ' ἐκκόψω, ἐκτεμῶ καὶ
τὰ ἡδονῆς καὶ ἐπιθυμίας ὀργῆς τε καὶ θυμοῦ καὶ
τῶν παραπλησίων παθῶν, κἂν ἄχρις οὐρανοῦ
μηκύνηται,[1] τὰ φυτά, ἐπικαύσω καὶ τὰς ῥίζας αὐτῶν
ἐφιεῖσ' ἄχρι τῶν ὑστάτων τῆς γῆς φλογὸς ῥιπήν,
[303] ὡς μηδὲν | μέρος ἀλλὰ μηδ' ἴχνος ἢ σκιὰν ὑπολει-
18 φθῆναι τὸ παράπαν. ἀνελῶ μὲν δὴ ταῦτα, φυτεύσω
δὲ ταῖς μὲν ἐν ἡλικίᾳ παιδικῇ ψυχαῖς μοσχεύματα,
ὧν ὁ καρπὸς αὐτὰς τιθηνήσεται—ἔστι δὲ ταῦτα ἡ
τοῦ γράφειν καὶ ἀναγινώσκειν εὐτρόχως ἐπιτήδευσις,
ἡ τῶν παρὰ σοφοῖς ποιηταῖς ἀκριβὴς ἔρευνα,
γεωμετρία καὶ ἡ περὶ τοὺς ῥητορικοὺς λόγους
μελέτη καὶ ἡ σύμπασα τῆς ἐγκυκλίου παιδείας
μουσική—, ταῖς δὲ νεανιευομέναις καὶ ἀνδρουμέναις
ἤδη τὰ ἀμείνω καὶ τελεώτερα, τὸ φρονήσεως φυτόν,
τὸ ἀνδρείας, τὸ σωφροσύνης, τὸ δικαιοσύνης, τὸ
19 ἀρετῆς ἁπάσης. ἂν μέντοι τι καὶ τῶν τῆς ἀγρίας
λεγομένης ὕλης[2] ἐδώδιμον μὲν μὴ φέρῃ καρπόν,
δύνηται δὲ ἐδωδίμου φραγμὸς εἶναι καὶ φυλακτήριον,
καὶ τοῦτο ταμιεύσομαι, οὐ δι' ἑαυτό, ἀλλ' ὅτι
ὑπηρετεῖν ἀναγκαίῳ καὶ χρησίμῳ σφόδρα πέφυκε.

---

[1] mss. μηκύνῃ.   [2] mss. μούσης.

perfectly clear and unmistakable language and adducing proofs which admit of no doubt destroys plausible falsehood, that greatest snare and pest of the soul, it makes the mind like smoothed wax ready to receive the impressions made by the science that explores existence and that which aims at building character, impressions free from flaw and aught that is not genuine.

IV. These, then, are the offers held out by soul-17 husbandry in its inaugural proclamation : " The trees of folly and licentiousness, of injustice and cowardice I will wholly cut down ; I will moreover extirpate the plants of pleasure and desire, of anger and wrath and of like passions, even though they be grown up to heaven ; I will burn up their very roots, letting the rush of fire pursue them even to the depths of the earth, that no part or trace or shadow of them whatever be left behind. These I will destroy, but 18 I will plant for souls in their childhood suckers whose fruit shall feed them. These suckers are the learning to write easily and read fluently ; the diligent search of what wise poets have written ; geometry and the practice of rhetorical composition ; and the whole of the education embraced in school-learning. For souls at the stage of youths and of those now growing into men I will provide the better and more perfect thing suited to their age, the plant of sound sense, that of courage, that of temperance, that of justice, that of all virtue. If, again, some tree among those 19 that belong to what is called wild wood does not bear edible fruit, but can be a fence and protection of such fruit, this tree also will I keep in store, not for its own sake, but because it is adapted to do service to another that is indispensable and most useful."

117

PHILO

20 V. Διὰ τοῦτο ὁ πάνσοφος Μωυσῆς τῷ μὲν δικαίῳ τὴν τῆς ψυχῆς γεωργικὴν ὡς ἐναρμόνιον καὶ ἐπιβάλλουσαν τέχνην ἀνατίθησι λέγων '' ἤρξατο Νῶε ἄνθρωπος εἶναι γεωργός,'' τῷ δὲ ἀδίκῳ τὴν ἄνευ ἐπιστήμης φέρουσαν ἄχθη βαρύτατα γῆς ἐργασίαν· 21 '' Κάιν '' γάρ φησιν '' ἦν ἐργαζόμενος τὴν γῆν,'' καὶ μικρὸν ὕστερον, ἡνίκα τὸ ἐπὶ τῇ ἀδελφοκτονίᾳ ἄγος ἐργασάμενος καταφωρᾶται, λέγεται· '' ἐπικατάρατος σὺ ἀπὸ τῆς γῆς, ἣ ἔχανε τὸ στόμα αὐτῆς δέξασθαι τὸ αἷμα τοῦ ἀδελφοῦ σου ἐκ τῆς χειρός σου, ᾗ ἐργᾷ τὴν γῆν, καὶ οὐ προσθήσει τὴν ἰσχὺν 22 αὐτῆς δοῦναί σοι.'' πῶς οὖν ἄν τις περιφανέστερον ἐπιδείξαι δύναιτο, ὅτι γῆς ἐργάτην ἀλλ' οὐ γεωργὸν ὁ νομοθέτης νομίζει τὸν φαῦλον, ἢ τὸν τρόπον τοῦτον; οὐ μὴν ὑποληπτέον ἢ περὶ ἀνθρώπου χερσὶ καὶ ποσὶ καὶ τῇ ἄλλῃ δυνάμει τοῦ σώματος ἐνεργεῖν ἱκανοῦ ἢ περὶ γῆς ὀρεινῆς καὶ πεδιάδος εἶναι τὸν λόγον, ἀλλὰ περὶ τῶν καθ' ἕκαστον ἡμῶν δυνάμεων· τὴν γὰρ τοῦ φαύλου ψυχὴν περὶ οὐδὲν ἄλλο πραγματεύεσθαι συμβέβηκεν ἢ τὸ γήινον 23 σῶμα καὶ τὰς τοῦ σώματος ἁπάσας ἡδονάς. ὁ γοῦν πολὺς ὅμιλος ἀνθρώπων τὰ γῆς ἐπιὼν κλίματα καὶ ἄχρι τῶν περάτων φθάνων αὐτῆς καὶ τὰ πελάγη περαιούμενος καὶ τὰ ἐν μυχοῖς θαλάττης ἀναζητῶν καὶ μηδὲν μέρος ἐῶν τοῦ παντὸς ἀδιερεύνητον ἀεὶ καὶ πανταχοῦ πορίζει ταῦτα, δι' ὧν ἡδονὴν συναυ- 24 ξήσει· καθάπερ γὰρ οἱ ἁλιευόμενοι δίκτυα καθιᾶσιν ἔστιν ὅτε μήκιστα πολλὴν ἐν κύκλῳ περιβαλλόμενοι

---

a Or "earned from his working." Philo plays with ἐργάζομαι which can mean either "to work" (till) or "gain by work." So, too, ἄγος (pollution) carries with it the idea of a curse and explains the ἐπικατάρατος of the text.

V. It is for this reason that Moses, the all-wise, 20
ascribes to the righteous man soul-husbandry as a
science in keeping with him and rightly pertaining
to him, saying " Noah began to be a husbandman,"
whereas to the unrighteous man he ascribes that
working of the ground which is without scientific
knowledge and carries very heavy loads. For he 21
says, " Cain was one working the ground " (Gen. iv.
2), and, a little later, when he is discovered to have
incurred *a* the pollution of fratricide, it is said : " Cursed
art thou from the ground, which hath opened her
mouth to receive thy brother's blood from thy hand,
with which thou shalt work the ground, and it shall
not yield *b* its strength to give it thee " (Gen. iv.
12 f.). How, I ask, could anyone shew more clearly 22
than in this manner that the lawgiver considers the
bad man a worker of the soil and not an husbandman ? We must not, however, suppose that what is
here spoken of is either a man able to work with
hands and feet and the other powers of the body, or
that it is soil on hill or plain. No, the subject dealt
with is the faculties of each one of us ; for the soul
of the bad man has no other interest than his earthy
body, and all the body's pleasures. At all events 23
the majority of mankind traversing all the quarters
of the earth and finding their way to its utmost
bounds, and crossing its oceans, and seeking what is
hidden in far-reaching creeks of the sea, and leaving
no part of the whole world unexplored, are always
and everywhere procuring the means of increasing
pleasure. For even as fishermen let down nets, 24
sometimes very long, taking in a large extent of sea,

b Or " add."   *Cf. Quod Det.* 112.

θάλατταν, ἵν᾽ ὡς πλείστους ἐντὸς ληφθέντας ἀρκύων
οἷα τειχήρεις γεγονότας ἰχθύας συλλάβωσι, τὸν αὐτὸν τρόπον ἡ πλείστη μοῖρα ἀνθρώπων οὐκ ἐπὶ
[304] μέρος θαλάττης μόνον, | ἀλλ᾽ ἐφ᾽ ἅπασαν τὴν
ὕδατος καὶ γῆς καὶ ἀέρος φύσιν τὰ πάναγρα, ὡς
οἱ ποιηταί πού φασι, λίνα τείνασ᾽ ἅπαντα παντα-
25 χόθεν δι᾽ ἡδονῆς ἀπόλαυσίν τε καὶ χρῆσιν ἀγκι-
στρεύεται· καὶ γὰρ γῆν μεταλλεύουσι καὶ τὰ πελάγη
διαβαίνουσι καὶ τἆλλα πάντα ὅσα εἰρήνης καὶ
πολέμου ἔργα δρῶσιν, ὕλας ἀφθόνους ὡς βασιλίδι
ἡδονῇ πορίζοντες, οἱ γεωργίας μὲν ἀμύητοι ψυ-
χικῆς, ἣ σπείρουσα καὶ φυτεύουσα τὰς ἀρετὰς
καρπὸν δρέπεται τὸν εὐδαίμονα βίον ἀπ᾽ αὐτῶν,
ἐργασάμενοι δὲ καὶ μεθοδεύοντες τὰ φίλα τῇ
σαρκὶ καὶ τὸν σύνθετον χοῦν, τὸν πεπλασμένον
ἀνδριάντα, τὸν ψυχῆς ἔγγιστα οἶκον,[1] ὃν ἀπὸ
γενέσεως ἄχρι τελευτῆς, ἄχθος τοσοῦτον, οὐκ
ἀποτίθεται νεκροφοροῦσα, μετὰ σπουδῆς τῆς
πάσης οἰκειούμενοι.

26 VI. Ὡς μὲν οὖν γεωργίας ἐργασία γῆς καὶ
γεωργοῦ γῆς ἐργάτης διαφέρουσιν, εἴρηται. σκεπτέον δέ, μὴ καὶ ἄλλαι τινές εἰσιν ἰδέαι συγγενεῖς
τῶν εἰρημένων, διὰ τὴν ἐν τοῖς ὀνόμασι κοινωνίαν
ἐπικρύπτουσαι τὰς ἐν τοῖς πράγμασι διαφοράς·
εἰσι δέ γε ἃς ἀναζητοῦντες εὕρομεν διτταί, περὶ
27 ὧν τὰ προσήκοντα, ἐὰν οἷόν τε ᾖ, λέξομεν. αὐτίκα
τοίνυν ὡς γεωργὸν καὶ γῆς ἐργάτην δόξαντας
ἀδιαφορεῖν ἀλλήλων εὕρομεν ἐν τοῖς κατὰ διάνοιαν

---

[1] Mangey ὄγκον, which perhaps may be right. For οἶκον
cf. Quod Deus 150.

in order that they may enclose within the toils as many fish as possible imprisoned as though by a wall : in just the same fashion the larger part of mankind stretching what the poets call, I think, " all-capturing nets," not only over every part of the sea but over the whole realm of water, earth and air, ensnares from all quarters things of all sorts to satisfy and indulge Pleasure. They dig into the ground and 25 cross the seas and do all works incidental to war or peace to provide lavish materials for Pleasure as for a queen. These people have not learned the secrets of soul-husbandry, which sows and plants the virtues and reaps as their fruit a happy life. They have made the objects dear to the flesh their business,[a] and these they pursue methodically. With all earnestness they seek to make their own that composition of clay, that moulded statue, that house so close to the soul, which it never lays aside but carries as a corpse from birth to death, ah ! how sore a burden !

VI. We have stated how working of the soil differs 26 from husbandry and a worker of the soil from an husbandman. But we must consider whether there are not other cases like those which have been mentioned, in which the difference between the things signified is obscured by their passing under the same name. There are two such instances which we have found by careful search, and concerning which we will say, if we can, what ought to be said. For example, then, as in the case of " husbandman " 27 and " soil-worker," by resorting to allegory we found a wide difference in meaning to underly apparent

[a] Or "their work," still continuing the thought of γῆς ἐργασία.

ἀλληγοροῦντες μακρῷ διεστηκότας, οὕτως ποιμένα
καὶ κτηνοτρόφον· μέμνηται γὰρ ποτὲ μὲν κτηνο-
28 τροφίας ποτὲ δ' αὖ ποιμενικῆς ὁ νομοθέτης. καὶ οἵ
γε μὴ λίαν ἠκριβωμένοι τάχα που τῆς αὐτῆς ἐπι-
τηδεύσεως συνωνυμούσας ὑπολήψονται προσρήσεις
εἶναι, εἰσὶ δέ γε πραγμάτων διαφερόντων ἐν ταῖς
29 δι' ὑπονοιῶν ἀποδόσεσι· καὶ γὰρ εἰ τοῖς θρεμμάτων
προεστηκόσιν ἀμφότερα ἐπιφημίζειν ἔθος κτηνοτρόφων καὶ ποιμένων ὀνόματα, ἀλλ' οὔ γε τῷ τὴν
ψυχῆς ἀγέλην ἐπιτετραμμένῳ λογισμῷ· φαῦλος
μὲν γὰρ ὢν ὁ ἀγελάρχης οὗτος καλεῖται κτηνο-
τρόφος, ἀγαθὸς δὲ καὶ σπουδαῖος ὀνομάζεται
30 ποιμήν. ὃν δὲ τρόπον, ἐπιδείξομεν αὐτίκα· VII. ἡ
φύσις ἡμῶν ἑκάστῳ κτήνη συγγεγέννηκε, τῆς
ψυχῆς ὥσπερ ἀπὸ μιᾶς ῥίζης ἔρνη διττὰ ἀνα-
βλαστούσης, ὧν τὸ μὲν ἄτμητον ὅλον δι' ὅλων
ἐαθὲν ἐπεφημίσθη νοῦς, τὸ δ' ἑξαχῇ σχισθὲν εἰς
ἑπτὰ φύσεις πέντε τῶν αἰσθήσεων καὶ δυεῖν ἄλλων
31 ὀργάνων, φωνητηρίου τε καὶ γονίμου. αὕτη δὲ
πᾶσα ἡ πληθὺς ἄλογος οὖσα κτήνεσιν ἀπεικάζεται,
πληθύι δὲ νόμῳ φύσεως ἡγεμόνος ἐξ ἀνάγκης δεῖ.[1]
[305] ἐπειδὰν μὲν οὖν ἄπειρος ἀρχῆς ἅμα καὶ | πλούσιος
ἐξαναστὰς ἄρχοντα ἑαυτὸν ἀποφήνῃ, μυρίων αἴτιος
32 κακῶν γίνεται τοῖς θρέμμασιν· αὐτὸς μὲν γὰρ
ἄφθονα παρέχει τὰ ἐπιτήδεια, τὰ δὲ ἀμέτρως
ἐμφορούμενα ὑπὸ πλεοναζούσης τροφῆς ἐξυβρίζει
—κόρου γὰρ ὕβρις ἔγγονον γνήσιον—, ἐξυβρίζοντα

---

[1] MSS. ἀεί et alia.

---

[a] Cf. De Op. 117 and note.

identity, so shall we find it to be with " shepherd " and " cattle-rearer." For the lawgiver speaks in some places of " cattle-rearing," in others of " shep- 28 herding," and people who have not acquired real accuracy will perhaps suppose that these are synonym- ous descriptions of the same pursuit, whereas they denote different things when words are rendered in the light of their deeper meaning. For though it is 29 customary to apply to those who have charge of animals both names, calling them " cattle-rearers " and " shepherds " indiscriminately, yet we may not do so when we are speaking of the reasoning faculty to which the flock of the soul has been entrusted : for this ruler of a flock is called a " cattle-rearer " when he is a bad ruler, but, when a good and sterling one, he receives the name of " shepherd." How this is, we will at once shew. VII. Nature has produced 30 each one of us with " cattle " as part of our being. The living soul puts forth, as it were, from one root two shoots, one of which has been left whole and undivided and is called " Mind," while the other by a sixfold division is made into seven growths, five those of the senses and (two) of two other organs, that of utterance and that of generation.[a] All this 31 herd being irrational is compared to cattle, and by nature's law a herd cannot do without a governor. Now when a man at once without experience in ruling and possessed of wealth rises up and con- stitutes himself a ruler, he becomes the author of a multitude of evils to his charges. For he on his 32 part supplies provender lavishly, and the animals gorging themselves beyond measure wax wanton from abundance of food, wantonness being the true offspring of excess, and in their wantonness they

μέντοι σκιρτᾷ καὶ ἀφηνιάζει καὶ κατὰ μέρος
σκιδνάμενα διαλύει τὸ τῆς ἀγέλης συντεταγμένον
33 στῖφος. ὁ δὲ τέως ἡγεμὼν καταλειφθεὶς ὑπὸ τῶν
ἀρχομένων ἰδιώτης ἀνεφάνη, καὶ ἐπιτρέχει μὲν
σπουδάζων, εἴ τι δύναιτο συλλαβεῖν ἐξ ὑπαρχῆς
καὶ ὑπαγαγέσθαι· ὅταν δὲ ἀδυνατῇ, στένει καὶ
κλαίει τὴν ἰδίαν κακίζων εὐχέρειαν καὶ ἑαυτὸν τῶν
34 συμβεβηκότων αἰτιώμενος. τοῦτον δὴ τὸν τρόπον καὶ τὰ τῶν αἰσθήσεων θρέμματα, ἐπειδὰν ὁ
νοῦς ὑπτίως καὶ ῥαθύμως ἔχῃ, τῆς τῶν αἰσθητῶν
ἀπλήστως ἐμφορούμενα ἀφθονίας ἀπαυχενίζει τε
καὶ σκιρτᾷ καὶ πλημμελῶς ὅπῃ τύχοι φέρεται, καὶ
ὀφθαλμοὶ πρὸς πάντα ἀναπεπταμένοι τὰ ὁρατά,
καὶ ἃ μὴ θέμις ὁρᾶν, ἐξώκειλαν, καὶ ἀκοαὶ πάσας
φωνὰς παραδεχόμεναι καὶ μηδέποτε πληρούμεναι,
διψῶσαι δὲ ἀεὶ περιεργίας καὶ φιλοπραγμοσύνης,
ἔστι δὲ ὅπου καὶ ἀνελευθέρου χλεύης ἐκπεφοιτή-
35 κασιν. VIII. ἐπεὶ πόθεν ἄλλοθεν τὰ πανταχοῦ
τῆς οἰκουμένης θέατρα νομίζομεν ἀμυθήτων μυ-
ριάδων ἀνὰ πᾶσαν ἡμέραν πληροῦσθαι; οἱ γὰρ
ἀκουσμάτων καὶ θεαμάτων ἥττους καὶ ὦτα καὶ
ὀφθαλμοὺς χωρὶς ἡνιῶν ἐάσαντες φέρεσθαι καὶ
κιθαριστὰς καὶ κιθαρῳδοὺς καὶ πᾶσαν τὴν κεκλα-
σμένην καὶ ἄνανδρον μουσικὴν περιέποντες, ἔτι δὲ
ὀρχηστὰς καὶ τοὺς ἄλλους μίμους ἀποδεχόμενοι, ὅτι
σχέσεις καὶ κινήσεις ἐκτεθηλυμμένας ἴσχονται καὶ
κινοῦνται, τὸν ἐπὶ σκηνῆς ἀεὶ πόλεμον συγκρο-
τοῦσι μήτε τῆς τῶν ἰδίων μήτε τῆς τῶν κοινῶν

ᵃ Or " actively promoting the warfare of the stage," *i.e.*
encouraging by their partisanship the rivalries and intrigues
of the actors. Mangey "factiones theatricas instaurant."

124

become frolicsome and refuse to be controlled, and getting separated in scattered groups they break up the compact array of the flock. The erstwhile 33 ruler, forsaken by his subjects, is shewn to be a raw hand, and runs after them anxious if possible to get hold of some animal and bring it under control again. Finding that he cannot do this, he weeps and groans, cursing his own rashness, and blaming himself for what has happened. Precisely in this way does that 34 other herd, our senses, act; whenever the mind gets lazy and careless, they gorge themselves insatiably with the lavish food brought in by the objects of sense, shake off restraint, and get unruly, going at random where they have no business to go. The eyes wide open to all things visible, even those which it is not right to look upon, meet with disaster. The ears welcome all sounds and are never satisfied; they are athirst all the time for particulars about other people's business, in some cases for topics for vulgar jesting, and go far and wide on these errands. VIII. From 35 what other quarter can we suppose that the theatres all over the world are filled every day with countless myriads? Those whom spectacles and musical per- formances have made their slaves, allowing ears and eyes to wander about unbridled; taken up with flute-players and harpers and the whole range of unmanly and effeminate music; delighting in dancers and other actors, because they put themselves into indelicate positions and make indelicate movements; ever organizing a warfare as mimic as that on the stage *a* without a thought for their own betterment or

Philo frequently uses συγκροτέω with πόλεμον in the sense of "organize" or "wage"; otherwise it might be taken as = "applaud."

PHILO

ἐπανορθώσεως πεφροντικότες, ἀλλὰ τὸν ἑαυτῶν οἱ
δυστυχεῖς διά τε ὀφθαλμῶν καὶ ὤτων ἀνατρέποντες
36 βίον. ἄλλοι δέ εἰσιν οἱ τούτων ἀθλιώτεροι καὶ
κακοδαιμονέστεροι, οἳ τὴν γεῦσιν ὥσπερ ἐκ δεσμῶν
ἔλυσαν· ἡ δὲ πρὸς πᾶσαν σιτίων τε καὶ ποτῶν
‹ἀπόλαυσιν› ἄφετος εὐθὺς ὁρμήσασα τά τε ἤδη
εὐτρεπισθέντα ἐπιλέγεται καὶ πεῖναν ἄληκτον καὶ
ἄπληστον ἴσχει τῶν ἀπόντων, ὡς, κἂν αἱ τῆς
γαστρὸς ἀποπληρωθῶσι δεξαμεναί, σπαργῶσαν ἔτι
καὶ μαιμῶσαν τὴν ἀεὶ κενὴν ἐπιθυμίαν περι-
βλέπεσθαι καὶ περιφοιτᾶν, μή τί που παρορᾶθὲν
λείψανον ἀφεῖται, ἵνα καὶ τοῦτο παμφάγου πυρὸς
37 δίκην ἐπιλιχμήσηται. γαστριμαργίᾳ τοίνυν ἡ ὀπα-
δὸς ἐκ φύσεως ἀκολουθεῖ συνουσίας ἡδονὴ μανίαν
ἔκτοπον καὶ οἶστρον ἀνεπίσχετον καὶ λύτταν
ἀργαλεωτάτην ἐπιφέρουσα· ὅταν γὰρ ὑπὸ ὀψο-
[306] φαγίας καὶ ἀκράτου καὶ πολλῆς | μέθης ἄνθρωποι
πιεσθῶσιν, οὐκέτι κρατεῖν ἑαυτῶν δύνανται, πρὸς
δὲ τὰς ἐρωτικὰς μίξεις ἐπειγόμενοι κωμάζουσι καὶ
θυραυλοῦσι, μέχρις ἂν τὸν πολὺν τοῦ πάθους ἀπ-
38 οχετευσάμενοι βρασμὸν ἠρεμῆσαι δυνηθῶσιν. οὗ
χάριν καὶ ἡ φύσις ὡς ἔοικεν ὑπογάστρια τὰ
συνουσίας ὄργανα ἐδημιούργησε, προλαβοῦσα ὅτι
λιμῷ μὲν οὐ χαίρει, πλησμονῇ δὲ ἕπεται καὶ πρὸς
τὰς ἰδίας ἐνεργείας ὑπανίσταται.
39 IX. Τοὺς οὖν τοῖς θρέμμασι τούτοις ἐπιτρέ-
ποντας ἀθρόων ὧν ὀρέγονται πάντων ἐμφορεῖσθαι
κτηνοτρόφους λεκτέον, ποιμένας δ᾽ ἔμπαλιν ὅσοι
τά τε ἀναγκαῖα καὶ αὐτὰ μόνα τὰ ἐπιτήδεια παρ-
έχουσι περιτεμνόμενοι καὶ ἀποκόπτοντες τὴν περιτ-

126

for that of the commonweal, but overthrowing (the poor wretches !), by means of eyes and ears their own life itself. Others there are more miserable 36 and ill-starred than these, who have let loose their appetite like an animal which had been tied up. Thus left at large it at once makes for all kinds of enjoyment of eatables and drinkables, takes its pick of what has already been served up, and develops a ceaseless and insatiable craving for what is not on the table. So, even if the receptacles of the belly have been completely filled, taste still empty and still swelling and panting goes about looking everywhere to see whether haply there are any leavings that have been overlooked and let pass, that like an all-devouring fire it may pick up this as well. Glut- 37 tony is naturally followed by her attendant, sexual indulgence, bringing on extraordinary madness, fierce desire and most grievous frenzy. For when men have been loaded up with overeating and strong drink and heavy intoxication, they are no longer able to control themselves, but in haste to indulge their lusts they carry on their revels and beset doors until they have drained off the great vehemence of their passion and find it possible to be still. This is 38 apparently the reason why Nature placed the organs of sexual lust where she did, assuming that they do not like hunger, but are roused to their special activities when fulness of food leads the way.

IX. So we must give the name of cattle-rearers to 39 those who permit these creatures to gorge themselves wholesale with all that they crave after. The title of shepherds we must give on the other hand to such as supply them with the necessaries of life only and nothing more, pruning and cutting off all excessive

τὴν καὶ ἀλυσιτελῆ πᾶσαν ἀφθονίαν, ἥτις ἀπορίας
καὶ ἐνδείας οὐχ ἥκιστα βλάπτει, πρόνοιάν τε
πολλὴν ἔχουσι τοῦ μὴ ἐξ ἀμελείας καὶ ῥᾳθυμίας
νοσῆσαι τὴν ἀγέλην εὐχόμενοι μηδὲ τὰς ἔξωθεν
40 εἰωθυίας κατασκήπτειν νόσους ἐπιγενέσθαι. στοχά-
ζονται δὲ οὐδὲν ἧττον καὶ τοῦ μὴ διασπασθεῖσαν
αὐτὴν σποράδην διασκεδασθῆναι, φόβον ἐπανα-
τεινόμενοι τὸν σωφρονιστὴν τῶν λόγῳ μηδέποτε
πειθομένων καὶ κολάσει χρώμενοι συνεχεῖ, μετρίᾳ
μὲν κατὰ τῶν ἰάσιμα νεωτεριζόντων, ἀφορήτῳ δὲ
κατὰ τῶν ἀνίατα· τὸ γὰρ εἶναι δοκοῦν ἀπευκτὸν
μέγιστον ἀγαθὸν ἀφραίνουσιν, ἡ κόλασις, ὥσπερ τοῖς
41 τὰ σώματα κάμνουσιν αἱ ἰατρικαὶ ὗλαι. X. ταῦτα
τὰ ἐπιτηδεύματα ποιμένων ἐστίν, οἳ τῶν σὺν ἡδονῇ
βλαβερῶν τὰ μετὰ ἀηδίας προτιμῶσιν ὠφέλιμα.
οὕτως γοῦν σεμνὸν καὶ λυσιτελὲς νενόμισται τὸ
ποιμαίνειν, ὥστε τὸ μὲν ποιητικὸν γένος τοὺς
βασιλέας ποιμένας λαῶν εἴωθε καλεῖν, ὁ δὲ νομοθέτης τοὺς σοφούς, οἳ μόνοι πρὸς ἀλήθειαν βασιλεῖς
εἰσιν· ἄρχοντας γὰρ αὐτοὺς ὡς ἂν ποίμνης εἰσάγει
τῆς ἀνθρώπων ἁπάντων ἀλόγου φορᾶς.
42 Διὰ τοῦτο καὶ τῷ τελειωθέντι ἐξ ἀσκήσεως
Ἰακὼβ τὴν ποιμενικὴν ἐπιστήμην περιῆψε· ποιμαίνει γὰρ οὗτος τὰ πρόβατα Λάβαν, τῆς τοῦ
ἄφρονος ψυχῆς τὰ αἰσθητὰ μόνα καὶ φαινόμενα
νομιζούσης ἀγαθά, χρώμασι καὶ σκιαῖς ἡπατη-
μένης καὶ δεδουλωμένης· λευκασμὸς γὰρ ἑρμηνεύε-
43 ται Λάβαν. καὶ Μωυσεῖ τῷ πανσόφῳ τὴν αὐτὴν

ᵃ See App. p. 490.

and hurtful luxuriance, a thing which does no less harm than straitness and dearth. " Shepherds " too are those who exercise much forethought that the flock may not contract disease as the result of negligence and laziness, praying too that there may be no occurrence of such plagues as are wont to come as a visitation which cannot be guarded against. No less 40 do they make it their aim that the flock may not be broken up and scattered about. Fear is the corrector of those who never obey reason. This they hold over them, and have recourse to constant punishment, a mild form in the case of those whose rebellion is capable of being cured, but very severe in the case of those whose wrongdoings defy curative treatment. For that which is apparently much to be deprecated is a very great boon to people who act senselessly, just as physic is to people in bad bodily health. X. These are the practices and ways of shepherds, 41 who prefer what is distasteful but beneficial to what is pleasant but hurtful. So full of dignity and benefit has the shepherd's task been held to be, that poets are wont to give to kings the title of " shepherds of peoples," a title which the lawgiver bestows on the wise. They are the only real kings,[a] and he shews them to us ruling, as a shepherd does his flock, over the irrational tendency common to all mankind.

This is why he ascribed to Jacob, who was perfected 42 as the result of discipline, the shepherd's lore. For Jacob tends the sheep of Laban (Gen. xxx. 36), that is to say, of the soul of the foolish one which considers nothing good but sensible objects that meet the eye, and which is deceived and enslaved by colours and shadows ; for the meaning of " Laban " is " whitening." He ascribes the same profession to Moses, the 43

τέχνην ἀνατίθησι· καὶ γὰρ οὗτος ποιμὴν ἀπο-
δείκνυται διανοίας τῦφον πρὸ ἀληθείας ἀσπαζο-
[307] μένης καὶ πρὸ τοῦ εἶναι τὸ δοκεῖν | ἀποδεχομένης·
περισσὸς γὰρ Ἰοθὸρ ἑρμηνεύεται, περιττὸν δὲ καὶ
ἐπεισηγμένον ἀπλανεῖ βίῳ πρὸς ἀπάτην τῦφος, ᾧ
καὶ τὰ κατὰ πόλεις ἕτερα παρ' ἑτέροις, οὐ τὰ αὐτὰ
δίκαια παρὰ πᾶσιν, ἔθος εἰσηγεῖσθαι τὰ κοινὰ τῆς
φύσεως καὶ ἀκίνητα νόμιμα οὐδ' ὄναρ ἰδόντι·
λέγεται γὰρ ὅτι " Μωυσῆς ἦν ποιμαίνων τὰ πρό-
44 βατα Ἰοθὸρ τοῦ ἱερέως Μαδιάμ." ὁ δ' αὐτὸς οὗτος
εὔχεται, μὴ ὡς ἀνεπιτρόπευτον ποίμνην τὸν ὄχλον
καὶ λεὼν[1] ἅπαντα τῆς ψυχῆς ἀφεθῆναι, τυχεῖν δὲ
ἀγαθοῦ ποιμένος ἐξάγοντος μὲν ἀπὸ τῶν ἀφροσύνης
καὶ ἀδικίας καὶ πάσης κακίας δικτύων, εἰσάγοντος
δὲ εἰς τὰ παιδείας καὶ τῆς ἄλλης ἀρετῆς δόγματα·
" ἐπισκεψάσθω " γάρ φησι " κύριος ὁ θεὸς τῶν
πνευμάτων καὶ πάσης σαρκὸς ἄνθρωπον ἐπὶ τῆς
συναγωγῆς ταύτης." εἶτα ὀλίγα προσειπὼν ἐπι-
φέρει· " καὶ οὐκ ἔσται ἡ συναγωγὴ κυρίου ὡσεὶ
45 πρόβατα, οἷς οὐκ ἔστι ποιμήν." XI. ἀλλ' οὐκ
ἄξιον εὔχεσθαι μὴ χωρὶς ἐπιστάτου καὶ ἡγεμόνος
ἐαθῆναι τὸ συγγενὲς καὶ συμφυὲς ἡμῶν ἑκάστῳ
ποίμνιον, ὡς μὴ τῆς φαυλοτάτης τῶν κακο-
πολιτειῶν ὀχλοκρατίας, ἣ παράκομμα τῆς ἀρίστης
δημοκρατίας ἐστίν, ἀναπλησθέντες θορύβοις καὶ
ταραχαῖς καὶ ἐμφυλίοις στάσεσιν ἀεὶ χρώμενοι
46 διατελῶμεν; οὐ μὴν ἀναρχία μόνον ὀχλοκρατίαν
τίκτουσα δεινόν, ἀλλ' ἢ καὶ παρανόμου καὶ βιαίου

---

[1] mss. κλαίων et alia.

---

[a] See App. p. 490.

all-wise ; for he also is appointed shepherd of a mind that welcomes conceit in preference to truth, and approves seeming in preference to being. For " Jethro " or " Iothor " means " uneven,[a] " and self-conceit is an uneven and adventitious thing that comes in to beguile a fixed and steady life. It is a quality whose way is to introduce principles of right varying city by city ; of one kind in this city, of another kind in that ; not the same rule of right in all. The ordinances of nature that apply to all alike and are immovable it has never seen even in a dream. What we are told is that " Moses was shepherding the sheep of Jethro the priest of Midian " (Exod. iii. 1). This same Moses prays that the whole multi- 44 tude of the soul-folk may not be left as an untended flock, but may be given a good shepherd, leading them forth away from the snares of folly and injustice and all wickedness, and leading them in to imbibe all that discipline and virtue in its other forms would teach them. For he says, " Let the Lord, the God of the spirits and of all flesh, appoint a man over this congregation ; " then, after adding a few words, he continues, " And the congregation of the Lord shall not be as sheep that have no shepherd " (Numb. xxvii. 16 f.). XI. Is it not well to pray that the flock linked 45 to each one of us by a common birth and a common growth may not be left without a ruler and guide ? So might mob-rule, the very worst of bad constitutions, the counterfeit of democracy, which is the best of them, infect us, while we spend our days in ceaseless experience of disorders, tumults and intestine broils. Anarchy, however, the mother of mob-rule, is not our 46 only danger. We have to dread also the uprising of some aspirant to sovereign power, forcibly setting law

PHILO

τινὸς ἐφ' ἡγεμονίαν ἐπανάστασις· τύραννος γὰρ ἐκ
φύσεως ἐχθρός, πόλεων μὲν ἄνθρωπος, σώματος
δὲ καὶ ψυχῆς καὶ τῶν καθ' ἑκάτερον πραγμάτων ὁ
τὴν ἀκρόπολιν ἐπιτετειχικὼς ἑκάστῳ θηριωδέ-
47 στατος νοῦς. ἀλυσιτελεῖς δὲ οὐχ αὗται μόνον αἱ
δεσποτεῖαι, ἀλλὰ καὶ τῶν λίαν ἐπιεικῶν ἀρχαί τε
καὶ προστασίαι· χρηστότης γὰρ πρᾶγμα εὐκατα-
φρόνητον καὶ ἑκατέροις, ἄρχουσί τε καὶ ὑπηκόοις,
βλαβερόν, τοῖς μὲν ἐκ τῆς τῶν ὑποτεταγμένων εἰς
αὐτοὺς ὀλιγωρίας μηδὲν μήτε ἴδιον μήτε κοινὸν
ἐπανορθώσασθαι δυναμένοις. ἔστι δ' ὅτε καὶ τὰς
ἡγεμονίας ἀναγκαζομένοις ἀποτίθεσθαι, τοῖς δὲ ἐκ
συνεχοῦς τῆς πρὸς τοὺς ἄρχοντας ὀλιγωρίας πειθοῦς
ἠμεληκόσι καὶ ἀδεῶς[1] ἐπὶ μεγάλου κακοῦ κτήσει
48 περιποιησαμένοις αὐθάδειαν. τούτους μὲν ⟨οὖν⟩
θρεμμάτων, ἐκείνους δὲ κτηνοτρόφων οὐδὲν νομι-
στέον διαφέρειν· οἱ μὲν γὰρ τρυφᾶν ἐν ἀφθόνοις
ὕλαις ἀναπείθουσιν, οἱ δὲ τὸν κόρον ἀδυνατοῦντες
φέρειν ἐξυβρίζουσι. χρὴ δὲ ὥσπερ αἰπόλον ἢ
βουκόλον ἢ ποιμένα ἢ κοινῶς νομέα τὸν ἡμέτερον
[308] ἄρχειν νοῦν τὸ | συμφέρον πρὸ τοῦ ἡδέος ἑαυτῷ τε
καὶ τοῖς θρέμμασιν αἱρούμενον.

49   XII. Ἡ δὲ τοῦ θεοῦ ἐπίσκεψις πρῶτον σχεδὸν
καὶ μόνον αἴτιον τοῦ τὰ μέρη τῆς ψυχῆς μὴ ἀν-
επιτρόπευτα ἀφεθῆναι, τυχεῖν δὲ ἀνυπαιτίου καὶ
πάντα ἀγαθοῦ ποιμένος· οὗ κατασταθέντος ἀμή-

---

[1] MSS. καταδεὲς or κατὰ δέος.

132

at naught. For a tyrant is a natural enemy. In cities this enemy is man ; to body and soul and all the interests of each of these, it is an utterly savage mind, that has turned our inner citadel into a fortress from which to assail us. Nor is it only from these 47 tyrannies that we derive no benefit. We gain nothing from the rule and governance of men who are too good and gentle. For kindness is a quality open to contempt, and injurious to both sides, both rulers and subjects. The former, owing to the slight esteem in which they are held by those placed under their authority, are powerless to set right anything that is wrong either with individual citizens or with the commonwealth. In some instances they are actually compelled to abdicate. Their subjects, as the result of habitual contempt for their rulers, have come to disregard their moral suasion, and undeterred by fear, have, at the cost of incurring a great evil, made the acquisition of stubbornness. These, therefore, we 48 must regard as differing in no respect from cattle, nor their rulers from cattle-rearers. The latter induce them to luxuriate in abundance of material comforts ; the former, powerless to bear the overfeeding, wax wanton. But our mind ought to rule as a goat-herd, or a cow-herd, or a shepherd, or, to use a general term, as a herdsman, as one who chooses both for himself and the creatures he tends what is advantageous in preference to what is agreeable.

XII. That which brings it about that the different 49 parts of the soul are not left to drift with no one to watch over them, is, we may say, mainly, nay solely, God's care and oversight. It secures for the soul the benefit of a blameless and perfectly good shepherd. When He has been set over it there is no possibility

χανον τὴν σύνοδον τῆς διανοίας γενέσθαι σποράδα.
ὑπὸ γὰρ μίαν καὶ τὴν αὐτὴν σύνταξιν ἐξ ἀνάγκης
φανεῖται πρὸς τὴν ἑνὸς ἐπιστασίαν ἀφορῶσα, ἐπεὶ
τό γε πολλαῖς ὑπακούειν ἀρχαῖς ἀναγκάζεσθαι
βαρύτατον ἄχθος.

50   Οὕτως μέντοι τὸ ποιμαίνειν ἐστὶν ἀγαθόν, ὥστε
οὐ βασιλεῦσι μόνον καὶ σοφοῖς ἀνδράσι καὶ ψυχαῖς
τέλεια κεκαθαρμέναις ἀλλὰ καὶ θεῷ τῷ πανηγεμόνι
δικαίως ἀνατίθεται. τούτου δὲ ἐγγυητὴς οὐχ ὁ
τυχὼν ἀλλὰ προφήτης ἐστίν, ᾧ καλὸν πιστεύειν, ὁ
τὰς ὑμνῳδίας ἀναγράψας· λέγει γὰρ ὧδε· " κύριος
51 ποιμαίνει με, καὶ οὐδέν με ὑστερήσει." τοῦτο
μέντοι τὸ ᾆσμα παντὶ φιλοθέῳ μελετᾶν ἐμπρεπές,
τῷ δὲ δὴ κόσμῳ καὶ διαφερόντως· καθάπερ γάρ
τινα ποίμνην γῆν καὶ ὕδωρ καὶ ἀέρα καὶ πῦρ καὶ
ὅσα ἐν τούτοις φυτά τε αὖ καὶ ζῷα, τὰ μὲν θνητὰ
τὰ δὲ θεῖα, ἔτι δὲ οὐρανοῦ φύσιν καὶ ἡλίου καὶ
σελήνης περιόδους καὶ τῶν ἄλλων ἀστέρων τροπάς
τε αὖ καὶ χορείας ἐναρμονίους ὁ ποιμὴν καὶ
βασιλεὺς θεὸς ἄγει κατὰ δίκην καὶ νόμον, προστησά-
μενος τὸν ὀρθὸν αὑτοῦ λόγον καὶ πρωτόγονον υἱόν,
ὃς τὴν ἐπιμέλειαν τῆς ἱερᾶς ταύτης ἀγέλης οἷά
τις μεγάλου βασιλέως ὕπαρχος διαδέξεται· καὶ γὰρ
εἴρηταί που· " Ἰδοὺ ἐγώ εἰμι, ἀποστέλλω ἄγγελόν
μου εἰς πρόσωπόν σου τοῦ φυλάξαι σε ἐν τῇ
52 ὁδῷ." λεγέτω τοίνυν καὶ ὁ κόσμος ἅπας, ἡ
μεγίστη καὶ τελεωτάτη τοῦ ὄντος θεοῦ ποίμνη·
" κύριος ποιμαίνει με, καὶ οὐδέν με ὑστερήσει."
53 λεγέτω καὶ ἕκαστος τῶν ἐν μέρει τὸ αὐτὸ τοῦτο
μὴ τῇ διὰ γλώττης καὶ στόματος ῥεούσῃ φωνῇ
πρὸς βραχεῖαν ἀέρος ἐξικνουμένη μοῖραν, ἀλλὰ τῇ
τῆς διανοίας εὐρυνομένη καὶ τῶν τοῦ παντὸς

of the union of the mind's parts being dissolved. For, having been brought under one and the same direction, it will evidently have to look only to the guidance of a single chief. For to be compelled to give heed to many authorities is a very heavy burden.

Indeed, so good a thing is shepherding that it is 50 justly ascribed not to kings only and wise men and perfectly cleansed souls but also to God the All-Sovereign. The authority for this ascription is not any ordinary one but a prophet, whom we do well to trust. This is the way in which the Psalmist speaks : "The Lord shepherds me and nothing shall be lacking to me" (Ps. xxiii. 1). It well befits every lover of 51 God to rehearse this Psalm. But for the Universe it is a still more fitting theme. For land and water and air and fire, and all plants and animals which are in these, whether mortal or divine, yea and the sky, and the circuits of sun and moon, and the revolutions and rhythmic movements of the other heavenly bodies, are like some flock under the hand of God its King and Shepherd. This hallowed flock He leads in accordance with right and law, setting over it His true Word and Firstborn Son Who shall take upon Him its government like some viceroy of a great king ; for it is said in a certain place : "Behold I AM, I send My Angel before thy face to guard thee in the way" (Exod. xxiii. 20). Let therefore even the whole 52 universe, that greatest and most perfect flock of the God who IS, say, "The Lord shepherds me, and nothing shall fail me." Let each individual person 53 too utter this same cry, not with the voice that glides forth over tongue and lips, not reaching beyond a short space of air, but with the voice of the understanding that has wide scope and lays hold on the

[309] ἁπτομένη περάτων· | ἀμήχανον γὰρ τῶν ἐπι-
βαλλόντων ἔνδειαν εἶναί τινος ἐπιστατοῦντος θεοῦ
πλήρη καὶ τέλεια τἀγαθὰ τοῖς οὖσιν ἅπασιν
54 εἰωθότος χαρίζεσθαι. XIII. παγκάλη δὲ εἰς ὁσιότητα παραίνεσις ἡ διὰ τοῦ λεχθέντος ᾄσματος· τῷ
γὰρ ὄντι ὁ μὲν πάντα τὰ ἄλλα δοκῶν ἔχειν, τῇ δὲ
ἑνὸς προστασίᾳ δυσχεραίνων, ἀτελὴς καὶ πένης·
ἥτις δὲ ὑπὸ θεοῦ ποιμαίνεται ψυχὴ τὸ ἓν καὶ μόνον
ἔχουσα, οὗ τὰ πάντα ἐκκρέμαται, ἀπροσδεὴς
εἰκότως ἐστὶν ἄλλων, οὐ τυφλὸν πλοῦτον, βλέποντα δὲ καὶ σφόδρα ὀξυδορκοῦντα θαυμάζουσα.
55 Τούτου πάντες οἱ μαθηταὶ εἰς σύντονον καὶ
δυσαπάλλακτον ἔρωτα ἦλθον, διὸ κτηνοτροφίαν
γελάσαντες ἐξεπόνησαν ποιμενικὴν ἐπιστήμην.
56 τεκμήριον δέ· ὁ τὴν περὶ σῶμα καὶ τὰς κενὰς
δόξας ὑπόθεσιν ἀεὶ μελετῶν Ἰωσήφ, ἄρχειν μὲν
καὶ ἐπιστατεῖν ἀλόγου φύσεως οὐκ ἐπιστάμενος—
πρεσβύταις γὰρ ἔθος ἐπὶ τὰς ἀνυπευθύνους[1] ἀρχὰς
καλεῖσθαι, νέος δέ ἐστιν οὗτος ἀεί, κἂν τὸ χρόνου
μήκει γῆρας ἐπιγινόμενον ἐνέγκηται—, τρέφειν
δὲ εἰωθὼς καὶ συναύξειν ὑπολαμβάνει καὶ τοὺς
φιλαρέτους πεῖσαι δυνήσεσθαι μεταβάλλειν ὡς
αὑτόν, ἵνα τῶν ἀλόγων καὶ ἀψύχων περιεχόμενοι
μηκέτ' ἐνευκαιρεῖν δύνωνται τοῖς λογικῆς ψυχῆς
57 ἐπιτηδεύμασι· φησὶ γάρ· ἂν ὁ βασιλεὺς νοῦς τῆς
σωματικῆς χώρας πυνθάνηται, τί τὸ ἔργον ὑμῶν,
ἀποκρίνεσθε· ἄνδρες κτηνοτρόφοι ἐσμέν. τοῦτο

---

[1] MSS. ἀνυπαιτίους.

ends of the universe. For it cannot be that there should be any lack of a fitting portion, when God rules, whose wont it is to bestow good in fullness and perfection on all that is.. XIII. Magnificent is the 54 call to holiness sounded by the psalm just quoted ; for the man is poor and incomplete in very deed, who, while seeming to have all things else, chafes at the sovereignty of One ; whereas the soul that is shepherded of God, having the one and only thing on which all depend, is naturally exempt from want of other things, for it worships no blind wealth, but a wealth that sees and that with vision surpassingly keen.

An intense and unquenchable love for this wealth 55 was entertained by all who belonged to its school, and this made them laugh cattle-rearing to scorn and spend labour on the lore of shepherding. The history of Joseph affords proof of this. Joseph, always having 56 as the object of his thought and aim the rule of life based on the body and on the surmises of vain imagination, does not know how to govern and direct irrational natures. To offices such as this which are subject to no higher control older men are generally called ; but he is always a young man, even if he have attained the old age that comes on us by mere lapse of time. Being accustomed to feed and fatten irrational natures instead of ruling them, he imagines that he will be able to win the lovers of virtue also to change over to his side in order that, devoting themselves to irrational and soulless creatures, they may no longer be able to find time for the pursuits of a rational soul. For he says, " If that Mind, whose realm is the body, 57 inquire what your work is, tell him in reply, We are cattle-rearers " (Gen. xlvi. 33 f.). On hearing this

ἀκούσαντες κατὰ τὸ εἰκὸς δυσχεραίνουσιν, εἰ
ἡγεμόνες ὄντες ὑπηκόων τάξιν ἔχειν ὁμολογή-
58 σουσιν· οἱ μὲν γὰρ τροφὰς ταῖς αἰσθήσεσι διὰ τῆς
τῶν αἰσθητῶν ἀφθονίας εὐτρεπιζόμενοι δοῦλοι
γίνονται τῶν τρεφομένων καθάπερ δεσποίναις
οἰκέται φόρον τελοῦντες καθ᾽ ἑκάστην ἡμέραν
ἀναγκαῖον, ἄρχοντες δὲ οἱ τούτων ἐπιστατοῦντες
καὶ τὰ περιττὰ τῆς εἰς ἀπληστίαν ὁρμῆς αὐτῶν
59 ἐπιστομίζοντες. τὸ μὲν οὖν πρῶτον καίτοι τοῦ
λεχθέντος οὐ καθ᾽ ἡδονὴν ἀκούσαντες ἐχεμυθήσουσι
περιττὸν ἡγούμενοι τὸ μὴ μαθησομένοις διαφορὰν
κτηνοτροφίας καὶ ποιμενικῆς ὑφηγεῖσθαι, αὖθις δὲ
ὅταν ὁ περὶ τούτων ἀγὼν ἐνστῇ, διαγωνιοῦνται
πάσῃ δυνάμει καί, πρὶν ἀνὰ κράτος ἑλεῖν, οὐκ
ἀνήσουσι τὸ τῆς φύσεως ἐλεύθερόν τε καὶ εὐγενὲς
καὶ ἡγεμονικὸν τῷ ὄντι ἐπιδειξάμενοι· πυνθανο-
μένου γοῦν τοῦ βασιλέως "τί τὸ ἔργον ὑμῶν;"
ἀποκρίνονται· "ποιμένες ἐσμέν, καὶ οἱ πατέρες
60 ἡμῶν." XIV. εἶτ᾽ οὐκ ἂν δόξαιεν ἐπὶ ποιμενικῇ
τοσοῦτον αὐχεῖν, ὅσον οὐδὲ ἐπὶ τῷ τοσούτῳ κράτει
τῆς ἀρχῆς ὁ προσομιλῶν αὐτοῖς βασιλεύς; οἵ γε
οὐχ αὑτοῖς μόνοις τὴν προαίρεσιν τοῦ βίου τούτου
μαρτυροῦσιν, ἀλλὰ καὶ τοῖς πατράσιν αὐτῶν, ὡς
61 σπουδῆς καὶ ἐπιμελείας ἁπάσης | ἀξίου· καίτοι γε,
[310] εἰ μὲν ἦν περὶ αἰγῶν ἢ προβάτων ἐπιμελείας ὁ
λόγος, κἂν ἴσως ᾐδέσθησαν ὁμολογεῖν ἀτιμίαν
φυγόντες· ἄδοξα γὰρ καὶ ταπεινὰ τὰ τοιαῦτα παρὰ
τοῖς ὄγκον μὲν εὐτυχίας τὸν ἄνευ φρονήσεως περι-
βεβλημένοις καὶ μάλιστα βασιλεῦσι νενόμισται·

they are vexed, as we might expect, that, being rulers, they are to admit that they occupy the position of subjects ; for those, who prepare food for the senses 58 by means of the lavish abundance of sensible objects, become slaves of those whom they feed, compelled day by day, like household servants to mistresses, to render the appointed due ; whereas the place of rulers is held by those who exercise authority over the senses, and check their excessive impulse to greed. At first his brethren, though far from pleased at 59 hearing what was said to them, will hold their peace, deeming it superfluous trouble to set forth to those who will not learn the difference between cattle-feeding and shepherding ; but afterwards when the contest regarding these matters is upon them, they will engage in it with all their might, and, until they have carried the day, they will never relax their efforts to make manifest the free and noble and truly princely character that pertains to their nature. When the king asks them " What is your work ? " they answer " We are shepherds, as were our fathers " (Gen. xlvii. 3). XIV. Aye indeed ! Does it not seem 60 as though they were more proud of being shepherds than is the king, who is talking to them, of all his sovereign power ? They proclaim that not they only but their fathers also deliberately chose this course of life as worthy of entire and enthusiastic devotion. And yet, if the care of literal goats or sheep was what 61 was meant, they would perhaps, in their shrinking from disgrace, have been actually ashamed to own what they were ; for such pursuits are held mean and inglorious in the eyes of those who have compassed that importance, wholly devoid of wisdom, that comes with prosperity, and most of all in the eyes of mon-

PHILO

62 τὸ δὲ Αἰγυπτιακὸν ἐκ φύσεως καὶ διαφερόντως
ἐστὶν ὑπέραυχον, ὁπότε μικρά τις αὐτὸ μόνον αὔρα
καταπνεύσειεν εὐπραγίας, ὡς χλεύην καὶ πλατὺν
γέλωτα ἡγεῖσθαι τὰς τῶν δημοτικωτέρων ἀνθρώπων
63 περὶ βίον σπουδάς τε καὶ φιλοτιμίας. ἐπειδὴ δὲ
περὶ τῶν ἐν ψυχῇ δυνάμεων λογικῶν τε αὖ καὶ
ἀλόγων πρόκειται σκοπεῖν, εἰκότως αὐχήσουσιν οἱ
πεπεισμένοι ὅτι δύνανται κρατεῖν τῶν ἀλόγων
64 συμμάχοις χρώμενοι ταῖς λογικαῖς. ἐὰν μέντοι τις
βάσκανος καὶ φιλεγκλήμων αἰτιώμενος φάσκῃ·
πῶς οὖν ποιμενικὴν τέχνην διαπονοῦντες καὶ τῆς
συμφυοῦς ποίμνης ἐπιμέλειαν ἔχειν καὶ προστασίαν
ἐπαγγελλόμενοι προσορμίσασθαι τῇ σώματος καὶ
παθῶν χώρᾳ διενοήθητε, Αἰγύπτῳ, ἀλλ᾽ οὐχ
ἑτέρωσε τὸν πλοῦν ἐποιήσασθε; μετὰ παρρησίας
αὐτῷ λεκτέον, ὅτι "παροικεῖν, οὐ κατοικεῖν
65 ἤλθομεν." τῷ γὰρ ὄντι πᾶσα ψυχὴ σοφοῦ πατρίδα
μὲν οὐρανόν, ξένην δὲ γῆν ἔλαχε, καὶ νομίζει τὸν
μὲν σοφίας οἶκον ἴδιον, τὸν δὲ σώματος ὀθνεῖον,
66 ᾧ καὶ παρεπιδημεῖν οἴεται. οὐκοῦν ἐπειδὰν ὁ
ἀγελάρχης νοῦς παραλαβὼν τὴν ψυχῆς ἀγέλην
νόμῳ φύσεως διδασκάλῳ χρώμενος εὐτόνως ἀφ-
ηγῆται, δόκιμον αὐτὴν καὶ σφόδρα ἐπαινετὴν ἀπεργ-
άζεται, ὅταν δὲ παρανομίᾳ ῥαθύμως καὶ ἀνειμένως
προσφερόμενος, ψεκτήν. εἰκότως τοίνυν ὁ μὲν
βασιλέως ὄνομα ὑποδύσεται ποιμὴν προσαγο-
ρευθείς, ὁ δ᾽ ὀψαρτυτοῦ τινος ἢ σιτοπόνου κτηνο-

archs. The spirit of the Egyptians too is by nature 62
arrogant even beyond that of other men, whenever
a feeble breath only of good fortune has blown over
it, and this arrogance makes them treat the aims in
life and the ambitions of more common people as
matter for rude jesting and loud ridicule. But seeing 63
that the subject propounded for consideration is that
of the rational and irrational faculties in the soul,
those will have ground for boasting who are convinced
that they are able by employing the rational faculties
as their allies to get the better of those which are
irrational. If, however, some malignant and con- 64
tentious person find fault with them and say, " How
is it, then, that, devoting your labour to the science
of shepherding, and professing to bestow the care of
leaders on the flock that lives and grows with your
life and growth, you conceived the idea of coming to
anchor in Egypt, the land of the body and the passions, instead of voyaging to some different port ? "
—we may confidently say to him " We came to
sojourn (Gen. xlvii. 4)—not to settle there "; for in 65
reality a wise man's soul ever finds heaven to be his
fatherland and earth a foreign country, and regards
as his own the dwelling-place of wisdom, and that of
the body as outlandish, and looks on himself as a
stranger and sojourner in it. Accordingly when 66
Mind, the ruler of the flock, taking the flock of the
soul in hand with the law of Nature as his instructor
shews it the way with vigorous leadership, he renders
it well worthy of praise and approval, even as he
subjects it to blame if he disregard Nature's law and
behave slackly and carelessly. With good reason,
then, will the one take on him the name of king and
be hailed " shepherd ," but the other that of a sort

141

τρόφος ἐπιφημισθείς, εὐωχίαν καὶ θοίνην ἀδηφαγεῖν
θρέμμασιν εἰωθόσιν εὐτρεπιζόμενος.

67 XV. Ὃν δὴ τρόπον γεωργὸς μὲν ἐργάτου γῆς,
ποιμὴν δὲ κτηνοτρόφου διενήνοχεν, οὐκ ἀμελῶς
ἐπιδέδειχα. καὶ τρίτον δ' ἐστὶ συγγένειάν τινα ἔχον
πρὸς τὰ λεχθέντα, περὶ οὗ νῦν ἐροῦμεν· ἱππέα τε
γὰρ καὶ ἀναβάτην οὐ μόνον ἄνθρωπον ἐποχούμενον
ἐποχουμένου χρεμετιστικῷ ζῴῳ μακρῷ διαφέρειν
68 ἡγεῖται, ἀλλὰ καὶ λογισμὸν λογισμοῦ. ὁ μὲν
τοίνυν ἄνευ τέχνης ἱππικῆς ἐπιβεβηκὼς λέγεται
μὲν εἰκότως ἀναβάτης, ἐκδέδωκε δὲ ἑαυτὸν ἀλόγῳ
καὶ σκιρτητικῷ θρέμματι, ὥσθ' ὅπη ἂν ἐκεῖνο
[311] χωρῇ | ᾽κεῖσε πάντως ἀναγκαῖον φέρεσθαι καὶ μὴ
προϊδόμενον χάσμα γῆς ἢ βαθύν τινα βόθρον ὑπὸ
τῆς ἐν τῷ δρόμῳ ῥύμης κατακρημνισθῆναι [συν-
69 ηνέχθη] καὶ συγκαταποθῆναι τὸν φερόμενον. ὁ
δ' ἱππεὺς πάλιν, ὅταν ἀνέρχεσθαι μέλλῃ, χαλινὸν
ἐντίθησι κἄπειτ' ἐφαλλόμενος τῆς περιαυχενίου
χαίτης ἐνείληπται καὶ φέρεσθαι δοκῶν αὐτός, εἰ
δεῖ τἀληθὲς εἰπεῖν, ἄγει τὸ κομίζον τρόπον
κυβερνήτου· καὶ γὰρ ἐκεῖνος ἄγεσθαι δοκῶν ὑπὸ
νεὼς τῆς κυβερνωμένης ἄγει πρὸς ἀλήθειαν αὐτὴν
70 καὶ ἐφ' οὓς ἐπείγεται παραπέμπει λιμένας. ὅταν
μὲν οὖν εὐηνίως προέρχηται, καταψήχει ὁ ἱππεὺς
ὡς ἂν ἐπαινῶν τὸν ἵππον, ὅταν δὲ σὺν πλείονι
ὁρμῇ πέραν ἐκφέρηται τοῦ μετρίου, μετὰ βίας
εὐτόνως ἀναχαιτίζει, ὡς ὑπανεῖναι τοῦ τάχους·
ἐὰν δὲ ἀπειθῶν ἐπιμένῃ, λαβὼν τοῦ χαλινοῦ ὅλον
ἀντέσπασε καὶ ἀντιπεριήγαγεν αὐτοῦ τὸν αὐχένα,

ᵃ Or "mounted man."
ᵇ Or "the man mounted on him."

of cook or baker and be entitled " cattle-feeder,"
serving up rich fare as a feast for beasts who make a
habit of gluttony.

XV. I have taken some pains to shew in what way 67
a husbandman differs from a worker on the soil, and
a shepherd from a feeder of cattle. There is a third
head akin to those that have been dealt with, and of
it we will now speak. For the lawgiver holds that a
horseman differs greatly from a rider, not only when
each is a man seated on a neighing animal but when
each is a process of reasoning. Well then, he who
being without skill in horsemanship is on a horse's
back is naturally called a rider.[a] He has given him- 68
self over to an irrational and capricious beast, the
consequence being that, wherever the creature goes,
thither he must of absolute necessity be carried, and
that the animal, not having caught sight in time of an
opening in the ground or of some deep trench, is
hurled headlong owing to the violence of his pace,
and his rider [b] is borne to destruction with him. The 69
horseman, on the other hand, when he is about to
mount, puts the bit in the horse's mouth and then as
he leaps on its back, seizes hold of its mane, and,
though seeming to be borne along, himself in actual
fact leads, as a pilot does, the creature that is carrying
him. For the pilot also, while seeming to be led by
the ship which he is steering, in reality leads it, and
convoys it to the ports which he is anxious to reach.
When the horse goes ahead in obedience to the rein, 70
the horseman strokes him as though he were praising
him, but when he gets too impetuous and exceeds
the suitable pace, he uses force and pulls back his head
strongly, so as to lessen his speed. If he goes on
being refractory, he grips the bit and pulls his whole

71 ὡς ἐξ ἀνάγκης στῆναι· καὶ πρὸς σκιρτήσεις μὲν
καὶ τοὺς συνεχεῖς ἀφηνιασμούς εἰσι μάστιγες καὶ
μύωπες εὐτρεπεῖς καὶ τἄλλ' ὅσα πωλοδάμναις
ἵππων κατεσκεύασται κολαστήρια. καὶ θαυμαστὸν
οὐδέν· ἀνιόντος γὰρ τοῦ ἱππέως καὶ ἱππικὴ τέχνη
συνανέρχεται,[1] ὥστε δύο ὄντες καὶ ἐποχούμενοι καὶ
ἐπιστήμονες εἰκότως ἑνὸς καὶ ὑποβεβλημένου καὶ
ἀπαραδέκτου τέχνης ζῴου περιέσονται.

72 XVI. Μεταβὰς τοίνυν ἀπὸ τῶν χρεμετιζόντων
καὶ τῶν ἐποχουμένων αὐτοῖς τὴν σαυτοῦ ψυχὴν εἰ
θέλεις ἐρεύνησον· εὑρήσεις γὰρ ἐν τοῖς μέρεσιν
αὐτῆς καὶ ἵππους καὶ ἡνίοχον καὶ ἀναβάτην, ὅσαπερ
73 καὶ ἐν τοῖς ἐκτός. ἵπποι μὲν οὖν ἐπιθυμία καὶ
θυμός εἰσιν, ὁ μὲν ἄρρην, ἡ δὲ θήλεια. διὰ τοῦθ'
ὁ μὲν γαυριῶν ἄφετος εἶναι βούλεται καὶ ἐλεύθερος
καὶ ἔστιν ὑψαύχην ὡς ἂν ἄρρην, ἡ δ' ἀνελεύθερος
καὶ δουλοπρεπὴς καὶ πανουργία χαιρουσα οἰκόσιτος,
οἰκοφθόρος· θήλεια γάρ. ἀναβάτης δὲ καὶ ἡνίοχος
εἷς ὁ νοῦς· ἀλλ' ἡνίκα μὲν μετὰ φρονήσεως ἄνεισιν,
ἡνίοχος, ὁπότε δὲ μετ' ἀφροσύνης, ἀναβάτης.
74 ἄφρων μὲν οὖν ὑπὸ ἀμαθίας κρατεῖν ἀδυνατεῖ τῶν
ἡνιῶν, αἱ δὲ τῶν χειρῶν ἀπορρυεῖσαι χαμαὶ
πίπτουσι, τὰ δὲ ζῷα εὐθὺς ἀφηνιάσαντα πλημ-
75 μελῆ καὶ ἄτακτον ποιεῖται τὸν δρόμον. ὁ δ'
ἐπιβεβηκὼς οὐδενὸς ἐνειλημμένος, ὑφ' οὗ στη-
ριχθήσεται, πίπτει, περιδρυπτόμενος δὲ γόνυ καὶ
χεῖρας καὶ πρόσωπα μεγάλα κλαίει τὴν ἰδίαν
κακοπραγίαν ὁ δείλαιος, πολλάκις δὲ καὶ τὰς

---

[1] MSS. συνέρχεται.

[a] The figure is based on *Phaedrus* 246 ff. *Cf.* note to
Leg All. 70, Vol. I. p. 478.
[b] *i.e.* " eats you out of house and home." See App. p. 490.

neck round the other way, so that he is forced to stop. To counter rearings and constant unruliness there are **71** whips and spurs ready at hand and all the other contrivances with which breakers-in of colts are provided for punishing them. There is nothing to wonder at in all this, for when the horseman gets on the horse's back, skill in horsemanship gets up with him, so that there are really two, a seated man on the horse and an expert, and they will naturally get the better of a single animal who is not only underneath them but is incapable of acquiring skill.

XVI. Passing then from the neighing animals and **72** those that ride upon them, search, if you please, your own soul; for you will find among its constituent parts both horses and one who wields the reins and one who is mounted, all just as in the outside world. Desire and high spirit are horses, the one male, the **73** other female.ᵃ For this reason the one prances and wants to be free and at large and has a high neck, as you might expect of a male. The other is mean and slavish, up to sly tricks, keeps her nose in the manger and empties it in no time,ᵇ for she is a female. The Mind is alike mounted man and wielder of the reins; a wielder of the reins, when he mounts accompanied by good sense, a mere mounted man when folly is his companion. The foolish man, since he has never learnt, **74** cannot keep hold of the reins. They slip from his hand and drop on the ground; and straightway the animals are out of control, and their course becomes erratic and disorderly. The fool behind them does **75** not take hold of anything to steady him, but tumbles out barking knee and hands and face, and loudly bewails, poor miserable fellow, his own misfortune. Many a time his feet catch in the board, and he hangs

βάσεις πρὸς τὸν δίφρον ἐξημμένος ἀνατραπεὶς
[312 ὕπτιος ἐπὶ νῶτα | ἀπηώρηται καὶ ἐν ἁρματοτροχιαῖς
αὐταῖς κεφαλήν τε καὶ αὐχένα καὶ ὤμους ἀμ-
φοτέρους περιθραύεται κατασυρόμενος, εἶθ᾽ ὧδε
κἀκεῖσε φορούμενος καὶ πᾶσι τοῖς ἐν ποσὶ προσ-
76 αραττόμενος οἰκτρότατον ὑπομένει θάνατον. τῷ
μὲν δὴ τοιοῦτον ἀποβαίνει τὸ τέλος, τὸ δὲ ὄχημα
ἀνακουφιζόμενον καὶ ἐξαλλόμενον μετὰ βίας, ὅταν
ἐπὶ γῆν παλίσσυτον ἐνεχθῇ, ῥᾷστα κατάγνυται,
ὡς μηκέτ᾽ αὖθις ἁρμοσθῆναι καὶ παγῆναι δύνασθαι·
τὰ δὲ ζῷα πάντων τῶν συνεχόντων ἀφειμένα
παρακινεῖται καὶ οἰστρᾷ καὶ οὐ παύεται φερόμενα,
πρὶν ὑποσκελισθέντα πεσεῖν ἢ κατά τινος ἐνεχθέντα
77 κρημνοῦ βαθέος παραπολέσθαι. XVII. τοῦτον οὖν
ἔοικε τὸν τρόπον αὐτοῖς ἐπιβάταις τὸ τῆς ψυχῆς
ὄχημα σύμπαν διαφθείρεσθαι πλημμελῆσαν τὴν
ἡνιόχησιν. τοὺς δὴ τοιούτους ἵππους καὶ τοὺς
ἐποχουμένους ἄνευ τέχνης αὐτοῖς λυσιτελὲς καθ-
αιρεῖσθαι, ἵνα τὰ ἀρετῆς ἐγείρηται· πιπτούσης
γὰρ ἀφροσύνης ἀνάγκη φρόνησιν ὑπανίστασθαι.
78 Διὰ τοῦτ᾽ ἐν προτρεπτικοῖς Μωυσῆς φησιν· "ἐὰν
ἐξέλθῃς εἰς πόλεμον ἐπ᾽ ἐχθρούς σου καὶ ἴδῃς ἵππον
καὶ ἀναβάτην καὶ λαὸν πλείονα, οὐ φοβηθήσῃ, ὅτι
κύριος ὁ θεὸς μετὰ σοῦ." θυμοῦ γὰρ καὶ ἐπιθυμίας καὶ συνόλως ἁπάντων παθῶν, καὶ τῶν
ὅλων ἐποχουμένων ὥσπερ ἵπποις ἑκάστοις λογισμῶν, κἂν ἀμάχῳ ῥώμῃ κεχρῆσθαι νομισθῶσιν,
ἀλογητέον τοὺς ἔχοντας τὴν τοῦ μεγάλου βασιλέως
θεοῦ δύναμιν ὑπερασπίζουσαν καὶ προαγωνιζομένην
79 αἰεὶ καὶ πανταχοῦ. στρατὸς δὲ θεῖος αἱ ἀρεταὶ
φιλοθέων ὑπέρμαχοι ψυχῶν, αἷς, ἐπειδὰν ἴδωσι τὸν

―――――――――――

ᵃ One of Philo's names for Deuteronomy; *cf.* § 172.

suspended turned over back-downwards, and as he is dragged along in the very wheel tracks he gets head and neck and both shoulders battered and crushed, and in the end, tossed after this fashion in every direction and knocking up against everything that comes in his way, he undergoes a most pitiable death. For 76 him such is the end that results, but the vehicle lifting itself up and making violent springs, when it reaches the ground in its rebound, too easily becomes a wreck, so that it is quite beyond being mended and made strong again. The horses, released from all that kept them in, become distracted and maddened and never stop tearing along until they trip and fall, or are swept down some steep precipice and perish. XVII. It is to be expected that the entire vehicle of 77 the soul with all who are on it should come to ruin in this manner, if it has gone wrong in the matter of the driving. It is a gain that such horses and those who drive them without skill should be destroyed, that the products of virtue may be exalted ; for when folly has a fall, wisdom is bound to rise up.

This is why Moses in his "hortatory discourse" [a] 78 says : "If thou shalt go out to war against thine enemies and see horse and rider and much people, thou shalt not be afraid, because the Lord thy God is with thee" (Deut. xx. 1). For high spirit and craving lust and all passions generally, and the whole array of reasoning faculties seated upon each of them as upon horses, even though they be held to have at their disposal resistless might, may be disregarded by those who have the power of the Great King acting always and everywhere as their shield and champion. There 79 is a divine army consisting of the virtues who fight on behalf of souls that love God, whom it befits

PHILO

ἀντίπαλον ἡττημένον, ἁρμόττει πάγκαλον καὶ πρε-
πωδέστατον ὕμνον ᾄδειν τῷ νικηφόρῳ καὶ καλλι-
νίκῳ θεῷ. δύο δὲ χοροί, ὁ μὲν τῆς ἀνδρωνίτιδος,
ὁ δὲ τῆς γυναικωνίτιδος ἑστίας, στάντες ἄντηχον
80 καὶ ἀντίφωνον ἀναμέλψουσιν ἁρμονίαν. χρήσεται
δ᾽ ὁ μὲν τῶν ἀνδρῶν χορὸς ἡγεμόνι Μωυσεῖ, νῷ
τελείῳ, ὁ δὲ τῶν γυναικῶν Μαριάμ, αἰσθήσει
κεκαθαρμένῃ· δίκαιον γὰρ καὶ νοητῶς καὶ αἰσθητῶς
τοὺς εἰς τὸ θεῖον ὕμνους καὶ εὐδαιμονισμοὺς
ἀνυπερθέτως ποιεῖσθαι καὶ τῶν ὀργάνων ἐμμελῶς
κρούειν ἑκάτερον, τό τε νοῦ καὶ αἰσθήσεως, ἐπὶ
81 τῇ τοῦ μόνου σωτῆρος εὐχαριστίᾳ καὶ τιμῇ. τὴν
γοῦν παράλιον ᾠδὴν ᾄδουσι μὲν πάντες ἄνδρες,
οὐ μὴν τυφλῇ διανοίᾳ, ἀλλ᾽ ὀξὺ καθορῶντες Μωυσέως ἐξάρχοντος, ᾄδουσι δὲ καὶ γυναῖκες αἱ
πρὸς ἀλήθειαν ἄρισται, τῷ τῆς ἀρετῆς ἐγγεγραμ-
μέναι πολιτεύματι, Μαριὰμ ἀφηγουμένης αὐταῖς.
82 XVIII. ὕμνος δὲ ὁ αὐτὸς ἀμφοτέροις ᾄδεται τοῖς
χοροῖς ἐπῳδὸν ἔχων θαυμασιώτατον, ὃν ἐφ-
υμνεῖσθαι καλόν· ἔστι δὲ τοιόσδε· '' ἄσωμεν τῷ
[313] κυρίῳ, ἐνδόξως γὰρ | δεδόξασται· ἵππον καὶ
83 ἀναβάτην ἔρριψεν εἰς θάλασσαν.'' ἀμείνονα γὰρ
καὶ τελειοτέραν οὐκ ἄν τις εὕροι σκοπῶν νίκην ἢ
καθ᾽ ἣν τὸ τετράπουν καὶ σκιρτητικὸν καὶ ὑπέραυχον ἥττηται παθῶν τε καὶ κακιῶν ἀλκιμώτατον
στῖφος—καὶ γὰρ κακίαι τῷ γένει τέτταρες καὶ
πάθη ταύταις ἰσάριθμα—, πρὸς δὲ καὶ ὁ ἐπιβάτης
αὐτῶν μισάρετος καὶ φιλοπαθὴς νοῦς καταπεσὼν

---

[a] See App. p. 490.
[b] The four vices are folly, cowardice, intemperance, injustice (corresponding to the four virtues). Diog. Laert. vii.
92. For the four passions, grief, fear, desire, pleasure, see
S.V.F. iii. 381 ff.

when they see the adversary vanquished, to sing to God, gloriously triumphant and giver of victory, a hymn of beauty and wholly befitting Him. And two choirs, one from the quarters of the men, one from those of the women, with answering note and voice shall raise harmonious chant. The choir of the 80 men shall have Moses for its leader, that is Mind in its perfection, that of the women shall be led by Miriam, that is sense-perception made pure and clean [a] (Exod. xv. 1, 20). For it is right with both mind and sense to render hymns and sing blessings to the Godhead without delay, and tunefully to strike each of our instruments, that of mind and that of sense perception, in thanksgiving and honour paid to the only Saviour. So we find [a] the Song by the seashore 81 sung by all that are men, with no blind understanding but with keenest vision, with Moses as their leader ; it is sung also by the women who in the true sense are the best, having been enrolled as members of Virtue's commonwealth, with Miriam to start their song. XVIII. The same hymn is sung by both 82 choirs, and it has a most noteworthy refrain, the recurrence of which is strikingly beautiful. It is this : " Let us sing unto the Lord, for gloriously hath He been glorified ; horse and rider He threw into the sea " (Exod. xv. 1, 21). No one who looks 83 into the matter could find a more perfect victory than one in which that most doughty array of passions and vices, four-footed, restless, boastful beyond measure, has been defeated. So it is, for vices are four in kind and passions equal to these in number. [b] It is a victory, moreover, in which their rider has been thrown and dispatched, even virtue-hating and

οἴχεται, ὃς ἡδοναῖς καὶ ἐπιθυμίαις, ἀδικίαις τε καὶ
πανουργίαις, ἔτι δὲ ἁρπαγαῖς καὶ πλεονεξίαις καὶ
τοῖς παραπλησίοις θρέμμασιν ἐγεγήθει.

84 Παγκάλως οὖν ὁ νομοθέτης ἐν ταῖς παραινέσεσιν
ἐκδιδάσκει μηδ' ἄρχοντα χειροτονεῖν ἱπποτρόφον,
ἀνεπιτήδειον οἰόμενος εἶναι πρὸς ἡγεμονίαν πάνθ'
ὃς ἂν περὶ ἡδονὰς καὶ ἐπιθυμίας καὶ ἔρωτας
ἀκαθέκτους μεμηνὼς οἷα ἀχαλίνωτος καὶ ἀφηνια-
στὴς ἵππος οἰστρᾷ· λέγει γὰρ ὧδε· " οὐ δυνήσῃ
καταστῆσαι ἐπὶ σεαυτὸν[1] ἄνθρωπον ἀλλότριον, ὅτι
οὐκ ἀδελφός σού ἐστι· διότι οὐ πληθυνεῖ ἑαυτῷ
ἵππον, οὐδὲ μὴ ἀποστρέψῃ τὸν λαὸν εἰς Αἴγυπτον."

85 οὐκοῦν τῶν ἱπποτρόφων πρὸς ἀρχὴν πέφυκεν
οὐδεὶς κατὰ τὸν ἱερώτατον Μωυσῆν· καίτοι φαίη
τις ἂν ἴσως, ὅτι μεγάλη χεὶρ ἐστι βασιλέως ἱππικὴ
δύναμις οὔτε πεζῆς οὔτε ναυτικῆς ἀποδέουσα,
πολλαχοῦ δὲ καὶ λυσιτελεστέρα καὶ μάλιστα ἐν οἷς
ἀνυπερθέτου καὶ συντόνου τάχους[2] τῆς ἐπεξόδου
δεῖ τῶν καιρῶν μέλλειν οὐκ ἐπιτρεπόντων, ἀλλ'
ἐπ' αὐτῆς ἱσταμένων ἀκμῆς, ὡς μὴ ἀναβάλλεσθαι
τοὺς ὑστερηκότας μᾶλλον ἢ ἀποτυχεῖν ἂν εἰκότως
εἰσάπαν νομισθῆναι, φθάντων παρελθεῖν ὥσπερ

86 νέφους ἐκείνων. XIX. εἴποιμεν δ' ἂν αὐτοῖς·
οὐδεμίαν, ὦ γενναῖοι, φρουρὰν ἄρχοντος ὁ νομοθέτης ὑποτέμνεται οὐδὲ τὸ συλλεχθὲν αὐτῷ στράτευμα ἀκρωτηριάζει τῆς δυνάμεως τὸ ἀνυσιμώ-
τερον, τὴν ἱππικὴν δύναμιν, ἀποκόπτων, ἀλλ' ὡς

---

[1] MSS. ἐπ' αὐτόν.
[2] MSS. ἀνυπερθέτῳ καὶ συντόμῳ τάχει.

---

a Another of Philo's names for Deuteronomy.

passion-loving mind, whose delight was in pleasures and cravings, acts of injustice and rascality, as well as in exploits of plundering and overreaching and all that stable.

Right well therefore does the lawgiver in his 84 Charges *a* give directions not to appoint a horse-rearer to be a ruler, regarding as unsuited for such high authority any man who resembles an unbridled and unruly horse, and, in his wild excitement over pleasures, lusts and amours, knows no restraint. These are the lawgiver's words, " Thou mayest not appoint over thyself a foreigner, because he is not thy brother ; for the reason that he shall not multiply to himself horses, nor turn the people back into Egypt" (Deut. xvii. 15 f.). According, therefore, to 85 Moses, that most holy man, a rearer of horses is by nature unfit to hold rule ; and yet it might be urged that strength in cavalry is a great asset to a king, and not a whit less important than infantry and the naval force ; nay, in many cases of greater service than these. These arms are especially important when it is requisite that the offensive should be instantaneous and vigorously pressed ; when the state of affairs does not admit of delay, but is in the highest degree critical ; so that those who are behindhand would fairly be considered not so much to have been slow to gain the advantage as to have failed for good and all, since the other side has been too quick for them, and gone by them like a cloud. XIX. We would say in answer to these criticisms, 86 " My good sirs, the lawgiver is not curtailing any ruler's garrison, nor is he incapacitating the army which he has collected by cutting off the more effective part of the force, the cavalry. He is trying

οἷόν τε πειρᾶται συναύξειν, ἵν᾿ εἴς τε ἰσχὺν καὶ
πλῆθος ἐπιδόντες οἱ σύμμαχοι ῥᾷστα τοὺς ἐναντίους
87 καθαιρῶσι. τίνι γὰρ οὕτω λοχίσαι στράτευμα καὶ
τάξαι καὶ κατὰ φάλαγγας διανεῖμαι καὶ λοχαγοὺς
καὶ ταξιάρχους καὶ τοὺς ἄλλους πλείονων ἢ ἐλαττόνων ἡγεμόνας καταστῆσαι ἢ ὅσα τακτικὰ καὶ
στρατηγικὰ εὕρηται [καὶ] τοῖς ὀρθῶς χρησομένοις
ὑφηγήσασθαι κατὰ πολλὴν τῆς ἐν τούτοις ἐπι-
88 στήμης περιουσίαν ἐξεγένετο; ἀλλὰ γὰρ οὐκ ἔστι
νῦν ὁ λόγος αὐτῷ περὶ δυνάμεως ἱππικῆς, ἣν
συγκροτεῖσθαι πρὸς ἄρχοντος ἐπ᾿ ἀναιρέσει δυσ-
μενῶν καὶ σωτηρίᾳ φίλων ἀναγκαῖον, ἀλλὰ περὶ
τῆς κατὰ ψυχὴν ἀλόγου καὶ ἀμέτρου καὶ ἀπειθοῦς
φορᾶς, ἣν ἐπιστομίζειν λυσιτελές, μή ποτε τὸν
λαὸν αὐτῆς ἅπαντα εἰς Αἴγυπτον, τὴν τοῦ σώματος
χώραν, ἀποστρέψῃ καὶ φιλήδονον καὶ φιλοπαθῆ
μᾶλλον ἢ φιλάρετον καὶ φιλόθεον ἀνὰ κράτος |
[314] ἐργάσηται, ἐπειδὴ τὸν πλῆθος ἵππων παρ᾿ ἑαυτῷ
κτώμενον ἀνάγκη τὴν εἰς Αἴγυπτον, ὡς αὐτὸς
89 ἔφη, βαδίζειν ὁδόν. ὅταν γὰρ καθ᾿ ἑκάτερον
τοῖχον τῆς ψυχῆς νεὼς τρόπον, τόν τε νοῦ καὶ
αἰσθήσεως, ὑπὸ βίας τῶν καταπνεόντων εἰς αὐτὴν
παθῶν τε καὶ ἀδικημάτων ἀντιρρεπούσης καὶ
κλινομένης ἐξαιρόμενον ἐπιβαίνῃ τὸ κῦμα, τόθ᾿ ὡς
εἰκὸς ὑπέραντλος ὁ νοῦς γινόμενος καταποντοῦται·
βυθὸς δέ ἐστιν, εἰς ὃν καταποντοῦται καὶ κατα-
δύεται, σῶμα αὐτὸ τὸ ἀπεικασθὲν Αἰγύπτῳ.
90 XX. μή ποτ᾿ οὖν περὶ τοῦτο σπουδάσῃς τῆς
ἱπποτροφίας τὸ εἶδος. οἱ μὲν γὰρ θάτερον μετιόντες ψεκτοὶ μὲν καὶ αὐτοί· πῶς γὰρ οὔ; παρ᾿
οἷς ἄλογα ζῷα μᾶλλον τετίμηται, ὧν ἐκ τῆς οἰ-

his best to improve it, that by an increase, both in strength and numbers, those who are fighting side by side may most easily overcome their enemies. For who was so capable as he, in virtue of abundant 87 acquaintance with these matters, to marshal an army by phalanxes and draw it up in order of battle and to appoint captains and corps-commanders and the other leaders of larger or smaller bodies of men, or to impart to those who would make a right use of it all that has been found out in the way of tactics and strategy ? But the fact is that he is not talking 88 in this passage about a cavalry force, which a sovereign has to organize for the overthrow of an unfriendly power and for the safety of his friends. He is speaking about that irrational and unmeasured and unruly movement in the soul to check which is in her interest, lest some day it turn back all her people to Egypt, the country of the body, and forcibly render it a lover of pleasure and passion rather than of God and virtue. For he who acquires a multitude of horses cannot fail, as the lawgiver himself said, to take the road to Egypt. For when the 89 soul is swaying and tossing like a vessel, now to the side of the mind now to that of body, owing to the violence of the passions and misdeeds that rage against her, and the billows rising mountains high sweep over her, then in all likelihood the mind becomes waterlogged and sinks ; and the bottom to which it sinks is nothing else than the body, of which Egypt is the figure. XX. Never then give 90 your mind to this kind of horse-rearing. Blameworthy indeed are those also who make a business of it in its literal form. To be sure they are so. With them irrational beasts are of greater value than human

κίας ἵππων μὲν ἀγέλαι κατευωχημένων ἀεὶ προ-
έρχονται, ἀνθρώπων δὲ ἑπομένων οὐδὲ εἷς ἔρανον
εἰς ἐπανόρθωσιν ἐνδείας, οὐ δωρεὰν εἰς περιουσίαν
91 εὑρισκόμενος. ἀλλ' ὅμως κουφότερα ἀδικοῦσιν·
ἀθλητὰς γὰρ ἵππους ἀνατρέφοντες τούς τε ἱεροὺς
ἀγῶνας καὶ τὰς πανταχῇ πανηγύρεις ἀγομένας φασὶ
κοσμεῖν καὶ οὐχ ἡδονῆς μόνον [ἀλλὰ] καὶ τῆς περὶ
τὴν θέαν τέρψεως αἴτιοι γίνεσθαι τοῖς ὁρῶσιν, ἀλλὰ
καὶ τῆς τῶν καλῶν¹ ἀσκήσεώς τε καὶ μελέτης· οἱ
γὰρ τὸν τοῦ νικηφορῆσαι πόθον ἐνιδόντες² θηρίοις,
διὰ τιμῆς ἔρωτα καὶ ζῆλον ἀρετῆς ἀλέκτῳ τινὶ
προτροπῇ καὶ προθυμίᾳ χρησάμενοι, πόνους ἡδεῖς
ὑποστάντες τῶν οἰκείων καὶ ἐπιβαλλόντων οὐκ ἀφ-
92 έξονται, πρὶν ἢ ἐπὶ τέλος ἐλθεῖν αὐτῶν. ἀλλ' οὗτοι
μὲν εὑρεσιλογοῦσιν ἀδικοῦντες, οἱ δ' ἄνευ ἀπολογίας
διαμαρτάνοντές εἰσιν οἱ τὸν ἀναβάτην νοῦν ἔποχον
ἀποφαίνοντες ἄπειρον ἱππικῆς ἐπιστήμης κακίᾳ
93 καὶ πάθει τετράποδι. ἐὰν μέντοι τέχνην τὴν
ἡνιοχικὴν ἀναδιδαχθεὶς ἐπὶ πλέον ἐνομιλήσῃς καὶ
ἐνδιατρίψῃς αὐτῇ καὶ ἤδη νομίσῃς ἱκανὸς εἶναι
δύνασθαι κρατεῖν ἵππων, ἀναβὰς ἔχου τῶν ἡνιῶν·
οὕτως γὰρ οὔτε ἀνασκιρτώντων αὐτὸς ἀποπίπτων
μετὰ τραυμάτων δυσιάτων γέλωτα παρ' ἐπιχαιρε-
κακοῦσιν ὀφλήσεις θεαταῖς οὔτ' ἐξ ἐναντίας ἢ
κατόπιν ἐπιτρεχόντων ἐχθρῶν ἁλώσῃ, τοὺς μὲν
τάχει φθάνων τῷ προεκδραμεῖν διώκοντας, τῶν

¹ mss. κακῶν.   ² mss. ἐνδιδόντες.

ᵃ Whether ἡδεῖς is taken as nom. or acc., it is doubtful
Greek in this sense. Mangey's ἡδέως is more natural.
154

beings. From their mansions there continually come troops of well-fed horses leading the way, while of the human beings that come behind these not one can get out of them a contribution to supply his need, or a gift to provide him with some spare cash. Nevertheless the wrong done by these people is less 91 heinous. For they contend that by training race-horses they both add lustre to the sacred race-meetings, and to the national festivals which are held universally ; that they not only give the spectators pleasure and provide them with the enjoyment of the sight, but promote the cultivation and study of noble aims ; for men (they say) who behold in animals the desire to carry off the victory, find themselves filled, by reason of their love of honour and enthusiasm for excellence, with an urgency and readiness beyond words, and so readily *a* submit to exertions in such contests as properly belong to them, and will not desist till they achieve their object. While these people find arguments in favour of their 92 ill-doing, those who sin without excuse are those who take Mind, that rider who is a tyro in the science of horsemanship, and put him on the back of four-footed vice and passion. If, however, you have 93 been taught the art of driving, and having become fairly familiar with it by persistent practice, have come to the conclusion that you can now manage horses, mount and hold on to the reins. By this means you will escape two disasters. If the horses rear you will not fall off, get badly hurt, and incur the ridicule of malicious spectators ; nor, if enemies make a rush at you from in front or from behind, will you be caught ; you will be too quick for those who come from behind and outstrip their pursuit ; and you will

δὲ προσιόντων ἀλογῶν διὰ τὴν τοῦ δύνασθαι
ἐξαναχωρεῖν ἀσφαλῶς ἐπιστήμην.

94 XXI. Οὐκ εἰκότως οὖν Μωυσῆς ἐπὶ τῇ τῶν
ἀναβατῶν ᾄδων ἀπωλείᾳ τοῖς ἱππεῦσιν εὔχεται
σωτηρίαν παντελῆ; δύνανται γὰρ οὗτοι χαλινὸν
ταῖς ἀλόγοις δυνάμεσιν ἐμβαλόντες αὐτῶν ἐπιστομίζειν τῆς πλεοναζούσης τὴν φορὰν ὁρμῆς.
τίς οὖν ἡ εὐχή, λεκτέον· " γενέσθω " φησί " Δὰν
ὄφις ἐφ' ὁδοῦ, ἐγκαθήμενος ἐπὶ τρίβου, δάκνων
πτέρναν ἵππου, καὶ πεσεῖται ὁ ἱππεὺς εἰς τὰ ὀπίσω,
95 τὴν σωτηρίαν περιμένων κυρίου." ὃ δ' αἰνίττεται
διὰ τῆς εὐχῆς, μηνυτέον· ἑρμηνεύεται Δὰν κρίσις.
[315] τὴν | οὖν ἐξετάζουσαν καὶ ἀκριβοῦσαν καὶ δια-
κρίνουσαν καὶ τρόπον τινὰ δικάζουσαν ἕκαστα τῆς
ψυχῆς δύναμιν ὡμοίωσε δράκοντι—ζῷον δ' ἐστὶ
καὶ τὴν κίνησιν ποικίλον καὶ συνετὸν ἐν τοῖς
μάλιστα καὶ πρὸς ἀλκὴν ἕτοιμον καὶ τοὺς χειρῶν
ἄρχοντας ἀδίκων ἀμύνασθαι δυνατώτατον—, οὐ
μὴν τῷ φίλῳ καὶ συμβούλῳ ζωῆς—Εὔαν πατρίῳ
γλώττῃ καλεῖν αὐτὴν ἔθος,[b] ἀλλὰ τῷ πρὸς
Μωυσέως ἐξ ὕλης χαλκῆς δημιουργηθέντι, ὃν οἱ
δηχθέντες ὑπὸ τῶν ἰοβόλων ὄφεων καίτοι μέλλοντες
τελευτήσειν ὁπότε κατίδοιεν ἐπιβιοῦν καὶ μηδέποτε
96 ἀποθνήσκειν λέγονται. XXII. ταῦτα δ' οὕτως
μὲν λεγόμενα φάσμασιν ἔοικε καὶ τέρασι, δράκων
ἀνθρώπου προϊέμενος φωνὴν καὶ ἐνσοφιστεύων
ἀκακωτάτοις ἤθεσι καὶ πιθανότησιν εὐπαραγώγοις
γυναῖκα ἀπατῶν, καὶ ἕτερος αἴτιος σωτηρίας γενό-
97 μενος παντελοῦς τοῖς θεασαμένοις. ἐν δὲ ταῖς δι'

---

[a] See App. p. 491.
[b] Or "playing the sophist with innocent ways."

make light of the frontal attack owing to your knowing the trick of backing without risk.

XXI. Does not Moses, then, when celebrating the 94 destruction of the riders, naturally pray for complete salvation for the horsemen? For these are able [a] by applying bit and bridle to the irrational faculties to curb the excessive violence of their movement. We must say, then, what his prayer is : " Let Dan," he says, " be a serpent on the road, seated upon the track, biting the heel of the horse ; and the horseman shall fall backwards, waiting for the salvation of the Lord" (Gen. xlix. 17 f.). What he intimates by the 95 prayer, we must point out. " Dan [a] " means " judgement " or " sifting." The faculty, then, which tests and investigates and determines and, in a manner, judges all the soul's concerns, he likened to a serpent. This is a creature tortuous in its movements, of great intelligence, ready to shew fight, and most capable of defending itself against wrongful aggression. He did not liken the faculty to the serpent that played the friend and gave advice to " Life "—whom in our own language we call " Eve "—but to the serpent made by Moses out of material brass. When those who had been bittten by the venomous serpents looked upon this one, though at the point of death, they are said to have lived on and in no case to have died (Numb. xxi. 8). XXII. Told in this way, these 96 things are like prodigies and marvels, one serpent emitting a human voice and using quibbling arguments to an utterly guileless character,[b] and cheating a woman with seductive plausibilities ; and another proving the author of complete deliverance to those who beheld it. But when we interpret words by the 97

PHILO

ὑπονοιῶν ἀποδόσεσι τὸ μὲν μυθῶδες ἐκποδὼν
οἴχεται, τὸ δ' ἀληθὲς ἀρίδηλον εὑρίσκεται· τὸν μὲν
οὖν τῆς γυναικὸς ὄφιν, αἰσθήσεως καὶ σαρκῶν
ἐκκρεμαμένης ζωῆς, ἡδονὴν εἶναί φαμεν, ἰλυσπω-
μένην καὶ πολυπλοκωτάτην, ἀνεγερθῆναι μὴ δυναμένην, αἰεὶ καταβεβλημένην, ἐπὶ μόνα τὰ γῆς
ἕρπουσαν ἀγαθά, καταδύσεις τὰς ἐν τῷ σώματι
ζητοῦσαν, ὥσπερ ὀρύγμασιν ἢ χάσμασιν ἑκάστῃ
τῶν αἰσθήσεων ἐμφωλεύουσαν, σύμβουλον ἀνθρώπου, φονῶσαν κατὰ τοῦ κρείττονος, ἰοβόλοις
καὶ ἀνωδύνοις γλιχομένην δήγμασιν ἀποκτεῖναι·
τὸν δὲ Μωυσέως ὄφιν τὴν ἡδονῆς ἐναντίαν διάθεσιν,
καρτερίαν, παρὸ καὶ τῆς χαλκοῦ κραταιοτάτης
98 ὕλης κατεσκευασμένος εἰσάγεται. τὸν οὖν ἄκρως
καταθεασάμενον τὸ καρτερίας εἶδος, κἂν εἰ δεδηγ-
μένος πρότερον ὑπὸ τῶν φίλτρων ἡδονῆς τυγχάνοι,
ζῆν ἀναγκαῖον· ἡ μὲν γὰρ ἐπανατείνεται ψυχῇ
θάνατον ἀπαραίτητον, ἐγκράτεια δ' ὑγείαν καὶ
σωτηρίαν προτείνει βίου. ἀντιπαθὲς δ' ἀκολασίας
99 φάρμακον ἢ ἀλεξίκακος σωφροσύνη. παντὶ δὲ
[316] σοφῷ τὸ καλὸν φίλον, ὃ καὶ πάντως ἐστὶ | σω-
τήριον. ὥσθ' ὅταν εὔχηται Μωυσῆς γενέσθαι τῷ
Δὰν ἢ αὐτὸν ἐκεῖνον ὄφιν—ἑκατέρως γὰρ ἔστιν
ἐκδέξασθαι—, παραπλήσιον τῷ ὑπ' αὐτοῦ κατα-
σκευασθέντι, ἀλλ' οὐχ ὅμοιον τῷ τῆς Εὔας εὔχεται·
τὴν γὰρ εὐχὴν ἀγαθῶν αἴτησιν εἶναι συμβέβηκε.
100 τὸ μὲν οὖν τῆς καρτερίας γένος ἀγαθὸν καὶ οἰστικὸν
ἀφθαρσίας, ἀγαθοῦ τελείου, τὸ δὲ τῆς ἡδονῆς κακὸν

---

[a] *Cf.* the lxx in Gen. iii. 20 καὶ ἐκάλεσεν Ἀδὰμ τὸ ὄνομα τῆς γυναικὸς αὐτοῦ, Ζωή.

[b] This seems strange here, notwithstanding " friend and counsellor " above, §95. Mangey proposed ἐπίβουλον, Wend. ⟨κακὸν⟩ σύμβουλον.

158

meanings that lie beneath the surface, all that is mythical is removed out of our way, and the real sense becomes as clear as daylight. Well then, we say that the woman is Life [a] depending on the senses and material substance of our bodies ; that her serpent is pleasure, a crawling thing with many a twist, powerless to raise itself upright, always prone, creeping after the good things of earth alone, making for the hiding-places afforded to it by the body, making its lair in each of the senses as in cavities or dug-outs, giving advice to a human being,[b] athirst for the blood of anything better than itself, delighting to cause death by poisonous and painless bites. We say that the serpent of Moses is the disposition quite contrary to pleasure, even stedfast endurance, which explains why it is represented as being made of very strong material like brass. He, then, who has looked with 98 fixed gaze on the form of patient endurance, even though he should perchance have been previously bitten by the wiles of pleasure, cannot but live ; for, whereas pleasure menaces the soul with inevitable death, self-control holds out to it health and safety for life ; and self-mastery, that averter of ills, is an antidote to licentiousness. And the thing that is 99 beautiful and noble, which assuredly brings health and salvation, is dear to every wise man. So when Moses prays, either that there may be for Dan, or that Dan himself may be, a serpent (for the words may be taken either way), he prays for a serpent corresponding to the one made by him, but not like Eve's ; for prayer is an asking for good things. And 100 we know that endurance is of a good kind that brings immortality, a perfect good, while pleasure is

159

τὴν μεγίστην τιμωρίαν ἐπιφέρον, θάνατον. διὸ
λέγει· " γενέσθω Δὰν ὄφις " οὐχ ἑτέρωθι μᾶλλον ἢ
101 " ἐφ᾽ ὁδοῦ "· τὰ μὲν γὰρ τῆς ἀκρασίας καὶ λαιμαργίας καὶ ὅσα ἄλλα αἱ ἀμέτρητοι καὶ ἄπληστοι,
πληρούμεναι πρὸς τῆς τῶν ἐκτὸς ἀφθονίας, ὠδίνουσι
καὶ τίκτουσιν ἡδοναί, κατὰ λεωφόρου καὶ εὐθυ-
τενοῦς βαίνειν οὐκ ἐπιτρέπει ψυχήν, φάραγξι δὲ
καὶ βαράθροις ἐμπίπτειν ἄχρι τοῦ καὶ διαφθεῖραι
παντελῶς αὐτὴν ἀναγκάζει· τὰ δὲ καρτερίας καὶ
σωφροσύνης καὶ τῆς ἄλλης ἀρετῆς * * * ἐχόμενα
μόνα,¹ μηδενὸς ὄντος ἐν ποσὶν ὀλισθηροῦ, ᾧ προσ-
πταίσασα κλιθήσεται.   προσφυέστατα οὖν ἔχεσθαι τῆς ὀρθῆς ὁδοῦ σωφροσύνην εἶπε, διότι καὶ
τὴν ἐναντίαν ἕξιν ἀκολασίαν ἀνοδίᾳ χρῆσθαι συμ-
102 βέβηκε.   XXIII. τὸ δὲ " καθήμενος ἐπὶ
τρίβου " τοιοῦτον ὑποβάλλει νοῦν, ὥς γε ἐμαυτὸν
πείθω· τρίβος ἐστὶν ἡ τετριμμένη πρός τε ἀνθρώπων καὶ ὑποζυγίων ἱππήλατος καὶ ἀμαξήλατος
103 ὁδός. ταύτῃ φασὶν ἡδονὴν ἐμφερεστάτην εἶναι·
σχεδὸν γὰρ ἀπὸ γενέσεως ἄχρι τοῦ μακροῦ γήρως
ἐπιβαίνουσι καὶ ἐμπεριπατοῦσι καὶ μετὰ σχολῆς
καὶ ῥᾳστώνης ἐνδιατρίβουσι τῇ ὁδῷ ταύτῃ, οὐκ
ἄνθρωποι ⟨μόνον⟩, ἀλλὰ καὶ ὅσαι ἄλλαι ἰδέαι τῶν
ζῴων εἰσίν· ἐν γὰρ οὐδέν ἐστιν ὃ μὴ πρὸς ἡδονῆς
δελεασθὲν εἵλκυσται καὶ ἐμφέρεται τοῖς πολυπλοκω-
τάτοις δικτύοις αὐτῆς, ἃ πολὺς διεκδῦναι πόνος.
104 αἱ δὲ φρονήσεως καὶ σωφροσύνης καὶ τῶν ἄλλων
ἀρετῶν ὁδοί, καὶ εἰ μὴ ἄβατοι, ἀλλά τοι πάντως

¹ The passage is evidently corrupt. Wendland's conjecture that there is a lacuna after ἀρετῆς which he supplies
with ⟨εὐοδίαν ψυχῇ παρ⟩έχεται μόνα has been followed in the

of an evil kind that inflicts the greatest penalty, even death. Wherefore it says, " Let Dan become a serpent " not elsewhere than " on the road." For 101 lack of self-control, and gluttony, and all else that issues from the womb of those immoderate and insatiate pleasures that ever conceive by the abundance of external comforts, never allow the soul to go along the straight course by the highway, but compel it to fall into pits and clefts, until they have utterly destroyed it. But only the practice of endurance and temperance and other virtue secures for the soul a safe journey where there is no slippery object under foot upon which the soul must stumble and be laid low. Most fitly therefore did he say that temperance keeps to the right road, since the opposite condition, that of licentiousness, finds no road at all.

XXIII. The sense suggested by the words "sitting on 102 the track " is, I am convinced, something of this kind. By " track " is meant the road for horses and carriages trodden both by men and by beasts of burden. They say that pleasure is very like this road ; for 103 almost from birth to late old age this road is traversed and used as a promenade and a place of recreation in which to spend leisure hours not by men only but by every other kind of living creatures. For there is no single thing that does not yield to the enticement of pleasure, and get caught and dragged along in her entangling nets, through which it is difficult to slip and make your escape. But the roads of sound-sense 104 and self-mastery and of the other virtues, if not untrodden, are at all events unworn ; for scanty is the

---

translation, but it is a mere guess ; and the ἔχεσθαι τῆς ὁδοῦ in the next sentence rather suggests that ἐχόμενα should be kept.

ἄτριπτοι· ὀλίγος γὰρ ἀριθμός ἐστι τῶν αὐτὰς
βαδιζόντων, οἳ πεφιλοσοφήκασιν ἀνόθως καὶ πρὸς
μόνον τὸ καλὸν ἑταιρίαν ἔθεντο, τῶν ἄλλων
105 ἁπάντων ἅπαξ ἀλογήσαντες. " ἐγκάθηται " οὖν,
καὶ οὐχ ἅπαξ, ὅτῳ ζῆλος καὶ φροντὶς εἰσέρχεται
καρτερίας, ἵν᾽ ἐξ ἐνέδρας ἐπιθέμενος τὴν ἑθάδα
ἡδονήν, πηγὴν ἀεννάων κακῶν, ἐπιφράξῃ καὶ ἐκ
106 τοῦ τῆς ψυχῆς ἀνέλῃ χωρίου. τότε, ὡς φησιν
ἀκολουθίᾳ χρώμενος, ἀναγκαίως " δήξεται πτέρναν
ἵππου "· καρτερίας γὰρ καὶ σωφροσύνης ἴδιον τὰς
τῆς ὑψαυχενούσης κακίας καὶ τοῦ παρατεθηγμένου
107 καὶ ὀξυκινήτου καὶ σκιρτητικοῦ πάθους ἐπιβάθρας
[317] διασεῖσαι | καὶ ἀνατρέψαι. XXIV. τὸν μὲν οὖν
τῆς Εὔας ὄφιν εἰσάγει κατ᾽ ἀνθρώπου φονῶντα—
λέγει γὰρ ἐν ταῖς ἀραῖς· " αὐτός σου τηρήσει
κεφαλήν, καὶ σὺ τηρήσεις αὐτοῦ πτέρναν "—, τὸν
δὲ τοῦ Δάν, περὶ οὗ νῦν ἐστιν ὁ λόγος, ἵππου
108 πτέρναν, ἀλλ᾽ οὐκ ἀνθρώπου δάκνοντα· ὁ μὲν γὰρ
τῆς Εὔας ἡδονῆς ὢν σύμβολον, ὡς ἐδείχθη πρότερον, ἀνθρώπῳ τῷ καθ᾽ ἕκαστον ἡμῶν ἐπιτίθεται
λογισμῷ—φθορὰ γὰρ διανοίας πλεοναζούσης ἡδονῆς
109 ἀπόλαυσίς τε καὶ χρῆσις—· ὁ δὲ τοῦ Δάν, εἰκών
τις ὢν ἐρρωμενεστάτης ἀρετῆς καρτερίας, ἵππον,
τὸ πάθους καὶ κακίας σύμβολον, δήξεται, διότι
σωφροσύνη τὴν τούτων καθαίρεσίν τε καὶ φθορὰν
μελετᾷ. δηχθέντων μέντοι καὶ ὀκλασάντων " ὁ
110 ἱππεύς " φησί " πεσεῖται."   ὃ δ᾽ αἰνίττεται, τοιοῦτόν ἐστι· καλὸν καὶ περιμάχητον εἶναι

---

a *i.e.* "and remains there."
b Or "according to the natural sequence of the thought"
(perhaps, as Mangey, read ἀναγκαίᾳ).

162

number of those that tread them, that have genuinely devoted themselves to the pursuit of wisdom, and entered into no other association than that with the beautiful and noble, and have renounced everything else whatever. To continue. There " lies in am- 105 bush," and that not once only,^{a} everyone into whom a zeal and care for endurance enters, in order that making his onslaught from his lurking-place he may block the way of familiar pleasure, the fountain of ever-flowing ills, and rid the domain of the soul of her. Then, as he goes straight on to say,^{b} he will as 106 a matter of course " bite the horse's heel " ; for it is characteristic of endurance and self-mastery to disturb and upset the means by which vaunting vice and passion, keen and swift and unruly, make their approach. XXIV. Eve's serpent is represented by 107 the lawgiver as thirsting for man's blood, for he says in the curses pronounced on it, " He shall lie in wait for thy head, and thou shalt lie in wait for his heel " (Gen. iii. 15) ; whereas Dan's serpent, of which we are now speaking, is represented as biting, not a man's, but a horse's heel. For Eve's serpent, being, 108 as was shewn before, a symbol of pleasure, attacks a man, namely, the reasoning faculty in each of us ; for the delightful experience of abounding pleasure is the ruin of the understanding ; whereas the serpent 109 of Dan, being a figure of endurance, a most sturdy virtue, will be found to bite a horse, the symbol of passion and wickedness, inasmuch as temperance makes the overthrow and destruction of these its aim. When these have been bitten and brought to their knees, " the horseman," he says, " shall fall."

What he conveys by a figure is this. 110 He regards it as no worthy object of ambition for

νομίζει¹ μηδενὶ τῶν ἐκ πάθους ἢ κακίας τὸν ἡμέτερον ἐποχεῖσθαι νοῦν, ἀλλ' ὁπότ' ἐπιβῆναί τινι
αὐτῶν βιασθείη, σπουδάζειν καθάλλεσθαι καὶ ἀπο-
πίπτειν· τὰ γὰρ τοιαῦτα πτώματα φέρει τὰς εὐκλεε-
στάτας νίκας. διὸ καὶ τῶν πάλαι τις προκληθεὶς
ἐπὶ λοιδορίας ἅμιλλαν οὐκ ἂν εἰς τοιοῦτον ἀγῶνα
ἔφη ποτὲ παρελθεῖν, ἐν ᾧ χείρων ὁ νικῶν ἐστι τοῦ
111 ἡττωμένου. XXV. καὶ σὺ τοίνυν, ὦ οὗτος, μηδέ-
ποτ' εἰς κακῶν παρέλθῃς ἅμιλλαν μηδὲ περὶ
πρωτείων τῶν ἐν τούτοις διαγωνίσῃ, ἀλλὰ μάλιστα
μέν, ἐὰν οἷόν τε ᾖ, σπούδασον ἀποδρᾶναι· ἐὰν δέ
που πρὸς ἐρρωμενεστέρας δυνάμεως βιασθεὶς ἀναγ-
κασθῇς διαγωνίσασθαι, μὴ μελλήσῃς ἡττᾶσθαι·
112 τότε γὰρ εὖ μὲν ἔσῃ νενικηκὼς ὁ ἡττώμενος,
ἡττώμενοι δ' οἱ νενικηκότες. καὶ μὴ ἐπιτρέψῃς
μηδὲ κήρυκι κηρῦξαι μηδὲ βραβευτῇ στεφανῶσαι
τὸν ἐχθρόν, ἀλλ' αὐτὸς παρελθὼν τὰ βραβεῖα καὶ
τὸν φοίνικα ἀνάδος καὶ στεφάνωσον, εἰ θέλει, καὶ
ταῖς ταινίαις ἀνάδησον καὶ κήρυξον αὐτὸς μεγάλῃ
καὶ ἀρρήκτῳ φωνῇ κήρυγμα τοιοῦτον· τὸν ἐπιθυμίας καὶ θυμοῦ καὶ ἀκολασίας ἀφροσύνης τε αὖ
καὶ ἀδικίας προτεθέντα ἀγῶνα, ὦ θεαταὶ καὶ
ἀθλοθέται, ἥττημαι μὲν ἐγώ, νενίκηκε δ' οὑτοσί,²
καὶ οὕτως ἐκ πολλοῦ τοῦ περιόντος νενίκηκεν,
ὥστε καὶ παρὰ τοῖς ἀνταγωνισταῖς ἡμῖν, οὓς
113 εἰκὸς³ ἦν βασκαίνειν, μὴ φθονεῖσθαι. τὰ μὲν οὖν
τῶν ἀνιέρων τούτων ἀγώνων ἆθλα παραχώρησον
ἄλλοις, τὰ δὲ τῶν ἱερῶν ὄντως αὐτὸς ἀνάδησαι·
ἱεροὺς δὲ μὴ νομίσῃς ἀγῶνας, οὓς αἱ πόλεις ἐν ταῖς

¹ MSS. νομίζειν.   ² MSS. οὗτος εἶ.   ³ MSS. ὡς νῖκος.

ᵃ Demosthenes; see Stobaeus, Flor. xix. 4.

our mind to ride on any of the progeny of passion
or wickedness, but, should it ever be forced to mount
one of them, he considers that it is best for it to
make haste to jump down and tumble off; for such
falls bring the noblest victories. This explains what
was meant by one of the ancients [a] when challenged
to a reviling match. He said that he would never
come forward for such a contest, for in it the victor
is worse than the vanquished. XXV. Do you then 111
also, my friend, never come forward for a rivalry in
badness, nor contend for the first place in this, but,
best of all, if possible make haste to run away, but
if in any case, under the pressure of strength greater
than your own, you are compelled to engage in the
contest, do not hesitate to be defeated; for then 112
you, the defeated combatant, will have won a grand
victory, and those who have won will be suffering
defeat. And do not allow either the herald to
announce or the judge to crown the enemy as victor,
but come forward yourself and present the prizes
and the palm, and crown him (" by your leave, sir "),
and bind the headband round his head, and do you
yourself make with loud and strong voice this
announcement : " In the contest that was proposed
in lust and anger and licentiousness, in folly also and
injustice, O ye spectators and stewards of the sports,
I have been vanquished, and this man is the victor,
and has proved himself so vastly superior, that even
we, his antagonists, who might have been expected
to grudge him his victory, feel no envy." Yield, 113
then, to others the prizes in these unholy contests,
but bind upon your own head the wreaths won in
the holy ones. And count not those to be holy contests which the states hold in their triennial Festivals,

τριετηρίσιν ἄγουσι θέατρα ἀναδειμάμεναι πολλὰς
[318] ἀνθρώπων δεξόμενα¹ μυριάδας· ἐν | γὰρ τούτοις ἢ
ὁ καταπαλαίσας τινὰ καὶ ὕπτιον ἢ πρηνῆ τείνας
ἐπὶ γῆν ἢ ὁ πυκτεύειν² καὶ παγκρατιάζειν δυνάμενος καὶ μηδεμιᾶς μήτε ὕβρεως μήτε ἀδικίας ἀπ-
114 εχόμενος φέρεται τὰ πρωτεῖα· XXVI. εἰσὶ δ' οἳ
σφόδρα καὶ κραταιότατα σιδηροῦν τροπὸν³ ἀκονη-
σάμενοι καὶ στομώσαντες ἑκατέραν τῶν χειρῶν
περιάψαντες κεφαλὰς καὶ πρόσωπα τῶν ἀντιπάλων
ἀποσκάπτουσι καὶ τἆλλα, ἐπὰν τύχωσι τὰς πληγὰς
ἐνεγκόντες, ἀποθραύουσιν, εἶτα βραβείων καὶ στε-
φάνων τῆς ἀνηλεοῦς ὠμότητος ἕνεκα μεταποιοῦν-
115 ται. τὰ μὲν γὰρ ἄλλα ἀγωνίσματα δρομέων ἢ
πεντάθλων τίς οὐκ ἂν γελάσαι τῶν εὖ φρονούντων,
ἐπιτετηδευκότων μήκιστα ἐξάλλεσθαι καὶ μετρου-
μένων τὰ διαστήματα καὶ περὶ ποδῶν ὠκύτητος
ἁμιλλωμένων; οὓς οὐ μόνον τῶν ἁδροτέρων ζῴων
δορκὰς ἢ ἔλαφος ἀλλὰ καὶ τῶν βραχυτάτων
σκυλάκιον ἢ λαγωδάριον μὴ σφόδρα ἐπειγόμενον
116 ῥύμῃ καὶ ἀπνευστὶ θέοντας παραδραμεῖται. τούτων
μὲν δὴ τῶν ἀγώνων πρὸς ἀλήθειαν ἱερὸς οὐδείς,
κἂν πάντες ἄνθρωποι μαρτυρῶσιν, οὓς ἀνάγκη
πρὸς ἑαυτῶν ψευδομαρτυριῶν ἁλίσκεσθαι· οἱ γὰρ
ταῦτα θαυμάζοντες τοὺς νόμους τοὺς καθ' ὑβριστῶν
καὶ τιμωρίας τὰς ἐπὶ ταῖς αἰκίαις ἔθεσαν καὶ
δικαστὰς τοὺς περὶ ἑκάστων διαγνωσομένους ἀπ-
117 εκλήρωσαν. πῶς οὖν εἰκός ἐστι τοὺς αὐτοὺς ἐπὶ
μὲν τοῖς ἰδίᾳ τινὰς αἰκισαμένοις ἀγανακτεῖν καὶ
δίκας κατ' αὐτῶν ἀπαραιτήτους ὡρικέναι, ἐπὶ δὲ
τοῖς δημοσίᾳ καὶ ἐν πανηγύρεσι καὶ θεάτροις

---

¹ MSS. δεξάμεναι (-α).   ² MSS. παλαίειν.
³ Conj. Tr.: MSS. and Wend. σιδήρου τρόπον.

and have built for them theatres to hold many myriads of men ; for in these prizes are carried away either by the man who has out-wrestled someone and laid him on his back or on his face upon the ground, or by the man who can box or combine boxing with wrestling, and who stops short at no act of outrage or unfairness. XXVI. Some give a sharp, strong 114 edge to an iron-bound thong,[a] and fasten it round both hands and lacerate the heads and faces of their opponents, and, when they succeed in planting their blows, batter the rest of their bodies, and then claim prizes and garlands for their pitiless savagery. As 115 for the other contests, of sprinters or of those who enter for the five exercises, what sensible person would not laugh at them, at their having practised to jump as far as possible, and getting the several distances measured, and making swiftness of foot a matter of rivalry ? And yet not only one of the larger animals, a gazelle or a stag, but a dog or hare, among the smaller ones, will, without hurrying much, outstrip them when running full pelt and without taking breath. Of these contests, in sober truth, 116 none is sacred, and even if all men testify to that effect, they cannot escape being convicted of false witness by themselves. For it was the admirers of these things who passed the laws against overbearing persons, and fixed the punishments to be awarded to acts of outrage, and allotted judges to investigate the several cases. How, then, are these two things compatible ? How can the very same persons be 117 indignant at outrages committed in private and have affixed to them inexorable penalties, and at the same time have by law awarded garlands and public

* See App. p. 491.

στεφάνους καὶ κηρύγματα καὶ ἄλλα τινὰ νομο-
118 θετῆσαι; δυεῖν γὰρ ἐναντίων καθ' ἑνὸς εἴτε
σώματος εἴτε πράγματος ὁρισθέντων ἢ εὖ ἢ
κακῶς ἐξ ἀνάγκης ἂν ἔχοι θάτερον· ἄμφω γὰρ
ἀμήχανον. πότερον οὖν ἐπαινοῖτ'[1] ἂν δεόντως;
ἆρ' οὐ τὸ τοὺς χειρῶν ἄρχοντας ἀδίκων κολάζεσθαι; ψέγοιτ' ἂν οὖν εἰκότως τὸ ἐναντίον, τὸ
τιμᾶσθαι· ψεκτὸν δ' οὐδὲν τῶν ἱερῶν, ἀλλὰ πάντως
119 εὐκλεές. XXVII. ὁ τοίνυν Ὀλυμπιακὸς ἀγὼν
μόνος ἂν λέγοιτο ἐνδίκως ἱερός, οὐχ ὃν τιθέασιν
οἱ τὴν Ἦλιν οἰκοῦντες, ἀλλ' ὁ περὶ κτήσεως τῶν
θείων καὶ ὀλυμπίων ὡς ἀληθῶς ἀρετῶν. εἰς
τοῦτον τὸν ἀγῶνα οἱ ἀσθενέστατοι τὰ σώματα
ἐρρωμενέστατοι δὲ τὰς ψυχὰς ἐγγράφονται πάντες,
εἶτα ἀποδυσάμενοι καὶ κονισάμενοι πάνθ' ὅσα καὶ
τέχνης καὶ δυνάμεως ἔργα δρῶσι, παραλιπόντες
120 οὐδὲν ὑπὲρ τοῦ νικηφορῆσαι. τῶν μὲν οὖν ἀντιπάλων οἱ ἀθληταὶ περίεισιν οὗτοι, πρὸς ἀλλήλους
δὲ πάλιν περὶ πρωτείων διαφέρονται[2]· οὐ γὰρ ὁ
αὐτὸς τῆς νίκης τρόπος ἅπασιν, ἀλλὰ πάντες ἄξιοι
τιμῆς ἀργαλεωτάτους καὶ βαρεῖς ἀνατρέψαντες
121 καὶ καταβαλόντες ἐχθρούς. θαυμασιώτατος δὲ καὶ
τούτων ὁ διενεγκών, ᾧ καὶ τὰ πρῶτα τῶν ἄθλων[3] |
[319] οὐ φθονητέον λαμβάνοντι. οἳ δὲ κἂν δευτερείων
ἢ τρίτων ἀξιωθῶσι, μὴ κατηφείτωσαν· καὶ γὰρ
ταῦτα ἐπ' ἀρετῆς κτήσει προτίθεται, τοῖς δὲ μὴ

---

[1] MSS. πότερον συνεπαινοῖτ' ἂν.
[2] MSS. διαλέγονται.   [3] MSS. ἀθλητῶν.

---

[a] See App. p. 491.   [b] Or "as a reward for."

announcements and other honours to those who have
done so publicly and at State festivals and in theatres?
For if two things, contrary the one to the other, have 118
been determined against one person or one action,
one or other must of necessity be right and the other
wrong; for it is out of the question that they should
both be right or both wrong. Which then, rightly,
would you praise? Would you not approve the
punishment of those who are guilty of unprovoked
violence and wrong? In that case you would censure,
as a matter of course, the opposite treatment of them,
the shewing honour to them. XXVII. And, since 119
nothing sacred is censurable, but wholly of good
report, it follows that the Olympic contest *a* is the
only one that can rightly be called sacred; not the
one which the inhabitants of Elis hold, but the contest for the winning of the virtues which are divine
and really Olympian. For this contest those who
are very weaklings in their bodies but stalwarts in
their souls all enter, and proceed to strip and rub
dust over them and do everything that skill and
strength enables them to do, omitting nothing that
can help them to victory. So these athletes prevail 120
over their opponents, but they are also competing
among themselves for the highest place. For they
do not all win the victory in the same way, though
all deserve honour for overthrowing and bringing
down most troublesome and doughty opponents.
Most worthy of admiration is the one who excels 121
among these, and, as he receives the first prizes, no
one can grudge them to him. Nor let those be down-
cast who have been held worthy of the second or
third prize. For these, like the first, are prizes offered
with a view to *b* the acquisition of virtue, and those

τῶν ἄκρων ἐφικέσθαι δυναμένοις ἡ τῶν μέσων
κτῆσις ὠφέλιμος, λέγεται δὲ ὅτι καὶ βεβαιοτέρα
τὸν ἐμφυόμενον ἀεὶ τοῖς ὑπερέχουσιν ἐκφεύγουσα
122 φθόνον. παιδευτικώτατα οὖν εἴρηται τὸ '' πεσεῖται
ὁ ἱππεύς,'' ἵν' εἴ τις ἀποπίπτοι [μὲν] κακῶν,
ἐγείρηται [δὲ] ἀγαθοῖς ἐπερειδόμενος καὶ συν-
ορθιασθῇ. διδασκαλικώτατον δὲ κἀκεῖνο, μὴ πρόσω
φάναι, κατόπιν δὲ πίπτειν, ἐπειδὴ κακίας καὶ
123 πάθους ὑστερίζειν ἀεὶ λυσιτελέστατον· φθάνειν μὲν
γὰρ τὰ καλὰ δρῶντα δεῖ, τὰ δὲ αἰσχρὰ μέλλειν
[καὶ] ἔμπαλιν, κἀκείνοις μὲν προσέρχεσθαι, τούτων
δὲ ὑστερίζειν καὶ μακρὸν ὅσον ἀπολείπεσθαι· ᾧ
⟨γὰρ⟩ τῶν ἁμαρτημάτων ἐγγίνεται ⟨καὶ⟩ παθῶν
ὑστερίζειν, ἄνοσος διατελεῖ. τὴν γοῦν '' παρὰ τοῦ
θεοῦ σωτηρίαν περιμένειν '' φησὶν αὐτόν, ἵνα ἐφ'
ὅσον ἀπελείφθη τοῦ ἀδικεῖν, ἐπὶ τοσοῦτον τῷ
δικαιοπραγεῖν ἐπιδράμῃ.

124 XXVIII. Περὶ μὲν οὖν ἱππέως καὶ ἀναβάτου,
κτηνοτρόφου τε καὶ ποιμένος, ἔτι δὲ γῆν ἐργαζο-
μένου καὶ γεωργοῦ τὰ προσήκοντα εἴρηται, καὶ αἱ
καθ' ἑκάστην συζυγίαν ὡς οἷόν τε ἦν ἠκρίβωνται
125 διαφοραί. πρὸς δὲ τὰ ἀκόλουθα καιρὸς ἤδη τρέ-
πεσθαι. τὸν οὖν ἐφιέμενον ἀρετῆς οὐ παντελῆ
κεκτημένον τὴν γεωργικὴν¹ ψυχῆς ἐπιστήμην εἰσάγει, ἀλλ' αὐτὸ μόνον περὶ τὰς ἀρχὰς αὐτῆς πεπονη-
μένον· λέγει γάρ· '' ἤρξατο Νῶε ἄνθρωπος εἶναι

---

¹ mss. γεωργικῆς; cf. ἡ γεωργικὴ ψυχῆς τέχνη Quod Det. 111.

ᵃ Or '' meaning that he should be as eager for right-doing
as he was backward for wrong-doing,'' the ἵνα expressing
the purpose of the prophet's words, rather than that of the
horseman, as in § 122.

who cannot reach the topmost virtues are gainers by the acquisition of the less lofty ones, and theirs is actually, as is often said, a more secure gain since it escapes the envy which ever attaches itself to pre-eminence. There is, then, a very instructive purpose 122 in the words, " the horseman shall fall," namely, that if a man fall off from evil things, he may get up supporting himself upon good things and be set upright. Another point full of teaching is his speaking of falling not forwards, but backwards, since to be behindhand in vice and passion is always most to our advantage ; for we ought to be beforehand when 123 doing noble deeds, but on the contrary to be tardy about doing base deeds : we should go to meet the former, but be late for the latter, and fall short of them by the greatest possible distance ; for he, whose happiness it is to be late for sinful deeds and passion's promptings, abides in freedom from soul-sickness. You see, it says that he is "waiting for the salvation that comes from God." He looks out for it, to the end that he may run as far to meet right-doing as he was late for wrongdoing.[a]

XXVIII. All that is pertinent to horseman and 124 rider, cattle-rearer and shepherd, as well as to soil-worker and husbandman, has now been said, and the differences between the members of each pair have been stated with such minuteness as was possible. It is time to turn to what comes afterwards. Well, 125 the lawgiver represents the aspirant to virtue as not possessing in its completeness the science of soul-husbandry, but as having done no more than spend some labour on the elements of that science ; for he says, " Noah began to be an husbandman." Now

γεωργός." ἀρχὴ δ', ὁ τῶν παλαιῶν λόγος, ἥμισυ
τοῦ παντὸς ὡς ἂν ἡμίσει πρὸς τὸ τέλος ἀφ-
εστηκυῖα,[1] οὗ μὴ προσγενομένου καὶ τὸ ἄρξασθαι
126 πολλάκις μεγάλα πολλοὺς ἔβλαψεν. ἤδη γοῦν τινες
καὶ τῶν οὐκ εὐαγῶν τῆς διανοίας κατὰ τὰς συνεχεῖς
μεταβολὰς στροβουμένης ἔννοιαν χρηστοῦ τινος
ἔλαβον, ἀλλ' οὐδὲν ὤνηντο· ἔστι γὰρ μὴ πρὸς τὸ
τέλος ἠξάντων φορὰν ἀθρόον τῶν ἐναντίων καταρ-
ραγεῖσαν ἐπικλύσαι καὶ τὸ χρηστὸν ἐκεῖνο δια-
127 φθαρῆναι νόημα.   XXIX. οὐ διὰ τοῦτο
μέντοι δόξαντι θυσίας ἀμέμπτους ἀναγαγεῖν τῷ
Κάιν λόγιον ἐξέπεσε μὴ θαρρεῖν ὡς κεκαλλιερη-
κότι; μὴ γὰρ ἐφ' ἱεροῖς καὶ τελείοις βουθυτῆσαι·
τὸ δὲ λόγιόν ἐστι τοιόνδε· "οὐκ ἐὰν ὀρθῶς προσ-
128 ενέγκῃς, ὀρθῶς δὲ μὴ διέλῃς." ὀρθὸν μὲν οὖν ἡ
τοῦ θεοῦ τιμή, τὸ δὲ ἀδιαίρετον οὐκ ὀρθόν. ὃν
δ' ἔχει καὶ τοῦτο λόγον, ἴδωμεν· εἰσί τινες οἱ τὸ
εὐσεβὲς ἐν τῷ πάντα φάσκειν ὑπὸ θεοῦ γενέσθαι,
129 τά τε καλὰ καὶ τὰ ἐναντία, περιγράφοντες· πρὸς
[320] οὓς ἂν λέγοιμεν, ὅτι τὸ μὲν ὑμῶν | ἐπαινετόν ἐστι
τῆς δόξης, τὸ δ' ἔμπαλιν ψεκτόν, ἐπαινετὸν μέν,
ὅτι τὸ μόνον θαυμάζετε τίμιον, ψεκτὸν δὲ αὖ,
παρόσον ἄνευ τομῆς καὶ διαιρέσεως· ἔδει γὰρ μὴ

---

[1] MSS. ὃς ἂν . . . ἀφέστηκεν.

---

[a] Cf. Quod Det. 64.
[b] The main links of the thought from here to § 168 may be
given as follows: Good ideas are often spoilt for want of
proper analysis or " distinguishing," but (§ 134) distinguishing
by itself is useless, without remembering and meditating on
what has been learnt (cf. De Sac. 82 ff.).   In connexion with
this we have the tirade against futile and exaggerated distinguishing (cf. §§ 136-141).   The two together will give perfection, but till this is gained the beginner must not attempt

" a beginning is half of the whole," or " begun is half done," [a] as was said by the men of old, as being half-way towards the end, whereas if the end be not added as well, the very making of a beginning has many a time done many people much harm.[b] It has, 126 as we all know, happened before now that even people far from guiltless, as their mind kept turning about in perpetual change, have hit upon an idea of something wholesome, but have got no good from it ; for it is possible that ere they have come to the end, a strong current of contrary tendencies has swept over them like a flood, and that wholesome idea has come to nothing.   XXIX. Was it not owing to 127 this, that, when Cain imagined that he had presented faultless sacrifices, a divine intimation was made to him not to be confident that his offering had met with God's favour ; for that the conditions of his sacrifice had not been holy and perfect ?   The divine message is this : " ⟨All is⟩ not ⟨well⟩, if thou offerest rightly, but dost not rightly distinguish "[c] (Gen. iv. 7).   So 128 the honour paid to God is a right act, but the failure to divide is not right.   What this means, let us see. There are some whose definition of reverence is that it consists in saying that all things were made by God, both beautiful things and their opposites.   We 129 would say to these, one part of your opinion is praise-worthy, the other part on the contrary is faulty.   It is praiseworthy that you regard with wonder and reverence that which is alone worthy of honour ; on the other hand, you are to blame for doing so without clear-cut distinctions.   You ought never to have

things beyond his capacity (§§ 146-165), or he will find himself supplanted by others (§§ 166-168).

[c] For Philo's way of taking this text see note on *De Sobr.* 50.

173

φῦραι καὶ συγχέαι πάντων ἀθρόως ἀποφήναντας
αἴτιον, ἀλλὰ μετὰ διαστολῆς μόνον ὁμολογῆσαι
130 τῶν ἀγαθῶν. ἄτοπον γὰρ ἱερέων μὲν πρόνοιαν
ἔχειν, ὡς ὁλόκληροι τὰ σώματα καὶ παντελεῖς
ἔσονται, τῶν τε καταθυομένων ζῴων, ὡς οὐδὲν
οὐδεμιᾷ τὸ παράπαν ἀλλ' οὐδὲ τῇ βραχυτάτῃ
χρήσεται λώβῃ, καί τινας διόπους[1] ἐπ' αὐτὸ τοῦτο
χειροτονεῖν τὸ ἔργον, οὓς ἔνιοι μωμοσκόπους
ὀνομάζουσιν, ἵνα ἄμωμα καὶ ἀσινῆ προσάγηται τῷ
βωμῷ τὰ ἱερεῖα, τὰς δὲ περὶ θεοῦ δόξας ἐν ταῖς
ἑκάστων ψυχαῖς ὑποσυγκεχύσθαι[2] καὶ μὴ κανόνι
131 ὀρθοῦ λόγου διακεκρίσθαι.   XXX. τὸν
κάμηλον οὐχ ὁρᾷς ὅτι ἀκάθαρτον εἶναι φησι ζῷον
ὁ νόμος, ἐπειδὴ μηρυκᾶται μέν, οὐ διχηλεῖ δέ;
καίτοι γε πρὸς τὴν ῥητὴν ἐπίσκεψιν οὐκ οἶδ' ὃν
ἔχει λόγον ἡ προσαποδοθεῖσα ⟨αἰτία⟩, πρὸς δὲ τὴν
132 δι' ὑπονοιῶν ἀναγκαιότατον· ὥσπερ γὰρ τὸ μηρυκώ-
μενον τὴν προκαταβληθεῖσαν ὑπαναπλέουσαν αὖθις
ἐπιλεαίνει τροφήν, οὕτως ἡ ψυχὴ τοῦ φιλομαθοῦς,
ἐπειδάν τινα δι' ἀκοῆς δέξηται θεωρήματα, λήθη
μὲν αὐτὰ οὐ παραδίδωσιν, ἠρεμήσασα δὲ καθ'
ἑαυτὴν ἕκαστα μεθ' ἡσυχίας τῆς πάσης ἀναπολεῖ
133 καὶ εἰς ἀνάμνησιν τῶν πάντων ἔρχεται. μνήμη δ'
οὐ πᾶσα ἀγαθόν, ἀλλ' ἡ ἐπὶ μόνοις τοῖς ἀγαθοῖς,
ἐπεὶ τό γε ἄληστα εἶναι τὰ κακὰ βλαβερώτατον·
οὗ ἕνεκα πρὸς τελειότητα χρεία τοῦ διχηλεῖν, ἵνα

---

[1] MSS. δεῖ ὅσους.
[2] MSS. ἐπισυγκεχύσθαι.

---

^a See App. p. 491.

174

mixed and confused the matter by representing Him as Author of all things indiscriminately, but to have drawn a sharp line and owned Him Author of the good things only.[a] It is a senseless thing to be 130 scrupulous about priests being free from bodily defect or deformity and about animals for sacrifice being exempt from the very slightest blemish, and to appoint inspectors (called by some " flaw-spiers ") on purpose to provide that the victims may be brought to the altar free from flaw or imperfections ; and at the same time to suffer the ideas about God in their several souls to be in confusion, with no distinctions made between true and false by the application to them of the rule and standard of right principles.

XXX. Do you not see that the Law 131 says that the camel is an unclean animal, because, though it chews the cud, it does not part the hoof (Lev. xi. 4) ? And yet, if we fix our eyes on the literal way of regarding the matter, I do not know what principle there is in the reason given for the camel's uncleanness ; but, if we look to the way suggested by latent meanings there is a most vital principle. For as the animal that chews the cud 132 renders digestible the food taken in before as it rises again to the surface,[a] so the soul of the keen learner, when it has by listening taken in this and that pro-position, does not hand them over to forgetfulness, but in stillness all alone goes over them one by one quite quietly, and so succeeds in recalling them all to memory. Not all memory, however, is a good thing, 133 but that which is brought to bear upon good things only, for it would be a thing most noxious that evil should be unforgettable. That is why, if perfection is to be attained, it is necessary to divide the hoof,

τοῦ μνημονικοῦ δίχα τμηθέντος ὁ λόγος διὰ στόματος, οὗ πέρατα¹ ἡ φύσις διττὰ εἰργάσατο χείλη,
ῥέων διαστείλῃ τό τε ὠφέλιμον καὶ τὸ ἐπιζήμιον
134 μνήμης γένους εἶδος. ἀλλ' οὐδὲ τὸ διχηλεῖν ἄνευ
τοῦ μηρυκᾶσθαι καθ' ἑαυτὸ φαίνεταί τινα ἔχειν
ὄνησιν ἐξ αὐτοῦ. τί γὰρ ὄφελος τὰς φύσεις τῶν
πραγμάτων τέμνειν ἄνωθεν ἀρξάμενον μέχρι τῶν
λεπτοτάτων, εἰς τοὔσχατον ⟨δὲ⟩ αὐτὸ μηκέτι
γίνεσθαι μηδὲ ἔχειν διαιρετὰ² τὰ μέρη, ἅπερ ἄτομα
καὶ ἀμερῆ πρὸς ἐνίων εὐθυβόλως ὀνομάζεται;
135 ταῦτα γὰρ συνέσεως μὲν καὶ περιττῆς ἀκριβείας
ἠκονημένης εἰς ὀξυτάτην ἀγχίνοιαν ἐναργῆ δείγματ'
ἐστίν, ὄνησιν δὲ οὐδεμίαν πρὸς καλοκἀγαθίαν καὶ
[321] | ἀνεπιλήπτου βίου διέξοδον ἔχει.
136 XXXI. καθ' ἑκάστην γοῦν ἡμέραν ὁ πανταχοῦ
τῶν σοφιστῶν ὅμιλος ἀποκναίει τὰ ὦτα τῶν παρα-
τυγχανόντων ἀκριβολογούμενος καὶ τὰς διπλᾶς καὶ
ἀμφιβόλους λέξεις ἀναπτύσσων καὶ τῶν πραγμάτων ὅσα δοκεῖ μεμνῆσθαι—πέπηγε δὲ καὶ πλειόνων
—διακρίνων. ἢ οὐχ οἱ μὲν τὰ στοιχεῖα τῆς ἐγγραμμάτου φωνῆς εἴς τε ἄφωνα καὶ φωνήεντα τέμνουσιν;
ἔνιοι δὲ τὸν λόγον εἰς τὰ ἀνωτάτω τρία, ὄνομα,
137 ῥῆμα, σύνδεσμον; μουσικοὶ δὲ τὴν ἰδίαν ἐπιστήμην εἰς ῥυθμόν, εἰς μέτρον,³ εἰς μέλος, καὶ τὸ
μέλος εἴς τε τὸ χρωματικὸν καὶ ἐναρμόνιον καὶ
διατονικὸν εἶδος καὶ διὰ τεσσάρων καὶ διὰ πέντε

---

¹ mss. ὥσπερ ἄττα.
² Perhaps read ἀδιαίρετα, *i.e.* " *never* finding that the parts
we come to are incapable of division." See App. p. 492.
³ mss. μέρος.

ᵃ Lit. "no longer to reach," *i.e.* "to fail to do what we do
in other undertakings," a common extension of meaning in
οὐκέτι or μηκέτι. ᵇ See App. p. 491.

176

in order that, the faculty of memory being cut in twain, language as it flows through the mouth, for which Nature wrought lips as twin boundaries, may separate the beneficial and the injurious forms of memory. But neither does dividing the hoof by 134 itself apart from chewing the cud appear to have any-thing advantageous on its own account. For what use is there in dissecting the natures of things, beginning from the beginning and going on to the minutest particles, and yet failing to reach [a] the absolute end, and finding before you defying division those parts which are happily named by some " atoms " or " partless " ? [b] For such a course is clear proof of 135 sagacity and nicety of precision whetted to keenest edge of shrewdness ; but it is of no advantage to-wards promoting nobility of character and a blame-less passage through life. XXXI. See 136 how true this is. Day after day the swarm of sophists to be found everywhere wears out the ears of any audience they happen to have with disquisitions on minutiae, unravelling phrases that are ambiguous and can bear two meanings and distinguishing among circumstances such as it is well to bear in mind—and they are set on bearing in mind a vast number.[c] Do not some of them divide the letters of written speech into consonants and vowels ? And do not some of them break up language into its three ultimate [d] parts. noun, verb, conjunction ? Do not musicians divide 137 their own science into rhythm, metre, tune ; and the tune or melody into the chromatic, harmonic and diatonic form, and into intervals of a fourth, a fifth

---

[c] Or "such as they think well . . . and even more " (*i.e.* than they themselves think worth remembering).

[d] Or "main parts," as γενικώτατα § 138.

καὶ διὰ πασῶν, συνημμένων τε καὶ διεζευγμένων
138 μελῳδίας; γεωμέτραι δὲ εἰς τὰς γενικωτάτας δύο
γραμμὰς εὐθεῖάν τε καὶ περιφέρειαν; καὶ οἱ ἄλλοι
τεχνῖται εἰς τὰς καθ᾽ ἑκάστην ἐπιστήμην ἰδέας τὰς
139 ἀπὸ τῶν πρώτων ἄχρι τῶν ὑστάτων; ᾧ συνεπ-
ηχείτω μέντοι καὶ τῶν φιλοσοφούντων χορὸς ἅπας
τὰ εἰωθότα διεξιών, ὅτι τῶν ὄντων τὰ μέν ἐστι
σώματα, τὰ δ᾽ ἀσώματα· καὶ τὰ μὲν ἄψυχα, τὰ δὲ
ψυχὴν ἔχοντα· καὶ τὰ μὲν λογικά, τὰ δ᾽ ἄλογα·
καὶ τὰ μὲν θνητά, τὰ δὲ θεῖα· καὶ τῶν θνητῶν τὸ
140 μὲν ἄρρεν, τὸ δὲ θῆλυ, τὰ ἀνθρώπου τμήματα· καὶ
πάλιν τῶν ἀσωμάτων τὰ μὲν τέλεια, τὰ δὲ ἀτελῆ·
καὶ τῶν τελείων τὰ μὲν ἐρωτήματα καὶ πύσματα
ἀρατικά[1] τε αὖ καὶ ὁρκικὰ καὶ ὅσαι ἄλλαι τῶν
κατ᾽ εἶδος ἐν ταῖς περὶ τούτων στοιχειώσεσιν ἀνα-
γράφονται διαφοραί, τὰ δὲ πάλιν ἃ διαλεκτικοῖς
141 ἔθος ὀνομάζειν ἀξιώματα· καὶ τούτων τὰ μὲν ἁπλᾶ,
τὰ δ᾽ οὐχ ἁπλᾶ· καὶ τῶν οὐχ ἁπλῶν τὰ μὲν συν-
ημμένα, τὰ δὲ παρασυνημμένα τὸ μᾶλλον ἢ ἧττον,[2]
καὶ προσέτι δὲ διεζευγμένα καὶ ἄλλα τοιουτότροπα,
ἔτι δ᾽ ἀληθῆ τε καὶ ψευδῆ καὶ ἄδηλα, δυνατά τε
καὶ ἀδύνατα [καὶ τὰ μὲν φθαρτὰ καὶ ἄφθαρτα]
καὶ ἀναγκαῖα καὶ οὐκ ἀναγκαῖα, καὶ εὔπορά τε
καὶ ἄπορα καὶ ὅσα συγγενῆ τούτοις· πάλιν δὲ τῶν
ἀτελῶν αἱ εἰς τὰ λεγόμενα κατηγορήματα καὶ

[1] mss. ἐρωτικά.
[2] Perhaps (as in Diog. Laert. vii. 69) ⟨τὰ διασαφοῦντα⟩ (or
some equivalent participle) τὸ μᾶλλον καὶ ἧττον.

---

[a] Or "from the primary (divisions) to the ultimate."
[b] The Stoics admitted four kinds of "incorporeal" things,
viz. time, place, void, and λεκτόν or σημαινόμενον, *i.e.* the
meaning conveyed by speech as opposed to the actual sound

or an octave, and into melodies with united or dis-
joined tetrachords ? Do not geometricians put all 138
lines under two main heads, the straight line and the
curve ? Do not other experts place everything in
the principal categories that their several sciences
suggest, categories that start with the elements of
the science and go on until they have dealt with their
last and highest achievements [a] ? With their com- 139
pany let the whole choir of philosophers chime in,
harping on their wonted themes, how that of existences some are bodies, some incorporeal [b]; and of
bodies, some lifeless, some having life ; some rational,
some irrational, some mortal, some divine ; and of
mortal beings, some male, some female ; a distinction which applies to man ; and of things incorporeal 140
again, some complete, some incomplete [c]; and of those
that are complete, some questions and inquiries, im-
precations and adjurations, not to mention all the
other particular differences, all of which are set forth
in the elementary handbooks which deal with them.
Again, there are what dialecticians are accustomed to
call propositions. Of these, some are simple, some 141
not so ; and of the non-simple, some hypothetical,
some inferential, some ⟨indicating⟩ more or less,
some moreover disjunctive; and suchlike distinctions.
They distinguish further things true, false, and doubtful ; possible and impossible ; conclusive and in-
conclusive ; [d] soluble and insoluble ; and all kindred
antitheses. Again, applying to incorporeal things
which are incomplete there are the subdivisions into

which was corporeal. See *S.V.F.* ii. 331. Philo ignores the
first three and deals with the subdivisions of λεκτόν.

[c] For the explanation of these and the following terms
see App. p. 492.

[d] Or " necessarily and not necessarily true."

συμβεβηκότα καὶ ὅσα τούτων ἐλάττω διαιρέσεις
142 προσεχεῖς. XXXII. κἂν ἔτι παρα-
θήξας ὁ νοῦς εἰς τὸ λεπτότερον ἑαυτόν, καθάπερ
ἰατρὸς τὰ σώματα, τὰς τῶν πραγμάτων φύσεις
ἀνατέμνῃ, πλέον οὐδὲν πρὸς ἀρετῆς κτῆσιν ἐργά-
σεται, ἀλλὰ διχηλήσει μὲν διαστέλλειν καὶ δια-
κρίνειν ἕκαστα δυνάμενος, οὐ μηρυκηθήσεται δέ,
ὡς ὠφελίμῳ χρῆσθαι τροφῇ κατὰ τὰς ὑπομνήσεις
[322] τὴν ἐξ ἁμαρτημάτων ἐπιγεγενημένην τραχύτητα
143 ψυχῇ λεαινούσῃ καὶ | προσηνῆ καὶ λείαν τῷ ὄντι
κίνησιν ἀπεργαζομένῃ. μυρίοι οὖν τῶν λεγομένων
σοφιστῶν θαυμασθέντες κατὰ πόλεις καὶ τὴν οἰκουμένην σχεδὸν ἅπασαν ἐπὶ τιμὴν ἐπιστρέψαντες
ἕνεκα ἀκριβολογίας καὶ τῆς περὶ τὰς εὑρέσεις
δεινότητος ἀνὰ κράτος τοῖς πάθεσι ἐγκατεγήρασαν
καὶ ἐγκατέτριψαν[1] τὸν βίον οὐδὲν ἰδιωτῶν ἠμελημένων καὶ φαυλοτάτων διενεγκόντες ἀνθρώπων·
144 διὸ καὶ παγκάλως τοὺς οὕτω βιοῦντας τῶν σοφιστῶν ὁ νομοθέτης τῷ συῶν παραβάλλει γένει
διαυγεῖ μὲν οὐδενὶ καὶ καθαρῷ θολερῷ δὲ καὶ
βορβορώδει[2] βίῳ καὶ τοῖς αἰσχίστοις ἐμφερομένους.[3]
145 τὸν γὰρ σῦν ἀκάθαρτον εἶναί φησιν, ὅτι διχηλεῖ
μέν, οὐ μηρυκᾶται δέ, ὡς τὸν κάμηλον διὰ τὴν
ἐναντίαν πρόφασιν, ὅτι μηρυκώμενος οὐ διχηλεῖ.
ὅσα μέν<τοι> τῶν ζῴων ἀμφοτέρων μετέχει,
καθαρὰ εἰκότως ἀναγράφεται, ὅτι τὴν περὶ ἑκάτερον[4] τῶν λεχθέντων ἀτοπίαν ἐκπέφευγε. καὶ γὰρ
διαίρεσις ἄνευ μνήμης καὶ μελέτης καὶ διεξόδου

---

[1] mss. κατεγήρασαν καὶ κατέτριψαν, which perhaps might be
retained and a participle like χρώμενοι inserted to govern
πάθεσι. [2] mss. βαραθρώδει.
[3] So mss.: perhaps ἐμφερομένων. [4] mss. θατέραν (-α).

180

" predicates " and " complements " and still **more** minute refinements. XXXII. And if the 142 mind putting a still finer edge upon itself dissect the natures of things, as a surgeon does men's bodies, he will effect nothing that is of advantage for the acquiring of virtue. It is true that, by reason of his power to distinguish and discriminate in each case, he will " divide the hoof," but he will not " chew the cud " so as to have at his service beneficial nourishment with its wholesome reminders, smoothing out the roughness that had accrued to the soul as the result of errors, and producing an easy and truly smooth movement.[a]   And so multitudes of those who 143 are called sophists, after winning the admiration of city after city, and after drawing wellnigh the whole world to honour them for their hair-splitting and their clever inventiveness, have with all their might worn their life out, and brought it to premature old age, by the indulgence of their passions, differing not at all from neglected nobodies and the most worthless of mankind. Excellently, therefore, does the law- 144 giver compare the race of sophists who live in this way to swine. Such men are at home in a mode of life not bright and luminous but thick and muddy and in all that is most ugly. For he says that the 145 pig is unclean, because, though it divide the hoof, it does not chew the cud (Lev. xi. 7). He pronounces the camel unclean for the opposite reason, because though chewing the cud he does not divide the hoof. But such animals as do both are, as we might expect, set down as clean, since they have escaped the unnatural development in each of the directions named. For indeed distinguishing without memory and with-

* See App. p. 493.

τῶν ἀρίστων * * *[1] ἀγαθὸν ἀτελές, ἡ δ' ἀμφοῖν εἰς
ταὐτὸ σύνοδός τε καὶ κοινωνία τελειότατον.

146   XXXIII. Τελειότητα δὲ καὶ οἱ δυσμενεῖς τῆς
ψυχῆς καταπτήσσουσιν, ὧν μηκέτι ἐπανίστασθαι
δυναμένων ἡ ἀψευδὴς εἰρήνη κρατεῖ. ἡμιέργου
δ' ὅσοι σοφίας ἢ πάλιν ἡμιπαγοῦς ἔλαχον, ἀσθενέ-
στεροι ἢ ὥστε ἁμαρτημάτων ἐκ πολλοῦ συγκεκροτη-
μένων καὶ πρὸς ἀλκὴν ἐπιδεδωκότων ἐναντιοῦσθαι
147 στίφεσι. διὰ τοῦθ' ὅταν ἐν τῷ τοῦ πολέμου καιρῷ
ποιῆται τῆς στρατιᾶς κατάλογον, οὐχ ἅπασαν
καλεῖ τὴν νεότητα, κἂν μετὰ προθυμίας τῆς πάσης
αὐτοκελεύστῳ χρῆται πρὸς ἐχθρῶν ἄμυναν ἑτοιμό-
τητι, προστάττει δὲ ἀπιόντας οἴκοι καταμεῖναι,
ὡς ἂν ἐκ συνεχοῦς μελέτης τὴν τοῦ ποτὲ δύνασθαι
νικᾶν ἀνὰ κράτος ἰσχύν τε καὶ ἐμπειρίαν εὕρωνται
148 κραταιοτάτην. ἡ δὲ πρόσταξις διὰ τῶν τῆς στρατιᾶς
γραμματέων γίνεται, ὅταν ὁ πόλεμος ἐγγὺς καὶ
ἐπὶ θύραις ὢν ἤδη τυγχάνῃ· ταυτὶ δὲ φήσουσι·
" τίς ὁ ἄνθρωπος ὁ οἰκοδομήσας οἰκίαν καινὴν
καὶ οὐκ ἐνεκαίνισεν αὐτήν; πορευέσθω καὶ ἀποστραφήτω εἰς τὴν οἰκίαν αὐτοῦ, μὴ ἀποθάνῃ ἐν τῷ
πολέμῳ καὶ ἄνθρωπος ἕτερος ἐγκαινιεῖ αὐτήν.
καὶ τίς ὃς ἐφύτευσεν ἀμπελῶνα καὶ οὐκ εὐφράνθη
ἐξ αὐτοῦ; πορευέσθω καὶ ἀποστραφήτω εἰς τὴν
οἰκίαν αὐτοῦ, μὴ ἀποθάνῃ ἐν τῷ πολέμῳ καὶ
ἄνθρωπος ἕτερος εὐφρανθήσεται ἐξ αὐτοῦ. καὶ
τίς ἐμνηστεύσατο γυναῖκα καὶ οὐκ ἔλαβεν αὐτήν;
πορευέσθω καὶ ἀποστραφήτω εἰς τὴν οἰκίαν αὐτοῦ,
μὴ ἀποθάνῃ ἐν τῷ πολέμῳ καὶ ἄνθρωπος ἕτερος

---

[1] The translation follows Wend., who supplies after ἀρίστων
some such words as καὶ μνήμη χωρὶς διαιρέσεως τῶν ἀγαθῶν καὶ
τῶν ἐναντίων; but see App. 493.

out conning and going over of the things that are best is an incomplete good (as is memory without distinguishing between good things and their opposites), but the meeting and partnership of both in combination is a good most complete and perfect.

XXXIII. Now even men of ill will cower before 146 perfection of soul, and, when they can no longer resist it, genuine peace prevails. But men that have attained to a wisdom half-wrought or, to change the figure, half-baked, are too feeble to stand up against massed bodies of sins that have been long in training and have become increasingly formidable. This is 147 why, when in time of war the lawgiver is mustering the army, he does not summon all the youth, even though it be filled with the utmost zeal and shew readiness that requires no spurring to repel the enemy, but bids them depart and stay at home, that as the result of constant practice they may acquire overpowering strength and skill, such as shall enable them one day to win a decisive victory. The command is given through the marshals or 148 secretaries[a] of the army, when war is near and already at the very doors. What they are to say is this: "Who is the man that has built a new house and has not hanselled it? Let him go and turn back to his house, lest he be killed in the war and another man hansel it. And who is there that has planted a vineyard and not been made joyous by its fruits? Let him go his way and turn back to his house, lest he die in the war and another have joy from it. And to whom has a wife been promised, whom he has not taken? Let him go his way and turn back to his house, lest he die in the war and another take her"

a E.V. "officers."

PHILO

149
[323] | λήψεται αὐτήν." XXXIV. διὰ τί γάρ, εἴποιμ'
ἄν, ὦ θαυμασιώτατε, οὐχὶ τούτους μᾶλλον ἑτέρων
εἰς τὸν ἀγῶνα τοῦ πολέμου κατατάττειν ἀξιοῖς, οἳ
γύναια καὶ οἰκίας καὶ ἀμπελῶνας καὶ τὴν ἄλλην
κτῆσιν ἀφθονωτάτην περιπεποίηνται; τοὺς γὰρ
περὶ τῆς τούτων ἀσφαλείας κινδύνους, καὶ εἰ
πάντως εἶεν βαρύτατοι, κουφότατα οἴσουσιν· ἐπεὶ
οἷς γε τῶν λεχθέντων οὐδὲν πρόσεστιν, ἅτε μηδὲν
ἔχοντες ἀναγκαῖον ἐνέχυρον ὄκνῳ καὶ ῥᾳθυμίᾳ τὰ
150 πολλὰ χρήσονται. ἢ παρόσον οὐδενὸς τῶν κτηθέντων ἀπολελαύκασιν, εἶτα μηδ' ὕστερον δυνηθῶσιν
ἀπολαῦσαι; τοῖς γὰρ κρατηθεῖσι τῷ πολέμῳ τίς
ἀπολείπεται τῶν κτηθέντων ὄνησις; ἀλλ' οὐχ
ἁλώσονται.¹ εὐθὺς μὲν οὖν τό γε ἐπὶ τοῖς ἀστρατεύτοις πείσονται· οἴκοι γὰρ καθεζομένων καὶ τρυ-
φώντων ἀνάγκη τοὺς τὰ τοῦ πολέμου συντόνως
δρῶντας ἐχθροὺς οὐκ ἀναιμωτὶ μόνον ἀλλὰ καὶ
151 ἀκονιτὶ κρατεῖν. ἀλλὰ τὸ τῶν ἄλλων συμμάχων
πλῆθος καὶ τὸν ὑπὲρ τούτων ἀγῶνα προθύμως
ἀναδέξεται. πρῶτον μὲν ἄτοπον ἐπὶ ταῖς ἑτέρων
σπουδαῖς ἢ τύχαις ὁρμεῖν, καὶ μάλιστα ὅτε περὶ
ἀναστάσεως καὶ ἀνδραποδισμοῦ καὶ πορθήσεως
ἴδιός τε καὶ κοινὸς ἐπικρέμαται κίνδυνος, δυναμένους συνδιαφέρεσθαι τὰ τοῦ πολέμου καὶ μήθ'
ὑπὸ νόσου μηθ' ὑπὸ γήρως μήθ' ὑπ' ἄλλης κακο-
πραγίας μηδεμιᾶς κωλυομένους. ἁρπάσαντας γὰρ
δεῖ τὰ ὅπλα ἐν ταῖς πρώταις φάλαγξι τούτους καὶ

¹ Wend. prints a mark of interrogation here and in §151
after ἀναδέξεται. The translators have substituted full stops,
regarding the sentences in both cases as objections raised by
the other side.

ᵃ The elaborate argument which follows to show that
Moses must have intended an intellectual or spiritual warfare

184

(Deut. xx. 5-7).[a] XXXIV. " For what reason," I 149
should be inclined to say, " my good friend, do you
not think fit to assign these more than others to the
conflict of the war, who have secured for themselves
wives and houses and vineyards and other possessions
in lavish abundance ? They will bear very lightly, be
they ever so heavy, the dangers incurred to keep them
safe; while those who have none of the ties mentioned,
having nothing vital at stake, will for the most part
be sluggish and slack. Or, again, is the fact that they 150
have derived no enjoyment from any of their acquisitions a good reason for depriving them of the possibility of doing so in the future ? For what advantage
from their possessions remains to the vanquished ?

" Nay but," I think you urge, " *they* will not be
prisoners."

On the contrary, they will at once incur the fate of
non-combatants. For enemies vigorously carrying
on operations of war are quite sure to become masters
of men sitting at home at their ease, not merely
without bloodshed but without a struggle.

" Nay," you urge again, " the large forces on their 151
side will gladly undertake to fight for these as well."

In the first place, I reply, it is monstrous to rely
on the efforts or good fortune of others, especially
when there is the menace hanging over both individual citizens and the city itself of spoliation and
deportation and enslavement, and that when they
are able to do their part in bearing the burdens of
war and are hindered from doing so neither by
illness nor by old age nor by any other misfortune.
It behoves these people to snatch up their weapons

takes the form of a dialogue with the γραμματεῖς in which
they raise objections in §§ 150, 151, and 155.

PHILO

ὑπερέχειν τῶν συμμάχων τὰς ἀσπίδας ἐκθύμως
καὶ φιλοκινδύνως μαχομένους.   XXXV.

152 ἔπειτ' οὐ προδοσίας μόνον, ἀλλὰ καὶ πολλῆς ἀν-
αλγησίας ἐξενηνοχότες ἂν εἶεν δείγματα, εἰ οἱ μὲν
ἄλλοι προπολεμήσουσιν, αὐτοὶ δὲ πρὸς τοῖς οἰκείοις
πράγμασιν ἔσονται, καὶ οἱ μὲν τοὺς ὑπὲρ τῆς
ἐκείνων σωτηρίας ἀγῶνας ἀναρρίπτειν θελήσουσιν,
οἱ δὲ οὐδὲ τοὺς ὑπὲρ ἑαυτῶν ἀναδέξονται, καὶ οἱ
μὲν ἀσιτίας καὶ χαμευνίας καὶ τὰς ἄλλας σώματός
τε καὶ ψυχῆς κακώσεις ἄσμενοι διὰ τὸν τοῦ νικῆσαι
πόθον καρτερήσουσιν, οἱ δὲ κονιάματα καὶ λήρους,
κόσμον ἄψυχον, οἰκίαις περιτιθέντες ἢ τὴν κατ'
ἀγροὺς ὀπώραν δρεπόμενοι καὶ τἀπιλήνι' ἄγοντες
ἢ ταῖς ὁμολογηθείσαις ἔκπαλαι παρθένοις νῦν πρῶτον εἰς ὁμιλίαν ἐρχόμενοι καὶ συνευναζόμενοι ὡς
ἐν ἐπιτηδειοτάτῳ τοῦ γαμεῖν καιρῷ διατελοῦσι;

153 καλόν γε τοίχων ἐπιμελεῖσθαι, προσόδους ἐκλέγειν,
ἑστιᾶσθαι, μεθύειν, θαλαμεύεσθαι, νυμφοστολεῖσθαι
τὰς γεγηρακυίας καὶ σαπράς, τὸ λεγόμενον, ἀλλ'
εἰρήνης ἔργα, ἐν δ' ἔτι ἡβῶντός τε καὶ ἀνθοῦντος

154 ἀκμῇ πολέμου ἄτοπα[1] δρᾶν. ἢ τούτων οὐχ ὁ
πατήρ, οὐκ ἀδελφός, οὐ τῶν ἀφ' αἵματος οὐδείς,
οὐ γένους ἐστράτευται, ἀλλὰ πανοίκιος αὐτοῖς ἐμ-
[324] πεφώλευκεν | ἡ δειλία; ἀλλὰ πάντως εἰσὶ μυρίοι
τῶν συγγενῶν ἀγωνιζόμενοι. τούτων οὖν τὸν ὑπὲρ
τῆς ψυχῆς κίνδυνον αἰρομένων οἱ χλιδῶντες
καὶ ἁβροδιαίτως ζῶντες τίνας οὐκ ἂν ἀτιθάσους
θῆρας δι' ὑπερβολὴν ὠμότητος παραδράμοιεν;

155 ἀλλὰ χαλεπὸν τὸ ἑτέρους ἀπονητὶ τῶν ἡμετέρων

---

[1] Conj. Tr.: mss. πάντα: Cohn suggested ταῦτα δρᾶν
αἴσχιστον. Perhaps πολέμου ⟨πολέμου⟩ πάντα, i.e. in time of war

and taking their place in the front ranks to hold their shields over their comrades fighting with a courage that courts danger. XXXV. In the next 152 place, they would have given proof not only of treachery but of utter insensibility, if, while the others are to be fighting in their defence, they are to be about their private business ; and while the others are to be willing to stand the hazard of the conflict for their safety, they are not to take the trouble to fight for their own ; and, while the others in their desire for victory are gladly to put up with short rations and sleeping in the field and the other hardships of body and soul, they spend their time in decking their houses with stuccoes and trumperies, poor soulless display ; or getting in the fruit of their orchards and celebrating the vintage festival ; or now for the first time consummating their marriage with the maidens betrothed to them long before, as though this were an ideal season for weddings. 'Tis good to 153 look after walls, to collect rents, to attend banquets, to get tipsy, to indulge in sexual intercourse, for the aged and as the saying is, decayed dames, to be escorted to the bridal chamber, but they are works of peace, and monstrous things to do when war is in full course. Has not a father, has not a brother, has no blood- 154 relation, no member of the clan of these men enlisted ? Has cowardice made their whole family its lair ? Nay, there surely are a host of their kinsfolk at the front. Would not, then, those, who live in ease and luxury while these are imperilling their lives, far surpass in cruelty any savage beasts you can name ?

" It is hard," you are thinking, " that other 155

it is well that all that is done should be things of war. Possibly πολέμου ⟨ὅσα πολέμου⟩, cf. § 25 above.

ἀπολαῦσαι πόνων. καὶ πότερον χαλεπώτερον ἐχθροὺς ἔτι ζώντων ἢ φίλους καὶ συγγενεῖς τετε-
λευτηκότων ἐπὶ τὸν κλῆρον ἐλθεῖν; ἢ καὶ τὸ
συγκρίνειν τὰ οὕτως μακρὰν ἀφεστῶτα εὔηθες;
156 καὶ μὴν εὔλογον μὴ μόνον ὅσα τοῖς ἀστρατεύτοις
πρόσεστιν, ἀλλὰ καὶ αὐτοὺς ἐκείνους ἐχθρῶν κεκρα-
τηκότων γενέσθαι κτήματα· τοῖς δέ γε ἀπο-
θνῄσκουσιν ὑπὲρ τῆς κοινῆς σωτηρίας, καὶ εἰ
μηδενὸς ἀπώναντο[1] πρότερον τῶν κατὰ τὴν οὐσίαν,
ἡδίστη τελευτὴ γίνεται λογιζομένοις ὅτι πρὸς οὓς
ηὔξαντο διαδόχους τὴν οὐσίαν ἐλθεῖν ἔρχεται.

157 XXXVI. Τὸ μὲν οὖν τοῦ νόμου ῥητὸν τοσαύτας
καὶ ἔτι πλείους ἐπισκέψεις ἴσως ἔχει. ὡς δὲ
μηδεὶς εὑρεσιλογῶν θρασύνηται τῶν κακοτεχνούν-
των, ἀλληγοροῦντες φήσομεν ὅτι πρῶτον μὲν οὐ
μόνον οἴεται δεῖν ὁ νόμος περὶ τὴν τῶν ἀγαθῶν
πονεῖσθαί τινα κτῆσιν, ἀλλὰ καὶ περὶ τὴν τῶν
κτηθέντων ἀπόλαυσιν, καὶ τό γε εὐδαιμονεῖν
ἀρετῆς χρήσει τελείας περιγενέσθαι νομίζει σῷον
καὶ παντελῆ περιποιούσης βίον· ἔπειθ' ὅτι οὐ περὶ
οἰκίας ἢ ἀμπελῶνος ἢ τῆς καθ' ὁμολογίας ἐγγυη-
θείσης γυναικός ἐστιν ὁ λόγος αὐτῷ, ὅπως τὴν
μὲν ὡς μνηστὴρ ἀγάγηται, τοῦ δ' ἀμπελῶνος τὸν
καρπὸν ὁ φυτουργὸς ἀποδρεψάμενος καὶ ἀποθλίψας,
εἶτ' ἐμπιὼν μεθύσματος ἀκράτου γανωθῇ, τὴν δ'
οἰκίαν ὁ ἀναδειμάμενος οἰκήσῃ, ἀλλὰ περὶ τῶν

---

[1] mss. ἀφ' ὧν ἂν τό, which was formerly patched up by
reading εἰ μηδενὸς ἀπέλαυσαν ἀφ' ὧν ἂν τὸ πρότερον εἶχον.

people without doing any work should get the benefit
of our labours."

Pray, which is harder, that enemies should come
into the property while we are still alive, or that
friends and kinsfolk should do so when we are dead ?
Nay, 'tis silly even to compare things so wide apart.
Again, it is probable not only that all that belongs 156
to those who did not join up should become the
property of the victorious enemy, but that they
themselves should so become ; while to those who
are dying for the common salvation, even supposing
that they had in former days derived no benefit from
the family property, a happy ending comes as they
reflect that the property is falling to the heirs to
whom it was their prayer that it should fall.

XXXVI. The letter of the Law perhaps suggests 157
all these considerations and more than these. But
that no malicious critic may too daringly give rein to
his inventive talent, we will leave the letter, and
make one or two remarks about the inner meaning
of the Law. Firstly, it considers that a man ought
to concern himself not only with the acquisition of
good things, but with the enjoyment of what he has
acquired, and that happiness results from the practice of perfect excellence seeing that such excellence
secures a life sound and complete in every way.
Secondly, what the Law means is that a man's main
consideration is not house or vineyard or the wife
already betrothed to him ; how he is to take to wife
her whom he has wooed and won ; how the planter
of the vineyard is to cull and crush its fruit, and then
drink large draughts of the intoxicating beverage and
make his heart glad ; or how the man that has built
the house is to occupy it ; but that the faculties of a

κατὰ ψυχὴν δυνάμεων, δι' ὧν συμβέβηκεν ἀρχάς
τε λαμβάνειν καὶ προκοπὰς καὶ τελειότητας ἐν
158 πράξεσιν ἐπαινεταῖς· αἱ μὲν τοίνυν ἀρχαὶ περὶ
μνηστῆρα φιλοῦσι γίνεσθαι—καθάπερ γὰρ ὁ μνώ-
μενος γυναῖκα μέλλει ἔτι ἀνὴρ[1] οὐ γεγονὼς ἤδη,
τὸν αὐτὸν τρόπον ὁ εὐφυὴς εὐγενῆ μὲν καὶ καθαρὰν
ἄξεσθαι παρθένον, παιδείαν, ἐλπίζει, μνᾶται δ'
αὐτίκα—, αἱ δὲ προκοπαὶ περὶ γεωργόν—ὡς γὰρ
ἐπιμελὲς τῷ φυτουργῷ τὰ δένδρα αὔξεσθαι, καὶ
τῷ φιλομαθεῖ τὰ φρονήσεως θεωρήματα ποιῆσαι
μηκίστην λαβεῖν ἐπίδοσιν—, αἱ δὲ τελειότητες περὶ
δημιουργίαν οἰκίας τελειουμένης μέν, οὔπω δὲ
159 πῆξιν λαβούσης. XXXVII. ἁρμόττει δὴ πᾶσι
τούτοις, ἀρχομένοις, προκόπτουσι, τετελειωμένοις,
βιοῦν ἀφιλονείκως καὶ μὴ τῷ τῶν σοφιστῶν ἐπ-
αποδύεσθαι πολέμῳ δύσεριν ταραχὴν ἐπὶ νοθείᾳ
[325] τἀληθοῦς ἀεὶ μελετώντων· ἐπειδὴ τἀληθὲς εἰρήνῃ
160 φίλον, | ἢ δυσμενὴς αὐτοῖς. εἰ γὰρ εἰς τοῦτον
ἀφίξονται τὸν ἀγῶνα πρὸς ἐμπειροπολέμους ἰδιώ-
ται, παντελῶς ἁλώσονται· ὁ μὲν ἀρχόμενος, ⟨ὅτι⟩
ἄπειρος, ὁ δὲ προκόπτων, ὅτι ἀτελής, ὁ δὲ τέλειος,
ὅτι οὔπω ἄτριβος[2] ἀρετῆς· δεῖ δ' ὥσπερ τὰ κονιάματα στηριχθῆναι βεβαίως καὶ λαβεῖν πῆξιν, οὕτως

---

[1] Conj. Tr.: mss. μέλλων ἐπὰν ἀνήρ. Adler proposes μέλλων
ἐπαν⟨δροῦσθαι⟩ or ἔπαν⟨δρος εἶναι⟩. Wendland suggested
μέλλει γενέσθαι ἀνήρ.
[2] Sic mss. Emendations proposed are οὔπω ἐντριβὴς or ἔτι
ἀτριβὴς (? πω ἀτριβής, the usage being perhaps defensible with
the implied negative in ἀτριβής).

---

[a] Or the passage may be taken as follows : " The lawgiver
is not speaking of house or vineyard. . . . He does not wish
that he should take to wife . . . But he is speaking of the

man's soul are a man's main consideration.^a Through
these he can make a beginning, make progress, and
reach perfection in praiseworthy doings. Beginnings 158
are seen in a wooer, for, just as he who is wooing a
woman has wedlock still in futurity not being already
a husband, in the same way the well-constituted man
looks forward to one day marrying Discipline, a high-
born and pure maiden, but for the present he is her
wooer. Progress is seen in the work of the husbandman, for, as it is the planter's care that the trees
should grow, so is it the earnest student's care to
bring it about that the principles of sound sense shall
receive the utmost development. Perfection is to
be seen in the building of a house, which is receiving its finishing touches, but has not yet become
quite compact and firmly settled. XXXVII. It 159
befits all these, the beginners, those making progress,
and those who have reached perfection, to live without contention, refusing to engage in the war waged
by the sophists, with their unceasing practice of
quarrelsomeness and disturbance to the adulteration
of the truth : for the truth is dear to peace, and
peace has no liking for them. If our friends *do* come 160
into this conflict, mere unprofessionals engaging
trained and seasoned fighters, they will undoubtedly
get the worst of it ; the beginner because he lacks
experience, the man who is progressing, because he
is incomplete, the man who has reached completeness, because he is still unpractised in virtue. It is
requisite, just as it is that plaster should become
firm and fixed and acquire solidity,^b so too that the

faculties of a man's soul ; " *cf.* for this use of ὁ λόγος αὐτῷ,
" he is not speaking about," § 88 above.
^b See App. p. 493.

τὰς τῶν τελειωθέντων ψυχὰς κραταιωθείσας παγιώ-
τερον ἱδρυθῆναι μελέτῃ συνεχεῖ καὶ γυμνάσμασιν
161 ἐπαλλήλοις. οἱ δὲ μὴ τούτων τυγχάνοντες παρὰ
τοῖς φιλοσόφοις διαλεληθότες εἶναι λέγονται σοφοί·
τοὺς γὰρ ἄχρι σοφίας ἄκρας ἐληλακότας καὶ τῶν
ὅρων αὐτῆς ἄρτι πρῶτον ἀψαμένους ἀμήχανον
εἰδέναι φασὶ τὴν ἑαυτῶν τελείωσιν· μὴ γὰρ κατὰ
τὸν αὐτὸν χρόνον ἄμφω συνίστασθαι, τήν τε πρὸς
τὸ πέρας ἄφιξιν καὶ τὴν τῆς ἀφίξεως κατάληψιν,
ἀλλ᾽ εἶναι μεθόριον ἄγνοιαν, οὐ τὴν μακρὰν ἀπ-
εληλαμένην ἐπιστήμης, ἀλλὰ τὴν ἐγγὺς καὶ ἀγχί-
162 θυρον αὐτῇ. τοῦ μὲν οὖν καταλαμβάνοντος καὶ
συνιέντος καὶ τὰς ἑαυτοῦ δυνάμεις ἐπισταμένου
ἄκρως γένοιτ᾽ ἂν ἔργον πολεμῆσαι τῷ φιλέριδι
καὶ σοφιστικῷ στίφει· νικήσειν γὰρ τὸν τοιοῦτον
ἐλπίς. ᾧ δὲ ἔτι τὸ ἀγνοίας ἐπιπροσθεῖ σκότος,
μήπω τοῦ τῆς ἐπιστήμης ἀναλάμψαι φέγγους
ἰσχυκότος, ἀσφαλὲς οἴκοι καταμεῖναι, τουτέστιν
εἰς τὴν περὶ ὧν ἄκρως οὐ κατείληφε μὴ παρελθεῖν
163 ἅμιλλαν, ἀλλ᾽ ἠρεμῆσαί τε καὶ ἡσυχάσαι. ὁ δ᾽
ὑπ᾽ αὐθαδείας ἐξενεχθείς, τὰ παλαίσματα τῶν
ἀντιπάλων οὐκ εἰδὼς πρὶν δρᾶσαι παθεῖν φθή-
σεται καὶ τὸν ἐπιστήμης θάνατον ἐνδέξεται, ὅς
ἐστιν ἀργαλεώτερος τοῦ ψυχὴν καὶ σῶμα διακρίνον-
164 τος. ὀφείλει δὲ τοῦτο συμβαίνειν τοῖς πρὸς τῶν
σοφισμάτων ἀπατωμένοις· ὅταν γὰρ τὰς λύσεις
αὐτῶν εὑρεῖν μὴ δυνηθῶσιν, ὡς ἀληθέσι τοῖς

<hr />

ᵃ See App. p. 493.

souls of those that have been perfected should become more firmly settled, strengthened by constant practice and continual exercise. Those who do not enjoy 161 these advantages have the name among the philosophers of wise men unconscious of their wisdom.[a] For they say that it is out of the question that those who have sped as far as the edge of wisdom and have just come for the first time into contact with its borders should be conscious of their own perfecting, that both things cannot come about at the same time, the arrival at the goal and the apprehension of the arrival, but that ignorance must form a border-land between the two, not that ignorance which is far removed from knowledge, but that which is close at hand and hard by her door. It will, then, be the 162 business of him who fully apprehends and understands the subject and thoroughly knows his own powers, to go to war with the strife-loving band of sophists ; for there is ground for expecting that such an one will be the conqueror. But for him whose eyes are still covered by the darkness of ignorance, the light of knowledge not being strong enough as yet to shine out, it is safe to stay at home, that is, not to come forward for the contest about matters which he has not fully apprehended, but to keep still and be quiet. But he who has been carried away 163 by presumption, not knowing his opponents' grips and throws, before he can be an agent will quickly be a victim and experience the death of knowledge, which is a far more woeful death than that which severs soul and body. This is bound to befall those 164 who are cheated by sophistries ; for they fail to find the way to refute these, and owing to their having regarded false statements as true and given

PHILO

κατεψευσμένοις πεπιστευκότες ἀποθνήσκουσι βίον
τὸν τῆς ἐπιστήμης ταὐτὸν πεπονθότες τοῖς ὑπὸ
κολάκων φενακιζομένοις· καὶ γὰρ τούτων ἡ τῆς
ψυχῆς ὑγιαίνουσα καὶ ἀληθὴς ὑπὸ τῆς φύσει νοσερᾶς
165 ἐξωθεῖται καὶ ἀνατρέπεται φιλίας. XXXVIII.
συμβουλευτέον οὖν εἰς τοὺς τοιούτους ἀγῶνας μὴ
παρέρχεσθαι τοῖς τε ἀρχομένοις τοῦ μανθάνειν—
ἀνεπιστήμονες γάρ—καὶ τοῖς προκόπτουσι, διότι οὐ
τέλειοι, καὶ τοῖς πρῶτον τελειωθεῖσι, διότι λέληθεν
166 αὐτοὺς ἄχρι πῇ τελειότης. τῶν δὲ ἀπειθησάντων
ἄλλος, φησίν, ἄνθρωπος τὴν μὲν οἰκίαν οἰκήσει,
τὸν δ᾽ ἀμπελῶνα κτήσεται, τὴν δὲ γυναῖκα ἄξεται·
τὸ δ᾽ ἐστὶν ἴσον τῷ αἱ λεχθεῖσαι δυνάμεις σπουδῆς
[326] βελτιώσεως, τελειώσεως | ἐπιλείψουσι μὲν οὐδέ-
ποτε, ἄλλοτε δὲ ἄλλοις ἐνομιλήσουσιν ἀνθρώποις
ἐπιφοιτῶσαι καὶ τὰς ψυχὰς οὐ τὰς αὐτὰς * * *[1]
167 ἀμείβουσαι, σφραγῖσιν[2] ὁμοιούμεναι. καὶ γὰρ αὗται
τὸν κηρὸν ἐπειδὰν τυπώσωσι, παθοῦσαι μηδὲν ἀπ᾽
αὐτῶν εἶδος ἐγχαράξασαι μένουσιν ἐν ὁμοίῳ· κἂν
ὁ τυπωθεὶς συγχυθῇ κηρὸς καὶ ἀφανισθῇ, πάλιν
ἕτερος ὑποβληθήσεται. ὥστε, ὦ γενναῖοι, μὴ
νομίσητε φθειρομένοις συμφθείρεσθαι τὰς δυνάμεις
ὑμῖν· ἀθάνατοι γὰρ οὖσαι μυρίους ἄλλους πρὸ
ὑμῶν ἀσπάζονται τῆς ἀπ᾽ αὐτῶν εὐκλείας,[3] οὓς ἂν
αἴσθωνται μὴ ὥσπερ ὑμᾶς διὰ τὸ ῥιψοκίνδυνον
ἀποδεδρακότας τὴν ὁμιλίαν αὐτῶν, ἀλλὰ προσ-

---

[1] The translation follows Wend., who suggests οὐ τὰς
αὐτὰς ⟨ἀεὶ κατοικοῦσαι, ἀλλ᾽ ἐξ ἄλλων ἄλλας⟩ ἀμείβουσαι. An
alternative is to limit the corruption to ἀμείβουσαι. Mangey
ἀπομάττουσαι.   [2] mss. σφόδρα γ᾽ εἰσίν.
[3] The genitive is hardly defensible. Wend. proposes
ἀσπάζονται ⟨μεταδιδοῦσαι⟩, Cohn τῇ . . . εὐκλείᾳ.

them credence, they die so far as the life of knowledge is concerned. Their experience is the same as
that of those who are taken in by flatterers : for in
their case, too, the true and healthy friendship of
the soul is thrust out and overturned by the friendship that is essentially unwholesome. XXXVIII. 165
We must therefore advise those, who are beginning
to learn, to decline such contests, owing to their lack
of knowledge ; those who are making progress,
owing to their not being perfect ; and those who
have just attained perfection, because they are to
some extent unconscious of their perfectness. As 166
for those who disregard this bidding, it says of each
of them, another man shall live in his house, shall
become owner of his vineyard, shall marry his
betrothed. This is equivalent to saying, "the
faculties *a* mentioned of keenness to learn, of improvement, of becoming perfect, shall indeed never
fail, but they associate with one man at one time,
with another man at another time, going about and
not tenanting the same souls always and changing
from soul to soul. In this the faculties resemble 167
seals ; for these too, when they have stamped the
wax, unaffected by the impressions they have made,
after engraving an image on it remain as they
were, and if the impression on the wax gets blurred
and effaced, other wax will be substituted for it.
So do not imagine, good sirs, that the faculties
decay when you do. They are immortal, and ready
to welcome ten thousand others in preference to you
to the fame gained from them. These are all whom
they perceive not to have shunned their converse as
you did, owing to your foolhardiness, but to draw

a Or " talents."

168 ἰόντας καὶ θεραπευτικῶς ἀσφαλείας ἔχοντας. εἰ
δέ τις ἀρετῆς φίλος, εὐχέσθω τὰ καλὰ πάντα
ἐμφυτευθῆναί τε αὐτῷ καὶ ἐπὶ τῆς ἑαυτοῦ ψυχῆς
φανῆναι καθάπερ ἐν ἀνδριάντι καὶ γραφῇ τελείᾳ
τὰς εἰς εὐμορφίαν συμμετρίας, λογιζόμενος ὅτι
εἰσὶν ἔφεδροι μυρίοι, οἷς ἡ φύσις ἀντ᾽ αὐτοῦ
δωρήσεται ταῦτα πάντα, εὐμαθείας, προκοπάς,
τελειότητας. ἄμεινον δὲ πρὸ ἐκείνων αὐτὸν ἐκ-
λάμψαι ταμιευόμενον τὰς ὑπὸ τοῦ θεοῦ δοθείσας
ἀσφαλῶς χάριτας καὶ μὴ προενεγκόντα πόρθησιν
ἐχθροῖς ἀφειδοῦσιν ἑτοιμοτάτην λείαν παρασχεῖν.

169 XXXIX. Οὐκοῦν βραχὺ ὄφελος ἀρχῆς, ἣν τέλος
αἴσιον οὐκ ἐσφράγισται. πολλάκις μέντοι καὶ
τελειωθέντες τινὲς ἀτελεῖς ἐνομίσθησαν τῷ παρὰ
τὴν ἰδίαν προθυμίαν, ἀλλὰ μὴ κατ᾽ ἐπιφροσύνην
θεοῦ βελτιωθῆναι δόξαι, καὶ διὰ τοῦτο μέντοι ⟨τὸ⟩
δόξαι μετεωρισθέντες[1] καὶ ἐξαρθέντες ἐπὶ μήκιστον
ἀφ᾽ ὑψηλοτέρων χωρίων εἰς ἔσχατον κατενεχ-
170 θέντες βυθὸν ἠφανίσθησαν· " ἐὰν " γάρ φησιν
" οἰκοδομήσῃς οἰκίαν καινήν, καὶ ποιήσεις στε-
φάνην τῷ δώματί σου, καὶ οὐ ποιήσεις φόνον ἐν
τῇ οἰκίᾳ σου, ἐὰν πέσῃ ὁ πεσὼν ἀπ᾽ αὐτοῦ."
171 πτωμάτων γὰρ ἀργαλεώτατον θεοῦ τιμῆς ἀπο-
πεσεῖν ὀλισθόντα, στεφανώσαντα πρὸ ἐκείνου
ἑαυτὸν καὶ φόνον ἐμφύλιον ἐργασάμενον· κτείνει
γὰρ τὴν ἑαυτοῦ ψυχὴν ὁ μὴ τὸ ὂν τιμῶν, ὡς ἀνό-
νητον αὐτῷ γενέσθαι παιδείας τὸ οἰκοδόμημα.

[1] MSS. νεωτερισθέντες.

---

[a] So the lxx, which Philo takes to mean "for fear you
yourself fall." The E.V. "that thou bring not blood upon
thy house, if any man fall from thence " gives the real sense
better.

196

near and pay great heed to safety. If any man be 168
a lover of virtue, let him pray that all fair things may
not only be implanted in him, but may shew themselves upon the surface of his soul, as do the ex-
quisite proportions of beauty in a statue and a perfect
portrait. Let him consider that there are myriads
waiting to follow him, on whom in his stead Nature
will bestow all the boons of which we have been
thinking, the gift of quickness to learn, that of
making progress, that of attaining perfection. Is it
not better that, instead of leaving it to them, he
should himself shine out and be a retentive steward
of God's gracious gifts, and that he should not, by
gratuitously offering an opportunity for plunder, supply
ruthless foes with booty lying ready to their hand?

XXXIX. Little advantage, therefore, is there in a 169
beginning to which a right ending has not set its seal.
Quite frequently persons who had attained perfection
have been accounted imperfect owing to their fancy-
ing that their improvement was due to their own zeal
and not to the directing care of God. Owing to this
fancy they were lifted up and greatly exalted, and
so came to be borne down from lofty regions into the
lowest abyss and so lost to sight : for we read,
" If thou shalt build a new house, then shalt thou 170
also make a parapet round thy roof, and so thou
shalt not cause death in thy house, if the faller from
it falls "[a] (Deut. xxii. 8). For there is no fall so 171
grievous as to slip and fall away from rendering
honour to God, through ascribing the victory to one-
self instead of to Him, and so being the perpetrator
of the murder of one's kin. For he that fails to
honour That which IS slays his own soul, so that the
edifice of instruction ceases to be of use to him. In-

παιδεία δὲ φύσιν ἔλαχε τὴν ἀγήρω, διόπερ καινὴν
εἶπε τὴν οἰκίαν αὐτῆς· τὰ μὲν γὰρ ἄλλα χρόνῳ
φθείρεται, ἡ δ' ἐφ' ὅσον πρόεισιν, ἐπὶ μήκιστον
ἡβᾷ καὶ ἐπακμάζει τὸ ἀειθαλὲς εἶδος φαιδρυνομένη
172 καὶ ταῖς συνεχέσιν ἐπιμελείαις καινουμένη. κἂν
[327] τοῖς | προτρεπτικοῖς μέντοι παραινεῖ τοὺς κτῆσιν
ἀγαθῶν λαχόντας πλείστην μὴ ἑαυτοὺς ἀναγράψαι
τῆς κτήσεως αἰτίους, ἀλλὰ " μνησθῆναι θεοῦ τοῦ
173 διδόντος ἰσχὺν ποιῆσαι δύναμιν." τοῦτο μὲν οὖν
τὸ εὐπραγίας ἦν πέρας, ἀρχαὶ δ' ἐκεῖναι· ὥστε
τοὺς ἐκλανθανομένους τοῦ τέλους μηδὲ τῆς τῶν
κτηθέντων <ἀρχῆς> εὖ ἂν ἔτ' ἀπόνασθαι.[1] τούτοις μὲν οὖν ἑκούσια γίνεται διὰ φιλαυτίαν τὰ
σφάλματα οὐχ ὑπομένουσι τὸν φιλόδωρον[2] καὶ
τελεσφόρον θεὸν αἴτιον ἀποφῆναι τῶν ἀγαθῶν.
174 XL. εἰσὶ δ' οἳ πάντα κάλων εὐσεβείας ἀνασείσαντες
ἐνορμίσασθαι τοῖς λιμέσιν αὐτῆς ταχυναυτοῦντες
ἐσπούδασαν, κἄπειτ' οὐ μακρὰν ἀφεστηκότων,
ἀλλ' ἤδη μελλόντων προσέχειν, αἰφνίδιον ἐξ ἐναντίας καταρραγὲν πνεῦμα πλησίστιον[3] εὐθυδρομοῦν
τὸ σκάφος ἀνέωσεν, ὡς[4] ὑποκεῖραι πολλὰ τῶν πρὸς
175 εὔπλοιαν συνεργούντων. τούτους οὐκ ἄν τις ἔτι
θαλαττεύοντας αἰτιάσαιτο· ἀκούσιος γὰρ αὐτοῖς
ἐπειγομένοις[5] γέγονεν ἡ βραδυτής· τίς οὖν ἀπεικάζεται τούτοις ἢ ὁ τὴν μεγάλην λεγομένην εὐξάμενος

[1] mss. ἐπαπόνασθαι.   [2] mss. θεόφιλον.
[3] mss. πλησίον.   [4] mss. ἀνώσεως or ἀνέσεως.
[5] mss. ἐπιγιγνόμενος, -η.

---

a The vow of the Nazarite is called (as in *Leg. All.* i. 17)
"the great vow" from Numb. vi. 2 ὃς ἂν μεγάλως εὔξηται
εὐχήν (R.V. "a special vow"). For Philo's interpretation
cf. Quod Deus 89, 90, where also the contact with the corpse
is treated as an "involuntary" error.

struction has obtained the nature that never grows old, and for this reason her house is called " new." For whereas other things decay by lapse of time, she, however far she advances, retains the bloom of youth and is in her prime all along, radiant with unfailing loveliness, and renewing her freshness by her unceasing diligence.   Moreover in his Exhortations the 172 lawgiver charges those who have obtained large possession of good things not to inscribe themselves in their hearts as authors of their wealth, but " to remember God Who giveth strength to acquire power" (Deut. viii. 18).   This remembrance, then, 173 was in his eyes the goal of prosperity, the putting forth of power the beginning : the consequence of this being that those who forget the end of their acquisitions cannot any longer derive real benefit from their beginning.   The disasters which befall these men are self-chosen, the outcome of selfishness. They cannot bear to acknowledge as the Author of the good things which they enjoy the God Who brings to perfection the gifts which He loves to bestow. XL. But there are others who, with every stitch 174 of piety's canvas spread, have used every effort to make a quick voyage, and to come to anchor in her harbours, and then, when they were no distance away, but on the very point of coming to land, a violent head-wind has suddenly burst upon them, and driven the vessel straight back, stripping her of much of the gear on which her seaworthiness depended. No one would find fault with these men for being 175 still at sea ; for the delay was contrary to their wish and befell them when they were making all speed. Who, then, resembles these men ?   Who but he who vowed what is called the great Vow *a* ?   For he says :

199

εὐχήν; " ἐὰν γάρ τις " φησίν " ἀποθάνῃ ἐπ' αὐτῷ
αἰφνίδιον, παραχρῆμα μιανθήσεται ἡ κεφαλὴ εὐχῆς
αὐτοῦ, καὶ ξυρήσεται·" εἶτα ὀλίγα προσειπὼν ἐπι-
φέρει· " αἱ δ' ἡμέραι αἱ πρότεραι ἄλογοι ἔσονται,
176 ὅτι ἐμιάνθη κεφαλὴ εὐχῆς αὐτοῦ·" δι' ἀμφοτέρων
τοίνυν, τοῦ τε " αἰφνίδιον " καὶ τοῦ " παραχρῆμα " εἰπεῖν, ἡ ἀκούσιος παρίσταται τῆς ψυχῆς
τροπή· πρὸς μὲν ⟨γὰρ⟩ τὰ ἑκούσια τῶν ἁμαρτημάτων εἰς τὸ βουλεύσασθαι ποῦ καὶ πότε καὶ
πῶς πρακτέον χρόνου δεῖ, τὰ δὲ ἀκούσια ἐξαίφνης,
ἀπερισκέπτως καί, εἰ οἷόν τε τοῦτ' εἰπεῖν, ἀχρόνως
177 κατασκήπτει. χαλεπὸν γὰρ ὥσπερ τοὺς δρομεῖς
ἀρξαμένους ὁδοῦ τῆς πρὸς εὐσέβειαν ἀπταίστως
καὶ ἀπνευστὶ διευθῦναι τὸν δρόμον, ἐπειδὴ μυρία
178 ἐμποδὼν παντὶ τῷ γενομένῳ. πρότερον μὲν ⟨οὖν⟩,
ὃ ἓν καὶ μόνον εὐεργεσία, μηδενὸς τῶν κατὰ
γνώμην ἀδικημάτων ἐφάψασθαι πᾶσάν τε τὴν
ἀμήχανον τῶν ἑκουσίων[1] πληθὺν ἰσχῦσαι διώσασθαι·
δεύτερον δὲ τὸ μήτε πολλοῖς τῶν ἀκουσίων μήτ'
ἐπὶ μήκιστον χρόνον ἐνδιατρῖψαι.

179   Παγκάλως δὲ τὰς τῆς ἀκουσίου τροπῆς ἡμέρας
εἶπεν ἀλόγους, οὐ μόνον ἐπειδὴ τὸ ἁμαρτάνειν ἄλογον,
ἀλλ' ὅτι καὶ τῶν ἀκουσίων λόγον οὐκ ἔστιν ἀπο-
δοῦναι. παρὸ καὶ πυνθανομένων πολλάκις τὰς τῶν |
[328] πραγμάτων αἰτίας φαμὲν μήτ' εἰδέναι μήτ' εἰπεῖν
δύνασθαι· μήτε γὰρ γιγνομένων συμπαραληφθῆναι,

---

[1] So mss. Wend. ἀκουσίων, *i.e.* the ideal course is to avoid
both kinds of offence, the next best to avoid the " voluntary "
and to minimize the " involuntary." But since the " occasions
of the involuntary are infinite " (§ 179), the ideal can rarely
be reached (§ 180).

---

[a] In *Quod Deus* 90 they are not worth counting.

" If someone die suddenly beside him, the head of his vow shall forthwith be defiled, and he shall shave it." Then, after a few more words, he adds, " The former days shall be void, because the head of his vow was defiled " (Numb. vi. 9, 12). The involuntary nature 176 of the soul's failure is evidenced by both of the words which he uses, "sudden" and "forthwith," for whereas in the case of deliberate sins time is required for planning where and when and how the thing is to be done, unintentional sins swoop upon us suddenly, without thought, and if we may so say, in no time. For it is difficult for the runners, as we may call them, 177 after starting on the way to piety, to finish the whole course without stumbling, and without stopping to draw breath ; for every man born meets ten thousand obstacles. The first need then, which is the one 178 and only thing that is " well-doing," is never to put hand to any deliberate wrong-doing, and to have strength to thrust from us the countless host of voluntary offences ; the second not to fall into many involuntary offences, nor to continue long in the practice of them.

Right well did he say that the days of the involun- 179 tary failure were void (ἀλόγους) not only because to sin is void of reason (ἄλογον) but also because it is impossible to render an account (λόγον) of involuntary sins.[a] Accordingly, when people inquire after the motives for things that have been done,[b] we often say that we neither know nor are able to tell them : for that when they were being done we were not taken

---

[b] Apparently meaning " *our* motives for what *we* have done." Philo seems to be expressing in a curiously strong way the feeling that our " involuntary " errors are something quite independent of us. They treat us as strangers and we are taken aback when we find that they have happened.

180 ἀλλὰ καὶ τὴν ἄφιξιν αὐτῶν ἀγνοῆσαι. σπάνιον
οὖν εἴ τῳ δωρήσεται ὁ θεὸς ἀπ᾽ ἀρχῆς ἄχρι τέλους
σταδιεῦσαι τὸν βίον μήτ᾽ ὀκλάσαντι μήτ᾽ ὀλι-
σθόντι, ἀλλ᾽ ἑκατέραν φύσιν ἀδικημάτων, ἑκουσίων
τε καὶ ἀκουσίων, ῥύμῃ καὶ φορᾷ τάχους ὠκυ-
δρομωτάτου ὑπερπτῆναι.

181 Ταῦτα μὲν οὖν ἀρχῆς τε πέρι καὶ τέλους εἴρηται
διὰ Νῶε τὸν δίκαιον, ὃς τὰ πρῶτα καὶ στοιχειώδη
τῆς γεωργικῆς κτησάμενος τέχνης ἄχρι τῶν
περάτων αὐτῆς ἐλθεῖν ἠσθένησε· λέγεται γὰρ ὅτι
" ἤρξατο γῆς εἶναι γεωργός," οὐ τῶν ὅρων τῶν
ἄκρας ἐπιστήμης ἐλάβετο. τὰ δὲ περὶ τῆς φυτουρ-
γίας εἰρημένα αὐτοῦ λέγωμεν αὖθις.

into confidence, nay, that they arrived without our knowing it. 'Tis a rare event then if God shall vouch- 180 safe to a man to run life's course from beginning to end without slackening or slipping, and to avoid each kind of transgressions, voluntary and involuntary, by flying past them, in the vehement rush of matchless speed.

These remarks on beginning and end have been 181 made apropos of Noah the righteous man who, after making himself master of the elements of the science of husbandry, had not the strength to reach its final stages, for it is said that " he began to be a husband-man," not that he reached the furthest limits of full knowledge. What is said about his work as a planter let us tell at another time.

CONCERNING NOAH'S WORK
AS A PLANTER
(DE PLANTATIONE)

ANALYTICAL INTRODUCTION

THE first part of this treatise, extending to the end of § 139, treats firstly of God's planting and then of man learning to copy His work. The second part (§ 140 onwards) should be entitled Περὶ μέθης, for it deals with the vine only with respect to its fruit. The title of the treatise is, therefore, inappropriate.

A. 1-139

(a) 1-72. The first Planter and His plant.

(α) 1-27. The universe and its component parts planted.

(β) 28-31. Trees planted in man, the microcosm.

(γ) 32-46. The names of the two trees in Eden point to an allegorical interpretation. " Eden " is " delight " in the Lord. " Eastward " is " in the light." " The tree of Life " is the man of Gen. i. 27 in the image of God. The earthly man of Gen. ii. is placed in Paradise to be tested amid the virtues, the plants of a rational soul.

(δ) 47 ff. That Israel, God's special inheritance, may be planted in Eden is Moses' prayer.

(ε) 62-72. God the Portion of Inheritance of Levi and of those who have the Levite mind.

(*b*) Lessons learned from the First Planter, and copies of His planting (73-139).

(*a*) 74-93. Abraham's planting (Gen. xxi. 33). The *tree* the " hide " of 10,000 cubits ; the *place* the well, which is without water (Gen. xxvi. 32 LXX), and so symbolic of the fruitless search for knowledge, and of the discovery of our own ignorance ; the *fruit* the invocation of the Name " Eternal God," which connotes " Benefactor," whereas " Lord " connotes " Master."

(*β*) 94-139. Our planting (Lev. xix. 23-25). Ere we can plant *fruit* trees we must *migrate* to the God-given land, *i.e.* the mind must find the way of Wisdom. The beginner bidden to *prune*, *i.e.* cut out all hurtful things, *e.g.* the harlot and the toady from Friendship, superstition from Religion. Jacob's peeled rods and the leper's flesh, both white *all over*, serve as a pattern. Philo attempts to explain the command to prune the fruit itself.

The fourth year, in which the fruit is " holy for praise to the Lord " leads to a discourse on the number 4, on *praise* as the fruit of education, on *thanksgiving* as creation's chief duty, illustrated by the story of the birth of Mnemosyne. As the fifth year is ours for food, after the fourth year of thanksgiving, so " Issachar " or " Reward " was born next after " Judah " or " Praise."

B. 140-177

We now pass on to the vine-culture of Noah. As the vine is the means of Drunkenness (and the just man made himself drunk with it), we have to consider the subject of drunkenness. Moses' views will be given later (in *De Ebrietate*). Let us now examine what the philosophical schools say about it.[a] They put the question thus, " Will the wise man get drunk ? " (139-141). But before stating the arguments on either side, we note that the term " get drunk " ($\mu\epsilon\theta\acute{v}\epsilon\iota\nu$) may be used for hard drinking ($o\acute{\iota}\nuo\hat{v}\sigma\theta\alpha\iota$) simply,[b] or for drinking carried to the point of foolish behaviour ($\lambda\eta\rho\epsilon\hat{\iota}\nu$). All condemn the latter, but one school holds that if $\mu\epsilon\theta\acute{v}\epsilon\iota\nu$ is used in the less offensive sense, the wise man may freely indulge in it ; another,[c] " that he cannot safely do so, and will therefore avoid all carousals, unless social duties necessitate his participation in them."

---

[a] Various opinions have been held as to the provenance of the disquisition which follows. It of course definitely disclaims originality, though as a matter of fact parts of it (e.g. §§ 168 f.) are evidently comments interpolated by Philo himself. Pearson in *Journal of Philology* 1907 regarded it as Peripatetic. Arnim, who discussed it very fully in his *Quellen-Studien zu Philo*, believes that Philo is here representing the views of a contemporary Stoic, but a Stoic of a free-thinking type, who had taken over a good deal of Peripateticism. Some of his reasons for this will be found in the Notes to §§ 171 f. The translators are rather inclined to agree with Heinemann that the discourse, at least from § 149 onwards, is rather of the rhetorical and epideictic type. We would suggest that the writer or speaker whom Philo is quoting or adapting, though conversant with philosophical terms, is not propounding a definite philosophical opinion, but merely endeavouring by a series of ingenious quibbles to show that the Stoic maxim the wise man will drink freely ($o\acute{\iota}\nu\omega\theta\acute{\eta}\sigma\epsilon\tau\alpha\iota$), but will not get drunk ($\mu\epsilon\theta\upsilon\sigma\theta\acute{\eta}\sigma\epsilon\tau\alpha\iota$), will not hold water.

[b] *Cf.* St. John ii. 10 ὅταν μεθυσθῶσι, where the A.V. translated " when men have well drunk," the R. V. " have drunk freely."

[c] Arnim holds that three schools of thought are mentioned. See note on § 145.

PHILO

The arguments of the thesis : " The wise man will get drunk " are now stated.[a]

(1) As μέθυ and οἶνος are admittedly synonyms, their derivatives μεθύειν and οἰνοῦσθαι must be synonyms also. (This is preceded by a disquisition on " homonyms " and " synonyms.") (§§ 149-155.)

(2) μεθύειν is properly μετὰ τὸ θύειν, (" after sacrificing "), and the ancient and right use of wine was orderly and religious in marked contrast to present custom. If μεθύειν is used in this sense, it is suitable to the wise man (§§ 156-164).

(3) Another derivation of μεθύειν is from μέθεσις (relaxation), and the blessings of relaxation and cheerfulness are pointed out.

(4) A dialectical argument, that, as soberness is found in the fool as well as in the wise man, its opposite, drunkenness, is common to both (§ 172).

(5) An argument from the use of the term μέθη in various writers, showing that they identified μεθύειν with οἰνοῦσθαι, and did not associate it with λῆρος (§§ 173 f.).

At this point the disputant professes to meet the arguments of the other side. The first of these is

[a] It will be observed (a) that of these arguments 1, 2, 3, and 5 merely attempt to show that μεθύειν may be used in the milder sense : (β) that no attempt is made to defend λῆρος, which is definitely disclaimed in (5). The disputant, in fact, though professing to argue for the " wise man will get drunk," is really arguing for the *first half* of the Stoic maxim " the wise man will drink freely, but will *not* get drunk." Note further that little or no attempt is made to meet the view of the more rigid school described in § 143, which held that hard drinking, though not wrong in itself, might lead to evil.

the argument of Zeno, that, since no man could trust the drunken man with a secret, drunkenness is unsuitable to the wise man. This is refuted (§§ 175-177). The rest of the disquisition is lost.[a]

[a] It seems to be generally assumed that, after one or more further arguments had been disposed of, the debate ended ; in other words, that Philo only quotes one speech (or treatise) which, though it professed to meet the arguments of opponents, was throughout in support of the thesis : " that the wise man will get drunk." It seems to the translators more likely that not only the end of the supporter's speech, but also the whole of the opponent's answer has been lost. It is a favourite device of rhetoricians to choose out the weakest arguments on the opposite side and demolish them beforehand. It is noteworthy that the argument refuted in §§ 176 ff. is one which, though put forward by Zeno, was rejected by the later Stoics (see note on § 176).

ΠΕΡΙ ΦΥΤΟΥΡΓΙΑΣ ΝΩΕ ΤΟ ΔΕΥΤΕΡΟΝ

[329] I. | Ἐν μὲν τῷ προτέρῳ βιβλίῳ τὰ περὶ γεωρ-
γικῆς τέχνης γενικῆς, ὅσα καιρὸς ἦν, εἴπομεν, ἐν
δὲ τούτῳ περὶ τῆς κατ᾽ εἶδος ἀμπελουργικῆς, ὡς
ἂν οἷόν τε ᾖ, ἀποδώσομεν. τὸν γὰρ δίκαιον
οὐ γεωργὸν μόνον, ἀλλὰ καὶ ἰδίως ἀμπελουργὸν
εἰσάγει φάσκων· " ἤρξατο Νῶε ἄνθρωπος εἶναι
γεωργὸς γῆς καὶ ἐφύτευσεν ἀμπελῶνα."

2 προσήκει δὲ τὸν μέλλοντα περὶ τῶν κατὰ μέρος
φυτουργιῶν[1] τε καὶ γεωργιῶν διεξιέναι κατανοῆσαι
πρῶτον τὰ τελειότατα τοῦ παντὸς φυτὰ καὶ τὸν
μέγαν φυτουργὸν καὶ ἐπιστάτην αὐτῶν. ὁ μὲν
τοίνυν τῶν φυτουργῶν μέγιστος καὶ τὴν τέχνην
τελειότατος ὁ τῶν ὅλων ἡγεμών ἐστι, φυτὸν δὲ
αὖ[2] περιέχον ἐν ἑαυτῷ τὰ ἐν μέρει φυτὰ ἅμα[3]
παμμυρία καθάπερ κληματίδας ἐκ μιᾶς ἀνα-
3 βλαστάνοντα ῥίζης ὅδε ὁ κόσμος. ἐπειδὴ γὰρ τὴν
οὐσίαν ἄτακτον καὶ συγκεχυμένην οὖσαν ἐξ αὑτῆς
εἰς τάξιν ἐξ ἀταξίας καὶ ἐκ συγχύσεως εἰς διάκρισιν ἄγων ὁ κοσμοπλάστης μορφοῦν ἤρξατο,
[330] γῆν μὲν καὶ ὕδωρ ἐπὶ τὸ μέσον ἐρρίζου, τὰ | δὲ

---

[1] mss. φυτῶν. [2] mss. οὐ. [3] mss. ἀλλά.

212

CONCERNING NOAH'S WORK AS A PLANTER

BOOK II

I. We have said in the former book all that the 1 occasion called for regarding the husbandman's art in general. In this book we shall give such an account as we can of the art of a vine-dresser in particular. For Moses introduces the righteous man not as a husbandman only, but specially as a vine-dresser ; his words are : " Noah began to be a husbandman tilling the ground, and he planted a vineyard " (Gen. ix. 20). It is incumbent on one, 2 who is going to discourse on the work of planters and husbandmen as carried on in this or that place, to begin by marking well the plants set in the universe, those most perfect of all plants, and their great Planter and Overseer. It is the Lord of all things that is the greatest of planters and most perfect Master of His art. It is this World that is a plant containing in itself the particular plants all at once in their myriads, like shoots springing from a single root. For, when the Framer of the World, finding 3 all that existed confused and disordered of itself, began to give it form, by bringing it out of disorder into order, out of confusion into distinction of parts, He caused earth and water to occupy the position of

ἀέρος καὶ πυρὸς δένδρα πρὸς τὴν μετάρσιον
ἀνεῖλκεν ἀπὸ τοῦ μέσου χώραν, τὸν δὲ αἰθέριον
ἐν κύκλῳ τόπον ὠχυροῦτο τῶν ἐντὸς ὅρον
τε καὶ φυλακτήριον αὐτὸν τιθείς, ἀφ' οὗ καὶ
οὐρανὸς ὠνομάσθαι δοκεῖ· ⟨καὶ⟩ ὀχεῖσθαι μὲν
γῆν ὕδατι ξηρὰν οὖσαν, ἣν δέος ἦν ὕδατι δια-
λύεσθαι, πυρὶ δὲ ἀέρα θερμῷ φύσει τὸν ἐξ ἑαυτοῦ
ψυχρότατον, θαῦμα ἔκτοπον, ὁ θαυματοποιὸς
4 εἰργάζετο. πῶς γὰρ οὐ τεράστιον ὑπὸ μὲν τοῦ
λυομένου συνέχεσθαι τὸ λύον, πρὸς γῆς ὕδωρ, ἐπὶ
δὲ τῷ ψυχροτάτῳ τὸ θερμότατον ἄσβεστον ἱδρῦσθαι, πῦρ ἐπὶ ἀέρι;   καὶ ταῦτα μὲν τὰ
τέλεια τοῦ παντὸς ἦν μοσχεύματα, τὸ δὲ παμ-
μέγεθες καὶ παμφορώτατον ἔρνος ὁ κόσμος οὗτος,
5 οὗ παραφυάδες οἱ εἰρημένοι βλαστοί. II. Ὅπου
ποτ' οὖν ἄρα τὰς ῥίζας καθῆκε καὶ τίς ἐστιν αὐτῷ
βάσις, ἐφ' ἧς ὥσπερ ἀνδριὰς ἐρήρεισται, σκεπτέον.
σῶμα μὲν οὖν οὐδὲν ἀπολειφθὲν εἰκὸς ἔξω πλανᾶ-
σθαι πᾶσαν τὴν δι' ὅλων ὕλην ἐργασαμένου καὶ
6 διακοσμήσαντος θεοῦ· τελειότατον γὰρ ἥρμοττε
τὸ μέγιστον τῶν ἔργων τῷ μεγίστῳ δημιουργῷ
διαπλάσασθαι, τελειότατον δὲ οὐκ ἂν ἦν, εἰ μὴ
τελείοις συνεπληροῦτο μέρεσιν· ὥστε ἐκ γῆς
ἁπάσης καὶ παντὸς ὕδατος καὶ ἀέρος καὶ πυρός,
μηδενὸς ἔξω μηδὲ τοῦ βραχυτάτου καταλειφθέντος,
7 συνέστη ὅδε ὁ κόσμος. ἀνάγκη τοίνυν ἐκτὸς ἢ
κενὸν ἢ μηδὲν εἶναι. εἰ μὲν δὴ κενόν, πῶς τὸ

---

[a] Or from *both*. Cornutus i. 1 gives ὠρεύειν ὅ ἐστι
φυλάσσειν, as well as ὅρος for the originals from which οὐρανός
is derived.

[b] See App. p. 494.

roots at its centre ; the trees, that are air and fire, He drew up from the centre to the space on high ; the encircling region of ether He firmly established, and set it to be at once a boundary and guard of all that is within. (Apparently its name " Heaven " is derived from the former word.[a]) And (surpassing wonder !) this Doer of wondrous works caused earth, a dry substance in danger of being dissolved by water, to be held by [b] water, and air, of itself coldest of all things, to be held by fire whose very nature is heat. How can it be other than a prodigy that the 4 dissolving element should be held together by that which it dissolves, water by earth ; and that on the coldest element the hottest should be seated un-quenched, fire upon air ? The elements of which we have spoken are the perfect branches of the whole, but the stock, far greater and more productive than all of them, is this world, of which the growths that have been mentioned are offshoots. II. We must consider, therefore, where He caused its 5 roots to strike, and on what it rests as a statue on its pedestal. It is unlikely that any material body has been left over and was moving about at random out-side, seeing that God had wrought up and placed in orderly position all matter wherever found. For it 6 became the greatest artificer to fashion to full per-fection the greatest of constructions, and it would have come short of full perfection, had it not had a complement of perfect parts.[b] Accordingly this world of ours was formed out of all that there is of earth, and all that there is of water, and air and fire, not even the smallest particle being left outside. It 7 follows that outside there is either empty space or nothing at all. If there is empty space, how comes

πλῆρες καὶ ναστὸν καὶ τῶν ὄντων βαρύτατον οὐ
βρίθει ταλαντεῦον στερεοῦ μηδενὸς ἀπερείδοντος[1];
ἐξ οὗ φάσματι ἂν ἐοικέναι δόξαι, ζητούσης ἀεὶ
τῆς διανοίας βάσιν σωματικήν, ⟨ἣν⟩ πᾶν ἔχειν
εἰκός, ἐάν τι κενὸν μόνον[2] τυγχάνῃ, τὸν δὲ δὴ
κόσμον καὶ διαφερόντως, ὅτι τὸ μέγιστον σωμάτων
ἐστὶ καὶ πλῆθος ἄλλων σωμάτων ὡς οἰκεῖα ἐγ-
8 κεκόλπισται μέρη. τὰς δυσωπίας οὖν εἴ τις ἀπο-
διδράσκειν βούλοιτο τὰς ἐν τοῖς διαπορηθεῖσι,
λεγέτω μετὰ παρρησίας, ὅτι οὐδὲν τῶν ἐν ὕλαις
κραταιὸν οὕτως, ὡς τὸν κόσμον ἀχθοφορεῖν
ἰσχῦσαι, λόγος δὲ ὁ ἀΐδιος θεοῦ τοῦ αἰωνίου τὸ
[331] ὀχυρώτατον καὶ | βεβαιότατον ἔρεισμα τῶν ὅλων
9 ἐστίν. οὗτος ἀπὸ τῶν μέσων ἐπὶ τὰ
πέρατα καὶ ἀπὸ τῶν ἄκρων ἐπὶ τὰ μέσα ταθεὶς
δολιχεύει τὸν τῆς φύσεως δρόμον ἀήττητον συνάγων
τὰ μέρη πάντα καὶ σφίγγων· δεσμὸν γὰρ αὐτὸν
ἄρρηκτον τοῦ παντὸς ὁ γεννήσας ἐποίει πατήρ.
10 εἰκότως οὖν οὐδὲ γῆ πᾶσα διαλυθήσεται πρὸς
παντὸς ὕδατος, ὅπερ αὐτῆς οἱ κόλποι κεχωρήκασιν,
οὐδ' ὑπὸ ἀέρος σβεσθήσεται πῦρ, οὐδ' ἔμπαλιν ὑπὸ
πυρὸς ἀὴρ ἀναφλεχθήσεται, τοῦ θείου λόγου μεθόριον τάττοντος αὐτὸν καθάπερ φωνῆεν στοιχείων
ἀφώνων, ἵνα τὸ ὅλον ὥσπερ ἐπὶ τῆς ἐγγραμμάτου
μουσικῆς[3] συνηχήσῃ, τὰς τῶν ἐναντίων ἀπειλὰς
πειθοῖ τῇ συνόδῳ[4] μεσιτεύοντός τε καὶ διαιτῶντος.

---

[1] ἀπερείδοντος conj. Tr. for ἐπερείδοντος MSS.

[2] MSS. ἐάν τε κινούμενον: Wend. ἐάν τι κινούμενον.   Perhaps
ἐάν τε ⟨ἰσχύμενον, ἐάν τε⟩ κινούμενον.

[3] Mangey and Wend. φωνῆς, which is elsewhere coupled with
ἐγγραμμάτου, e.g. De Agr. 136. But the μούσης of the MSS. is reproduced in a quotation of the passage by Eusebius as μουσικῆς.

[4] MSS. and Eusebius συνόδῳ (sic): Wend. συναγωγῷ.

it that a thing that is full and dense and heaviest of all existences does not sink down by sheer weight, having nothing solid external to it to hold it up? This would seem to be of the nature of a phantom, since our understanding ever looks for a material basis, which it expects everything to have, even if it be but an empty thing, but above all the world, since it is the largest of material bodies, and holds in its bosom as parts of itself a mass of other material bodies. Let anyone then, who would fain escape the confusion 8 of face, which we all feel when we have to leave problems unsolved, say plainly that no material thing is so strong as to be able to bear the burden of the world; and that the everlasting Word of the eternal God is the very sure and staunch prop of the Whole.   He it is, who extending Himself 9 from the midst to its utmost bounds and from its extremities to the midst again, keeps up through all its length Nature's unvanquished course, combining and compacting all its parts. For the Father Who begat Him constituted His Word such a Bond of the Universe as nothing can break. Good reason, then, 10 have we to be sure that all the earth shall not be dissolved by all the water which has gathered within its hollows; nor fire be quenched by air; nor, on the other hand, air be ignited by fire. The Divine Word stations Himself to keep these elements apart, like a Vocal between voiceless elements of speech, that the universe may send forth a harmony like that of a masterpiece of literature.[a] He mediates between the opponents amid their threatenings, and reconciles them by winning ways to peace and con-

---

[a] See App. p. 494.

11   III. Οὕτως μὲν δὴ τὸ παμφορώτατον
φυτὸν ἐρριζοῦτο καὶ ῥιζωθὲν ἐκρατεῖτο· τῶν δὲ ἐν
μέρει καὶ βραχυτέρων φυτῶν τὰ μὲν μεταβατικῶς
κινητά, τὰ δὲ ἄνευ μεταβάσεως ὡς ἂν ἑστῶτα
12 κατὰ τὸν αὐτὸν τόπον ἐδημιουργεῖτο. τὰ μὲν
οὖν μεταβατικῇ κινήσει χρώμενα, ἃ δή φαμεν
ἡμεῖς ζῷα εἶναι, ταῖς τοῦ παντὸς ὁλοσχερεστέραις
προσεγένετο μοίραις, γῇ μὲν τὰ χερσαῖα, πλωτὰ
δὲ ὕδατι, τὰ δὲ πτηνὰ ἀέρι καὶ τὰ πυρίγονα πυρί,
ὧν τὴν γένεσιν ἀριδηλοτέραν κατὰ Μακεδονίαν
λόγος ἔχει προφαίνεσθαι, καὶ οἱ ἀστέρες[1] οὐρανῷ
—ζῷα γὰρ καὶ τούτους νοερὰ δι' ὅλων φασὶν οἱ
φιλοσοφήσαντες—, ⟨ὧν⟩ οἱ μὲν πλάνητες ἐξ
ἑαυτῶν, οἱ δ' ἀπλανεῖς τῇ τοῦ παντὸς συμπεριαγο-
μένοι φορᾷ τόπους ἐναλλάττειν δοκοῦσι.
13 τὰ δὲ ἀφαντάστῳ φύσει διοικούμενα, ἅπερ ἰδίως
λέγεται φυτά, μεταβατικῆς κινήσεως ἀμέτοχα.
14   IV. διττὰ δὲ ἔν τε γῇ καὶ ἀέρι γένη ὁ
ποιῶν ἐποίει. ἀέρι μὲν τὰ πτηνὰ καὶ αἰσθητὰ καὶ
δυνάμεις ἄλλας αἰσθήσει οὐδαμῇ οὐδαμῶς κατα-
λαμβανομένας— ψυχῶν ὁ θίασος οὗτος ἀσωμάτων
ἐστὶ διακεκοσμημένων οὐ ταῖς αὐταῖς ἐν τάξεσι·
τὰς μὲν γὰρ εἰσκρίνεσθαι λόγος ἔχει σώμασι
θνητοῖς καὶ κατά τινας ὡρισμένας περιόδους
ἀπαλλάττεσθαι πάλιν, τὰς δὲ θειοτέρας κατασκευῆς

---

[1] mss. τοὺς ἀστέρας ἐν.

---

a For the whole of this section cf. De Gig. 7 f.

cord.   III. On this wise was the tree 11
planted which yields all fruit that grows. On this
wise when planted was it held fast. Among lesser
plants, that did not partake of its universal character,
some were created with a capacity of moving from
one place to another, others, meant to be stationary,
lacked such capacity for change of place. Our name 12
for those which have the power of locomotion is
animals. These took to (*i.e.* were so made as naturally
to belong to) the several main divisions of our universe, land animals to earth, to water those that
swim, the winged creatures to air, and to fire the
fire-born. It is said that the production of these last
is more patent to observation in Macedonia than
elsewhere. The stars found their place in heaven.
Those who have made philosophy their study tell us
that these too are living creatures, but of a kind
composed entirely of Mind. Of these some, the
planets, appear to change their position by a power
inherent in themselves, others to do so as they are
swept along in the rush of our universe, and these
we call fixed stars.[a]   The creations en- 13
dowed with a nature incapable of taking in impressions, to which the name of " plants " is specially
given, do not share the power of locomotion.

IV. Of twofold kind were the beings which the great 14
Maker made as well in the earth as in the air. In
the air He made the winged creatures perceived by
our senses, and other mighty beings besides which
are wholly beyond apprehension by sense. This is
the host of the bodiless souls. Their array is made
up of companies that differ in kind. We are told that
some enter into mortal bodies, and quit them again
at certain fixed periods, while others, endowed with

λαχούσας ἄπαντος ἀλογεῖν τοῦ γῆς χωρίου, ἀνω-
[332] τάτω δ' εἶναι πρὸς αὐτῷ τῷ | αἰθέρι τὰς καθαρω-
τάτας, ἃς οἱ μὲν παρ' Ἕλλησι φιλοσοφήσαντες
ἥρωας καλοῦσι, Μωυσῆς δὲ ὀνόματι εὐθυβόλῳ
χρώμενος ἀγγέλους προσαγορεύει, πρεσβευομένας
καὶ διαγγελλούσας τά τε παρὰ τοῦ ἡγεμόνος τοῖς
ὑπηκόοις ἀγαθὰ καὶ τῷ βασιλεῖ ὧν εἰσιν οἱ
ὑπήκοοι χρεῖοι.   γῇ δὲ ζῷά τε χερσαῖα
καὶ φυτά, δύο πάλιν, προσένειμε, τὴν αὐτὴν μητέρα
15 τε βουληθεὶς εἶναι καὶ τροφόν· καθάπερ γὰρ
γυναικὶ καὶ παντὶ τῷ θήλει πηγαὶ πρὸς τῷ μέλλειν
ἀποκυΐσκειν ἀναχέονται[1] γάλακτος, ἵνα τοῖς γεννω-
μένοις ἄρδωσι τὰς ἀναγκαίας καὶ ἁρμοττούσας
τροφάς, τὸν αὐτὸν τρόπον καὶ τῇ χερσαίων ζῴων
μητρὶ γῇ πάσας φυτῶν προσένειμεν ἰδέας, ἵνα
συγγενέσι καὶ μὴ ὀθνείοις τροφαῖς τὰ γεννώμενα
16 χρήσηται.   καὶ μὴν τὰ μὲν φυτὰ κατωκάρα
ἀπειργάζετο τὰς κεφαλὰς αὐτῶν ἐν τοῖς βαθυγειο-
τάτοις γῆς μέρεσι πήξας, ζῴων δὲ τῶν ἀλόγων
τὰς κεφαλὰς ἀνελκύσας ἀπὸ γῆς ἐπὶ προμήκους
αὐχένος ἄκρας ἡρμόζετο τῷ αὐχένι ὥσπερ ἐπίβασιν
17 τοὺς ἐμπροσθίους πόδας θείς. ἐξαιρέτου δὲ τῆς
κατασκευῆς ἔλαχεν ἄνθρωπος· τῶν μὲν γὰρ ἄλλων
τὰς ὄψεις περιήγαγε κάτω κάμψας, διὸ νένευκε
πρὸς χέρσον, ἀνθρώπου δὲ ἔμπαλιν ἀνώρθωσεν,
ἵνα τὸν οὐρανὸν καταθεᾶται, φυτὸν οὐκ ἐπίγειον
ἀλλ' οὐράνιον, ὡς ὁ παλαιὸς λόγος, ὑπάρχων. V.
18 ἀλλ' οἱ μὲν ἄλλοι τῆς αἰθερίου φύσεως τὸν ἡμέτερον

[1] mss. ἀποχέονται.

a diviner constitution, have no regard for any earthly quarter, but exist on high nigh to the ethereal region itself. These are the purest spirits of all, whom Greek philosophers call heroes, but whom Moses, employing a well-chosen name, entitles " angels," for they go on embassies bearing tidings from the great Ruler to His subjects of the boons which He sends them, and reporting to the Monarch what His subjects are in need of.   Two kinds again did He assign to earth, land animals and plants. For He willed her to be at once both mother and nurse. For, even as in woman and all female 15 kind there well up springs of milk when the time of delivery draws near, that they may furnish necessary drink of a suitable kind to their offspring ; even so in like manner did the Creator bestow on earth, the mother of land animals, plants of all sorts, to the end that the new-born might have the benefit of nourishment not foreign but akin to them. Furthermore, 16 while He fashioned the plants head downwards, fixing their heads in the portions of the earth where the soil lay deepest, He raised from the earth the heads of the animals that are without reason and set them on the top of a long neck, placing the fore feet as a support for the neck. But the build allotted to man 17 was distinguished above that of other living creatures. For by turning the eyes of the others downwards He made them incline to the earth beneath them. The eyes of man, on the contrary, He set high up, that he might gaze on heaven, for man, as the old saying is, is a plant not earthly but heavenly.[a] V. Now while 18 others, by asserting that our human mind is a particle

---

[a] *Timaeus* 90 A ; *cf.* for the preceding section *ib.* 91 E. See note on *Quod Det*. 84.

νοῦν μοῖραν εἰπόντες εἶναι συγγένειαν ἀνθρώπῳ
πρὸς αἰθέρα συνῆψαν. ὁ δὲ μέγας Μωυσῆς οὐδενὶ
τῶν γεγονότων τῆς λογικῆς ψυχῆς τὸ εἶδος
ὡμοίωσεν, ἀλλ' εἶπεν αὐτὴν τοῦ θείου καὶ ἀοράτου
πνεύματος ἐκείνου δόκιμον εἶναι νόμισμα σημειωθὲν
καὶ τυπωθὲν σφραγῖδι θεοῦ, ἧς ὁ χαρακτήρ ἐστιν
19 ὁ ἀίδιος λόγος· " ἐνέπνευσε " γάρ φησιν " ὁ θεὸς
εἰς τὸ πρόσωπον αὐτοῦ πνοὴν ζωῆς," ὥστε
ἀνάγκη πρὸς τὸν ἐκπέμποντα τὸν δεχόμενον
ἀπεικονίσθαι· διὸ καὶ λέγεται κατ' εἰκόνα θεοῦ
τὸν ἄνθρωπον γεγενῆσθαι, οὐ μὴν κατ' εἰκόνα
20 τινὸς τῶν γεγονότων. ἀκόλουθον οὖν ἦν τῆς
ἀνθρώπου ψυχῆς κατὰ τὸν ἀρχέτυπον τοῦ αἰτίου
λόγον ἀπεικονισθείσης καὶ τὸ σῶμα ἀνεγερθὲν
πρὸς τὴν καθαρωτάτην τοῦ παντὸς μοῖραν, οὐρανόν,
τὰς ὄψεις ἀνατεῖναι, ἵνα τῷ φανερῷ τὸ ἀφανὲς
21 ἐκδήλως καταλαμβάνηται. ἐπειδὴ τοίνυν τὴν πρὸς
τὸ ὂν διανοίας ὁλκὴν ἀμήχανον ἦν ἰδεῖν ὅτι μὴ
τοὺς ἀχθέντας πρὸς αὐτοῦ μόνους—ὃ γὰρ πέπονθεν
ἕκαστος, αὐτὸς ἐξαιρέτως οἶδεν—, εἴδωλον ἐναργὲς
[383] | ἀειδοῦς ὄμματος τὰ τοῦ σώματος ποιεῖ δυνάμενα
22 πρὸς αἰθέρα ἀπονεύειν. ὁπότε γὰρ οἱ ἐκ φθαρτῆς
παγέντες ὕλης ὀφθαλμοὶ τοσοῦτον ἐπέβησαν, ὡς
ἀπὸ τοῦ τῆς γῆς χωρίου πρὸς τὸν μακρὰν οὕτως
ἀφεστῶτα ἀνατρέχειν οὐρανὸν καὶ ψαύειν τῶν
περάτων αὐτοῦ, πόσον τινὰ χρὴ νομίσαι τὸν πάντῃ
δρόμον τῶν ψυχῆς ὀμμάτων; ἅπερ ὑπὸ πολλοῦ
τοῦ τὸ ὂν κατιδεῖν τηλαυγῶς ἱμέρου πτερωθέντα
οὐ μόνον πρὸς τὸν ἔσχατον αἰθέρα τείνεται, παρα-

of the ethereal substance, have claimed for man a kinship with the upper air ; our great Moses likened the fashion of the reasonable soul to no created thing, but averred it to be a genuine coinage of that dread Spirit, the Divine and Invisible One, signed and impressed by the seal of God, the stamp of which is the Eternal Word. His words are " God in-breathed 19 into his face a breath of Life " (Gen. ii. 7) ; so that it cannot but be that he that receives is made in the likeness of Him Who sends forth the breath. Accordingly we also read that man has been made after the Image of God (Gen. i. 27), not however after the image of anything created. It followed then, as a 20 natural consequence of man's soul having been made after the image of the Archetype, the Word of the First Cause, that his body also was made erect, and could lift up its eyes to heaven, the purest portion of our universe, that by means of that which he could see man might clearly apprehend that which he could not see. Since, then, it was impossible for 21 any to discern how the understanding tends towards the Existent One, save those only who had been drawn by Him—for each one of us knows what he has himself experienced as no other can know it— He endows the bodily eyes with the power of taking the direction of the upper air, and so makes them a distinct representation of the invisible eye. For, 22 seeing that the eyes formed out of perishable matter obtained so great reach as to travel from the earthly region to heaven, that is so far away, and to touch its bounds, how vast must we deem the flight in all directions of the eyes of the soul ? The strong yearning to perceive the Existent One gives them wings to attain not only to the furthest region of the upper

μειψάμενα δὲ καὶ παντὸς τοῦ κόσμου τοὺς ὅρους
23 ἐπείγεται πρὸς τὸν ἀγένητον.   VI. διὰ
τοῦτο ἐν τοῖς χρησμοῖς οἱ σοφίας καὶ ἐπιστήμης
ἄπληστοι διατελοῦντες ἀνακεκλῆσθαι λέγονται·
πρὸς γὰρ τὸ θεῖον ἄνω καλεῖσθαι θέμις τοὺς ὑπ᾽
24 αὐτοῦ καταπνευσθέντας.   δεινὸν γάρ, εἰ τυφῶσι
μὲν καὶ ἁρπυίαις αὐτόπρεμνα δένδρα πρὸς ἀέρα
ἀνασπᾶται καὶ μυριάγωγα σκάφη βρίθοντα φόρτῳ
καθάπερ τινὰ τῶν κουφοτάτων ἐκ μέσων τῶν
πελαγῶν ἀναρπάζεται καὶ λίμναι καὶ ποταμοὶ
μετάρσιοι φέρονται, τοὺς γῆς κόλπους ἐκλιπόντος
τοῦ ῥεύματος, ὅπερ ἀνιμήσαντο αἱ τῶν ἀνέμων
κραταιόταται καὶ πολυπλοκώταται δῖναι, τῇ δὲ
τοῦ θείου πνεύματος καὶ πάντα δυνατοῦ καὶ τὰ
κάτω νικῶντος φύσει κοῦφον ὁ νοῦς ὢν οὐκ ἐπ-
ελαφρίζεται καὶ πρὸς μήκιστον ὕψος ἐξαίρεται, καὶ
25 μάλιστα ὁ τοῦ φιλοσοφήσαντος ἀνόθως.   οὗτος
γὰρ κάτω μὲν οὐ βρίθει πρὸς τὰ σώματος καὶ γῆς
φίλα ταλαντεύων, ὧν διάζευξιν καὶ ἀλλοτρίωσιν
ἀεὶ διεπόνησεν, ἄνω δὲ φέρεται τῶν μεταρσίων
καὶ ἱεροπρεπεστάτων καὶ εὐδαιμόνων φύσεων
26 ἀκορέστως ἐρασθείς.   τοιγαροῦν Μωυσῆς ὁ ταμίας
καὶ φύλαξ τῶν τοῦ ὄντος ὀργίων ἀνακεκλήσεται·
λέγεται γὰρ ἐν Λευιτικῇ βίβλῳ· '' ἀνεκάλεσε
Μωυσῆν.'' ἀνακεκλήσεται δὲ καὶ ὁ τῶν δευτερείων
ἀξιωθεὶς Βεσελεήλ· καὶ γὰρ τοῦτον ἀνακαλεῖ ὁ
θεὸς πρὸς τὴν τῶν ἱερῶν κατασκευήν τε καὶ
27 ἐπιμέλειαν ἔργων.   ἀλλ᾽ ὁ μὲν τὰ δευτερεῖα τῆς

air, but to overpass the very bounds of the entire
universe and speed away toward the Uncreate.

VI. This is why those who crave for 23
wisdom and knowledge with insatiable persistence are
said in the Sacred Oracles to have been called upwards ; for it accords with God's ways that those
who have received His down-breathing should be
called up to Him. For when trees are whirled up, 24
roots and all, into the air by hurricanes and tornadoes,
and heavily laden ships of large tonnage are snatched
up out of mid-ocean, as though objects of very little
weight, and lakes and rivers are borne aloft, and
earth's hollows are left empty by the water as it is
drawn up by a tangle of violently eddying winds,
it is strange if a light substance like the mind
is not rendered buoyant and raised to the utmost
height by the native force of the Divine spirit, over-
coming as it does in its boundless might all powers
that are here below. Above all is it strange if this
is not so with the mind of the genuine philosopher.
Such an one suffers from no weight of downward 25
pressure towards the objects dear to the body and
to earth. From these he has ever made an earnest
effort to sever and estrange himself. So he is borne
upward insatiably enamoured of all holy happy
natures that dwell on high. Accordingly Moses, 26
the keeper and guardian of the mysteries of the
Existent One, will be one called above ; for it is said
in the Book of Leviticus, " He called Moses up above"
(Lev. i. 1). One called up above will Bezeleel also
be, held worthy of a place in the second rank. For
him also does God call up above for the construction
and overseeing of the sacred works (Exod. xxxi. 2 ff.).
But while Bezeleel shall carry off the lower honours 27

ἀνακλήσεως, Μωυσῆς δὲ ὁ πάνσοφος οἴσεται τὰ
πρωτεῖα· ἐκεῖνος μὲν γὰρ τὰς σκιὰς πλάττει
καθάπερ οἱ ζωγραφοῦντες οἷς οὐ θέμις οὐδὲν
ἔμψυχον δημιουργῆσαι—Βεσελεὴλ γὰρ ἐν σκιαῖς
ποιῶν ἑρμηνεύεται—, Μωυσῆς δὲ οὐ σκιὰς ἀλλὰ
τὰς ἀρχετύπους φύσεις αὐτὰς τῶν πραγμάτων
ἔλαχεν ἀνατυποῦν. ἄλλως τε καὶ τὸ αἴτιον οἷς μὲν
τηλαυγέστερον καὶ ἀριδηλότερον ὡς ἂν ἐν ἡλίῳ
καθαρῷ, οἷς δὲ ἀμυδρότερον ὡς ἂν ἐν σκιᾷ τὰ
οἰκεῖα εἴωθεν ἐπιδείκνυσθαι.

28 VII. | Διεξεληλυθότες οὖν περὶ τῶν ὁλοσχερε-
[334] στέρων ἐν κόσμῳ φυτῶν ἴδωμεν ὃν τρόπον καὶ τὰ
ἐν τῷ ἀνθρώπῳ, τῷ βραχεῖ κόσμῳ, δένδρα ὁ
πάνσοφος ἐδημιούργει θεός. αὐτίκα τοίνυν ὡσ-
περβαθύγειον χωρίον σῶμα τὸ ἡμέτερον λαβὼν
29 δεξαμενὰς αὐτῷ τὰς αἰσθήσεις ἀπειργάζετο· κἄπειθ’
οἷα φυτὸν ἥμερον καὶ ὠφελιμώτατον ⟨εἰς⟩[1] ἑκάστην
αὐτῶν ἐνετίθει, ἀκοὴν μὲν εἰς οὖς, ὄψιν δ’ εἰς
ὄμματα καὶ εἰς μυκτῆρας ὄσφρησιν καὶ τὰς ἄλλας
εἰς τὰ οἰκεῖα καὶ συγγενῆ χωρία. μαρτυρεῖ δέ μου
τῷ λόγῳ ὁ θεσπέσιος ἀνὴρ ἐν ὕμνοις λέγων ὧδε·
“ὁ φυτεύων οὓς οὐκ ἀκούει; ὁ πλάσσων ὀφθαλ-
30 μοὺς οὐκ ἐπιβλέψει;” καὶ τὰς διηκούσας μέντοι
μέχρι σκελῶν τε καὶ χειρῶν καὶ τῶν ἄλλων τοῦ
σώματος μερῶν, ὅσα ἐντός τε καὶ ἐκτός, δυνάμεις
31 ἁπάσας εὐγενῆ μοσχεύματα εἶναι συμβέβηκε. τὰ
δὲ ἀμείνω καὶ τελειότερα τῷ μεσαιτάτῳ καὶ
καρποφορεῖν δυναμένῳ διαφερόντως ἡγεμονικῷ

---

[1] εἰς may easily have dropped out before ἐκ. Heinemann
translates as if it had. See App. p. 494.

conferred by the call above, Moses the all-wise shall bear away the primary honours. For the former fashions the shadows, just as painters do, to whom Heaven has not granted power to create aught that has life. " Bezeleel," we must remember, means " making in shadows." Moses on the other hand obtained the office of producing not shadows but the actual archetype of the several objects. Nor need we wonder at such distinctions. It is the wont of the Supreme Cause to exhibit the objects proper to each, to some in a clearer, more radiant vision, as though in unclouded sunshine, to others more dimly, as though in the shade.

VII. As we have now brought to a close our dis- 28 cussion of those objects on a larger scale which are set to grow in the field of the universe, let us note the way in which God the all-wise fashioned the trees that are in man, the microcosm. To begin with, then, He took our body, as though He were taking some deep-soiled plot of ground and made the organs of sense as tree-beds for it. Having done this He 29 set a sense in each of them, as a plant highly valuable for cultivation, hearing in the ear, sight in the eyes, in the nostrils scent, and the rest in their appropriate and congenial positions. I may cite as a witness to what I say the sacred poet, where he says " He that planteth the ear, doth He not hear ? He that fashioneth the eyes, shall He not behold ? " (Psalm xciv. 9). And all the other faculties of the body 30 including legs and hands and every part, whether inner or outer, are nothing else than noble shoots and growths. The better and more perfect growths He 31 planted in the dominant faculty, which holds the central position, and possesses in a pre-eminent

προσερρίζου· ταῦτα δέ εἰσι νόησις, κατάληψις,
εὐστοχία, μελέται, μνῆμαι, ἕξεις, διαθέσεις,
τεχνῶν ἰδέαι πολύτροποι, βεβαιότης ἐπιστημῶν,
τῶν ἀρετῆς ἁπάσης θεωρημάτων ἄληστος ἀνά-
ληψις. τούτων οὐδὲν οὐδεὶς θνητὸς ἱκανὸς φυτουρ-
γῆσαι, πάντων δὲ ἀθρόων εἷς ὁ ἀγένητος τεχνίτης,
οὐ πεποιηκὼς μόνον, ἀλλὰ καὶ ποιῶν ἀεὶ καθ᾽
ἕκαστον τῶν γεννωμένων τὰ φυτὰ ταῦτα.

32   VIII. Τοῖς εἰρημένοις ἐστὶν ἀκόλουθος καὶ ἡ
τοῦ παραδείσου φυτουργία· λέγεται γάρ· ‘‘ ἐφύτευσεν ὁ θεὸς παράδεισον ἐν Ἐδὲμ κατὰ ἀνατολάς,
καὶ ἔθετο ἐκεῖ τὸν ἄνθρωπον ὃν ἔπλασεν.’’ τὸ
μὲν οὖν ἀμπέλους καὶ ἐλαιῶν ἢ μηλεῶν ἢ
ῥοιῶν ἢ τῶν παραπλησίων δένδρα οἴεσθαι[1] πολλὴ
33 καὶ δυσθεράπευτος εὐήθεια. τίνος γὰρ ἕνεκα,
εἴποι τις ἄν; ἵνα ἐνδιαιτήσεις εὐαγώγους ἔχῃ;
ὁ γὰρ κόσμος ἅπας αὐταρκέστατον ἐνδιαίτημα ἂν
νομισθείη θεῷ τῷ πανηγεμόνι; ἢ οὐχὶ μυρίων
καὶ ἄλλων δόξαι ἂν ὑστερίζειν, ὡς πρὸς ὑποδοχὴν
τοῦ μεγάλου βασιλέως ἀξιόχρεων ὑποληφθῆναι
χωρίον; χωρὶς τοῦ[2] μηδὲ εὐαγὲς εἶναι οἴεσθαι τὸ
αἴτιον ἐν τῷ αἰτιατῷ περιέχεσθαι [τῷ] μηδὲ τὰ
34 δένδρα τοὺς ἐτησίους δήπου φέρειν καρπούς. πρὸς
τὴν τίνος οὖν ἀπόλαυσίν τε καὶ χρῆσιν καρπο-
φορήσει ὁ παράδεισος; ἀνθρώπου μὲν οὐδενός·
οὐδεὶς γὰρ εἰσάγεται τὸ παράπαν τὸν παράδεισον
οἰκῶν, ἐπεὶ καὶ τὸν πρῶτον διαπλασθέντα ἐκ γῆς
35 μεταναστῆναί φησιν ἐνθένδε, ὄνομα Ἀδάμ. καὶ

---

[1] No lacuna (as Wend.) An infinitive can be understood
after οἴομαι, e.g. Homer, *Odyssey* xxiv. 401.

[2] mss. χωρίον τοῦ : Wend. χωρὶς τοῦ.

[a] *Cf.* note on *De Cher.* 62.   [b] *Cf. L.A.* i. 43.

degree the capacity for yielding fruit. These growths are insight, apprehension, accurate judgement, constant practice, powers of memory, varying conditions, chronic dispositions,[a] scientific capacity taking many forms and directions, certainty of knowledge, ability to take in and retain the principles and implications of virtue in every shape. Not one of these is any mortal man whatever capable of growing. The One Grower of them all is the Uncreate Artificer, Who not only has made these plants once for all, but is ever making them in the case of each man who is from time to time begotten.

VIII. In agreement with what I have said is the 32 planting of the garden; for we read, " God planted a garden in Eden facing the sun-rising, and placed there the man whom He had moulded " (Gen. ii. 8). To imagine that he planted vines and olive and apple and pomegranate trees or the like, would be serious folly, difficult to eradicate. One would 33 naturally ask What for? To provide Himself with convenient places to live in?[b] Would the whole world be considered a sufficient dwelling for God the Lord of all? Would it not evidently fall short in countless other ways[c] of being deemed meet to receive the Great King? To say nothing of the irreverence of supposing that the Cause of all things is contained in that which He has caused, and to say nothing of the fact that the trees of His planting do not yield annual fruits as ours do.[d] For whose use 34 and enjoyment, then, will the Garden yield its fruits? Not for that of any man; for no one whatever is mentioned as dwelling in the garden, for we are told that Adam, the man first moulded out of the earth,

[c] *i.e.* than being without a garden.   [d] See App. p. 494.

μὴν ὅ γε θεὸς ὥσπερ τῶν ἄλλων καὶ τροφῆς
ἀνεπιδεής ἐστιν· ἀνάγκη γὰρ τὸν τροφῇ χρώμενον
δεῖσθαι μὲν τὸ πρῶτον, ἔπειτα δὲ ὄργανα εὐ-
τρεπίσθαι, δι' ὧν καὶ τὴν εἰσιοῦσαν παραδέξεται
[335] καὶ τὴν ἐκμασηθεῖσαν θύραζε ἀποπέμψει. | ταῦτα
δὲ μακαριότητος καὶ εὐδαιμονίας τῆς περὶ τὸ
αἴτιον ἀπάδει, τῶν ἀνθρωπόμορφον, ἔτι δὲ καὶ
ἀνθρωποπαθὲς αὐτὸ εἰσαγόντων ἐπ' εὐσεβείας καὶ
ὁσιότητος καθαιρέσει, μεγάλων ἀρετῶν, ἐκθεσμό-
36 τατα ὄντα εὑρήματα.   IX. ἰτέον οὖν
ἐπ' ἀλληγορίαν τὴν ὁρατικοῖς φίλην ἀνδράσι· καὶ
γὰρ οἱ χρησμοὶ τὰς εἰς αὐτὴν ἡμῖν ἀφορμὰς ἐναρ-
γέστατα προτείνουσι· λέγουσι γὰρ ἐν τῷ παραδείσῳ
φυτὰ εἶναι μηδὲν ἐοικότα τοῖς παρ' ἡμῖν, ἀλλὰ
ζωῆς, ἀθανασίας, εἰδήσεως, καταλήψεως, συνέσεως,
37 καλοῦ καὶ πονηροῦ φαντασίας. ταῦτα δὲ χέρσου
μὲν οὐκ ἂν εἴη, λογικῆς δὲ ψυχῆς ἀναγκαίως
φυτά, ἡ μὲν[1] πρὸς ἀρετὴν ὁδὸς αὐτῆς ζωὴν καὶ
ἀθανασίαν ἔχουσα τὸ τέλος, ἡ δὲ πρὸς κακίαν
φυγήν τε τούτων καὶ θάνατον. τὸν οὖν φιλόδωρον
θεὸν ὑποληπτέον ἐν τῇ ψυχῇ καθάπερ παράδεισον
ἀρετῶν καὶ τῶν κατ' αὐτὰς πράξεων ἐμφυτεύειν
πρὸς τελείαν εὐδαιμονίαν αὐτὴν ἄγοντα.

38   Διὰ τοῦτο καὶ τόπον οἰκειότατον προσένειμε
τῷ παραδείσῳ καλούμενον Ἐδέμ—ἑρμηνεύεται δὲ
τρυφή—, σύμβολον ψυχῆς τῆς ἄρτια βλεπούσης,
ἀρεταῖς ἐγχορευούσης καὶ ὑπὸ πλήθους καὶ μεγέ-
θους χαρᾶς ἀνασκιρτώσης, ἀπόλαυσμα ἓν ἀντὶ

---

[1] Or, with Wend., ⟨ἧς⟩ ἡ μὲν, "to which belongs the path"
etc.

migrated thence. As for God, *He* stands in no need of 35 food any more than of aught else. For one who uses food must in the first place experience need, and in the next place be equipped with organs by means of which to take the food that comes in, and to discharge that from which he has drawn its goodness. These things are not in harmony with the blessedness and happiness of the First Cause. They are utterly monstrous inventions of men who would overthrow great virtues like piety and reverence by representing Him as having the form and passions of mankind.

IX. So we must turn to allegory, the method dear 36 to men with their eyes opened. Indeed the sacred oracles most evidently afford us the clues for the use of this method. For they say that in the garden there are trees in no way resembling those with which we are familiar, but trees of Life, of Immortality, of Knowledge, of Apprehension, of Understanding, of the conception of good and evil. And 37 these can be no growths of earthly soil, but must be those of the reasonable soul, namely its path according to virtue with life and immortality as its end, and its path according to evil ending in the shunning of these and in death. We must conceive therefore that the bountiful God plants in the soul as it were a garden of virtues and of the modes of conduct corresponding to each of them, a garden that brings the soul to perfect happiness.

Because of this He assigned to the garden a site 38 most suitable, bearing the name of " Eden," which means " luxuriance," symbol of a soul whose eyesight is perfect, disporting itself in virtues, leaping and skipping by reason of abundance of great joy, having set before it, as an enjoyment outweighing thousands

231

μυρίων τῶν παρὰ ἀνθρώποις ἡδίστων προτεθει-
39 μένης τὴν τοῦ μόνου θεραπείαν σοφοῦ. τούτου
τοῦ γανώματος ἀκράτου τις σπάσας, ὁ τοῦ
Μωυσέως δὴ θιασώτης, ὃς οὐχὶ τῶν ἠμελημένων
ἦν, ἐν ὑμνῳδίαις ἀνεφθέγξατο πρὸς τὸν ἴδιον
νοῦν φάσκων " κατατρύφησον τοῦ κυρίου," παρα-
κεκινημένος πρὸς τὸν οὐράνιον καὶ θεῖον ἔρωτα
τῇ φωνῇ, τὰς μὲν ⟨ἐν⟩ τοῖς λεγομένοις καὶ
φαινομένοις ἀνθρωπίνοις ἀγαθοῖς χλιδὰς καὶ
θρύψεις ἀλήκτους[1] δυσχεράνας, ὅλον δὲ τὸν νοῦν
ὑπὸ θείας κατοχῆς συναρπασθεὶς οἴστρῳ καὶ
40 ἐνευφραινόμενος μόνῳ θεῷ.   X. καὶ
τὸ πρὸς ἀνατολαῖς μέντοι τὸν παράδεισον εἶναι
δεῖγμα τοῦ λεχθέντος ἐστί· σκοταῖον μὲν γὰρ
καὶ δυόμενον καὶ νυκτίφορον ἀφροσύνη, λαμπρότατον δὲ καὶ περιαυγέστατον καὶ ἀνατέλλον ὡς
ἀληθῶς φρόνησις. καὶ καθάπερ ἀνίσχων ἥλιος
ὅλον τὸν οὐρανοῦ κύκλον φέγγους ἀναπληροῖ, τὸν
αὐτὸν τρόπον αἱ ἀρετῆς ἀκτῖνες ἀναλάμψασαι τὸ
διανοίας χωρίον ὅλον μεστὸν αὐγῆς καθαρᾶς
ἀπεργάζονται.
41   Τὰ μὲν οὖν ἀνθρώπου κτήματα φρουροὺς ἔχει
καὶ φύλακας ἀγριωτάτους θῆρας εἰς τὴν τῶν
ἐπιόντων καὶ κατατρεχόντων ἄμυναν, τὰ δὲ τοῦ
θεοῦ κτήματα λογικὰς φύσεις· " ἔθετο " γάρ
φησιν " ἐκεῖ τὸν ἄνθρωπον ὃν ἔπλασεν," ὅ ἐστιν,
λογικῶν μόνον τῶν ἀρετῶν αἱ ἀσκήσεις τε καὶ
42 χρήσεις. ἐξαίρετον γέρας παρὰ τὰς τῶν ἀλόγων[2]
ψυχὰς τουτὶ παρὰ τοῦ θεοῦ ἔλαβον· διὸ καὶ
ἐμφαντικώτατα εἴρηται, ὅτι τὸν ἐν ἡμῖν πρὸς

---

[1] mss. ἀλέκτως *et alia.*

of those that men deem sweetest, the worship and service of the Only Wise. One, after taking a sheer 39 draught of this bright joy, a member indeed of Moses' fellowship, not found among the indifferent, spake aloud in hymns of praise, and addressing his own mind cried, " Delight in the Lord " (Psalm xxxvi. 4), moved by the utterance to an ecstasy of the love that is heavenly and Divine, filled with loathing for those interminable bouts of softness and debauchery amid the seeming and so-called good things of mankind, while his whole mind is snatched up in holy frenzy by a Divine possession, and he finds his gladness in God alone.   X. A proof of what I 40 have said is the nearness of the garden to the sunrising (Gen. ii. 8) ; for, while folly is a thing sinking, dark, night-bringing, wisdom is verily a thing of sunrise, all radiancy and brightness. And even as the sun, when it comes up, fills all the circle of heaven with light, even so do the rays of virtue, when they have shone out, cause the whole region of the understanding to be flooded with pure brilliancy.

Now, whereas man's possessions have animals of 41 great ferocity to watch and guard them against being attacked and overrun, the possessions of God are guarded by rational beings : for it says, " He stationed there the man whom He had fashioned," that is to say, the trainings in the virtues and exercises of the virtues belong to rational beings only. This they 42 received at the hands of God, as a pre-eminent privilege above the lives of the irrational creatures. And that is why it is stated in the most vivid manner

---

PHILO

[336] ἀλήθειαν ἄνθρωπον, | τουτέστι τὸν νοῦν, ἔθηκεν
ἐν ἱερωτάτοις καλοκἀγαθίας βλαστήμασι καὶ
φυτοῖς, ἐπεὶ [δὲ]¹ τῶν διανοίας ἀμετόχων ἱκανὸν
οὐδὲν ἀρετὰς γεωργῆσαι,² ὧν τὸ παράπαν λαμ-
43 βάνειν οὐ πέφυκε κατάληψιν.   XI. οὐκ
ἔστι δ' οὖν ἀπορητέον, τί δήποτε εἰς μὲν τὴν
κιβωτόν, ἣν ἐν τῷ μεγίστῳ κατακλυσμῷ κατα-
σκευασθῆναι συνέβη, πᾶσαι τῶν θηρίων αἱ ἰδέαι
εἰσάγονται, εἰς δὲ τὸν παράδεισον οὐδεμία· ἡ μὲν
γὰρ κιβωτὸς σύμβολον ἦν σώματος, ὅπερ ἐξ
ἀνάγκης κεχώρηκε τὰς παθῶν καὶ κακιῶν ἀτιθάσους κἀξηγριωμένας κῆρας, ὁ δὲ παράδεισος
ἀρετῶν· ἀρεταὶ δὲ οὐδὲν ἀνήμερον ἢ συνόλως
44 ἄλογον παραδέχονται.   παρατετηρη-
μένως δὲ οὐ τὸν κατὰ τὴν εἰκόνα τυπωθέντα
ἄνθρωπον, ἀλλὰ τὸν πεπλασμένον εἰσαχθῆναί
φησιν εἰς τὸν παράδεισον· ὁ μὲν γὰρ τῷ κατὰ τὴν
εἰκόνα θεοῦ χαραχθεὶς πνεύματι οὐδὲν διαφέρει
τοῦ τὴν ἀθάνατον ζωὴν καρποφοροῦντος, ὡς
ἔμοιγε φαίνεται, δένδρου—ἄμφω γὰρ ἄφθαρτα
καὶ μοίρας τῆς μεσαιτάτης καὶ ἡγεμονικωτάτης
ἠξίωται· λέγεται γὰρ ὅτι τὸ ξύλον τῆς ζωῆς
ἐστιν ἐν μέσῳ τοῦ παραδείσου—, ὁ δὲ τοῦ
πολυμιγοῦς καὶ γεωδεστέρου σώματος, ἀπλάστου
καὶ ἁπλῆς φύσεως ἀμέτοχος, ἧς ὁ ἀσκητὴς ἐπί-
σταται τὸν οἶκον καὶ τὰς αὐλὰς [τοῦ κυρίου] οἰκεῖν
μόνος—'Ἰακὼβ γὰρ "ἄπλαστος οἰκῶν οἰκίαν"
εἰσάγεται—, πολυτρόπῳ δὲ καὶ ἐκ παντοίων
συνηρημένῃ καὶ πεπλασμένῃ διαθέσει χρώμενος.

¹ mss. ἐπὶ δέ.   ² mss. ἀρετῆς (or ἄρα τις) ἐγεώργησεν.

ª Lit. "unfashioned."

234

possible that He set the mind, which is the real man in us, amid holiest shoots and growths of noble character, since among beings void of understanding there is not one capable of tilling virtues, for they are by nature utterly incompetent to apprehend these.   XI. We need, then, be at no loss **43** to know why there are brought in into the ark, which was built at the time of the great Flood, all the kinds of wild beasts, but into the Garden no kind at all. For the ark was a figure of the body, which has been obliged to make room for the savage and untamed pests of passions and vices, whereas the garden was a figure of the virtues ; and virtues entertain nothing wild, nothing (we may say outright) that is irrational.

It is with deliberate care that the law- **44** giver says not of the man made after God's image, but of the man fashioned out of earth, that he was introduced into the garden. For the man stamped with the spirit which is after the image of God differs not a whit, as it appears to me, from the tree that bears the fruit of immortal life : for both are imperishable and have been accounted worthy of the most central and most princely portion : for we are told that the tree of Life is in the midst of the Garden (Gen. ii. 9). Nor is there any difference between the man fashioned out of the earth and the earthly composite body.   He has no part in a nature simple and uncompounded, whose house and courts only the self-trainer knows how to occupy, even Jacob who is put before us as " a plain*a* man dwelling in a house " (Gen. xxv. 27). The earthy man has a disposition of versatile subtlety, fashioned and con- cocted of elements of all sorts   It was to be expected, **45**

45 τιθέναι οὖν ἐν τῷ παραδείσῳ, τῷ παντὶ κόσμῳ,
ῥιζωθέντα εἰκὸς ἦν τὸν μέσον νοῦν, ὁλκοῖς πρὸς
τἀναντία κεχρημένον δυνάμεσιν ἐπὶ τὴν διάκρισίν
τε αὐτῶν ἀνακληθέντα,[1] ἵνα πρὸς αἵρεσιν καὶ
φυγὴν ὁρμήσας, εἰ μὲν τὰ ἀμείνω δεξιώσαιτο,
ἀθανασίας καὶ εὐκλείας ἀπόναιτο, εἰ δ' αὖ τὰ
χείρω, ψεκτὸν θάνατον εὕρηται.

46 XII. Τοιαῦτα μὲν δὴ δένδρα ὁ μόνος σοφὸς ἐν
ψυχαῖς λογικαῖς ἐρρίζου. Μωυσῆς δὲ οἰκτιζό-
μενος τοὺς μετανάστας ἐκ τοῦ τῶν ἀρετῶν παραδείσου γεγονότας καὶ τὸ αὐτεξούσιον τοῦ θεοῦ
κράτος καὶ τὰς ἴλεως καὶ ἡμέρους αὐτοῦ[2] δυνάμεις
εὔχεται, ὅθεν ὁ γήινος νοῦς Ἀδὰμ πεφυγάδευται,
κεῖθι τοὺς ὁρατικοὺς ἐμφυτευθῆναι· λέγει γάρ·

47 " εἰσαγαγὼν καταφύτευσον αὐτοὺς εἰς ὄρος κληρονομίας[3] σου, εἰς ἕτοιμον κατοικητήριόν σου ὃ
κατειργάσω, κύριε, ἁγίασμα, κύριε, ὃ ἡτοίμασαν
αἱ χεῖρές σου· κύριος βασιλεύων τὸν αἰῶνα καὶ
48 ἐπ' αἰῶνα καὶ ἔτι." | οὐκοῦν σαφέστατα εἰ καὶ
[337] τις ἄλλος ἔμαθεν, ὅτι τὰ σπέρματα καὶ τὰς
ῥίζας ἁπάντων καθεὶς ὁ θεὸς αἴτιός ἐστι τοῦ τὸ
μέγιστον ἀναβλαστῆσαι φυτόν, τόνδε τὸν κόσμον,
ὃν καὶ νῦν ἔοικεν αἰνίττεσθαι δι' αὐτοῦ τοῦ
λεχθέντος ᾄσματος " ὄρος " αὐτὸν " κληρονομίας "
εἰπών· ἐπειδὴ τοῦ πεποιηκότος οἰκειότατον τὸ
49 γενόμενον κτῆμα καὶ κλῆρος. εὔχεται οὖν ἡμᾶς
ἐν τούτῳ φυτευθῆναι, οὐχ ἵνα ἄλογοι καὶ ἀφη-
νιασταὶ γενώμεθα τὰς φύσεις, ἀλλ' ἵνα ἑπόμενοι
τῇ τοῦ τελειοτάτου διοικήσει τὴν κατὰ τὰ

---

[1] So Wend.: mss. μετα κλη(κλι, βλη)θῆναι.
[2] αὐτοῦ is transposed with Cohn.   [3] mss. κληροδοσίας.

then, that God should plant and set in the garden,
or the whole universe, the middle or neutral mind,
played upon by forces drawing it in opposite directions and given the high calling to decide between
them, that it might be moved to choose and to shun,
to win fame and immortality should it welcome the
better, and incur a dishonourable death should it
choose the worse.

XII. Such, then, were the trees which He Who 46
alone is wise planted in rational souls. Moses,
lamenting over those who had become exiles from
the garden of the virtues, implores alike God's
absolute sovereignty and His gracious and gentle
powers, that the people endowed with sight may
be planted in on the spot whence the earthly mind,
called Adam, has been banished. This is what he
says : " Bring them in, plant them in the mountain 47
of Thine inheritance, in the place, O Lord, which is
ready, which Thou wroughtest for Thee to dwell in,
the sanctuary, O Lord, which Thy hands have made
ready : the Lord is sovereign for ever and ever "
(Exod. xv. 17 f.). So Moses, beyond all others, had 48
most accurately learned that God, by setting the
seeds and roots of all things, is the Cause of the
greatest of all plants springing up, even this universe.
It is at this evidently that he points in the present
instance by the words of the Song itself just quoted,
by calling the world " the mountain of Thine inheritance," since that which has been brought into being
is, in a peculiar degree, the possession and portion
of him who has made it. So he prays that in this 49
we may be planted. He would not have us become
irrational and unruly in our natures. Nay, he would
have us comply with the ordering of the All-perfect,

αὐτὰ καὶ ὡσαύτως ἔχουσαν αὐτοῦ διέξοδον
ἀπομιμούμενοι σώφρονι καὶ ἀπταίστῳ βίῳ χρώ-
μεθα· τὸ γὰρ ἀκολουθίᾳ φύσεως ἰσχῦσαι ζῆν
50 εὐδαιμονίας τέλος εἶπον οἱ πρῶτοι.   καὶ
μὴν τά γε αὖθις λεγόμενα συνάδει τῷ προτεθέντι,
τὸ¹ τὸν κόσμον εὐτρεπῆ καὶ ἕτοιμον αἰσθητὸν
οἶκον εἶναι θεοῦ, τὸ κατειργάσθαι καὶ μὴ ἀγένητον
εἶναι, ὡς ᾠήθησάν τινες, τὸ " ἁγίασμα," οἷον
ἁγίων ἀπαύγασμα, μίμημα ἀρχετύπου, ἐπεὶ τὰ
αἰσθήσει καλὰ τῶν νοήσει καλῶν εἰκόνες, τὸ
ἡτοιμάσθαι ὑπὸ χειρῶν θεοῦ, τῶν κοσμοποιῶν
51 αὐτοῦ δυνάμεων. ἀλλ' ὅπως μηδεὶς ὑπολάβοι τὸν
ποιητὴν χρεῖον εἶναί τινος τῶν γεγονότων, τὸ
ἀναγκαιότατον ἐπιφωνήσει· "βασιλεύων τὸν αἰῶνα
καὶ ἐπ' αἰῶνα καὶ ἔτι." βασιλέα² δὲ οὐδενὸς δεῖσθαι,
52 τὰ δὲ ὑπήκοα βασιλέως θέμις πάντα. τινὲς δὲ
ἔφασαν κλῆρον εἶναι καὶ λέγεσθαι θεοῦ τὸ ἀγαθόν,
οὗ τὴν χρῆσιν καὶ ἀπόλαυσιν εὔχεσθαι νυνὶ
Μωυσῆν προσγενέσθαι· εἰσαγαγών, γάρ φησιν,
ἡμᾶς οἷα παῖδας ἄρτι μανθάνειν ἀρχομένους διὰ
τῶν σοφίας δογμάτων καὶ θεωρημάτων καὶ μὴ
ἀστοιχειώτους ἐάσας ἐν ὑψηλῷ καὶ οὐρανίῳ λόγῳ
53 καταφύτευσον. κλῆρος γὰρ οὗτος ἑτοιμότατος
καὶ προχειρότατος οἶκος, ἐπιτηδειότατον ἐνδιαί-

---

¹ mss. τῷ.
² mss. βασιλεῖ, βασιλεύς.

ᵃ The argument seems to be that to be planted in the
Cosmos is to be planted in nature. Thus the text can be
harmonized with the Stoic doctrine of "living according
to nature."
ᵇ Lit. "bring in," "introduce," almost "apprentice."

and faithfully copying His constant and undeviating course, pursue without stumbling a life of self-mastery : for to attain the power to live as nature bids has been pronounced by the men of old supreme happiness.[a]   And mark how well the 50 epithets that follow harmonize with that which was put first. The world, we read, is God's house in the realm of sense-perception, prepared and ready for Him. It is a thing wrought, not, as some have fancied, uncreate. It is a " sanctuary," an out-shining of sanctity, so to speak, a copy of the original ; since the objects that are beautiful to the eye of sense are images of those in which the understanding recognizes beauty. Lastly, it has been prepared by the " hands " of God, his world-creating powers. And to the end that none may suppose that the 51 Maker is in need of those whom He has made, Moses will crown his utterance with the point that is vital beyond all others : " reigning for ever and ever." It is an established principle that a sovereign is dependent on no one, while subjects are in all respects dependent on the sovereign. Some have 52 maintained that that which is God's portion, and is spoken of here as such, is that which is good, and that Moses' prayer in this instance is for the obtaining of the experience and enjoyment thereof. For his prayer runs thus : " Initiate [b] us, the children just · beginning to learn, by means of the pronouncements and principles of wisdom, and leave us not un-grounded, but plant us in a high and heavenly doctrine.[c] " For this is a " portion " best prepared, 53 a " house " most ready, an abode most fitting, which

[c] Or " Reason," here identified with " the Good " ; " high " is added to bring in the " mountain."

τημα, ὃ " κατειργάσω ἅγιον "· ἀγαθῶν γὰρ καὶ
ἁγίων, ὦ δέσποτα, ποιητὴς ὢν τυγχάνεις, ὡς
ἔμπαλιν κακῶν καὶ βεβήλων γένεσις ἡ φθαρτή.
βασίλευε δὴ τὸν ἄπειρον αἰῶνα ψυχῆς τῆς ἱκέτιδος
μηδὲ ἀκαρὲς ἐῶν αὐτὴν ἀνηγεμόνευτον· ἡ γὰρ
ἀδιάστατος παρὰ σοὶ δουλεία τῆς μεγίστης ἀρχῆς,
54 οὐκ ἐλευθερίας μόνον ἀμείνων.   XIII. πολλοῖς
δὲ ἂν τάχα που ζήτησιν παράσχοι, τίνα ἔχει λόγον
τὸ " εἰς ὄρος κληρονομίας σου "· κληροδοτεῖν μὲν
θεὸν ἀναγκαῖον, κληρονομεῖν δὲ ἴσως οὐκ εὔλογον
55 πάντων αὐτοῦ κτημάτων ὄντων. ἀλλὰ μήποτε
τοῦτο λέγεται ἐπὶ τῶν κατὰ τὸν ἐξαίρετον οἰ-
κειώσεως λόγον δεσποζομένων πρὸς αὐτοῦ, καθάπερ
οἱ βασιλεῖς ἁπάντων μὲν ἄρχουσι τῶν ὑπηκόων,
[338] διαφερόντως δὲ τῶν οἰκετῶν, οἷς πρὸς | τὴν τοῦ
σώματος ἐπιμέλειαν καὶ τὴν ἄλλην δίαιταν ὑπηρέ-
56 ταις εἰώθασι χρῆσθαι.   οἱ δὲ αὐτοὶ καὶ
τῶν κατὰ τὴν χώραν ἁπάντων ὄντες κτημάτων
δεσπόται καὶ ὅσων ἐπικρατεῖν οἱ ἰδιῶται δοκοῦσι,
μόνα ταῦτα ἔχειν νομίζονται, ἅπερ ἐπιτρόποις καὶ
ἐπιμεληταῖς ἐγχειρίσαιεν, ἀφ' ὧν καὶ τὰς ἐτησίους
προσόδους ἐκλέγουσιν· εἰς ἃ πολλάκις ἀνέσεως καὶ
εὐθυμίας ἕνεκα προσέρχονται τὸ βαρύτατον τῶν
ἐν πολιτείᾳ καὶ βασιλείᾳ φροντίδων ἄχθος ἀπο-
τιθέμενοι· καὶ καλεῖται μέντοι ταῦτα τὰ κτήματα
57 αὐτοῖς βασιλικά. καὶ μὴν ἄργυρός τε καὶ χρυσὸς
καὶ ὅσα ἄλλα κειμήλια παρὰ τοῖς ἀρχομένοις
θησαυροφυλακεῖται τῶν ἡγουμένων μᾶλλον ἢ τῶν
ἐχόντων ἐστίν, ἀλλ' ὅμως ἴδιοι τῶν βασιλέων

"Thou hast wrought as a Holy Place"; for of things good and holy, O Master, Thou art Maker, as from the corruptible creation come things evil and profane. Reign through the age that has no limit over the soul that implores Thee, never leaving it for one moment without a sovereign Ruler: for never-ceasing slavery under Thee surpasses not freedom only but the highest sovereignty. XIII. It is 54 possible that the words "Into the mountain of Thine inheritance" may suggest to many an inquiry as to how to account for them: for that God *gives* portions is a necessary truth, but it may appear a con-tradiction that He should *obtain* a portion, since all things belong to Him. This expression would seem 55 to apply to those who are on a special footing of more intimate relationship with Him as their Master. So kings are rulers of all their subjects, but in an eminent degree of their household servants, of whose ministry they are accustomed to avail themselves for the care of their persons and their other require-ments. Again these same rulers, though 56 they are masters of all properties throughout the land, including those over which private citizens have apparent control, are reckoned to have those only which they place in the hands of bailiffs and agents, from which also they collect the yearly income. To these they frequently resort for holiday and enjoyment, laying aside the serious burden of the anxieties incident to government and sovereignty, and these estates of theirs go by the name of royal demesnes. Again, silver and gold, and other precious 57 things which are kept in the treasuries of subjects, belong to the rulers rather than to those who have them. But in spite of this we speak of sovereigns'

θησαυροὶ λέγονται, ἐν οἷς οἱ ταχθέντες τῶν φόρων
ἐκλογεῖς¹ ⟨τὰς⟩ ἀπὸ τῆς χώρας προσόδους κατα-
58 τίθενται. μηδὲν οὖν θαυμάσῃς, εἰ καὶ τοῦ πανηγεμόνος θεοῦ τὸ ἐφ᾽ ἅπασι κράτος εἰληχότος
ἐξαίρετος κλῆρος εἶναι λέγεται ψυχῶν σοφῶν ὁ
θίασος, ὁ² ὀξυωπέστατα ὁρῶν, ἀμέμπτῳ καὶ
ἀκραιφνεῖ κεχρημένος τῷ διανοίας ὄμματι, μύσαντι
μὲν οὐδέποτε, ἀεὶ δὲ ἀναπεπταμένῳ καὶ εὐθυτενῶς
59 βλέποντι. XIV. οὐ διὰ τοῦτο μέντοι καὶ ἐν
ᾠδῇ τῇ μείζονι λέγεται· '' ἐπερώτησον τὸν πατέρα
σου καὶ ἀναγγελεῖ σοι, τοὺς πρεσβυτέρους σου καὶ
ἐροῦσί σοι· ὅτε διεμέριζεν ὁ ὕψιστος ἔθνη, ὡς
διέσπειρεν υἱοὺς Ἀδάμ, ἔστησεν ὅρια ἐθνῶν κατὰ
ἀριθμὸν ἀγγέλων θεοῦ· καὶ ἐγένετο μερὶς κυρίου
60 λαὸς αὐτοῦ Ἰσραήλ''; ἰδοὺ γὰρ πάλιν μερίδα
καὶ κλῆρον εἴρηκε θεοῦ τὸν ὁρατικὸν αὐτοῦ καὶ
γνήσιον θεραπευτὴν τρόπον, τοὺς δὲ γῆς παῖδας,
οὓς Ἀδὰμ ὠνόμασεν υἱούς, ἐσπάρθαι καὶ ἀνα-
σκεδασθῆναι καὶ μηκέτι συναχθῆναι,³ στῖφος δὲ
γενέσθαι⁴ ἡγεμόνι χρήσασθαι ὀρθῷ λόγῳ μὴ δυναμένους. τῷ γὰρ ὄντι ἁρμονίας μὲν καὶ ἑνώσεως
αἴτιον ἀρετή, διαλύσεως δὲ καὶ διαρτήσεως ἡ
61 ἐναντία διάθεσις.   δεῖγμα μέντοι τῶν
εἰρημένων ἐστὶ τὸ γινόμενον ἀνὰ πᾶν ἔτος ἡμέρᾳ
τῇ λεγομένῃ τοῦ ἱλασμοῦ· τότε γὰρ διείρηται
'' δύο τράγους διακληροῦν, τὸν μὲν τῷ κυρίῳ,
[339] τὸν δὲ τῷ ἀποπομπαίῳ,'' | διττὸν λόγον, ὃν μὲν

---

¹ ἐκλογεῖς is read for ἐκλογισταί with Cohn in *Addenda*.
² MSS. ὃς or ὡς.   ³ MSS. καὶ ἐπισυνε(α)χθῆναι.
⁴ MSS. ἐγγενέσθαι.

private coffers in which the appointed collectors of dues deposit the revenues from the country. Marvel 58 not at all, then, if the title of special portion of God the universal Ruler, to whom sovereignty over all pertains, is bestowed upon the company of wise souls, whose vision is supremely keen, the eye of whose understanding is clear and flawless, closing never, ever open in a gaze direct and piercing. XIV. Is 59 not this the explanation of that utterance in the Greater Song : " Ask thy father, and he will proclaim it to thee, thy elders, and they will tell it thee ; when the Most High distributed the nations, when He dispersed the sons of Adam, He set up boundaries of the nations corresponding to the number of the angels of God, and His people Israel became the portion of the Lord " (Deut. xxxii. 7–9) ? Mark 60 how he has again given the name of " portion " and " lot " of God to the character that has eyes to see Him and accords Him genuine devotion, while he says that the children of earth, whom he entitles sons of Adam, have been dispersed and broken up and no more gathered together but are become a mob incapable of following the guidance of right reason. For virtue is in very deed the cause of harmony and unity, whereas the contrary disposition brings about dissolution and dismemberment. An 61 illustration of what has been said is afforded by that which is done year by year on the day called the " Day of Atonement." It is enjoined on that day " to assign by lot two goats, one for the Lord, and one for separation[a] (Lev. xvi. 8), a twofold description,[b]

---

[a] See App. p. 495.
[b] Or "two ways of thinking," the goats representing two different attitudes of mind.

θεῷ, ὃν δὲ γενέσει· ὁ ἀποσεμνύνων μὲν οὖν τὸ
αἴτιον [τιμὴν] αὐτῷ προσκληρώσεται, ὁ δὲ γένεσιν[1]
φυγαδευθήσεται, τῶν μὲν ἱερωτάτων ἐλαυνόμενος
χωρίων, εἰς δὲ ἄβατα καὶ βέβηλα καὶ βάραθρώδη[2]
ἐμπίπτων.

62 XV. Τοσαύτη μέντοι τῇ ⟨τοῦ⟩ θεοφιλοῦς περι-
ουσίᾳ χρῆται Μωυσῆς, ὥστε αὐτῷ τούτῳ μάλιστα
πεπιστευκὼς θερμοτέροις καὶ μείζοσιν ἢ κατὰ τὰς
ἀσθενεστέρων[3] ἡμῶν ἀκοὰς λόγοις τε καὶ δόγμασιν
εἴωθε χρῆσθαι· οὐ γὰρ μόνον ἀξιοῖ κληρονομεῖν
θεόν, ἀλλὰ καὶ αὐτόν, τὸ παραδοξότατον, κλῆρον
63 ἑτέρων εἶναι. φυλὴν γὰρ ὅλην πρόσφυγα καὶ
ἱκέτιν αὐτοῦ λῆξιν μὲν τῆς χώρας, καθάπερ τὰς
ἄλλας ἕνδεκα, οὐκ ἠξίωσε νείμασθαι, γέρας δὲ
ἐξαίρετον λαβεῖν ἱερωσύνην, οὐκ ἐπίγειον, ἀλλ'
ὀλύμπιον κτῆμα· "οὐ γὰρ ἔσται" φησί "τῇ
φυλῇ Λευὶ μερὶς οὐδὲ κλῆρος ἐν υἱοῖς Ἰσραήλ,
ὅτι κύριος αὐτὸς κλῆρος αὐτῶν." καὶ ἐκ προσώπου μέντοι τοῦ θεοῦ διὰ τῶν χρησμῶν ᾄδεται
τὸν τρόπον τοῦτον· "ἐγὼ μερίς σου καὶ κληρο-
64 δοσία." τῷ γὰρ ὄντι ὁ τελείως ἐκκεκαθαρμένος
νοῦς καὶ πάντα τὰ γενέσεως ἀπογινώσκων ἓν
μόνον οἶδε καὶ γνωρίζει τὸ ἀγένητον, ᾧ προσελήλυθεν, ὑφ' οὗ καὶ προσείληπται. τίνι γὰρ
ἔξεστιν εἰπεῖν "αὐτός μοι μόνος ἐστὶν ὁ θεός"
ἢ τῷ μηδὲν τῶν μετ' αὐτὸν ἀσπαζομένῳ; οὗτος
δ' ἐστὶν ὁ Λευίτης τρόπος· ἑρμηνεύεται γὰρ
"αὐτός μοι" διὰ τὸ ἄλλα ἄλλοις τετιμῆσθαι,

---

[1] mss. γενέσει.
[2] βαραθρώδη is Mangey's conj. for βάραθρα.
[3] ἀσθενεστέρων is Mangey's conj. for ἑτέρων.

one for God and one for created things. That which
exalts the First Cause shall be allotted to Him, while
that which exalts creation shall be banished, driven
from the most holy places, to find itself amid rocky
chasms in trackless and unhallowed regions.

XV. So fully does Moses take advantage of the 62
prerogative of one beloved of God, that, inspired with
confidence by this very fact, he is wont to use language
and utter teachings larger and more daring than suit
the ears of us feebler folk. For not only does he
think it in accordance with God's dignity to obtain
a portion, but, what is strangest of all, Himself to be
the portion of others. For he deemed it meet and 63
right that a whole tribe, which had taken refuge at
God's footstool, should be allotted no part of the
country, like the other eleven tribes, but should
receive the pre-eminent privilege of the priesthood,
a possession not earthly but heavenly. " The tribe
of Levi," he says, " shall have no lot or portion among
the children of Israel, for the Lord is their portion "
(Deut. x. 9) ; and there is an utterance rung out on
this wise by the holy oracles in the name of God,
" I am thy portion and inheritance " (Numb. xviii.
20) : for in reality the mind, which has been perfectly 64
cleansed and purified, and which renounces all things
pertaining to creation, is acquainted with One alone,
and knows but One, even the Uncreate, to Whom it
has drawn nigh, by Whom also it has been taken to
Himself. For who is at liberty to say " God Himself
is alone (and all) to me," save one who has no welcome
for aught that comes after Him ? And this is the
Levite attitude of mind, for the word means " He
(is precious) to me," the thought conveyed being that
while different things have been held precious by

μόνῳ δὲ αὐτῷ τὸ ἀνωτάτω καὶ πάντων ἄριστον
65 αἴτιον.   XVI. ἤδη τινὰ τῶν παλαιῶν φασι
καθάπερ ἐκπρεπεστάτης γυναικὸς τῷ σοφίας
ἐπιμανέντα κάλλει πολυτελεστάτης πομπῆς θεασάμενον παρασκευὴν ἄφθονον, ἀπιδόντα πρός τινας
τῶν συνήθων εἰπεῖν " ἴδετε, ὦ ἑταῖροι, ὅσων
χρείαν οὐκ ἔχω," καίτοι γε ἔξω τῶν ἀναγκαίων
οὐδὲν ἁπλῶς περιβεβλημένον, ὡς μηδὲ ὑποφυση-
θέντα πλούτου μεγέθει, ὃ μυρίοις συνέβη, δόξαι
66 τῷ λόγῳ καταλαζονεύεσθαι. τοῦθ'[1] ὁ νομοθέτης
ἐκδιδάσκει φρονεῖν δεῖν τοὺς μηδὲν χρῆμα τῶν ἐν
γενέσει πορίζοντας,[2] ἀπογινώσκοντας δὲ ὅσα γενητὰ
διὰ τὴν πρὸς τὸν ἀγένητον οἰκειότητα, ὃν μόνον
πλοῦτον καὶ εὐδαιμονίας ὅρον τελεωτάτης ἐνόμισαν.
67   μηκέτι νῦν οἱ τὰς βασιλείας καὶ
ἡγεμονίας ἀναψάμενοι μεγαλαυχείτωσαν, οἱ μὲν
ὅτι μίαν πόλιν ἢ χώραν ἢ ἔθνος ἐν ὑπηγάγοντο,
οἱ δὲ ὅτι πάντα μὲν γῆς κλίματα μέχρι τῶν
περάτων αὐτῆς, πάντα δὲ Ἑλληνικὰ καὶ βαρβαρικὰ
ἔθνη, πάντας δὲ ποταμοὺς καὶ τὰ ἄπειρα πλήθει[3]
68 καὶ μεγέθει πελάγη προσεκτήσαντο. καὶ γὰρ εἰ
μετὰ τούτων τῆς μεταρσίου φύσεως, ὃ μηδὲ εἰπεῖν
εὐαγές, ἣν μόνην ἐκ πάντων ἀδούλωτον καὶ
ἐλεύθερον ὁ ποιητὴς εἰργάσατο, ἐπεκράτησαν,
[340] ἰδιῶται νομισθεῖεν ἂν κατὰ σύγκρισιν | μεγάλων
βασιλέων, οἳ τὸν θεὸν κλῆρον ἔλαχον· ὅσῳ γὰρ ὁ

---

[1] mss. and Wend. καταλαζονεύεσθαι τοῦ θεοῦ δ: Heinemann's
punctuation and reading (τοῦθ' for τοῦ θ) are adopted.
[2] mss. πορίζοντας: Wend. γνωρίζοντας.   [3] mss. πλήθη.

---

[a] μόνον would make better sense.
[b] Or "highest."   [c] See note on *Quod Deus* 146.

different people, he is alone ^a in holding precious the original ^b and worthiest Cause of all things.   XVI. They say ^c that in olden time one who was en- 65 raptured by the beauty of wisdom, as by that of some distinguished lady, after watching the array of a procession pass by on which vast sums had been lavished, fastened his eyes on a group of his associates and said, " See, my friends, of how many things I have no need."   And yet he was wearing absolutely nothing beyond necessary clothing, so that he cannot be supposed to have been puffed up by his great riches, as countless thousands have been, and to have uttered the words as a boast.   This is the mind 66 which, as the lawgiver insists, should be that of those who provide themselves with no property that has its place among things created, but renounce all these on the ground of that intimate association with the Uncreate, to possess Whom, they are convinced, is the only wealth, the only gauge of consummate happiness.   In face of this let those cease 67 their proud boastings who have acquired royal and imperial sway, some by bringing under their authority a single city or country or nation, some by having, over and above these, made themselves masters of all earth's regions to its fullest bounds, all nations, Greek and barbarian alike, all rivers, and seas un- limited in number and extent.   For even had they, 68 besides controlling these, extended their empire, an idea which it were impious to utter, to the realm of the upper air, alone of all things made by the Creator to enjoy a freedom untouched by bondage—even then, they would be reckoned ordinary citizens when compared with great kings who received God as their portion ; for the kingship of these as far sur-

κτησάμενος τὸ κτῆμα τοῦ κτήματος ἀμείνων καὶ
τὸ πεποιηκὸς τοῦ γεγονότος, τοσούτῳ βασιλικώ-
69 τεροι ἐκεῖνοι.   XVII. τοὺς μὲν οὖν
πάντα τοῦ σπουδαίου φάσκοντας εἶναι παρα-
δοξολογεῖν ᾠήθησάν τινες ἀφορῶντες εἰς τὴν
ἐκτὸς ἔνδειάν τε καὶ περιουσίαν καὶ μηδένα τῶν
ἀχρημάτων ἢ ἀκτημόνων πλούσιον νομίζοντες.
Μωυσῆς δὲ οὕτως περίβλεπτον καὶ περιμάχητον
ἡγεῖται σοφίαν, ὥστε οὐ μόνον τὸν σύμπαντα
κόσμον ἀξιόχρεω κλῆρον αὐτῆς ἀλλὰ καὶ τὸν τῶν
70 ὅλων ἡγεμόνα νομίζειν. τὰ δὲ δόγματα οὐκ
ἐπαμφοτεριζόντων ταῦτ'[1] ἐστίν, ἀλλὰ βεβαίᾳ πίστει
κατεσχημένων· ἐπεὶ καὶ νῦν εἰσί τινες τῶν ἐπι-
μορφαζόντων εὐσέβειαν, οἳ τὸ πρόχειρον τοῦ
λόγου παρασυκοφαντοῦσι φάσκοντες οὔθ' ὅσιον
οὔτ' ἀσφαλὲς εἶναι λέγειν ἀνθρώπου θεὸν κλῆρον.
71   οὐ γὰρ ἀπὸ γνησίου τοῦ πάθους, ἀλλ'
ὑποβολιμαίου καὶ νόθου, πρὸς τὴν θεωρίαν τῶν
πραγμάτων, εἴποιμ' ἂν αὐτοῖς, ἥκετε· ἐν ἴσῳ γὰρ
ᾠήθητε τὰ ἀμπέλων ἢ ἐλαιῶν ἢ τῶν ὁμοιοτρόπων
κτήματα τῶν[2] ἐχόντων καὶ σοφῶν τὸν θεὸν κλῆρον
λέγεσθαι, καὶ οὐκ ἐνενοήσατε ὅτι καὶ ζωγράφοις
ζωγραφία καὶ συνόλως τέχνη τῷ τεχνίτῃ λέγεται
κλῆρος, οὐχ ὡς γήινον κτῆμα, ἀλλ' ὡς ὀλύμπιον
72 ἀγώνισμα. δεσπόζεται γὰρ τῶν τοιούτων οὐδέν,
ἀλλ' ὠφελεῖ τοὺς ἔχοντας· ὥστε καὶ τὸ ὂν κλῆρον
μὴ ὡς κτῆμα τούτοις ἐμφερὲς ἀκούετε τοῖς λεχ-

---

[1] mss. ἐπ' ἀμφοτέρων ταὐτόν.
[2] mss. κτημάτων or κτήματα (om. τῶν).

    * Or " press unduly."

passes theirs as he that has gained possession is better than the possession, and he that has made than that which he has made.   XVII.

Some, paying regard to outward want and outward 69 superfluity, and reckoning no one rich if found among those without money or possessions, have looked on the assertion that all things belong to the wise man as a paradox. But Moses considers wisdom an object of such admiration and emulation, that he thinks its worthy portion to be not merely the whole world, but the very Lord of all. These are not, we must 70 remember, opinions held by men who halt between two opinions, but by men possessed by stedfast faith ; for even now there are in the ranks of those who wear a semblance of piety, men who in a petty spirit find fault with *a* the literal sense of the word, urging that it is irreligious and dangerous to speak of God as the portion of man.   What I 71 would say to them is this : " The frame of mind in which you approached the consideration of the subject was not a genuine one, but spurious and illegitimate. You imagined that there is no difference between the way in which God is said to be the portion of the wise, and the way in which plantations of vines or olive trees or the like are said to be the possessions of their owners. You failed to notice that portrait-painting is spoken of as a lot or portion for portrait-painters, and generally any such pursuit for him who pursues it, not as an earthly possession to be owned, but as a heavenly prize to be striven for. For things 72 such as these bring benefit to those who have them, without being under them as masters. Pray, then, you petty fault-finders, when you hear the Existent One spoken of as Portion, do not take it to mean a

θεῖσιν, ὦ συκοφάνται, ἀλλ' ὡς ὠφελιμώτατον καὶ
μεγίστων[1] τοῖς θεραπεύειν ἀξιοῦσιν ἀγαθῶν αἴτιον.

73   XVIII. Εἰρηκότες οὖν περὶ τοῦ πρώτου φυτουργοῦ καὶ φυτοῦ τὰ ἁρμόζοντα μέτιμεν ἑξῆς
ἐπὶ τὰς τῶν μαθημάτων ἅμα καὶ μιμημάτων
ἐπιμελείας. εὐθέως τοίνυν ὁ σοφὸς Ἀβραὰμ
λέγεται "φυτεῦσαι ἄρουραν ἐπὶ τῷ φρέατι τοῦ
ὅρκου καὶ ἐπικαλέσαι τὸ ὄνομα κυρίου θεοῦ
αἰωνίου[2]"· καὶ οὐ δεδήλωται τῶν φυτῶν ἡ ἰδιότης,
74 ἀλλ' αὐτὸ μόνον τοῦ χωρίου τὸ μέγεθος. φασὶ
δὲ οἷς ἔθος ἐρευνᾶν τὰ τοιαῦτα, πάνθ'[3] ὅσα ἐν
κτήμασιν ἠκριβῶσθαι διαφερόντως, καὶ τὸ δένδρον
καὶ τὸ χωρίον καὶ τὸν τοῦ δένδρου καρπόν· τὸ
μὲν οὖν δένδρον αὐτὴν εἶναι τὴν ἄρουραν, ἀλλ'
οὐχ ὅμοιον[4] τοῖς βλαστάνουσιν ἀπὸ γῆς, ἀλλὰ
κατὰ τὴν τοῦ θεοφιλοῦς ῥιζωθὲν διάνοιαν, τὸ
δὲ χωρίον τὸ φρέαρ τοῦ ὅρκου, τὸν δὲ καρπὸν
τὴν τοῦ κυρίου ὀνόματος μετάληψιν εἰς θεὸν
75 αἰώνιον. τὸν δὲ περὶ ἑκάστου τῶν προταθέντων
εἰκότα λόγον ἀναγκαῖον προσαποδοῦναι· ἡ μὲν
[341] τοίνυν ἄρουρα μήκει πηχῶν | οὖσα ἑκατὸν καὶ
πλάτει τῶν ἴσων κατὰ τὴν τοῦ τετραγώνου φύσιν
πολυπλασιασθέντων εἰς μυρίων ἀριθμὸν ἐπιπέδων
76 συντίθεται πηχῶν. ἔστι δὲ ὅρος οὗτος τῶν ἀπὸ
μονάδος παραυξηθέντων ὁ μέγιστος καὶ τελειότατος, ὥστε ἀρχὴν μὲν ἀριθμῶν εἶναι μονάδα,
τέλος δὲ ἐν τοῖς κατὰ τὴν πρώτην σύνθεσιν μυριάδα.

---

[1] MSS. μέγιστον.
[2] MSS. θεοῦ αἰωνίου: Wend. θεὸς αἰώνιος.
[3] πάνθ' is read with Heinemann for πάντα θεοῦ in MSS.
[4] ὅμοιον and ῥιζωθὲν are Heinemann's conjj. for ὁμοίαν and ῥιζωθεῖσαν.

possession similar to those which have been mentioned, but to mean One bringing vast benefits and the Cause of exceeding great good to those who regard His service as their fit employment."

XVIII. Having said, then, what was called for about 73 the first Planter and that which He planted, we will pass on next to the industry of those who have learnt from the former and copied the latter. We come at once to the record [a] of Abraham the wise "planting a hide of land at the well of the oath, and invoking upon it the Name of the Lord as God eternal" (Gen. xxi. 33). No particulars are given as to the kind of plants meant, but simply the size of the plot of ground. Yet those whose habit it is to look closely 74 into such matters assure us that we have all the points of an estate laid down with extraordinary precision, the tree, the ground, and the fruit of the tree; the hide itself being the tree; not a tree like those which spring up from the earth, but one planted in the understanding of him that is beloved of God; the well of the oath, the plot of ground; and the change of the Name of the Lord into "God eternal," the Fruit. Each of these points requires further treat- 75 ment in the shape of such a reasoned account of them as may commend itself. Well, the hide, being 100 cubits long and as many broad, comes, by the rule of square measure, to 10,000 superficial cubits. This is the highest completest term in the series 76 which increases from unity: that is to say, while 1 is the starting-point of numbers, a myriad or 10,000 is the end,[a] if we adhere to the line of progress on which we set out.[b] Accordingly that comparison is

[a] See App. p. 495.
[b] See App. p. 496.

παρὸ καί τινες οὐκ ἀπὸ σκοποῦ βαλβῖδι μὲν μονάδα,
καμπτῆρι δὲ εἴκασαν μυριάδα, τοὺς δὲ μεθορίους
πάντας ἀριθμοὺς τοῖς δρόμον ἀγωνιζομένοις· ἀρχό-
μενοι γὰρ ὥσπερ ἀπὸ βαλβῖδος φέρεσθαι μονάδος
παρὰ μυριάδα τὸ τέλος ἵστανται.

77 Μετιόντες οὖν ἀπὸ τούτων τινὲς ὡσανεὶ συμβόλων ἔφασαν τὸν θεὸν ἀρχὴν καὶ πέρας εἶναι τῶν
ἁπάντων, δόγμα κατασκευαστικὸν εὐσεβείας· τοῦτο
τὸ δόγμα φυτευθὲν ἐν ψυχῇ κάλλιστον καὶ τρο-
φιμώτατον καρπόν, ὁσιότητα, τίκτει.

78 Τόπος ⟨δ'⟩ ἐστὶν οἰκειότατος τῷ φυτῷ τὸ
φρέαρ, ὃ κέκληται ὅρκος, ἐν ᾧ κατέχει λόγος μὴ
ἀνευρεθῆναι ὕδωρ· '' παραγενόμενοι'' γάρ φησιν
'' οἱ παῖδες Ἰσαὰκ ἀπήγγειλαν αὐτῷ περὶ τοῦ
φρέατος οὗ ὤρυξαν, καὶ εἶπον· οὐχ εὕρομεν ὕδωρ,
καὶ ἐκάλεσεν αὐτὸ ὅρκος.'' τοῦτο δὲ ἦν ἔχει
79 δύναμιν θεασώμεθα·   XIX. οἱ τὴν τῶν
ὄντων φύσιν διερευνῶντες καὶ τὰς περὶ ἑκάστων
ζητήσεις μὴ ὀλιγώρως ποιούμενοι παραπλήσια
ποιοῦσι τοῖς τὰ φρέατα ὀρύττουσι· καὶ γὰρ
ἐκεῖνοι τὰς ἐν ἀφανεῖ πηγὰς ἀναζητοῦσι. καὶ
κοινὸς μὲν πόθος ἅπασίν ἐστι ποτὸν ἀνευρεῖν,
ἀλλὰ τοῖς μὲν δι' οὗ σῶμα, τοῖς δὲ δι' οὗ ψυχὴ
80 πέφυκε τρέφεσθαι. ὥσπερ οὖν ἔνιοι τῶν ἀνα-
τεμνόντων τὰ φρέατα τὸ ζητούμενον ὕδωρ πολλάκις οὐχ εὗρον, οὕτως οἱ προσωτέρω χωροῦντες
τῶν ἐπιστημῶν καὶ ἐπὶ πλέον ἐμβαθύνοντες
αὐταῖς ἀδυνατοῦσι τοῦ τέλους ἐπιψαῦσαι. τοὺς
γοῦν πολυμαθεῖς φασιν ἀμαθίαν δεινὴν ἑαυτῶν

not wide of the mark which some have made between
1 and the post from which runners start, and 10,000
and the post at which they finish, all the intervening
numbers being like the competitors in the race;
for beginning their course from 1 as from a starting-
post they come to a stop at 10,000 as the finish.

Some have found symbols in these things and have 77
gone on with their help to proclaim God as the beginning and final goal of all things, a teaching on which
religion can be built; this teaching, when planted in
the soul, produces piety, a fruit most fair and full
of nourishment.

The well, entitled Oath, in which, as history says, 78
no water was found, is a place most appropriate to
that which grew there. What we read is this:
" The servants of Isaac came and brought word to
him concerning the well which they had dug, saying
' We found no water,' and he called it ' Oath ' "
(Gen. xxvi. 32 f.). Let us observe the force of
these words.   XIX. Those who thoroughly 79
investigate the nature of existing things, and prose-
cute their inquires into each one of them in no
indifferent spirit, act as those do who dig wells; for
the investigators, like the well-diggers, are in search
of hidden springs. And all have in common a desire
to find water, but in the one case it is water naturally
adapted to the nourishment of the body, in the other
to the nourishment of the soul. Now just as some 80
of those who open up wells often fail to find the water
of which they are in search, so those, who make more
than ordinary progress in various kinds of knowledge,
and go deeper into them than most of us, are often
powerless to reach the end they aim at. It is said
that men of great learning accuse themselves of

κατηγορεῖν, μόνον γὰρ ὅσον τοῦ ἀληθοῦς ὑστερί-
ζουσιν ᾖσθοντο. καί τινα τῶν παλαιῶν λόγος
ἔχει θαυμαζόμενον ἐπὶ σοφίᾳ εἰκότως φάναι
θαυμάζεσθαι· μόνον γὰρ εἰδέναι ὅτι οὐδὲν οἶδεν.[a]

81   ἑλοῦ δ' εἰ θέλεις ἣν ἂν διανοηθῇς
μικρὰν ἢ μείζονα τέχνην καὶ τὸν κατὰ ταύτην
γενόμενον ἄριστόν τε καὶ δοκιμώτατον, εἶτα κατα-
νόησον εἰ τὰ ἐπαγγέλματα τῆς τέχνης ἰσάζει τοῖς
ἔργοις τοῦ τεχνίτου· σκοπῶν γὰρ εὑρήσεις ταῦτα
ἐκείνων οὐ βραχέσιν ἀλλὰ μεγάλοις διαστήμασιν
ἀποδέοντα, σχεδὸν ἀδυνάτου καθεστῶτος πρὸς
ἡντινοῦν τελειωθῆναι τέχνην πηγῆς τρόπον ἀεὶ
καινουμένην[1] καὶ θεωρημάτων παντοίων ἰδέας ἀνομ-
82 βροῦσαν.   διὰ τοῦθ' ὅρκος ὠνομάσθη
προσφυέστατα τὸ πίστεως βεβαιοτάτης σύμβολον
[342] μαρτυρίαν θεοῦ περιεχούσης. | ὡς γὰρ ὁ ὀμνὺς
τῶν ἀμφισβητουμένων καλεῖ θεὸν μάρτυρα, ἐπ'
οὐδενὶ οὕτως ἔστιν εὐορκῆσαι ὡς ἐπὶ τῷ μηδεμιᾶς
ἐπιστήμης εὑρίσκεσθαι παρὰ τῷ τεχνίτῃ τέλος.
83 ὁ δὲ αὐτὸς λόγος καὶ ἐπὶ τὰς ἄλλας ὅσαι περὶ
ἡμᾶς δυνάμεις ὀλίγου δεῖν κεχώρηκεν· ὥσπερ γὰρ
ἐν τῷ λεχθέντι φρέατι ὕδωρ φασὶ μὴ εὑρεθῆναι,
οὕτως οὐδὲ ἐν ὀφθαλμοῖς τὸ ὁρατὸν[2] οὐδ' ἐν ὠσὶ
τὸ ἀκούειν οὐδ' ἐν μυκτῆρσι τὸ ὀσφραίνεσθαι οὐδὲ
συνόλως ἐν αἰσθήσεως ὀργάνοις τὸ αἰσθάνεσθαι,
κατὰ τὸ παραπλήσιον δὲ οὐδ' ἐν νῷ τὸ καταλαμ-

---

¹ MSS. κινουμένην.   ² Perhaps read ὁρᾶν or ὁρατικόν.

^a See Plato, *Apology* 21 A.

terrible ignorance, for all that they have come to perceive is how far they fall short of the truth. There is a story [a] that one of the men of the olden days, when people marvelled at his wisdom, said that he was rightly marvelled at; for that he was the only man who knew that he knew nothing.

Choose, if you will, whatever science or art you may 81 be minded to choose, be it a small one or a greater one, and the man who is best and most approved in this art or science. Then notice carefully whether the professions of the science are made good by what its votary does. If you look you will find that the one fails of the other not by short but by long distances. For it is practically impossible to attain perfection in respect of any science or art whatever, seeing that it is being continually replenished, as a spring is, and ever welling up results of thought and study of many a kind. That is why the 82 name of " Oath " given to it was so perfectly suitable : for an oath represents that surest form of trustworthiness which carries with it the testimony of God. For as the man who swears calls God as a witness of the points in dispute, there is no point on which it is more possible to take a sure oath than upon the fact that no subject of knowledge whatever is found to have reached the goal of perfection in the person of him who is an expert in it. The same 83 principle holds good for almost all the other faculties which we possess. For, just as in the well that we read of we are told that no water was found, so neither is sight found in eyes, nor hearing in ears, nor smelling in nostrils, nor, to say all at once, is sense-perception found in organs of sense ; and apprehension in like manner is not found in mind

84 βάνειν. πῶς γὰρ ἂν παρορᾶν ἢ παρακούειν ἢ
παρανοεῖν συνέβαινεν, εἴπερ ἐν τούτοις πάγιαι ἦσαν
αἱ ἀντιλήψεις ἑκάστου, ἀλλὰ μὴ ἐπ' αὐτῶν θεοῦ
σπείροντος τὸ βέβαιον ἐπεφύκεσαν;

85 XX. Ἱκανῶς οὖν καὶ περὶ τοῦ χωρίου διειλεγμένοι, ἐν ᾧ τὸ δένδρον ἀνθεῖ, καὶ περὶ τοῦ καρποῦ
τελευταῖον ἐξεργασώμεθα. τίς οὖν ὁ καρπὸς
αὐτοῦ, αὐτὸς ὑφηγήσεται· "ἐπεκάλεσε" γὰρ
86 "τὸ ὄνομα κυρίου[1] θεὸς αἰώνιος." αἱ τοίνυν
λεχθεῖσαι προσρήσεις τὰς περὶ τὸ ὂν ἐμφαίνουσι
δυνάμεις· ἡ μὲν γὰρ κύριος καθ' ἣν ἄρχει,
ἡ δὲ θεὸς καθ' ἣν εὐεργετεῖ· οὗ χάριν καὶ τῇ
κατὰ τὸν ἱερώτατον Μωυσῆν κοσμοποιίᾳ πάσῃ
τὸ τοῦ θεοῦ ὄνομα ἀναλαμβάνεται· ἥρμοττε γὰρ
τὴν δύναμιν, καθ' ἣν ὁ ποιῶν εἰς γένεσιν ἄγων
ἐτίθετο καὶ διεκοσμεῖτο, διὰ ταύτης καὶ [κατα]κλη-
87 θῆναι. καθὸ μὲν οὖν ἄρχων ἐστίν, ἄμφω δύναται,
καὶ εὖ καὶ κακῶς ποιεῖν, συμμεταβαλλόμενος πρὸς
τὴν τοῦ δράσαντος ἀπόδοσιν· καθὸ δὲ εὐεργέτης,
88 θάτερον μόνον βούλεται, τὸ εὐεργετεῖν. μέγιστον
δ' ἂν ψυχῆς γένοιτο ἀγαθὸν μηκέτι ἐνδοιάζειν περὶ
τῆς πρὸς ἑκάτερα τοῦ βασιλέως ἰσχύος, ἀλλ'
ἀνενδοιάστως τὸν μὲν ἕνεκα τοῦ κράτους τῆς
ἀρχῆς αὐτοῦ φόβον ἐπικρεμάμενον καταλύειν, τὴν
δὲ ἐκ τοῦ προαιρετικῶς εἶναι φιλόδωρον ἀγαθῶν
κτήσεως καὶ χρήσεως ἐλπίδα βεβαιοτάτην ζω-

---

[1] MSS. κύριος ὁ.

---

[a] τὴν δύναμιν ... διὰ ταύτης: an irregular construction
for καθ' ἣν δύναμιν ... διὰ ταύτης.

[b] πρὸς τὴν τοῦ δράσαντος ἀπόδοσιν: this genitive of the
person requited is very doubtful Greek. Mangey proposed
δρασθέντος, "the deed done."

either. For how would it ever happen that we 84
should see or hear or conceive amiss, if the power to
apprehend each object had been inherently fixed
in the several organs, instead of the power to apprehend springing from the seed of certitude sown upon
the organs by God ?

XX. Now that we have adequately dealt with the 85
further subject of the plot in which the tree blooms,
let us work out as our last point that of the fruit.
What its fruit is, then, Moses himself shall inform
us : for 'tis said " he called upon it the Name of the
Lord, as God eternal " (Gen. xxi. 33). The titles, 86
then, just mentioned exhibit the powers of Him that
IS ; the title " Lord " the power in virtue of which
He rules, that of "God" the power in virtue of which
He bestows benefits. This is why the name " God "
is employed throughout all the record of Creation
given by Moses, that most holy man. For it was
fitting that the Creator should be spoken of by a
title coming to Him through that power in virtue
of which,[a] when bringing the world into being, He
set and ordered it. In so far as He is Ruler, He has 87
both powers, both to bestow benefits and to inflict
evil, changing His dealing as the recompense due
to the doer [b] of every deed demands : but in so far as
He is Benefactor, He wills only the one, to bestow
benefits. Very great good would come to the soul 88
from ceasing to be of two minds in face of the King's
readiness to put forth His might in either direction,
and if it would resolutely break down the fear that
hangs over it owing to the dread force of His sovereignty, and kindle the flame of that most sure hope
of winning and enjoying good things, which is afforded
by the fact that to be bountiful is His choice and

89 πυρεῖν. τὸ δὴ " θεὸς αἰώνιος " ἴσον ἐστὶ τῷ ὁ
χαριζόμενος οὐ ποτὲ μὲν ποτὲ δὲ οὔ, ἀεὶ δὲ καὶ
συνεχῶς, ὁ ἀδιαστάτως εὐεργετῶν, ὁ τὴν τῶν
δωρεῶν ἐπάλληλον φορὰν ἀπαύστως συνείρων, ὁ
τὰς χάριτας ἐχομένας ἀλλήλων ἀνακυκλῶν δυνάμεσιν ἐνωτικαῖς καθαρμοσάμενος, ὁ μηδένα καιρὸν
τοῦ ποιεῖν εὖ παραλείπων, ὁ κύριος ὤν, ὡς

90 καὶ βλάπτειν δύνασθαι.   XXI. τοῦτο καὶ
ὁ ἀσκητὴς Ἰακὼβ ᾐτήσατο ἐπιτέλειαν[1] τῶν ἱεροπρεπεστάτων εὐχῶν· εἶπε γάρ που· " καὶ ἔσται
κύριος ἐμοὶ εἰς θεόν," ἴσον τῷ οὐκέτι μοι τὸ

[343] δεσποτικὸν ἐπιδείξεται τῆς αὐτοκράτορος | ἀρχῆς,
ἀλλὰ τὸ εὐεργετικὸν τῆς ἵλεω περὶ πάντα καὶ
σωτηρίου δυνάμεως, τὸν μὲν οἷα ἐπὶ δεσπότῃ
φόβον ἀναιρῶν, τὴν δὲ ὡς ἐπ' εὐεργέτῃ φιλίαν

91 καὶ εὔνοιαν τῇ ψυχῇ παρέχων.   τίς
ἂν οὖν τοῦθ' ὑπολάβοι ψυχή, ὅτι ὁ δεσπότης
καὶ ἡγεμὼν τῶν ὅλων οὐδὲν τῆς ἑαυτοῦ φύσεως
μεταβάλλων, μένων δὲ ἐν ὁμοίῳ, ἀγαθός ἐστι
συνεχῶς καὶ φιλόδωρος ἀνελλιπῶς, τῶν[2] ὄντως
ἀγαθῶν ἀφθόνων καὶ ἀεννάων αἴτιος τελειότατος

92 τοῖς εὐδαιμονοῦσι; βασιλεῖ δὲ πεπιστευκέναι μὴ
τῷ μεγέθει τῆς ἀρχῆς ἐπαιρομένῳ πρὸς βλάβας
τῶν ὑπηκόων, ἀλλὰ φιλανθρωπίᾳ τὸ ἐνδεὲς[3] ἑκάστῳ
ἐπανορθοῦσθαι προαιρουμένῳ, μέγιστόν ἐστι πρὸς
εὐθυμίαν καὶ ἀσφάλειαν ἕρκος.

---

[1] Conj. Tr.: mss. and Wend. ἐπὶ τέλει.
[2] τῶν is substituted for ὅθεν, and note of interrogation
placed after εὐδαιμονοῦσι on Mangey's conj.   [3] mss. ἀνενδεές.

---

[a] *i.e.* although at the same time He is Lord. But the
addition is strange in view of the emphasis laid on the
difference of the two names. Perhaps insert οὐχ or οὐ τῷ
before ὁ κύριος; *i.e.* the title God eternal is equivalent to

258

delight. The title " God Eternal " is equivalent to 89
" He that is, not sometimes gracious and sometimes
not so, but continuously and always ; He that with-
out intermission bestows benefits ; He that causes
His gifts to follow each other in ceaseless flow ;
He who makes His boons come round in unbroken
cycle, knitting them together by unifying forces ;
He who lets no opportunity of doing good go by ;
He who is Lord,[a] and so is able to hurt also."

XXI. This is what Jacob, the trainer of self, claimed 90
as the fulfilment of those vows of most sacred import.
He said, you remember, " And the Lord shall be to
me for God " (Gen. xxviii. 21), as much as to say,
He shall no longer exhibit towards me the masterful-
ness that characterizes the rule of an autocrat, but
the readiness to bless that marks the power that
is in every way kindly, and bent on the welfare of
men. He shall do away with the fear we feel before
Him as Master, and implant in the soul the loyalty
and affection that goes out to Him as Benefactor.

What soul, in fact, would imagine that 91
the Master and Sovereign of the Universe, without
undergoing any change in His own nature, but remaining as He is, is kind continuously and bountiful
incessantly, supreme Author of real good things
coming without stint in ceaseless flow to happy
souls ? It is a strong bulwark of cheerfulness of 92
spirit and freedom from danger to have reposed our
confidence in a King who is not urged by the greatness of His dominion to inflict injuries on His subjects, but whose love for man makes it His delight
to supply what is lacking to each one.

Benefactor etc., but not to Lord, which implies power to
hurt. Negatives are frequently omitted in the MSS. of Philo.

93 XXII. Ἃ τοίνυν ὑπεσχόμεθα, ἤδη σχεδὸν
ἀποδέδεικται, [τὸ] φυτὸν μὲν τὸ ἀρχήν τε καὶ
τέλος[1] λαμβάνεσθαι τῶν ἁπάντων εἶναι θεόν,
χωρίον δὲ τὸ ἀκόλουθον τὸ ἐν μηδενὶ τῶν ἐν
γενέσει τέλειον εὑρίσκεσθαι, ἐπ᾽ αὐτῷ δ᾽ ἔσθ᾽ ὅτε
χάρισι τοῦ αἰτίου προφαίνεσθαι, καρπὸς δὲ τὸ τὰς
τοῦ θεοῦ διαιωνίζειν χάριτας καὶ ὀμβρούσας
ἀπαύστως μηδέποτε λήγειν.

94 Οὕτως μὲν δὴ καὶ ὁ σοφὸς ἑπόμενος τῇ τοῦ
πρώτου καὶ μεγίστου φυτουργοῦ τέχνῃ τὴν γεωργικὴν ἐπιδείκνυται. βούλεται δὲ ὁ ἱερὸς λόγος
καὶ τοῖς μήπω τελειωθεῖσιν ἡμῖν, ἔτι δὲ ἐν μέσοις
ἀριθμοῖς τῶν λεγομένων καθηκόντων ἐξεταζο-
μένοις, διαπονηθῆναι τὰ γεωργικά· φησὶ γάρ·
95 " ὅταν εἰσέλθητε πρὸς τὴν γῆν, ἣν κύριος ὁ θεὸς
ὑμῶν δίδωσιν ὑμῖν, καὶ καταφυτεύσητε πᾶν ξύλον
βρώσεως, περικαθαριεῖτε τὴν ἀκαθαρσίαν αὐτοῦ·
ὁ καρπὸς[2] αὐτοῦ τρία ἔτη ἔσται ἀπερικάθαρτος,[3] οὐ
βρωθήσεται· τῷ δὲ ἔτει τῷ τετάρτῳ ἔσται πᾶς
καρπὸς αὐτοῦ ἅγιος, αἰνετὸς[4] τῷ κυρίῳ· τῷ δὲ ἔτει
τῷ πέμπτῳ φάγεσθε τὸν καρπόν, πρόσθεμα ὑμῖν
τὰ γεννήματα αὐτοῦ. ἐγώ εἰμι κύριος ὁ θεὸς
96 ὑμῶν." οὐκοῦν τῶν ξύλων τὰ ἐδώδιμα,
πρὶν εἰς τὴν ὑπὸ θεοῦ δοθεῖσαν χώραν μεταναστῆναι, φυτεύειν ἀδύνατον· " ὅταν γὰρ εἰσέλθητε
πρὸς τὴν γῆν, φυτεύσετε πᾶν ξύλον βρώσιμον "
φησίν, ὥστε ἔξω διατρίβοντες οὐκ ἂν δυναίμεθα
τὰ τοιαῦτα τῶν δένδρων γεωργεῖν· καὶ μήποτ᾽

---

¹ MSS. τινα κάλλιστον.   ² MSS. τὸν καρπὸν.
³ MSS. ἀκάθαρτος.   ⁴ MSS. ἐν ἔτος.

ᵃ See App. p. 496.
ᵇ Or "for giving praise to."   So from §§ 117 ff. it appears

XXII. We may take it, then, that the points which 93 we undertook to prove have now been demonstrated. That God be presupposed as Beginning and End of all things has been shewn to be the plant : as a corollary to this, that perfection is found in no part of creation, though by special grace ^{a} of the First Cause it is ever and anon displayed upon its face, has been shewn to be the plot of ground ; while the perpetuity and unceasing downpour of the gifts of God's grace has been shewn to be the fruit.

Of such sort, then, is husbandry as exhibited by 94 the sage also, treading in the steps of the first and greatest Planter. But the intention of the inspired Word is that we too who are not yet perfected, but are still classified as in the preliminary and un-developed stages of what are called natural duties,^{a} should make husbandry our serious business : for It says : "When ye shall have entered into the land, 95 which the Lord your God giveth you, and shall have planted any tree for food, ye shall cleanse away its uncleanness : for three years its fruit shall remain not cleansed away, it shall not be eaten : but in the fourth year all its fruit shall be holy for a thank-offering to the Lord ^{b} : but in the fifth year ye shall eat the fruit ; its crop ^{a} shall be added to your store. I am the Lord, your God " (Lev. xix. 23 – 25).

Accordingly it is impossible to grow 96 fruit-trees before migrating into the country given by God ; for the words are, " When ye shall have entered into the land, ye shall plant every tree yielding food," so that while staying outside we shall be unable to cultivate such trees. And this is what

that Philo takes the word, which elsewhere means " praise-worthy."

97 εἰκότως· ἕως μὲν γὰρ εἰς τὴν σοφίας ὁδὸν οὐ
προσελήλυθεν ὁ νοῦς, τετραμμένος δὲ πόρρω
πλανᾶται, τῶν τῆς ἀγρίας ὕλης ἐπιμελεῖται φυτῶν,
ἅπερ ἤτοι ἄγονα ὄντα ἐστείρωται ἢ γεννῶντα
98 ἐδωδίμων ἐστὶν ἄφορα. ὅταν δὲ εἰς τὴν φρονήσεως
[344] ἐμβὰς ὁδὸν συνεισέρχηται | τοῖς δόγμασι καὶ συν-
τρέχῃ πᾶσιν, ἄρξεται¹ τὴν ἥμερον καὶ καρπῶν
ἡμέρων οἰστικὴν ἀντὶ τῆς ἀγρίας ἐκείνης γεωργεῖν,
ἀπάθειαν ἀντὶ παθῶν καὶ ἀντὶ ἀγνοίας ἐπιστήμην
99 καὶ ἀντὶ κακῶν ἀγαθά. ἐπεὶ οὖν² ὁ ἄρτι³
εἰσαγόμενος μακρὰν τοῦ τέλους ἀφέστηκεν, εἰκότως φυτεύσαντι αὐτῷ προστέτακται περιελεῖν τὴν
ἀκαθαρσίαν τοῦ φυτευθέντος. τί δὲ τοῦτ' ἐστί,
100 συνεπισκεψώμεθα· XXIII. τὰ μέσα τῶν καθηκόντων ἡμέρων φυτῶν ἔχειν μοι δοκεῖ λόγον·
ἑκάτερα γὰρ ὠφελιμωτάτους φέρει καρπούς, τὰ
μὲν σώμασι, τὰ δὲ ψυχαῖς. πολλὰ δὲ ἐν τοῖς
μέσοις συναναβλαστάνοντα καὶ ἐπιφυόμενα τῶν
βλαβερῶν ἀναγκαίως ἂν τέμνοιτο⁴ τοῦ μὴ ζημιοῦ-
101 σθαι τὰ ἀμείνω χάριν. ἢ οὐκ ἂν εἴποιμεν φυτὸν
ἥμερον ψυχῆς παρακαταθήκης ἀπόδοσιν; ἀλλὰ
τοῦτό γε τὸ φυτὸν καθάρσεως δεῖται καὶ περιτ-
τοτέρας ἐπιμελείας. τίς οὖν ἡ κάθαρσις ἥδε;
παρὰ νήφοντος λαβὼν παρακαταθήκην μήτε μεθύοντι μήτ' ἀσώτῳ μήτε μεμηνότι ἀποδῷς — ὁ
γὰρ λαβὼν ὄνησιν ἐκ τοῦ κομίσασθαι οὐχ ἕξει

---

¹ MSS. ἄρξηται or αὔξητε.   ² MSS. οἰκείων.
³ MSS. ἀρετῆς.   ⁴ MSS. ἂν γένοιτο.

ᵃ See App. p. 496.

we might expect; for, so long as the mind has not 97
come near and entered the way of wisdom, but turns
in another direction and wanders away far off, its
attention is given to trees of wild growth, which are
either barren and yield nothing, or, though they are
productive, bear no edible fruit. But when the mind 98
has stepped on to the way of good sense, and in the
company of all its teachings comes into and runs along
that way, it will begin instead of those wild trees to
cultivate trees of the orchard bearing orchard fruits,
instead of passions freedom from them, knowledge
in place of ignorance, good things in the place of
evil things.   Since, then, the pupil just 99
beginning his course is a long way from the end, we
can quite understand why he is directed after
planting to remove the uncleanness of that which
he has planted. Let us get a good view of what it
is to do this. XXIII. Natural duties which are 100
indifferent [a] seem to me to correspond to garden or
orchard trees : for in each case most wholesome fruits
are borne, for bodies in one case, for souls in the other.
But many harmful shoots that spring together with
the trees of the preliminary stage and many harmful
growths that come on them have to be cut away, to
save the better parts from being injured. Might 101
we not speak of the returning of a sum entrusted to
us as a tree grown in the soul's orchard ? Yet this
tree at all events requires cleansing and more than
usual attention. What is the cleansing in this case ?
When you have received something in trust from a
man when he was sober, you should not return it to
him when he is drunk, or when playing fast and loose
with his money, or when mad, for the recipient will
not be in a fit condition to derive any real benefit

καιρὸν ὠφεληθῆναι—, μηδὲ χρεώσταις ἢ δούλοις
ἀποδῷς δανειστῶν καὶ δεσποτῶν ἐφεδρευόντων—
προδοσία γὰρ τοῦτ᾽ ἐστίν, οὐκ ἀπόδοσις—, μηδὲ
τὴν ἐν ὀλίγοις πίστιν φύλαττε ⟨ἐπὶ⟩ θήρᾳ¹ τῆς
102 ἐν πλείοσι πίστεως· δελέατά γε οἱ μὲν ἁλιευόμενοι μικρὰ καθιέντες ἐπὶ τῷ τοὺς μείζους
ἀγκιστρεύεσθαι τῶν ἰχθύων οὐ σφόδρα ἂν ⟨εἶεν⟩
ὑπαίτιοι τῆς κατ᾽ ἀγορὰν εὐετηρίας προνοεῖσθαι
φάσκοντες καὶ ὡς ἂν ἄφθονον τοῖς ἀνθρώποις τὴν
103 καθ᾽ ἑκάστην ἡμέραν ποιήσωνται δίαιταν· δέλεαρ
δὴ μηδεὶς ὀλιγοχρημάτου παρακαταθήκης ἀπόδοσιν ἐπ᾽ ἄγρᾳ μείζονος προφερέτω, χερσὶ μὲν
τὰ ἑνὸς καὶ ὀλίγα προτείνων, διανοίᾳ δὲ τὰ πάντων
καὶ ἀμύθητα νοσφιζόμενος. ἐὰν οὖν ὡς δένδρου
τῆς παρακαταθήκης περιέλῃς τὰ ἀκάθαρτα, τὰς
ἀπὸ τῶν ἐφεδρευόντων βλάβας, τὰς ἀκαιρίας, τὰς
ἐνέδρας, τὰ ὁμοιότροπα πάντα, ἡμερώσεις τὸ
μέλλον ἀγριαίνεσθαι.

104 XXIV. Κἂν τῷ φιλίας μέντοι φυτῷ τοιάδε² τὰ
παραβλαστάνοντα τεμεῖν καὶ ἀποκόψαι φυλακῆς
ἕνεκα τοῦ βελτίονος ἀναγκαῖον. τὰ δὲ παραβλαστάνοντα ταῦτ᾽ ἐστίν· ἑταιρῶν πρὸς ἐραστὰς
γοητεῖαι, πρὸς τοὺς κολακευομένους οἰκοσίτων
105 ἀπάται. τὰς γὰρ μισθαρνούσας ἐπὶ τῇ ὥρᾳ τοῦ
σώματος ἰδεῖν ἔστι περιεχομένας τῶν ἐραστῶν ὡς
δὴ σφόδρα φιλούσας—φιλοῦσι δὲ οὐκ ἐκείνους, ἀλλ᾽
ἑαυτὰς καὶ τοῖς καθ᾽ ἑκάστην ἡμέραν λήμμασιν
ἐπικεχήνασι—, τούς τε κόλακας ἄλεκτον μέν ἐστι
[345] ὅτε μῖσος πρὸς τοὺς | θεραπευομένους φυλάττοντας,

---

¹ mss. θήρας : Mang. ἐπὶ θήρᾳ.
² τοιάδε conj. Tr. for ταῦτα δή.

---

from recovering it. And do not return it to debtors or slaves,[a] when the creditors and masters are lying in wait for them. To do so is betrayal, not payment of a due. And do not be strict about a small sum entrusted to you, with a view to ensnaring people into trusting you with larger sums. It is true that 102 fishermen drop small baits with a view to hooking the bigger fish, and are not seriously to blame. They can plead that they are providing for a good market, and to secure people an abundant supply for the table every day. Then let no one parade the 103 payment of a trifling sum entrusted to him by way of a bait to get a larger deposit. To do so is to hold out in one's hands an insignificant amount belonging to one person, while in intention one is appropriating untold sums belonging to all men. If, then, you treat the deposit as a tree and remove its impurities, to wit payments entailing injurious treatment to the recipient, ill-timed payments, payments that are really ensnaring tricks, and everything of this kind, you will make fit for your orchard what was turning wild.

XXIV. In the tree of friendship there are out- 104 growths, such as I shall describe, to be pruned and cut off for the sake of preserving the better part. Such outgrowths are practices of courtesans for taking in their lovers, ways parasites [b] have of deceiving their dupes. You may see women, who earn money by 105 the prostitution of their bodily charms, clinging to those enamoured of them as though they intensely loved them. It is not these that they love; they love themselves and are greedy for their daily takings. You may note flatterers cherishing often enough hatred that words cannot express for those upon

ὀψοφαγιαν δὲ καὶ λαιμαργίαν ἀγαπῶντας, ὑφ᾽ ὧν
ἀναπείθονται τοὺς χορηγοὺς τῶν ἀμέτρων ἐπι-
106 θυμιῶν περιέπειν. τὸ δὲ τῆς ἀκιβδηλεύτου φιλίας[1]
δένδρον ἀποσεισάμενον καὶ μεθέμενον ταῦτα καρπὸν
τοῖς χρησομένοις ὠφελιμώτατον οἴσει, τὸ ἀδέκα-
στον. εὔνοια γάρ ἐστι βούλησις τοῦ τῷ πλησίον
εἶναι[2] τὰ ἀγαθὰ αὐτοῦ[3] χάριν ἐκείνου. αἱ δέ γε
χαμαιτύπαι καὶ οἱ κόλακες αὑτῶν ἕνεκα σπουδά-
ζουσιν, αἱ μὲν τοῖς ἐρασταῖς, οἱ δὲ τοῖς κολακευο-
μένοις τὰ ἀγαθὰ προσάγειν. τὰς οὖν εἰρωνείας
καὶ γοητείας καθάπερ ἐπιφυομένας κῆρας τῷ
φιλίας φυτῷ περικοπτέον.

107 XXV. Ἱερουργίαι γε μὴν καὶ ἡ περὶ τὰς θυσίας
ἁγιστεία[4] βλάστημα κάλλιστον, ἀλλὰ παραναπέφυκεν
αὐτῷ κακόν, δεισιδαιμονία, ἣν πρὶν χλοῆσαι
λυσιτελὲς ἐκτεμεῖν. ἔνιοι γὰρ ᾠήθησαν τὸ βου-
θυτεῖν εὐσέβειαν εἶναι, καὶ ἐξ ὧν ἂν κλέψωσιν ἢ
ἀρνήσωνται ἢ χρεωκοπήσωσιν ἢ ἁρπάσωσιν ἢ
λεηλατήσωσι μοίρας ἀπονέμουσι τοῖς βωμοῖς, οἱ
δυσκάθαρτοι, τὸ μὴ δοῦναι δίκην ἐφ᾽ οἷς ἐξήμαρτον
108 ὤνιον εἶναι νομίζοντες. ἀλλὰ γάρ, εἴποιμ᾽ ἂν
αὐτοῖς, ἀδέκαστόν ἐστιν, ὦ οὗτοι, τὸ θεοῦ δικα-
στήριον, ὡς τοὺς μὲν γνώμῃ κεχρημένους ὑπαιτίῳ,
κἂν καθ᾽ ἅπασαν ἡμέραν ἑκατὸν βόας ἀνάγωσιν,
ἀποστρέφεσθαι, τοὺς δ᾽ ἀνυπαιτίους, κἂν μηδὲν
θύωσι τὸ παράπαν, ἀποδέχεσθαι. βωμοῖς γὰρ
ἀπύροις, περὶ οὓς ἀρεταὶ χορεύουσι, γέγηθεν ὁ
θεός, ἀλλ᾽ οὐ πυρὶ πολλῷ φλέγουσιν, ὅπερ αἱ τῶν

---

[1] MSS. σοφίας.   [2] MSS. τούτων πλησίον γὰρ εἶναι.
[3] MSS. αὐτὰ.   [4] MSS. πίστις.

[a] See App. p. 496.
[b] Lit. "cutting debts."   Cf. Plutarch i. 87 в χρεοκοπίδης.

whom they fawn, in love with rich dishes and over-eating, and induced by nothing else than these to court those who glut their measureless greed. The 106 tree of genuine friendship will shake off and be quit of these things, and will bear fruit most beneficial to those who shall eat of it, namely honesty. For real goodwill is a desire that good *a* should befall your neighbour for his own sake, whereas it is to further objects of their own that harlots and toadies take such pains to offer the things that will please, the former in their designs upon their lovers, the latter upon their patrons. So we must treat everything that smacks of sham and quackery as we treat hurtful ongrowths, and cut it away from the tree of friendship.

XXV. Again, sacred ministrations and the holy 107 service of sacrifices is a plant most fair, but it has a parasitic growth that is evil, namely superstition, and it is well to apply the knife to this before its green leaves appear. For some have imagined that it is piety to slaughter oxen, and allot to the altars portions of what they have got by stealing, or by repudiating debts, or by defrauding creditors,*b* or by seizing property and cattle-lifting, thinking, in their gross defilement, that impunity for their offences is a thing that can be bought. "Nay, nay," I would 108 say to them, " no bribes, O foolish ones, can reach God's tribunal." He turns His face away from those who approach with guilty intent, even though they lead to His altar a hundred bullocks every day, and accepts the guiltless, although they sacrifice nothing at all. God delights in altars beset by a choir of Virtues, albeit no fire burn on them. He takes no delight in blazing altar fires fed by the unhallowed sacrifices of men to whose hearts sacrifice is unknown.

267

ἀνιέρων ἄθυτοι θυσίαι συνανέφλεξαν ὑπομιμνή-
σκουσαι τὰς ἑκάστων ἀγνοίας τε καὶ διαμαρτίας·
καὶ γὰρ εἶπέ που Μωυσῆν θυσίαν '' ἀναμιμνή-
109 σκουσαν ἁμαρτίαν.'' πάντ' οὖν τὰ τοιαῦτα
μεγάλης γιγνόμενα ζημίας αἴτια χρὴ περιαιρεῖν
καὶ ἀποκόπτειν ἑπομένους τῷ χρησμῷ, ἐν ᾧ
διείρηται περιαιρεῖν τὴν ἀκαθαρσίαν ξύλου τοῦ
110 φυτευθέντος ἐδωδίμου.   XXVI. ἀλλ'
ἡμεῖς μὲν οὐδὲ διδασκόμενοι πρὸς εὐμάθειαν
ἐπιδίδομεν· ἔνιοι δὲ αὐτοδιδάκτῳ τῇ φύσει χρησάμενοι τἀγαθὸν ἐξέδυσαν τῶν ἐνειλημμένων
βλαβῶν, καθάπερ ὁ ἀσκητὴς ἐπίκλην Ἰακώβ·
οὗτος γὰρ '' ῥάβδους ἐλέπισε λεπίσματα λευκὰ
περισύρων τὸ χλωρόν,'' ἵνα τῆς ἐν μέσοις ποικιλίας
σκοταίοις καὶ ζοφεροῖς πανταχοῦ ἀναιρεθείσης
τὸ μὴ τέχνῃ ποικιλλόμενον,[1] φύσει δὲ γεννώ-
μενον ἀδελφὸν αὐτῆς λευκὸν εἶδος ἀναδειχθῇ.
111 παρὸ καὶ ἐν τῷ περὶ τῆς λέπρας | τεθέντι νόμῳ
[346] διείρηται τὸν μηκέτι διηνθισμένον ποικιλίᾳ χρωμάτων ὅλον δὲ λευκωθέντα δι' ὅλων ἀπὸ κεφαλῆς
⟨ἄκρας⟩ ἕως ποδῶν ἐσχάτων καθαρὸν εἶναι, ἵνα
κατὰ τὴν ἀπὸ τοῦ σώματος μετάβασιν τὸ ποικίλον
καὶ πανοῦργον καὶ ἀντιρρέπον καὶ ἐπαμφοτερίζον
τῆς διανοίας μεθέμενοι πάθος τὸ ἀποίκιλον καὶ
ἀνενδοίαστον ἀληθείας ἁπλοῦν χρῶμα δεξώμεθα.
112   Τὸ μὲν οὖν τὸ ξύλον φάσκειν περικαθαίρεσθαι
λόγον ἔχει βεβαιούμενον ἀληθείᾳ, τὸ δὲ τὸν καρπὸν

---

[1] MSS. ποικιλλομένη.

[a] See App. p. 496.

Nay, these sacrifices do but put Him in remembrance of the ignorance and offences of the several offerers ; for Moses, as we know, speaks of sacrifice " bringing sin to remembrance " (Num. v. 15). All such defile- 109 ments entail great loss. We must clear the way and cut them off in obedience to the oracle, in which a command is given to clear away the uncleanness of the fruit-trees that have been planted.

XXVI. But, while we, even under teachers, fail to 110 make progress and become apt pupils, some, taking advantage of a nature which is its own teacher, have released the good in them from the hurtful growths which had fastened upon it. It was so with the trainer of self, whose name was Jacob, for he " peeled rods, stripping off the green bark, and causing them to shew white where they were peeled " (Gen. xxx. 37). His aim[a] was to do away entirely with the variety and changeableness of hue, which is associated with the misty darkness and gloom of the undeveloped stages ; and to bring into full view the whiteness, which is due to no artificial variegation, but is akin to Nature, to which it owes its birth. It is in accordance with this that in the law laid down regarding leprosy it is enjoined that the leper is clean whose body is no longer particoloured, shewing a variety of hues, but has turned white all over from head to foot (Lev. xiii. 12 f.). The aim of this ordinance is that, by way of leaving behind us bodily concerns,[a] we may abandon the condition of mind which is changeful and vacillating, ready to put its hand to any project and to face both ways, and may take the plain hue of truth with its freedom from changefulness and indecision.

The statement that the trees undergo a cleansing 112 is quite reasonable and accords with facts ; the

269

οὐ πάνυ τῷ ἐναργεῖ πεπίστωται[1]· σῦκα γὰρ ἢ
σταφυλὴν ἢ συνόλως καρπὸν οὐδεὶς γεωργῶν
113 περικαθαίρει.   XXVII. καὶ μήν φησί γε· " ὁ
καρπὸς αὐτοῦ τρία ἔτη ἔσται ἀπερικάθαρτος,[2]
οὐ βρωθήσεται," ὡς εἰωθότος δήπου περικαθαίρεσθαι ἀεί.   λεκτέον οὖν, ὅτι καὶ τοῦθ᾽ ἕν ἐστι
τῶν ἐν ὑπονοίαις ἀποδιδομένων, τοῦ ῥητοῦ μὴ
σφόδρα συνᾴδοντος. ἡ δὲ λέξις ἐστὶν ἀμφίβολος·
δηλοῖ γὰρ ἕν μέν τι τοιοῦτον " ὁ καρπὸς αὐτοῦ τρία
ἔτη ἔσται," εἶτα ἰδίᾳ τὸ " ἀπερικάθαρτος οὐ
βρωθώσεται," ἕτερον δὲ " ὁ καρπὸς αὐτοῦ τρία
ἔτη ἔσται ἀπερικάθαρτος," ἔπειθ᾽ οὕτως " ⟨οὐ⟩
114 βρωθήσεται." κατὰ μὲν οὖν τὸ πρότερον σημαινόμενον ταῦτα ἄν τις ἐκδέξαιτο, τῶν τριῶν ἐτῶν ἀντὶ
τοῦ τριμεροῦς χρόνου παραλαμβανομένων, ὃς εἰς
τὸν παρεληλυθότα καὶ ἐνεστῶτα καὶ μέλλοντα
τέμνεσθαι πέφυκεν,[3] ὁ τῆς παιδείας καρπὸς ἔσται
καὶ ὑποστήσεται καὶ μενεῖ σῷος κατὰ πάντα τὰ
χρόνου τμήματα, ἴσον τῷ δι᾽ αἰῶνος φθορὰν μὴ
δεχόμενος· ἄφθαρτος γὰρ ἡ τοῦ ἀγαθοῦ φύσις.
" ἀπερικάθαρτος δὲ καρπὸς οὐ βρωθήσεται,"
παρόσον οἱ μὲν κεκαθαρμένοι καὶ ὑγιαίνοντες
ἀστεῖοι λόγοι ψυχὴν τρέφουσι καὶ νοῦν αὔξουσιν,
οὐ τρόφιμοι δέ εἰσιν οἱ ἐναντίοι νόσον καὶ φθορὰν
115 ἐπιπέμποντες[4] αὐτῇ. κατὰ δὲ τὸ ἕτερον σημαινόμενον ὥσπερ ἀναπόδεικτος ⟨λόγος⟩[5] λέγεται διχῶς,

---

[1] MSS. πεπίστευται.   [2] MSS. ἀκάθαρτος.
[3] The first sentence of § 114 is punctuated after Mangey
and Heinemann.   [4] MSS. ἐπιλάμποντες.
[5] λόγος is inserted before λέγεται with Cohn (conj.).

statement that the fruit does so is by no means made good by what we see before our eyes ; for no gardener cleanses figs or grapes or any fruit at all. XXVII. And yet it says, " The fruit shall remain uncleansed for three years ; it shall not be eaten," as though it were the custom to cleanse it regularly as a matter of course. Let me say, then, that this again is one of the points to be interpreted allegorically, the literal interpretation being quite out of keeping with facts. The sentence can be taken in two ways. Read in one way, it means something of this kind, " Its fruit shall be for three years " ; then, as an independent sentence, " it shall not be eaten uncleansed." Read in another way, " Its fruit shall be uncleansed for three years," and then the words " it shall not be eaten." Led by the sense yielded 114 by the former punctuation, we arrive at this result. We take the three years to represent time in its natural threefold division into past, present, and future. The fruit of instruction—so we understand the words—shall be, subsist, remain free from interference, through all the divisions of time. This is equivalent to saying that throughout eternity it is exempt from corruption ; for the nature of good is incorruptible. " But uncleansed fruit shall not be eaten." This is due to the fact that right teaching, having submitted to a cleansing which makes it wholesome, nourishes the soul and makes the mind grow ; while teaching of a contrary sort is devoid of nourishment, and lets loose upon the soul corruption and disease. An illustration will help us to see the senses which the other arrangement of the words may convey. An argument is called " in- 115 demonstrable," either when it has such inherent

ὅ τε δυσκόλως ἀργαλεότητος ἕνεκα ἐπιδεικνύμενος
καὶ ὁ ἐνθένδε γνώριμος ἐξ αὐτοῦ, τὸ σαφὲς οὐκ
ἐκ τῆς ἑτέρου μαρτυρίας, ἀλλ' ἐκ τῆς ἐμφαινομένης
ἐναργείας αὐτῷ πιστούμενος, ᾧ[1] πρὸς τοὺς συλ-
λογιστικοὺς εἴωθεν ἡ διαλεκτικὴ λόγους χρῆσθαι,
οὕτως ἀπερικάθαρτος καρπὸς ὅ τε δεόμενος
καθάρσεως καὶ μὴ κεκαθαρμένος, καὶ ὁ τηλ-
116 αὐγέστατος.   τοιοῦτός ἐστιν ὁ παιδείας καρπὸς
"τρία ἔτη," τουτέστι τὸν τριμερῆ χρόνον, τὸν
σύμπαντα αἰῶνα, καθαρώτατος καὶ διαυγέστατος,
ὑπ' οὐδενὸς βλαβεροῦ συσκιαζόμενος, λουτρῶν καὶ
περιρραντηρίων ἢ συνόλως ἑτέρου τινὸς τῶν εἰς
κάθαρσιν τεινόντων οὐδαμῇ οὐδαμῶς χρεῖος ὤν.

117
[347]   XXVIII. "Τῷ | δὲ ἔτει" φησί "τῷ τετάρτῳ
ἔσται πᾶς ὁ καρπὸς αὐτοῦ ἅγιος, αἰνετὸς[2] τῷ
κυρίῳ." τὸν τέσσαρα ἀριθμὸν πολλαχοῦ μὲν τῆς
νομοθεσίας, μάλιστα δὲ ἐν τῷ καταλόγῳ τῆς τοῦ
παντὸς γενέσεως, ἀποσεμνύνειν ἔοικεν ὁ προ-
118 φητικὸς λόγος· τὸ γὰρ αἰσθητὸν καὶ τίμιον φῶς,
τὸ καὶ ἑαυτοῦ καὶ τῶν ἄλλων σαφέστατον γνώρισμα,
καὶ τοὺς τοκέας αὐτοῦ ἥλιον καὶ σελήνην καὶ τὸν
ἱερώτατον χορὸν τῶν ἀστέρων, οἳ νύκτα τε καὶ
ἡμέραν, ἔτι τε μῆνας καὶ ἐνιαυτοὺς ἀνατολαῖς καὶ
δύσεσιν ἐπεράτωσαν ἀριθμοῦ τε φύσιν ἀνέδειξαν,
119 οἷς τὸ μέγιστον ψυχῆς ἀγαθὸν[3] ἀνάκειται, ἡμέρα
τετάρτῃ φησὶ δημιουργηθῆναι. διαφερόντως δὲ
καὶ νῦν αὐτὸν ἐκτετίμηκεν, οὐκ ἐν ἑτέρῳ χρόνῳ
τὸν τῶν δένδρων καρπὸν ἀναθεὶς τῷ θεῷ ἢ ἐνιαυ-
120 τῷ τῆς φυτείας τετάρτῳ. λόγον γὰρ καὶ φυσι-

---

[1] mss. καὶ: Cohn conj. ᾧ καὶ.
[2] mss. ἐν ἔτος.   [3] mss. ἀπάτη.   See App. p. 497.

difficulties that it is hardly capable of demonstration, or when its force is recognized at once by its mere statement, when it relies for its certainty not on any proof drawn from elsewhere, but from its self-evident character ; the kind of argument which Logic usually employs in formal syllogisms. Just so can the word " without cleansing " be used either of fruit that needs cleansing and has not received it, or of fruit that is perfectly bright and brilliant. Such is the 116 fruit of education " through three years," that is through past, present, and future, that is all eternity, wholly pure and bright, bedimmed by no hurtful thing, utterly exempt from need of washings or lustrations or anything else whatever whose purpose is to cleanse.

XXVIII. " And in the fourth year," it says, " all 117 its fruit shall be holy, for giving praise unto the lord " (Lev. xix. 24). In many parts of the Lawgiving, but above all in the record of the creation of the universe, we see the prophetic word glorifying the number 4. For (Gen. i. 14) it ascribes to the fourth day the making of those things on which depends the soul's chiefest good[a] ; the precious light of the senses, 118 which gives us most sure knowledge of itself and all other objects ; light's parents, the sun and moon and that most holy choir of the stars ; these by their risings and settings determined the bounds of months and years, and revealed number's place in nature. And in the passage before us it has accorded 119 highest honour to the number 4, by making the fruit of the trees an offering to God at no other time than in the fourth year from their planting. The number indeed involves deep principles both 120

[a] See App. p. 496.

κώτατον καὶ ἠθικώτατον ἔχει· τάς τε γοῦν τοῦ
παντὸς ῥίζας, ἐξ ὧν ὁ κόσμος, τέτταρας εἶναι
121 συμβέβηκε, γῆν, ὕδωρ, ἀέρα, πῦρ, καὶ τὰς ἐτησίους
ὥρας ἰσαρίθμους χειμῶνα καὶ θέρος καὶ τὰς μεθορίους, ἔαρ τε καὶ μετόπωρον. πρεσβύτατός τε
αὖ τετραγώνων ὁ ἀριθμὸς ὢν ἐν ὀρθαῖς γωνίαις,
122 ὡς τὸ κατὰ γεωμετρίαν δηλοῖ σχῆμα, ἐξετάζεται·
αἱ δ' εἰσὶν ὀρθότητος λόγου σαφῆ δείγματα, πηγὴ
δὲ ἀέναος ἀρετῶν ὁ ὀρθὸς λόγος. ἀνάγκη μέντοι
τὰς τοῦ τετραγώνου πλευρὰς ἴσας εἶναι· δικαιοσύνην
δὲ ἰσότης τὴν ἔξαρχον καὶ ἡγεμονίδα τῶν ἀρετῶν
ἔτεκεν· ὥστε ἰσότητος καὶ δικαιοσύνης καὶ πάσης
123 ἀρετῆς χωρὶς τῶν[1] ἄλλων ἐπιδείκνυται τὸν ἀριθμὸν
εἶναι σύμβολον.

Καλεῖται δ' ἡ τετρὰς καὶ " πᾶς," ὅτι τοὺς ἄχρι
δεκάδος καὶ αὐτὴν δεκάδα περιέχει δυνάμει.
XXIX. ὅτι μὲν οὖν τοὺς πρὸ αὐτῆς, παντὶ τῳ
124 δῆλον· ὅτι δὲ καὶ τοὺς μετ' αὐτήν, ἐξ ἐπιλογισμοῦ
ῥᾴδιον ἰδεῖν [ἐν ἀριθμῷ μὲν ἕξ]. ἕν, δύο, τρία,
τέτταρα συντιθέντες ὃ ἠπορούμεν εὑρήσομεν. ἐκ
μὲν γὰρ ἑνὸς καὶ τεττάρων πεντὰς ἔσται, ἐκ δὲ
δυεῖν καὶ τεττάρων ἑξάς, ἑβδομὰς δὲ ἐκ τριῶν καὶ
τεττάρων· καὶ κατὰ τὴν διπλῆν σύνθεσιν ἐξ ἑνὸς
καὶ τριῶν καὶ τεττάρων ὀγδοάς, καὶ πάλιν ἐκ
125 δυεῖν καὶ τριῶν καὶ τεττάρων ὁ ἐννέα ἀριθμός,
δεκὰς δὲ ἐκ πάντων· ἓν γὰρ καὶ δύο καὶ τρία καὶ
τέτταρα δέκα γεννᾷ. διὰ τοῦτο καὶ Μωυσῆς
εἶπεν, ὅτι " ἔτει τῷ τετάρτῳ ἔσται πᾶς ὁ καρπὸς
αὐτοῦ ἅγιος"· ἄρτιον γὰρ καὶ ὁλόκληρον καὶ

---

[1] mss. ὧν, which might be translated "besides the other
things which it (*i.e.* the number four) displays."

of physics and ethics.[a] For the roots of the universe, out of which the world grows, are four— earth, water, air, fire. Of the same number are the seasons, Winter and Summer, and those that come between, Spring and Autumn. And, since it is the 121 first of all numbers produced by squaring another number, it is in right angles that it presents itself to view, as is made evident by the geometrical figure. And right angles are clear pictures of rightness of reasoned thought, and right reason is an everflowing spring of virtue. Again, the sides of the square are 122 necessarily equal : and equality is the mother of justice, empress and queen of the virtues. Thus the word of prophecy shews that this number is the symbol of equality, and righteousness, and every virtue in a way that the other numbers are not.

The number 4 is also called " all " or " totality " [b] 123 because it potentially embraces the numbers up to 10 and 10 itself. That it so embraces those which precede it is plain to everyone : and it is easy to see by further reckoning that it so embraces the numbers that come after it also. Add together $1 + 2 + 3 + 4$, 124 and we shall find what we wanted. For out of $1 + 4$ we shall get 5 ; out of $2 + 4$ we shall get 6 ; 7 out of $3 + 4$; and (by adding three instead of two numbers together) from $1 + 3 + 4$ we get 8 ; and again from $2 + 3 + 4$ we get the number 9 ; and from all taken together we get 10 ; for $1 + 2 + 3 + 4$ produces 10. This is why Moses said " In the fourth year *all* the 125 fruit shall be holy." For the number 4 is, in relation

---

[a] *Cf. Leg. All.* i. 39. The " ethical " interpretation begins at " right angles are pictures of rightness." What precedes is " physical " in Philo's sense of the word.

[b] See App. p. 497.

πλήρη, ὡς καὶ σύμπαντα, ὡς τύπῳ φάναι, λόγον
ἔχει, διὰ τὸ δεκάδα, ἣν τετρὰς ἐγέννησε, πρῶτον
καμπτῆρα τῶν ἀπὸ μονάδος συντιθεμένων ἀριθμῶν
[348] ἑστάναι· | δεκὰς δὲ καὶ τετρὰς " πᾶς " ἐν ἀριθμοῖς[1]
εἶναι λέγεται, ἀλλὰ δεκὰς μὲν ἀποτελέσματι, τετρὰς
δὲ δυνάμει.

126   XXX. Τόν τε παιδείας καρπὸν οὐ μόνον ἅγιον,
ἀλλὰ καὶ αἰνετὸν εἶναί φησι προσηκόντως· ἑκάστη
μέν γε τῶν ἀρετῶν ἐστι χρῆμα ἅγιον, εὐχαριστία
δὲ ὑπερβαλλόντως· θεῷ δὲ οὐκ ἔνεστι γνησίως
εὐχαριστῆσαι δι' ὧν νομίζουσιν οἱ πολλοὶ κατα-
σκευῶν ἀναθημάτων θυσιῶν—οὐδὲ γὰρ σύμπας
ὁ κόσμος ἱερὸν ἀξιόχρεων ἂν γένοιτο πρὸς τὴν τούτου τιμήν—, ἀλλὰ δι' ἐπαίνων καὶ ὕμνων, οὐχ
οὓς ἡ γεγωνὸς ᾄσεται φωνή, ἀλλὰ οὓς ὁ ἀειδὴς
καὶ καθαρώτατος νοῦς ἐπηχήσει καὶ ἀναμέλψει.
127   παλαιὸς γοῦν ᾄδεται λόγος ⟨ὃς⟩[2] ὑπὸ μὲν σοφῶν
εὑρεθείς, μνήμῃ δέ, οἷα φιλεῖ, κατὰ διαδοχὰς παρα-
δοθεὶς τοῖς μετέπειτα, οὐδὲ τὰς ἀεὶ παιδείας
λίχνους ἡμετέρας παρῆλθεν ἀκοάς. ἔστι δὲ τοιόσ-
δε· ἡνίκα, φασί, τὸν σύμπαντα κόσμον ὁ ποιητὴς
ἐτελεσφόρησεν, ἑνὸς τῶν ὑποφητῶν ἐπύθετο, εἴ τι
ποθεῖ μὴ γενόμενον τῶν ὅσα κατὰ γῆς καὶ καθ'
ὕδατος ἢ ὅσα κατὰ τὴν μετάρσιον ἀέρος ἢ τὴν
128   ἐσχάτην τοῦ παντὸς φύσιν οὐρανοῦ γέγονεν. ὁ
δὲ ἀπεκρίνατο τέλεια μὲν καὶ πλήρη πάντα διὰ
πάντων εἶναι, ἓν δὲ μόνον ζητεῖν, τὸν ἐπαινέτην
αὐτῶν λόγον, ὃς τὰς ἐν πᾶσι καὶ τοῖς βραχυτάτοις

---

[1] mss. μὲν ἀριθμός.   [2] ⟨ὃς⟩ conj. Tr.

---

[a] Or " prophets," " interpreters."

to other numbers, even and complete and full and, in a loose sense, universal, owing to the fact that 10, the offspring of 4, is fixed as first turning-point of the numbers from 1 onwards in a series. And 10 and 4 are said to be " all " or " totality " among numbers; 10 being so in realized actuality, and 4 potentially.

XXX. Quite appropriately does Moses speak of 126 the fruit of instruction as being not only " holy " but " for praise "; for each of the virtues is a holy matter, but thanksgiving is pre-eminently so. But it is not possible genuinely to express our gratitude to God by means of buildings and oblations and sacrifices, as is the custom of most people, for even the whole world were not a temple adequate to yield the honour due to Him. Nay, it must be expressed by means of hymns of praise, and these not such as the audible voice shall sing, but strains raised and re-echoed by the mind too pure for eye to discern. Indeed there is an old story on men's 127 lips, the invention of wise men, and handed down by memory to succeeding generations of posterity, which has not escaped my ears which are for ever greedy for teaching. It is to this effect. When, they say, the Creator had finished the whole world, He inquired of one of His subordinates [a] whether he missed as having failed to be created aught of created things beneath the earth or beneath the water, aught found in air's high realm or heaven's, furthest of all realms that are. He, it is said, 128 made answer that all were perfect and complete in all their parts, and that he was looking for one thing only, namely the word to sound their praises, which should make the surpassing excellence that

καὶ ἀφανεστάτοις δοκοῦσιν ὑπερβολὰς οὐκ ἐπαι-
νέσει μᾶλλον ἢ ἐξαγγελεῖ· τὰς γὰρ διηγήσεις τῶν
τοῦ θεοῦ ἔργων αὐταρκέστατον ἐκείνων ἔπαινον
εἶναι, προσθήκης οὐδεμιᾶς ἔξωθεν εἰς κόσμον δεομέ-
νων, ἀλλὰ τὸ ἀψευδὲς τῆς ἀληθείας τελειότατον
129 ἐχόντων ἐγκώμιον. ἀκούσαντα δὲ τὸν πατέρα τοῦ
παντὸς τὸ λεχθὲν ἐπαινέσαι, καὶ οὐκ εἰς μακρὰν τὸ
πάμμουσον καὶ ὑμνῳδὸν ἀναφανῆναι γένος ἐκ μιᾶς
δὴ τῶν περὶ αὐτὸν δυνάμεων παρθένου Μνήμης,
ἣν Μνημοσύνην παρατρέποντες οἱ πολλοὶ τοὔνομα
καλοῦσιν.
130 XXXI. Ὁ μὲν οὖν τῶν παλαιῶν μῦθος ὧδε
ἔχει. ἑπόμενοι δὲ ἡμεῖς αὐτῷ λέγομεν, ὅτι οἰκειό-
τατόν ἐστιν ἔργον θεῷ μὲν εὐεργετεῖν, γενέσει[1] δὲ
εὐχαριστεῖν μηδὲν ἔξω τούτου πλέον τῶν εἰς
ἀμοιβὴν ἀντιπαρασχεῖν δυναμένῃ[2]· ὃ γὰρ ἂν θελή-
σῃ τῶν ἄλλων ἀντιχαρίσασθαι, τοῦθ' εὑρήσεται τοῦ
πάντα πεποιηκότος ἀλλ' οὐ τῆς κομιζούσης φύσεως
131 κτῆμα ἴδιον. μαθόντες οὖν, ὡς ἓν ἔργον ἡμῖν ἐπι-
βάλλει μόνον ἐν τοῖς πρὸς τιμὴν θεοῦ, τὸ εὐ-
χάριστον, τοῦτο ἀεὶ καὶ πανταχοῦ μελετῶμεν
διὰ φωνῆς καὶ διὰ γραμμάτων ἀστείων καὶ
μηδέποτε ἐπιλείπωμεν μήτε λόγους ἐγκωμιαστι-
κοὺς μήτε ποιήματα συντιθέντες, ἵνα καὶ ἐμμελῶς καὶ χωρὶς μέλους καὶ καθ' ἑκατέραν φωνῆς
ἰδέαν, ᾗ τὸ λέγειν καὶ τὸ ᾄδειν ἀποκεκλήρωται, ὅ
τε κοσμοποιὸς καὶ ὁ κόσμος γεραίρηται, "ὁ μέν,"
[349] ὡς ἔφη τις, | "ἄριστος τῶν αἰτίων, ὁ δὲ τελειό-
τατος τῶν γεγονότων."

---

[1] mss. θεὸν . . . γένεσιν.   [2] mss. -ην or -ων.

marked even the most minute and inconspicuous among them the subject of announcement rather than of praise, seeing that the mere recounting of the works of God was in itself their all-sufficient praise, for they needed the embellishment of no extraneous additions, but possessed in the reality that could not lie their most perfect encomium. The story runs 129 that the Author of the universe on hearing this commended what had been said, and that it was not long before there appeared the new birth, the family of the Muses [a] and hymnody, sprung from the womb of one of His powers, even virgin Memory, whose name most people slightly change and call her "Mnemosyne."

XXXI. So runs the myth of the men of old. We 130 take the same line and say that the work most appropriate to God is conferring boons, that most fitting to creation giving thanks, seeing that it has no power to render in return anything beyond this; for, whatever else it may have thought of giving in requital, this it will find to be the property of the Maker of all things, and not of the being that brings it. Having learned, then, that, in all that has to do 131 with shewing honour to God, one work only is incumbent upon us, namely thanksgiving, let us always and everywhere make this our study, using voice and skilful pen. Let us never tire of composing eulogies in prose and poetry, to the end that, whether with or without musical accompaniment whichever of its appointed functions the voice may exercise, be it eloquent speech or song, high honour may be given both to the world and to the Creator of the world; the former, as one has said, [b] the most perfect of things produced, the latter the best of producers.

132 XXXII. Ἐπειδὰν οὖν ἔτει καὶ ἀριθμῷ τετάρτῳ πᾶς ὁ ψυχῆς ἀφιερωθῇ καρπός, τῷ πέμπτῳ τὴν ἀπόλαυσιν καὶ χρῆσιν ἡμεῖς αὐτοὶ σχήσομεν.[1] φησὶ γάρ· '' ἐν τῷ ἔτει τῷ πέμπτῳ φάγεσθε τὸν καρπόν,'' ἐπειδὴ τὸ γεγονὸς τοῦ πεποιηκότος ὕστερον ἐν ἅπασιν ἐξετάζεσθαι νόμος φύσεως ἀνεπίληπτος, ὥστε κἄν, εἰ τῶν δευτερείων ἀντιλαμβανοίμεθα, καὶ θαυμαστὸν ἡγεῖσθαι.

133 καὶ διὰ τοῦτο μέντοι τὸν καρπὸν τοῦ πέμπτου ἡμῖν ἀνατίθησιν, ὅτι αἰσθήσεως πεντὰς ἀριθμὸς οἰκεῖος καί, εἰ δεῖ τἀληθὲς εἰπεῖν, τὸ τρέφον τὸν νοῦν ἡμῶν ἐστιν αἴσθησις, ἢ δι' ὀφθαλμῶν τὰς χρωμάτων καὶ σχημάτων ποιότητας εὐτρεπίζουσα ἢ δι' ὤτων παντοδαπὰς τὰς τῶν φωνῶν ἰδιότητας ἢ διὰ μυκτήρων ὀσμὰς ἢ χυλοὺς διὰ στόματος ἢ μαλακότητας εὐενδότους καὶ σκληρότητας ἀντιτύπους ἢ λειότητας καὶ τραχύτητας, ⟨ψυχρότητάς⟩ τε αὖ καὶ θερμότητας διὰ τῆς ἀνὰ πᾶν τὸ σῶμα σκιδναμένης δυνάμεως ἣν ἔθος ὀνομάζειν ἁφήν.

134 XXXIII. Τῶν δὲ εἰρημένων παράδειγμα σαφέστατον οἱ Λείας υἱοί, τῆς ἀρετῆς, οὐχ ἅπαντες, ἀλλὰ τέταρτός τε καὶ πέμπτος. ἐπὶ μὲν γὰρ τοῦ τετάρτου φησὶ Μωυσῆς, ὅτι '' ἔστη τοῦ τίκτειν,'' καλεῖται δὲ Ἰούδας, ὃς ἑρμηνεύεται κυρίῳ ἐξομολόγησις. τὸν δὲ πέμπτον Ἰσσάχαρ προσαγορεύει, μισθὸς δὲ μεταληφθεὶς καλεῖται. καὶ τεκοῦσα τὸν τρόπον τοῦτον ἡ ψυχὴ ὃ ἔπαθεν εὐθὺς ἐξελάλησεν· '' ἐκάλεσε'' γάρ φησι '' τὸ ὄνομα αὐτοῦ Ἰσσάχαρ, ὅ

135 ἐστι μισθός.''   οὐκοῦν Ἰούδας ὁ εὐλογῶν τὸν

[1] MSS. αὐτοῖς χρήσομεν.

XXXII. When, therefore, in the fourth year and 132
in the number 4 all the soul's fruit shall have been
consecrated, in the fifth year and in the number 5
we ourselves shall get the enjoyment and use of it ;
for he says, " in the fifth year ye shall eat the fruit."
This accords with nature's incontrovertible law, that
the place of creation is in all things lower than that
of the Creator. That is why Moses treats it as a
marvel that we should be recipients even of secondary
privileges.   Again, the reason why he 133
ascribes to us the fruit of the fifth year and number
is that 5 is the number proper to sense-perception,
and that, if we are to face facts, we must own that it
is sense-perception that supplies food to our mind.
By means of the eyes, it serves up to it the varying
qualities of colours and forms ; through the ears, the
peculiarities of sounds in all their diversity ; scents
by way of the nostrils ; savours by the palate ;
smoothness and roughness, yielding softness and
resistent hardness, nay coldness and heat as well, by
means of the faculty distributed over all the body,
which we are in the habit of calling " touch."

XXXIII. A very clear illustration of what has been 134
said is found in the sons of Leah, who is Virtue ; not
indeed in all of them, but in the fourth and fifth.
For, after recording the birth of the fourth, Moses
says that " she ceased from bearing " (Gen. xxx. 35),
and his name is " Judah," which signifies " confession
of praise to the Lord." The fifth she calls " Issachar,"
a name which interpreted means " reward." And
the soul, upon giving birth to this character, at once
gave utterance to her experience ; for it says, " She
called his name Issachar, which is ' reward ' " (Gen.
xxx. 18).   It follows that Judah, the 135

PHILO

θεὸν νοῦς καὶ τὰς εἰς αὐτὸν εὐχαρίστους ὑμνῳδίας
ἀπαύστως μελετῶν αὐτὸς ὁ πρὸς ἀλήθειαν " ἅγιος
καὶ αἰνετὸς καρπὸς " ἦν, οὐχ ὑπὸ γῆς δένδρων,
ἀλλ' ὑπὸ φύσεως λογικῆς καὶ σπουδαίας ἐνεχθείς.
παρὸ καὶ ἡ τεκοῦσα αὐτὸν φύσις " στῆναι "
λέγεται " τοῦ τίκτειν," ἐπεὶ καὶ πῇ τράπηται
οὐκ εἶχεν ἔτι, πρὸς τὸν τελειότητος ὅρον ἐλθοῦσα·
τῶν γὰρ ἀποκυηθέντων κατορθωμάτων ἁπάντων
ἄριστον καὶ τελειότατον γέννημα ὁ εἰς τὸν πατέρα
136 τοῦ παντὸς ὕμνος.   ὁ δὲ πέμπτος υἱὸς
τῆς κατὰ τὸν πέμπτον ἐνιαυτὸν τῶν φυτευθέντων
ἀδιαφορεῖ χρήσεως· ὅ τε γὰρ γεωπόνος μισθὸν
τρόπον τινὰ λαμβάνει παρὰ τῶν δένδρων ἔτει
πέμπτῳ καὶ τὸ τῆς ψυχῆς γέννημα Ἰσσάχαρ [ὃς
μισθὸς ἐκαλεῖτο, καὶ σφόδρα εἰκότως, μετὰ τὸν
[350] εὐχάριστον Ἰούδαν ἀποκυηθείς· τῷ γὰρ | εὐχαρίστῳ
μισθὸς αὐτὸ τὸ εὐχαριστεῖν αὐταρκέστατος.
137 οἱ μὲν οὖν τῶν δένδρων καρποὶ γεννήματα λέγονται
τῶν ἐχόντων, ὁ δὲ παιδείας καὶ φρονήσεως οὐκέτι
ἀνθρώπου, μόνου δέ, ὥς φησι Μωυσῆς, τοῦ
πανηγεμόνος· εἰπὼν γὰρ " τὰ γεννήματα αὐτοῦ "
ἐπιφέρει· " ἐγώ εἰμι κύριος ὁ θεὸς ὑμῶν," ἐναρ-
γέστατα παριστὰς ὅτι οὗ τὸ γέννημα καὶ ὁ τῆς
138 ψυχῆς καρπός, εἷς ἐστιν ὁ θεός. τούτῳ καὶ παρά
τινι τῶν προφητῶν χρησθὲν συνάδει τόδε· " ἐξ
ἐμοῦ ὁ καρπός σου εὕρηται. τίς σοφὸς καὶ συνήσει
ταῦτα; συνετὸς καὶ γνώσεται αὐτά;" οὐ γὰρ
παντὸς ἀλλὰ μόνου σοφοῦ τὸ γνῶναι, τίνος
ὁ διανοίας καρπός ἐστι.

---

a Or " right (truly virtuous) actions." See note on *Quod Deus* 100.

b See App. p. 497.

282

mind that blesses God, and is ceaselessly engaged in conning hymns of thanksgiving to Him, was himself the fruit that is really " holy and for praise to God," fruit borne not by earth's trees but by those of a rational and virtuous nature. Accordingly the nature which gave birth to him is said to have " ceased from bearing," because she had no longer any way to turn, having reached the utmost bound of perfectness ; for of all successful accomplishments[a] ever brought to the birth the best and most perfect is the hymn of praise to the Father of the universe.

The fifth son is identical with the using 136 in the fifth year of the trees that had been planted ; for, on the one hand, the husbandman does receive a sort of pay or reward from the trees in the fifth year, and, on the other, the offspring of the soul was called Issachar, " pay " or " reward." He was very naturally so called, having been born next after Judah the thanksgiver ; for the thanksgiver finds in thanksgiving itself an all-sufficient reward.

Now, whereas fruits borne by trees are called pro- 137 ducts of the persons who own them, the fruit of instruction and good sense is not like these spoken of as being a man's, but as belonging, as Moses says, to no other than the Ruler of all. For after the words, "His products,[b]" he adds, "I am the Lord your God," affording most clear proof that He to whom the product and the fruit of the soul pertains is One, even God. In harmony with this is the oracle given in 138 one of the prophets : " From Me is thy fruit found. Who is wise, and he shall understand these things ? understanding, and he shall know them ? " (Hosea xiv. 9 f.). For not everybody, but only the wise man knows, Whose is the fruit of intelligence.

139 XXXIV. Περὶ μὲν οὖν γεωργίας τῆς πρεσβυτάτης καὶ ἱερωτάτης, ᾗ τὸ αἴτιον πρὸς τὸν κόσμον, τὸ παμφορώτατον φυτῶν, χρῆται, καὶ περὶ τῆς ἑπομένης, ἣν ὁ ἀστεῖος ἐπιτηδεύει, καὶ περὶ τῆς φερομένης τετράδος τῶν ἄθλων[1] ἃ κατὰ προστάξεις καὶ ὑφηγήσεις νόμων συνεκροτεῖτο, ὡς 140 οἷόν τε ἦν εἴπομεν.   τὴν δὲ τοῦ δικαίου Νῶε ἀμπελουργικήν, εἶδος γεωργικῆς οὖσαν, ἐπισκεψώμεθα. λέγεται γὰρ ὅτι " ἤρξατο Νῶε ἄνθρωπος εἶναι γεωργὸς γῆς· καὶ ἐφύτευσεν ἀμπελῶνα, καὶ 141 ἔπιε τοῦ οἴνου, καὶ ἐμεθύσθη." οὐκοῦν τὸ μέθης φυτὸν ἐξεργάζεται τεχνικῶς καὶ ἐπιστημόνως ὁ δίκαιος τῶν ἀφρόνων ἄτεχνον καὶ πλημμελῆ ποιουμένων αὐτοῦ τὴν ἐπιστασίαν, ὥστε ἀναγκαῖον τὰ προσήκοντα περὶ μέθης εἰπεῖν· εὐθὺς γὰρ εἰσόμεθα καὶ τὴν δύναμιν τοῦ παρέχοντος αὐτῇ τὰς ἀφορμὰς φυτοῦ. τὰ μὲν οὖν εἰρημένα τῷ νομοθέτῃ περὶ μέθης εἰσόμεθα ἐπ' ἀκριβείας αὖθις, νυνὶ δὲ ἐξερευνήσωμεν ὅσα καὶ τοῖς ἄλλοις ἔδοξεν.

142 XXXV. Ἐσπουδάσθη δὲ παρὰ πολλοῖς τῶν φιλοσόφων ἡ σκέψις οὐ μετρίως. προτείνεται δὲ οὕτως, εἰ μεθυσθήσεται ὁ σοφός. ἔστι τοίνυν τὸ μεθύειν διττόν, ἓν μὲν ἴσον τι τῷ οἰνοῦσθαι, ἕτερον 143 δὲ ἴσον τῷ ληρεῖν ἐν οἴνῳ. τῶν δὲ ἐπιχειρησάντων τῇ προτάσει οἱ μὲν ἔφασαν μήτε ἀκράτῳ πλείονι χρήσεσθαι[2] τὸν σοφὸν μήτε ληρήσειν· τὸ μὲν γὰρ

---

[1] καὶ is omitted before ἃ κατὰ from Wendland's conj.
[2] mss. χρῆσθαι.

---

[a] See App. p. 497.
[b] Or "the word μεθύειν is used in two senses."
[c] See App. p. 498.

XXXIV. We have discoursed to the best of our 139 ability concerning the earliest and most sacred husbandry, plied by the First Cause in dealing with the world, that most fertile of plants ; and concerning the husbandry that comes next in order, carried on by the man of worth ; and concerning the number 4 [a] which carries off the prizes conferred upon it by the injunctions and directions found in laws. Let us now turn our attention to the righteous 140 Noah's work on his vineyard, which is a special form of husbandry. The account runs : " Noah began to be a husbandman, a tiller of the soil : and he planted a vineyard and drank of the wine, and became drunk " (Gen. ix. 20 f.). We see from these words that the righteous man tills the tree, that is the means of drunkenness, with skill and knowledge, while those who are devoid of good sense tend it in an unskilful and faulty way. This 141 renders it necessary for us to make some pertinent remarks regarding drunkenness; for, as we treat of it, we shall ascertain also the powers and properties of the tree which furnishes it with the material which produces it. The Lawgiver's words regarding drunkenness we shall acquaint ourselves with another time : let us at present engage in a thorough investigation of the sentiments of other persons.

XXXV. Many philosophers have given no slight 142 attention to the question ; which is propounded in the form " Will the wise man get drunk ? " Now, there are two ways of getting drunk [b] ; one is equivalent to drinking heavily, the other to being silly in your cups.[c] Among those who have tackled the 143 problem some have maintained that the wise man will neither take strong drink in excess nor become

ἁμάρτημα, τὸ δὲ ἁμαρτήματος εἶναι ποιητικόν,
144 ἑκάτερον δὲ ἀλλότριον κατορθοῦντος· οἱ δὲ τὸ μὲν
οἰνοῦσθαι καὶ σπουδαίῳ προσῆκον ἀπεφήναντο, τὸ
δὲ ληρεῖν ἀνοίκειον· τὴν γὰρ ἐν αὐτῷ φρόνησιν
ἱκανὴν εἶναι τοῖς βλάπτειν ἐπιχειροῦσιν ἀντι-
στατῆσαι καὶ τὸν ἐπὶ τῇ ψυχῇ[1] νεωτερισμὸν αὐτῶν
καθελεῖν· δύναμιν δὲ περιβεβλῆσθαι φρόνησιν
παθῶν σβεστήριον εἴτε ὑπὸ φλεγμαίνοντος ἔρωτος
οἴστρῳ[2] ἀνερριπισμένων εἴτε ὑπὸ πολλοῦ καὶ
ζέοντος ἐξημμένων οἴνου, δι' ἣν ὑπεράνω στήσεται·
[351] ἐπεὶ | καὶ τῶν κατὰ ποταμοῦ βαθέος ἢ θαλάττης
δυομένων οἱ μὲν ἄπειροι τοῦ ναυτίλλεσθαι διαφθεί-
ρονται, οἱ δὲ τοῦ πράγματος ἐπιστήμονες τάχιστα
διασῴζονται· καὶ μὴν ὥσπερ χειμάρρους ὁ πολὺς
ἄκρατος ἐπικλύζων τὴν ψυχὴν τοτὲ μὲν βρίθουσαν
εἰς ἀμαθίας ἔσχατον βυθὸν κατέρριψε, τοτὲ δὲ
ὑπὸ τῆς σωτηρίου παιδείας ἐπικουφιζομένην καὶ
ἐπελαφριζομένην οὐδὲν ἴσχυσε βλάψαι.
145 οἱ δὲ τὸ μέγεθος τῆς περὶ τὸ πάθος ὑπερβολῆς οὐ
κατανοήσαντες, οἶμαι, τοῦ σοφοῦ μετεωροπολοῦντα
αὐτὸν ὥσπερ οἱ τὰ πτηνὰ θηρῶντες ἐπὶ γῆν ἀπ'
οὐρανοῦ κατεβίβασαν, ἵν' εἰς τὰς ὁμοίας κῆρας
ἀγάγωσιν, οὐδ' ἱδρύοντες[3] ἀρετῆς εἰς ὕψος ἔφασαν,
ὅτι χρησάμενος οἴνῳ πλείονι τοῦ μετρίου πάντως
ἀκράτωρ αὐτὸς ἑαυτοῦ γενόμενος διαμαρτήσεται
καὶ οὐ χεῖρας μόνον ὑπ' ἀσθενείας οἷα τῶν ἀθλητῶν
οἱ νενικημένοι καθείς, ἀλλὰ καὶ αὐχένα καὶ κεφαλὴν
παραβαλὼν καὶ ὀκλάσας καὶ ὅλον τὸ σῶμα κατα-

---

[1] τῇ ψυχῇ is kept with mss.: Wend. τὴν ψυχήν.
[2] mss. οἴστρῳ: Wend. οἴστρων.
[3] ἱδρύοντες conj. Tr.: U ἱδρῶντες, MGF ἱδρῶτες.

ᵃ See App. p. 498.

silly and maudlin; the latter being a sin, and the former productive of sin, and both alike alien to him whose standard of conduct is the highest. Others, while regarding a condition of silliness as 144 foreign to a man of moral excellence, have pronounced heavy drinking to befit him, seeing that the good sense which resides in him is capable of holding its own against everything that attempts to injure him, and of baffling their efforts to change the constitution of his soul. They hold that good sense is an armour which has power to quench passions, whether fanned by the stinging blasts of inflaming love, or kindled by the heat of much wine; and that in virtue of his good sense he will come off victorious. They point out that, when people sink in a deep river or in the sea, those who cannot swim are drowned, while those who know how to swim escape at once; and that a quantity of strong drink is like a torrent washing over the soul; in one case, as it sinks, plunging it into the lowest depth of ignorance, in another case, as it is buoyed up and kept afloat by salutary instruction, altogether powerless to hurt it.   The others,[a] 145 failing, as I think, to recognize the completeness of the wise man's superiority to every passion, have brought him down to earth from heaven whose skies he haunts, treating him as fowlers treat the birds they catch, and being bent on bringing him into as evil a plight, and not setting him on virtue's lofty summit, have declared that after taking an immoderate quantity of wine he will certainly lose self-control and commit sin, and not only, like vanquished athletes, let his hands fall from sheer weakness, but let his neck and head drop and his knees give way, and, collapsing in

PHILO

146 συρεὶς ἀναπεσεῖται. XXXVI. τοῦτο μέντοι προ-
μαθὼν οὐκ ἄν ποτε ἀξιώσειεν ἑκὼν εἰς πολυοινίας
ἀγῶνα ἐλθεῖν, εἰ μὴ μεγάλα εἴη τὰ διαφέροντα,
σωτηρία πατρίδος ἢ τιμὴ γονέων ἢ τέκνων καὶ
τῶν οἰκειοτάτων σωμάτων ἀσφάλεια ἢ συνόλως
147 ἰδίων τε καὶ κοινῶν ἐπανόρθωσις πραγμάτων. οὐδὲ
γὰρ θανάσιμον φάρμακον προσενέγκαιτο ἄν, εἰ μὴ
πάνυ βιάζοιντο οἱ καιροὶ καθάπερ ἐκ πατρίδος
μετανίστασθαι τοῦ βίου· φάρμακον δέ, εἰ καὶ οὐ
θανάτου, μανίας γοῦν ἄκρατον εἶναι αἴτιον συμβέβηκε. διὰ τί δ' οὐχὶ καὶ μανίαν λεκτέον
θάνατον, ᾧ τὸ κράτιστον ἀποθνήσκει τῶν ἐν ἡμῖν,
ὁ νοῦς; ἀλλά μοι δοκεῖ τις ἄν εἰκότως τὸν δια-
κρίνοντα καὶ διαλύοντα ψυχήν τε καὶ σῶμα ὡς
κουφότερον ἀντὶ βαρυτέρου τοῦ κατὰ τὴν ἔκστασιν,
148 εἴ τις ἦν αἵρεσις, ἀνενδοιάστως ἑλέσθαι. διὰ τοῦτο
μέντοι καὶ τὸν εὑρετὴν τῆς περὶ τὸν οἶνον ἐργασίας
μαινόλην ἐκάλεσαν οἱ πρῶτοι καὶ τὰς ἐξ αὐτοῦ
κατασχέτους γενομένας βάκχας μαινάδας, ἐπεὶ
μανίας καὶ παραφροσύνης αἴτιος τοῖς ἀπλήστως
ἐμφορουμένοις ὁ οἶνος.

149 XXXVII. Τὰ μὲν οὖν ὡσανεὶ προοίμια τῆς
σκέψεως τοιαῦτά ἐστι, τὸν δὲ περὶ αὐτῆς λόγον
ἤδη περαίνωμεν διπλοῦν ὡς εἰκὸς ὄντα, τὸν μὲν
ὅτι ὁ σοφὸς μεθυσθήσεται κατασκευάζοντα, τὸν
δὲ τοὐναντίον ὅτι οὐ μεθυσθήσεται βεβαιούμενον.
150 τοῦ δὲ προτέρου τὰς πίστεις ἁρμόττον λέγειν
πρότερον, ποιησαμένους ἐνθένδε τὴν ἀρχήν· τῶν

---

a Or "entirely lose heart."

every part, sink to the ground.[a] XXXVI. Having 146
learned this beforehand he will never think fit
voluntarily to engage in a drinking-contest, unless
the matters at issue are of great moment, a fatherland's deliverance, respect for parents, children's
safety or that of the persons of those very near and
dear, or, in a word, a putting on a right footing
of private and public concerns. No more would a wise 147
man take a deadly poison, unless the crisis were such
as absolutely to compel him to depart from life as
though he were leaving his country. And strong
drink *is* a poison bringing about not death indeed but
madness. And yet why should we not call madness
death, seeing that by it mind dies, the noblest part
of us ? Nay it appears to me that, were a choice
offered, a man would be likely to choose without
hesitation the death that separates and dissolves
the union of soul and body, in preference to that of
going out of one's senses, feeling that he was choosing
the lighter in place of the heavier. It was for this 148
reason that the earliest inhabitants of the world
called the inventor of the culture of the vine Maenoles
and the Bacchants whom its frenzy seized Maenads,
since wine is the cause of madness and loss of sound
sense in those who imbibe it over freely.

XXXVII. Such then is what we may call the pre- 149
lude to our inquiry. It is time for us to state in
full the argument bearing upon it. That argument
obviously admits of two contentions, one establishing
the thesis that the wise man will get drunk, the
other maintaining the contrary, that he will not get
drunk. It will be convenient to take first the 150
proofs by which the former thesis is supported. We
will begin by remarking that some things are

πραγμάτων τὰ μὲν ὁμώνυμα, τὰ δὲ συνώνυμα
εἶναι συμβέβηκεν. ὁμωνυμία δὲ καὶ συνωνυμία
[352] τἀναντία ὁμολογεῖται, | ὅτι ὁμωνυμία μὲν κατὰ
πολλῶν ὑποκειμένων ἓν ὄνομα, συνωνυμία δὲ καθ᾿
151 ἑνὸς ὑποκειμένου <πολλά>.   ἡ κυνὸς
φωνὴ πάντως ὁμώνυμος ἐμφερομένων πλειόνων
ἀνομοίων, ἃ δι᾿ αὐτῆς σημαίνεται· τό τε γὰρ
χερσαῖον ὑλακτικὸν ζῷον κύων καὶ θὴρ ὁ θαλάττιος
καὶ ὁ οὐράνιος ἀστήρ, ὃν ὀπωρινὸν οἱ ποιηταὶ
καλοῦσιν, ὅτι τῆς ὀπώρας ἄρτι ἡβώσης ἐπιτέλλει
τοῦ τελεσφορηθῆναί τε χάριν αὐτὴν καὶ πεπανθῆναι,
καὶ προσέτι ὁ ἀπὸ τῆς κυνικῆς αἱρέσεως ὁρμηθεὶς
φιλόσοφος, Ἀρίστιππος καὶ Διογένης καὶ ἄλλων
οἳ τὰ αὐτὰ ἐπιτηδεύειν ἠξίωσαν ἀπερίληπτος
152 ἀριθμὸς ἀνθρώπων.   ἄλλαι δ᾿ εἰσὶ προσρήσεις διάφοροι κατὰ σημαινομένου ἑνὸς ὡς ἰός,
ὀϊστός, βέλος— τὸ γὰρ διὰ τῆς τόξου νευρᾶς ἐπὶ
τὸν σκοπὸν ἀφιέμενον πάντα ταῦτα λέγεται—· καὶ
πάλιν εἰρεσία, κώπη, πλάτη, τὸ πρὸς πλοῦν
ἰσοδυναμοῦν ἱστίοις· ὁπότε γὰρ μὴ δύναιτο χρῆσθαι
ναῦς κατὰ νηνεμίας ἢ ἀντιπνοίας ἱστίοις, πρόσκωποι
καθίσαντες οἷς ἐπιμελὲς καὶ οἷα ταρσοὺς ἑκατέρω-
θεν ἀποτείναντες ὑπόπτερον αὐτὴν φέρεσθαι βιά-
ζονται, ἡ δὲ ἐξαιρομένη πρὸς ὕψος, ἐπιτρέχουσα
τοῖς κύμασι μᾶλλον ἢ ἐντέμνουσα ταῦτα, τρο-
χάζουσα ταχυναυτεῖ καὶ ναυλοχωτάτοις ὑποδρόμοις
153 ἐνορμίζεται.   καὶ μὴν πάλιν σκίπων,
βακτηρία, ῥάβδος ἑνὸς ὑποκειμένου διάφοροι

---

[a] ἐμφέρεσθαι, here used of different senses being *implied*
in one word, is found in § 154 in the sense of "occur,"
"be used."

homonymous and others synonymous. Everyone will allow that homonymy and synonymy are opposites, homonymy meaning one name applied to many objects, synonymy many names applied to one object. The word " dog " is certainly 151 homonymous, several dissimilar objects being included under it,*a* all of which it is used to signify. The barking animal on the land is a " dog "; so is the monster found in the sea ; and the star in the heavens which the poets call the fruit star, because just when the summer fruit has reached its prime this star rises to bring it to perfection and to ripen it. The name " dog " is applied moreover to the man whose philosophy takes its colour from the Cynic school, Aristippus, Diogenes, and ever so many others who found it congenial to conform themselves to their principles.

There are other names which are different though 152 one thing is meant by them, as " arrow," " shaft," " dart "; for the thing discharged at the mark from the string of the bow is called by all these names. Again, the instrument which does as well as sails for propelling a vessel is called an " oar," " scull," " rowing-sweep." For when, owing to a calm or head wind, a vessel cannot make use of sails, the men, whose business it is, take their seats at the oars, and stretching out from each side wing-like blades, force the vessel to be borne along as though it were flying. The vessel, lifted high out of the water, not so much cutting the waves as coursing over them, makes a quick run, and is soon safely moored in harbour.

Once more " staff," " walking-stick," 153 " rod " are different names by which we call one object, with which we can beat someone, on which

κλήσεις, ᾧ τύπτειν καὶ ἀκραδάντως σκηρίπτεσθαι
καὶ ἐπερείδεσθαι καὶ ἄλλα πλείω ποιεῖν ἔνεστι.
ταῦτα δ' οὐ μακρολογοῦντες ὅλως εἴπομεν, ἀλλ'
ὑπὲρ τοῦ σαφέστερον γνῶναι τὸ ζητούμενον.

154 XXXVIII. τὸν ἄκρατον ὥσπερ οἶνον,
οὕτως καὶ μέθυ οἱ παλαιοὶ ἐκάλουν· πολλαχοῦ γοῦν
τῆς ποιήσεώς ἐστι τουτὶ τοὔνομα ἐμφερόμενον,
ὥστ' εἰ τὰ συνωνυμοῦντα καθ' ἑνὸς ὑποκειμένου
λέγεται, οἶνος καὶ μέθυ, καὶ τὰ ἀπὸ τούτων οὐδὲν
ὅτι μὴ φωναῖς διοίσει μόνον, τό τε οἰνοῦσθαι καὶ
155 τὸ μεθύειν [ἕν]· ἑκάτερον δὲ πλείονος οἴνου χρῆσιν
ἐμφαίνει, ἣν πολλῶν ἕνεκα αἰτιῶν οὐκ ἂν ἀπο-
στρέφοιτο ὁ σπουδαῖος. εἰ δὲ οἰνωθήσεται, καὶ
μεθυσθήσεται, χεῖρον οὐδὲν ἐκ τῆς μέθης διατεθείς,
ἀλλὰ ταὐτὸν ὅπερ καὶ [ὁ] ἐκ ψιλῆς τῆς οἰνώσεως
παθών.

156 Μία μὲν ἀπόδειξις περὶ τοῦ τὸν σοφὸν μεθυσθῆναι
λέλεκται, δευτέρα δ' ἐστὶ τοιαύτη· σχεδὸν οἱ νῦν
ἄνθρωποι τοῖς προτέροις ἔξω μέρους βραχέος
οὐδὲν ὁμοιότροπον ζηλοῦν ἀξιοῦσιν, ἀλλὰ καὶ ἐν
λόγοις καὶ ἐν ἔργοις τὸ μὴ συνῳδὸν καὶ διαφωνοῦν
157 ἐπιδείκνυνται· τοὺς μὲν γὰρ λόγους ὑγιαίνοντας
καὶ ἐρρωμένους εἰς πάθος ἀνήκεστον καὶ φθορὰν
περιήγαγον ἀντὶ σφριγώσης καὶ ἀθλητικῆς ὄντως
[353] | εὐεξίας οὐδὲν ὅτι μὴ νοσοῦν κατασκευάσαντες
καὶ τὸν πλήρη καὶ ναστόν, ὡς ἔφη τις, ὑπ' εὐ-
τονίας ὄγκον εἰς παρὰ φύσιν οἰδούσης καχεξίας

---

[a] *i.e.* "in many cases the wise man would see no reason
for avoiding this."

we can firmly support ourselves, on which we can lean, and with which we can do several other things. I have given these examples, not just because my tongue runs on, but that we may get a clearer idea of the subject which we are investigating.

XXXVIII. The ancients called strong 154 drink " wine " and an " intoxicant " indifferently : as we see from the frequency with which this last word occurs in poetry. If, then, " wine " and " intoxicant " are used as synonyms of one object, their derivatives " to be filled with wine " and " to be intoxicated" will differ only in word; for either 155 term denotes taking more wine than usual, a thing which several motives[a] might induce a really excellent man to do. But if such an one will get filled with wine, he will get drunk, and be in no worse plight for being drunk, but in precisely the same state as he was brought to by being filled with wine.

One proof of the wise man's getting drunk has 156 been mentioned ; there is a second to the following effect. Broadly speaking, the men of the present day, apart from a small fraction of them, do not resemble those of former times in their aims and enthusiasms, but both in language and in action exhibit tendencies wholly out of harmony with theirs. Language that was once healthy and robust they 157 have turned into a jargon hopelessly depraved. For a style sound and full of vitality as an athlete's frame they have substituted a sickly form of speech. A full and massive type, possessed, as someone has said, of a solidity due to its firmness of fibre, they debase into a bloated mis-growth of disease, to which they give a seeming loftiness and grandeur by

ἀγαγόντες καὶ κενῷ φυσήματι μόνον ἐπαίροντες,
ὃ δι' ἔνδειαν τῆς συνεχούσης δυνάμεως, ὅταν
158 μάλιστα περιταθῇ, ῥήγνυται. τὰς δὲ πράξεις ἐπ-
αινέσεως[1] καὶ σπουδῆς ἀξίας καὶ αὐτάς, ὡς ἔπος
εἰπεῖν, ἄρρενας ἐξεθήλυναν αἰσχρὰς ἀντὶ καλῶν
ἐργαζόμενοι, ὡς ὀλίγους εἶναι παντάπασιν ἑκατέροις, ἔργοις τε καὶ λόγοις, ἀρχαιοτρόπου ζηλώσεως
159 ἐρῶντας.   τοιγαροῦν ἐπ' ἐκείνων ποιηταὶ
καὶ λογογράφοι καὶ ὅσοι περὶ τὰ ἄλλα μουσικῆς
ἐσπούδαζον ἤνθουν, οὐ τὰς ἀκοὰς διὰ τῆς ἐν
ῥυθμοῖς φωνῆς ἀφηδύνοντές τε καὶ θρύπτοντες,
ἀλλὰ εἴ τι τῆς διανοίας κατεαγὸς καὶ κεκλασμένον
ἐγείροντες καὶ ὅσον ἐμμελὲς αὐτῆς ἁρμοζόμενοι
φύσεως καὶ ἀρετῆς ὀργάνοις[2]· ἐφ' ἡμῶν δὲ ὀψαρ-
τυταὶ καὶ σιτοπόνοι καὶ ὅσοι τῆς ἐν βαφικῇ καὶ
μυρεψικῇ τεχνῖται περιεργίας, ἀεί τι καινὸν χρῶμα
ἢ σχῆμα ἢ ἀτμὸν ἢ χυλὸν ἐπιτειχίζοντες ταῖς
αἰσθήσεσιν, ὅπως τὸν ἡγεμόνα πορθήσωσι νοῦν.

160 XXXIX. Τίνος δὴ χάριν τούτων ἐμνήσθην;
ἵν' ἐπιδείξω, ὅτι καὶ τὸν ἄκρατον οὐχ ὁμοίως οἱ
νῦν τοῖς πάλαι προσφέρονται. νῦν μὲν γὰρ ἄχρι
τοῦ σῶμα καὶ ψυχὴν παρεθῆναι πίνουσιν ἀθρόως
καὶ ἀπνευστί, χαίνοντες ἔτι καὶ προσεπιφέρειν
τοῖς οἰνοχοουμένοις κελεύοντες, κἂν διαμέλλωσιν
ἀγανακτοῦντες, ὅτι τὸν θερμὸν λεγόμενον παρ' αὐτοῖς πότον[3] παραψύχουσι, καὶ τὸ παράκομμα τῶν

---

[1] mss. γενέσεως.   [2] mss. ὀργίοις.
[3] mss. ποτόν.

empty puffing and blowing, which, in default of any
confining power, bursts when distention has reached
its limit.   Actions, meriting praise and calling out 158
enthusiasm, and, if the expression may be permitted,
masculine, they have rendered effeminate, and in
performing them made them base instead of noble.
The result is that whether on the side of action
or of speech, there are very few indeed who take
delight in the objects that kindled the ardour of
the men of old.   Consequently in their 159
times poets and chroniclers flourished and all who
engaged in literary work of other kinds, and they
did not at once charm and enervate men's ears by
the rhythm of their language, but they revived any
faculty of the mind that had broken down and
lost its tone, and every true note of it they kept in
tune with the instruments of nature and of virtue.
But in our days it is chefs and confectioners that
flourish, and experts in making dyes and concocting
unguents.   These are ever aiming at sacking the
citadel of Mind, by bringing to bear upon the senses
some novelty in shade of colour or shape of dress
or perfume or savoury dish.

XXXIX. What has been my object in recalling 160
these things ?   My object has been to make it clear
that the modern way of taking strong drink is not
the same as the ancient way.   For nowadays men go
on till body and soul are unstrung, drinking huge
draughts without stopping, open-mouthed for more,
and ordering the servants to replenish the cups they
have just filled and shewing arrogance if they delay,
because all such delay cools what they are pleased
to call the "heat" of the carousal.   They give an
exhibition to their fellow-guests of that counterfeit

γυμνικῶν, τὸν παροίνιον ἀγῶνα, πρὸς τοὺς συν-
όντας ἐπιδείκνυνται, ἐν ᾧ μεγάλα καὶ καλὰ
ἀλλήλους ἀντιδρῶσιν, ὦτα καὶ ῥῖνας καὶ χειρῶν
ἄκρους δακτύλους καὶ ὁποῖα δ' ἂν τύχῃ μέρη τοῦ
161 σώματος ἀπεσθίοντες. ταῦτ' ἐστὶ τῆς
ἡβώσης καὶ νεωτέρας καὶ ἄρτι ἀκμαζούσης ἆθλα,
ὡς ἔοικεν, εὐφροσύνης, τῆς δὲ ἀρχαίας καὶ πρεσβυτέρας τἀναντία· πάσης γὰρ καλῆς πράξεως
ἀφ' ἱερῶν τελείων οἱ πρότεροι κατήρχοντο, νομίζοντες μάλιστα οὕτως αἴσιον ἀποβήσεσθαι τὸ
τέλος αὐτοῖς, καὶ πρὶν εὔξασθαί τε καὶ θῦσαι, καὶ
εἰ σφόδρα τοῦ πράττειν ἐπέσπευδον οἱ καιροί,
πάντως ἀνέμενον οὐκ ἀεὶ τὸ ταχὺ τοῦ βραδέος
ἡγούμενοι κρεῖττον· οὐ προμηθὲς μὲν γὰρ τάχος
βλαβερόν, βραδυτὴς δὲ μετ' εὐελπιστίας ὠφέλιμον.
162 εἰδότες οὖν, ὅτι καὶ ἡ τοῦ οἴνου
ἀπόλαυσίς τε καὶ χρῆσις δεῖται πολλῆς ἐπιμελείας,
[354] οὔτε ἄδην¹ | οὔτε ἀεὶ προσεφέροντο τὸν ἄκρατον,
ἀλλ' ἔν τε κόσμῳ καὶ καιρῷ προσήκοντι. πρότερον γὰρ εὐξάμενοι καὶ θυσίας ἀναγαγόντες καὶ
ἱλασάμενοι τὸ θεῖον, σώματα καὶ ψυχὰς καθηρά-
μενοι, τὰ μὲν λουτροῖς, τὰ δὲ νόμων καὶ παιδείας
ὀρθῆς ῥεύμασι, φαιδροὶ καὶ γεγηθότες πρὸς ἀν-
ειμένην δίαιταν ἐτρέποντο, μηδὲ οἴκαδε πολλάκις
ἀφικόμενοι, ἀλλ' ἐν οἷς ἔθυσαν ἱεροῖς διατελοῦντες,
ἵνα καὶ τῶν θυσιῶν μεμνημένοι καὶ τὸν τόπον
αἰδούμενοι ἱεροπρεπεστάτην ὡς ἀληθῶς ἄγωσιν
εὐωχίαν, μήτε λόγῳ μήτε ἔργῳ διαμαρτάνοντες.²
163 ἀπὸ τούτου γέ τοι φασὶ τὸ μεθύειν

---

¹ mss. ἄρδην. ² mss. διαπατοῦντες.

parody of the athletic games, namely the tipsy contest. In this they practise on one another magnificent passes, gnawing off ears and noses and tops of fingers and any parts of the body that come handy.

These are, apparently, the contests indulged in by the gladness of these later times, which flourishes to-day and is just reaching its full growth; but far other were those of the more lofty gladness of old. For our forefathers inaugurated every noble business with sacrifices duly offered, deeming that an auspicious result would by this means be ensured. However urgently the crisis might call for immediate action, they never failed to tarry to pray and offer sacrifices beforehand, deeming that what is rapid is not always superior to what is slow; for rapidity without forethought is hurtful, while slowness prompted by the prospect of a happy issue is beneficial. Knowing, then, that, like other things, the use and enjoyment of wine needs great care, they took strong drink neither in great quantity nor at all times, but in such order and season as was befitting. For after having first prayed and presented sacrifices and implored the favour of the Deity, when they had cleansed their bodies by ablutions and their souls by streams of holy ordinances and instructions in the right way, radiant and gladsome they turned to relaxation and enjoyment, in many cases not after returning home, but remaining in the temples in which they had sacrificed in order that both the recollection of their sacrifices and their reverence for the place might lead them to celebrate a festivity in actual truth most holy, sinning neither in word nor deed. You must know that it was from this, so it is said, that " getting drunk "

ὠνομάσθαι, ὅτι μετὰ τὸ θύειν ἔθος ἦν τοῖς πρότερον οἰνοῦσθαι. τίσι δὴ μᾶλλον οἰκεῖος ἂν εἴη
τῆς τοῦ ἀκράτου χρήσεως ὁ λεχθεὶς τρόπος ἢ
σοφοῖς ἀνδράσιν, οἷς καὶ τὸ πρὸ τῆς μέθης ἔργον
164 ἁρμόττει τὸ θύειν; σχεδὸν γὰρ οὐδὲ εἷς τῶν
φαύλων πρὸς ἀλήθειαν ἱερουργεῖ, κἂν ἐνδελεχεῖς
μυρίους βόας ἀνὰ πᾶσαν ἡμέραν ἀνάγῃ[1]· τὸ γὰρ
ἀναγκαιότατον ἱερεῖον αὐτῷ λελώβηται, ὁ νοῦς,
λώβας δὲ οὐ θέμις βωμῶν προσάψασθαι.

165 Δεύτερος μὲν δὴ λόγος οὗτος εἴρηται, δεικνὺς
ὅτι οὐκ ἀλλότριον σπουδαίου τὸ μεθύειν, XL.
τρίτος δ᾽ ἐστὶν ἀπὸ διαφερούσης τῆς πρὸς τὴν
ἐτυμολογίαν πιθανότητος ἠρτημένος· τὴν γὰρ
μέθην οὐ μόνον, ἐπειδὴ μετὰ θυσίας ἐπιτελεῖται,
νομίζουσί τινες εἰρῆσθαι, ἀλλ᾽ ὅτι καὶ μεθέσεως
166 ψυχῆς αἰτία γίγνεται.   μεθίεται δὲ ὁ μὲν
τῶν ἀφρόνων λογισμὸς εἰς πλειόνων χύσιν[2] ἁμαρτημάτων, ὁ δὲ τῶν ἐμφρόνων εἰς ἀνέσεως καὶ
εὐθυμίας καὶ ἱλαρότητος ἀπόλαυσιν· ἡδίων γὰρ
αὐτὸς ἑαυτοῦ νήφοντος οἰνωθεὶς ὁ σοφὸς γίγνεται,
ὥστε οὐδ᾽ ἂν ταύτῃ διαμαρτάνοιμεν φάσκοντες ὅτι
167 μεθυσθήσεται.   πρὸς δὲ τούτοις κἀκεῖνο
λεκτέον, ὅτι οὐ σκυθρωπὸν καὶ αὐστηρὸν[3] τὸ τῆς
σοφίας εἶδος, ὑπὸ συννοίας καὶ κατηφείας ἐσταλ-
μένον, ἀλλ᾽ ἔμπαλιν ἱλαρὸν καὶ γαληνίζον, μεστὸν
γηθοσύνης καὶ χαρᾶς· ὑφ᾽ ὧν πολλάκις προήχθη

---

[1] mss. ἀγάγῃ.   [2] mss. ἴσχυσιν.   [3] mss. αὐχμηρὸν.

[a] See App. p. 498.
[b] Or "based on another and different form of the argument
from etymology." See App. p. 498.

got its name, because it was the custom of the men of earlier times to indulge in wine "after sacrificing."[a] Now with whom, I ask, would the mode of using strong drink just described be more in keeping than with wise men, with whose character the act which precedes the drunkenness, namely the act of sacrificing, is also in perfect accord ? For we may venture to say that there is not a single 164 bad man who really performs a sacrificial act, even though he lead to the altar in unceasing procession ten thousand bullocks every day ; for in his case the mind, the most essential victim, is a blemished thing, and no blemish may come into contact with an altar.

Such is a second argument put forward to shew 165 that getting drunk is not a thing inconsistent with moral excellence. XL. There is a third, possessing etymological plausibility[b] in a very high degree. For some hold that drunkenness is so termed, not only because it follows the performance of sacrifice, but because it is also the cause of a letting go or release of soul. It is to 166 give vent to many sins that the reasoning faculty of fools is let go, but that of sensible men for the enjoyment of relaxation, cheerfulness, and good spirits ; for the wise man becomes a more genial person after indulging in wine than when he is sober, and accordingly we should not be wrong in asserting on this ground as well as on those others that he will get drunk. We must re- 167 mark furthermore that the countenance of wisdom is not scowling and severe, contracted by deep thought and depression of spirit, but on the contrary cheerful and tranquil, full of joy and gladness, feelings which often prompt a man to be sportive and

τις οὐκ ἀμούσως παῖξαί τι καὶ χαριεντίσασθαι,
παιδιὰν μέντοι τῇ σεμνότητι καὶ σπουδῇ καθάπερ
ἐν ἡρμοσμένῃ λύρᾳ φθόγγοις ἀντιφώνοις εἰς ἑνὸς
168 μέλους κρᾶσιν συνηχοῦσαν.   κατὰ γοῦν
τὸν ἱερώτατον Μωυσῆν τέλος ἐστὶ σοφίας παιδιὰ
καὶ γέλως, ἀλλ' οὐχ ἃ τοῖς νηπίοις ἄνευ φρονήσεως πᾶσι μελετᾶται, ἀλλ' ἃ τοῖς ἤδη πολιοῖς οὐ
χρόνῳ μόνον ἀλλὰ καὶ βουλαῖς ἀγαθαῖς γεγονό-
σιν. οὐχ ὁρᾷς ὅτι τὸν αὐτήκοον καὶ αὐτομαθοῦς
καὶ αὐτουργοῦ τῆς ἐπιστήμης ἀρυσάμενον οὐ μετ-
έχοντα γέλωτος, ἀλλ' αὐτὸν γέλωτα εἶναί φησιν;
169 οὗτός ἐστιν Ἰσαάκ, ὃς ἑρμηνεύεται γέλως, ᾧ
παίζειν μετὰ τῆς ὑπομονῆς, ἣν Ῥεβέκκαν Ἑβραῖοι
[355] καλοῦσιν, ἁρμόττει. XLI. τὴν δὲ | θείαν παιδιὰν τῆς
ψυχῆς ἰδιώτῃ μὲν οὐ θέμις ἰδεῖν, βασιλεῖ δὲ ἔξεστιν,
ᾧ πάμπολυν χρόνον παρῴκησεν, εἰ καὶ μὴ πάντ'
ἐνῴκησε τὸν αἰῶνα, σοφία. προσαγορεύεται οὗτος
Ἀβιμέλεχ, ὃς διακύψας τῇ θυρίδι, τῷ διοιχθέντι
καὶ φωσφόρῳ τῆς διανοίας ὄμματι, τὸν Ἰσαὰκ εἶδε
παίζοντα μετὰ Ῥεβέκκας τῆς γυναικὸς αὐτοῦ.
170   τί γὰρ ἄλλο ἐμπρεπὲς[1] ἔργον
σοφῷ ἢ τὸ παίζειν καὶ γανοῦσθαι καὶ συνευφραί-
νεσθαι τῇ τῶν καλῶν ὑπομονῇ; ἐξ ὧν ὅτι καὶ
μεθυσθήσεται δῆλόν ἐστι τῆς μέθης ἠθοποιούσης
καὶ ἄνεσιν καὶ ἀφέλειαν[2] ἐργαζομένης· ὁ γὰρ
171 ἄκρατος τὰ τῇ φύσει προσόντα ἐπιτείνειν καὶ

---

[1] mss. ἐμπρέπει.
[2] mss. ὠφέλειαν: so Wend.: ἀφέλειαν is Mangey's conjecture.

jocular in a perfectly refined way. Such sportiveness is in harmony with a dignified self-respect, a harmony like that of a lyre tuned to give forth a single melody by a blending of answering notes.

Moses, at all events, holiest of men, 168 shews us that sport and merriment is the height of wisdom, not the sport which children of all sorts indulge in, paying no heed to good sense, but such as is seen in those who are now become grey-headed not only in respect of age but of thoughtfulness. Do you not observe that when he is speaking of the man who drew directly from the well of knowledge, listening to no other, learning through no other, resorting to no agency whatever, he does not say that he had a part in laughter, but that he was laughter itself? I am speaking of Isaac, whose name means 169 "laughter," and whom it well befits to sport with "patient waiting," who is called in Hebrew "Rebecca." XLI. For the sacred sporting of the soul is a sight not permissible to an ordinary citizen, but it is open to a king, with whom wisdom was for a very long time a guest, if indeed she did not make him her permanent abode. The name of this king is Abimelech. He looked out at the window, the mind's eye wide-opened and admitting light, and saw Isaac sporting with Rebecca his wife (Gen. xxvi. 8). What other occupation is 170 seemly for a wise man rather than bright sportiveness and making merry in the company of one who waits patiently for all that is beautiful? Hence it is evident that he will get drunk also, seeing that drunkenness benefits the character, saving it from overstrain and undue intensity. For strong drink is likely to intensify natural tend- 171

σφοδρύνειν ἔοικεν εἴτε καλὰ εἴτε καὶ τὰ ἐναντία,
καθάπερ καὶ πολλὰ τῶν ἄλλων· ἐπεὶ καὶ χρήματα
αἴτια μὲν ἀγαθῶν ⟨ἀγαθῷ⟩, κακῷ δέ, ὡς ἔφη
τις, κακῶν· καὶ πάλιν δόξα τοῦ μὲν ἄφρονος τὴν
κακίαν ἐπιφανεστέραν, τοῦ δὲ δικαίου τὴν ἀρετὴν
εὐκλεεστέραν ἐπιφαίνει. οὕτως οὖν καὶ ὁ ἄκρατος
ἀναχυθεὶς τὸν μὲν πάθεσι κεχρημένον ἐμπαθέστερον,[1]
τὸν δὲ εὐπαθείαις εὐμενέστερον καὶ ἵλεω μᾶλλον
ἀπειργάσατο.   τίς γε μὴν οὐκ οἶδεν,
172 ὅτι δυεῖν ἐναντίων ἐπειδὰν θάτερον εἶδος ἐφαρμόζῃ
πλείοσι, καὶ θάτερον ἐξ ἀνάγκης συμβήσεται;
οἷον λευκοῦ καὶ μέλανος ἐναντίων ὄντων, εἰ τὸ
λευκὸν ἀστείοις τε καὶ φαύλοις, καὶ τὸ μέλαν ἐξ
ἴσου δήπουθεν ἀμφοτέροις, οὐχὶ μόνοις προσέσται
τοῖς ἑτέροις. καὶ μὴν τό γε νήφειν καὶ τὸ μεθύειν
ἐναντία, μετέχουσι δὲ τοῦ νήφειν, ὡς ὁ τῶν προτέρων λόγος, ἀγαθοί τε καὶ φαῦλοι· ὥστε καὶ τὸ
μεθύειν ἑκατέρῳ τῶν εἰδῶν ἐφαρμόττει. μεθυσθήσεται τοιγάρτοι καὶ ὁ ἀστεῖος μηδὲν τῆς ἀρετῆς
ἀποβαλών.

XLII. Εἰ δ' ὥσπερ ἐν δικαστηρίῳ μὴ μόνον
173 ταῖς ἐντέχνοις ἀποδείξεσιν, ἀλλὰ καὶ ταῖς ἀτέχνοις
λεγομέναις χρηστέον, ὧν μία ἐστὶν ἡ διὰ τῶν
μαρτυριῶν, πολλοὺς καὶ εὐδοκίμους μαρτυροῦντας
παρεξόμεθα παῖδας ἰατρῶν καὶ φιλοσόφων, οὐ
λόγοις μόνον ἀλλὰ καὶ γράμμασι τὴν μαρτυρίαν
σημαινομένους. μυρίας γὰρ ἀπολελοίπασι συν-
174 τάξεις ἐπιγράψαντες περὶ μέθης, ἐν αἷς περὶ ψιλῆς
αὐτὸ μόνον χρήσεως οἴνου σκοποῦσιν, οὐδὲν περὶ

---

[1] mss. εὐπαθέστερον.

---

[a] See App. p. 498.   [b] See App. p. 499.

encies, whether good or the reverse, just as many other things do. Money, it has been said, is the cause of good things to a good man, of evil things to a bad man. Fame again makes the fool's badness more conspicuous, while it causes a brighter glory to rest upon the virtue of the righteous man. On this principle, therefore, a lavish use of strong drink places the man who has given the rein to his passions more completely at their mercy, while it makes him who has cherished right feelings *a* more kindly and well disposed. Again, all 172 know that when one of two opposite predicates is applicable to two or more sets of people, it cannot but be that the other is applicable also. For instance, black and white are opposites. If white is predicable of bad and good, black too will of course be equally so of both, not only of one of the two sets. So too soberness and drunkenness are opposites, and both bad and good men, so our forefathers said, partake of soberness. It follows that drunkenness also is predicable of both sorts. Accordingly the man of moral worth will get drunk as well as other people without losing any of his virtue.

XLII. If, just as in a court of law, we are to make 173 use, not only of the logical or dialectical proofs, but also of the modes of persuasion that are called "inartistic,*b*" one of which is that which employs evidence, we shall call as witnesses many distinguished physicians and philosophers, who ratify their evidence by writings as well as by words. For 174 they have left behind them innumerable treatises bearing the title "Concerning drunkenness," in which they deal with nothing but the subject of drinking wine at all, without adding a word of inquiry

τῶν ληρεῖν εἰωθότων προσεξετάζοντες, ἀλλ᾽ ὅλον
τὸ παροινίας παραπέμψαντες εἶδος· ὥστε καὶ
παρὰ τούτοις σαφέστατα ἀνωμολογῆσθαι, ὅτι τὸ
μεθύειν ἦν τὸ οἰνοῦσθαι. οἴνου δὲ σπάσαι πλείονος
οὐκ ἂν εἴη χεῖρον ἐν καιρῷ σοφόν· οὐ τοίνυν
[356] διαμαρτησόμεθα | λέγοντες ὅτι μεθυσθήσεται.

175 Ἐπεὶ δὲ οὐδεὶς καθ᾽ αὑτὸν ἀγωνιζόμενος ἀναγράφεται νικῶν, εἰ δὲ ἀγωνίζεται, σκιαμαχεῖν μᾶλλον
ἂν εἰκότως δόξαι, ἀνάγκη καὶ τοὺς τὸ ἐναντίον
κατασκευάζοντας λόγους εἰπεῖν, ἵνα δικαιοτάτη
γενηθῇ κρίσις, μηδετέρου μέρους ἐξ ἐρήμου κατα-
176 δικασθέντος.   ἔστι δὲ πρῶτος καὶ δυ-
νατώτατος οὗτος· εἰ τῷ μεθύοντι οὐκ ἄν τις
εὐλόγως λόγον ἀπόρρητον παρακατάθοιτο, ⟨τῷ
δὲ ἀστείῳ παρακατατίθεται⟩, οὐκ ἄρα μεθύει ὁ
ἀστεῖος. ἀλλ᾽ οὖν[1] πρὶν ἢ τοὺς ἄλλους ἑξῆς συν-
είρειν, ἄμεινον καθ᾽ ἕκαστον τῶν προτεινομένων
ἀντιλέγειν, ἵνα μὴ μακρηγοροῦντες ἐπὶ πλέον
177 διοχλεῖν δοκῶμεν.   φήσει δή τις ἐναντιούμενος, ὅτι κατὰ τὸν λεχθέντα λόγον ὁ σοφὸς
οὔτε μελαγχολήσει ποτὲ οὔτε κοιμηθήσεται οὔτε
συνόλως ἀποθανεῖται· ᾧ δὲ μὴ συμβαίνει τι τοιοῦτον, ἄψυχόν ἐστιν ἢ θεῖον, ἄνθρωπος δὲ οὐκ ἂν
εἴη τὸ παράπαν. τὴν γὰρ ἀγωγὴν[2] τοῦ λόγου
μιμησάμενος ἐφαρμόσει τὸν τρόπον τοῦτον τῷ
μελαγχολῶντι ἢ κοιμωμένῳ ἢ ἀποθνήσκοντι· οὐκ
ἄν τις εὐλόγως λόγον ἀπόρρητον τῷ τοιούτῳ παρακατάθοιτο, τῷ δὲ σοφῷ εὐλόγως· οὔτ᾽ ἄρα[3] μελαγ-
χολᾷ οὔτε κοιμᾶται οὔτε ἀποθνήσκει ὁ σοφός.

---

¹ MSS. ἆρ᾽ οὖν.   ² MSS. τὴν παραγωγήν.
                  ³ MSS. οὐ γάρ.

ᵃ See App. p. 499.

regarding those who are in the habit of losing their heads ; thus giving the go-by altogether to intoxication as an aspect of the subject. Thus we find in these men too the most explicit acknowledgement that drunkenness was suffering from the effects of wine. But there would be nothing amiss in a wise man quaffing wine freely on occasion : we shall not be wrong, then, in saying that he will get drunk.

But, since no one is registered as victor if he has no 175 antagonist, and anyone engaged in such a contest would naturally be considered rather to be fighting a shadow, we must needs mention the arguments maintaining the contrary, in order that a perfectly fair decision may be reached, neither side being condemned by default. Of such argu- 176 ments the first and most weighty is this.[a] If one would not act reasonably in entrusting a secret to a drunken man, and does entrust secrets to a good man, it follows that a good man does not get drunk. Well now, instead of the whole series of arguments one after another, it will be better, as each is advanced, to answer it, that we may not seem tedious through making too long a story of it. A man may 177 counter the arguments just mentioned by saying that according to it the wise man will never be melancholy, never fall asleep, in a word, never die. But he whom nothing of this sort befalls would be an inanimate thing or a Divine Being, certainly not a man. For reproducing the conduct of the argument, he will apply it in this way to the case of the melancholy or sleeping or dying man : No one would act reasonably in entrusting a secret to one in such case, but would act reasonably in doing so to a wise man : therefore a wise man never falls into melancholy, or goes to sleep, or dies.

ON DRUNKENNESS
(DE EBRIETATE)

ANALYTICAL INTRODUCTION

THIS treatise [a] like its two predecessors is founded on Gen. ix. 20-29, particularly the last words, " And (Noah) drank of the wine and was drunken." Philo, however, from the first breaks away from this text and, having discussed at the end of the *De Plantatione* the various philosophical views on drunkenness, proceeds to consider the views of Moses on the subject. He lays down that Moses uses wine as a symbol for five things : (1) foolishness or foolish talking ; (2) complete " insensibility " [b] ; (3) greediness [c] ; (4) cheerfulness and gladness ; (5) nakedness (1-5). He then gives a short introductory explanation of each of these, dwelling particularly on one aspect of

[a] Both Jerome and Eusebius state that there were two treatises περὶ μέθης. Whether ours is the second of them, the *De Plant.* being the first (or perhaps *De Plant.* 134-end together with what has evidently been lost at the end of that treatise) or ours is the first, and the second contained the discussion of γυμνότης (see note b on opposite page) is an open question. The general opinion is in favour of the latter alternative. Adler, however, in his *Studien zu Philon von Alexandreia* has recently argued for the former.

[b] This word, though by no means wholly satisfactory, seems the best equivalent for ἀναισθησία with which Philo generally couples παντελής. Literally ἀναισθησία is the stupor of complete intoxication, but " stupor " is not appropriate when the ἀναισθησία is transferred to the moral or mental sphere.

[c] Presumably, in general, any insatiable desire. But Philo in his later treatment reduces it to γαστριμαργία or gluttony.

ON DRUNKENNESS

" nakedness " as the truth which strips off all disguises from virtue and vice, and this leads to a short digression on the mutually exclusive nature of these two (6-10), a thought evidently suggested by Socrates' fable of Pleasure and Pain in the *Phaedo*. He then proceeds to a detailed consideration of these five,[a] though as a matter of fact only the first three are treated in what has come down to us.[b]

I. First, "folly " or "foolish talking." This with its digressions occupies from § 11 to § 153. Its chief cause is ἀπαιδευσία, that is defiance of or unsusceptibility to all educating influences (11-12). How abhorrent this is to Moses is shewn by the law in Deut. xxi. that the parents of a rebellious and profligate son must bring him for judgement before the elders. The development of this illustration occupies sections 13-98. This rebellious son, the type of the ἀπαίδευτος, has four charges brought against him by his parents, disobedience, contentiousness, " riotous feasting " and wine-bibbing (13-14). The two first are distinguished as being the one passive, the other active (15-19). In dealing with the third Philo ignores the derived meaning—riotous feasting—of the obscure

---

[a] The first three are clearly evil, while the fourth (gladness) is wholly good. As for " nakedness," if the reading adopted in the text of § 4 is right, it is regarded as applicable to folly and ignorance and this will agree with *Leg. All.* ii. 54. On the other hand it is to be noted that the " causes " of nakedness in § 8 are either good or neutral.

[b] But not only does Philo promise to discuss all the five, but the opening words of *De Sobrietate* shew that there actually was such a discussion. Whether, however, " gladness " was treated at any length may be doubted. Philo may have passed it over rapidly, noting that while Moses used wine as a symbol for it, it could not be associated with drunkenness. Indeed there is a hint of such a view in § 223.

PHILO

word συμβολοκοπεῖν and confines himself to what he
supposes to be the original meaning. Of the two
elements of which it is compounded he takes the first
συμβολαί to represent " contributions " or " combinations " for evil, while the other (κόπτειν) shews
the " cutting " or destructive force of these contributions (20-24), against which we are warned in the
words, " Thou shalt not follow a multitude to do
evil " (25). The fourth charge that he is " fired with
wine " (οἰνοφλυγεῖ) represents a state in which the
ἀπαιδευσία is inflaming the man's whole nature (27).
That his natural protectors, his parents, should be
his accusers is the just punishment of such a one
(28-29). But " parents " means more than the literal
father and mother. In one sense our father is God
and our mother God's Wisdom, parents whose mercies and judgements alike are greater than we can
receive (30-32). In another sense the father is
" right reason " or philosophy, while the mother is
custom, convention and secular education (33-34).[a]
This idea Philo proceeds to develop (33-92) in what is,
in spite of minor extravagances, a really fine allegory
and does much to redeem the general inferiority of
this treatise. These parents have four kinds of
children, (1) and (2) those who obey one parent but
not the other, (3) those who obey both, (4) those
who obey neither (35). We first deal with those who
disregard the father and love the mother, *i.e.* the
votaries of convention. They are typified, first by
Jethro here, as always in Philo, " the man of super-

[a] Philo's conception of the " Encyclia " here seems to
differ somewhat from his general view. Usually they are
to be valued as an introduction to the higher παιδεία, *i.e.*
philosophy. Here they are mainly a training in the conventional life.

310

fluity" or " unevenness " (36). The special sayings
of his selected here are his advice to Moses on the
conduct of his business in Exod. xviii. and his refusal
to follow Israel in Num. x., and even his saying, " Now
I know that the Lord is great above all gods " is
turned to his discredit on the grounds that " now "
should be " always " and that he still ascribes reality
to non-existent gods (37-45). The second example
of this class is Laban, the admirer, as always, of the
material and external, but his special error is his
saying " it is not our custom to give the younger
(Rachel) before the elder (Leah)," for the younger
daughter, the learning of the schools, should precede
in time the elder, philosophy—and Jacob's reply to
Laban is perversely construed to mean that he will
never leave Leah (46-53). Some other texts are
enlisted to shew the inferiority of the feminine
element in mankind, as exemplified in Rachel, and
her words about the " manner of women " in Gen.
xxxi. (54-64), and we pass on to the next class, the
father-lovers, the despisers of convention and followers of right reason only. These are especially represented by the Levites, who ignore and even as in
Exod. xxxii. slay their kinsfolk and thus are murderers
in the eyes of the conventional world, though not in
the eyes of divine reason (65-67). The kinsfolk, etc.,
are interpreted to mean the body, the senses and
rhetorical eloquence, all of which are sacrificed by the
father-lover, and the final example of this class is
Phinehas who slew the Midianitish woman (Num.
xxv.) and whose story is interpreted in the same
allegorical way with a short meditation on the rewards
he received of " peace and priesthood " (73-76).

The class of those who reject both parents receives

the appropriate denunciation (77-79) and we finally come to those who reverence both. Here we may be surprised to find that Philo after all regards this as the perfect way, in spite of his high praise of the pure philosopher (80-81). This obedience to both right reason and custom is held to deserve the name of Israel which supersedes that of Jacob (82-84), and Moses has approved this twofold excellence, in his institution of an external as well as an internal altar, and the two different robes for the priest. These robes are respectively simple and ornate, and the second shews us that life has many aspects (85-87). For true wisdom shews itself in various forms not only in religion, but also in the physical sciences, in ethics and politics and in social activities (88-92). That the two parents have other children besides the disobedient one is deduced from the phrase " this our son " and Philo takes various examples of such children from the great names of the Pentateuch (73-94).

Philo now once more denounces the wickedness of the disobedient son and compares him to the degenerate Israelites who worshipped the golden calf, and thus he is led to quote the words of Joshua on that occasion, " There is a voice of war in the camp . . ." And Moses' reply, " that the sounds are not those of victory or defeat, but those of the wine-feast of men who shout over the wine that I hear " (95-96). This quotation carries Philo away at once to a disquisition on its various phrases. " There is a voice in the camp " signifies the tumult of passion in the camp of human life (97-104), and some illustrations of this thought are given (97-104). " It is not the voice of might (or " victory ") " suggests a comparison with the words of Abraham after his victory over the nine

312

kings (*i.e.* the four passions and the five senses), and this involves an explanation of Abraham's refusal to accept reward from the King of Sodom, as the wise soul's refusal to accept from any but God and a rebuke to idolaters (105-110). Another song of victory is that of Moses over Pharaoh's host (111) and the " Song of the Well " in Num. xxi. (112-113) which in its turn leads to a discussion of the allegorical meaning of various phrases in the speech of the victorious captains in Num. xxxi., particularly of " each one gave what he had found " (114-120). The " voice of the defeated " is passed over rapidly as indicating weakness rather than wickedness, and contrasted with the voice of those who shout over (or " lead ") the wine, which voice indicates the deliberate madness of evil (121-123). Thus we are brought back for a moment to the main thought of drunkenness as moral folly, and reminded that freedom from this is true priesthood (124-126). This was the inner meaning of the command to Aaron to abstain from wine when he approached the tabernacle or the altar (127-129). In the literal sense this is sound enough, for what can be worse than a drunken worshipper (130-131), but in the deeper sense the tabernacle is the " idea " of incorporeal virtue, and the altar that of the particular virtues, and to him who approaches either of these folly is not so much forbidden as impossible (132-139). Similar morals are drawn from the concluding words of the same passages (140-143), and also from Samuel's lifelong abstinence (143-144), and the mention of Samuel leads to some thoughts on the words of Hannah (*i.e.* Grace) to those who thought her drunk, " I have drunk no wine and I will pour out my soul before

PHILO

the Lord," in which we have a parable of the truth that the " joy " of grace is as the Bacchant's inspiration and that freedom from folly makes the soul a fitting libation to God (145-152). This concludes the discussion of drunkenness as spiritual folly produced by ἀπαιδευσία (153).

II. The second thing for which wine stood as a symbol was, we saw, " stupor " or " insensibility," and in the mental or moral sphere this is ignorance, which stands to the mind as blindness or deafness to the body, while knowledge is the eye and ear of the soul (154-161). But we must distinguish two kinds of ignorance, one mere non-knowledge, the other the belief that we know, when we do not (162-163). This last is represented by Lot with his wife, who is " Custom " ever looking back upon the past, and his two daughters who are " Deliberation " and " Assent." The statement that their daughters " gave their father wine to drink " means that the mind is hypnotized with the belief that it can by deliberation find out the truth and give a right judgement or assent, whereas in reality nothing of the sort is possible even to the educated [a] (164-168). The

---

[a] The sections which follow are very extraordinary. Philo seems to jettison his general dogmatic principles and to enrol himself in the school of the Sceptics. In fact he reproduces so clearly several of the " ten tropes " of the famous sceptic Aenesidemus, as given by Diogenes Laertius and Sextus Empiricus, that he enables the historians of philosophy to lay down a *terminus ad quem* for the date of that philosopher, of which, till the attention of scholars was called to these chapters, nothing more was known than that he must have preceded Diogenes and Sextus. It will be seen that in 193-202 he extends ἀκαταληψία or impossibility of apprehension to moral questions, and thus seems to overthrow the basis of his philosophy.

fact that the same objects produce at different times different impressions on the mind shews that we cannot base certain judgements on these impressions (162-170). Philo then proceeds to enumerate the causes or rather " modes " of these uncertainties. The first is the difference in the habits and constitution of animals, which argues that they too receive different impressions from the same things, and with this he joins the changes which some of them, *e.g.* the chameleon and the elk, are supposed to exhibit in different environments (171-175). The second mode is the various feelings, likes and dislikes shewn by mankind, in which not only does one man differ from another, but even the individual from himself (175-180). The third mode is the optical illusions produced by the distances or situations of objects, such as " the straight staff bent in a pool " (181-183). The fourth is the observation that any two or more things, while remaining the same in substance, produce totally different results according to the proportions in which they are combined (184-185). The fifth is relativity, for since we only know one thing with reference to another, we cannot be said to know them at all (186-189). This is illustrated by the fact that colour, smell and the like are really the effect of the combination of something in the object with something in ourselves (190-191). Further, we are warned against forming moral judgements by the fact that on all such questions there is an infinite difference of opinion among various nations, states and individuals which forbids us to assert with certainty that any particular act is virtuous or not (192-197). Philo goes on to say that while he is not surprised that the vulgar should form positive judgements, he is sur-

315

prised to find that philosophers can still be dogmatists and yet come to totally different opinions on vital questions, and he enumerates some of these, such as whether the universe is infinite or not, created or uncreated, ruled by providence or not, and whether morality is the only good or whether there are numerous goods (198-202). True indeed are the words of the text " he knew not when they (the daughters) slept and rose up," for both the counsels and the assents of the mind are utterly untrustworthy (203-205).

III. The third idea suggested by wine or drunkenness, viz. greediness or gluttony, is treated by Philo in a comparatively literal manner. Such allegory as there is is chiefly drawn from the story of Pharaoh in Genesis (Egypt as usual representing the body), who on his birthday was reconciled with his chief butler, thereby representing the tendency of the sated sensualist to return to his excesses as soon as possible (206-209). From the statement (in the LXX) that all the three officers of Pharaoh's table—the chief butler, the chief baker and the chief cook *a*—were eunuchs, he draws the lesson that the ministers of pleasure are incapable of begetting wisdom, and this is also implied in the banishment by Moses of eunuchs from the congregation (210-213). Further the prefix of " chief " applied in Genesis to these three indicates the gourmand's excessive indulgence as compared with simple living, and Philo takes the opportunity to give a rhetorical description of these refinements of luxury (214-220). Also it was the chief cupbearer (not the other two) with whom Pharaoh was reconciled, and this shews that the

---

a In the LXX Potiphar is called the " chief cook."

passion for wine is the most persistent form which bodily indulgence takes (220-221). A text which he quotes in connexion with this from the Song of Moses, in which the phrase " the vine of Sodom " occurs, brings him back to the allegorical view of drunkenness as the symbol of folly in general. For the fool's " vine " or his foolish desires do not produce the gladness of true wine, but its roots are as ashes, and the treatise concludes with the prayer that our " vine " may be rather that of true and fruit-bearing instruction (222-end).

ΠΕΡΙ ΜΕΘΗΣ

I. Τὰ μὲν τοῖς ἄλλοις φιλοσόφοις εἰρημένα περὶ
1 μέθης, ὡς οἷόν τε ἦν, ἐν τῇ πρὸ ταύτης ὑπεμνήσαμεν
βίβλῳ, νυνὶ δὲ ἐπισκεψώμεθα τίνα τῷ πάντα μεγάλῳ
καὶ σοφῷ νομοθέτῃ περὶ αὐτῆς δοκεῖ. πολλαχοῦ
2 γὰρ τῆς νομοθεσίας οἴνου καὶ τοῦ γεννῶντος φυτοῦ
τὸν οἶνον ἀμπέλου διαμέμνηται· καὶ τοῖς μὲν
ἐμπίνειν ἐπιτρέπει, τοῖς δ' οὐκ ἐφίησι, καὶ τοῖς
αὐτοῖς ἔστιν ὅτε προστάττει τἀναντία, οἴνῳ χρῆσθαί
τε καὶ μή. οὗτοι μὲν οὖν εἰσιν οἱ τὴν μεγάλην
εὐχὴν εὐξάμενοι, οἷς δὲ ἀκράτῳ χρῆσθαι ἀπείρηται
οἱ λειτουργοῦντες ἱερεῖς, οἱ δὲ προσφερόμενοι τὸν
οἶνον μυρίοι τῶν ἐπ' ἀρετῇ μάλιστα καὶ παρ' αὐτῷ
τεθαυμασμένων.   πρὶν δὲ περὶ τούτων
3 ἄρξασθαι λέγειν, τὰ συντείνοντα πρὸς τὰς κατα-
σκευὰς αὐτῶν ἀκριβωτέον. ἔστι δ' ὥς γ' οἶμαι
τάδε· II. σύμβολον τὸν ἄκρατον Μωυσῆς οὐχ
4 ἑνὸς ἀλλὰ πλειόνων εἶναι νομίζει, τοῦ ληρεῖν καὶ
παραπαίειν, ἀναισθησίας παντελοῦς, ἀπληστίας
ἀκορέστου καὶ δυσαρέστου, εὐθυμίας[1] καὶ εὐφροσύνης, τῆς τἄλλα περιεχούσης καὶ πᾶσι τοῖς

---

[1] Wendland ἐπιθυμίας. In this case δυσαρέστου would
agree with ἐπιθυμίας, and τῆς τἄλλα περιεχούσης with εὐφροσύνης. See App. p. 500.

[a] See App. p. 500.

ON DRUNKENNESS

I. The views expressed by the other philosophers 1
on drunkenness have been stated by me to the best
of my ability in the preceding book. Let us now
consider what the great lawgiver in his never-failing
wisdom holds on this subject. In many places of 2
his legislation he mentions wine and the plant whose
fruit it is—the vine. Some persons he permits,
others he forbids, to drink of it, and sometimes he
gives opposite orders,[a] at one time enjoining and at
another prohibiting its use to the same persons.
These last are those who have made the great vow
(Num. vi. 2), while those who are forbidden the use
of strong drink are the ministering priests (Lev. x. 9) ;
while of persons who take wine there are numberless
instances among those whom he too holds in the
highest admiration for their virtue.
But before we begin to discuss these matters, we 3
must carefully investigate the points which bear
on our exposition. These points, I think, are the
following. II. Moses uses strong liquor as a symbol 4
for more than one, in fact for several, things : for
foolish talking and raving, for complete insensibility,
for insatiable and ever-discontented greediness, for
cheerfulness and gladness, for the nakedness which
embraces the rest and manifests itself in all the

[358] εἰρημένοις ἐμφαινομένης γυμνότητος ᾗ τὸν Νῶε |
μεθυσθέντα φησὶ χρήσασθαι. τὸν μὲν οὖν οἶνον
5 λέγεται ταῦτα ἐργάζεσθαι. μυρίοι δὲ καὶ τῶν οὐ
προσαψαμένων ἀκράτου νήφειν ὑπολαμβάνοντες
τοῖς ὁμοίοις ἁλίσκονται· καὶ ἔστιν ἰδεῖν τοὺς μὲν
αὐτῶν ἀφραίνοντάς τε καὶ ληροῦντας, τοὺς δ᾽
ἀναισθησίᾳ παντελεῖ κατεσχημένους, τοὺς δὲ
μηδέποτε πληρουμένους, αἰεὶ δὲ τῶν ἀνηνύτων
διψῶντας διὰ χηρείαν ἐπιστήμης, τοὺς δ᾽ ἔμπαλιν
γανουμένους καὶ εὐφραινομένους, τοὺς δὲ τῷ ὄντι
6 γυμνουμένους.   τοῦ μὲν οὖν ληρεῖν αἴτιον
ἡ ἐπιζήμιος ἀπαιδευσία—λέγω δ᾽ οὐ τὴν παιδείας ἀν-
επιστημοσύνην, ἀλλὰ τὴν πρὸς αὐτὴν ἀλλοτρίωσιν—,
τοῦ δ᾽ ἀναισθητεῖν ἡ ἐπίβουλος καὶ πηρὸς ἄγνοια,
ἀπληστίας δὲ ἡ ἀργαλεωτάτη παθῶν ψυχῆς ἐπιθυμία, εὐφροσύνης δὲ κτῆσις ὁμοῦ καὶ χρῆσις
ἀρετῆς, γυμνότητος μέντοι πολλά, ἄγνοια τῶν
ἐναντίων, ἀκακία καὶ ἀφέλεια ἠθῶν, ἀλήθεια ἡ
τὰ τῶν συνεσκιασμένων πραγμάτων ἀνακαλυπτήρια
ἄγουσα δύναμις, τῇ μὲν ἀπαμπίσχουσα ἀρετήν, τῇ
7 δὲ κακίαν ἐν μέρει· ἅμα μὲν γὰρ οὐχ οἷον ἀπο-
δύσασθαι, ἀλλ᾽ οὐδ᾽ ἐνσκευάσασθαι ταύτας δυνατόν·
ἐπειδὰν δέ τις ἀπορρίψῃ τὴν ἑτέραν, ἐξ ἀνάγκης
τὴν ἐναντίαν ἀναλαβὼν ἐπαμπίσχεται.
8 ὥσπερ γὰρ ἡδονὴν καὶ ἀλγηδόνα φύσει μαχομένας,
ὡς ὁ παλαιὸς λόγος, εἰς μίαν κορυφὴν συνάψας ὁ

---

a Cf. Leg. All. ii. 54, where three kinds of nakedness are
distinguished : (a) that of the soul stripped of passion, a
state which to Philo is true joy ; (b) foolishness, as in the
case of Noah (60 f.); (c) ignorance of good and evil, as in
Adam and Eve (64 f.).
b The two epithets are explained in §§ 150-163. Ignorance
320

qualities just mentioned,[a] in which condition Noah was, we read, when intoxicated. All these we are told are produced by wine. Yet thousands of those 5 who never touch strong drink and consider themselves sober are mastered by similar emotions. We may see them in some cases mad and foolish, in others under the dominion of complete insensibility, in others never filled but always thirsting for impossibilities through lack of knowledge, or on the other hand full of gladness and exultation, finally in the true sense naked.   The folly is caused by 6 indiscipline in its noxious form, by which I mean not the mere unacquaintance with discipline but aversion to it ; insensibility is caused by ignorance (always) blind and (often) with a will for evil [b] ; greediness by that most painful of the soul's passions, lust ; while gladness arises both from the winning and the practice of virtue. Nakedness has many causes : incapacity for distinguishing between moral opposites, innocence and simplicity of manners, truth, that is, the power which unveils [c] what is wrapped in obscurity. At one moment it is virtue that she uncovers, at another vice in its turn. For we cannot 7 doff both of these at the same moment any more than we can don them. When we discard the one we necessarily adopt and assume its opposite. The old story [d] tells us that God when He fastened 8 the naturally conflicting sensations of pleasure and

is always blindness, but when under the delusion that it is knowledge it is actually mischievous (§ 163).

[c] Lit. " celebrating the unveiling " (of the bride), v. Dict. of Ant. (" Matrimonium ").

[d] i.e. the fable suggested by Socrates (*Phaedo* 60 B) where we have much the same phrase as here, ἐκ μιᾶς κορυφῆς συνημμένω δύ' ὄντε, v. note (App.) on *De Gig.* 56.

θεὸς ἑκατέρας αἴσθησιν οὐκ ἐν ταὐτῷ, διαλλάττουσι
δὲ χρόνοις ἐνειργάσατο κατὰ τὴν φυγὴν τῆς ἑτέρας
κάθοδον τῇ ἐναντίᾳ ψηφισάμενος, οὕτως ἀπὸ μιᾶς
ῥίζης τοῦ ἡγεμονικοῦ τά τε ἀρετῆς καὶ κακίας
διττὰ ἀνέδραμεν ἔρνη μήτε βλαστάνοντα μήτε
9 καρποφοροῦντα ἐν ταὐτῷ· ὁπότε μὲν γὰρ φυλλορ-
ροεῖ καὶ ἀφαυαίνεται θάτερον, ἄρχεται ἀναβλα-
στάνειν καὶ χλοηφορεῖν τὸ ἐναντίον, ὡς ὑπολαβεῖν,
ὅτι ἑκάτερον τῇ θατέρου δυσχεραῖνον εὐπραγίᾳ
στέλλεται.   δι᾽ ἣν αἰτίαν φυσικώτατα[1]
τὴν Ἰακὼβ ἔξοδον εἴσοδον Ἠσαῦ παρίστησιν·
"ἐγένετο" γάρ φησιν "ὅσον ἐξῆλθεν Ἰακώβ, ἧκεν
10 Ἠσαῦ ὁ ἀδελφὸς αὐτοῦ." μέχρι μὲν γὰρ ἐνσχολάζει
καὶ ἐμπεριπατεῖ τῇ ψυχῇ φρόνησις, ὑπερόριος πᾶς
ὁ ἀφροσύνης ἑταῖρος ἐκτετόξευται· ἐπειδὰν δὲ
μεταναστῇ, γεγηθὼς κάτεισιν ἐκεῖνος, τῆς πολεμίου
καὶ δυσμενοῦς δι᾽ ἣν ἠλαύνετο καὶ ἐφυγαδεύετο
μηκέτι τὸν αὐτὸν χῶρον οἰκούσης.

11   III. Τὰ μὲν οὖν ὡσανεὶ προοίμια τῆς γραφῆς
ἀρκούντως λέλεκται, τὰς δ᾽ ἀποδείξεις ἑκάστων
προσαποδώσομεν, ἀπὸ τοῦ πρώτου πρῶτον ἀρξά-
[359] μενοι διδάσκειν· τὴν τοίνυν ἀπαιδευσίαν ⟨τοῦ⟩ |
ληρεῖν καὶ ἁμαρτάνειν αἰτίαν ἔφαμεν εἶναι καθάπερ
12 μυρίοις τῶν ἀφρόνων τὸν πολὺν ἄκρατον. ἀπαιδευσία γὰρ τῶν ψυχῆς ἁμαρτημάτων, εἰ δεῖ τἀληθὲς
εἰπεῖν, τὸ ἀρχέκακον, ἀφ᾽ ἧς ὥσπερ ἀπὸ πηγῆς
ῥέουσιν αἱ τοῦ βίου πράξεις, πότιμον μὲν καὶ
σωτήριον οὐδὲν οὐδενὶ νᾶμα ἐκδιδοῦσαι[2] τὸ παράπαν,
ἁλμυρὸν δὲ νόσου καὶ φθορᾶς τοῖς χρησομένοις

____

[1] mss. φυσικωτάτην.
[2] Wendland ἐκδιδοῦσα with some mss. See App. p. 500.

pain under a single head, caused them to be felt at different times and not at the same moment, and thus decreed that the banishment of the one should involve the restoration of the other. Just in the same way, from a single root in our dominant part spring the two shoots of vice and virtue, yet never sprouting or bearing fruit at the same moment. For when one 9 sheds its leaves and withers, its opposite begins to exhibit new life and verdure, so that we might suppose that each shrinks and shrivels in resentment at the thriving of the other. And so it is in full agreement with philosophical truth that Moses represents the outgoing of Jacob as being the incoming of Esau. "It came to pass," he says, "that as soon as Jacob went out Esau his brother came in" (Gen. xxvii. 30).[a] For so long as prudence has its 10 lodging and scene of action in the soul, so long is every friend of folly an outcast from her borders. But when prudence has changed her quarters, the other returns with glee now that the bitter enemy, who caused his expulsion and life of exile, no longer dwells where he did.

III. So much then for what we may call the pre- 11 liminaries of our treatise. I will now proceed to the demonstration of each head beginning with the first. Well, we agreed that indiscipline was the cause of folly and error, as wine when taken in large quantities is to so many foolish persons. Indiscipline is 12 indeed the prime cause of the soul's errors, and from it as from a spring flow those actions of our lives which give to none any sweet and salutary stream, but only briny waters fraught with plague and destruction to those who use them.

---

[a] We have the same use of the text in *De Sac.* 135.

13 αἴτιον.   οὕτως γοῦν κατὰ ἀναγώγων
καὶ ἀπαιδεύτων ὁ νομοθέτης φονᾷ, ὡς κατ' οὐδενὸς
ἴσως ἑτέρου. τεκμήριον δέ· τίνες εἰσὶν οἱ μὴ
ἐπιτηδεύσει μᾶλλον ἢ φύσει σύμμαχοι παρά τε
ἀνθρώποις καὶ ἐν τοῖς ἄλλοις γένεσι τῶν ζῴων;
ἀλλ' οὐδὲ μανεὶς ἑτέρους ἂν εἴποι τις ἢ τοὺς τοκέας
εἶναι· κήδεται γὰρ ἀδιδάκτῳ τῇ φύσει τὸ πεποιηκὸς
αἰεὶ τοῦ γενομένου, καὶ σωτηρίας αὐτοῦ καὶ διαμονῆς τῆς εἰσάπαν πρόνοιαν ἔχει.

14 IV. τοὺς οὖν ἐκ φύσεως συναγωνιστὰς ὑπάρχοντας
εἰς ἐχθρῶν μετελθεῖν τάξιν ἐσπούδασε κατηγόρους
ἐπιστήσας τοὺς δεόντως ἂν συναγορεύοντας, πατέρα
καὶ μητέρα, ἵν' ὑφ' ὧν εἰκὸς ἦν σῴζεσθαι μόνων[a]
παραπόλωνται· "ἐὰν γάρ τινι" φησίν "υἱὸς ᾖ
ἀπειθὴς καὶ ἐρεθιστὴς οὐχ ὑπακούων φωνῆς πατρὸς
καὶ μητρός, καὶ παιδεύωσιν αὐτὸν καὶ μὴ εἰσακούῃ
αὐτῶν, συλλαβόντες αὐτὸν ὁ πατὴρ αὐτοῦ καὶ ἡ
μήτηρ ἐξάξουσιν εἰς τὴν γερουσίαν τῆς πόλεως
αὐτοῦ καὶ ἐπὶ τὴν πύλην τοῦ τόπου αὐτοῦ, καὶ
ἐροῦσι τοῖς ἀνδράσι τῆς πόλεως αὐτῶν· ὁ υἱὸς
ἡμῶν οὗτος ἀπειθεῖ καὶ ἐρεθίζει, οὐκ εἰσακούει
τῆς φωνῆς ἡμῶν, συμβολοκοπῶν[b] οἰνοφλυγεῖ. καὶ
λιθοβολήσουσιν αὐτὸν οἱ ἄνδρες τῆς πόλεως, καὶ
ἐξαρεῖς τὸν πονηρὸν ἐξ ὑμῶν αὐτῶν."

15 οὐκοῦν αἱ κατηγορίαι ἀριθμῷ τέτταρες, ἀπείθεια
καὶ ἐρεθισμὸς καὶ συμβολῶν εἰσφορὰ[c] καὶ μέθη.
μεγίστη δ' ἡ τελευταία παραύξησιν ἀπὸ τῆς πρώτης
ἀπειθείας λαβοῦσα· ἀρξαμένη γὰρ ἀφηνιάζειν ἡ

---

[a] Or "should be the sole workers of his ruin"; μόνων may
perhaps be taken with both verbs.
[b] See App. p. 500.
[c] Lit. "paying of contributions."

Thus it is against the untrained and undisciplined 13
more perhaps than against any other person that the
lawgiver breathes slaughter. Here is our proof.
Who play the part of protectors not so much by
acquired habit as by nature amongst humankind and
every other kind of animal ? Surely it is the parents.
Not even a madman would give a different answer.
For nature ever instinctively prompts the maker to
care for what he has made, and to take thought for
its preservation and perpetual maintenance.

IV. Now when Moses set up those who would prop- 14
erly plead the cause of an offender, namely his father
and mother, to appear as his accusers, thus providing
that those who might be expected to preserve him
against all others should actually work his ruin,[a] he
shewed his desire that these natural supporters should
be converted into enemies. " For if anyone," he
says, " has a disobedient and contentious son who
does not listen to the voice of his father and mother,
and they discipline him and he does not hearken to
them, his father and mother shall take him and bring
him forth to the assembly of the elders of his city
and to the gate of his place, and shall say to the men
of their city, ' This our son is disobedient and contentious, he does not listen to our voice, he is a
riotous liver [b] and a wine-bibber,' and the men of the
city shall stone him with stones and thou shalt
remove the evil one from among yourselves " (Deut.
xxi. 18-21). We see then that the accusa- 15
tions are four in number, disobedience, contentiousness, participation in riotous feasting [c] and drunkenness. But the last is the chief, rising to a climax
from the first, disobedience. For when the soul has
begun to cast off the reins and taken its onward

ψυχὴ καὶ προελθοῦσα διὰ ἔριδος καὶ φιλονεικίας
ἐπὶ ὕστατον ὅρον ἔρχεται, μέθην, τὴν ἐκστάσεως
καὶ παραφροσύνης αἰτίαν. ἑκάστης δὲ τῶν κατη-
γοριῶν τὴν δύναμιν ἰδεῖν ἀναγκαῖον τὴν ἀρχὴν
ἀπὸ τῆς πρώτης λαβόντας.

16 V. Ἀνωμολόγηται τοίνυν περιφανῶς, ὅτι τὸ
εἴκειν καὶ πειθαρχεῖν ἀρετῇ καλὸν καὶ συμφέρον,
ὥστε τὸ ἀπειθεῖν ἔμπαλιν αἰσχρὸν καὶ οὐ μετρίως
ἀλυσιτελές· τὸ δὲ δὴ καὶ ἐρεθίζειν ὑπερβολὴν πᾶσαν
κεχώρηκε τοῦ δεινοῦ· ὁ γὰρ ἀπειθὴς τοῦ φιλέριδος
ἧττον μοχθηρός ἐστιν, ὁ μὲν αὐτὸ μόνον τῶν προσ-
ταττομένων ἀλογῶν, ὁ δὲ καὶ τοῖς ἐναντίοις
17 ἐγχειρεῖν σπουδὴν πεποιημένος.   φέρε
δ᾽ ὡς ἔχει τοῦτο θεασώμεθα· νόμου κελεύοντος, εἰ
[360] τύχοι, τοὺς | γονεῖς τιμᾶν, ὁ μὲν μὴ τιμῶν ἀπειθής,
ὁ δ᾽ ἀτιμάζων φίλερις. καὶ πάλιν τοῦ τὴν πατρίδα
σῴζειν ὄντος δικαίου τὸν μὲν πρὸς αὐτὸ τοῦτο
ὄκνῳ χρώμενον ἀπειθῇ, τὸν δ᾽ ἔτι καὶ προδιδόναι
18 διεγνωκότα δύσεριν καὶ φιλόνεικον λεκτέον. ὅ τε
μὴ χαριζόμενός τισιν ἐναντιούμενος τῷ φάσκοντι
δεῖν ὠφελεῖν ἀπειθεῖ, ὁ δὲ πρὸς τῷ μὴ χαρίζεσθαι
καὶ ὅσα βλάβης ἐστὶν ἐμποιῶν ἔριδι ἐπαιρόμενος
ἀνίατα ἐξαμαρτάνει. καὶ μὴν ὅ γε ἱερουργίαις
καὶ τοῖς ἄλλοις ὅσα πρὸς εὐσέβειαν ἀναφέρεται μὴ
χρώμενος ἀπειθεῖ προστάξεσιν, ἃς ὁ νόμος εἴωθε
περὶ τούτων προστάττειν, ἀνερεθίζει δ᾽ ὁ πρὸς
τοὐναντίον, ἀσέβειαν, ἀποκλίνας καὶ ἀθεότητος

course through strife and dissension, it reaches its utmost limit in drunkenness, which produces frenzy and madness. We must take these accusations one by one and observe their full meaning, beginning with the first.

V. We have it as a clear and admitted fact that 16 submission and obedience to virtue is noble and profitable, and the converse follows, that disobedience is disgraceful and in a high degree unprofitable. But if contentiousness is added to disobedience, it involves a vast increase of the evil. The disobedient man is not on so low a moral level as the quarrelsome and strife-loving man, since he merely disregards the commands he receives and nothing more, while the other takes active pains to carry out what is opposed to these commands. Let us consider how 17 this shews itself. The law, to take one instance, bids us honour our parents ; he then who does not honour them is disobedient, he who actively dishonours them is a strife-lover. Again, it is a righteous action to save one's country. He who shirks this particular duty is to be classed as disobedient, he who actually purposes to betray it as a man of strife and contention. So too one who fails to do a kind- 18 ness to his neighbour, in opposition to another who tells him that it is his duty to give help, is disobedient. But one who, besides withholding his kindness, works all the harm he can is moved by the spirit of strife to deadly error. And again the man who fails to make use of the holy rites and all else that relates to piety is disobedient to the commandments which law and custom regularly prescribe in these matters, but rebellious or strife-stirrer is the name for him who turns aside to their direct opposite, impiety, and

19 εἰσηγητής. VI. οἷος ἦν ὁ φάσκων
"τίς ἐστιν οὗ ὑπακούσομαι;" καὶ πάλιν "οὐκ οἶδα
τὸν κύριον"· διὰ μὲν οὖν τῆς προτέρας φωνῆς
παρίστησιν, ὅτι οὐκ ἔστι τὸ θεῖον, διὰ δὲ τῆς
ἔπειτα, ὅτι, εἰ καὶ ἔστιν, ἀλλά τοι ἀγνοεῖται, ὅπερ
ἐκ τοῦ μὴ προνοεῖν συνάγεται· εἰ γὰρ προὐνόει,
κἂν ἐγινώσκετο.

20 Συμβολάς γε μὴν καὶ ἐράνους φέρειν ἐπὶ μὲν
τῇ τοῦ ἀρίστου κτήματος μετουσίᾳ, φρονήσεως,
ἐπαινετὸν καὶ συμφέρον, ἕνεκα δὲ τῆς τοῦ ἀκρο-
τάτου πάντων ⟨κακοῦ⟩, ἀφροσύνης, ἀλυσιτελές
21 τε καὶ ψεκτόν. αἱ μὲν οὖν πρὸς τὸ ἄριστον συμ-
βολαὶ πόθος ἀρετῆς, τῶν καλῶν ζῆλος, μελέται
συνεχεῖς, ἀσκήσεις ἐπίμονοι,[1] ἄτρυτοι καὶ ἀκμῆτες
πόνοι, αἱ δὲ πρὸς τὸ ἐναντίον ἄνεσις, ῥαθυμία,
22 τρυφή, θρύψις, παντελὴς ἐκδιαίτησις. ἰδεῖν μέντοι
καὶ τοὺς ἐπαποδυομένους πολυοινίᾳ καὶ καθ᾽
ἑκάστην ἡμέραν γυμναζομένους καὶ ἀθλοῦντας
τοὺς ἐπ᾽ ἀπληστίᾳ γαστρὸς ἄθλους ἔστι συμβολὰς
μὲν ὡς ἐπί τινι τῶν λυσιτελῶν εἰσφέροντας, ζημιου-
μένους δὲ πάντα, χρήματα, σώματα, ψυχάς· τὰ
μὲν γὰρ εἰσφέροντες μειοῦσι τὴν οὐσίαν, τῶν δὲ
σωμάτων διὰ τὸ ἁβροδίαιτον κατακλῶσι καὶ
θρύπτουσι τὰς δυνάμεις, τὰς δὲ ψυχὰς ποταμοῦ
χειμάρρου τρόπον ἀμετρίᾳ τροφῶν ἐπικλύζοντες
23 εἰς βυθὸν ἀναγκάζουσι δύεσθαι. τὸν
αὐτὸν δὴ τρόπον καὶ ὅσοι φέρουσιν ἐράνους ἐπὶ
καθαιρέσει παιδείας, τὸ κυριώτατον τῶν ἐν αὐτοῖς
ζημιοῦσι, διάνοιαν, ἀποκόπτοντες αὐτῆς τὰ σωτήρια,

---

[1] MSS. ἐπίπονοι.

---

[a] Or "who is it, whom I am to obey?"
[b] See App. p. 500.

becomes a leader in godlessness.   VI. Such 19
was he who said, " who is He that I should obey
Him," *a* and again, " I know not the Lord " (Exod.
v. 2).   In the first of these utterances he asserts that
there is no God ; in the second that even if there is a
God he is not known to us, and this conclusion pre-
supposes the assumption that there is no divine
providence.   For if there were such a thing as providence, God too would be known.

As for contributions or club subscriptions, when 20
the object is to share in the best of possessions, prudence, such payments are praiseworthy and profitable ;
but when they are paid to obtain that supreme evil,
folly, the practice is unprofitable and blameworthy.
We contribute to the former object by desire for 21
virtue, by zeal for things noble, by continuous study
therein, by persistent self-training, by unwearied and
unflagging labour.   We contribute to the opposite
by slackness, indolence, luxury, effeminacy, and by
complete irregularity of life.*b*   We can see indeed 22
people preparing themselves to compete in the arena
of wine-bibbing and every day exercising themselves
and contending in the contests of gluttony.   The
contributions they make are supposed to be for a
profitable purpose, but they are actually mulcting
themselves in everything, in money, body and soul.
Their substance they diminish by the actual payments, their bodily powers they shatter and enfeeble
by the delicate living, and by excessive indulgence
in food they deluge their souls as with a winter torrent
and submerge them perforce in the depths.
In just the same way those who pay their contri- 23
butions only to destroy training and education are
mulcting their most vital element, the understanding,

φρόνησιν καὶ σωφροσύνην, ἔτι δὲ ἀνδρείαν καὶ
δικαιοσύνην. διό μοι δοκεῖ καὶ αὐτὸς ὀνόματι
συνθέτῳ χρῆσθαι τῷ " συμβολοκοπῶν " πρὸς δήλωσιν ἐναργεστέραν τοῦ σημαινομένου, διότι τὰ
κατὰ ἀρετῆς ἐπιχειρήματα ὥσπερ τινὰς συμβολὰς
καὶ ἐράνους εἰσφέροντες τιτρώσκουσι καὶ διαιροῦσι
καὶ συγκόπτουσι μέχρι παντελοῦς φθορᾶς τὰς
φιληκόους καὶ φιλομαθεῖς ψυχάς.   VII.

24 ὁ μὲν οὖν σοφὸς Ἀβραὰμ ἐπανελθεῖν λέγεται " ἀπὸ
τῆς κοπῆς τοῦ Χοδολλαγόμορ καὶ τῶν βασιλέων
τῶν μετ' αὐτοῦ," ὁ δ' Ἀμαλὴκ ἔμπαλιν τοῦ ἀσκητοῦ
" τὴν οὐραγίαν κόπτειν " ἀκολουθίᾳ φύσεως· ἐχθρὰ
[361] γὰρ | τὰ ἐναντία καὶ τὸν ἐπ' ἀλλήλοις ὄλεθρον ἀεὶ
25 μελετῶντα.   τὸν δὲ κομίζοντα τὰς συμβολὰς καὶ ταύτῃ μάλιστ' ἄν τις αἰτιάσαιτο, ὅτι
οὐ μόνον ἀδικεῖν, ἀλλὰ καὶ συναδικεῖν ἔγνωκεν
ἑτέροις ἀξιῶν τὰ μὲν αὐτὸς εἰσηγεῖσθαι, τὰ δ'
εἰσηγουμένων ἄλλων ἀκροᾶσθαι, ὅπως καὶ φύσει
καὶ μαθήσει διαμαρτάνων μηδεμίαν εἰς σωτηρίαν
ὑπολείπηται χρηστὴν ἐλπίδα ἑαυτῷ, καὶ ταῦτα
νόμου διειρηκότος " μὴ γίνεσθαι μετὰ πολλῶν
26 ἐπὶ κακίᾳ." τῷ γὰρ ὄντι πολύχουν μὲν καὶ πολυ-
φορώτατον ἐν ἀνθρώπων ψυχαῖς τὸ κακόν, ἐσταλ-
μένον δὲ καὶ σπάνιον τἀγαθόν. παραίνεσις οὖν
ὠφελιμωτάτη μὴ τοῖς πολλοῖς, μεθ' ὧν τὸ ἀδικεῖν,
ἀλλὰ τοῖς ὀλίγοις, μεθ' ὧν τὸ δικαιοπραγεῖν, συμ-
φέρεσθαι.

---

^a κοπή, " rout," literally is " cutting."

and cut away therefrom its safeguards, prudence and
self-control, and indeed courage and justice to boot.
It was for this reason, I think, that Moses himself
used a compound word, "contribution cutting," to
bring out more clearly the nature of the thing he was
describing, because when men bring their efforts like
contributions or club-money, so to speak, to bear
against virtue, they wound and divide and cut in
pieces docile and knowledge-loving souls, till they
bring them to utter destruction.   VII.
Thus we read that the wise Abraham returned from 24
the "cutting"^a of Chedorlaomer and his fellow kings
(Gen. xiv. 17), while on the other hand Amalek "cuts
the rearguard" of the Practiser (Deut. xxv. 18).
Both these are in accordance with natural truth, for
there is a hostility between opposites and they are
always meditating destruction of each other.
There is another charge, and that the greatest, which 25
could be brought against the provider of the contributions. He purposes not only to wrong, but to
join with others in wrongdoing. He consents to
initiate evil himself, and also to comply with what
others initiate, that thus he may leave himself no
ray of hope that may serve for his redemption, since
his sin lies both in his nature and in what he has
learnt from others. And this in spite of the direct
injunction of the law, not "to go with the many to
do evil" (Exod. xxiii. 2). For in very truth manifold 26
are the aspects and the products of evil in men's
souls, while the good is narrowly confined and scanty.
And so most excellent is the advice that we should
not keep company with the many but with the few;
for wrongdoing is the associate of the former, but
right action of the latter.

27 VIII. Τέταρτον τοίνυν καὶ μέγιστον ἔγκλημα
ἦν τὸ μεθύειν, οὐκ ἀνειμένως, ἀλλὰ σφόδρα
συντόνως· τὸ γὰρ οἰνοφλυγεῖν ἴσον ἐστὶ τῷ τὸ
παραίτιον ἀφροσύνης φάρμακον, ἀπαιδευσίαν, ἐν-
τύφεσθαι καὶ ἀνακαίεσθαι καὶ ἀναφλέγεσθαι μηδέποτε σβεσθῆναι δυναμένην, ἀλλ' ὅλην δι' ὅλων
αἰεὶ τὴν ψυχὴν ἐμπιπρᾶσάν τε καὶ πυρπολοῦσαν.

28 εἰκότως οὖν ἕψεται δίκη πάντα μοχθηρὸν τρόπον
ἐκκαθαίρουσα διανοίας· λέγεται γὰρ "ἐξαρεῖς τὸν
πονηρόν," οὐκ ἐκ πόλεως ἢ χώρας ἢ ἔθνους, ἀλλ'
"ἐξ ὑμῶν αὐτῶν"· ἡμῖν γὰρ αὐτοῖς ἐνυπάρχουσι
καὶ ἐμφωλεύουσιν οἱ ὑπαίτιοι καὶ ἐπίληπτοι
λογισμοί, οὕς, ὁπότε ἀνιάτως ἔχοιεν, ἀποκόπτειν

29 καὶ διαφθείρειν ἀναγκαῖον.   τὸν οὖν
ἀπειθῆ καὶ φίλεριν καὶ λόγων πιθανότητας ὥσπερ
τινὰς συμβολὰς καὶ ἐράνους ἐπὶ καθαιρέσει τοῦ
καλοῦ πορίζοντα καὶ ἀκράτῳ φλεγόμενον καὶ
καταμεθύοντα ἀρετῆς καὶ παροινίας ἐκτόπους[1] εἰς
αὐτὴν παροινοῦντα δίκαιον ἦν κατηγόρους μὲν
τοὺς ἄλλοις συμμάχους λαβεῖν, πατέρα καὶ μητέρα,
⟨φθορὰν⟩ δὲ ἐνδέξασθαι παντελῆ πρὸς νουθεσίαν
καὶ σωφρονισμὸν τῶν οἴων τε σῴζεσθαι.

30   Πατρὸς δὲ καὶ μητρὸς κοιναὶ μὲν αἱ κλήσεις,
διάφοροι δ' αἱ δυνάμεις.   τὸν γοῦν τόδε τὸ πᾶν
ἐργασάμενον δημιουργὸν ὁμοῦ καὶ πατέρα εἶναι
τοῦ γεγονότος εὐθὺς ἐν δίκῃ φήσομεν, μητέρα δὲ

[1] MSS. ἐκτόπως.

---

[a] Philo connects -φλυγεῖν with φλέγω, though the word
is rather to be connected with φλύζω, "bubble."

[b] Philo has in mind the (unquoted) conclusion of Deut. xxi.
21, "and the rest when they hear it shall fear." *Cf.* also
S.V.F. ii. 1175, where the Stoic idea of punishment as a
deterrent of others is brought out.

VIII. The fourth and greatest charge was that of 27 drunkenness—and drunkenness not of the milder but of the most intense sort. For the phrase here used, " fired with wine," [a] is as much as to say that the poison which causes folly, indiscipline, smoulders within the man, then bursts into fire and flame impossible to quench, and consumes the soul through its whole being with the conflagration. Naturally, 28 therefore, will punishment follow, purging every base tendency out of the mind. For it says, " thou shalt remove the evil one," not out of a city or a country or a nation but " out of yourselves " (Deut. xxi. 21). For it is in ourselves that the vicious and culpable thoughts exist and have their lair, thoughts which we must cut away and destroy when their state is incurable.   We see then this man as dis- 29 obedient, as strife-loving, as providing in the form of persuasive arguments " contributions " and " club-money " for the subversion of morality, and finally inflamed with strong drink and making drunken assaults on virtue and directing his monstrous orgies against her. Surely it were just that such a one as he should find his accusers in those in whom others find their allies, namely in his father and mother, and be visited with complete destruction, to admonish and bring to their senses those who can be saved.[b]

Now " father and mother " is a phrase which can 30 bear different meanings.[c] For instance we should rightly say and without further question that the Architect who made this universe was at the same time the father of what was thus born, whilst its mother was the knowledge possessed by its Maker.

[c] Lit. " the titles are common but the meanings different." See App. p. 500.

τὴν τοῦ πεποιηκότος ἐπιστήμην, ᾗ συνὼν ὁ θεὸς
οὐχ ὡς ἄνθρωπος ἔσπειρε γένεσιν. ἡ δὲ παρα-
δεξαμένη τὰ τοῦ θεοῦ σπέρματα τελεσφόροις ὠδῖσι
[362] τὸν μόνον καὶ ἀγαπητὸν αἰσθητὸν υἱὸν | ἀπεκύησε,
31 τόνδε τὸν κόσμον. εἰσάγεται γοῦν παρά τινι τῶν
ἐκ τοῦ θείου χοροῦ ἡ σοφία περὶ αὑτῆς λέγουσα
τὸν τρόπον τοῦτον· '' ὁ θεὸς ἐκτήσατό με πρωτίστην
τῶν ἑαυτοῦ ἔργων, καὶ πρὸ τοῦ αἰῶνος ἐθεμελίωσέ
με·'' ἦν γὰρ ἀναγκαῖον τῆς μητρὸς καὶ τιθήνης τῶν
ὅλων πάνθ' ὅσα εἰς γένεσιν ἦλθεν εἶναι νεώτερα.
32 IX. τούτων οὖν τῶν γονέων τίς ἱκανὸς ὑποστῆναι
κατηγορίαν; ἀλλ' οὐδὲ μετρίαν ἀπειλὴν ἢ ἐλα-
φροτάτην κατάμεμψιν. οὐδὲ γὰρ τῶν δωρεῶν
ἱκανὸς οὐδεὶς χωρῆσαι τὸ ἄφθονον πλῆθος, ἴσως
δὲ οὐδ' ὁ κόσμος, ἀλλ' οἷα βραχεῖα δεξαμενὴ
μεγάλης ἐπιρρεούσης τῶν τοῦ θεοῦ χαρίτων πηγῆς
τάχιστα ἀποπληρωθήσεται, ὡς ἀναβλύσαι τε καὶ
ὑπερεκχεῖσθαι. εἰ δὲ τὰς εὐεργεσίας ἀδυνατοῦμεν
δέχεσθαι, τὰς κολαστηρίους δυνάμεις πῶς ἐπι-
33 φερομένας οἴσομεν;   τοὺς μὲν δὴ τοῦ
παντὸς γονεῖς ὑπεξαιρετέον τοῦ παρόντος λόγου,
τοὺς δὲ φοιτητὰς καὶ γνωρίμους αὐτῶν τὴν ἐπιμέλειαν καὶ προστασίαν εἰληχότας ψυχῶν, ὅσαι
μὴ ἀνάγωγοι καὶ ἄμουσοι, νῦν ἐπισκεψώμεθα.
πατέρα τοίνυν εἶναί φαμεν τὸν ἄρρενα καὶ τέλειον
καὶ ὀρθὸν λόγον, μητέρα δὲ τὴν μέσην[1] καὶ
ἐγκύκλιον χορείαν τε καὶ παιδείαν· οἷς καλὸν καὶ
34 συμφέρον ὡς ἂν ἔκγονον τοκεῦσι πείθεσθαι. τοῦ
μὲν οὖν πατρός, ὀρθοῦ λόγου, παράγγελμα ἔπεσθαι

---

[1] MSS. ἴσην.

[a] Because there is another son not αἰσθητός, i.e. the νοητὸς
κόσμος, cf. Quod Deus 31.   [b] See App. p. 501.

With His knowledge God had union, not as men have it, and begat created being. And knowledge, having received the divine seed, when her travail was consummated bore the only beloved son who is apprehended by the senses,^a the world which we see. Thus 31 in the pages of one of the inspired company, wisdom is represented as speaking of herself after this manner : " God obtained ^b me first of all his works and founded me before the ages " (Prov. viii. 22). True, for it was necessary that all that came to the birth of creation should be younger than the mother and nurse of the All. IX. If *these* parents accuse, who 32 is able to withstand their accusation, or even a mild threat or the lightest chiding ? Why, even their gifts are so boundless in number that no one, not even, one may say, the world, can contain them, but like some small cistern it will quickly be filled to the brim by the influx from the fountain of God's gracious boons, and discharge the rest in an overflow. And if we are unable to contain their benefits. how shall we endure the visitation of their powers to chastise ? But in the present discussion, 33 we must leave out of consideration the parents of the universe, and rather turn our eyes to the disciples, who have followed in their company,^b to whom has been committed the care and guidance of such souls as are not without training or incapable of culture. I suggest, then, that the father is reason, masculine, perfect, right reason and the mother the lower learning of the schools, with its regular course or round of instruction. These two stand to us in the relation of parents to children, and it is good and profitable to obey them.

Now right reason, the father, bids us follow in the 34

καὶ ἀκολουθεῖν τῇ φύσει γυμνὴν καὶ ἀπημφιασμένην ἀλήθειαν μεταδιώκοντας, παιδείας δέ, τῆς μητρός, θέσει δικαίοις προσέχειν, ἃ κατὰ πόλεις καὶ ἔθνη καὶ χώρας ἔθεντο οἱ πρῶτοι δόκησιν
35 πρὸ ἀληθείας ἀσπασάμενοι. τοῖς γονεῦσι τούτοις τέτταρες παίδων εἰσὶ τάξεις, ἡ μὲν ἀμφοτέροις καταπειθής, ἡ δ᾽ οὐδετέρῳ προσέχουσα, ἐναντία τῇ προτέρᾳ· τῶν δ᾽ ἄλλων ἡμιτελὴς ἑκατέρα, ἡ μὲν γὰρ αὐτῶν φιλοπάτωρ σφόδρα γεγονυῖα τῷ μὲν προσέχει, μητρὸς δὲ καὶ τῶν ἐπισκήψεων[1] αὐτῆς ἀλογεῖ, ἡ δ᾽ ἔμπαλιν φιλομήτωρ εἶναι δοκοῦσα τῇ μὲν πάντα ὑπηρετεῖ, τῶν δὲ τοῦ πατρὸς ἥκιστα φροντίζει. ἡ μὲν οὖν πρώτη τὰ κατὰ πάντων ἆθλα οἴσεται νικητήρια, ἡ δ᾽ ἀντίπαλος ἧτταν ὁμοῦ καὶ φθορὰν ἀναδέξεται, τῶν δ᾽ ἄλλων ἑκατέρα, ἡ μὲν δευτερείων, ἡ δὲ τρίτων ἄθλων μεταποιήσεται, δευτερείων μὲν ἡ πειθαρχοῦσα πατρί, τρίτων δ᾽ ἡ τῇ μητρί.

36 X. Τῆς μὲν οὖν φιλομήτορος ταῖς τῶν πολλῶν δόξαις ὑπεικούσης καὶ κατὰ τὰς πολυτρόπους τοῦ βίου ζηλώσεις παντοδαπὰς μεταβαλλούσης ἰδέας |
[363] Αἰγυπτίου Πρωτέως τὸν τρόπον, ὃς τῷ πάνθ᾽ ὅσα ἐν τῷ παντὶ πεφυκέναι γίνεσθαι τὸ ἀληθὲς ἀδηλούμενον ἔσχεν εἶδος, τύπος ἐναργέστατος Ἰοθόρ, πλάσμα τύφου, πρὸς πόλιν καὶ πολιτείαν συγκλύδων καὶ μιγάδων ἀνθρώπων κεναῖς αἰωρουμένων δόξαις
37 μάλιστα ἁρμόττων. Μωυσέως γὰρ τοῦ σοφοῦ τὸν λεὼν ἅπαντα τῆς ψυχῆς πρὸς εὐσέβειαν καὶ τιμὴν θεοῦ μετακαλοῦντος καὶ τάς τε προστάξεις

---

[1] mss. ἐπισκέψεων.

a Or " opinion."
b See App. p. 501.

steps of nature and pursue truth in her naked and undisguised form. Education, the mother, bids us give ear to rules laid down by human ordinance, rules which have been made in different cities and countries and nations by those who first embraced the apparent [a] in preference to the true. These 35 parents have four classes of children. The first is obedient to both ; the second is the direct opposite, and gives heed to neither, while each of the other two lacks its half. One of them is heartily devoted to the father and gives ear to him, but disregards the mother and her injunctions. The other, on the contrary, appears devoted to the mother, and serves her in every way, but pays no heed to the words of the father. Of these four the first will carry off the palm of victory over all comers, while the second its opposite will receive defeat accompanied by destruction. Each of the others will claim a prize, one the second, the other the third ; the second belongs to the class which obeys the father, the third to the class which obeys the mother.

X. [b] This last kind which loves the mother, which 36 bows down to the opinions of the multitude and undergoes all manner of transformations in conformity with the ever-varying aspirations of human life, like the Egyptian Proteus, whose true form remained a matter of uncertainty through his power to become everything in the universe, is most clearly typified by Jethro. Jethro is a compound of vanity, closely corresponding with a city or commonwealth peopled by a promiscuous horde, who swing to and fro as their idle opinions carry them. See how he deals 37 with Moses. He in his wisdom was recalling the whole people of the soul to piety and to honouring

PHILO

καὶ τοὺς ἱερωτάτους νόμους ἀναδιδάσκοντος—
φησὶ γὰρ ὅτι " ἐπειδὰν γένηται αὐτοῖς ἀντιλογία
καὶ ἔλθωσι πρὸς μέ, διακρίνω ἕκαστον καὶ συμ-
βιβάζω τὰ προστάγματα τοῦ θεοῦ καὶ τὸν νόμον
αὐτοῦ"—, παρελθὼν ὁ δοκησίσοφος Ἰοθόρ, τῶν
μὲν θείων ἀμύητος ἀγαθῶν, τοῖς δὲ ἀνθρωπείοις
καὶ φθαρτοῖς μάλιστ' ἐνωμιληκὼς δημαγωγεῖ καὶ
νόμους ἐναντίους τοῖς τῆς φύσεως ἀναγράφει, πρὸς
τὸ δοκεῖν ἀφορῶν ἐκείνων ἀναφερομένων πρὸς τὸ
38 εἶναι. καίτοι καὶ τοῦτον ἐλεήσας καὶ οἰκτισά-
μενος τοῦ πολλοῦ πλάνου μεταδιδάσκειν οἴεται δεῖν
καὶ ἀναπείθειν ἀποστῆναι μὲν τῶν κενῶν δοξῶν,
39 ἀκολουθῆσαι δὲ παγίως τῷ ἀληθεῖ· " ἐξάραντες,"
γάρ φησιν, ἡμεῖς καὶ ἀποκόψαντες τῆς διανοίας
τὸν κενὸν τῦφον μετανιστάμεθα εἰς τὸν ἐπιστήμης
τόπον, ὃν χρησμοῖς καὶ ὁμολογίαις θείαις λαμ-
βάνομεν· " ἴθι δὴ μεθ' ἡμῶν καὶ εὖ σε ποιήσομεν."
ἀποβαλεῖς μὲν γὰρ τὴν βλαβερωτάτην δόκησιν,
40 κτήσῃ δὲ τὴν ὠφελιμωτάτην ἀλήθειαν. ἀλλὰ γὰρ
τοιαῦτα κατεπασθεὶς ἀλογήσει τῶν εἰρημένων καὶ
ἐπιστήμῃ μὲν οὐδαμῇ οὐδαμῶς ἕψεται, ἀναχωρήσει
δὲ καὶ ἀναδραμεῖται πρὸς τὸν ἴδιον καὶ κενὸν τῦφον·
λέγεται γὰρ ὅτι εἶπε πρὸς αὐτόν· " οὐ πορεύσομαι
ἀλλ' εἰς τὴν γῆν μου καὶ τὴν γενεάν μου," τουτέστι
τὴν συγγενῆ ψευδοδοξοῦσαν[1] ἀπιστίαν, ἐπειδὴ τὴν
ἀληθεύουσαν[1] ἀνδράσι φίλην πίστιν οὐκ ἔμαθε.
41   XI. καὶ γὰρ ὅταν ἐπίδειξιν εὐσεβείας
βουλόμενος ποιήσασθαι λέγῃ· " νῦν ἔγνων ὅτι μέγας

---

[1] Or ψευδοδοξοῦσιν . . . ἀληθεύουσιν (Adler).

---

[a] The LXX has ἐξαίρομεν ἡμεῖς εἰς τὸν τόπον ὃν εἶπε Κύριος,
where ἐξαίρω, as often, is used intransitively. Philo, however,

338

God, and was teaching them the commandments and holy laws. His words are, " when they have a dispute and come to me, I judge between each of them and instruct them in the commandments of God and His law " (Exod. xviii. 16). And then comes forward Jethro the seeming wise, who has never learnt the secrets of the divine blessings, but his concern has been with little else than things human and corruptible. He plays the demagogue, and the laws which he lays down contradict the laws of nature ; for his eyes are fixed on semblance, while they relate to real existence. Yet even on him Moses has com- 38 passion, and pities him for his great delusion ; he feels that he should teach him a better lesson, and persuade him to depart from his empty opinions and follow truth stedfastly. We have " removed," [a] he 39 says in effect, and excised from the mind its empty vanity and are passing over to the place of knowledge, which is ours through the oracles and promises of God. " Come with us and we will do thee good " (Num. x. 29). For you will lose the most harmful of evils, mere seeming, and gain the most profitable of blessings, truth. But even to words of such charm 40 as these Jethro will pay no heed, nor ever follow knowledge in any way, but will hasten to return to the empty vanity which is indeed his own. For we read that he said to Moses, " I will not go, but I will go to my land and my generation " (Num. x. 30) ; that is, to the unfaith of false opinion which is his kinsman, since he has not learnt the true faith, so dear to real men.   XI. For when he 41 wishes to make a shew of piety and says " now I

for his allegory uses it transitively. The English " remove " gives the double usage.

κύριος παρὰ πάντας τοὺς θεούς," ἀσέβειαν παρὰ
δικάζειν ἐπισταμένοις ἀνδράσιν ἑαυτοῦ κατηγορεῖ.
42 φήσουσι γὰρ αὐτῷ· νῦν ἔγνως, ἀνόσιε, πρότερον
δ' οὐκ ἠπίστασο τὸ μέγεθος τοῦ παντὸς¹ ἡγεμόνος;
ἦν γάρ τι πρεσβύτερον θεοῦ, ᾧ προεντετύχηκας;
ἢ τοῖς ἐκγόνοις οὐχ αἱ τῶν γονέων ἀρεταὶ πρὸ τῶν
ἄλλων ἅπαξ ἁπάντων γνώριμοι; τοῦ δὲ παντὸς
οὐκ ἄρα ἀρχηγέτης ὁ κτίστης καὶ πατὴρ αὐτοῦ;
ὥστ' εἰ νῦν ἐγνωκέναι φῇς σύ, οὐδὲ νῦν ἔγνωκας,
43 ὅτι οὐκ ἀπὸ γενέσεως ἀρχῆς. ἐλέγχῃ δ' οὐδὲν
ἧττον ἐπιμορφάζων, ὅταν συγκρίνῃς τὰ ἀσύγκριτα
καὶ λέγῃς παρὰ πάντας τοὺς θεοὺς τὸ μεγαλεῖον
τοῦ ὄντος ἐγνωκέναι· εἰ γὰρ ᾔδεις ἀληθείᾳ τὸ ὄν,
οὐδένα ἂν τῶν ἄλλων ὑπέλαβες εἶναι θεὸν αὐτεξού-
44 σιον. ὥσπερ γὰρ ἀνατείλας ὁ ἥλιος ἀποκρύπτει |
[364] τοὺς ἀστέρας τῶν ἡμετέρων ὄψεων ἀθρόον τὸ ἑαυτοῦ
καταχέας φέγγος, οὕτως ὅταν τῷ τῆς ψυχῆς ὄμματι
ἀμιγεῖς καὶ καθαρώταται καὶ τηλαυγέσταται τοῦ
φωσφόρου θεοῦ νοηταὶ ἐναστράψωσιν αὐγαί, κατιδεῖν
οὐδὲν ἕτερον δύναται· ἐπιλάμψασα γὰρ ἡ τοῦ ὄντος
ἐπιστήμη πάντα περιαυγάζει, ὡς καὶ τοῖς λαμπρο-
τάτοις ἐξ ἑαυτῶν εἶναι δοκοῦσιν ἐπισκοτεῖν. θεοῖς
45 οὖν τοῖς ψευδωνύμοις οὐκ ἄν τις τὸν² ἀληθῆ θεὸν
συγκρίνειν ὑπέμενεν, εἴπερ ἀψευδῶς ἐγίνωσκεν αὐτόν·
ἀλλ' ἡ ἀνεπιστημοσύνη τοῦ ἑνὸς τὴν ἐπὶ πολλοῖς ὡς ὑπ-
άρχουσι, πρὸς ἀλήθειαν οὐκ οὖσι, δόξαν εἰργάσατο.

---

¹ παντὸς is suspected on the grounds that while Philo often
uses πάντων without the article, he regularly uses it with the
singular. Perhaps read πάντων ἡγεμόνος, or πανηγεμόνος, or
τοῦ τοῦ παντὸς ἡγεμόνος.   ² MSS. πιστὸν.

ᵃ See App. p. 501.
ᵇ Or "notwithstanding (all your professions)"; *cf.* the use
of οὐχ ἧττον in § 64 and § 195.
340

know that the Lord is great beyond all the gods "
(Exod. xviii. 11), he does but charge himself with
impiety in the eyes of men who knew how to judge.
They will say to him " Blasphemer ! is it now that 42
you know this, and have you never till now understood
the greatness of the ruler of all ? Did your past
experience shew you anything more ancient or more
venerable than God ? Are not the excellences of the
parents known to the children, before those of any
others ? Is not the Maker and Father of the Universe He who presided at its beginning ?*a* So if you
say that you now know, not even now have you true
knowledge, since it does not date from the beginning
of your own existence. And you stand no less *b* con- 43
victed of mere feigning, when you compare two in-
comparables, and say that you know that the greatness of the Existent is beyond all the Gods. For if
you had true knowledge of that which IS, you would
not have supposed that any other god had power of
his own.' The sun when it rises hides from our sight 44
the light of the other stars by pouring upon them
the flood of its own beams ; even so, when the rays
of the Divine Day-star, rays visible to the mind only,
pure from all defiling mixture and piercing to the
furthest distance, flash upon the eye of the soul, it can
descry nothing else. For when the knowledge of the
Existent shines, it wraps everything in light, and thus
renders invisible even bodies which seemed brightest
in themselves. No one, then, could have the boldness 45
to compare the true God with those falsely so called,
if he had any knowledge of Him which was free
from falsehood. But your ignorance of the One produced your opinion of the existence of the Many
whereas in real truth they had no existence.

46 XII. τῆς αὐτῆς προαιρέσεώς ἐστι πᾶς, ὅτῳ τὰ
μὲν ψυχῆς ἀπέγνωσται, τὰ δὲ περὶ σῶμά τε[1] καὶ
ἐκτὸς χρώμασι καὶ σχήμασι πεποικιλμένα πρὸς
ἀπάτην αἰσθήσεως εὐπαραγώγου θαυμάζεται.
47 καλεῖ δὲ τὸν τοιοῦτον ὁ νομοθέτης Λάβαν, ὃς τοὺς
ἀληθεῖς τῆς φύσεως νόμους οὐ κατιδὼν ψευδο-
γραφεῖ τοὺς παρὰ ἀνθρώποις φάσκων· " οὐκ ἔστιν
οὕτως ἐν τῷ τόπῳ ἡμῶν, δοῦναι τὴν νεωτέραν
48 πρὶν ἢ τὴν πρεσβυτέραν." οὗτος μὲν γὰρ τὴν ἐν
χρόνοις τάξιν φυλάττειν οἴεται δεῖν, τὰ πρεσβύτερα
πρότερον καὶ τὰ νεώτερα αὖθις εἰς κοινωνίαν
ἄγεσθαι δικαιῶν. ὁ δὲ σοφίας ἀσκητὴς εἰδὼς καὶ
φύσεις ἀχρόνους ὑπαρχούσας ἐφίεται καὶ νεωτέρων
προτέρων καὶ πρεσβυτέρων ὑστέρων.
ἔχει δὲ καὶ τὸν ἠθοποιὸν λόγον ἑαυτῷ συνᾴδοντα·
τοῖς γὰρ ἀσκηταῖς ἀνάγκη πρότερον ἐντυχεῖν τῇ
νεωτέρᾳ παιδείᾳ, ἵνα τῆς τελειοτέρας αὖθις ἀπ-
49 όνασθαι βεβαίως δυνηθῶσι. παρὸ καὶ μέχρι νῦν
οἱ καλοκαγαθίας ἐρασταὶ οὐ πρότερον ἐπὶ τὰς τῆς
πρεσβυτέρας ἀφικνοῦνται θύρας φιλοσοφίας, πρὶν
ἢ ταῖς νεωτέραις ἐντυχεῖν, γραμματικῇ καὶ γεω-
μετρίᾳ καὶ τῇ συμπάσῃ τῶν ἐγκυκλίων μουσικῇ·
αὗται γὰρ σοφίαν προξενοῦσιν. ὁ δ' ἀντισοφίζεται βουλό-
50 μενος τὴν πρεσβυτέραν ἡμᾶς ἀγαγέσθαι προτέραν,
οὐχ ἵνα βεβαίως ἔχωμεν, ἀλλ' ἵνα τοῖς τῆς νεωτέρας φίλτροις δελεασθέντες αὖθις τὸν ἐπ' ἐκείνῃ
51 πόθον ἐκλύσωμεν. XIII. καὶ σχεδὸν τοῦτο συνέβη πολλοῖς τῶν ἀνοδίᾳ πρὸς παιδείαν χρησα-
μένων. ἔτι γάρ, ὡς ἔπος εἰπεῖν, ἀπ' αὐτῶν σπαρ-

[1] MSS. σώματα.

---

[a] See App. p. 501.　　　　　[b] See App. p. 502.

XII. The same creed and rule is followed by every- 46
one who has rejected the things of the soul and set
his admiration on the things of the body, and outside
the body, with shapes and colours rife, decked out to
deceive the senses which are so easily seduced.   Such 47
a one is called by the lawgiver Laban, who, being
blind to the true laws of nature, proclaims with false
lips man-made law.   " It is not so in our place," he
says, " to give the younger in marriage before the
elder " (Gen. xxix. 26).   For Laban thinks that he 48
should maintain the order of time.   He holds that
older things should first be taken into our company,
and younger things only later.   But the Practiser
of Wisdom, knowing that the timeless also exists in
nature,[a] desires what is younger first and the elder
afterwards.   And the laws of human character [a] as well as of nature agree with him in this ;
for Men of Practice must first take up with the
younger culture, that afterwards they may be able
to have secure enjoyment of that which is more
perfect.   And therefore to this day the lovers of true 49
nobility do not attend at the door of the elder sister,
philosophy, till they have taken knowledge of the
younger sisters, grammar and geometry and the
whole range of the school culture.   For these ever
secure the favours of wisdom to those who woo her in
guilelessness and sincerity.   But Laban with his so- 50
phistry will have it otherwise, and wishes us to wed
the elder first, not that we may possess her in security,
but that afterwards snared by the love-charms of the
younger sister, we may abandon our desire of the elder.
XIII. [b]And this or something very like it happens 51
to many who have left the right path [b] in their search
for culture.   For from the very cradle, we may say,

γάνων πρὸς τελειότατον ἐπιτήδευμα, φιλοσοφίαν,
ἐλθόντες, ἀμύητοι τῶν ἐγκυκλίων εἰσάπαν οὐ
δικαιώσαντες γενέσθαι ὀψὲ καὶ μόλις αὐτῶν
ἅψασθαι διενοήθησαν. κἄπειτα ἀπὸ τῆς μείζονος
καὶ πρεσβυτέρας ἐπὶ τὴν τῶν ἐλαττόνων καὶ
νεωτέρων θέαν καταβάντες ἐνεγήρασαν αὐτοῖς,
ὡς μηκέτ' ἀναδραμεῖν ὅθεν ὥρμησαν ἰσχῦσαι.
52   διὰ τοῦτ' οἶμαί φησι· "συντέλεσον
[365] τὰ ἕβδομα ταύτης," ἴσον τῷ | μὴ ἀτελεύτητον
ἔστω σοι τὸ τῆς ψυχῆς ἀγαθόν, ἀλλ' ὅρον ἐχέτω
καὶ πέρας, ἵνα καὶ τῇ νεωτέρᾳ τάξει τῶν ἀγαθῶν
ἐντύχῃς, ἣν σώματος κάλλος καὶ δόξα καὶ πλοῦτος
53 καὶ τὰ ὁμοιότροπα κεκλήρωται. ὁ δὲ συντελέ-
σειν μὲν οὐχ ὑπισχνεῖται, "ἀναπληρώσειν" δ'
αὐτὴν ὁμολογεῖ, τουτέστι μηδέποτε ἐπιλείψειν τὰ
πρὸς αὔξησιν καὶ συμπλήρωσιν αὐτῆς ἐπιτηδεύων,
ἀλλ' ἀεὶ καὶ πανταχοῦ περιέξεσθαι,[1] κἂν μυρία τὰ
54 ἀντισπῶντα καὶ ἀνθέλκοντα ᾖ.   πάνυ
δ' ἐκδήλως τὸ τὰ ἔθη γυναιξὶ μᾶλλον ἢ ἀνδράσιν
ἐπιτηδεύεσθαι δοκεῖ μοι παρίστασθαι διὰ τῶν
Ῥαχὴλ τῆς μόνα τὰ αἰσθητὰ θαυμαζούσης λόγων·
φησὶ γὰρ πρὸς τὸν πατέρα ἑαυτῆς· "μὴ βαρέως
φέρε, κύριε· οὐ δύναμαι ἀναστῆναι ἐνώπιόν σου,
ὅτι τὰ κατ' ἐθισμὸν τῶν γυναικῶν μοί ἐστιν."
55 οὐκοῦν γυναικῶν ἴδιον τὸ ἔθεσι πείθεσθαι· καὶ γὰρ
τῷ ὄντι ἀσθενεστέρας καὶ θηλυτέρας ψυχῆς τὸ
ἔθος· ἀνδρῶν γάρ τοι ἡ φύσις, καὶ ἐρρωμένου καὶ
ἄρρενος ὡς ἀληθῶς λογισμοῦ ἕπεσθαι φύσει.

[1] MSS. περιέσεσθαι.

they betake themselves to the most perfect of studies, philosophy, and afterwards deeming it wrong that they should have no tincture at all of the school subjects, bethink themselves to make a belated and painful effort to grasp them. And then having made their descent from the greater and older branch, philosophy, to the contemplation of the lesser and younger branches, they grow old in their company and thus lose all power of retracing their course to the place from which they started. And 52 this, I think, is why Laban says, " bring to a consummation her week " (Gen. xxix. 27), meaning " let not the true good of the soul be thine unendingly, but let it have its term and limit, that so you may keep company with the younger order of goods in which are classed bodily beauty and glory and riches and the like." But Jacob does not promise to bring 53 her to a consummation, but agrees to "fulfil" (Gen. xxix. 28) her, that is never to cease pursuing what tends to her growth and completeness and always and everywhere to cleave to her, however great be the host of influences which draw and pull him in the opposite direction. That the rule of 54 custom is followed by women more than men is, I think, quite clearly shewn by the words of Rachel, who looks with admiration only on that which is perceived by the senses. For she says to her father, " Be not wroth, sir ; I cannot rise before thee, because the custom of women is upon me " (Gen. xxxi. 35). So we see that obedience to custom is the 55 special property of women. Indeed, custom is the rule of the weaker and more effeminate soul. For nature is of men, and to follow nature is the mark of a strong and truly masculine reason.

56 XIV. καταπέπληγμαι δὲ τὸ ἀψευδὲς τῆς ψυχῆς τῆς ἐν τοῖς ἑαυτῆς διαλόγοις ὁμολογούσης, ὅτι οὐ δύναται τῶν φαινομένων ἀγαθῶν κατεξαναστῆναι, ἀλλ᾽ ἕκαστον αὐτῶν τέθηπε καὶ τιμᾷ καὶ

57 μονονοὺχ ἑαυτῆς προκέκρικεν. ἐπεὶ τίς ἡμῶν ἀντιστατεῖ πλούτῳ; τίς δὲ πρὸς δόξαν κονίεται; τίς δὲ τιμῆς ἢ ἀρχῆς καταπεφρόνηκε σχεδὸν τῶν ἔτι φυρομένων ἐν κεναῖς δόξαις; οὐδὲ εἷς τὸ

58 παράπαν. ἀλλ᾽ ἕως μὲν οὐδὲν τούτων πάρεστιν, ὑψηγοροῦμεν ὡς ὀλιγοδεᾶς ἑταῖροι τὸν αὐταρκέστατον καὶ δικαιότατον καὶ ἐλευθέροις καὶ εὐγενέσιν ἁρμόττοντα περιποιούσης βίον· ἐπειδὰν δέ τινος τῶν εἰρημένων ἐλπὶς ἢ ἐλπίδος αὐτὸ μόνον αὖρα βραχεῖα καταπνεύσῃ, διελεγχόμεθα· ὑπείκοντες γὰρ εὐθὺς ἐνδίδομεν καὶ ἀντιβῆναι καὶ ἀντισχεῖν οὐ δυνάμεθα, προδοθέντες δ᾽ ὑπὸ τῶν φίλων αἰσθήσεων ὅλην τὴν ψυχῆς συμμαχίαν ἐκλείπομεν καὶ οὐκέτι λανθάνοντες ἀλλ᾽ ἤδη φανερῶς αὐτο-

59 μολοῦμεν· καὶ μήποτ᾽ εἰκότως· ἔτι γὰρ ἡμῖν ἔθη τὰ γυναικῶν ἐπιπεπόλακεν οὔπω δυνηθεῖσι τὰ μὲν ἐκνίψασθαι, πρὸς δὲ τὴν ἀνδρωνῖτιν μεταδραμεῖν ἑστίαν, καθάπερ λόγος ἔχει τὴν φιλάρετον διάνοιαν,

60 ὄνομα Σάρραν· αὕτη γὰρ εἰσάγεται διὰ τῶν χρησμῶν " τὰ γυναικεῖα πάντ᾽ ἐκλιποῦσα," ἡνίκα τὸ αὐτομαθὲς γένος ὠδίνειν καὶ ἀποτίκτειν

61 ἔμελλεν, ἐπίκλησιν Ἰσαάκ. λέγεται δὲ καὶ ἀμήτωρ γενέσθαι τὴν ἐκ πατρός, οὐ πρὸς μητρός, αὐτὸ μόνον κληρωσαμένη συγγένειαν, θήλεος γενεᾶς

ᵃ See App. p. 502.
ᵇ Or " all those who are allies of the soul."

XIV. And how striking is the frank truthfulness of 56
that soul who, discoursing with herself,^a confesses that
she cannot rise up against apparent goods, but stands
amazed before each of them, and honours them and
continues to prefer them almost to her own self. For 57
which of us stands up to oppose riches ? Who pre-
pares himself to wrestle with glory ? How many of
those who still live in the mazes of empty opinions
have come to despise honour and office ? Not a single
one. So long, indeed, as none of these things is with 58
us, we talk loftily as though our hearts were given to
that frugal contentment which is the secret of a life
completely self-sufficient and righteous, the life which
befits the free and nobly born. But when we feel
upon our cheeks the breath of hope for such things,
though it be but the slightest breath and nothing
more, we are shewn in our true colours, we straightway submit and surrender and can make no effort
of resistance. Betrayed by the senses which we love,
we abandon all comradeship with the soul ^b ; we
desert and that no longer secretly, but without con-
cealment. And surely that is natural. For the 59
customs of women still prevail among us, and we
cannot as yet cleanse ourselves from them, or flee to
the dwelling-place where the men are quartered,
as we are told that it was with the virtue-loving
mind, named Sarah. For the oracles 60
represent her as having left all the things of
women (Gen. xviii. 11), when her travail was at
hand and she was about to bring forth the self-
taught nature, named Isaac. She is declared, too, to 61
be without a mother, and to have inherited her kinship only on the father's side and not on the mother's,
and thus to have no part in female parentage. For

PHILO

ἀμέτοχος. εἶπε γάρ πού τις· "καὶ γὰρ ἀληθῶς
[366] ἀδελφή | μού ἐστιν ἐκ πατρός, ἀλλ' οὐκ ἐκ μητρός."
οὐ γὰρ ἐξ ὕλης τῆς αἰσθητῆς συνισταμένης ἀεὶ
καὶ λυομένης, ἣν μητέρα καὶ τροφὸν καὶ τιθήνην
τῶν ποιητῶν ἔφασαν, οἷς πρώτοις σοφίας ἀν-
εβλάστησεν ἔρνος, ἀλλ' ἐκ τοῦ πάντων αἰτίου καὶ
62 πατρός. αὕτη μὲν οὖν ὑπερκύψασα τὸν σωμα-
τοειδῆ πάντα κόσμον ὑπὸ τῆς ἐν θεῷ χαρᾶς γανω-
θεῖσα γέλωτα τὰς ἀνθρώπων θήσεται σπουδάς,
ὅσαι περὶ τῶν κατὰ πόλεμον ἢ κατ' εἰρήνην
63 πραγμάτων εἰσίν.   XV. ἡμεῖς δὲ ἔτι
ὑπὸ τῆς ἀνάνδρου καὶ γυναικώδους συνηθείας τῆς
περὶ τὰς αἰσθήσεις καὶ τὰ πάθη καὶ τὰ αἰσθητὰ
νικώμενοι τῶν φανέντων οὐδενὸς κατεξαναστῆναι
δυνάμεθα, πρὸς πάντων δὲ καὶ τῶν ἐπιτυχόντων
64 οἱ μὲν ἄκοντες οἱ δὲ καὶ ἑκόντες ἑλκόμεθα. κἂν
τὸ στῖφος ἡμῶν τοῖς τοῦ πατρὸς ἐπιτάγμασιν
ἀδυνατοῦν ὑπηρετεῖν ἁλίσκηται, σύμμαχον οὐδὲν
ἧττον ἕξει τὴν μητέρα, παιδείαν μέσην τὰ νομιζόμενα καὶ δοκοῦντα εἶναι δίκαια γράφουσαν κατὰ
πόλεις καὶ ἄλλα ἄλλοις νομοθετοῦσαν.
65 Εἰσὶ δέ τινες, οἳ τῶν μητρῴων ὑπερορῶντες
περιέχονται παντὶ σθένει τῶν πατρῴων, οὓς καὶ
τῆς μεγίστης τιμῆς, ἱερωσύνης, ὁ ὀρθὸς λόγος
ἠξίωσε. κἂν τὰς πράξεις αὐτῶν διέλθωμεν, ἐφ'
αἷς τὸ γέρας τοῦτο εὕραντο, χλεύην ἴσως παρὰ

___
ᵃ i.e. Plato. The allusion is to the *Timaeus*, where ὕλη
is described as the μητὴρ τοῦ γεγονότος 51 A, cf. 50 D, and
as τιθήνη 49 A and 52 D.
ᵇ An allusion to Sarah laughing in Gen. xviii. 12; cf. a

348

we find it said, "Indeed she is my sister, the daughter of my father but not of my mother" (Gen. xx. 12). She is not born of that material substance perceptible to our senses, ever in a state of formation and dissolution, the material which is called mother or foster-mother or nurse of created things by those in whom first the young plant of wisdom grew[a]; she is born of the Father and Cause of all things. And 62 so, soaring above the whole world of bodily forms, and exulting in the joy that is in God, she will count as a matter for laughter[b] those anxious cares of men which are expended on human affairs, whether in war or peace. XV. But we who are still under 63 the sway of habit, the unmanly and womanish habit, whose concern is with the senses and the objects of sense and the passions, cannot stand up against phenomena in any form, but all of them, even those of the common sort, draw us on sometimes with our free will, sometimes without it. Yet if our battalion 64 be unable to do service to the father's commands and thus suffer defeat,[c] it will none the less have an ally in the mother, the lower education, who enacts from city to city the ordinances which custom and opinion approve, her legislation differing with the different peoples.

But there are also some who despise the mother's 65 bidding, but cling with all their might to the father's words, and these right reason has judged worthy of the highest honour, the priesthood. And if we describe their deeds, for which they were thus rewarded, we shall perhaps incur the mockery of many, who are

similar use of the incident, in defiance of its context, *Leg. All.* iii. 219.
^c Or " be convicted as incapable of doing service."

πολλοῖς ὀφλήσομεν τοῖς ταῖς προχείροις φαντασίαις
ἀπατωμένοις, τὰς δὲ ἀφανεῖς καὶ συνεσκιασμένας
66 δυνάμεις οὐ κατανοοῦσιν· οἱ γὰρ εὐχὰς καὶ
θυσίας καὶ πᾶσαν τὴν περὶ τὸ ἱερὸν ἁγιστείαν ἐγ-
χειρισθέντες εἰσί, τὸ παραδοξότατον, ἀνδροφόνοι,
ἀδελφοκτόνοι, τῶν οἰκειοτάτων καὶ φιλτάτων
σωμάτων αὐτόχειρες, οὓς ἐχρῆν καθαροὺς καὶ ἐκ
καθαρῶν, μηδενὸς ἄγους προσαψαμένους, ἑκουσίου
μὲν ἄπαγε, ἀλλὰ μηδ᾽ ἀκουσίου χειροτονεῖσθαι·
67 λέγεται γάρ· "ἀποκτείνατε ἕκαστος τὸν ἀδελφὸν
αὑτοῦ καὶ ἕκαστος τὸν πλησίον αὑτοῦ καὶ ἕκαστος
τὸν ἔγγιστα αὑτοῦ. καὶ ἐποίησαν οἱ υἱοὶ Λευί,
καθὰ ἐλάλησε Μωυσῆς, καὶ ἔπεσον ἐκ τοῦ λαοῦ
ἐν ἐκείνῃ τῇ ἡμέρᾳ εἰς τρισχιλίους ἄνδρας." καὶ
τοὺς τοσαύτην ἀνῃρηκότας πληθὺν ἐπαινεῖ φάσκων·
"ἐπληρώσατε τὰς χεῖρας σήμερον κυρίῳ, ἕκαστος
ἐν τῷ υἱῷ ἢ τῷ ἀδελφῷ, δοθῆναι ἐφ᾽ ὑμᾶς εὐλογίαν."
68 XVI. τί οὖν λεκτέον ἢ ὅτι οἱ τοιοῦτοι τοῖς μὲν
κοινοῖς ἀνθρώπων ἔθεσιν ἁλίσκονται κατήγοροι
ἔχοντες τὴν πολιτευομένην καὶ δημαγωγὸν μητέρα
συνήθειαν, τοῖς δὲ τῆς φύσεως διασῴζονται συμ-
μάχῳ χρώμενοι ὀρθῷ λόγῳ, τῷ πατρί;
69 καὶ γὰρ οὐδ᾽, ὥσπερ νομίζουσί τινες, ἀνθρώπους
ἀναιροῦσιν οἱ ἱερεῖς, ζῷα λογικὰ ἐκ ψυχῆς καὶ
σώματος συνεστῶτα, ἀλλ᾽ ὅσα οἰκεῖα καὶ φίλα τῇ σαρκὶ
[367] ἀποκόπτουσι τῆς διανοίας ἑαυτῶν,| εὐπρεπὲς εἶναι
νομίζοντες τοῖς θεραπευταῖς τοῦ μόνου σοφοῦ
γενησομένοις πάντων ὅσα γένεσιν εἴληχεν ἀλλοτριοῦ-
σθαι καὶ πᾶσιν ὡς ἐχθροῖς καὶ δυσμενεστάτοις
70 προσφέρεσθαι. διὰ τοῦτο καὶ "ἀδελφόν," οὐκ
ἄνθρωπον, ἀλλὰ τὸ ψυχῆς ἀδελφὸν σῶμα ἀποκτενοῦμεν, τουτέστι τοῦ φιλαρέτου καὶ θείου τὸ

350

deceived by the semblances that lie ready before their eyes but do not descry the values which are unseen and wrapt in shadow. For they into whose charge 66 the work of prayer and sacrifice and all the worship of the temple was given, are actually—strange paradox— homicides, fratricides, slayers of the bodies which are nearest and dearest to them, though they should have come to their office, pure in themselves and in their lineage, having had no contact with any pollution even involuntary, far less voluntary. For 67 we read " slay each his brother and each his neighbour and each him that is nearest to him. And the children of Levi did as Moses spake, and there fell of the people on that day up to three thousand men " (Exod. xxxii. 27, 28). And he praises those who had slain this great multitude with these words, " ye have filled your hands to-day unto the Lord, each in his son or in his brother, that blessing should be given upon you " (Exod. xxxii. 29). XVI. What, then, can we 68 say but that such as these are condemned by the rules that obtain among men, for they have for their accuser their mother, custom, the politician and demagogue, but are acquitted by the laws of nature, for they have the support of their father, right reason ?

For it is not human beings, as some suppose, who are 69 slain by the priests, not living reasoning animals composed of soul and body. No, they are cutting away from their own hearts and minds all that is near and dear to the flesh. They hold that it befits those who are to be ministers to the only wise Being, to estrange themselves from all that belongs to the world of creation, and to treat all such as bitter and deadly foes. Therefore we shall kill our " brother "—not a 70 man, but the soul's brother, the body ; that is, we shall

PHILO

φιλοπαθὲς καὶ θνητὸν διαζεύξομεν. ἀποκτενοῦμεν
καὶ τὸν " πλησίον," πάλιν οὐκ ἄνθρωπον, ἀλλὰ τὸν
‹αἰσθήσεων› χορὸν καὶ θίασον· οὗτος[1] γὰρ ψυχῆς
ἐστιν ὁμοῦ καὶ οἰκεῖος καὶ δυσμενής, δελέατα καὶ
παγίδας ἐπ' αὐτῇ τιθείς, ἵνα τοῖς ἐπιρρέουσιν
αἰσθητοῖς κατακλυζομένη μηδέποτε πρὸς οὐρανὸν
ἀνακύψῃ μηδὲ τὰς νοητὰς καὶ θεοειδεῖς φύσεις
ἀσπάσηται. ἀποκτενοῦμεν καὶ " τὸν ἔγγιστα"· ὁ
δ' ἐγγυτάτω διανοίας ὁ κατὰ προφορὰν ἐστι λόγος,
εὐλόγοις καὶ εἰκόσι καὶ πιθανότησι δόξας ψευδεῖς
ἐντιθεὶς ἐπ' ὀλέθρῳ τοῦ κρατίστου κτήματος
71 ἀληθείας. XVII. διὰ τί οὖν οὐχὶ καὶ τοῦτον
σοφιστὴν ὄντα καὶ μιαρὸν ἀμυνούμεθα τὸν ἁρμόττοντα αὐτῷ καταψηφισάμενοι θάνατον, ἡσυχίαν—
λόγου γὰρ ἡσυχία θάνατος—, ἵνα μηκέτ' ἐν-
σοφιστεύοντος ὁ νοῦς μεθέλκηται, δύνηται δ'
ἀπηλλαγμένος πάντως τῶν κατὰ τὸ " ἀδελφὸν"
σῶμα ἡδονῶν, τῶν κατὰ τὰς " πλησίον" καὶ
ἀγχιθύρους αἰσθήσεις γοητειῶν, τῶν κατὰ τὸν
" ἔγγιστα" λόγον σοφιστειῶν ἐλεύθερος καὶ ἄφετος
ἐαθεὶς καθαρῶς τοῖς νοητοῖς ἅπασιν ἐπιβάλλειν;
72   οὗτός ἐστιν ὁ " λέγων τῷ πατρὶ καὶ
τῇ μητρί," τοῖς θνητοῖς γονεῦσιν, " οὐχ ἑώρακα
ὑμᾶς," ἀφ' οὗ τὰ θεῖα εἶδον, ὁ " μὴ γνωρίζων τοὺς
υἱούς," ἀφ' οὗ γνώριμος σοφίας ἐγένετο, ὁ " ἀπογινώσκων τοὺς ἀδελφούς," ἀφ' οὗ μὴ ἀπεγνώσθη
παρὰ θεῷ, ἀλλὰ σωτηρίας ἠξιώθη παντελοῦς.
73   οὗτός ἐστιν ὁ " τὸν σειρομάστην
λαβών," τουτέστιν ὁ μαστεύσας καὶ ἀναζητήσας

[1] Or perhaps, as Mangey, τὸν χορὸν αἰσθήσεων· οὗτος.

[a] See App. p. 502.
[b] Lit. " pit-searcher "; see footnote to De Post. 182.
352

dissever the passion-loving and mortal element from the virtue-loving and divine. We shall kill, too, our " neighbour," again no man, but the troop and company of the senses. That company is at once the close intimate and the enemy of the soul, spreading its gins and snares for her, in order that, overwhelmed by the flood of sense-perceived objects, she may never lift her head heavenwards nor welcome those natures whose divine forms are grasped only by the mind. Again we shall kill our " nearest "; and nearest to the understanding is the uttered word,[a] which through the specious, the probable and the persuasive implants in us false opinions for the destruction of our noblest possession, truth. XVII. Why, then, should 71 we not at once take vengeance on him too, sophist and miscreant that he is, by sentencing him to the death that befits him—that is to silence, for silence is the death of speech ? Thus will he no longer ply his sophistries within the mind, nor will that mind be led astray, but absolutely released from the pleasures of his " brother," the body, and from the witcheries of the senses, the " neighbours " at his gates, and from the sophistries of the speech which is " nearest " to him, he will be able to devote his unhampered liberty to the world of mental things.   It is this 72 Mind who " says to his father and mother "—his mortal parents—" I have not seen you," from the day when I saw the things of God ; it is this Mind who no longer knows his sons, ever since he came to the knowledge of wisdom ; it is this Mind who renounces his brethren (Deut. xxxiii. 9), ever since he was not renounced before God, but judged worthy of full salvation.   It is this same Mind who 73 " took the lance," [b] that is probed and searched the

τὰ τῆς φθαρτῆς γενέσεως, ἧς ἐν σιτίοις καὶ ποτοῖς
τὸ εὔδαιμον τεθησαύρισται, καὶ " εἰς τὴν κάμινον,"
ὥς φησι Μωυσῆς, " εἰσελθών," τὸν καιόμενον
καὶ φλεγόμενον ὑπερβολαῖς ἀδικημάτων καὶ μηδέποτε σβεσθῆναι δυνάμενον ἀνθρώπων βίον, κἄπειτα
ἰσχύσας καὶ τὴν " γυναῖκα διὰ τῆς μήτρας " ἀνα-
τεμεῖν, ὅτι αἰτία τοῦ γεννᾶν ἔδοξεν εἶναι πάσχουσα
πρὸς ἀλήθειαν μᾶλλον ἢ δρῶσα, καὶ πάντα " ἄνθρωπον " καὶ λογισμὸν τὸν ἐπακολουθήσαντα τῇδε
τῇ δόξῃ τῇ ⟨τὰ⟩ τοῦ μόνου τῶν γινομένων αἰτίου
θεοῦ περιαπτούσῃ παθηταῖς οὐσίαις.   XVIII.
74 ἆρ' οὐχὶ καὶ οὗτος ἀνδροφόνος παρὰ πολλοῖς ἂν
[368] εἶναι νομισθείη τοῖς | πρὸς γυναικῶν ἔθεσιν ἁλισκό-
μενος[1]; ἀλλὰ παρά γε θεῷ τῷ πανηγεμόνι καὶ
πατρὶ μυρίων ἐπαίνων καὶ ἐγκωμίων καὶ ἀναφ-
αιρέτων ἄθλων ἀξιωθήσεται· τὰ δ' ἆθλα μεγάλα
75 καὶ ἀδελφά, εἰρήνη καὶ ἱερωσύνη.   τό
τε γὰρ τὴν ἐν τῷ σπουδαζομένῳ παρὰ τοῖς πολλοῖς
ἀνθρώποις βίῳ δυσάλωτον στρατείαν καὶ τὸν ἐν
ψυχῇ τῶν ἐπιθυμιῶν ἐμφύλιον πόλεμον καταλῦσαι
δυνηθέντα εἰρήνην βεβαιώσασθαι μέγα καὶ λαμπρὸν
ἔργον, τό τε μηδὲν ἄλλο, μὴ πλοῦτον, μὴ δόξαν,
μὴ τιμήν, μὴ ἀρχήν, μὴ κάλλος, μὴ ἰσχύν, μὴ ὅσα
σώματος πλεονεκτήματα, μηδ' αὖ γῆν ἢ οὐρανὸν
ἢ τὸν σύμπαντα κόσμον, ἀλλὰ τὸ πρεσβύτατον τῶν
αἰτίων τὸ πρὸς ἀλήθειαν θεραπείας καὶ τῆς ἀνωτάτω

---

[1] Wendland τοῖς τρόπον γυναικῶν ἔθεσιν ἁλισκομένοις.   See
App. p. 503.

---

[a] A.V. " tent," R.V. " pavilion " (marg. " alcove "). No
reason seems to be known for the LXX translation. κάμινος
elsewhere always means " furnace," a sense impossible in this
context.   [b] See App. p. 502.

secrets of corruptible creation, which finds in food and drink the treasure-house of its happiness; who " entered," as Moses tells us, " the furnace " ᵃ—the furnace of human life, which burns so fiercely and unquenchably, fed with the exceeding multitude of our transgressions; who then received strength to " pierce " both the woman and the man—" the woman through the womb," because she believed herself to be the cause of generation, though in reality her part is passive rather than active—" the man " as representing every thought which followed this belief—the belief which invests the natures which are but the subjects of God's action with the dues which belong only to Him who alone is the cause of all that comes into being (Num. xxv. 7, 8).ᵇ

XVIII. Surely such a one must pass for a murderer 74 in the judgement of the multitude, and be condemned by custom the woman-like, but in the judgement of God the all-ruling Father he will be held worthy of laud and praise beyond reckoning and of prizes that cannot be taken from him—two great and sister prizes, peace and priesthood (Num. xxv. 2, 13).

For to be able to stay the fierce per- 75 sistent warfare of the outward life which the multitude so eagerly pursues, and the intestine battling of lust against lust in the soul, and there establish peace, is a great and glorious feat. And to have learnt that nothing else, neither wealth, nor glory, nor honour, nor office, nor beauty, nor strength, nor all bodily advantages, nor earth nor heaven, nor the whole world, but only the true cause, the Cause supreme among causes, deserves our service and highest honour, and thereby to have attained the rank of

τιμῆς ἀξιώσαντα μόνον τὴν ἱερωσύνης λαβεῖν τάξιν
76 θαυμαστὸν καὶ περιμάχητον. ἀδελφὰ δ᾽ ἔφην τὰ
ἆθλα οὐκ ἀπὸ σκοποῦ, ἀλλ᾽ εἰδὼς ὅτι οὔτ᾽ ἂν ἱερεὺς
γένοιτο πρὸς ἀλήθειαν ἔτι τὴν ἀνθρωπίνην καὶ
θνητὴν στρατευόμενος στρατείαν, ἐν ᾗ ταγματαρ-
χοῦσιν αἱ κεναὶ δόξαι, οὔτ᾽ ἂν εἰρηνικὸς ἀνὴρ μὴ
τὸ μόνον ἀμέτοχον πολέμου καὶ τὴν αἰώνιον
εἰρήνην ἄγον ἀψευδῶς καὶ ἁπλῶς θεραπεύων.
77 XIX. Τοιοῦτοι μέν εἰσιν οἱ τὸν πατέρα καὶ
τὰ τοῦ πατρὸς τιμῶντες, μητρὸς δὲ καὶ τῶν
ἐκείνης ἥκιστα φροντίζοντες. τὸν δ᾽ ἀμφοτέροις
πολεμωθέντα τοῖς γονεῦσι διασυνίστησιν εἰσαγαγὼν
λέγοντα· "οὐκ οἶδα τὸν κύριον, καὶ τὸν Ἰσραὴλ
οὐκ ἐξαποστέλλω·" οὗτος γὰρ ἔοικε καὶ τοῖς πρὸς
θεὸν ὀρθῷ λόγῳ βραβευομένοις καὶ τοῖς πρὸς
γένεσιν παιδείᾳ βεβαιουμένοις ἐναντιοῦσθαι καὶ
78 συγχεῖν πάντα διὰ πάντων. εἰσὶ δὲ καὶ ἔτι νῦν—
οὔπω γὰρ τὸ ἀνθρώπων γένος τὴν ἄκρατον κακίαν
ἐκαθήρατο—μήτε τῶν εἰς εὐσέβειαν μήτε τῶν
εἰς κοινωνίαν μηδὲν ἁπλῶς δρᾶν ἐγνωκότες, ἀλλὰ
τοὐναντίον ἀσεβείας μὲν καὶ ἀθεότητος ἑταῖροι,
79 πρὸς δὲ τοὺς ὁμοίους ἄπιστοι. καὶ περινοστοῦσιν
αἱ μέγισται τῶν πόλεων κῆρες οὗτοι, τὰ ἴδια καὶ
τὰ κοινὰ ὑπὸ φιλοπραγμοσύνης διέποντες, μᾶλλον
δ᾽, εἰ χρὴ τἀληθὲς εἰπεῖν, ἀνατρέποντες· οὓς ἐχρῆν
ὥσπερ μεγάλην νόσον, λιμὸν ἢ λοιμὸν ἤ τι κακὸν
ἄλλο θεήλατον, εὐχαῖς καὶ θυσίαις ἀποτρέπεσθαι·
φθοραὶ γὰρ οὗτοι μεγάλαι τοῖς ἐντυχοῦσι. παρὸ
καὶ Μωυσῆς τὸν ὄλεθρον αὐτῶν ᾄδει πρὸς τῆς

ᵃ Apparently the thought is that the sea which blocked
the way of the Israelites was Pharaoh's ally. For " swallowed
up " cf. Ex. xv. 4 (lxx κατεπόθησαν).

priesthood—this is a privilege as marvellous as it is worthy of all our efforts. But when I called these 76 two prizes sisters, I did not miscall them. I knew that none could be a true priest, who was still a soldier in that war of mortal men, in which the ranks are led by vain opinions, and that none could be a man of peace who did not worship in truth and sincerity that Being who alone is exempt from war and dwells in eternal peace.

XIX. Such are they who honour the father and 77 what is his, but disregard the mother and what is hers. But the son who is at enmity with both his parents is shewn to us by Moses, when he represents him as saying, " I know not the Lord and I do not send Israel forth " (Exod. v. 2). Such a one, we may expect, will oppose both what right reason rules to be our duty to God and what training and education establish for our dealings with the world of creation ; and thus he will work universal confusion. The 78 human race has never purged itself of the wickedness which is unmixed with good, and there are still those whose will and purpose is to do no action whatever that can tend to piety or human fellowship, who on the contrary keep company with impiety and godlessness, and also keep no faith with their fellows. And 79 these are the chief pests which haunt cities, controlling or, to speak more truly, upsetting private and public life with their restless intrigues. We might well treat them like some great plague or famine or murrain, or any other heaven-sent curse, and endeavour to avert them by prayers and sacrifices. For great is the havoc they work among those whom they meet. And therefore Moses sings of their destruction ; how they fell through their own allies [a]

ἰδίου συμμαχίας ἁλόντων καὶ ὥσπερ τρικυμίαις
ταῖς ἰδίαις δόξαις ἐγκαταποθέντων.

80   XX. Λέγωμεν τοίνυν ἑξῆς καὶ περὶ τῶν τούτοις
μὲν ἐχθρῶν, παιδείαν δὲ καὶ ὀρθὸν λόγον ἐκτετι-
μηκότων, ὧν ἦσαν οἱ τῷ ἑτέρῳ τῶν γονέων προσ-
[369] κείμενοι τὴν ἀρετὴν | ἡμιτελεῖς χορευταί.[1] οὗτοι
τοίνυν καὶ νόμων, οὓς ὁ πατήρ, ὁ ὀρθὸς λόγος,
ἔθηκεν, ἄριστοι φύλακες καὶ ἐθῶν πιστοὶ ταμίαι,
81 ἅπερ ἡ παιδεία, μήτηρ αὐτῶν, εἰσηγήσατο. ἐδιδά-
χθησαν δὲ ὑπὸ μὲν ὀρθοῦ λόγου, πατρός, τὸν πατέρα
τῶν ὅλων τιμᾶν, ὑπὸ δὲ παιδείας, τῆς μητρός,
τῶν θέσει καὶ νομιζομένων παρὰ πᾶσιν εἶναι
82 δικαίων μὴ ὀλιγωρεῖν.   ἡνίκα γοῦν ὁ
ἀσκητὴς Ἰακὼβ καὶ τοὺς ἀρετῆς ἄθλους διαθλῶν
ἔμελλεν ἀκοὰς ὀφθαλμῶν ἀντιδιδόναι καὶ λόγους
ἔργων καὶ προκοπὰς τελειότητος, τοῦ φιλοδώρου
θεοῦ βουληθέντος αὐτοῦ τὴν διάνοιαν ἐνομματῶσαι,
ἵνα ταῦτ' ἐναργῶς ἴδῃ ἃ πρότερον ἀκοῇ παρελαμ-
βανε—πιστοτέρα γὰρ ὄψις ὤτων—, ἐπήχησαν
οἱ χρησμοί· "οὐ κληθήσεται τὸ ὄνομά σου Ἰακώβ,
ἀλλ' Ἰσραὴλ ἔσται σου τὸ ὄνομα, ὅτι ἴσχυσας
μετὰ θεοῦ καὶ μετὰ ἀνθρώπων δυνατός." Ἰακὼβ
μὲν οὖν μαθήσεως καὶ προκοπῆς ὄνομα, ἀκοῆς
ἐξηρτημένων δυνάμεων, Ἰσραὴλ δὲ τελειότητος·
83 ὅρασιν γὰρ θεοῦ μηνύει τοὔνομα. τελειότερον δὲ
τί ἂν εἴη τῶν ἐν ἀρεταῖς ἢ τὸ ὄντως ὂν ἰδεῖν;
ὁ δὴ κατιδὼν τἀγαθὸν τοῦτο παρ' ἀμφοτέροις

---

[1] Wendland suggested ⟨ὑστέρ⟩ησαν, and τῆς ἀρετῆς, but
Adler's argument for the ms. text, taking ὧν as dependent on
χορευταί and ἀρετὴν as acc. of respect, is convincing. The
phrase ἡμιτελεῖς τὴν ἀρετήν recurs De Decal. 110.

---

[a] The connexion lies in the words " strong with God and

and were swallowed up by the heavy sea of their own imaginations.

XX. Let us then speak next of those who are the 80 enemies of these last, but have given due honour to both education and right reason, of whom those who attach themselves to one parent only were but half-hearted followers in virtue. This fourth class are valiant guardians of the laws which their father, right reason, has laid down, and faithful stewards of the customs which their mother, instruction, has introduced. Their father, right reason, has taught them 81 to honour the Father of the all; their mother, instruction, has taught them not to make light of those principles which are laid down by convention and accepted everywhere. Consider the case 82 of Jacob.[a] The Man of Practice was now in the last bout of his exercises in virtue, about to exchange hearing for eyesight, words for deeds, and progress for perfection, since God in his bounty had willed to plant eyes in his understanding that he might see clearly what before he had grasped by hearing, for sight is more trustworthy than the ears. Then it was that the oracles rang out their proclamation, " Thy name shall not be called Jacob, but Israel shall be thy name, because thou hast been strong with God and mighty with men " (Gen. xxxii. 28). Now Jacob is a name for learning and progress, gifts which depend upon the hearing; Israel for perfection, for the name expresses the vision of God. And 83 what among all the blessings which the virtues give can be more perfect than the sight of the Absolutely Existent? He who has the sight of this blessing has

mighty with men." Philo equates God with the father " reason " and men with the mother " convention."

ἀνωμολόγηται τοῖς γονεῦσιν εὐδόκιμος, ἰσχὺν
μὲν τὴν ἐν θεῷ, δύναμιν δὲ τὴν παρὰ ἀνθρώποις
84 εὑράμενος.   εὖ μοι δοκεῖ καὶ ἐν Παροι-
μίαις εἰρῆσθαι "προνοούντων[1] καλὰ ἐνώπιον κυρίου
καὶ ἀνθρώπων," ἐπειδὴ δι' ἀμφοτέρων παντελὴς
ἡ κτῆσις τἀγαθοῦ περιγίνεται· διδαχθεὶς γὰρ
φυλάσσειν νόμους πατρὸς καὶ μὴ ἀπωθεῖσθαι
θεσμοὺς μητρὸς θαρρήσεις ἐπισεμνυνόμενος εἰπεῖν·
"υἱὸς γὰρ ἐγενόμην κἀγὼ πατρὶ ὑπήκοος καὶ
ἀγαπώμενος ἐν προσώπῳ μητρός." XXI. ἀλλ'
οὐκ ἔμελλες, εἴποιμ' ἂν αὐτῷ, στέργεσθαι φυλάττων
μὲν τὰ παρὰ γενητοῖς καθεστῶτα νόμιμα διὰ πόθον
κοινωνίας, φυλάττων δὲ καὶ τοὺς τοῦ ἀγενήτου
θεσμοὺς δι' εὐσεβείας ἔρωτα καὶ ζῆλον;
85 τοιγάρτοι καὶ θεοπρόπος Μωυσῆς διὰ τῆς τῶν
κατὰ τὸν νεὼν δημιουργίας ἱερῶν τὴν ἐν ἀμφοτέροις
τελειότητα διαδείξει· οὐ γὰρ ἀπερισκέπτως ἡμῖν
τὴν κιβωτὸν ἔνδοθέν τε καὶ ἔξωθεν χρυσῷ περιαμ-
πίσχει, οὐδὲ στολὰς τῷ ἀρχιερεῖ διττὰς ἀναδίδωσιν,
οὐδὲ βωμοὺς δύο, τὸν μὲν ἔξω πρὸς τὰ ἱερεῖα, τὸν
δὲ πρὸς τὸ ἐπιθυμιᾶν ἔνδον δημιουργεῖ, ἀλλὰ
βουλόμενος διὰ συμβόλων τούτων τὰς καθ' ἑκάτερον
86 εἶδος ἀρετὰς παραστῆσαι.   τὸν γὰρ
σοφὸν κἂν τοῖς κατὰ ψυχὴν ἔνδον ἀοράτοις κἂν
τοῖς ἔξω περιφαινομένοις δεῖ τῇ παντὸς τιμιωτέρα
χρυσοῦ φρονήσει κεκοσμῆσθαι, καὶ ὁπότε μὲν τῶν
ἀνθρωπείων σπουδασμάτων ὑποκεχώρηκε τὸ ὂν
θεραπεύων μόνον, τὴν ἀποίκιλον ἀληθείας ἐνδύεσθαι

---

[1] The lxx has προνοοῦ, which perhaps should be read here.

---

a See App. p. 503.
b Or " we must not fail to observe that he did."
360

his fair fame acknowledged in the eyes of both parents, for he has gained the strength which is in God and the power which avails among men.

Good also, I think, is that saying in the Proverbs, 84 "Let them provide things excellent in the sight of the Lord and men" (Prov. iii. 4), since it is through both these that the acquisition of excellence is brought to its fullness. For if you have learnt to observe the laws of your father and not to reject the ordinances of your mother,[a] you will not fear to say with pride, "For I too became a son obedient to my father and beloved before the face of my mother" (Prov. iv. 3). XXI. Aye indeed, I would say to such a one, "How could you fail to win affection, if in your desire for human fellowship you observe the customs that hold among created men, and in your zeal and passion for piety observe also the ordinances of the Uncreated? And therefore Moses, God's 85 interpreter, will use the sacred works that furnished the tabernacle to shew us the twofold perfection. For it is not without a well-thought purpose for us [b] that he covers the ark both inside and outside with gold (Exod. xxv. 10) and gives two robes to the high-priest (Exod. xxviii. 4), and builds two altars, one without for the sacrificial ritual, the other within for burning incense (Exod. xxvii. 1, xxx. 1). No, he wished by these symbols to represent the virtues of either kind. For the wise man must be 86 adorned with the prudence that is more precious than all gold, both in the inward invisible things of the soul and in the outward which are seen of all men. Again, when he has retired from the press of human pursuits and worships the Existent only, he must put on the unadorned robe of truth which nothing mortal

361

[370] στολήν, ἧς | οὐδὲν ἐφάψεται θνητόν—καὶ γὰρ
ἔστι λινῆς ὕλης ἐξ οὐδενὸς τῶν πεφυκότων ἀποθνήσκειν γεννωμένης—, ὁπότε δὲ μέτεισι πρὸς
πολιτείαν, τὴν μὲν ἔνδον ἀποτίθεσθαι, ποικιλωτάτην
δὲ καὶ ὀφθῆναι θαυμασιωτάτην ἑτέραν ἀναλαμ-
βάνειν· πολύτροπος γὰρ ὢν ὁ βίος ποικιλωτάτου
δεῖται τὴν σοφίαν τοῦ πηδαλιουχήσοντος κυβερνή-

87 του. οὗτος κατὰ μὲν τὸν περιφανῆ βωμὸν ἢ βίον
καὶ δορᾶς καὶ σαρκῶν καὶ αἵματος καὶ πάντων
ὅσα περὶ σῶμα δόξει πολλὴν ποιεῖσθαι πρόνοιαν,
ὡς μὴ μυρίοις ἀπέχθοιτο κρίνουσιν ἀγαθὰ μετὰ
τὰ ψυχῆς δευτερείοις τετιμημένα τὰ περὶ σῶμα,
κατὰ δὲ τὸν ἔνδον πᾶσιν ἀναίμοις, ἀσάρκοις,
ἀσωμάτοις, τοῖς ἐκ λογισμοῦ μόνοις χρήσεται,
ἃ λιβανωτῷ καὶ τοῖς ἐπιθυμιωμένοις ἀπεικάζεται·
ὡς γὰρ ταῦτα ῥῖνας, ἐκεῖνα τὸν ψυχῆς ἅπαντα

88 χῶρον εὐωδίας ἀναπίμπλησι. XXII.
χρὴ μέντοι μηδὲ τοῦτ' ἀγνοεῖν, ὅτι ἡ σοφία τέχνη
τεχνῶν οὖσα δοκεῖ μὲν ταῖς διαφόροις ὕλαις
ἐναλλάττεσθαι, τὸ δ' αὐτῆς ἀληθὲς εἶδος ἄτρεπτον
ἐμφαίνει τοῖς ὀξυδορκοῦσι καὶ μὴ τῷ περι-
κεχυμένῳ τῆς οὐσίας ὄγκῳ μεθελκομένοις, ἀλλὰ
τὸν ἐνεσφραγισμένον ὑπὸ τῆς τέχνης αὐτῆς χα-

89 ρακτῆρα διορῶσι. τὸν ἀνδριαντοποιὸν Φειδίαν
ἐκεῖνον καὶ χαλκὸν λαβόντα φασὶ καὶ ἐλέφαντα καὶ
χρυσὸν καὶ ἄλλας διαφόρους ὕλας ἀνδριάντας
ἀπεργάσασθαι καὶ ἐν ἅπασι τούτοις μίαν καὶ τὴν
αὐτὴν ἐνσημήνασθαι τέχνην, ὡς μὴ μόνον ἐπι-
στήμονας, ἀλλὰ καὶ λίαν ἰδιώτας τὸν δημιουργὸν

90 ἀπὸ τῶν δημιουργηθέντων γνωρίσαι· καθάπερ γὰρ

ᵃ i.e. not of wool. The same contrast is made De Spec. Leg.
i. 84.

shall touch. For the stuff of which it is made is linen, not the produce of animals whose nature is to perish.[a] But when he passes to the citizen's life, he must put off that inner robe and don another,[b] whose manifold richness is a marvel to the eye. For life is many-sided, and needs that the master who is to control the helm should be wise with a wisdom of manifold variety. Again, that master as he stands at the outer, 87 the open and visible altar, the altar of common life, will seem to pay much regard to skin and flesh and blood and all the bodily parts lest he should offend the thousands who, though they assign to the things of the body a value secondary to the things of the soul, yet do hold them to be good. But when he stands at the inner altar, he will deal only with what is bloodless, fleshless, bodiless and is born of reason, which things are likened to the incense and the burnt spices. For as the incense fills the nostrils, so do these pervade the whole region of the soul with fragrance. XXII. This too we must not fail 88 to know, that wisdom which is the art of arts[c] seems to change with its different subject matters, yet shews its true form unchanged to those who have clearness of vision and are not misled by the dense and heavy wrappings which envelop its true substance, but descry the form impressed by the art itself. They say 89 that the great sculptor Pheidias would take brass and ivory and gold and various other materials to make his statues, and yet on all these he so stamped the impress of one and the same art, that not only adepts, but those who were totally ignorant of such matters, recognized the artist from his work. For as nature 90

---

[b] The reference is to Lev. xvi. 4 and 23, 24.
[c] See App. p. 503.

ἐπὶ τῶν διδύμων ἡ φύσις χρησαμένη τῷ αὐτῷ
πολλάκις χαρακτῆρι παρὰ μικρὸν ἀπαραλλάκτους
ὁμοιότητας ἐτύπωσε, τὸν αὐτὸν τρόπον καὶ ἡ τελεία
τέχνη, μίμημα καὶ ἀπεικόνισμα φύσεως οὖσα,
ὅταν διαφόρους ὕλας παραλάβῃ, σχηματίζει καὶ
ἐνσφραγίζεται τὴν αὐτὴν ἁπάσαις ἰδέαν, ὡς ταύτῃ
μάλιστα συγγενῆ καὶ ἀδελφὰ καὶ δίδυμα τὰ δη-
91 μιουργηθέντα γενέσθαι.   ταὐτὸν οὖν καὶ
ἡ ἐν τῷ σοφῷ δύναμις ἐπιδείξεται· πραγματευομένη
γὰρ τὰ περὶ τοῦ ὄντος εὐσέβεια καὶ ὁσιότης
ὀνομάζεται, τὰ δὲ περὶ οὐρανοῦ καὶ τῶν κατ' αὐτὸν
φυσιολογία, μετεωρολογικὴ δὲ τὰ περὶ τὸν ἀέρα
καὶ ὅσα κατὰ τὰς τροπὰς αὐτοῦ καὶ μεταβολὰς
ἔν τε ταῖς ὁλοσχερέσιν ἐτησίοις ὥραις καὶ ταῖς ἐν
μέρει κατά τε μηνῶν καὶ ἡμερῶν περιόδους πέφυκε
συνίστασθαι, ἠθικὴ δὲ τὰ πρὸς ἀνθρωπίνων ἐπανόρθωσιν ἠθῶν, ἧς ἰδέαι πολιτική τε ἡ περὶ[1] πόλιν
καὶ ἡ περὶ οἰκίας ἐπιμέλειαν οἰκονομική, συμποτικὴ
[371] | τε ἡ περὶ τὰ συμπόσια καὶ τὰς εὐωχίας, ἔτι δ' αἱ
ἡ μὲν περὶ ἀνθρώπων ἐπιστασίαν βασιλική, ἡ δὲ περὶ
92 προστάξεις καὶ ἀπαγορεύσεις νομοθετική· πάντα
γὰρ ταῦτα ὁ πολύφημος ὡς ἀληθῶς καὶ πολυώνυμος
σοφὸς κεχώρηκεν, εὐσέβειαν, ὁσιότητα, φυσιολογίαν
μετεωρολογίαν, ἠθοποιίαν, πολιτείαν, οἰκονομίαν
βασιλικήν, νομοθετικήν, ἄλλας μυρίας δυνάμεις, καὶ
ἐν ἁπάσαις ἓν εἶδος καὶ ταὐτὸν ἔχων ὀφθήσεται.
93   XXIII. Διειλεγμένοι δὲ περὶ τῶν ἐν τοῖ
ἐκγόνοις τεττάρων τάξεων οὐκ ἂν οὐδὲ ἐκεῖν
παρίδοιμεν, ὃ γένοιτ' ἂν τῆς διαιρέσεως καὶ τομῆ
τῶν κεφαλαίων ἐναργεστάτη πίστις· τοῦ γὰ
μετεωρισθέντος καὶ φυσηθέντος ὑπ' ἀνοίας παιδὸ

---

[1] MSS. πρός.

364

so often in the case of twins by using the same stamp shapes likenesses which are almost identical, so too that perfect art, which is the copy and effigies of nature, may take different materials and yet mould them and impress on them all the same form, and this it is which chiefly makes the products of its work to be as kinsfolk, brothers, twins to each other.

We shall find the same thing happening with the 91 power which resides in the Sage. Under the name of piety and holiness it deals with the attributes of the Really Existent; under that of nature-study, with all that concerns the heavens and the heavenly bodies; as meteorology, with the air and the consequences which result through its changes and variations both at the main seasons of the year and those particular ones which follow cycles of months and days; as ethic, with what tends to the improvement of human conduct, and this last takes various forms; politic, dealing with the state; economic, with the management of a house; sympotic, or the art of conviviality, with banquets and festivities; and further we have the kingly faculty dealing with the control of men, and the legislative with commands and prohibitions. All these—piety, holiness, nature-study, 92 meteorology, ethic, politic, economic, king-craft, legislator-craft and many other powers—find their home in him who is in the truest sense many-voiced and many-named, even the Sage, and in all he will be seen to have one and the same form.

XXIII. After discussing the four classes of sons, 93 we must not overlook the following point, which will be the clearest proof that our classification is based on a correct division. The son who is puffed up and carried away by his folly is denounced by his

οἱ γονεῖς τὸν τρόπον τοῦτον κατηγόρησαν εἰπόντες
" ὁ υἱὸς ἡμῶν οὗτος," δεικνύντες τὸν ἀπειθῆ καὶ
94 ἀπαυχενίζοντα. διὰ γὰρ τῆς δείξεως τῆς " οὗτος "
ἐμφαίνουσιν ὅτι καὶ ἑτέρους ἐγέννησαν, τοὺς μὲν
τῷ ἑτέρῳ, τοὺς δ' ἀμφοτέροις καταπειθεῖς, λογισμοὺς εὐφυεῖς, ὧν παράδειγμα Ῥουβήν· φιληκόους
καὶ φιλομαθεῖς ἑτέρους, ὧν ἐστι Συμεών, ἀκοὴ
γὰρ οὗτος ἑρμηνεύεται· πρόσφυγας καὶ ἱκέτας
θεοῦ, Λευιτῶν ὁ θίασος οὗτος· τὸν εὐχαριστητικὸν
ὕμνον ᾄδοντας οὐ γεγωνῷ φωνῇ μᾶλλον ἢ διανοίᾳ,
ὧν ἔξαρχος Ἰούδας· διὰ τὴν μετὰ πόνων ἀρετῆς
κτῆσιν ἑκούσιον μισθῶν καὶ δωρεῶν ἀξιωθέντας,
ὥσπερ Ἰσσάχαρ· μετανάστας ἀπὸ τῆς Χαλδαϊκῆς
μετεωρολογικῆς θεωρίας γεγονότας εἰς τὴν περὶ
τοῦ ἀγενήτου σκέψιν, ὡς Ἀβραάμ· αὐτήκοον καὶ
αὐτομαθῆ κτησαμένους ἀρετήν, ὥσπερ Ἰσαάκ·
λήματος καὶ ἰσχύος πλήρεις καὶ φίλους τῷ θεῷ,
καθάπερ Μωυσῆν τὸν τελειότατον.

95 XXIV. Εἰκότως οὖν τὸν ἀπειθῆ καὶ ἐρεθιστὴν
καὶ συμβολὰς εἰσφέροντα, τουτέστι συμβάλλοντα
καὶ συνάπτοντα ἁμαρτήματα ἁμαρτήμασι, μεγάλα
μικροῖς, νέα παλαιοῖς, ἑκούσια ἀκουσίοις, καὶ
ὥσπερ ὑπ' οἴνου φλεγόμενον ἄληκτον καὶ ἀνεπίσχετον μέθην τοῦ βίου παντὸς καταμεθύοντα καὶ
παροινοῦντα διὰ τὸ τοῦ τῆς ἀφροσύνης πόματος
ἀκράτου καὶ πολλοῦ σπάσαι καταλεύειν ὁ ἱερὸς
λόγος δικαιοῖ, ὅτι καὶ τὰς ὀρθοῦ λόγου προστάξεις
τοῦ πατρὸς καὶ τὰς παιδείας τῆς μητρὸς νομίμους
ὑφηγήσεις ἀνεῖλε καὶ παράδειγμα ἔχων τὸ καλο-

ᵃ Lit. " injunctions conforming to law or custom."

parents as " this son of ours," and it is in these words that they indicate his disobedience and recalcitrance. By using the word " this " in thus indicating him, 94 they suggest that they have other children, who are obedient either to one or both of their parents. Such are the reasonings of the naturally gifted, of which Reuben is a type ; the docile scholar, as Simeon, for his name means " hearing " ; the suppliants who take refuge with God, and this is the company of the Levites ; those who raise the hymn of thankfulness with their hearts rather than with their voices, and the leader of that choir is Judah ; those who have been judged worthy of rewards and prizes because of their own free will they have toiled in the acquisition of virtue, as Issachar ; those who have abandoned the Chaldean research of the supra-terrestrial to engage in the contemplation of the Uncreated, as Abraham ; those who have acquired virtue through no other voice but their own and no teacher but themselves, as Isaac ; those who are full of courage and strength and are dear to God, as Moses the most perfect of men.

XXIV. It is with good reason, then, that the dis- 95 obedient and contentious man who " brings contributions," that is contributes and adds sins to sins, great to small, new to old, voluntary to involuntary, and as though inflamed by wine drowns the whole of life in ceaseless and unending drunkenness, sodden with drinking deep of the unmixed cup of folly, is judged by the holy word to be worthy of stoning. Yes, for he has made away with the commands of right reason, his father and the observances enjoined by instruction,[a] his mother, and though he had before him the example of true nobility in his brothers

κἀγαθίας, τοὺς τοῖς γονεῦσιν εὐδοκίμους ἀδελφούς, τὴν τούτων ἀρετὴν οὐκ ἐμιμήσατο, τοὐναντίον δὲ καὶ προσεπιβαίνειν ἠξίωσεν, ὡς θεοπλαστεῖν μὲν τὸ σῶμα, θεοπλαστεῖν δὲ τὸν παρ' Αἰγυπτίοις μάλιστα τιμώμενον τῦφον, οὗ σύμβολον ἡ τοῦ

[372] χρυσοῦ ταύρου | κατασκευή, περὶ ὃν χοροὺς ἱστάντες οἱ φρενοβλαβεῖς ᾄδουσι καὶ ἐξάρχουσιν, οὐ παροίνιον καὶ κωμαστικὸν οἷα ἐν ἑορταῖς καὶ θαλίαις ἥδιστον μέλος, ἀλλὰ τὸν ὡς ἐπὶ τεθνεῶσιν ἀληθῆ θρῆνον αὑτοῖς, ὥσπερ ἔξοινοι καὶ τῆς ψυχῆς τὸν τόνον ὑπεκλύσαντές τε καὶ φθείραντες·

96 λέγεται γὰρ ὅτι " ἀκούσας Ἰησοῦς ⟨τῆς φωνῆς⟩ τοῦ λαοῦ κεκραγότων εἶπε πρὸς Μωυσῆν· φωνὴ πολέμου ἐν τῇ παρεμβολῇ. καὶ λέγει· οὐκ ἔστι φωνὴ ἐξαρχόντων κατ' ἰσχὺν οὐδὲ φωνὴ ἐξαρχόντων τροπῆς, ἀλλὰ φωνὴν ἐξαρχόντων οἴνου ἐγὼ ἀκούω. καὶ ἡνίκα ἤγγιζε τῇ παρεμβολῇ, ὁρᾷ τὸν μόσχον καὶ τοὺς χορούς." ἃ δὲ διὰ τούτων αἰνίττεται, παραστήσωμεν, ὡς ἂν οἷοί τε ὦμεν.

97 XXV. Τὰ περὶ ἡμᾶς τοτὲ μὲν ἠρεμεῖ, τοτὲ δὲ ὁρμαῖς καὶ ἐκβοήσεσιν ἀκαίροις ὡσανεὶ χρῆται· καὶ ἔστιν ἡ μὲν ἡσυχία τούτων εἰρήνη βαθεῖα, τὰ δὲ ἐναντία πόλεμος ἄσπονδος. μάρτυς δ' ὁ

98 πεπονθὼς ἀψευδέστατος· ἀκούσας γὰρ τῆς φωνῆς τοῦ λαοῦ κεκραγότων λέγει πρὸς τὸν σκεπτικὸν καὶ ἐπίσκοπον τῶν πραγμάτων· " φωνὴ πολέμου ἐν τῇ παρεμβολῇ." ἕως μὲν γὰρ οὐκ ἐκινοῦντο καὶ ἐκεκράγεσαν ἐν ἡμῖν αἱ ἄλογοι ὁρμαί, σταθερώ-

---

a See App. p. 503.

b ἔξοινος is contrasted with παροίνιος, a word which has not necessarily any unfavourable sense, in this differing from παροινεῖν and παροινία.

whom the parents honoured, he did not imitate their virtue, but contrariwise determined to be the aggressor in wickedness.[a] And thus he made a god of the body, a god of the vanity most honoured among the Egyptians,[a] whose symbol is the image of the golden bull. Round it the frenzied worshippers make their dances and raise and join in the song, but that song was not the sweet wine-song of merry revellers as in a feast or banquet, but a veritable dirge, their own funeral chant, a chant as of men maddened by wine,[b] who have loosened and destroyed the tone and vigour which nerved their souls.   For we 96 are told that " when Joshua heard the voice of the people as they shouted, he said to Moses : ' There is a voice of war in the camp, and he [a] said ' It is not the voice of men raising the shout [c] through might, nor of those who raise it for being overcome, but it is the voice of men who raise the shout over the wine that I hear.' And when he drew nigh to the camp, he saw the calf and the dances " (Exod. xxxii. 17-19). Let us shew as well as we can what he shadows forth under this figure.   XXV. Our being 97 is sometimes at rest, at other times is subject to impulses or, as we may call them, ill-timed outcries. When these are still we have profound peace, when it is otherwise we have relentless wars. To this 98 there can be no testimony so certain as that of personal experience. Such a person hears the voice of the people shouting and says to the one who watches and observes the course of events,[a] " There is a voice of war in the camp." For so long as the unreasoning impulses did not stir and " shout " within us, the

 [c] Or, as the allegorical treatment implies, " raise (or lead) the song."

τερον ὁ νοῦς ἵδρυτο· ἐπειδὴ δὲ ἤρξαντο πολύφωνον
καὶ πολύηχον ἀπεργάζεσθαι τὸ ψυχῆς χωρίον τὰ
πάθη συγκαλοῦσαι καὶ ἀνεγείρουσαι, στάσιν ἐμ-
99 φύλιον ἐγέννησαν.   ἐν δὲ τῷ στρατοπέδῳ
ὁ πόλεμος, φυσικώτατα· ποῦ γὰρ ἀλλαχόθι ἔριδες,
μάχαι, φιλονεικίαι, πάνθ᾽ ὅσα ἔργα ἀκαθαιρέτου
πολέμου, πλὴν ἐν τῷ μετὰ σώματος βίῳ, ὃν
ἀλληγορῶν καλεῖ στρατόπεδον; τοῦτον εἴωθεν
ἀπολιπεῖν ὁ νοῦς, ὅταν θεοφορηθεὶς πρὸς αὐτῷ
τῷ ὄντι γένηται καταθεώμενος τὰς ἀσωμάτους
100 ἰδέας· " λαβὼν " γάρ φησι " Μωυσῆς τὴν ἑαυτοῦ
σκηνὴν ἔπηξεν ἔξω τῆς παρεμβολῆς," καὶ οὐ
πλησίον, ἀλλὰ πορρωτάτω καὶ " μακρὰν ἀπὸ τῆς
παρεμβολῆς." αἰνίττεται δὲ διὰ τούτων, ὅτι ὁ
σοφὸς μέτοικος καὶ μετανάστης ἐστὶν ἀπὸ πολέμου
πρὸς εἰρήνην καὶ ἀπὸ τοῦ θνητοῦ καὶ πεφυρμένου
στρατοπέδου πρὸς τὸν ἀπόλεμον καὶ εἰρηναῖον
λογικῶν καὶ εὐδαιμόνων ψυχῶν βίον θεῖον.
101 XXVI. λέγει δὲ καὶ ἑτέρωθι ὅτι " ἐπειδὰν ἐξέλθω
τὴν πόλιν, ἐκπετάσω τὰς χεῖρας πρὸς τὸν κύριον,
καὶ αἱ φωναὶ παύσονται." μὴ νομίσῃς δὲ τὸν
διαλεγόμενον ἄνθρωπον εἶναι, τὸ ψυχῆς καὶ σώματος
ὕφασμα ἢ πλέγμα ἢ κρᾶμα ἢ ὅ τι ποτὲ χρὴ καλεῖν
τουτὶ τὸ σύνθετον ζῷον, ἀλλὰ νοῦν εἰλικρινέστατον
καὶ καθαρώτατον, ὃς ἐν μὲν τῇ πόλει τοῦ σώματος
καὶ τοῦ θνητοῦ βίου περιεχόμενος ἔσταλται καὶ
συνείληπται καὶ ὥσπερ ἐν δεσμωτηρίῳ καθειργ-
μένος μηδὲ ἐλευθέρου δύνασθαι σπᾶν ἀέρος ἄντικρυς
ὁμολογεῖ, ἐπειδὰν δὲ ἐξέλθῃ τὴν πόλιν ταύτην,
καθάπερ πόδας καὶ χεῖρας οἱ δεσμῶται τὰς ἐννοίας
[373] | αὐτὸς καὶ διανοήσεις λυθεὶς ἀφέτοις καὶ ἀπ-
ελευθεριαζούσαις χρήσεται ταῖς ἐνεργείαις, ὡς τὰς

mind stood firm and stedfast. But when they begin to fill the region of the soul with manifold sounds and voices, when they summon the passions and rouse them to action, they create the discord of civil war. "The war is in the camp." True **99** indeed. For where else do we find contentions, combats, hostilities and all the works that go with bitter and persistent war, but in the life of the body which in his parable he calls the camp? That camp the mind is wont to leave, when, filled with the divine, it finds itself in the presence of the Existent Himself and contemplates the incorporeal ideas. For **100** "Moses," we read, "took his tent and pitched it outside the camp," not near, but very far, "at a distance from the camp" (Exod. xxxiii. 7). Under this figure he suggests that the Sage is a pilgrim who travels from peace to war, and from the camp of mortality and confusion to the divine life of peace where strife is not, the life of reasonable and happy souls. XXVI. Elsewhere he says "When **101** I have gone out of the city I will spread out my hands to the Lord and the sounds shall cease" (Exod. ix. 29). Do not suppose that the person who speaks thus in a man—this compound animal in which soul and body are woven or twined or mingled (use any word you will). No, it is the mind pure and unalloyed. While it is cooped up in the city of the body and mortal life, it is cabined and cribbed and like a prisoner in the gaol declares roundly that it cannot even draw a breath of free air ; but when it has gone out of this city, its thoughts and reflections are at liberty, like the hands and feet of the unbound prisoner, and it finds free scope and range for the employment of its active powers, so that the

102 ἐπικελεύσεις τῶν παθῶν εὐθὺς ἐπισχεθῆναι. ἢ
οὐχ ἡδονῆς μὲν ἀνατεταμέναι αἱ ἐκβοήσεις, δι᾽ ὧν
τὰ ἑαυτῇ φίλα εἴωθε προστάττειν, ἐπιθυμίας δὲ
ἄρρηκτος ἡ φωνὴ χαλεπὰς ἀπειλὰς κατὰ τῶν μὴ
ὑπηρετούντων ἀπειλούσης, καὶ τῶν ἄλλων ἑκάστου
103 πολύηχος καὶ μεγαλόφωνός τις ἡ γῆρυς; ἀλλὰ
γὰρ οὐδ᾽ εἰ μυρίοις στόμασι καὶ γλώτταις ἕκαστον
τῶν παθῶν ⟨ἐν⟩ τῷ κατὰ τοὺς ποιητὰς λεγομένῳ
χρήσαιτο ὁμάδῳ, τὰς τοῦ τελείου δύναιτ᾽ ἂν ἀκοὰς
συγχέαι μετεληλυθότος ἤδη καὶ τὴν αὐτὴν ἐκείνοις
πόλιν μηκέτ᾽ οἰκεῖν ἐγνωκότος.

104   XXVII. Φαμένου δὴ τοῦ πεπονθότος, ὅτι ἐν τῷ
σωματικῷ στρατοπέδῳ τὰς τοῦ πολέμου φωνὰς
εἶναι πάσας συμβέβηκε τῆς εἰρήνη φίλης ἡσυχίας
μακρὰν ἀπεληλαμένης, ὁ ἱερὸς συναινεῖ λόγος· οὐ
γὰρ λέγει μὴ εἶναι πολέμου φωνήν, ἀλλὰ μὴ
τοιαύτην, ὁποίαν ἔνιοι νομίζουσιν ἢ νενικηκότων
ἢ κεκρατημένων, ἀλλ᾽ ἥτις ἂν γένοιτο βεβαρημένων
105 καὶ πεπιεσμένων οἴνῳ· τὸ γὰρ "οὐκ ἔστι φωνὴ
ἐξαρχόντων κατ᾽ ἰσχὺν" ἴσον ἐστὶ τῷ περι-
γεγενημένων τῷ πολέμῳ· ἰσχὺς γὰρ τοῦ κρατεῖν
αἴτιον.   οὕτως τὸν σοφὸν Ἀβραὰμ μετὰ
τὴν τῶν ἐννέα καθαίρεσιν βασιλέων, παθῶν μὲν
τεττάρων, πέντε δὲ αἰσθητικῶν δυνάμεων, αἳ παρὰ
φύσιν ἐκινοῦντο, εἰσάγει τὸν εὐχαριστητικὸν ὕμνον
ἐξάρχοντα καὶ φάσκοντα ταυτί· "ἐκτενῶ τὴν
χεῖρά μου πρὸς τὸν θεὸν τὸν ὕψιστον, ὃς ἔκτισε
τὸν οὐρανὸν καὶ τὴν γῆν, εἰ ἀπὸ σπαρτίου ἕως
σφαιρωτῆρος ὑποδήματος λήψομαι ἀπὸ πάντων
106 τῶν σῶν." δείκνυσι δ᾽, ὥς γ᾽ ἐμοὶ δοκεῖ, τὸ
γεγονὸς πᾶν, οὐρανόν, γῆν, ὕδωρ, πνεῦμα, ζῷα

clamours of the passions are at once restrained. How shrill are the outcries of pleasure, wherewith 102 it is wont to command what it wills! How continuous is the voice of desire, when it thunders forth its threats against those who do not minister to its wants! How full-toned and sonorous is the call of each of the other passions! Yet though each of 103 them should have a thousand tongues and mouths with which to swell the war-shout, to use the poet's phrase, yet it could not confuse the ears of the perfect Sage, who has passed elsewhere and resolved no longer to dwell in the same city as they.

XXVII. When the subject of that experience says 104 that he feels that in the camp of the body all the sounds are sounds of war, and that the quietness which is so dear to peace has been driven far away, the holy word does not dissent. For it does not say that the sound is not the sound of war but that it is not such a sound as some think it to be, such as would be made by the victorious or the defeated, but such as would proceed from those who are overpressed and weighed down by wine. For in the phrase "it is not the sound 105 of those who raise the song through might" the last words mean "those who have been victorious in war." For might is what causes victory. Thus wise Abraham, when he had routed the nine kings, the four passions that is and the five sense-faculties, which were rising in unnatural rebellion, is represented as raising the hymn of thanksgiving in these words, "I will stretch forth my hand to the most high God who made heaven and earth, if I will take from a rope to a shoe's latchet of all that is thine" (Gen. xiv. 22, 23). He points in these last words, I 106 think, to the whole of creation, heaven, earth, water,

PHILO

ὁμοῦ καὶ φυτά· ἑκάστῳ γὰρ αὐτῶν ὁ τὰς τῆς ψυχῆς
ἐνεργείας πρὸς θεὸν τείνας καὶ παρ' αὐτοῦ μόνου
τὰς ὠφελείας ἐπελπίζων δεόντως ἂν εἴποι· <παρ'>
οὐδενὸς λήψομαι τῶν σῶν, οὐ παρ' ἡλίου τὸ
μεθημερινόν, οὐ παρὰ σελήνης καὶ τῶν ἄλλων
ἀστέρων τὸ νυκτὶ φέγγος, οὐ παρὰ ἀέρος καὶ
νεφελῶν ὑετούς, οὐ παρὰ ὕδατος καὶ γῆς ποτὰ καὶ
σιτία, οὐ παρὰ ὀφθαλμῶν τὸ ὁρᾶν, οὐ τὸ ἀκούειν
παρὰ ὤτων, οὐ παρὰ μυκτήρων ὀσμάς, οὐ παρ'
ἐνστομίου χυλοῦ τὸ γεύεσθαι, οὐ παρὰ γλώττης
τὸ λέγειν, οὐ παρὰ χειρῶν τὸ διδόναι καὶ λαμβάνειν, οὐ τὸ προσέρχεσθαι καὶ ἐξαναχωρεῖν παρὰ
ποδῶν, οὐκ ἀναπνοὴν παρὰ πνεύμονος, οὐ πέψιν
παρ' ἥπατος, οὐ παρὰ τῶν ἄλλων σπλάγχνων τὰς
καθ' ἕκαστον οἰκείους ἐνεργείας, οὐ παρὰ δένδρων
καὶ σπαρτῶν τοὺς ἐτησίους καρπούς, ἀλλὰ πάντα
παρὰ τοῦ μόνου σοφοῦ τὰς αὐτοῦ χαριστηρίους
δυνάμεις πάντῃ τείναντος καὶ διὰ τούτων ὠφελοῦν-
τος. XXVIII. ὁ μὲν οὖν τοῦ ὄντος | ὁρατικὸς
τὸν αἴτιον ἐπιστάμενος τὰ ὧν ἐστιν αἴτιος δεύτερα
μετ' ἐκεῖνον τετίμηκεν ὁμολογῶν ἀκολακεύτως
τὰ προσόντα αὐτοῖς. ἡ δὲ ὁμολογία δικαιοτάτη·
παρ' ὑμῶν μὲν οὐδέν, παρὰ δὲ τοῦ θεοῦ λήψομαι,
οὗ κτήματα τὰ πάντα, δι' ὑμῶν δὲ ἴσως· ὄργανα
γὰρ ὑπηρετήσοντα ταῖς ἀθανάτοις αὐτοῦ χάρισι
γεγένησθε. ὁ δὲ ἀπερίσκεπτος διάνοιαν τυφλωθείς,
ᾗ τὸ ὂν μόνῃ καταληπτόν ἐστιν, αὐτὸ μὲν οὐδαμῇ
οὐδαμῶς εἶδε, τὰ δὲ ἐν κόσμῳ σώματα αἰσθήσεσι
ταῖς ἑαυτοῦ, ἃ δὴ πάντων ἐνόμισε γινομένων αἴτια.

107
[374]

108

374

the air we breathe, to animals and plants alike. To each of them he who has braced the activities of his own soul to stretch Godwards, and who hopes for help from Him alone, would rightly say, " I will take nothing from aught of thy creatures, not the light of day from the sun, nor the light of night from the moon and the other stars, nor rain from the air or the clouds, nor drink and food from water and earth, nor sight from the eyes, nor hearing from the ears, nor smell from the nostrils, nor taste from the juices of the palate, nor speech from the tongue, nor giving and receiving from the hands, nor moving forwards and backwards from the feet, nor respiration from the lungs, nor digestion from the liver, nor from the other inward parts the functions proper to each, nor their yearly fruits from the trees and seedlings, but I will take them all from the only wise Being who has extended His beneficent power every whither, and through them renders me help." XXVIII. He then 107 who has the vision of the Existent knows Him who is the Cause, and honours the things of which He is the cause only as second to Him. He will use no words of flattery, yet acknowledges what is their due. This acknowledgement is most just. I will take nothing *from* you, but I will take from God, the possessor of all things ; yet it may be that I will take *through* you, for you have been made instruments to minister to His undying acts of grace. But the man 108 of no discernment, whose understanding, by which alone the Existent can be comprehended, is blinded, has never anywhere seen that Existence, but only the material contents of this world as shewn to him by his senses, and these material things he believes to be the causes of all that comes into being.

109   παρὸ καὶ θεοπλαστεῖν ἀρξάμενος ἀγαλμάτων καὶ ξοάνων καὶ ἄλλων μυρίων ἀφιδρυμάτων
ὕλαις διαφόροις τετεχνιτευμένων κατέπλησε τὴν
οἰκουμένην, γραφεῦσι καὶ πλάσταις, οὓς ὑπερορίους
ὁ νομοθέτης τῆς κατ' αὐτὸν πολιτείας ἤλασεν,
ἆθλά τε μεγάλα καὶ τιμὰς ὑπερβαλλούσας ἰδίᾳ τε
καὶ κοινῇ ψηφισάμενος, ⟨καὶ⟩ κατειργάσατο
τοὐναντίον οὗ προσεδόκησεν, ἀντὶ ὁσιότητος ἀ-
110 σέβειαν· τὸ γὰρ πολύθεον ἐν ταῖς τῶν ἀφρόνων
ψυχαῖς ἀθεότητα ⟨κατασκευάζει⟩, καὶ θεοῦ τιμῆς
ἀλογοῦσιν οἱ τὰ θνητὰ θειώσαντες· οἷς οὐκ ἐξήρ-
κεσεν ἡλίου καὶ σελήνης, εἰ δὲ ἐβούλοντο, καὶ γῆς
ἁπάσης καὶ παντὸς ὕδατος εἰκόνας διαπλάσασθαι,
ἀλλ' ἤδη καὶ ἀλόγοις ζῴοις καὶ φυτοῖς τῆς τῶν
ἀφθάρτων τιμῆς μετέδοσαν. ὁ δὴ τούτοις ἐπιτιμῶν
τὸν ἐπινίκιον ὕμνον ἐξάρχων ἐδείχθη.
111 XXIX. καὶ Μωυσῆς μέντοι κατὰ ταῦτα, ἐπειδὰν
ἴδῃ τὸν βασιλέα τῆς Αἰγύπτου, τὸν ὑπέραυχον νοῦν,
σὺν τοῖς ἑξακοσίοις ἅρμασι, ταῖς τοῦ ὀργανικοῦ
σώματος ἓξ κινήσεσιν ἡρμοσμέναις τοῖς ἐπι-
βεβηκόσι τριστάταις, οἳ μηδενὸς τῶν κατὰ γένεσιν
πεφυκότος ἑστάναι περὶ πάντων οἴονται δεῖν ὡς
ἂν παγίως ἱδρυμένων καὶ μηδεμίαν δεχομένων
μεταβολὴν ἀποφαίνεσθαι, δίκην ἀξίαν τῆς ἀσεβείας
ὑποσχόντα καὶ τὸν ἀσκητικὸν ἔμπαλιν τὰς ἐπι-
δρομὰς τῶν πολεμίων ἐκφυγόντα καὶ ἀνὰ κράτος
ἀπροσδοκήτως διασωθέντα, τὸν δίκαιον καὶ ἀληθῆ
βραβευτὴν ὑμνεῖ θεὸν τὰ πρεπωδέστατα καὶ οἰ-
κειότατα ταῖς συντυχίαις ἐξάρχων ᾄσματα, διότι
" ἵππον καὶ ἀναβάτην ῥίψας εἰς θάλασσαν," τὸν

─────────

[a] In Philo's elastic philosophy of numbers 600 easily = 6.
For the six movements see *Leg. All.* i. 4.

And therefore he started fashioning gods and filled 109
the inhabited world with idols of stone and wood and
numberless other figures wrought in various materials,
and decreed great prizes and magnificent honours
public and private to painters and sculptors, whom
the lawgiver had banished from the boundaries of
his commonwealth. He expected to produce piety ;
what he accomplished was its opposite, impiety.
For polytheism creates atheism in the souls of the 110
foolish, and God's honour is set at naught by those
who deify the mortal. For it did not content them
to fashion images of sun or moon, or, if they would
have it so, of all the earth and all the water, but they
even allowed irrational plants and animals to share the
honour which belongs to things imperishable. Such
persons did Abraham rebuke and we shewed that it
was with this thought that he raised his hymn of
victory. XXIX. So, too, with the song 111
of Moses. He has seen the king of Egypt, the boastful mind with his six hundred [a] chariots (Exod. xiv. 7),
that is the six movements of the organic body, adjusted for the use of the princes who ride upon them
(Exod. xv. 4) who, though no created object can be
stable, think it right to aver that all such are firmly
established and unsusceptible of change. He has
seen that mind suffer the penalty due to its impiety
while the Votary of Practice has escaped the onset of
his enemies and been brought with might to un-
looked-for safety. So then he hymns God the
righteous and true dispenser of events and the song
which he raises is most fitting and suited to the
occasion. " The horse and his rider He has thrown
into the sea " (Exod. xv. 1), that is, He has buried

ἐποχούμενον νοῦν ταῖς τοῦ τετράποδος καὶ ἀφη-
νιαστοῦ πάθους ἀλόγοις ὁρμαῖς ἀφανίσας, βοηθὸς
καὶ ὑπερασπιστὴς ἐγένετο τῆς ὁρατικῆς ψυχῆς, ὡς
112 χαρίσασθαι παντελῆ σωτηρίαν αὐτῇ.   ὁ
δὲ αὐτὸς καὶ ἐπὶ τοῦ φρέατος ἐξάρχει, οὐκέτι
μόνον ἐπὶ καθαιρέσει τῶν παθῶν, ἀλλὰ καὶ ἐπὶ τῷ
τὸ κάλλιστον κτημάτων, σοφίαν, ἀνανταγώνιστον
ἰσχῦσαι λαβεῖν, ἣν ἀπεικάζει φρέατι· βαθεῖα γὰρ
[375] καὶ οὐκ ἐπιπόλαιος, γλυκὺ ἀναδιδοῦσα νᾶμα καλο-
κἀγαθίας | διψώσαις ψυχαῖς, ἀναγκαιότατον ὁμοῦ
113 καὶ ἥδιστον ποτόν· ἰδιώτῃ δὲ οὐδενὶ παιδείας
ἐφεῖται τοῦτο τὸ φρέαρ ὀρύττειν, μόνοις δὲ βασι-
λεῦσιν, ᾗ φησιν· '' ἐλατόμησαν αὐτὸ βασιλεῖς ''.
μεγάλων γὰρ ἡγεμόνων ἀναζητῆσαι καὶ κατερ-
γάσασθαι σοφίαν, οὐχὶ τῶν ὅπλοις γῆν καὶ θάλατταν ὑπηγμένων, ἀλλὰ τῶν ψυχῆς δυνάμεσι τὸν
πολύτροπον αὐτῆς καὶ μιγάδα καὶ πεφορημένον
114 ὄχλον κατηγωνισμένων.   XXX. τούτων
φοιτητὰς καὶ γνωρίμους εἶναι συμβέβηκε τοὺς
λέγοντας· '' οἱ παῖδές σου εἰλήφασι τὸ κεφάλαιον
τῶν ἀνδρῶν τῶν πολεμιστῶν τῶν μεθ' ἡμῶν, οὐ
διαπεφώνηκεν ἀπ' αὐτῶν οὐδὲ εἷς· προσαγηόχαμεν
115 τὸ δῶρον κυρίῳ ἀνήρ, ὃ εὗρεν·'' ἐοίκασι γὰρ καὶ
οὗτοι πάλιν ἐπινίκιον ᾆσμα ἐξάρχειν τελείων καὶ
ἡγεμονικῶν δυνάμεων ἐφιέμενοι—τὸν γὰρ συντι-
θέντα τὸ κεφάλαιον καὶ πλεῖστον ἀριθμὸν τῶν κατ'
ἀνδρείαν λόγων φασὶ λαβεῖν—, οὓς ἐκ φύσεως
εἶναι πολεμικοὺς συμβέβηκε δυσὶν ἀντιτεταγμένους
τέλεσιν, ἑνὶ μὲν οὖ ἡ δυσθεράπευτος[1] ἀφηγεῖται

---

[1] mss. δυσθήρατος.

---

[a] See App. p. 503.   [b] See App. p. 504.
[c] i.e. learning from the leaders to be leaders themselves.

out of sight the mind which rode upon the unreasoning impulses of passion, that four-footed beast which
knows not the rein, and has shewn Himself the
helper and champion of the soul which can see, to
bestow on it full salvation.   Again Moses 112
leads the song at the well, and this time his theme is
not only the rout of the passions, but the strength
invincible which can win that most beautiful of
possessions, wisdom, which he likens to a well.   For
wisdom lies deep below the surface and gives forth a
sweet stream of true nobility for thirsty souls, and
that draught is at once needful and delicious above
all things.   But to none of those who in instruction 113
are but of the common herd is it permitted to dig this
well, only to kings, as he says " kings hewed it "
(Num. xxi. 16-18).[a]   For it belongs to great leaders to
search for and accomplish wisdom, not leaders who
have subdued sea and land with arms, but those who
through the powers of the soul have conquered the
medley and confusion of the multitude which beset
it.   XXX. [b] These leaders prove to have 114
followers and disciples [b] in those who say " thy servants have taken the sum of the warriors who were
with us.   Not one of them is in discord.   We have
brought our gift to the Lord, every man what he
found " (Num. xxxi. 49, 50).   It would seem that 115
these too are raising a song of victory in their desire
for the perfect powers that befit the leaders.   For
they say that they have taken the largest number,
that which completes the sum, of the different aspects
of courage.   They are by nature combatants, mar-
shalled to fight against two battalions [b] of the enemy,
one led by cowardice, a quality so difficult to cure,
the other by rashness inspired by the frenzy of battle,

379

δειλία, ἑτέρῳ δὲ οὗ ἡ ἀρειμάνιος θρασύτης· ἀμφό-
116 τεραι δὲ γνώμης ἀγαθῆς ἀμέτοχοι. παγκάλως δ᾽
εἴρηται τὸ μηδένα διαπεφωνηκέναι πρὸς ὁλο-
κλήρου καὶ παντελοῦς μετουσίαν ἀνδρείας· καθάπερ
⟨γὰρ⟩ λύρα καὶ πᾶν μουσικῆς ὄργανον ἐκμελὲς
μέν, κἂν εἷς αὐτὸ μόνον ἀπῳδὸς ᾖ φθόγγος, ἡρμο-
σμένον δ᾽, ὅταν μιᾷ πλήξει συνηχῶσι τὴν αὐτὴν
συμφωνίαν ἀποτελοῦντες, τὸν αὐτὸν τρόπον καὶ
τὸ ψυχῆς ὄργανον ἀσύμφωνον μέν, ὅταν ἢ θράσει
σφόδρα ἐπιτεινόμενον πρὸς τὸ ὀξύτατον βιάζηται
ἢ δειλίᾳ πλέον τοῦ μετρίου ἀνιέμενον πρὸς τὸ
βαρύτατον χαλᾶται, σύμφωνον δ᾽, ὅταν οἱ τῆς
ἀνδρείας καὶ πάσης ἀρετῆς τόνοι πάντες ἀνα-
117 κραθέντες ἐν εὐάρμοστον ἀπογεννήσωσι μέλος. τῆς
δὲ συμφωνίας καὶ εὐαρμοστίας μέγα τεκμήριον τὸ
προσαγηοχέναι τὸ δῶρον τῷ θεῷ, τοῦτο δ᾽ ἐστὶ
τιμῆσαι πρεπόντως τὸ ὂν διὰ τοῦ σαφέστατα ὡμο-
λογηκέναι, ὅτι δῶρόν ἐστιν αὐτοῦ τόδε τὸ πᾶν·
118 λέγει γὰρ φυσικώτατα· '' ἀνὴρ ὃ εὗρε, τοῦτο προσ-
ήνεγκε δῶρον.'' ἕκαστος δ᾽ ἡμῶν γενόμενος εὐθὺς
εὑρίσκει τὸ μέγα δῶρον θεοῦ τὸν παντελῆ κόσμον,
⟨ὃν⟩ αὐτὸν[1] ἑαυτῷ καὶ τοῖς ἀρίστοις μέρεσιν
119 [ὄρεσιν] ἐχαρίσατο.   XXXI. εἰσὶ δὲ καὶ
[376] ἐν μέρει δωρεαί, ἃς θεῷ τε | δοῦναι καὶ λαβεῖν
ἀνθρώποις ἐμπρεπές. αὗται δ᾽ ἂν εἶεν ἀρεταὶ καὶ
αἱ κατ᾽ αὐτὰς ἐνέργειαι, ὧν τὴν εὕρεσιν σχεδὸν
ἄχρονον οὖσαν διὰ τὸ ὑπερβάλλον τοῦ χαριζομένου
τάχος ἐν οἷς εἴωθε δωρεῖσθαι πᾶς καταπέπληκται,
120 καὶ ὅτῳ μηδὲν μέγα τῶν ἄλλων ὑπείληπται. διὸ
καὶ πυνθάνεται· '' τί τοῦτο ὃ ταχὺ εὗρες, ὦ τέκνον;''

---

[1] Or, as Adler, αὐτὸν γὰρ. Wendland proposed ὃν, omitting

and neither has any element of good judgement. Now it is a fine saying that " none is at discord " or **116** thus failing to partake of courage perfect and complete. For as the lyre or any musical instrument is out of harmony if even a single note and nothing more be out of tune, but in harmony when, under a single stroke of the bow, the strings join in yielding the same symphony, so it is with the instrument of the soul. It is out of harmony when it is strained too far by rashness and forced to the highest pitch of the scale, or when it is relaxed too much by cowardice and weakened to the lowest. It is in harmony when all the strings of courage and every virtue combine to produce a single tuneful melody. The harmony and **117** tunefulness in this case is mightily attested by the words which say that they have offered their gift to God, that is, that they have duly honoured the Existent by clearly acknowledging that this universe **118** is His gift. For it says in words most agreeable to the truth of things, " what a man found, this he offered as a gift." Each of us, that is, finds at our birth that great gift of God, the complete universe which He bestowed on itself and on its highest **119** members. XXXI. There are also partial and particular gifts which it is fitting for God to give and for man to receive. These we shall find are the virtues and the activities which correspond to them. Our discovery of them one may almost say is timeless, because of the exceeding swiftness with which the Donor bestows His wonted gifts to the amazement of all, even of those who find nothing great in other **120** things. Thus Isaac asks, " what is this which thou

---

αὐτὸν, but the juxtaposition of αὐτὸν to ἑαυτῷ is very common and emphasis would be lost by its omission.

PHILO

τεθαυμακὼς τῆς σπουδαίας διαθέσεως τὴν ὀξύτητα·
ὁ δὲ εὖ παθὼν εὐθυβόλως ἀποκρίνεται· " ὃ παρέδωκε κύριος ὁ θεός." παραδόσεις γὰρ καὶ ὑφηγήσεις
βραδεῖαι μὲν αἱ δι᾽ ἀνθρώπων, ὀξύταται δ᾽ αἱ διὰ
θεοῦ, φθάνουσαι καὶ τὴν ὀξυτάτην χρόνου κίνησιν.

121 Οἱ μὲν οὖν κατ᾽ ἰσχὺν καὶ δύναμιν ἔξαρχοι καὶ
ἡγεμόνες τοῦ τὸν ἐπινίκιον καὶ εὐχαριστικὸν ὕμνον
ᾄδοντος χοροῦ οἱ λεχθέντες εἰσίν, οἱ δὲ κατὰ τροπὴν
καὶ ἀσθένειαν τοῦ τὸν ἐφ᾽ ἥτταις θρῆνον σφαδάζοντος
ἕτεροι, οὓς οὐ κακίζειν μᾶλλον ἢ οἰκτίζεσθαι χρὴ
καθάπερ τοὺς τὰ σώματα ἐκ φύσεως ἐπικήρως
ἔχοντας, οἷς καὶ ἡ τυχοῦσα νόσου πρόφασις
μέγα ἐμπόδιον πρὸς τὸ σῴζεσθαι.

122 ἔνιοι δ᾽ οὐ τῷ μαλθακωτέροις τοῖς ψυχῆς κεχρῆσθαι
τόνοις ἀνέπεσον ἄκοντες ὑπ᾽ ἐρρωμενεστέρας τῶν
ἀντιπάλων ἰσχύος πιεσθέντες, ἀλλὰ μιμησάμενοι
τοὺς ἐθελοδούλους ἑκόντες ἑαυτοὺς πικροῖς δεσπόταις ὑπέρριψαν γένος ὄντες ἐλεύθεροι· διὸ μὴ
δυνάμενοι πεπρᾶσθαι, τὸ παραλογώτατον, αὐτοὶ
δεσπότας ὠνούμενοι προσεκτῶντο, ταὐτὸ δρῶντες
τοῖς ἐμφορουμένοις ἀπλήστως πρὸς μέθην οἴνου—

123 καὶ γὰρ ἐκεῖνοι γνώμῃ τὸν ἄκρατον, οὐ βιασθέντες
προσφέρονται—, ὥστε καὶ γνώμῃ τὸ μὲν νηφάλιον
ἐκτέμνουσι τῆς ψυχῆς, τὸ δὲ παράληρον αἱροῦνται·
" φωνὴν " γάρ φησιν " ἐξαρχόντων [ὑπ᾽] οἴνου

ᵃ Between ἀσθένειαν and τοῦ understand ἔξαρχοι καὶ ἡγεμόνες.
ᵇ Or " with whom any trifling occasion of sickness is a
mighty obstacle to their well-being."
ᶜ Here begins the description of those " who raise the
song over the wine."
382

hast found quickly, my son ? " marvelling at the speed with which the virtuous disposition has been attained. The receiver of God's benefit answered rightly, " it is what the Lord God delivered to me " (Gen. xxvii. 20). For the instructions and injunctions delivered through men are slow, but those that come through God are exceeding swift, outrunning even the swiftest movement of time.

Now those described above are those who lead the 121 song of prevailing might, the precentors of the choir which sings the hymn of victory and thanksgiving, while they who raise the song of weakness and defeat,[a] leaders of the choir which sobs forth the wailing of the routed, are of another sort, men who deserve pity rather than reproaches, even as we pity those whose bodies are fatally stricken by nature, with whom the misfortune of their malady ever stands to prevent their finding health and safety.[b]

But some[c] have failed not involuntarily, not because 122 the nerves of their souls were feebler and because they were overpressed by the stouter might of their opponents, but because imitating those who hug their chains, they have voluntarily laid themselves at the feet of cruel masters, though they were born to freedom. And since in virtue of their free birth they could not be sold, they have—strange contrast—purchased and taken to them masters. Thus they are on a level with those who swill themselves insatiably with wine to the pitch of intoxication. For such de- 123 liberately and under no compulsion put the cup of strong drink to their lips, and so it is also with full deliberation that these men eliminate soberness from their soul and choose madness in its place. For so runs the text, " It is the voice of those who raise

ἐγὼ ἀκούω," τουτέστιν οὐκ ἀκούσιον ἐνδεδεγ-
μένων¹ μανίαν, ἀλλ' ἑκουσίῳ φρενοβλαβείᾳ βε-
124 βακχευμένων.　　　　XXXII. πᾶς δ' ὁ συν-
εγγίζων τῇ παρεμβολῇ " τὸν μόσχον ὁρᾷ καὶ τοὺς
χορούς," ᾗ καὶ αὐτὸς διασυνίστησι· τύφῳ γὰρ καὶ
τοῖς τύφου χορευταῖς ἐντυγχάνομεν, ὅσοι πλησίον
ἵστασθαι τοῦ σωματικοῦ στρατοπέδου διανοούμεθα
γνώμῃ· ἐπεὶ τοῖς τε φιλοθεάμοσι καὶ τὰ ἀσώματα
ὁρᾶν γλιχομένοις, ἅτε ἀτυφίας οὖσιν ἀσκηταῖς,
πορρωτάτω τοῦ σώματος ἔθος διοικίζεσθαι.

125 εὔχου δὴ τῷ θεῷ μηδέποτε ἔξαρχος οἴνου γενέσθαι,
τουτέστι μηδέποτε ἑκὼν ἀφηγήσασθαι τῆς εἰς
ἀπαιδευσίαν καὶ ἀφροσύνην ἀγούσης ὁδοῦ· τὰ γὰρ
ἀκούσια ἡμίσεα κακῶν καὶ κουφότερα, καθαρῷ τῷ
126 τοῦ συνειδότος ἐλέγχῳ μὴ βαρυνόμενα. τελεσ-
φορηθεισῶν δέ σοι τῶν εὐχῶν ἰδιώτης μὲν ἔτι
μένειν οὐκ ἂν δύναιο, τὴν δὲ μεγίστην ἡγεμονιῶν
ἀρχήν, ἱερωσύνην, κτήσῃ.　　　　σχεδὸν γὰρ
ἱερέων καὶ θεραπευτῶν θεοῦ μόνον τὸ ἔργον |
[377] νηφάλια θύειν, οἴνου καὶ παντὸς ὃ τοῦ ληρεῖν αἴτιον
127 βεβαιότητι διανοίας κατεξανισταμένων· " ἐλάλησε "
γάρ φησι " κύριος τῷ Ἀαρὼν λέγων· οἶνον καὶ
σίκερα οὐ πίεσθε σὺ καὶ οἱ υἱοί σου μετὰ σέ,²
ἡνίκα ἂν εἰσπορεύηθε εἰς τὴν σκηνὴν τοῦ μαρτυρίου
ἢ προσπορεύησθε τῷ θυσιαστηρίῳ, καὶ οὐ μὴ
ἀποθάνητε· νόμιμον αἰώνιον εἰς τὰς γενεὰς ὑμῶν
διαστεῖλαι ἀνὰ μέσον ἁγίων καὶ βεβήλων καὶ ἀνὰ

¹ MSS. ἐνδεδειγμένων.
² Possibly μετὰ σοῦ as in LXX, and also in § 138.

ᵃ The translation takes καθαρός in the sense of "unmixed,"
i.e. with nothing to lighten its force. Possibly " in all its
purity."

the song of wine that I hear," that is, not the song of those on whom insanity has fallen through no will of their own, but of those who are possessed with the frenzy which they themselves have willed.

XXXII. Now everyone who comes near to the camp 124 "sees the calf and the dance" (Exod. xxxii. 19), as Moses himself shews. For all of us who have the deliberate purpose to stand close to the camp of the body find themselves in the company of vanity and its band of revellers. Whereas those who yearn for the Vision and long to behold things incorporeal are practisers of simplicity, and therefore it is their custom to make their dwelling as far as may be from the body. Pray then to God that thou 125 mayest never become a leader in the wine song, never, that is, voluntarily take the first steps on the path which leads to indiscipline and folly. Voluntarily, I say, for involuntary evils are but half evils and lighter matters, since they have not upon them the sheer [a] weight of convicting conscience. But if thy 126 prayers are fulfilled thou canst no longer remain a layman, but wilt obtain the office which is the greatest of headships, the priesthood.

For it is the task of priests and ministers of God alone, or of hardly any others, to make the offering of sobriety, and in stedfastness of mind to resist the wine-cup and everything which causes folly. For 127 "the Lord spake unto Aaron," we read, "saying, Wine and strong liquor ye shall not drink, thou and thy sons after thee, whenever ye enter into the tabernacle of testimony, or approach the altar, and ye shall not die. It is an everlasting ordinance unto your generations, to make a difference between the holy and the profane and between the clean and the un-

PHILO

128 μέσον καθαρῶν καὶ ἀκαθάρτων." Ἀαρὼν δέ ἐστιν
ὁ ἱερεύς, καὶ τοὔνομα ὀρεινὸς ἑρμηνεύεται, μετέωρα
καὶ ὑψηλὰ φρονῶν λογισμός, οὐ διὰ μεγαλαυχίας
κενοῦ φυσήματος ὑπόπλεων ὄγκον, ἀλλὰ διὰ
μέγεθος ἀρετῆς, ἣ τὸ φρόνημα ἐξαίρουσα πέραν
οὐρανοῦ ταπεινὸν οὐδὲν ἐᾷ λογίζεσθαι. διακείμενος
129 δ᾽ οὕτως ἄκρατον καὶ πᾶν ἀφροσύνης φάρμακον
ἑκὼν οὔποτε προσήσεται. ἀνάγκη γάρ ἐστιν ἢ
ἀρρηφοροῦντα αὐτὸν εἰς τὴν σκηνὴν εἰσιέναι τὰς
ἀοράτους ἐπιτελέσοντα τελετὰς ἢ τῷ βωμῷ προσιόντα θυσίας ὑπέρ τε τῶν ἰδίων καὶ κοινῶν
130 χαριστηρίους ἀναγαγεῖν· νήψεως δὲ καὶ περιττῆς
ἀγχινοίας ταῦτα δεῖται.   XXXIII. θαυ-
μάσαι μὲν οὖν εἰκότως ἄν τις καὶ τὸ ῥητὸν τῆς
προστάξεως. πῶς γὰρ οὐ σεμνὸν νήφοντας καὶ ἐν
ἑαυτοῖς ὄντας πρὸς εὐχὰς καὶ ἱερουργίας χωρεῖν,
131 ὡς ἔμπαλιν ἀμφότερα, σῶμα καὶ ψυχήν, παρει-
μένους ὑπὸ οἴνου καταγέλαστον; ἢ δεσπόταις μὲν
καὶ γονεῦσι καὶ ἄρχουσιν οἰκέται καὶ υἱοὶ καὶ
ὑπήκοοι μέλλοντες προσέρχεσθαι πρόνοιαν ἕξουσι
τοῦ νήφειν, ὡς μήτε ἐν τοῖς λεγομένοις καὶ πραττο-
μένοις διαμάρτοιεν μήθ᾽ ὡς καταπεφρονηκότες
τῆς ἐκείνων ἀξιώσεως κολασθεῖεν ἤ, τὸ γοῦν
ἐπιεικέστατον, χλεύην ὄφλοιεν· τὸν δὲ τοῦ παντὸς
ἡγεμόνα καὶ πατέρα τις θεραπεύειν δικαιῶν οὐ καὶ
σιτίων καὶ ποτῶν καὶ ὕπνου καὶ πάντων ὅσα
ἀναγκαῖα τῇ φύσει περιέσται, ἀλλὰ πρὸς τὸ
ἁβροδίαιτον ἀποκλίνας τὸν τῶν ἀσώτων ζηλώσει
βίον, καὶ βεβαρημένος τοὺς ὀφθαλμοὺς ἀπ᾽ οἴνου
καὶ τὴν κεφαλὴν παραβάλλων καὶ τὸν αὐχένα
ἐγκάρσιον πλαγιάζων καὶ ὑπ᾽ ἀμετρίας ἐρευγόμενος
καὶ ὅλῳ διαρρέων τῷ σώματι χέρνιβος ἢ βωμῶν
386

clean " (Lev. x. 8-10).   Now Aaron is the 128
priest and his name means " mountainous." He is
the reason whose thoughts are lofty and sublime, not
with the empty inflated bigness of mere vaunting,
but with the greatness of virtue, which lifts his thinking above the heaven and will not let him cherish any
reasoning that is mean and low. And being so
minded he will never willingly allow strong wine or
any potion which breeds folly to approach him. For 129
he must either himself enter the tabernacle in mystic
procession to accomplish the unseen rites, or come to
the altar and there offer sacrifices of thanksgiving
for private and public blessings. And these need
sober abstinence and a close and ready attention.

XXXIII. In a literal sense too, this 130
command deserves our admiration. For surely it is
seemly that men should come to prayers and holy
services sober and with full control of themselves,
just as on the other hand to come with both body and
soul relaxed with wine is a matter for scorn and
ridicule. We know that when servants are about 131
to approach their masters, or sons their parents, or
subjects their rulers, they will take careful thought
to be sober that they may not transgress in word and
deed, and thus either receive punishment for having
shewn contempt for the dignity of their betters, or
at the best become an object of scorn. And shall he
who claims to serve the Lord and Father of all, instead of rising superior to food and drink and all other
natural necessities, fall away to luxury and affect the
life of the dissolute ? Shall he, with his eyes heavy
with wine and his head lolling and his neck bent awry,
come belching from his intemperance, limp and flabby
in every limb, to touch the holy water or the altars or

ἢ θυσιῶν προσάψεται; ἀλλ' οὐδὲ τὴν ἱερὰν ἐξ
ἀπόπτου φλόγα θεάσασθαι τῷ τοιούτῳ θέμις.

132   εἰ μέντοι μήτε σκηνὴν μήτε θυσια-
στήριον ὑπολάβοι τις λέγεσθαι τὰ ὁρώμενα ἐκ τῆς
ἀψύχου καὶ φθαρτῆς δημιουργηθέντα ὕλης, ἀλλὰ τὰ
[378] ἀόρατα καὶ [τὰ] νοητὰ | θεωρήματα, ὧν αἰσθηταὶ
ταῦτα εἰκόνες, καταπλαγήσεται μᾶλλον τὴν ὑφ-

133 ήγησιν. ἐπειδὴ γὰρ παντὸς τὸ μὲν παράδειγμα,
τὸ δὲ μίμημα ὁ ποιῶν ἐποίει, καὶ ἀρετῆς τὴν μὲν
ἀρχέτυπον σφραγῖδα εἰργάζετο, τὸν δὲ ἀπὸ ταύτης
ἐνεσημαίνετο ἐμφερέστατον χαρακτῆρα· ἡ μὲν οὖν
ἀρχέτυπος σφραγὶς ἀσώματός ἐστιν ἰδέα, ἡ δὲ
χαραχθεῖσα εἰκὼν σῶμα ἤδη, φύσει μὲν αἰσθητόν,
οὐ μὴν εἰς αἴσθησιν ἐρχόμενον· καθάπερ καὶ τὸ
ἐν τῷ βαθυτάτῳ τοῦ Ἀτλαντικοῦ πελάγους ξύλον
εἴποι τις ἂν πεφυκέναι μὲν πρὸς τὸ καίεσθαι,
μηδέποτε δ' ὑπὸ πυρὸς ἀναλωθήσεσθαι διὰ τὴν
134 τῆς θαλάττης ἀνάχυσιν.   XXXIV. τὴν
οὖν σκηνὴν καὶ τὸν βωμὸν ἐννοήσωμεν ἰδέας,[1] τὴν
μὲν ἀρετῆς ἀσωμάτου, τὸν δὲ αἰσθητῆς εἰκόνος
εἶναι σύμβολον. τὸν μέν γε βωμὸν καὶ τὰ ἐπ'
αὐτοῦ ῥάδιον ἰδεῖν—ἔξω τε γὰρ ἔχει τὴν κατα-
σκευὴν καὶ ἀσβέστῳ πυρὶ . . . ἀναλίσκεται, ὡς
μὴ μεθ' ἡμέραν μόνον, ἀλλὰ καὶ νύκτωρ περιλάμ-
135 πεσθαι—, ἡ δὲ σκηνὴ καὶ τὰ ἐν αὐτῇ πάντα ἀθέατα,
οὐχὶ τῷ μόνον ἐσωτάτω καὶ ἐν ἀδύτοις ἱδρῦσθαι,
ἀλλὰ καὶ τῷ τὸν προσαψάμενον ἢ διὰ περιεργίαν

---

[1] Or perhaps, as Adler, the comma may be placed before
ἰδέας, which will then be taken as gen. sing.; see App. p. 505.

---

[a] See App. p. 504.
[b] The lacuna in the text may be filled up with some such
words as τὰ ἱερουργούμενα.

the sacrifices ? Nay, for such a one it were a sacrilege that he should even from a distance behold the sacred fire.   But if we suppose that no actual 132 tabernacle or altar is meant, that is the visible objects fashioned from lifeless and perishable material, but those invisible conceptions perceived only by the mind, of which the others are copies ^{a} open to our senses, he will be still more lost in admiration at the ordinance. For since the Creator made both the 133 pattern and the copy in all that He made, virtue was not excepted : He wrought its archetypal seal, and He also stamped with this an impression which was its close counterpart. The archetypal seal is an incorporeal idea, but the copy which is made by the impression is something else—a material something, naturally perceptible by the senses, yet not actually coming into relation with them ; just as we might say that a piece of wood buried in the deepest part of the Atlantic ocean has a natural capacity for being burnt, though actually it will never be consumed by fire because the sea is around and above it.

XXXIV. ^{a} Let us conceive, then, of the tabernacle 134 and altar as " ideas," the first being a symbol of incorporeal virtue, the other of its sensible image. Now the altar and what is on it can be easily seen. For it is constructed out of doors, and the fire which consumes the offerings is never extinguished,^{b} and thus by night as well as by day it is in bright light. But the tabernacle and all its contents are unseen, 135 not only because they are placed right inside and in the heart of the sanctuary, but because anyone who touched them, or with a too curious eye looked upon them, was punished with death according to the

ὀφθαλμῶν ἰδόντα ἀπαραιτήτῳ δίκῃ θανάτου κατὰ
πρόσταξιν νόμου κολάζεσθαι, πλὴν εἰ μή τις
ὁλόκληρος καὶ παντελὴς εἴη, περὶ μηδέν, μὴ μέγα,
μὴ μικρόν, ἁπλῶς κηραίνων πάθος, ἀλλ' ἀρτίῳ
καὶ πλήρει καὶ πάντα τελειοτάτῃ κεχρημένος τῇ
136 φύσει. τούτῳ γὰρ ἐπιτέτραπται δι' ἔτους ἅπαξ
εἰσιόντι ἐπισκοπεῖν τὰ ἀθέατα ἄλλοις, ἐπειδὴ καὶ
ἐξ ἁπάντων μόνῳ ὁ τῶν ἀσωμάτων καὶ ἀφθάρτων
ἀγαθῶν πτηνὸς καὶ οὐράνιος ἔρως ἐνδιαιτᾶται.
137 ὅταν οὖν ὑπὸ τῆς ἰδέας πληχθεὶς ἕπηται τῇ τὰς
κατὰ μέρος ἀρετὰς τυπούσῃ σφραγῖδι κατανοῶν
καὶ καταπληττόμενος αὐτῆς τὸ θεοειδέστατον
κάλλος ἤ τινι προσέρχεται δεξαμένῃ τὸν ἐκείνης
χαρακτῆρα, λήθη μὲν ἀμαθίας καὶ ἀπαιδευσίας,
μνήμη δὲ παιδείας καὶ ἐπιστήμης εὐθὺς ἐγγίνεται.
138   διὸ λέγει· " οἶνον καὶ σίκερα οὐ
πίεσθε, σὺ καὶ οἱ υἱοί σου μετὰ σέ, ἡνίκα ἂν
εἰσπορεύησθε εἰς τὴν σκηνὴν τοῦ μαρτυρίου ἢ
προσπορεύησθε τῷ θυσιαστηρίῳ." ταῦτα δ' οὐκ
ἀπαγορεύων μᾶλλον ἢ γνώμην ἀποφαινόμενος
διεξέρχεται· τῷ μέν γε ἀπαγορεύοντι οἰκεῖον ἦν
εἰπεῖν· οἶνον, ὅταν ἱερουργῆτε, μὴ πίνετε, τῷ δὲ
γνώμην ἀποφαινομένῳ τὸ " οὐ πίεσθε." καὶ γάρ
ἐστιν ἀμήχανον τὸ μέθης καὶ παροινίας ψυχῆς
αἴτιον, ἀπαιδευσίαν, προσίεσθαι τὸν ταῖς γενικαῖς
καὶ κατ' εἶδος ἀρεταῖς ἐμμελετῶντα καὶ ἐγ-
139 χορεύοντα.   τὴν δὲ σκηνὴν " μαρτυρίου "
καλεῖ πολλάκις, ἤτοι παρόσον ὁ ἀψευδὴς θεὸς
ρετῆς ἐστι μάρτυς, ᾧ καλὸν καὶ σύμφορον

ordinance of the law, and against that sentence there was no appeal. The only exception made is for one who should be free from all defects, not wasting himself with any passion great or small, but endowed with a nature sound and complete and perfect in every respect. To him it is permitted to enter once 136 a year and behold the sights which are forbidden to others, because in him alone of all resides the winged and heavenly yearning for those forms of good which are incorporeal and imperishable. And so, when 137 smitten by its ideal beauty he follows that archetype which creates by impress the particular virtues, beholding with ecstasy its most divine loveliness, or when he approaches some virtue which has received its impress, ignorance and the condition of the uninstructed are forgotten, and knowledge and instruction are at once remembered. And there- 138 fore he says "Wine and strong liquor ye shall not drink, thou and thy sons after thee, when ye enter into the tabernacle of testimony or approach the altar." In these words he speaks not so much by way of prohibition as stating what he thinks will happen. If a prohibition were intended, it would have been natural to say "do not drink wine when you perform the rites"; the phrase "you shall not" or "will not" drink is naturally used, when the speaker is stating what he thinks. For it is impossible that anyone, whose study and association lie among the general and specific virtues, should let indiscipline, which is the cause of drunkenness and the symptoms which follow it in the soul, have entry to him. And he frequently calls the tabernacle "the taber- 139 nacle of testimony," either because God who cannot lie gives His testimony to virtue, a testimony to

PHILO

προσέχειν, ἢ παρόσον ἡ ἀρετὴ βεβαιότητα ταῖς
ψυχαῖς ἐντίθησι τοὺς ἐνδοιάζοντας καὶ ἐπαμφο-
τερίζοντας λογισμοὺς ἀνὰ κράτος ἐκτέμνουσα καὶ
[379] ὥσπερ ἐν δικαστηρίῳ | τῷ βίῳ τἀληθὲς ἀνα-
140 καλύπτουσα.   XXXV. λέγει δὲ ὅτι
οὐδ' ἀποθανεῖται ὁ νηφάλια θύων, ὡς ἀπαιδευσίας
μὲν θάνατον ἐπιφερούσης, παιδείας δὲ ἀφθαρσίαν·
καθάπερ γὰρ ἐν τοῖς σώμασιν ἡμῶν νόσος μὲν
διαλύσεως, ὑγεία δὲ σωτηρίας αἰτία, τὸν αὐτὸν
τρόπον καὶ ἐν ταῖς ψυχαῖς τὸ μὲν σῷζόν ἐστι
φρόνησις—ὑγεία γάρ τις αὕτη διανοίας—, τὸ
δὲ φθεῖρον ἀφροσύνη νόσον ἀνίατον ⟨ἐγ⟩κατα-
141 σκήπτουσα.¹   τοῦτο δὲ " νόμιμον αἰώνιον
εἶναι " φησιν, ἄντικρυς ἀποφαινόμενος· ὑπολαμβάνει γὰρ νόμον ἀθάνατον ἐν τῇ τοῦ παντὸς
ἐστηλιτεῦσθαι φύσει ταυτὶ περιέχοντα, ὅτι ὑγιεινὸν
μὲν καὶ σωτήριον χρῆμα παιδεία, νόσου δὲ καὶ
142 φθορᾶς αἴτιον ἀπαιδευσία. παρεμφαίνει δέ τι καὶ
τοιοῦτον· τὸ πρὸς ἀλήθειαν νόμιμον εὐθύς ἐστιν
αἰώνιον, ἐπεὶ καὶ ὁ ὀρθὸς λόγος, ὃς δὴ νόμος ἐστίν,
οὐ φθαρτός· καὶ γὰρ αὖ τοὐναντίον ⟨τὸ⟩ παρά-
νομον ἐφήμερόν τε καὶ εὐδιάλυτον ἐξ ἑαυτοῦ παρὰ
143 τοῖς εὖ φρονοῦσιν ἀνωμολόγηται.   νόμου
δὲ καὶ παιδείας ἴδιον βέβηλα ἁγίων καὶ ἀκάθαρτα
καθαρῶν " διαστέλλειν," ὡς ἔμπαλιν ἀνομίας καὶ
ἀπαιδευσίας εἰς ταὐτὸν ἄγειν τὰ μαχόμενα βιά-
ζεσθαι² φυρούσης τὰ πάντα καὶ συγχεούσης.

¹ The uncompounded verb κατασκήπτω is not found in this
sense.
² Wend. wished to omit βιάζεσθαι, but the construction may
be paralleled by βλάψαι βιαζόμενον § 185. Cf. also De Sobr. 6.

ᵃ Lit. " declaring (his opinion) outright." The thought

which it is excellent and profitable to give ear, or because virtue implants constancy in the souls of men, eradicating with a strong hand the reasonings which doubt and waver, and thus witness-like revealing the truth in the court of human life.

XXXV. Again, he says that he whose offerings are 140 wineless shall not even die ; meaning that instruction entails immortality, but its absence entails death. For as in our bodies disease is the cause of dissolution, while health preserves them, so in our souls the preserving element is prudence, which is, so to speak, mental health, while the destroying element is folly inflicting incurable malady.   This, he says, 141 is " an eternal statute," and the words mean what they say.[a] For he does hold that there is a deathless law engraved in the nature of the universe which lays down this truth, that instruction is a thing which gives health and safety, while its absence is the cause of disease and destruction. But there is also a 142 further explanation in the words to this effect. A statute which is law in the true sense is thereby eternal, since right reason, which is identical with law,[b] is not destructible ; for that its opposite, the unlawful, is ephemeral and of itself subject to dissolution is a truth acknowledged by men of good sense.   Again, it is the special task of law 143 and instruction to " distinguish " the profane from the sacred and the impure from the pure, just as conversely it is the way of lawlessness and indiscipline to mix and confuse everything and thus force under the same head things which are in conflict with each other.

seems to be that we may learn from the words not only that this particular law is eternal, but that all law in the true sense is necessarily ($εὐθύς$) so.   [b] See App. p. 505.

PHILO

XXXVI. διὰ τοῦτο ὁ καὶ βασιλέων καὶ προφητῶν μέγιστος Σαμουὴλ " οἶνον καὶ μέθυσμα," ὡς ὁ ἱερὸς λόγος φησίν, " ἄχρι τελευτῆς οὐ πίεται"· τέτακται γὰρ ἐν τῇ τοῦ θείου στρατοπέδου τάξει, ἣν οὐδέποτε λείψει προμηθείᾳ τοῦ σοφοῦ ταξιάρχου. Σαμουὴλ δὲ γέγονε μὲν ἴσως ἄνθρωπος, παρείλη-
144 πται δ' οὐχ ὡς σύνθετον ζῷον, ἀλλ' ὡς νοῦς λατρείᾳ καὶ θεραπείᾳ θεοῦ μόνῃ χαίρων· ἑρμηνεύεται γὰρ τεταγμένος θεῷ διὰ τὸ τὰς πράξεις ὅσαι κατὰ κενὰς δόξας συνίστανται χαλεπὴν ἀταξίαν εἶναι νομίζειν. οὗτος μητρὸς γέγονεν Ἄννης,
145 ἧς τοὔνομα μεταληφθέν ἐστι χάρις· ἄνευ γὰρ θείας χάριτος ἀμήχανον ἢ λιποτακτῆσαι τὰ θνητὰ ἢ τοῖς ἀφθάρτοις ἀεὶ παραμεῖναι· χάριτος δ' ἥτις ἂν
146 πληρωθῇ ψυχή, γέγηθεν εὐθὺς καὶ μειδιᾷ καὶ ἀνορχεῖται· βεβάκχευται γάρ, ὡς πολλοῖς τῶν ἀνοργιάστων μεθύειν καὶ παρακινεῖν[1] καὶ ἐξ-εστάναι ἂν δόξαι. διὸ καὶ λέγεται πρὸς αὐτὴν ὑπὸ παιδαρίου τινός, οὐχ ἑνός, ἀλλ' ὑπὸ παντὸς τοῦ νεωτερίζειν καὶ τὰ καλὰ χλευάζειν ἀκμὴν ἔχοντος· " ἕως πότε μεθυσθήσῃ; περιελοῦ | τὸν οἶνόν σου"
[380] φιλεῖ γὰρ τοῖς θεοφορήτοις οὐχ ἡ ψυχὴ μόνον
147 ἐγείρεσθαι καὶ ὥσπερ ἐξοιστρᾶν, ἀλλὰ καὶ τὸ σῶμα ἐνερευθὲς εἶναι καὶ πεπυρωμένον τῆς ἔνδον ἀναχεούσης καὶ χλιαινούσης χαρᾶς τὸ πάθος εἰς τὸ ἔξω διαδιδούσης· ὑφ' οὗ πολλοὶ τῶν ἀφρόνων ἀπατηθέντες τοὺς νήφοντας μεθύειν ὑπετόπασαν.

---

[1] Wendland corrected to παροινεῖν, but see App. p. 505.

---

[a] In what sense is Samuel a king? Perhaps as the hero of the First Book of Kings and the king-maker.

[b] So the lxx. The words οἶνον καὶ μέθυσμα οὐ πίεται have nothing corresponding to them in the Hebrew.

394

XXXVI. Therefore Samuel too, the greatest of kings[a] and prophets, " will never," as the scripture tells us, " drink wine or intoxicating liquor till his dying day " (1 Sam. i. 11).[b] For his place has been ordered in the ranks of the divine army, and through the providence of the wise commander he will never leave it. Now 144 probably there was an actual man called Samuel ; but we conceive of the Samuel of the scripture, not as a living compound of soul and body, but as a mind which rejoices in the service and worship of God and that only. For his name by interpretation means " appointed or ordered to God," because he thinks that all actions that are based on idle opinions are grievous disorder. His mother is Hannah, 145 whose name means in our language " grace." For without divine grace it is impossible either to leave the ranks of mortality, or to stay for ever among the immortal. Now when grace fills the soul, that 146 soul thereby rejoices and smiles and dances, for it is possessed and inspired, so that to many of the unenlightened it may seem to be drunken, crazy and beside itself. And therefore she is addressed by a " boy," [c] not meaning a single boy, but everyone whose age is ripe for restlessness and defiance and mockery of excellence, in these words : " How long wilt thou be drunken ? put away thy wine from thee " (1 Sam. i. 14). For with the God-possessed not only 147 is the soul wont to be stirred and goaded as it were into ecstasy but the body also is flushed and fiery, warmed by the overflowing joy within which passes on the sensation to the outer man, and thus many of the foolish are deceived and suppose that the sober

[c] So the LXX. In the Hebrew the words are spoken by Eli.

148   καίτοι γε ἐκεῖνοι μὲν τρόπον τινὰ
μεθύουσιν οἱ νήφοντες τὰ ἀγαθὰ ἀθρόα ἠκρατι-
σμένοι καὶ τὰς προπόσεις παρὰ τελείας ἀρετῆς
δεξάμενοι, οἱ δὲ τὴν ἀπὸ οἴνου μεθύοντες μέθην
ἄγευστοι φρονήσεως διετέλεσαν νηστείαν συνεχῆ
149 καὶ λιμὸν αὐτῆς ἄγοντες. εἰκότως οὖν ἀποκρίνεται
πρὸς τὸν νεωτεροποιὸν καὶ γέλωτα τίθεσθαι οἰό-
μενον[1] τὸν σεμνὸν καὶ αὐστηρὸν αὐτῆς βίον· ὦ
θαυμάσιε, " γυνὴ ἡ σκληρὰ ἡμέρα ἐγώ εἰμι, καὶ
οἶνον καὶ μέθυσμα οὐ πέπωκα, καὶ ἐκχεῶ τὴν
ψυχήν μου ἐνώπιον κυρίου "· παμπόλλη γε παρ-
ρησία τῆς ψυχῆς, ἧ τῶν χαρίτων τοῦ θεοῦ πε-
150 πλήρωται. πρῶτον μέν γε " σκληρὰν ἡμέραν "
εἶπεν ἑαυτὴν πρὸς τὸ χλευάζον ἀπιδοῦσα παιδάριον
—τούτῳ γὰρ καὶ παντὶ ἄφρονι τραχεῖα καὶ δύσ-
βατος καὶ ἀργαλεωτάτη νενόμισται ἡ ἐπ᾽ ἀρετὴν
ἄγουσα ὁδός, καθὰ καὶ τῶν παλαιῶν τις ἐμαρ-
τύρησεν εἰπών·

τὴν μέντοι κακότητα καὶ ἰλαδὸν ἔστιν ἑλέσθαι.
τῆς δ᾽ ἀρετῆς ἱδρῶτα θεὸς προπάροιθεν ἔθηκεν
ἀθάνατος, μακρὸς δὲ καὶ ὄρθιος οἶμος ἐς αὐτὴν
καὶ τρηχὺς τὸ πρῶτον· ἐπὴν δ᾽ εἰς ἄκρον ἵκηαι,
ῥηιδίη δὴ ᾽πειτα πέλει χαλεπή περ ἐοῦσα—.

151   XXXVII. εἶτα οἶνον καὶ μέθυσμα οὐ
φησι προσενέγκασθαι τῷ συνεχῶς καὶ παρὰ πάντα
τὸν βίον νήφειν ἐπαυχοῦσα· καὶ γὰρ ὄντως ἀφέτῳ
καὶ ἐλευθεριάζοντι καὶ καθαρῷ χρῆσθαι λογισμῷ
πρὸς μηδενὸς πάθους παροινουμένῳ μέγα καὶ
152 θαυμαστὸν ἦν ἔργον. ἐκ τούτου δὲ συμβαίνει νή-

---

[1] Wendland corrects unnecessarily to τιθέμενον.

are drunk.   Though, indeed, it is true **148**
that these sober ones are drunk in a sense, for all good
things are united in the strong wine on which they
feast, and they receive the loving-cup from perfect
virtue ; while those others who are drunk with the
drunkenness of wine have lived fasting from prudence
without ceasing, and no taste of it has come to their
famine-stricken lips. Fitly, then, does she answer **149**
the reckless one who thinks to mock her stern
and austere life, Sirrah, " I a woman am the hard
day,[a] I have drunk no wine or strong drink, and I will
pour out my soul before the Lord " (1 Sam. i. 15).
How vast is the boldness of the soul which is filled
with the gracious gifts of God ! First, we see, she **150**
calls herself a " hard day," taking the view of the
varlet who thought to make a mock of her, for
to him and to every fool the way to virtue seems
rough and painful and ill to tread, and to this one of
the old writers has testified in these words :

> Vice you may take by squadrons ; but there lies
> 'Twixt you and virtue (so hath God ordained)
> Sore travail. Long and steep the road to her,
> And rough at first ; but—reach the top—and she,
> So hard to win, is now an easy prize.[b]

XXXVII. Secondly, she declares that she **151**
has not partaken of wine or strong liquor, glorying
that her whole life has been one of unbroken abstinence. And rightly, for indeed it was a great and
wonderful feat to follow reason, the free, the unshackled, the pure, which no passion inebriates. And **152**

---

[a] Or, as Philo may have understood the words, " hard and
easy," taking ἡμέρα from ἥμερος, see App. p. 505. The E.V.
has " of a sorrowful spirit."
[b] Hesiod, *Works and Days*, 287, 289-292.

ψεως ἀκράτου τὸν νοῦν ἐμφορηθέντα σπονδὴν ὅλον
δι' ὅλων γίνεσθαί τε καὶ σπένδεσθαι θεῷ· τί γὰρ
ἦν τὸ '' ἐκχεῶ¹ τὴν ψυχήν μου ἐναντίον κυρίου ''
ἢ σύμπασαν αὐτὴν ἀνιερώσω, δεσμὰ μὲν οἷς
πρότερον ἐσφίγγετο, ἃ περιῆψαν αἱ τοῦ θνητοῦ
βίου κεναὶ σπουδαί, πάντα λύσας, προαγαγὼν δὲ
ἔξω καὶ τείνας καὶ ἀναχέας τοσοῦτον, ὡς καὶ τῶν
τοῦ παντὸς ἅψασθαι περάτων καὶ πρὸς τὴν τοῦ
ἀγενήτου παγκάλην καὶ ἀοίδιμον θέαν ἐπειχθῆναι;
153   Νηφόντων μὲν οὖν ὁ | χορὸς οὗτος παιδείαν προ-
[381] στησαμένων ἡγεμονίδα, μεθυόντων δ' ὁ πρότερος,
154 οὗπερ ἦν ἔξαρχος ἀπαιδευσία.   XXXVIII. ἐπεὶ
δὲ τὸ μεθύειν οὐ μόνον ἐδήλου τὸ ληρεῖν, ὃ δημιουργὸν ἀπαιδευσίαν εἶχεν, ἀλλὰ καὶ τὸ παντελῶς
ἀναισθητεῖν, ἀναισθησίας δὲ τῆς μὲν κατὰ τὸ
σῶμα δημιουργὸς οἶνος, τῆς δὲ κατὰ ψυχὴν ἄγνοια
τούτων ὧν εἰκὸς ἦν ἐπιστήμην ἀνειληφέναι,
λεκτέον καὶ περὶ ἀγνοίας βραχέα αὐτὰ τὰ καίρια
155 ὑπομιμνήσκοντας. τίνι οὖν ἀπεικάσωμεν τῶν ἐν
τῷ σώματι τὸ ἐν ψυχῇ πάθος ὃ κέκληται ἄγνοια
ἢ τῇ τῶν αἰσθητηρίων πηρώσει; οὐκοῦν ὅσοι
ὀφθαλμοὺς καὶ ὦτα ἐβλάβησαν, οὐδὲν ἔτι ⟨οὔτ'⟩
ἰδεῖν οὔτ' ἀκοῦσαι δύνανται, ἡμέραν μὲν καὶ φῶς,
ὧν ἕνεκα μόνων, εἰ χρὴ τἀληθὲς εἰπεῖν, τὸ ζῆν
αἱρετόν, οὐκ εἰδότες, μακρῷ δὲ σκότῳ καὶ νυκτὶ
αἰωνίῳ συνοικοῦντες, πρὸς πάντα καὶ μικρὰ καὶ
μείζω κεκωφημένοι, οὓς εἰκότως ὁ βίος ἀδυνάτους
156 εἴωθε καλεῖν· κἂν γὰρ αἱ τοῦ ἄλλου σώματος
ἅπασαι δυνάμεις ἐπ' αὐτὸ δὴ τὸ πέρας ἰσχύος

---

¹ The lxx has ἐκχέω.   But that Philo read the future is
shewn by ἀνιερώσω.

the result of this is that the mind, which has drunk deep of abstinence unmixed, becomes a libation in its whole being, a libation which is poured out to God. What else was meant by the words, " I will pour out my soul before the Lord " but " I will consecrate it all to him, I will loosen all the chains that bound it tight, which the empty aims and desires of mortal life had fastened upon it ; I will send it abroad, extend and diffuse it, so that it shall touch the bounds of the All, and hasten to that most glorious and loveliest of visions—the Vision of the Uncreated " ?

This, then, is the company of the sober who have 153 set before them instruction as their head, while the former was the company of the drunken, whose leader was indiscipline. XXXVIII. But drunken- 154 ness, we saw, does not only signify folly, which is the work of this rejection of discipline, but it also signifies complete insensibility. In the body this is produced by wine, but in the soul by ignorance of things of which we should naturally have acquired knowledge. Consequently on the subject of ignorance I must say a few words, only just what is needful, by way of reminder. Now what we call ignorance is an affection of the soul. To what affec- 155 tion of the body can we liken it, but to the incapacitation of the sense-organs ? All who have lost the use of eyes and ears can no longer see or hear and have no knowledge of day and light, which alone in truth make life desirable, but are surrounded by enduring darkness and everlasting night, thus rendered helpless in regard to every issue great or small. These persons are in common life generally and with good reason called " incapable." For even if all the 156 faculties of the rest of the body should attain the

ἔλθωσι καὶ ῥώμης, ὑποσκελισθεῖσαι πρὸς ὀφθαλμῶν
καὶ ὤτων πηρώσεως μέγα πτῶμα πίπτουσιν, ὡς
μηκέτ' ἀναστῆναι δύνασθαι· τὰ γὰρ ὑπερείδοντα
καὶ στηρίζοντα ἄνθρωπον λόγῳ μὲν αἱ βάσεις
εἰσίν, ἔργῳ δὲ ἀκοαί τε καὶ ὄψεις, ἃς ἔχων μέν τις
ὁλοκλήρους ἐγήγερται καὶ ἀνώρθωσαι, στερόμενος
δὲ αὐτῶν κλίνεται καὶ εἰσάπαν καθαιρεῖται.

157   τὸ παραπλήσιον οὖν ἐν ψυχῇ πάντως[1]
ἄγνοια ἐργάζεται τὰ βλέποντα καὶ ἀκούοντα αὐτῆς
λυμαινομένη καὶ μήτε φῶς μήτε λόγον παρεισ-
ελθεῖν ἐῶσα, τὸν μέν, ἵνα μὴ διδάξῃ, τὸ δέ, ἵνα μὴ
δείξῃ τὰ ὄντα, βαθὺ δὲ σκότος καὶ πολλὴν ἀλογίαν
καταχέασα κωφὴν λίθον τὸ περικαλλέστατον εἶδος
158 ψυχῆς εἰργάσατο. XXXIX. καὶ γὰρ τῇ ἀγνοίᾳ
τὸ ἐναντίον, ἡ ἐπιστήμη, τρόπον τινὰ ψυχῆς καὶ
ὀφθαλμοὶ καὶ ὦτά ἐστι· καὶ γὰρ τοῖς λεγομένοις
προσέχει τὸν νοῦν καὶ καταθεᾶται τὰ ὄντα καὶ
οὐδὲν οὔτε παρορᾶν οὔτε παρακούειν ὑπομένει,
πάντα δ' ὅσα ἀκοῆς καὶ θέας ἄξια περισκοπεῖ καὶ
περιβλέπεται, κἂν εἰ πεζεύειν καὶ πλεῖν δεῖ, γῆς
καὶ θαλάττης ἄχρι τῶν περάτων ἀφικνεῖται, ἵνα
159 ἴδῃ τι πλέον ἢ ἀκούσῃ καινότερον. ἀοκνότατον
γὰρ ὁ ἐπιστήμης ἔρως, ἐχθρὸς μὲν ὕπνου, φίλος
δὲ ἐγρηγόρσεως· διανιστὰς οὖν καὶ ἀνεγείρων καὶ
παραθήγων ἀεὶ διάνοιαν πανταχόσε περιφοιτᾶν
ἀναγκάζει λίχνον ἀκοῆς ἐργαζόμενος καὶ μαθήσεως
160 δίψαν ἄληκτον ἐντήκων.   οὐκοῦν ἐπιστήμη μὲν τὸ βλέπειν καὶ ἀκούειν περιποιεῖ, δι'
ὧν αἱ κατορθώσεις· ὁ γὰρ ἰδὼν καὶ ἀκούσας, γνοὺς
[382] | τὸ συμφέρον, τὸ μὲν ἑλόμενος, τὸ δὲ ἐναντίον

        [1] MSS. πάνθ' ὅσα.

---

   [a] Or "word . . . wordlessness." See App. p. 505.

utmost limit of strength and capacity, yet if they **are** handicapped by the crippling of eyes and ears they fall, and great is that fall, making any reinstatement impossible. For, though we speak of the feet as the support which upholds the man, in reality that is done by the faculties of sight and hearing : possessed of these in their fullness, the man stands uprisen and erect ; deprived of them, he gives way and is utterly prostrated. An exactly similar result in 157 the soul is produced by ignorance, which destroys its powers of seeing and hearing, and suffers neither light, which might shew it realities, nor reason,[a] which might be its teacher, to find their way in ; but sheds about it profound darkness and a flood of unreason,[a] and turns the soul's fair and lovely form into a senseless block of stone. XXXIX. Similarly know- 158 ledge, the opposite of ignorance, may be called the eyes and the ears of the soul. For it fixes the attention on what is said and contemplates what is, and allows no mis-seeing or mis-hearing,[b] but surveys and observes all that is worthy to be heard and seen. And if it be necessary to travel or take ship, it makes its way to the ends of the earth or ocean, to see something more or hear something new. For nothing 159 is so active as the passion for knowledge ; it hates sleep and loves wakefulness. So it ever arouses and excites and sharpens the intellect, and compelling it to range in every direction makes it greedy to hear, and instils an incessant thirst for learning.

Knowledge, then, provides[c] that sight or hearing, to 160 which we owe each case of right conduct. For he who sees and hears in the moral sense, knows what is good for him, and by choosing this and rejecting

---

[b] See App. p. 505.   [c] Or " preserves."

ἀποστραφεὶς ὠφέληται. ἄγνοια δὲ χαλεπωτέραν
τῆς ἐν τῷ σώματι πηρώσιν ἐπιφέρουσα τῇ ψυχῇ
πάντων ἁμαρτημάτων αἰτία γίνεται, μηδὲν μήτ᾽
ἐκ τοῦ προϊδέσθαι μήτ᾽ ἐκ τοῦ προακοῦσαι δυνα-
μένη λαβεῖν ἔξωθεν βοήθημα· διὰ γοῦν τὴν πολλὴν
ἐρημίαν ἑαυτῆς ἀφρούρητος καὶ ἀφύλακτος ἐαθεῖσα
[καὶ] πρὸς τῶν ἐπιτυχόντων ἀνθρώπων τε ὁμοῦ
161 καὶ πραγμάτων ἐπιβουλεύεται. μηδέποτ᾽ οὖν μήτ᾽
ἄκρατον προσενεγκώμεθα τοσοῦτον, ὡς ἀπραξίαν
ἐμποιῆσαι ταῖς αἰσθήσεσι, μήτε τοσοῦτον ἐπιστήμης ἀλλοτριωθῶμεν, ὡς ἄγνοιαν, τὸ μέγα καὶ
βαθὺ σκότος, τῆς ἑαυτῶν ψυχῆς κατασκεδάσαι.

162   XL. Διττὸν δὲ τὸ ἀγνοίας γένος, τὸ μὲν ἁπλοῦν,
ἢ παντελὴς ἀναισθησία, τὸ δὲ διπλοῦν, ὅταν μὴ
μόνον ἀνεπιστημοσύνη τις συνέχηται, ἀλλὰ καὶ
οἴηται εἰδέναι ἃ μηδαμῶς οἶδε δόξῃ ψευδεῖ σοφίας
163 ἐπαιρόμενος. τὸ μὲν οὖν πρότερον κακὸν ἔλαττον—
κουφοτέρων γὰρ ἁμαρτημάτων καὶ τάχα ἀκουσίων
αἴτιον—, τὸ δὲ δεύτερον μεῖζον· μεγάλα γὰρ
ἀποτίκτει καὶ οὐκ ἀκούσια μόνον ἀλλ᾽ ἤδη κὰκ
164 προνοίας ἀδικήματα.   περὶ ταῦτά μοι
δοκεῖ Λὼτ ὁ θυγατροποιὸς μάλιστα κηραίνειν
ἄρρεν καὶ τέλειον ἐν ψυχῇ φυτὸν ἀναθρέψαι μὴ
δυνάμενος· δύο γὰρ θυγατέρας ἐκ τῆς λιθουμένης
γυναικὸς ἔσχηκεν, ἣν εὐθυβόλῳ χρησάμενος ὀνόματι καλέσειεν ἄν τις συνήθειαν, ἐχθρὰν φύσιν
ἀληθείας, καὶ ὁπότε ἄγοι τις αὐτήν, ὑστερίζουσαν
καὶ περιβλεπομένην τὰ ἀρχαῖα καὶ σύντροφα καὶ
ἀψύχου τρόπον στήλης ἐν μέσοις αὐτοῖς κατα-
165 μένουσαν.   τῶν δὲ θυγατέρων ἡ μὲν
πρεσβυτέρα κεκλήσεται βουλή, συναίνεσις δὲ ἡ

its opposite, finds himself benefited. But ignorance entails a more severe disablement to the soul than the disablement of the body, and thus is the cause of all its wrongdoing, since it cannot draw help from outside itself through the warnings which seeing and hearing might give it. Thus, standing utterly alone, and left unguarded and unprotected, it is a butt for the haphazard hostility of men and circumstances alike. Let us, then, never drink so deep of strong 161 liquor as to reduce our senses to inactivity, nor become so estranged from knowledge as to spread the vast and profound darkness of ignorance over our soul.

XL. Now ignorance as a whole is of two different 162 kinds; one single, that is complete insensibility, the other twofold, that is when a man is not merely the victim of a want of knowledge, but also, encouraged by a false idea of his own wisdom, thinks he knows what he does not know at all. The former is the 163 lesser evil, for it is the cause of less serious and perhaps involuntary errors, and the second is the greater, for it is the parent of great iniquities, not only those which are involuntary, but such as are actually premeditated. It was this especially which 164 brought trouble to Lot—Lot who was the parent of daughters only and could rear no male or perfect growth within his soul. Two daughters he had and their mother was she who was turned into stone, whom we might call "custom," if we gave her her right name; her nature is hostile to truth, and if we take her with us, she lags behind and gazes round at the old familiar objects and remains among them like a lifeless monument. The elder of these 165 daughters will bear the name of Deliberation, and

νεωτέρα· τῷ μὲν γὰρ βουλεύσασθαι τὸ συναινεῖν
ἕπεται, συναινέσας δ' οὐδὲ εἷς ἔτι βουλεύεται.
καθίσας οὖν ὁ νοῦς ἐν τῷ ἑαυτοῦ συνεδρίῳ διακινεῖν
ἄρχεται τὰς θυγατέρας καὶ μετὰ μὲν τῆς πρεσβυτέρας, βουλῆς, σκοπεῖσθαί τε καὶ διερευνᾶν
ἕκαστα, μετὰ δὲ τῆς νεωτέρας, συναινέσεως,
ἐπινεύειν ῥᾳδίως τοῖς ἐπιτυχοῦσι καὶ ὡς φίλα τὰ
ἐχθρὰ ἀσπάζεσθαι, δέλεαρ εἴ τι μικρὸν ἡδονῆς
166 αὐτὸ μόνον ἀφ' ἑαυτῶν ἐνδιδώῃ. ταῦτα δὲ νήφων
μὲν λογισμὸς οὐκ ἀνέχεται, μέθῃ δὲ κατεσχημένος
καὶ ὥσπερ ἔξοινος ὤν· XLI. διὸ λέγεται· '' ἐπό-
τισαν τὸν πατέρα οἶνον.''   ἀναισθησία
παντελής, ἱκανὸν δοκεῖν εἶναι βουλεύεσθαι τὸν
νοῦν ἀφ' ἑαυτοῦ τὰ συμφέροντα ἢ τοῖς ὁπωσοῦν
φανεῖσιν, ὡς τὸ ἀληθὲς πάγιον ἐν ἑαυτοῖς ἔχουσι,
συναινέσαι, τῆς ἀνθρωπίνης φύσεως μηδαμῇ μηδαμῶς ἱκανῆς οὔσης ἢ ἐκ περισκέψεως τὸ σαφὲς
εὑρεῖν ἢ τὰ μὲν ὡς ἀληθῆ καὶ συμφέροντα ἑλέσθαι,
[383] τὰ δ' ὡς[1] ψευδῆ καὶ βλάβης αἴτια | ἀποστραφῆναι.
167 πολὺ γὰρ σκότος τῶν ὄντων καὶ σωμάτων καὶ
πραγμάτων κατακεχυμένον οὐκ ἐᾷ τὴν ἑκάστου
φύσιν ἰδεῖν, ἀλλὰ κἂν βιασάμενός τις ὑπὸ περιεργίας
ἢ τοῦ φιλομαθοῦς ἐθελήσῃ διακῦψαι, καθάπερ οἱ
πεπηρωμένοι προσπταίων τοῖς ἐν ποσί, πρίν τι
λαβεῖν, ἀναπεσὼν ὑστερίζει ἢ ταῖς χερσὶν ἐφαπτό-
μενος τὰ ἄδηλα εἰκάζει στοχασμῷ πρὸ ἀληθείας
168 κτώμενος. οὐδὲ γὰρ εἰ δᾳδουχοῦσα παιδεία παρα-
πέμποι τὸν νοῦν φῶς ἁψαμένη τὸ οἰκεῖον ἐπὶ τὴν
τῶν ὄντων θέαν, ὀνῆσαι δύναιτ' ἂν μᾶλλον ἢ
βλάψαι· τὸ γὰρ βραχὺ φέγγος ὑπὸ πολλοῦ σκότους

---

[1] MSS. ἢ ὡς.

[a] Or " to examine."

the younger of Assent. For assent follows deliberation, and no one who has given his assent continues
to deliberate. The mind then taking his seat in his
council begins to make his daughters busy.[a] With
the elder, Deliberation, he proceeds to discuss and
examine every point ; with the younger, Assent, he
readily agrees to every suggestion, giving a friendly
welcome to any however hostile, if what they have to
give offers any enticement of pleasure however small.
In its sober condition the mind does not tolerate this, 166
only when it has succumbed to intoxication and is as
though overcome by wine. XLI. And so we read,
" They gave their father wine to drink " (Gen. xix.
33).   Now this is complete insensibility,
that the mind should think itself competent to deliberate by itself on what is to its interests, or to
assent to presentations of any kind as though they
were a vehicle of solid truth, for human nature is
ever quite unable, either by circumspection to dis-
cover certainty, or to choose some things as true and
profitable, and to reject others as false and injurious.
For the vastness of the darkness which overspreads 167
the world of bodies and affairs forbids us to see the
nature of each ; and though curiosity or love of
learning may give us the wish to force our way and
peer through the curtain, we shall like blind men
stumble over the obstacles before us, lose our footing
and miss our object, or if our hands do lay hold of it,
we are but guessing at uncertainties and it is not
truth but conjecture that is in our grasp. For even 168
if instruction, torch in hand, should go before the
mind, shedding her own particular light to give it
sight of realities, it would do more harm than good.
For its little beam is bound to be extinguished by

σβέννυσθαι πέφυκε, σβεσθέντος δὲ ἀνωφελὴς πᾶσα
169 ὄψις.   τὸν μέντοι σεμνυνόμενον ἢ ἐπὶ
τῷ βουλεύεσθαι ἢ ἐπὶ τῷ τὰ μὲν αἱρεῖσθαι τὰ δὲ
φεύγειν ἱκανῶς δύνασθαι διὰ τούτων ὑπομνηστέον·
εἰ μὲν ἀπὸ τῶν αὐτῶν τὰς αὐτὰς ἀεὶ συνέβαινε
προσπίπτειν ἀπαραλλάκτους φαντασίας, ἣν ἴσως
ἀναγκαῖον τά τε ἐν ἡμῖν αὐτοῖς φύσει κατασκευα-
σθέντα διττὰ κριτήρια, αἴσθησίν τε καὶ νοῦν, ὡς
ἀψευδῆ καὶ ἀδέκαστα θαυμάζειν καὶ περὶ μηδενὸς
ἐνδοιάζοντας ἐπέχειν, ἀλλὰ τοῖς ἅπαξ φανεῖσι
πιστεύοντας τὰ μὲν αἱρεῖσθαι, τὰ δὲ ἔμπαλιν
170 ἀποστρέφεσθαι. ἐπειδὴ δὲ διαφόρως ἀπ᾽ αὐτῶν
εὑρισκόμεθα κινούμενοι, βέβαιον περὶ οὐδενὸς
οὐδὲν ἂν ἔχοιμεν εἰπεῖν, ἅτε μὴ ἑστῶτος τοῦ
φανέντος, ἀλλὰ πολυτρόποις καὶ πολυμόρφοις
χρωμένου ταῖς μεταβολαῖς. XLII. ἀνάγκη γὰρ
ἀνιδρύτου τῆς φαντασίας οὔσης ἀνίδρυτον εἶναι
καὶ τὴν ἐπ᾽ αὐτῇ κρίσιν.

171 Αἴτια δὲ τούτου πολλά· πρῶτον μὲν αἱ ἐν τοῖς
ζῴοις οὐ καθ᾽ ἓν μέρος ἀλλὰ σχεδὸν περὶ πάντα
ἀμύθητοι διαφοραί, αἱ περὶ τὴν γένεσιν καὶ κατα-
σκευὴν αὐτῶν, αἱ περὶ τὰς τροφὰς καὶ διαίτας, αἱ
περὶ τὰς αἱρέσεις καὶ φυγάς, αἱ περὶ τὰς αἰσθη-
τικὰς ἐνεργείας τε καὶ κινήσεις, αἱ περὶ τὰς τῶν
κατὰ σῶμα καὶ ψυχὴν ἀμυθήτων παθῶν ἰδιότητας.
172   χωρὶς γὰρ τῶν κρινόντων ἴδε καὶ τῶν
κρινομένων ἔνια, οἷα τὸν χαμαιλέοντα, τὸν πολύ-

―――――――――――――――
^a See App. p. 505.   ^b See App. p. 506.

the vast darkness, and when it is extinguished all
power of sight is useless.   He who prides 169
himself on his judgement in deliberation, or flatters
himself that he is competent to choose this and shun
that, should be brought to a recollection of the truth
by the following thoughts.   If it were always the case
that the same objects produced the same impressions
on the mind without any variation, it would perhaps
be necessary that the two instruments of judgement
which nature has established in us, sense and mind,
should be held in high esteem as veracious and incorruptible, and that we should not suspend our
judgement on any point through doubt but accept a
single presentation of two different objects, and on the
faith of this choose one and reject the other.   But 170
since we prove to be differently affected by them at
different times, we can say nothing with certainty
about anything, because the picture presented to us
is not constant, but subject to changes manifold and
multiform.   XLII. Since the mental picture is variable, the judgement we form of it must be variable
also.   There are many reasons for this.[a]

In the first place[b] there are the innumerable differ- 171
ences in living creatures, differences concerned not
with a single aspect, but practically with all ; differences in birth, in structure and equipment ; differences in food and mode of life ; differences in pre-
dilections and aversions ; differences in their sense-
activities and sense-movements ; differences in the
peculiarities which arise from the innumerable ways
in which body and soul are affected.   For 172
leaving out of sight for the moment those who form
judgements,[b] consider examples[b] among the objects
of such judgements. Take for instance the chameleon

ποδα· τὸν μέν γέ φασι τὴν χρόαν ἀλλάττοντα τοῖς
ἐδάφεσιν ὁμοιοῦσθαι καθ' ὧν εἴωθεν ἕρπειν, τὸν δὲ
ταῖς κατὰ θαλάττης πέτραις, ὧν ἂν περιδράξηται,
τάχα που τῆς σωτηρίου φύσεως ἀλεξίκακον
συλλήψεως δωρησαμένης τὴν εἰς τὸ πολυχρώματον
173 αὐτοῖς τροπὴν φάρμακον. τὸν δε αὐχένα τῆς
περιστερᾶς ἐν ἡλιακαῖς αὐγαῖς οὐ κατενόησας
μυρίας χρωμάτων ἀλλάττοντα ἰδέας; ἢ οὐχι
φοινικοῦν καὶ κυανοῦν, πυρωπόν τε αὖ καὶ ἀν-
θρακοειδές, ἔτι δὲ ὠχρὸν καὶ ἐρυθρὸν καὶ ἄλλα
παντοδαπὰ ἴσχει χρώματα, ὧν οὐδὲ τὰς κλήσεις
174 ῥᾴδιον ἀπομνημονεῦσαι; φασὶ μέντοι καὶ ἐν Σκύ-
[384] θαις τοῖς | καλουμένοις Γελώοις θαυμασιώτατόν τι
γίνεσθαι σπανίως μέν, γίνεσθαι δ' ὅμως θηρίον, ὃ
καλεῖται τάρανδρος, μέγεθος μὲν βοὸς οὐκ ἀποδέον,
ἐλάφῳ δὲ τὸν τοῦ προσώπου τύπον ἐμφερέστατον·
λόγος ἔχει τοῦτο μεταβάλλειν ἀεὶ τὰς τρίχας πρός
τε τὰ χωρία καὶ τὰ δένδρα καὶ πάνθ' ἁπλῶς οἷς
ἂν ἐγγὺς ἱστῆται, ὡς διὰ τὴν τῆς χρόας ὁμοιότητα
λανθάνειν τοὺς ἐντυγχάνοντας καὶ ταύτῃ μᾶλλον ἢ τῇ
175 περὶ σῶμα ἀλκῇ δυσθήρατον εἶναι. ταῦτα δὴ καὶ τὰ
τούτοις ὅμοια πίστεις ἐναργεῖς ἀκαταληψίας εἰσίν.

XLIII. Ἔπειτα δὲ αἱ μηκέτι τῶν ζῴων
ἁπάντων, ἀλλὰ καὶ ἀνθρώπων ἰδίᾳ πρὸς ἀλλήλους
176 περὶ πάντα ποικιλίαι. οὐ γὰρ μόνον ἄλλοτε ἄλλως
τὰ αὐτὰ κρίνουσιν, ἀλλὰ καὶ ἑτέρως ἕτεροι, ἡδονὰς
τε καὶ ἀηδίας ἔμπαλιν τῶν αὐτῶν λαμβάνοντες·
οἷς γὰρ δυσηρέστησαν ἔνιοι, ἐτέρφθησαν ἄλλοι, καὶ
κατὰ τοὐναντίον ἅπερ ὡς φίλα καὶ οἰκεῖα ἐπισπασάμενοι[1] τινες ἐδεξιώσαντο, ταῦθ' ἕτεροι ὡς

---

[1] Perhaps, as Adler, ἀσπασάμενοι. See App. p. 507.

[a] See App. p. 506.   [b] See App. p. 507.

and the polypus. The former, we are told, changes its colour and grows like the kinds of soil over which it is its habit to crawl; the latter grows like the rocks to which it clings in the sea, and we may fairly suppose that this power of changing to various colours is given them by protecting nature as a remedy against the danger of capture. Again, have we not 173 seen the dove's neck[a] change in the sun's rays into a thousand different hues, sometimes scarlet and dark blue, or fiery or like red-hot coal, again yellow and then ruddy, and all other kinds of colour, so numerous that it would be difficult to give even their names in full? Indeed it is said that in the land of the 174 Scythians who are known as the Geloans a most extraordinary animal is actually, though no doubt rarely, found called the elk, in size equal to an ox, but with a face shaped very like a deer. The account given of this creature is that it always changes the colour of its hair into that of the places, trees, or any imaginable thing near which it stands, and owing to this similarity of colour, we are told, it is not observed by passers-by, and this fact rather than its bodily strength makes it difficult to catch. These and similar phenomena are clear proofs of the 175 impossibility of apprehension.[a]

XLIII. Secondly,[b] there are the diversities on all subjects which, to pass from animals in general, we find also in men in particular. Not only do their judge- 176 ments [b] on the same objects vary at different times, but different persons receive different impressions of pleasure or its reverse from the same things. For what is disliked by some is enjoyed by others, and contrariwise what some receive with open arms as acceptable and agreeable to their nature is utterly

ἀλλότρια καὶ δυσμενῆ μακρὰν ἀφ' ἑαυτῶν ἐσκο-
177 ράκισαν. ἤδη γοῦν ἐν θεάτρῳ πολλάκις παρα-
τυχὼν εἶδον ὑφ' ἑνὸς μέλους τῶν ἀγωνιζομένων ἐπὶ
τῆς σκηνῆς τραγῳδῶν ἢ κιθαρῳδῶν τοὺς μὲν οὕτως
ἀχθέντας, ὡς ἀνεγειρομένους καὶ συνηχοῦντας ἄκον-
τας τὰ πρὸς ἔπαινον ἐκφωνεῖν, τοὺς δὲ οὕτως ἀτρώ-
τως ἔχοντας, ὡς μηδὲν τῶν ἀψύχων βάθρων ἐφ' οἷς
καθέζονται ταύτῃ γοῦν διαφέρειν ἂν νομισθῆναι,
ἐνίους δ' οὕτως ἀλλοτριωθέντας, ὡς καὶ τὴν θέαν
οἴχεσθαι καταλιπόντας, ἔτι καὶ προσαποκλειο-
μένους[1] ἑκατέρᾳ τῶν χειρῶν τὰ ὦτα, μὴ ἄρα τι
ἔναυλον ἀπολειφθὲν ἀηδίαν ὑπηχοῦν δυσκόλοις καὶ
δυσαρέστοις ψυχαῖς ἐργάσηται.

178   Καίτοι τί ταῦτά φαμεν; αὐτός τις εἷς ὢν ἕκαστος
ἐφ' ἑαυτοῦ, τὸ παραδοξότατον, μυρίας μεταβολὰς
καὶ τροπὰς δεχόμενος κατά τε σῶμα καὶ ψυχὴν
τοτὲ μὲν αἱρεῖται, τοτὲ δ' ἀποστρέφεται οὐδαμῶς
μεταβάλλοντα, μένειν δ' ἐπὶ τῆς αὐτῆς πεφυκότα
179 κατασκευῆς· οὐ γὰρ τὰ αὐτὰ ὑγιαίνουσι καὶ νοσοῦσι
προσπίπτειν φιλεῖ, οὐδὲ ἐγρηγορόσι καὶ κοιμω-
μένοις, οὐδὲ ἡβῶσι καὶ γεγηρακόσι· καὶ ἑστὼς
μέντοι καὶ κινούμενός τις ἑτέρας ἔλαβε φαντασίας, καὶ θαρρῶν καὶ δεδιὼς ἔμπαλιν, ἔτι
μέντοι λυπούμενός τε καὶ χαίρων, καὶ φιλῶν καὶ
180 τοὐναντίον μισῶν. καὶ τί δεῖ μακρηγοροῦντα περὶ
τούτων ἐνοχλεῖν; συνελόντι γὰρ φράσαι πᾶσα ἡ
σώματος καὶ ψυχῆς κατὰ φύσιν τε αὖ καὶ παρὰ |
[385] φύσιν κίνησις αἰτία τῆς περὶ τὰ φαινόμενα ἀστάτου

---

[1] MSS. προσαποσειομένους, which Wendland defends on the
strange ground that "shaking off their ears" may describe
the action of men trying to brush away the sound of the
music out of their ears. Cohn preferred ἀποσαττομένους,
which would give the same sense as ἀποκλειομένους (Mangey).

scouted by others as alien and repugnant. For 177
example, I have often when I chanced to be in the
theatre noticed the effect produced by some single
tune sung by the actors on the stage or played by the
musicians. Some of the audience are so moved, that
in their excitement they cannot help raising their
voices in a chorus of acclamation.[a] Others are so
unstirred that, as far as this is concerned, you might
suppose them on a level of feeling with the senseless
benches on which they sit. Others, again, are so
repelled that they are off and away from the performance, and indeed, as they go, block their ears
with both hands for fear that some echo of the music
should remain to haunt them and produce a sense of
discomfort to irritate and pain their souls.

[b] But it is needless to quote such cases as these. 178
Every single individual in his own person is subject,
extraordinary though it be, to numberless changes
and variations in body and soul, and chooses at one
time and rejects at another things which do not
change, but retain the natural constitution which
they have had throughout. The same feelings are 179
not experienced in health as in sickness, in wakefulness as in sleep, in youth as in age. And people
receive different mental impressions according as
they are standing or moving, confident or affrighted,
sad or joyful, loving or hating. And why tediously 180
pursue the subject? For to put it shortly, our
bodies and souls are in a state of motion, natural or
unnatural, which considered as a whole produces
that ceaseless change in the mental pictures pre-

---

[a] Or (not so probably) ἀνεγειρομένους "starting from their
seats," συνηχοῦντας "taking up the tune."
[b] See App. p. 507.

φορᾶς γίνεται μαχόμενα καὶ ἀσύμφωνα προσβαλλούσης ὀνείρατα.

181 XLIV. Γίνεται δ' οὐχ ἥκιστα τὸ περὶ[1] τὰς φαντασίας ἄστατον καὶ παρὰ τὰς θέσεις καὶ παρὰ τὰ διαστήματα καὶ παρὰ τοὺς τόπους, οἷς ἕκαστα

182 ἐμπεριέχεται. ἢ τοὺς κατὰ θαλάττης ἰχθῦς οὐχ ὁρῶμεν, ὁπότε τὰς πτέρυγας διατείνοντες ἐννήχοιντο, μείζους ἀεὶ τῆς φύσεως προφαινομένους; καὶ τὰς εἰρεσίας μέντοι, κἂν σφόδρα ὦσιν εὐθυτενεῖς, κεκλασμένας ὁρᾶσθαι συμβαίνει καθ' ὕδατος.

183 τά γε μὴν πορρωτάτω ψευδεῖς προσβάλλοντα φαντασίας τὸν νοῦν εἴωθεν ἀπατᾶν· ἄψυχα γὰρ ἔστιν ὅτε ὄντα ὑπετοπήθη ζῷα εἶναι καὶ τοὐναντίον τὰ ἔμψυχα ἄψυχα, ἔτι δὲ τὰ ἑστῶτα κινεῖσθαι καὶ τὰ κινούμενα ἑστάναι καὶ τὰ μὲν προσιόντα ἐξαναχωρεῖν, τὰ δὲ ἀπιόντα πάλιν προσέρχεσθαι, καὶ βραχύτατα μὲν τὰ περιμηκέστατα, περιφερῆ δ' αὖ τὰ πολυγώνια. καὶ μυρία ἄλλα ὑπὸ τῆς φανερᾶς ὄψεως ψευδογραφεῖται, οἷς οὐκ ἄν τις εὖ φρονῶν ὡς βεβαίοις συνεπιγράψαιτο.

184 XLV. Τί δ' αἱ ἐν τοῖς σκευαζομένοις ποσότητες; παρὰ γὰρ τὸ πλέον ἢ ἔλαττον αἵ τε βλάβαι καὶ ὠφέλειαι συνίστανται, καθάπερ ἐπὶ μυρίων ἄλλων καὶ μάλιστα τῶν κατὰ τὴν ἰατρικὴν ἐπιστήμην

185 ἔχει φαρμάκων· ἡ γὰρ ἐν ταῖς συνθέσεσι ποσότης ὅροις καὶ κανόσι μεμέτρηται, ὧν οὔτε ἐντὸς κάμψαι οὔτε περαιτέρω προελθεῖν ἀσφαλές—τὸ μὲν γὰρ ἔλαττον χαλᾷ, τὸ δὲ πλέον ἐπιτείνει τὰς δυνάμεις· βλαβερὸν δ' ἑκάτερον, τὸ μὲν ἀδυνατοῦν ἐνεργῆσαι δι' ἀσθένειαν, τὸ δὲ βλάψαι βιαζόμενον διὰ καρ-

---

[1] MSS. παρά.

sented to us which makes us the victim of conflicting [a] and incongruous dreams.

XLIV. [b] But the inconstancy of impressions is par- 181 ticularly caused by the positions and surroundings of the several objects and their distances from the observer. We see that fishes in the sea, when they 182 swim with their fins stretched, always look larger than nature has made them, and oars, however straight they are, appear bent below the water. Still more—the mind is often misled by distant objects which create false impressions. Sometimes we 183 suppose lifeless objects to be living objects or the converse. And we have similar illusions about things stationary and moving, advancing and receding, short and long, circular and multilateral. And numberless other distortions of the truth are produced even when sight is unimpeded, which no sane person would accept as trustworthy.

XLV. [b] What again of quantities in prepared mix- 184 tures? Their powers of benefiting or injuring depend on the relative quantity of the various ingredients, as we see in numberless cases and particularly in the drugs used by medical science. For 185 quantity in compounds is measured by regular standards, and we cannot with safety stop short of or go beyond what they prescribe; for anything smaller or greater than this respectively overweakens or overstrains the force of the preparation. In both cases harm is done. In the former case the medicine is incapable through its weakness of producing any effect, while in the latter its high degree of potency makes it a force of active mischief. And again accord-

[a] Or " which act upon us like conflicting," etc.
[b] See App. p. 507.

τερωτάτην ἰσχύν—, λειότησί τε αὖ καὶ τραχύτησι,
πυκνότησί τε αὖ καὶ πιλήσεσι καὶ τοὐναντίον
μανότησι καὶ ἐξαπλώσεσι τὸν εἰς βοήθειαν καὶ
βλάβην ἔλεγχον ἐναργῶς διασυνίστησιν.

186 Ἀλλὰ μὴν οὐδὲ ἐκεῖνό τις ἀγνοεῖ, ὅτι τῶν ὄντων
σχεδὸν ἐξ αὑτοῦ καὶ καθ' αὑτὸ νενόηται τὸ παράπαν
οὐδέν, τῇ δὲ πρὸς τὸ ἐναντίον παραθέσει δοκιμάζεται, οἷον τὸ μικρὸν παρὰ τὸ μέγα, τὸ ξηρὸν
παρὰ τὸ ὑγρόν, παρὰ τὸ ψυχρὸν τὸ θερμόν, παρὰ
τὸ βαρὺ τὸ κοῦφον, τὸ μέλαν παρὰ τὸ λευκόν, τὸ
ἀσθενὲς παρὰ τὸ ἰσχυρόν, τὰ ὀλίγα παρὰ τὰ πολλά.

187 κατὰ τὸ παραπλήσιον μέντοι καὶ ὅσα ἐπ' ἀρετὴν
ἢ κακίαν ἀναφέρεται, τὰ ὠφέλιμα διὰ τῶν βλαβερῶν γνωρίζεται, τὰ καλὰ τῇ τῶν αἰσχρῶν
ἀντιθέσει, τὰ δίκαια καὶ κοινῶς ἀγαθὰ τῇ τῶν
ἀδίκων καὶ κακῶν παραθέσει, καὶ πάντα μέντοι
τὰ ἄλλα ὅσα ἐν κόσμῳ σκοπῶν ἄν τις εὕροι κατὰ
τὸν αὐτὸν τύπον λαμβάνοντα τὴν ἐπίκρισιν· ἐξ
ἑαυτοῦ μὲν γὰρ ἕκαστον ἀκατάληπτον, ἐκ δὲ τῆς

188 πρὸς ἕτερον συγκρίσεως γνωρίζεσθαι δοκεῖ. τὸ
[386] δὲ μὴ ἑαυτῷ μαρτυρεῖν | ἱκανόν, τῆς δὲ ἀφ' ἑτέρου
χρῇζον συνηγορίας, ἀβέβαιον εἰς πίστιν· ὥστε
καὶ ταύτῃ τοὺς εὐχερῶς ὁμολογοῦντας ἢ ἀρνου-
μένους περὶ παντὸς οὑτινος⟨οῦν⟩ ἐλέγχεσθαι.

189 Καὶ τί θαυμαστόν; προσωτέρω γάρ τις χωρήσας
τῶν πραγμάτων καὶ εἰλικρινέστερον αὐτὰ αὐγασά-
μενος εἴσεται τοῦθ', ὅτι ἓν οὐδὲν καθ' ἁπλῆν ἡμῖν
τὴν ἑαυτοῦ προσπίπτει φύσιν, ἀλλὰ πάντα μίξεις
πολυπλοκωτάτας ἔχοντα καὶ κράσεις.

190 XLVI. αὐτίκα τῶν χρωμάτων ἀντιλαμβανόμεθα
πῶς; ἆρ' οὐ σὺν ἀέρι καὶ φωτί, τοῖς ἐκτός,
καὶ τῷ κατ' αὐτὴν τὴν ὄψιν ὑγρῷ; γλυκὺ δὲ καὶ

ing to its roughness or smoothness, and its density and compactness on the one hand, or its sponginess and dilatation on the other, it exhibits clearly the means of testing its power of helping or harming.

[a] Again, everyone knows that practically nothing at 186 all which exists is intelligible by itself and in itself, but everything is appreciated only by comparison with its opposite ; as small by comparison with great, dry with wet, hot with cold, light with heavy, black with white, weak with strong, few with many. The same rule holds with all that concerns virtue and vice. We only know the profitable through the hurtful, the 187 noble by contrast with the base, the just and the good in general by comparison with the unjust and evil. And indeed if we consider we shall see that everything else in the world is judged on the same pattern. For in itself each thing is beyond our apprehension, and it is only by bringing it into relation with something else that it seems to be known. Now that which is 188 incapable of attesting itself and needs to be vouched for by something else, gives no sure ground for belief. And it follows that on this principle we can estimate at their true value lightly-made affirmations and negations on any subject whatever.

Nor is this strange. For anyone who penetrates 189 deeper into things and views them in a purer light, will recognize that no single thing presents itself to us in its own absolute nature but all contain inter-lacings and intermixtures of the most complicated kind. XLVI. [a] For instance, how do we 190 apprehend colours ? Surely by means of the exter-nals, air and light, and the internal moisture in the eye itself. How do we discriminate between sweet

[a] See App. p. 508.

πικρὸν τίνα τρόπον δοκιμάζεται; μὴ δίχα τῶν
καθ᾽ ἡμᾶς αὐτοὺς ἐνστομίων χυλῶν ὅσοι κατὰ
φύσιν ἢ παρὰ φύσιν; οὐ δήπου. τί δ᾽; αἱ ἀπὸ
τῶν ἐπιθυμιωμένων ὀσμαὶ μὴ τὰς ἁπλᾶς ⟨καὶ⟩
εἰλικρινεῖς τῶν σωμάτων φύσεις παριστᾶσιν; ἢ
τὰς κεκραμένας ἔκ τε αὐτῶν καὶ ἀέρος, ἔστι δ᾽
ὅτε καὶ τοῦ τήκοντος τὰ σώματα πυρὸς καὶ τῆς
191 κατὰ τοὺς μυκτῆρας δυνάμεως; ἐκ δὴ τούτων
συνάγεται, ὅτι οὔτε χρωμάτων ἀντιλαμβανόμεθα,
ἀλλὰ τοῦ συνισταμένου κράματος ἔκ τε τῶν
ὑποκειμένων καὶ φωτός, οὔτε ὀσμῶν, ἀλλὰ μίγ-
ματος, ὅπερ συνέστη διά τε τοῦ ῥυέντος ἀπὸ τῶν
σωμάτων καὶ τοῦ πανδεχοῦς ἀέρος, οὔτε χυλῶν,
ἀλλὰ τοῦ γενομένου διά τε τοῦ προσιόντος γευστοῦ
καὶ τῆς κατὰ τὸ στόμα ὑγρᾶς οὐσίας.
192 XLVII. τούτων δὴ τοῦτον ἐχόντων τὸν τρόπον
εὐήθειαν ἢ προπέτειαν ἢ ἀλαζονείαν ἄξιον κατα-
γινώσκειν τῶν ἢ ὁμολογεῖν ἢ ἀρνεῖσθαι περὶ παντὸς
οὑτινοσοῦν ῥᾳδίως ὑπομενόντων. εἰ μὲν γὰρ αἱ
ἁπλαῖ δυνάμεις ἐκποδών, αἱ δὲ μικταὶ καὶ ἐκ
πλειόνων συνηρανισμέναι προῦπτοι, ἀμήχανον δὲ
καὶ τὰς ἀοράτους ἰδεῖν καὶ διὰ τῶν κεκραμένων
τὸν ἑκάστης τῶν συνερανισθεισῶν τύπον ἰδίᾳ
κατανοῆσαι, τί ἂν εἴη λοιπὸν ἢ τὸ ἐπέχειν [ἀναγ-
καῖον];
193 Ἐκεῖνα[1] δ᾽ ἡμᾶς οὐ παρακαλεῖ μὴ λίαν τοῖς
ἀφανέσι προπιστεύειν, ἃ σχεδὸν κατὰ πᾶσαν τὴν
οἰκουμένην ἀνακέχυται κοινὸν Ἕλλησιν ὁμοῦ καὶ
βαρβάροις ἐπάγοντα τὸν ἐκ τοῦ κρίνειν ὄλισθον;
τίνα οὖν ταῦτ᾽ ἐστίν; ἀγωγαὶ δήπουθεν αἱ ἐκ

---

[1] mss. ἐκεῖνο or ἐκεῖ.

[a] See App. p. 508.

and bitter ? Can we do so without the juices in the mouth, both those which are in accord with nature [a] and those which are not ? Surely not. Again, do the odours produced by burning incense present to us the natures of the substances in a pure and simple form, or in a combination, in which themselves and air, or sometimes also the fire which dissolves the material, are joined with the faculty possessed by the nostrils ? From this we deduce that we do not apprehend 191 colours, but only the combination produced by the light and the material substances to which the colours belong, nor smells, but only the mixture of the emanation from the substances with the all-admitting air ; nor flavours, but only the something produced by the application of what we taste to the moisture in our mouths.   XLVII. Since these things are 192 so, those who do not shrink from facile affirmation or negation of anything whatsoever deserve to be held guilty of folly or rashness or imposture. For if the properties of things by themselves are beyond our ken, and if it is only the mixture formed by the contribution of many factors which is open to our vision ; if, once more, it is as impossible to discern through the combinations the particular form of each of the contributing factors as it is to see them in their invisibility, what course is left to us but to suspend our judgement ?

[a]And are we not warned against giving over-ready 193 credence to uncertainties by other considerations ? I allude to certain facts, the evidence for which is found practically over the whole world as known to us—facts which entail on Greek and barbarian alike the universal tendency to error which positive judgement brings. By these I mean of course ways of life [a]

417

παίδων καὶ ἔθη πάτρια καὶ παλαιοὶ νόμοι, ὧν ἓν
οὐδὲν ὁμολογεῖται ταὐτὸν εἶναι παρὰ πᾶσιν, ἀλλὰ
κατὰ χώρας καὶ ἔθνη καὶ πόλεις, μᾶλλον δὲ καὶ
κατὰ κώμην καὶ οἰκίαν ἑκάστην, ἄνδρα μὲν οὖν
καὶ γυναῖκα καὶ νήπιον παῖδα τοῖς ὅλοις δια-
194 κέκριται· τὰ γοῦν αἰσχρὰ παρ᾽ ἡμῖν ἑτέροις καλά,
καὶ τὰ πρέποντα ἀπρεπῆ, καὶ τὰ δίκαια ἄδικα, καὶ
ἀνόσια μὲν τὰ ὅσια, νόμιμα δ᾽ αὖ τὰ παράνομα,
ἔτι δὲ ψεκτὰ τὰ ἐπαινετὰ καὶ ὑπόδικα τὰ τιμῆς
ἄξια καὶ ὅσα ἄλλα ἐναντία ταῦτα νομίζουσι.
195
[387] καὶ τί δεῖ μακρηγορεῖν τὸν ὑπὸ | ἑτέρων ἀναγ-
καιοτέρων μεθελκόμενον; εἰ μέντοι βουληθείη τις
ὑπὸ μηδεμιᾶς ἄλλης καινοτέρας θέας ἀγόμενος,
ἐνευκαιρήσας τῷ προτεθέντι κεφαλαίῳ τὰς ἑκάστων
ἀγωγὰς καὶ ἔθη καὶ νόμους ἐπιέναι χωρῶν, ἐθνῶν,
πόλεων, τόπων, ὑπηκόων ἡγεμόνων, ἐνδόξων
ἀδόξων, ἐλευθέρων οἰκετῶν, ἰδιωτῶν ἐπιστημόνων,
οὐχ ἡμέραν μίαν οὐδὲ δύο, ἀλλὰ οὐδὲ μῆνα ἢ
ἐνιαυτόν, τὸν δὲ ἅπαντα ἑαυτοῦ κατατρίψει βίον,
κἂν αἰῶνι χρήσηται μακρῷ, καὶ οὐδὲν ἧττον πολλὰ
ἀδιερεύνητα καὶ ἀπερίσκεπτα καὶ ἄφωνα λήσει
196 καταλιπών. οὐκοῦν ἄλλων παρ᾽ ἄλλοις οὐ βραχεῖ
μόνον διεστηκότων, ἀλλὰ καὶ τοῖς ὅλοις ἀπ-
ᾳδόντων, ὡς ἀντιστατεῖν καὶ διαμάχεσθαι, ἀνάγκη
καὶ τὰς προσπιπτούσας διαφέρειν φαντασίας καὶ
τὰς κρίσεις ἀλλήλαις πεπολεμῶσθαι. XLVIII.
197 ὧν ὑπαρχόντων τίς οὕτως ἔκφρων ἐστὶ καὶ παρά-
ληρος, ὡς φάναι παγίως, ὅτι τὸ τοιόνδε ἐστὶ
δίκαιον ἢ φρόνιμον ἢ καλὸν ἢ συμφέρον; ὃ γὰρ

ᵃ Lit. " accepted to be the same with all."
ᵇ The last words, if expressed in full, would run ὅσα ἄλλα
ἐναντία τῶν ὑφ᾽ ἡμῶν νομιζομένων ταῦτα νομίζουσ᾽.

from boyhood upwards, traditional usages, ancient laws, not a single one of which is regarded in the same light universally,[a] but every country, nation and city, or rather every village and house, indeed every man, woman and infant child takes a totally different view of it. As a proof of this we see that what is base 194 with us is noble with others, what is seemly and just with us is unseemly or unjust with them, our holy is their unholy, our lawful their unlawful, our laudable their blameworthy, our meritorious their criminal, and in all other matters their judgement is the opposite of ours.[b]   And why prolong the 195 subject when our attention is called elsewhere by more vital matters ? Still if anyone undistracted by some newer subject of contemplation should care to devote his leisure to the subject which has been be-fore us, and to examine the ways of life, usages and customs of different countries, nations, cities and places, subjects and rulers, high and low, freemen and slaves, ignorant and learned, it will occupy not only a day or two, not only a month or a year, but his whole lifetime, even though his years be many, and all the same he will leave behind him many such questions, which he knows not of, unexamined, unconsidered and unheard. Since then the divers customs of divers 196 persons are not distinguished merely by some slight difference, but exhibit an absolute contrast, amount-ing to bitter antagonism, it is inevitable that the im-pressions made upon the mind should differ and that the judgements formed should be at war with each other. XLVIII. In view of these facts, who is so 197 senseless and deranged as to assert positively that any particular thing is just or prudent or honourable or profitable ? For what one determines to be such,

ἂν οὗτος ὁρίσῃ, τἀναντία μεμελετηκὼς ἐκ παίδων
ἕτερος ἀκυρώσει.

198 Ἐγὼ δ᾽ οὐ τεθαύμακα, εἰ πεφορημένος καὶ μιγὰς
ὄχλος, ἐθῶν καὶ νόμων τῶν ὁπωσοῦν εἰσηγμένων
ἀκλεὴς δοῦλος, ἀπ᾽ αὐτῶν ἔτι σπαργάνων ὑπακούειν
ὡς ἂν δεσποτῶν ἢ τυράννων ἐκμαθών, κατακεκον-
δυλισμένος τὴν ψυχὴν καὶ μέγα καὶ νεανικὸν
φρόνημα λαβεῖν μὴ δυνάμενος πιστεύει τοῖς ἅπαξ
παραδοθεῖσι καὶ τὸν νοῦν ἐάσας ἀγύμναστον
ἀδιερευνήτοις καὶ ἀνεξετάστοις συναινέσεσί τε
καὶ ἀρνήσεσι χρῆται, ἀλλ᾽ εἰ καὶ τῶν λεγομένων
φιλοσόφων ἡ πληθὺς τὸ ἐν τοῖς οὖσι σαφὲς καὶ
ἀψευδὲς ἐπιμορφάζουσα θηρᾶν κατὰ στίφη καὶ
λόχους διακέκριται, καὶ δόγματα ἀσύμφωνα πολλάκις δὲ καὶ ἐναντία οὐ περὶ ἑνὸς τίθεται τοῦ
τυχόντος, ἀλλὰ σχεδὸν περὶ πάντων μικρῶν τε καὶ
199 μεγάλων, ἐν οἷς αἱ ζητήσεις συνίστανται· οἱ
γὰρ ἄπειρον τὸ πᾶν εἰσηγούμενοι τοῖς πεπερα-
σμένον εἶναι λέγουσιν ἢ οἱ τὸν κόσμον ἀγένητον
τοῖς γενητὸν ἀποφαινομένοις ἢ οἱ χωρὶς ἐπιστάτου
καὶ ἡγεμόνος ἀλόγου καὶ ἀπαυτοματιζούσης ἐξ-
άψαντες φορᾶς τοῖς ὑπολαμβάνουσι πρόνοιαν καὶ
ἐπιμέλειαν ὅλου καὶ τῶν μερῶν θαυμαστήν τιν᾽
εἶναι ἡνιοχοῦντος καὶ κυβερνῶντος ἀπταίστως καὶ
σωτηρίως θεοῦ πῶς ἂν δύναιντο τὰς αὐτὰς κατα-
λήψεις τῶν ὑποκειμένων ποιεῖσθαι πραγμάτων;
200 αἱ δὲ περὶ τὴν τἀγαθοῦ σκέψιν φαν-
τασίαι ἆρ᾽ οὐκ ἐπέχειν μᾶλλον ἢ ὁμολογεῖν βιά-

---

[a] See App. p. 508.
[b] Or " whatever their source " (or " authority ").
[c] It should be observed that the datives throughout this
sentence are governed by τὰς αὐτάς at the end.

420

will be repudiated by another who has practised the opposite from childhood.

[a] Now I for my part do not wonder that the chaotic 198 and promiscuous multitude who are bound in inglorious slavery to usages and customs introduced anyhow,[b] and who are indoctrinated from the cradle with the lesson of obedience to them, as to masters and despots, with their souls buffeted into subjection and incapable of entertaining any high or generous feeling, should give credence to traditions delivered once for all, and leaving their minds unexercised, should give vent to affirmations and negations without inquiry or examination. But I do wonder that the multitude of so-called philosophers, who feign to be seeking for exact and absolute certainty in things, are divided into troops and companies and propound dogmatic conclusions widely different and often diametrically opposite not on some single chance point, but on practically all points great or small, which constitute the problems which they seek to solve.

[a] When some assert that the universe 199 is infinite, others that it is finite, and some declare it to be created, others uncreated; when some refuse to connect it with any ruler or governor, but make it dependent on the automatic action of an unreasoning force, while others postulate a marvellous providence, caring for the whole and each part, exerted by a deity who guides and steers it and makes safe its steps, it is impossible that the substance of things should be apprehended by them in the same form.[c] Again, when the nature of the good is the subject 200 of inquiry, do not the ideas which present themselves compel us to withhold judgement rather than give

ζονται τῶν μὲν ἀγαθὸν εἶναι νομιζόντων μόνον τὸ
καλὸν καὶ θησαυριζομένων αὐτὸ ἐν ψυχῇ, τῶν δὲ
πρὸς πλείω κατακερματιζόντων καὶ ἄχρι σώματος
201 καὶ τῶν ἐκτὸς ἀποτεινόντων; οὗτοι λέγουσι τὰς
μὲν τυχηρὰς εὐπραγίας δορυφόρους εἶναι σώματος,
[388] ὑγείαν δὲ καὶ ἰσχὺν καὶ τὸ | ὁλόκληρον καὶ ἀκρί-
βειαν αἰσθητηρίων καὶ ὅσα ὁμοιότροπα τῆς βασι-
λίδος ψυχῆς· τρισὶ γὰρ τῆς τἀγαθοῦ φύσεως κεχρη-
μένης τάξεσι τὴν μὲν τρίτην καὶ ἐξωτάτην τῆς
δευτέρας καὶ ὑπεικούσης[1] πρόμαχον εἶναι, τὴν δὲ
δευτέραν τῆς πρώτης μέγα πρόβλημα καὶ φυ-
202 λακτήριον γεγενῆσθαι. καὶ περὶ αὐτῶν τούτων
μέντοι καὶ βίων διαφορᾶς καὶ τελῶν πρὸς ἃ χρὴ
τὰς πράξεις ἁπάσας ἀναφέρεσθαι καὶ μυρίων ἄλλων
ὅσα τε ἡ λογικὴ καὶ ἠθικὴ καὶ φυσικὴ πραγματεία
περιέχει γεγόνασι σκέψεις ἀμύθητοι, ὧν ἄχρι τοῦ
παρόντος οὐδεμία παρὰ πᾶσι τοῖς σκεπτικοῖς
συμπεφώνηται.

203 XLIX. Οὐκ εἰκότως οὖν τῶν δυεῖν θυγατέρων,
βουλῆς τε καὶ συναινέσεως, ἁρμοσθεισῶν καὶ
συνευνασθεισῶν ὁ νοῦς ἀγνοίᾳ ἐπιστήμης[2] χρώμενος
εἰσάγεται; λέγεται γὰρ ὅτι " οὐκ ᾔδει ἐν τῷ
204 κοιμηθῆναι αὐτὰς καὶ ἀναστῆναι ". οὔτε γὰρ ὕπνον
οὔτε ἐγρήγορσιν οὔτε σχέσιν οὔτε κίνησιν ἔοικε
σαφῶς καὶ παγίως καταλαμβάνειν, ἀλλὰ καὶ
ὁπότε ἄριστα βεβουλεῦσθαι δοκεῖ, τότε μάλιστα
ἀβουλότατος ὢν εὑρίσκεται τῶν πραγμάτων μὴ

---

[1] mss. ὑπ(ἀπ)ειλούσης. The correction ὑπεικούσης has been
universally accepted, but the phrase, "the second and yielding one," is odd. The translator suggests ὑπ᾿ εἶλ⟨αρ⟩ οὔσης,
i.e. "which is thus under shelter." The word εἶλαρ as used
in Iliad ii. 338 etc. is very appropriate to the context, and
Philo is fond of introducing Homeric words.

assent ? For some hold that the morally beautiful
is the only good and make the soul its repository, while
others split up the good into subdivisions and extend
it to include the body and things outside the body.
These persons say that fortunate circumstances are 201
the guards and attendants of the body, and that
health and strength and soundness and exactness of
perception in the sense-organs and all other things of
the kind serve the same purpose to the sovereign
soul. The nature of the good, they hold, divides
itself into three classes, of which the third and outermost protects the weakness of the second, which again
proves to be a strong bulwark and safeguard of the
first. And with regard to these, as well as to the 202
relative value of different ways of living, and the ends
to which all our actions should be referred, and
numberless other points, which are included in the
study of logic, ethics and physics, a host of questions
have arisen on none of which hitherto have the inquirers arrived at unanimity.

XLIX. We see then that the mind is fitly repre- 203
sented as labouring under absence of knowledge,
when its two daughters, Deliberation and Assent,
are in contact with it and become its bed-fellows.
For we are told, " He knew not when they slept and
rose up " (Gen. xix. 33, 35). The mind, it seems, 204
does not grasp clearly or firmly either sleeping or
waking, or yet rest or motion,[a] but it is just when it
thinks it has shewn its powers of deliberation at their
best, that it proves to be most lacking in that power,

[a] Or "that is, either rest or motion."

---

[2] "ignorance of knowledge" is a strange expression.
Adler proposes χηρούμενος for χρώμενος. Perhaps ἀγνοίᾳ ⟨ἀντ'⟩
ἐπιστήμης.

ὅμοιον τοῖς προσδοκηθεῖσι λαβόντων τὸ τέλος·
205 καὶ ὁπότε συνεπιγράφεσθαί τισιν ὡς ἀληθέσιν
ἔδοξε, τὴν ἐπ' εὐχερείᾳ καρποῦται κατάγνωσιν,
ἀπίστων καὶ ἀβεβαίων, οἷς πρότερον ὡς βε-
βαιοτάτοις ἐπίστευε, φαινομένων· ὥστε εἰς τὰ
ἐναντία, ὧν ὑπετόπησέ τις, εἰωθότων περιίστασθαι
τῶν πραγμάτων ἀσφαλέστατον τὸ ἐπέχειν εἶναι.

206 L. Διειλεγμένοι δὴ περὶ τούτων ἱκανῶς ἐπὶ τὰ
ἀκόλουθα τῷ λόγῳ τρεψώμεθα. ἔφαμεν τοίνυν
ἐκ τοῦ μεθύειν καὶ τὴν πολλοὺς πολλάκις μεγάλα
βλάπτουσαν γαστριμαργίαν δηλοῦσθαι, ἧ τοὺς
χρωμένους ἔστιν ἰδεῖν, κἂν τὰς τοῦ σώματος
δεξαμενὰς ἀποπληρωθῶσι πάσας, ἔτι κενοὺς τὰς
207 ἐπιθυμίας ὄντας· οὗτοι κἂν ὑπὸ πλήθους ὧν
ἐνεφορήσαντο διακορεῖς γενόμενοι πρὸς ὀλίγον
χρόνον καθάπερ οἱ πεπονηκότες ἀθληταὶ τὰ
σώματα διαπνεύσωσι, πάλιν ἐπαποδύονται τοῖς
208 αὐτοῖς ἀγωνίσμασιν.   ὁ γοῦν βασιλεὺς
τῆς Αἰγυπτίας χώρας, τοῦ σώματος, τῷ μέθης
ὑπηρέτῃ δόξας οἰνοχόῳ δυσχερᾶναι πάλιν οὐκ εἰς
μακρὰν καταλλαττόμενος ἐν ταῖς ἱεραῖς βίβλοις
εἰσάγεται τοῦ τὰς ἐπιθυμίας ἀναρρηγνύντος πάθους
ὑπομνησθεὶς ἐν ἡμέρᾳ γενέσεως φθαρτῆς, οὐκ ἐν
ἀφθάρτῳ τοῦ ἀγενήτου φωτός[1]· λέγεται γὰρ ὅτι
" ἡμέρα γενέσεως ἦν Φαραώ," ἡνίκα ἐκ τοῦ δεσμωτηρίου τὸν ἀρχιοινοχόον ἐπὶ σπονδαῖς μετ-
209 επέμψατο· τοῦ γὰρ φιλοπαθοῦς ἴδιον λαμπρὰ τὰ
[389 | γενητὰ καὶ φθαρτὰ ἡγεῖσθαι διὰ τὸ νυκτὶ καὶ

---

[1] Adler proposes φωτί.

[a] See App. p. 509.

for the issue of events bears no resemblance to its expectations. And again when it has been pleased 205 to subscribe to anything as true, it earns the condemnation passed on reckless thinking, for it appears that what it once believed in and thought to be most firmly established is really untrustworthy and insecure. The conclusion is that since things so often turn out the opposite of what we expect, the safest course is to suspend judgement.

L. This topic has now been sufficiently discussed. 206 Let us turn our discussion to what follows next. We said that one thing signified by drunkenness is that gluttony [a] whose great power for mischief is so widespread and constant, which leaves those who indulge in it, as we may see, with a void in their desires, even though they have every vacant place in their bodies filled. Such persons, when glutted and satiated by the 207 quantities they have engorged, may for a while like weary-limbed athletes give their bodies a breathing-space, but ere long they make themselves ready to take part in the same encounter. So we 208 see the King of Egypt, that is of the body, though he seemed to be angry with the cup-bearer who ministered to his drunkenness, represented in the holy books as being reconciled to him after a short time. He remembered the passion which excited his desires on his birthday—the day of his birth into a being destined to perish—not on the day of the light, which has no birth, a day which perishes not. For we are told that it was Pharaoh's birthday (Gen. xl. 20) when he sent for the chief cup-bearer from the prison to pour the cup of reconciliation.[a] It is characteristic of 209 the friend of passion that things created and perishable seem to him bright and shining, because in re-

σκότῳ κεχρῆσθαι βαθεῖ πρὸς τὴν τῶν ἀφθάρτων
ἐπιστήμην· οὗ χάριν εὐθὺς τὴν ἐξάρχουσαν ἡδονῆς[1]
μέθην καὶ τὸν ὑπηρέτην αὐτῆς δεξιοῦται.

210 LI. τρεῖς δ᾽ εἰσὶν οἱ τῆς ἀκολάστου καὶ ἀκράτορος ψυχῆς ἑστιοῦχοί τε καὶ θεραπευταί, ἀρχισιτοποιός, ἀρχιοινοχόος, ἀρχιμάγειρος, ὧν ὁ θαυμασιώτατος μέμνηται Μωυσῆς διὰ τούτων· " καὶ
ὠργίσθη Φαραὼ ἐπὶ τοῖς δυσὶν εὐνούχοις, ἐπὶ τῷ
ἀρχιοινοχόῳ καὶ ἐπὶ τῷ ἀρχισιτοποιῷ, καὶ ἔθετο
αὐτοὺς ἐν φυλακῇ παρὰ τῷ ἀρχιδεσμοφύλακι.[2]"
ἔστι δὲ καὶ ὁ ἀρχιμάγειρος εὐνοῦχος· λέγεται γὰρ
ἑτέρωθι· " κατήχθη δὲ Ἰωσὴφ εἰς Αἴγυπτον, καὶ
ἐκτήσατο αὐτὸν εὐνοῦχος Φαραώ, ἀρχιμάγειρος,"
καὶ πάλιν· " ἀπέδοντο τὸν Ἰωσὴφ τῷ σπάδοντι
211 Φαραώ, ἀρχιμαγείρῳ." τίνος δὴ χάριν
οὔτ᾽ ἀνὴρ οὔτε γυνὴ τῶν λεχθέντων οὐδὲν ἁπλῶς
ἐπιτέτραπται; ἢ ὅτι σπείρειν μὲν ἄνδρες γονὰς
ὑποδέχεσθαι δὲ γυναῖκες ἐκ φύσεως πεπαίδευνται,
ὧν τὴν εἰς ταὐτὸ σύνοδον αἰτίαν γενέσεως καὶ
τῆς τοῦ παντὸς διαμονῆς εἶναι συμβέβηκεν, ἀγόνου
δὲ καὶ ἐστειρωμένης, μᾶλλον δὲ ἐξευνουχισμένης
ψυχῆς σιτίοις πολυτελέσι καὶ ποτοῖς καὶ ὄψων
περιέργοις παραρτύσεσι χαίρειν μήτε τὰ ἀρετῆς
ἄρρενα ὡς ἀληθῶς σπέρματα καταβάλλεσθαι δυνα-
μένης μήτε τὰ καταβληθέντα παραδέξασθαι καὶ
ἀναθρέψασθαι, ἀλλ᾽ οἷα λυπρὰν ἄρουραν καὶ λιθώδη
πρὸς διαφθορὰν μόνον πεφυκέναι τῶν ἀεὶ ζῆν
212 ὀφειλόντων; δόγμα δὴ τίθεται κοινωφελέστατον,
ὅτι πᾶς ὁ δημιουργὸς ἡδονῆς σοφίας ἐστὶν ἄγονος
οὔτε ἄρρην ὢν οὔτε θήλεια, διὰ τὸ μήτε διδόναι

lation to knowledge of things imperishable, he dwells in night and profound darkness, and therefore at once he welcomes the drunkenness which brings pleasure in its train and him who is the minister of drunkenness. LI. The weak-willed incontinent soul has 210 three servants who provide its feasts, the chief baker, the chief butler and the chief cook, whom our most admirable Moses mentions in these words, " And Pharaoh was wroth with his two eunuchs, with the chief butler and the chief baker, and he put them in prison under the chief gaoler " (Gen. xl. 2, 3). But the chief cook is also a eunuch, for we have in another place, " and Joseph was brought down into Egypt and became the property of the eunuch of Pharaoh, the chief cook " (Gen. xxxix. 1), and again " they sold Joseph to the eunuch of Pharaoh, the chief cook " (Gen. xxxvii. 36). Why is it that not a 211 single one of these offices is entrusted to a real man or woman ? Is it not because nature has trained men to sow the germs of life and women to receive them, and the mating of these two is the cause of generation and of the permanence of the All, while on the other hand it is the nature of the soul which is impotent and barren, or rather has been made so by emasculation, to delight in costly bakemeats and drinks and dishes elaborately prepared ? For such a soul is neither able to drop the truly masculine seeds of virtue nor yet to receive and foster what is so dropped, but like a sorry stony field is only capable of blighting the successive growths, which were meant to live. In fact we have a doctrine laid down 212 most profitable to us all, that every craftsman whose work is to produce pleasure can produce no fruit of wisdom. He is neither male nor female, for he is in-

μήτε λαμβάνειν τὰ πρὸς ἀφθαρσίαν ἱκανὸς εἶναι
σπέρματα, μελετᾶν δ᾽ αἰσχίστην κατὰ τοῦ βίου
μελέτην, φθείρειν τὰ ἄφθαρτα καὶ σβεννύναι τὰ
213 μένοντα τῆς φύσεως λαμπάδια ἄσβεστα. τῶν
τοιούτων οὐδενὶ ἐπιτρέπει Μωυσῆς εἰς ἐκκλησίαν
ἀφικνεῖσθαι θεοῦ· λέγει γὰρ ὅτι " θλαδίας καὶ
ἀποκεκομμένος οὐκ εἰσελεύσεται εἰς ἐκκλησίαν
κυρίου." LII. τί γὰρ τῷ σοφίας ἀγόνῳ λόγῳ
ἀκροάσεως ἱερῶν ὄφελος ἐκτετμημένῳ πίστιν καὶ
παρακαταθήκην βιωφελεστάτων δογμάτων φυλάξει
214 μὴ δυναμένῳ;   τρεῖς δ᾽ ἄρ᾽ εἰσὶν ἀνθρώπων γένους ἑστιάτορες, σιτοποιός,[1] οἰνοχόος,
ὀψαρτυτής, εἰκότως, ἐπειδὴ τριῶν χρήσεώς τε
καὶ ἀπολαύσεως ἐφιέμεθα, σιτίων, ὄψου, ποτῶν·
ἀλλ᾽ οἱ μὲν μόνων τῶν ἀναγκαίων, οἷς πρός τε
τὸ ὑγιεινῶς καὶ μὴ ἀνελευθέρως ζῆν ἐξ ἀνάγκης
χρώμεθα, οἱ δὲ ἀμέτρων καὶ σφόδρα περιττῶν,
ἃ τὰς ὀρέξεις ἀναρρηγνύντα καὶ τὰς τοῦ σώματος
δεξαμενὰς πλήθει βαρύνοντα καὶ πιέζοντα μεγάλα
[390] καὶ | παντοδαπὰ τίκτειν νοσήματα φιλεῖ. οἱ μὲν
215 οὖν ἡδονῆς καὶ ἐπιθυμίας καὶ παθῶν ἰδιῶται
καθάπερ οἱ ἐν ταῖς πόλεσι δημοτικοὶ ἀμισῆ καὶ
ἀνεπαχθῆ βίον ζῶντες, ἅτε ὀλιγοδεεῖς ὄντες, οὐ
ποικίλων καὶ περιέργων τὴν τέχνην δέονται
ὑπηρετῶν, ἀλλ᾽ ἀποικίλῳ χρωμένων ὑπηρεσίᾳ,
216 μαγείρων, οἰνοχόων, σιτοποιῶν· οἱ δὲ ἡγεμονίαν
καὶ βασιλείαν νομίζοντες εἶναι τὸ ἡδέως ζῆν καὶ
πάντα καὶ μικρὰ καὶ μείζω πρὸς τοῦτ᾽ ἀναφέροντες

---

[1] σιτοποιός Tr. : mss. and Wendland ἀρχισιτοποιός.

[a] See App. p. 509.

capable of either giving or receiving the seeds whence spring the growth that perishes not, and the base craft he practises is aimed against human life. He destroys the indestructible and quenches the unquenchable ever-abiding lamps of nature. None 213 such does Moses permit to enter the congregation of God, for he says, " He who has lost the organs of generation [a] shall not come into the congregation of the Lord "(Deut. xxiii. 1). LII. For what use can he find in listening to holy words, who can beget no offspring of wisdom, when the knife has cut away the power of faith, and the store of truths which might best profit human life he cannot keep in his charge ?

Now mankind, as we have seen, has 214 three caterers, the baker, the cup-bearer and the cook. This is natural enough since we desire the use and enjoyment of these three things, bread, flesh and drink. But some desire only the bare necessities, the use of which is needed to keep life from being unhealthy and sordid ; while others seek them in luxurious forms, which excite the cravings of the appetite, and in extravagant quantities, which oppress and overload the receptacles of the body, and often produce grave disorders of every kind. The first of 215 these classes who are not specialists in pleasure or voluptuousness or passion are like the ordinary public in a city who live an inoffensive and innocuous life, who have few wants and therefore do not require versatile and highly-skilled artists to serve them, but only those who attempt no more than a plain and simple form of service, just cooks, cup-bearers and bakers. But the second class, holding that pleasant 216 living is sovereignty and kingship, and judging all things great and small by this standard, consider it

ἀρχιμαγείροις καὶ ἀρχιοινοχόοις καὶ ἀρχισιτο
ποιοῖς ὑπηρέταις ἀξιοῦσι χρῆσθαι, τουτέστιν ἄκρως
ἐκπεπονηκόσιν ἕκαστον ὧν ἐπετήδευσαν.

217 τὰ μὲν γὰρ ἀμήτων καὶ μελιπήκτων καὶ ἄλλων
ἀμυθήτων πεμμάτων ποικιλώτατα γένη οὐ μόνον
ταῖς τῆς ὕλης διαφοραῖς, ἀλλὰ καὶ τῷ τρόπῳ τῆς
κατασκευῆς καὶ τοῖς σχήμασι πρὸς οὐ μόνον τὴν
γεύσεως ἀλλὰ καὶ τὴν ὄψεως ἀπάτην περιεργα
σμένα οἱ περὶ σιτοποιίαν ἄκροι μελετῶσι.

218 τὰ δὲ περὶ ἐξέτασιν οἴνου θᾶττον ἀναδιδομένου
καὶ μὴ κεφαλαλγοῦς καὶ τοὐναντίον ἀνθίμου καὶ
εὐωδεστάτου, πολλὴν ἢ ὀλίγην ἀναδεχομένου τὴν
μεθ᾽ ὕδατος κρᾶσιν εἰς σφοδρὸν καὶ σύντονον ἢ
πρᾷον καὶ ἀνειμένον ἐπιτηδείου πότον[1] καὶ ὅσα
τοιουτότροπα ἀρχιοινοχόων ἐπιτηδεύματα ἐπ᾽ αὐτὸ
δὴ τῆς τέχνης ἀφιγμένων τὸ τέλος·

219 ἰχθύας δὲ καὶ ὄρνεις καὶ τὰ παραπλήσια ποικίλως
ἀρτῦσαι καὶ κατασκευάσαι καὶ ὅσα ἄλλα ὄψα
ἡδῦναι περιττοὶ τὴν ἐπιστήμην εἰσὶν εὐτρεπεῖς
ὀψαρτυταί, μυρία χωρὶς ὧν ἤκουσαν ἢ εἶδον ἀλλ᾽
ἐκ τῆς συνεχοῦς μελέτης καὶ τριβῆς τῶν εἰς
ἁβροδίαιτον καὶ τεθρυμμένον τὸν ἀβίωτον βίον
ἐπινοῆσαι δεινοί.

220 LIII. Ἀλλὰ γὰρ οὗτοι πάντες ἐδείχθησαν
εὐνοῦχοι, σοφίας ἄγονοι· πρὸς ὃν δὲ συμβατηρίους
τίθεται σπονδὰς ὁ γαστρὸς βασιλεὺς νοῦς οἰνο
χόος ἦν· φίλοινον γὰρ ὑπερφυῶς τὸ ἀνθρώπων
γένος καὶ πρὸς μόνον τοῦτο διαφερόντως ἀκό
ρεστον, εἴ γε ὕπνου μὲν καὶ ἐδωδῆς καὶ συνουσίας
καὶ τῶν ὁμοίων ἀπλήρωτος οὐδείς, ἀκράτου δὲ

---

[1] mss. ποτὸν (drink), which Adler would retain.

their due to employ chief cooks, chief butlers, chief
bakers, that is those who have worked up to a high
pitch of refinement the arts which they severally
profess.   Milk cakes, honey cakes, num- 217
berless other kinds of bakemeats in the greatest
possible variety, elaborately calculated to beguile the
eye as well as the palate, not only with diversities of
material, but also by the way in which the constituents
are proportioned and the shapes in which they appear,
engage the care and attention of the master-hands
in confectionery.   As for wine, whether 218
it is such as is quickly digested and leaves no head-
ache, whether on the other hand it has a fine bouquet [a]
and fragrance, whether it needs a small or great
dilution to fit it for a fierce and heated carousal or a
mild and quiet festivity, these and all such questions
are the study of chief butlers, who have reached the
very summit of their art.   Again, the 219
skilful dressing and preparation of fishes, birds and
the like, and the flavouring of other savoury dishes,
is a task readily accomplished by highly scientific
professionals, whose constant drill and practice in
catering for the life, which all its voluptuous luxury
cannot make worth living, has given them the
ingenuity to invent hundreds of other delicacies
besides those which they have seen and heard of.

LIII. Observe that while all these three were 220
shewn to be eunuchs and unable to beget wisdom, it
was the butler with whom the mind, whose kingdom
is the belly, made his compact of peace. For the
passion for wine is extraordinarily strong in mankind,
and is unique in this, that it does not produce satiety.
For whereas everyone is satisfied with a certain
amount of sleep and food and sexual intercourse and

σχεδὸν ἅπαντες καὶ μάλισθ' οἷς τὸ πρᾶγμα ἀσκεῖται·
221 πιόντες γὰρ ἔτι διψῶσι καὶ ἄρχονται μὲν ἀπὸ τῶν
βραχυτέρων κυάθων, προϊόντες δὲ ταῖς μείζοσιν
οἰνοχόαις ἐγχεῖν παραγγέλλουσιν· ἐπειδὰν ⟨δ'⟩
ἀκροθώρακες γενόμενοι χλιανθῶσιν, οὐκέτι κρατεῖν
ἑαυτῶν δυνάμενοι τὰς οἰνηρύσεις καὶ τὰς ἀμύστεις
καὶ τοὺς κρατῆρας ὅλους προσενεγκάμενοι ἀκράτου
[391] σπῶσιν ἀθρόως, | μέχρις ἂν ἢ βαθεῖ ὕπνῳ δαμα-
σθῶσιν ἢ τῶν ὄγκων ἀποπληρωθέντων ὑπερβλύσῃ
222 τὸ ἐπεισχεόμενον.   ἀλλὰ καὶ τότε ὅμως
ἡ ἄπληστος ἐν αὐτοῖς ὄρεξις ὥσπερ ἔτι λιμώττουσα
μαιμάζει[1]· "ἐκ γὰρ τῆς ἀμπέλου Σοδόμων ἡ
ἄμπελος αὐτῶν" ἦ φησι Μωυσῆς "καὶ ἡ κληματὶς
αὐτῶν ἐκ Γομόρρας· ἡ σταφυλὴ αὐτῶν σταφυλὴ
χολῆς, βότρυς πικρίας αὐτοῖς· θυμὸς δρακόντων
ὁ οἶνος αὐτῶν, καὶ θυμὸς ἀσπίδων ἀνίατος."
Σόδομα μέντοι στείρωσις καὶ τύφλωσις ἑρμηνεύεται,
ἀμπέλῳ δὲ καὶ τοῖς ἐξ αὐτῆς γινομένοις ἀπεικάζει
τοὺς οἰνοφλυγίας καὶ λαιμαργίας καὶ τῶν αἰσχίστων
223 ἡδονῶν ἥττους.   ἃ δὲ αἰνίττεται, τοιαῦτ'
ἐστίν· εὐφροσύνης μὲν ἀληθοῦς οὐδὲν ἐμπέφυκε
τῇ τοῦ φαύλου ψυχῇ φυτὸν ἅτε οὐχ ὑγιαινούσαις
κεχρημένη ῥίζαις, ἀλλὰ ἐμπεπρησμέναις καὶ τεφρω-
θείσαις, ὁπότε ἀνθ' ὕδατος τὰς κεραυνίους φλόγας
θεοῦ τὴν κατὰ ἀσεβῶν καλῶς δικάσαντος δίκην
ὁ οὐρανὸς ἀσβέστους ἔνιφεν, ἀκράτορος δὲ ἐπιθυμίας τῆς ἐστειρωμένης τὰ καλὰ καὶ πεπηρω-
μένης πρὸς πάντα τὰ θέας ἄξια, ἣν ἀμπέλῳ παρα-
βέβληκεν, οὐχὶ τῇ καρπῶν ἡμέρων μητρί, ἀλλὰ
ἥτις πικρίας καὶ πονηρίας καὶ πανουργίας ὀργῆς
τε καὶ θυμοῦ καὶ ἀκραχολωτάτων ἠθῶν οἰστικὴ

[1] MSS. μαιράζει.

the like, this is rarely so with strong drink, particularly among practised topers. They drink but do not 221 slake their thirst and, while they begin with smaller cups, as they advance they call for the wine to be poured in larger goblets. And when they get mellow and well warmed, they lose all control of themselves, and put beakers and cans and whole basins to their lips and drain them at a draught until either they are overcome with deep sleep, or the influx of the liquor fills up the cavities[a] and overflows. But even then the insatiable craving within them rages 222 as if it were still starving. "For their vine is of the vine of Sodom," as Moses says, "and their tendrils of Gomorrah, their grapes are grapes of gall, a cluster of bitterness to them. Their wine is the wrath of dragons and the incurable wrath of asps" (Deut. xxxii. 32, 33). Sodom is indeed by interpretation barrenness and blindness, and Moses here likens to a vine and its produce those who are under the thrall of wine-bibbing and gluttony and the basest of pleasures. His inner meaning is of 223 this kind. No plant of true gladness grows in the soul of the wicked, since it has no healthy roots, but such as were burnt to ashes, when God passed well-deserved sentence upon the impious, and the heavens rained instead of water the unquenchable flames of the thunderbolt. In such a soul all that grows is the lust which is barren of excellence, and blinded to all that is worthy of its contemplation, and this lust he compares to a vine; not that which is the mother of kindly fruits, but a vine which proves to be the bearer of bitterness and wickedness and villainy and wrath and anger and savage moods and tempers, the

[a] See App. p. 509.

γέγονε, δάκνουσα τὴν ψυχὴν ἔχεων καὶ ἀσπίδων τρόπον ἰοβόλων καὶ παντελῶς ἀνίατα.

224 ὧν ἀποτροπὴν εὐχώμεθα γενέσθαι τὸν πάντα ἵλεω ποτνιώμενοι θεόν, ἵνα καὶ τὴν ἀγρίαν ταύτην ἄμπελον διολέσῃ καὶ τοῖς εὐνούχοις καὶ πᾶσιν ἀγόνοις ἀρετῆς ἀίδιον ψηφίσηται φυγήν, ἀντὶ δὲ τούτων ἥμερα μὲν ταῖς ψυχαῖς ἡμῶν δένδρα τὰ παιδείας ὀρθῆς ἐμφυτεύσῃ, γενναίους δὲ καὶ ἄρρενας ὡς ἀληθῶς καρποὺς καὶ λόγους χαρίσηται δυναμένους μὲν σπείρειν καλὰς πράξεις, δυναμένους δὲ συναύξειν ἀρετάς, ἱκανοὺς δὲ τὴν εὐδαιμονίας ἅπασαν συνέχειν καὶ διαφυλάττειν εἰς ἀεὶ συγγένειαν.

vine which stings the soul like vipers and venomous asps, and that sting none can cure.   Let 224 us pray that these may be averted, and implore the all-merciful God to destroy this wild vine and decree eternal banishment to the eunuchs and all those who do not beget virtue, and that while in their stead He plants in the garden of our souls the trees of right instruction, He may grant us fruits of genuine worth and true virility, and powers of reason, capable of begetting good actions and also of bringing the virtues to their fullness, gifted too with the strength to bind together and keep safe for ever all that is akin to real happiness.

ON THE PRAYERS AND CURSES
UTTERED BY NOAH WHEN
HE BECAME SOBER

(DE SOBRIETATE)

ANALYTICAL INTRODUCTION

In this short treatise Philo concludes his discussion of Gen. ix. 20-27, which describe Noah's husbandry, vine-planting, drinking the wine, intoxication and nakedness, return to sobriety, and cursing or blessing his children. The verses here treated (24-27) run as follows :

I. (sections 1-20 of this treatise) And Noah returned to soberness from the wine and knew what his younger son had done to him.

II. (30-50) And he said, "Cursed be Canaan; a servant and bondman shall he be to his brethren."

III. (51-58) And he said, " Blessed be the Lord God of Shem ; and Canaan shall be a servant, a bondman of him."

IV. (59-end) And he said, " May God widen for Japhet, and let him dwell in the houses of Shem and let Canaan become his servant."

I. This raises two points, the meaning of " becoming sober " and that of the " younger son." The former is treated briefly. Sobriety is conceived of mainly as sobriety of soul, which takes the same place in the soul as clear vision in the body, and thus provides it with thoughts which in their turn lead to good actions (1-5).

The word " younger " starts Philo on a discussion of the use made in the Pentateuch of words literally denoting age, to shew moral relations. Ham is "younger" because his unfilial and indecent action proved his spirit of (youthful) [a] rebelliousness (νεωτεροποιία) (6). And so Ishmael is called a "child" when, as a little calculation will shew, he was twenty years old, because as a type of the falsely wise or sophist, he is, compared with the wise Isaac, a mere child (7-9). So too Moses calls the rebellious Israelites "blameworthy children" (10-11). Rachel (bodily beauty) is called younger than Leah (beauty of soul) (12). Joseph's "youth" in the moral sense is shewn by his staying in Egypt (the body) and his association with his illegitimate brethren (12-15). Conversely the wise Abraham is called the "elder," though the history represents him as less long-lived than his ancestors (16-18). The elders Moses is directed to choose mean those whose sterling worth he has proved (19-20). In particular the enactment forbidding the disinheritance of the firstborn son of the hated wife in favour of the younger son of the beloved wife, which gave rise to the long allegory of *De Sacrificiis*, 19-44 is audaciously pressed into service. As in *De Sacrificiis* the beloved wife is Pleasure, the hated Virtue, but as Moses mentioned the parenthood of Pleasure first, her child is firstborn in point of time and the name only belongs to the child of virtue in consideration of his moral superiority (21-26). So the younger in age Jacob takes the birthright from the elder Esau, and Jacob sets Ephraim who represents the faculty of memory, which comes later and is therefore younger, above Manasseh, who represents the more childish faculty of recollection, which is earlier and therefore older

[a] See note on § 6.

(27-29). This division ends with a statement of the justice of cursing the " younger " (30).

II. But why did Noah curse Ham's son Canaan, against whom nothing is alleged, instead of Ham? (31-33). Because while Ham is evil potential or " in rest," Canaan is evil active or " in motion." To understand this we must consider these terms " rest " and " motion " with their respective congeners, " habit " or " faculty " ($\xi\xi\iota\varsigma$) and " activity " (33-34). Now every workman or artist is called by such a name, even when he is not making anything, because he still has the faculty. But it is only when he is actually plying his trade or art that he incurs praise or blame (35-37). So too in the moral sphere. The possessor of good or bad qualities may have no opportunity for displaying them, but the qualities are still there (38-43). Ham means " heat," *i.e.* the latent disease in the soul, Canaan means " tossing," which represents the same in active motion. As no ruler punishes qualities till they actually produce crimes, Canaan properly incurs the curse, though, as one passes into the other, one may say that Ham is cursed through Canaan (44-47). Actual sin is the child of potential sin, and this is the real meaning of " visiting the sins of the fathers upon the children " (48). The same lesson is taught by the law of leprosy that only when the " bright spot " ceases to be stationary does the man become unclean (49), and also by God's word to Cain, " thou hast sinned, be still " (50).

III. The prayer for Shem speaks of the " Lord, the God of Shem." Shem is " the good " in its generic not in any of its special forms, and therefore to assert that God is Shem's God is to put the good man on a level with God's work, the Universe (51-54). And since " God " indicates the loving side of the Divine Nature, to say that the Lord is " Shem's God " is to say that, like Abraham, he is God's friend (55). And here Philo, adapting the well-known Stoic paradox, lays down that such a one alone is noble, rich, king and free (56-57). Finally the word " blessed " applied to God means that he who is thus blest can only repay God by blessing Him (58).

IV. In interpreting the prayer for Japhet Philo passes for a moment into one of his less austere moods. He suggests that the word " widen " means that Japhet may find good not only in the morally beautiful (τὸ καλόν) but in the " preferable indifferents " of the Stoics, bodily and external advantages (59-61). As to the last half, " let him dwell in the houses of Shem," the " him " may be God (Philo ignores the fact that in this case it could not be a prayer for Japhet), for God's fitting dwelling is in the good man's soul in the sense that it is especially under His care (62-64). And so in the literal narrative Shem is very properly represented as the ancestor of the Twelve Tribes who are called God's " palace " (65-66). If " him " is Japhet we may see a correction of the prayer for his " widening," a prayer that though for a time he may find good elsewhere, his final home may be the excellence of the soul (67-68). The treatise concludes with a few lines on " Canaan shall be their servant." The fool is indeed the slave of the virtues, if possible, for his reformation and emancipation, if otherwise, for chastisement (69).

441

ΠΕΡΙ ΩΝ ΝΗΨΑΣ Ο ΝΩΕ ΕΥΧΕΤΑΙ ΚΑΙ ΚΑΤΑΡΑΤΑΙ

I. Τὰ περὶ μέθης καὶ τῆς ἑπομένης αὐτῇ γυμνότητος εἰρημένα τῷ νομοθέτῃ διεξεληλυθότες πρότερον ἀρξώμεθα τοῖς λεχθεῖσι τὸν ἑξῆς προσαρμότ-
τειν λόγον· περίεστι τοίνυν ἐν τοῖς χρησμοῖς
ἀκόλουθα τάδε· " ἐξένηψε δὲ Νῶε ἀπὸ τοῦ οἴνου
καὶ ἔγνω ὅσα ἐποίησεν αὐτῷ ὁ υἱὸς αὐτοῦ ὁ νεώ-
2 τερος." τὸ νήφειν οὐ μόνον ψυχαῖς ἀλλὰ καὶ
σώμασιν ὠφελιμώτατον ἀνωμολόγηται· τάς τε γὰρ
ἐξ ἀμέτρου πλησμονῆς γινομένας νόσους ἀπωθεῖται
καὶ τὰς αἰσθήσεις πρὸς ἄκρας ὀξύτητας ἀκονᾷ καὶ
ὅλα μέντοι τὰ σώματα οὐκ ἐᾷ βαρυνόμενα πίπτειν,
ἀλλ' ἐξαίρει καὶ ἐπικουφίζει καὶ πρὸς τὰς οἰκείους
ἐνεργείας ἀνακαλεῖ πᾶσι τοῖς μέρεσιν ἑτοιμότητα
ἐντίκτον· καὶ συνόλως ὅσων δημιουργὸς κακῶν ἡ
μέθη, τοσούτων ἔμπαλιν ἀγαθῶν τὸ νηφάλιον.
3 ὁπότ' οὖν καὶ σώμασιν, οἷς ἡ οἴνου
πόσις οἰκεῖον, λυσιτελέστατον τὸ νήφειν, οὐ πολὺ
μᾶλλον ψυχαῖς, ὧν φθαρτὴ τροφὴ πᾶσα ἀλλότριον ;
νηφούσης γὰρ διανοίας τί τῶν παρὰ ἀνθρώποις
μεγαλειότερον; τίς δόξα; τίς πλοῦτος; τίς δυνα-

ON THE PRAYERS AND CURSES UTTERED BY NOAH WHEN HE BECAME SOBER

I. Having in the foregoing pages dealt fully with the **1** words of the lawgiver on drunkenness and the nakedness which followed it,[a] let us proceed to carry on the thread of our discussion by treating of the topic which comes next in order, " And Noah returned to soberness from the wine and knew what his younger son had done to him " (Gen. ix. 24). We are all agreed that soberness is most profitable **2** not only to souls but to bodies. For it repels the diseases which arise from excessive self-indulgence ; it sharpens the senses to their utmost acuteness and acts indeed upon the whole of our bodies by engendering readiness in every part and thus prevents them from succumbing in weariness, and lifts them up and relieves them and recalls them to their proper activities. In fact, every evil which has drunkenness for its author has its counterpart in some good which is produced by soberness.   Since **3** then sobriety is a source of the greatest profit to our bodies, to which the use of wine is a natural practice, how much more is it profitable to our souls, which have no relation to any perishable food ? What human gift or possession is greater than a sober understanding ? What form of glory—or of wealth

443

στεία; τίς ἰσχύς; τί τῶν πάντων ὅσα θαυμάζεται;
φέρε μόνον τὸ ψυχῆς ὄμμα ὅλον ἰσχῦσαι δι' ὅλων
διοιχθῆναι καὶ μηδὲν οἷα ὑπὸ ῥεύματος συγχυθῆναι
μέρος ἢ καταμῦσαι· τότε γὰρ μάλιστα ὀξυωπῆσαν,
σύνεσιν καὶ φρόνησιν αὐτὴν ἐμβλέπον, τοῖς νοητοῖς |
[393] ἀγάλμασιν ἐντεύξεται, ὧν ἡ θέα ψυχαγωγοῦσα πρὸς
οὐδὲν ἔτι τῶν αἰσθητῶν ἀπονεύειν ἐάσει.

4 καὶ τί θαυμάζομεν, εἰ τῷ νηφαλίῳ τῆς ψυχῆς καὶ
βλέποντι ὀξυωπέστατα τῶν γένεσιν λαχόντων
μηδέν ἐστιν ἰσότιμον; καὶ γὰρ οἱ τοῦ σώματος
ὀφθαλμοὶ καὶ τὸ αἰσθητὸν φῶς περιττῶς πρὸς
ἡμῶν πάντων τετίμηται· πολλοὶ γοῦν τῶν τὰς
ὄψεις ἀποβαλόντων καὶ τὸ ζῆν ἑκουσίως προσαπ-
έβαλον κουφότερον κακὸν πηρώσεως θάνατον εἶναι
5 δικάσαντες ἑαυτοῖς. ὅσῳ τοίνυν ψυχὴ σώματος
κρείττων, τοσούτῳ καὶ νοῦς ὀφθαλμῶν ἀμείνων.
ὃς εἴπερ ἀπήμων εἴη καὶ ἀζήμιος πρὸς μηδενὸς
τῶν μέθην παράφορον ἐργαζομένων ἀδικημάτων
ἢ παθῶν πιεσθείς, ὕπνῳ μὲν ἀποτάξεται λήθην
καὶ ὄκνον ἐμποιοῦντι τῶν πρακτέων, ἐγρήγορσιν
δὲ ἀσπασάμενος πρὸς τὰ θέας ἄξια πάντα ὀξυ-
δορκήσει, μνήμαις μὲν ὑποβαλλούσαις ἐγειρόμενος,
πράξεσι δὲ τοῖς γνωσθεῖσιν ἑπομέναις χρώμενος.

6 II. Τοῦ μὲν δὴ νήφοντος κατάστασίς ἐστι
τοιαύτη. " νεώτερον " δ' ὅταν φῇ " υἱόν," οὐχ
ἡλικίας ὄνομα ἀναγράφει, νεωτεροποιίαν δὲ ἀγα-

or of political power—or bodily strength—or what among all the objects of human admiration, if only we may assume that the soul's eye is nowhere suffused as by rheum or closed, but is able to open itself fully and completely ? For at such times when with clarity of vision it gazes upon good sense and prudence in their true selves, it will have within its ken those ideal forms which are intelligible only to the mind, and in the contemplation of these will find a spell which will not suffer it to turn aside any more to aught of the objects of sense.   And why should 4 we wonder that sobriety and clear-sightedness in the soul is of higher worth than anything whose lot is cast among things created, for the bodily eyes and the light which our senses perceive are valued above measure by us all? We know indeed that many who have lost their eyes have lost their lives as well by their own free action, because they judged that death was a lighter evil to them than blindness. Well then, the mind has the same superiority to the 5 eyes, as the soul has to the body. And if the mind be safe and unimpaired, free from the oppression of the iniquities or passions which produce the frenzy of drunkenness, it will renounce the slumber which makes us forget and shrink from the call of duty and welcoming wakefulness will gaze clear-eyed on all that is worthy of contemplation. The suggestions of memory will arouse it to decision and the actions to which these decisions lead will become its employment.

II. Such then is the condition of the sober. But 6 when Moses speaks of the " younger son," the words do not denote any particular degree of age, but suggest the tendency of the temperament which

445

PHILO

πῶντος ἐμφαίνει τρόπου διάθεσιν. ἐπεὶ πῶς ἂν ἢ
τὰ ἀθέατα κατιδεῖν παρὰ νόμον καὶ δίκην ἐβιάσατο ἢ
ἐκλαλῆσαι τὰ ὀφείλοντα ἡσυχάζεσθαι ἢ εἰς τοὐμ-
φανὲς προενεγκεῖν τὰ δυνάμενα οἴκοι συσκιάζε-
σθαι καὶ τοὺς ψυχῆς ὅρους μὴ ὑπερβαίνειν, εἰ μὴ
νεωτέρων πραγμάτων ἥπτετο γελῶν τὰ ἑτέροις
συμπίπτοντα, δέον ἐπιστένειν καὶ μὴ χλευάζειν ἐφ'
οἷς εἰκὸς ἦν καὶ εὐλαβούμενον τὸ μέλλον σκυθρω-
7 πάζειν;   πολλαχοῦ μέντοι τῆς νομοθεσίας καὶ τοὺς ἡλικίᾳ προήκοντας νέους καὶ τοὺς
μηδέπω γεγηρακότας ἔμπαλιν ὀνομάζει πρεσβυτέρους, οὐκ εἰς πολυετίαν ⟨καὶ ὀλιγοετίαν⟩ ἀφορῶν
ἢ βραχὺν καὶ μήκιστον χρόνον, ἀλλ' εἰς ψυχῆς
8 δυνάμεις κινουμένης εὖ τε καὶ χεῖρον· τὸν γοῦν
Ἰσμαὴλ εἰκοσαετίαν ἤδη που βεβιωκότα σχεδὸν
κατὰ τὴν πρὸς τὸν ἐν ἀρεταῖς τέλειον Ἰσαὰκ
σύγκρισιν ὀνομάζει παιδίον· "ἔλαβε" γάρ φησιν
"ἄρτους καὶ ἀσκὸν ὕδατος καὶ ἔδωκεν Ἄγαρ, καὶ
ἐπέθηκεν ἐπὶ τὸν ὦμον καὶ τὸ παιδίον," ἡνίκα
αὐτοὺς οἴκοθεν Ἀβραὰμ ἐξέπεμψε, καὶ πάλιν
"ἔρριψε τὸ παιδίον ὑποκάτω μιᾶς ἐλάτης," καὶ
"οὐ μὴ ἴδω τὸν θάνατον τοῦ παιδίου"· καίτοι πρὸ
μὲν τῆς γενέσεως Ἰσαὰκ τρισκαίδεκα γεγονὼς
ἐτῶν Ἰσμαὴλ περιτέτμηται, περὶ δὲ τὴν ἑπταέτιν
ἡλικίαν παυσαμένου τῆς ἐν γάλακτι τροφῆς ἐκείνου
τῷ τὴν ἐν παιδιαῖς ἰσότητα φέρεσθαι νόθος γνησίῳ
[394] | φυγαδεύεται σὺν τῇ τεκούσῃ. ἀλλ' ὅμως παιδίον
9

---

[a] Philo reads into νεωτεροποιία, in which νεωτερο- means
"innovation," the idea of νεώτερος, "younger."
[b] βιάζεσθαι followed by the inf. is used by Philo in the
sense of "to do a thing violently," *cf.* note on *De Ebr.* 143.
446

loves rebelliousness and defiance.[a] For how could
Ham thus roughly [b] defying custom and right have
looked where he should not look, or how could he
loudly proclaim what ought to be passed in silence,
or expose to public view what might well be hidden
in the secrecy of the home and never pass the boundaries of his inward thoughts, if he had not set his
hand to deeds of defiance, if he had not mocked at
the troubles of another, when he should rather
bewail, instead of jeering at sights which call for the
gloomy face that dreads the worse to come?

Often indeed does Moses in his laws give the name of 7
the " younger " to those who are advanced in years,
and the name of " elders " on the other hand to
those who have not yet reached old age, for he does
not consider whether the years of men are many or
few, or whether a period of time is short or long, but
he looks to the faculties of the soul whether its movements are good or ill. Accordingly when Ishmael 8
had apparently lived about twenty years, Moses
calls him a child by comparison with Isaac, who is
full grown in virtues. For we read that when
Abraham sent Hagar and Ishmael from his home,
" he took loaves and a skin of water, and gave them
to Hagar and put also the ' child ' on her shoulder,"
and again " she cast down the ' child ' under a single
pine," and " I will not see the death of the ' child ' "
(Gen. xxi. 14-16). And yet Ishmael was circum-
cised at the age of thirteen years, before the birth of
Isaac, and when the latter at about the age of seven
ceased to be fed with milk, we find Ishmael banished
with his mother, because he, the bastard, claimed to
play on equal terms with the true-born. Still all 9
the same, grown up as he was, he is called a child,

νεανίας ὢν ἤδη καλεῖται ὁ σοφιστὴς ἀντεξεταζό-
μενος σοφῷ· σοφίαν μὲν γὰρ Ἰσαάκ, σοφιστείαν
δὲ Ἰσμαὴλ κεκλήρωται, ὥς, ἐπειδὰν ἑκάτερον
χαρακτηρίζωμεν, ἐν τοῖς ἰδίᾳ λόγοις ἐπιδείκνυμεν.
ὃν γὰρ ἔχει λόγον κομιδῇ νήπιον παιδίον πρὸς
ἄνδρα τέλειον, τοῦτον καὶ σοφιστὴς πρὸς σοφὸν καὶ
τὰ ἐγκύκλια τῶν μαθημάτων πρὸς τὰς ἐν ἀρεταῖς
10 ἐπιστήμας.   III. καὶ ἐν ᾠδῇ μέντοι μείζονι τὸν λεὼν ἅπαντα, ὁπότε νεωτερίζοι, τὸ τῆς
ἄφρονος καὶ νηπίας ὄνομα ἡλικίας, τέκνα, καλεῖ·
" δίκαιος " γάρ φησι " καὶ ὅσιος ὁ κύριος· ἥμαρτον
οὐκ αὐτῷ τέκνα μωμητά; γενεὰ σκολιὰ καὶ δι-
εστραμμένη, ταῦτα κυρίῳ ἀνταποδίδοτε; οὕτως λαὸς
11 μωρὸς καὶ οὐχὶ σοφός; " οὐκοῦν τέκνα ἐναργῶς
ὠνόμακε τοὺς μώμους ἔχοντας ἄνδρας ἐν ψυχῇ καὶ
μωρίᾳ καὶ ἀνοίᾳ τὰ πολλὰ σφαλλομένους ἐν ταῖς
κατὰ τὸν ὀρθὸν βίον πράξεσιν, οὐκ εἰς τὰς ἐν παισὶ
σώματος ἡλικίας ἀπιδών, ἀλλ᾽ εἰς τὸ τῆς διανοίας
ἀλόγιστον καὶ πρὸς ἀλήθειαν βρεφῶδες.
12 οὕτως μέντοι καὶ Ῥαχήλ, ἡ σώματος εὐμορφία,
νεωτέρα Λείας, τοῦ κατὰ ψυχὴν κάλλους, ἀνα-
γράφεται· ἡ μὲν γὰρ θνητή, τὸ δ᾽ ἐστὶν ἀθάνατον,
καὶ ὅσα μέντοι τίμια πρὸς αἴσθησιν, ἑνὸς μόνου
τοῦ κατὰ ψυχὴν κάλλους ἀτελέστερα.
οἷς ἀκολουθεῖ καὶ τὸν Ἰωσὴφ νέον τε καὶ νεώτατον
αἰεὶ λέγεσθαι· καὶ γάρ, ὅταν ἐπιστατῇ τῆς ποίμνης
μετὰ τῶν νόθων ἀδελφῶν, νέος προσαγορεύεται,
καὶ ὅταν εὔχηται ὁ πατὴρ αὐτῷ φησίν· " υἱὸς

---

[a] Exod. xv. being the " lesser song " of Moses; cf. De Plant.
59.   [b] See App. p. 510.

thus marking the contrast between the sophist and the sage. For wisdom is Isaac's inheritance and sophistry Ishmael's, as we propose to shew in the special treatise, when we deal with the characteristics of the two. For the mere infant bears the same relation to the full-grown man as the sophist does to the sage, or the school subjects to the sciences which deal with virtues. III. And indeed in the 10 Greater Song,[a] he calls the whole people when they shew a rebellious spirit, by the name which belongs to the age of folly and babyhood, that is "bairns." "The Lord is just and holy," he says; "have not the blameworthy bairns sinned against him? a crooked and perverse generation, is it thus that ye requite the Lord? Are ye a people thus foolish and not wise?" (Deut. xxxii. 4-6). We see clearly that he has 11 given the name of "bairns" or "children" to men within whose souls are grounds for blame, men who so often fall through folly and senselessness and fail to do what the upright life requires. And in this he had no thought of literal age in the sense in which we use it of the bodies of the young, but of their truly infantine lack of a reasonable understanding.

Thus Rachel, who is comeliness of the 12 body, is described as younger than Leah, that is beauty of soul. For the former is mortal, the latter immortal, and indeed all the things that are precious to the senses are inferior in perfection to beauty of soul,[b] though they are many and it but one.
It is in accordance with this that Joseph is always called the young and youngest. For when he is keeping the flock with his bastard brothers,[b] he is spoken of as young (Gen. xxxvii. 2), and when his father prays for him he says, "my youngest son,

449

13 ηὐξημένος νεώτατος πρὸς μὲ ἀνάστρεψον." οὗτος
δέ ἐστιν ὁ τῆς περὶ τὸ σῶμα ἁπάσης ὑπέρμαχος
δυνάμεως καὶ ὁ τῆς τῶν ἐκτὸς ἀφθονίας ἀκολά-
κευτος ἑταῖρος, ὁ ⟨τὸ⟩ τῆς πρεσβυτέρας ψυχῆς
πρεσβύτερον καὶ τιμιώτερον ἀγαθὸν μήπω τέλειον
εὑρημένος. εἰ γὰρ εὕρητο, κἂν ὅλην Αἴγυπτον
ἀμεταστρεπτὶ φεύγων ᾤχετο· νυνὶ δὲ ἐπὶ τῷ
τρέφειν αὐτὴν καὶ τιθηνοκομεῖν μάλιστα σεμνύ-
νεται, ἧς τὸ μάχιμον καὶ ἡγεμονεῦον ὅταν ἴδῃ ὁ
ὁρῶν καταπεποντωμένον καὶ διεφθαρμένον, ὕμνον
14 εἰς τὸν θεὸν ᾄδει. νέος μὲν οὖν τρόπος ὁ μήπω
δυνάμενος μετὰ τῶν γνησίων ἀδελφῶν¹ ποιμαίνειν,
τὸ δ' ἐστὶ τῆς κατὰ ψυχὴν ἀλόγου φύσεως ἄρχειν
τε καὶ ἐπιτροπεύειν, ἀλλ' ἔτι μετὰ τῶν ⟨νόθων, οἷς
τῶν⟩ ἀγαθῶν τὰ δοκήσει² πρὸ τῶν γνησίων καὶ τῷ
15 εἶναι παραριθμουμένων τετίμηται. νεώτατος δέ,
κἂν ἐπίδοσιν καὶ αὔξησιν πρὸς τὸ ἄμεινον λάβῃ,
παρὰ τῷ τελείῳ νενόμισται μόνον ἀγαθὸν ἡγουμένῳ
τὸ καλόν· οὗ χάριν προτρέπων φησί· '' πρὸς μὲ
ἀνάστρεψον," ἴσον τῷ πρεσβυτέρας γνώμης ὀρέχ-
θητι, μὴ πάντα νεωτέριζε, ἤδη ποτὲ τὴν ἀρετὴν δι'
[395] αὐτὴν μόνην | στέρξον, μὴ καθάπερ παῖς ἄφρων τῇ
τῶν τυχηρῶν λαμπρότητι περιαυγαζόμενος ἀπάτης
καὶ ψευδοῦς δόξης ἀναπίμπλασο.
16 IV. Ὡς μὲν τοίνυν πολλαχοῦ νέον οὐκ εἰς τὴν

---

¹ mss. ἀρετῶν or εὑρετῶν: Adler suggests ἀρετῆς υἱῶν.
² Wendland reads for the μετὰ τῶν ἀγαθῶν τὰ δοκήσει of
the mss. μετὰ τῶν νόθων ⟨οἷς⟩ τὰ δοκήσει and inserts ἀγαθῶν
after παραριθμουμένων, producing the same meaning as the
text here printed (after Adler), but with less transcriptional
probability.

ᵃ So, with slight differences, the lxx. The Hebrew is
entirely different.

though grown, return to me " (Gen. xlix. 22).[a]
Now Joseph is the champion of bodily ability of 13
every kind, and the staunch and sincere henchman
of abundance in external things, but the treasure
which ranks in value and seniority above these, the
seniority of the soul, he has never yet gained in its
fullness. For if he had gained it, he would have fled
quite away from the length and breadth of Egypt,
and never turned to look back. But as it is, he finds
his chief glory in cherishing and fostering it—this
Egypt over which the Man of Vision sings his hymn
of triumph to God when he sees its fighters and its
leaders sunk in the sea and sent to perdition. The 14
" young " disposition, then, is one which cannot as
yet play the part of shepherd with its true-born
brothers, that is, rule and keep guard over the unreasoning element in the soul, but still consorts with
the base-born, who honour as goods such things as
are good in appearance rather than the genuine
goods which are reckoned as belonging to true
existence. And " youngest " too this youth is held 15
to be, even though he has received improvement and
growth to something better,[b] when compared with
the perfect or full-grown mind which holds moral
beauty to be the only good. And therefore Jacob
uses words of exhortation : " return to me," he says,
that is, desire the older way of thinking. Let not
your spirit in all things be the spirit of restless youth.
The time is come that you should love virtue for its
own sake only. Do not like a foolish boy be dazzled
by the brightness of fortune's gifts and fill yourself
with deceit and false opinion.

IV. We have shewn, then, that it is Moses' wont 16

[b] These words interpret the ηὐξημένος of the quotation.

σώματος ἀκμήν, ἀλλ᾽ εἰς τὴν ψυχῆς νεωτεροποιίαν
ἀφορῶν εἴωθε καλεῖν, ἐπιδέδεικται. ὡς δὲ καὶ
πρεσβύτερον οὐ τὸν γήρᾳ κατεσχημένον, ἀλλὰ τὸν
17 γέρως καὶ τιμῆς ἄξιον ὀνομάζει, δηλώσομεν. τίς
οὖν ἀγνοεῖ τῶν ἐντετυχηκότων ταῖς ἱερωτάταις
βίβλοις, ὅτι σχεδὸν τῶν προγόνων ἑαυτοῦ πάντων
ὁ σοφὸς Ἀβραὰμ ὀλιγοχρονιώτατος εἰσάγεται;
κἀκείνων μέν, οἶμαι, οἳ μακροβιώτατοι γεγόνασιν,
οὐδὲ εἷς, οὑτοσὶ δὲ ἀναγέγραπται πρεσβύτερος·
φασὶ γοῦν οἱ χρησμοί, ὅτι " Ἀβραὰμ ἦν πρεσβύτερος προβεβηκὼς καὶ κύριος εὐλόγησε τὸν
18 Ἀβραὰμ κατὰ πάντα." τοῦτό μοι δοκεῖ τὸ προ-
κείμενον αἰτίας ἀπόδοσις εἶναι, δι᾽ ἣν πρεσβύτερος ἐλέχθη ὁ σοφός· ἐπιφροσύνη γὰρ θεοῦ τὸ
λογικὸν τῆς ψυχῆς μέρος ὅταν εὖ διατεθῇ καὶ μὴ
καθ᾽ ἓν εἶδος ἀλλὰ κατὰ πάσας τὰς ἐπιβολὰς
εὐλογιστῇ, πρεσβυτέρα χρώμενον γνώμῃ καὶ αὐτὸ
19 δήπου πρεσβύτερόν ἐστιν. οὕτως καὶ
τοὺς συνέδρους τοῦ θεοφιλοῦς τὸν δέκα[1] ἑβδομάδων
ἀριθμὸν εἰληχότας πρεσβυτέρους ὀνομάζειν ἔθος·
λέγεται γάρ· " συνάγαγέ μοι ἑβδομήκοντα ἄνδρας
ἀπὸ τῶν πρεσβυτέρων Ἰσραήλ, οὓς αὐτὸς σὺ
20 οἶδας ὅτι οὗτοί εἰσι πρεσβύτεροι." οὐκοῦν οὐ
τοὺς ὑπὸ τῶν τυχόντων γέροντας νομιζομένους ὡς
ἱεροφάντας, ἀλλ᾽ οὓς ὁ σοφὸς οἶδε μόνος, τῆς τῶν

---

[1] MSS. ἕνδεκα.

---

[a] There is a play here on γῆρας and γέρας. If it is worth
keeping, we might translate " by advance of years—of
advance in honour." Cf. Quis Rer. Div. Her. 291, where
γῆρας is said to be τὸ γέρως ἀδελφὸν καὶ παρώνυμον.
[b] See App. p. 510.
[c] The sense would be clearer without ὡς ἱεροφάντας.

in many places to call a person young, thinking not of
his bodily vigour, but only of his soul, and the spirit
of rebelliousness which it displays. And now we
will go on to shew that he applies the name of elder
not to one who is bowed down with old age, but to
one who is worthy of precedence *a* and honour.
Everyone who is versed in the sacred books knows 17
that the wise Abraham is represented as more short-
lived than almost all his forefathers. And yet, I
think, to not a single one of these, long though their
span of life beyond comparison was, is the term elder
applied, but only to Abraham. This is seen by the
words of the oracles, " Abraham was an elder advanced in years, and God blessed him in everything "
(Gen. xxiv. 1). The phrase thus set before us *b* seems 18
to me to be an explanation of the reason why the
Sage is called elder. For when through the watchful
care of God the rational part of the soul is brought
into a good condition and reasons rightly not merely
in one direction, but wherever it applies itself, the
thoughts which it thinks are " older " and itself must
needs be older also. Thus too it is Moses' 19
way to give the name of " elder " to those counsellors
of the God-beloved, whose apportioned number was
that of seven times ten. For we find " gather to
me seventy men from the elders of Israel, whom thou
thyself knowest that these are elders " (Numb. xi.
16). We see then that not the men of senior age, 20
whom the common herd regard as initiators to the
holy mysteries, *c* but those whom the Sage alone
knows were held worthy by God of the title of

As it stands, it must mean that the common opinion looks
upon the old in age as the proper persons for such high
functions. But νομίζειν ὡς is a rare construction.

πρεσβυτέρων ἠξίωσε προσρήσεως· οὓς μὲν γὰρ ἂν
οὗτος ἀποδοκιμάσῃ καθάπερ ἀργυραμοιβὸς ἀγαθὸς
ἐκ τοῦ τῆς ἀρετῆς νομίσματος, κεκιβδηλευμένοι
νεωτεροποιοὶ τὰς ψυχὰς ἅπαντες· οὓς δ᾽ ἂν
γνωρίμους ἐθελήσῃ ποιήσασθαι, δόκιμοί τε καὶ τὸ
φρόνημα πρεσβύτεροι κατὰ τὸ ἀναγκαῖόν εἰσιν.

21   V. ἑνὶ μέντοι νόμου διατάγματι τοῖς
ἀκούειν ἐπισταμένοις ἑκάτερον ὧν εἶπον ἐναργέστερον φανεῖται δεδηλωκώς· " ἐὰν γὰρ γένωνται "
φησίν " ἀνθρώπῳ δύο γυναῖκες, ἠγαπημένη καὶ
μισουμένη, καὶ τέκωσιν αὐτῷ ἡ ἠγαπημένη καὶ ἡ
μισουμένη, καὶ γένηται υἱὸς πρωτότοκος τῆς
μισουμένης, ᾗ ἂν ἡμέρᾳ κληροδοτῇ τοῖς υἱοῖς τὰ
ὑπάρχοντα, οὐ δυνήσεται πρωτοτοκεῦσαι τῷ υἱῷ
τῆς ἠγαπημένης ὑπεριδὼν τὸν υἱὸν τῆς μισουμένης
τὸν πρωτότοκον· ἀλλὰ τὸν πρωτότοκον υἱὸν τῆς
μισουμένης ἐπιγνώσεται, δοῦναι αὐτῷ διπλᾶ ἀπὸ
πάντων ὧν ἐὰν εὑρεθῇ αὐτῷ, ὅτι οὗτός ἐστιν ἀρχὴ
τέκνων αὐτοῦ καὶ τούτῳ καθήκει τὰ πρωτοτόκια."

22
[396] | παρατετήρηκας ἤδη, ὅτι τὸν μὲν τῆς στεργομένης
υἱὸν οὐδέποτε πρωτότοκον ἢ πρεσβύτερον καλεῖ,
τὸν δὲ τῆς μισουμένης πολλάκις· καίτοι τοῦ μὲν
τὴν γένεσιν προτέρου, τοῦ δὲ ἐκ τῆς στυγουμένης
ὑστέρου δεδήλωκεν εὐθὺς ἀρχόμενος τῆς προσ-
τάξεως· " ἐὰν γὰρ τέκωσι " φησίν " ἡ ἠγαπημένη
καὶ ἡ μισουμένη." ἀλλ᾽ ὅμως τὸ μὲν τῆς προτέρας
γέννημα, κἂν πολυχρονιώτερον ᾖ, νεώτερον παρ᾽
ὀρθῷ λόγῳ δικάζοντι νενόμισται, τὸ δὲ τῆς ὑστέρας,

---

^a Or " take as his familiars."
^b Philo argues that the age (in the literal sense) of the
two sons is shewn by the *order* in which the motherhood of
454

" elders." For those whom the Sage like a good money-changer rejects from the currency of virtue are all men of dross, men with the spirit of youth-like rebellion in their souls. But those whom he has willed to consider as known to him [a] are tested and approved and must needs be elders in heart and mind. V. Indeed there is one command- 21 ment of the law in which those who have ears to hear will perceive that he sets before us still more clearly the two truths of which I have spoken. For we read " if a man has two wives, one loved and the other hated, and the beloved and the hated each bear a son to him, and the son of her that is hated is the firstborn, it shall be that on the day on which he allots his goods to his sons, he shall not be able to give the right of the firstborn to the son of her whom he loves, and set aside the firstborn, the son of her whom he hates, but he shall acknowledge the firstborn, the son of her whom he hates, to give him a double portion of all that he has gotten ; for he is the beginning of his children and to him belong the rights of the firstborn " (Deut. xxi. 15-17). You observe at once that the son of the beloved wife 22 is never called by him " firstborn " or " elder," but the son of the hated wife is so called often. And yet at the very beginning of the commandment he has shewn us that the birth of the former comes first and the birth of the latter afterwards.[b] For he writes, " if the beloved and the hated bear children." But all the same the issue of the wife mentioned first, though his years be more, is counted as younger in the judgement of right reason, while the child of

the two wives is mentioned. This meaning would come out more clearly if we read προτέραν . . ὑστέραν.

κἂν ἐν τοῖς κατὰ τὴν γένεσιν χρόνοις ὑστερίζῃ,
τῆς μείζονος καὶ πρεσβυτέρας μοίρας ἠξίωται.
23 διὰ τί; ὅτι τῶν γυναικῶν τὴν μὲν στεργομένην
ἡδονῆς, τὴν δὲ στυγουμένην φρονήσεως εἶναί φαμεν
σύμβολον· τῆς μὲν γὰρ ὁ πολὺς ὅμιλος ἀνθρώπων
τὴν συνουσίαν ὑπερφυῶς ἀγαπᾷ δελέατα καὶ
φίλτρα ἐξ ἑαυτῆς ἐπαγωγότατα ἐνδιδούσης ἀπὸ
γενέσεως ἀρχῆς ἄχρι πανυστάτου γήρως, τῆς δὲ
ἐκτόπως τὸ αὐστηρὸν καὶ περίσεμνον διαμεμίσηκε
καθάπερ οἱ ἄφρονες παῖδες τὰς τῶν γονέων καὶ
τρεφόντων ὠφελιμωτάτας μὲν ἀτερπεστάτας δὲ
24 ὑφηγήσεις. τίκτουσι δ' ἀμφότεραι, ἡ μὲν τὸν
φιλήδονον, ἡ δ' αὖ τὸν φιλάρετον ἐν ψυχῇ τρόπον.
ἀλλ' ὁ μὲν φιλήδονος ἀτελὴς καὶ ὄντως ἀεὶ παῖς
ἐστι, κἂν εἰς πολυετίας αἰῶνα μήκιστον ἀφίκηται,
ὁ δ' αὖ φιλάρετος ἐν γερουσίᾳ τῆς φρονήσεως ἐξ
ἔτι σπαργάνων, τὸ τοῦ λόγου δὴ τοῦτο, ἀγήρως
25 ὧν τάττεται· παρὸ καὶ λίαν ἐμφαντικῶς εἴρηκεν
ἐπὶ τοῦ τῆς μισουμένης ὑπὸ τῶν πολλῶν ἀρετῆς
γεγονότος, ὅτι " οὗτός ἐστιν ἀρχὴ τέκνων," καὶ
τάξει καὶ ἡγεμονίᾳ δήπου πρῶτος ὤν, " καὶ τούτῳ
καθήκει τὰ πρωτοτόκια " νόμῳ φύσεως, οὐκ
ἀνομίᾳ τῇ παρ' ἀνθρώποις.
26 VI. Ἑπόμενος οὖν αὐτῷ καὶ ὥσπερ ἐπὶ προτεθέντα σκοπὸν ἀφιεὶς εὐστόχως τὰ βέλη κατὰ
ἀκολουθίαν εἰσάγει τὸν Ἰακὼβ γενέσει μὲν τοῦ
Ἡσαῦ νεώτερον—ὅτι ἀφροσύνη μὲν ἐκ πρώτης
ἡλικίας ἐστὶν ἡμῖν σύντροφος, ὀψίγονος δ' ὁ τοῦ
καλοῦ ζῆλος—, δυνάμει δὲ πρεσβύτερον· παρὸ καὶ

ᵃ See *De Ebr.* 48 (and note).

the wife mentioned afterwards, though he be later in the date of his birth, is held worthy of the greater 23 and senior portion. Why? Because we declare that in the beloved wife we have a figure of pleasure and in the hated wife a figure of prudence. For pleasure's company is beloved beyond measure by the great mass of men, because from the hour of their birth to the utmost limits of old age she produces and sets before them such enticing lures and love-charms; while for prudence, severe and august as she is, they have a strange and profound hatred, as foolish children hate the most wholesome but most distasteful directions of their parents and those who 24 have the charge of them. Both are mothers; pleasure of the pleasure-loving, prudence of the virtue-loving tendency in the soul. But the former is never full grown but always in reality a child, however long and never-ending the tale of years to which he attains. But the other—the virtue-lover— is exempt from old age, yet " from the cradle," as the phrase goes, he ranks as an elder in the senate 25 of prudence. And therefore he says—and very forcible are his words—of the son of the hated wife— virtue who is hated by the multitude—that he is " the beginning of his children," and truly so, because he is first in rank and precedence—and again, " to him belong the rights of the firstborn," by the law of nature,[a] not by the no-law which prevails among men.

VI. Following this law consistently and aiming 26 his arrows skilfully at the mark he has set before him, Moses shews us Jacob as younger in years than Esau, but older in worth and value, since folly is congenital to us from our earliest years, but the desire for moral excellence is a later birth, and

τῶν πρωτοτοκίων ὁ μὲν Ἡσαῦ ἐξίσταται, μετα-
27 ποιεῖται δ' οὗτος εἰκότως. τούτοις
συνᾴδει καὶ τὰ ἐπὶ τῶν υἱῶν Ἰωσὴφ ἐκ πολλῆς
περισκέψεως ἀνεζητημένα, ἡνίκα ἐνθουσιῶν ὁ
σοφὸς ἀντικρὺς παρεστηκότων οὐκ ἐπιτίθησι ταῖς
κεφαλαῖς ἐξ ἐναντίας καὶ κατ' εὐθὺ τὰς χεῖρας
ἐπενεγκών, ἀλλ' ἐναλλάξας, ὅπως τῇ μὲν εὐωνύμῳ
τοῦ πρεσβυτέρου δοκοῦντος εἶναι, τοῦ δὲ νεωτέρου
28 τῇ δεξιᾷ ψαύσῃ. καλεῖται δ' ὁ μὲν [ἐν] γενέσει
πρεσβύτερος Μανασσῆς, ὁ δὲ νεώτερος Ἐφραΐμ·
ταῦτα δ' εἰ μεταληφθείη τὰ ὀνόματα εἰς Ἑλλάδα
γλῶτταν, μνήμης καὶ ἀναμνήσεως εὑρεθήσεται
[397] σύμβολα· ἑρμηνεύεται γὰρ | Μανασσῆς μὲν " ἐκ
λήθης "—τὸ δ' ἐστὶν ὀνόματι ἑτέρῳ καλούμενον
ἀνάμνησις· ὁ γὰρ ὧν ἐπελάθετο εἰς ἀνάμνησιν
ἐρχόμενος ἔξω πρόεισι τῆς λήθης—, Ἐφραΐμ δὲ
καρποφορία, μνήμης πρόσρησις οἰκειοτάτη, διότι
καρπὸς ὠφελιμώτατος καὶ τῷ ὄντι ἐδώδιμος
ψυχαῖς τὸ ἄληστον ἐν ταῖς ἀδιαστάτοις ⟨μνήμαις⟩.[1]
29 μνῆμαι μὲν οὖν ἠνδρωμένοις ἤδη καὶ παγίοις
συντυγχάνουσι, παρὸ καὶ νεώτεραι ἐνομίσθησαν
ὀψὲ φυόμεναι· λήθη δὲ καὶ ἀνάμνησις ἐπαλλήλως
σχεδὸν ἐκ πρώτης ἡλικίας ἑκάστῳ σύνεισιν, οὗ
ἕνεκα τὰ χρόνου πρεσβεῖα εὕρηνται καὶ ἐπ'
εὐωνύμοις παρὰ σοφῷ ταξιαρχοῦντι τάττονται·
τῶν δὲ ἀρετῆς αἱ μνῆμαι κοινωνήσουσι πρεσβείων,
ἃς ὁ θεοφιλὴς δεξιωσάμενος τῆς ἀμείνονος παρ'
ἑαυτῷ μοίρας ἀξιώσει.
30 Νήψας οὖν ὁ δίκαιος καὶ γνοὺς ὅσα " ἐποίησεν

---

[1] Wendland ἐν μνήμαις ἀδιαστάτοις.

therefore Esau is forced to surrender the inheritance of the firstborn to the rightful claims of Jacob.

The same truth is borne out by the 27 story of the sons of Joseph, a story which shews rich and careful thought.[a] The sage, we read, under inspiration lays his hands on the heads of the boys who stood opposite him, but lays them not straight in front but crosswise, meaning to touch with his left hand the boy who seemed the elder and the younger with his right (Gen. xlviii. 13, 14). Now the 28 elder boy is called Manasseh and the younger Ephraim—and if these names are translated into Greek we shall find they represent " reminiscence " and " memory." For Manasseh is by interpretation " from forgetfulness," another name for which is reminiscence, since anyone who is reminded of what he has forgotten, issues from a state of forgetfulness. Ephraim on the other hand is " fruit-bearing," a very suitable title for memory ; since truth unforgotten, because memory has been unbroken, is a fruit most profitable, a real food to souls. Now memories belong to those who have 29 reached settled manhood and therefore as being late-born are accounted younger. But forgetfulness and recollection follow in succession in each of us almost from our earliest years. And therefore theirs is the seniority in time and a place on the left, when the Sage marshals his ranks. But in seniority of virtue memories will have their share, and the God-beloved will lay on them his right hand and adjudge them worthy of the better portion which is his to give.

To resume. When the just man has returned to 30

[a] *Cf. Leg. All.* iii. 90-93.

αὐτῷ ὁ νεώτερος αὐτοῦ υἱὸς " ἀρὰς χαλεπωτάτας
τίθεται· τῷ γὰρ ὄντι ὅταν ὁ νοῦς νήψῃ, κατὰ τὸ
ἀκόλουθον εὐθὺς αἰσθάνεται ὅσα ἡ νεωτεροποιὸς
ἐν αὐτῷ κακία πρότερον εἰργάζετο, ἃ μεθύων
31 ἀδυνάτως καταλαβεῖν εἶχε. VII. τίνι μέντοι κατ-
αρᾶται, σκεπτέον· ἐν γάρ τι καὶ τοῦτο τῶν ἐρεύνης
ἀξίων ἐστίν, ἐπειδήπερ οὐ τῷ δοκοῦντι ἡμαρτη-
κέναι παιδί, ἀλλὰ τῷ ἐκείνου μὲν υἱῷ, ἑαυτοῦ δὲ
υἱωνῷ, οὗ φανερὸν οὐδὲν εἴς γε τὸ παρὸν ἀδίκημα,
32 οὐ μικρὸν οὐ μέγα, δεδήλωκεν· ὁ μὲν γὰρ ἐκ
περιεργίας ἰδεῖν τὸν πατέρα γυμνὸν ἐθελήσας καὶ
γελάσας ἃ εἶδε καὶ ἐκλαλήσας[1] τὰ δεόντως ἡσυχα-
σθέντα ὁ υἱὸς ἦν τοῦ Νῶε Χάμ, ὁ δὲ ἐφ' οἷς ἕτερος
ἠδίκησε τὰς αἰτίας ἔχων καὶ τὰς ἀρὰς καρπούμενος
Χανάαν ἐστι· λέγεται γὰρ " ἐπικατάρατος Χανάαν·
παῖς οἰκέτης [δοῦλος δούλων][2] ἔσται τοῖς ἀδελφοῖς
33 αὐτοῦ."   τί γὰρ ἡμάρτηκεν, ὡς ἔφην,
οὗτος; ἀλλ' ἐσκέψαντο μὲν ἐφ' ἑαυτῶν ἴσως οἷς
ἔθος ἀκριβοῦν τὰς ῥητὰς καὶ προχείρους ἀποδόσεις
ἐν τοῖς νόμοις· ἡμεῖς δὲ πειθόμενοι τῷ ὑπο-
βάλλοντι ὀρθῷ λόγῳ τὴν ἐγκειμένην ἀπόδοσιν δι-
ερμηνεύσωμεν ἐκεῖνα ἀναγκαίως προειπόντες·
34   VIII. σχέσις καὶ κίνησις διαφέρουσιν ἀλλήλων·
ἡ μὲν γάρ ἐστιν ἠρεμία, φορὰ δὲ ἡ κίνησις· ἧς
εἴδη δύο, τὸ μὲν μεταβατικόν, τὸ δὲ περὶ τὸν αὐτὸν
τόπον εἰλούμενον. σχέσει μὲν οὖν | ἀδελφὸν ἕξις,
[398] κινήσει δ' ἐνέργεια.   τὸ δὲ λεγόμενον
35 παραδείγματι οἰκείῳ γνωριμώτερον γένοιτ' ἄν·

---

[1] MSS. ἐκ(έγ)γελάσας.   [2] See App. p. 510.

* See App. p. 511.

soberness and knows " what his younger son has done to him," he utters curses stern and deep. For indeed when the mind becomes sober, it must follow that it at once perceives the former doings of the young rebellious wickedness within it, doings which in its drunken state it was incapable of comprehending. VII. But who is it that he curses? Let us con- 31 sider this, for this too is one of the questions which deserve our careful search, seeing that the person cursed is not the apparent sinner, Noah's son, but that son's son, Noah's grandson, though up to this point no clear wrongdoing great or small on his part has been indicated by Moses. It was Noah's son 32 Ham, who from idle curiosity wished to see his father naked, and laughed at what he saw and proclaimed aloud what it was right to leave untold. But it is Canaan who is charged with another's misdeeds and reaps the curses. For it is said, " Cursed be Canaan; a servant, a bondman shall be be to his brethren " (Gen. ix. 25). What, I repeat, 33 was his offence? Perhaps this question has been considered on their own principles by those who are used to discuss in details the literal and outward interpretation of the laws. Let us rather in obedience to the suggestions of right reason expound in full the inward interpretation. Something, however, must be said by way of preface. VIII. The 34 state of rest [a] and the state of motion differ from each other. While the former is static, the latter is dynamic and is of two kinds, one passing from point to point, the other revolving round a fixed place. Habit is akin to rest, as activity is to motion. These remarks might be made 35 more intelligible by a suitable illustration. The car-

τέκτονα καὶ ζωγράφον καὶ γεωργὸν καὶ μουσικὸν
καὶ τοὺς ἄλλους τεχνίτας, κἂν ἡσυχίαν ἄγωσι
μηδὲν τῶν κατὰ τὰς τέχνας ἐνεργοῦντες, οὐδὲν
ἧττον τοῖς εἰρημένοις ἔθος καλεῖν ὀνόμασιν, ἐπεὶ
τὴν ἐν ἑκάστοις ἐμπειρίαν καὶ ἐπιστήμην ἀνειλη-
36 φότες ἔχουσιν. ἐπειδὰν δὲ ὁ τεκτονικὸς ξύλων
ὕλην ἐργάζηται λαβών, ὁ δὲ ζωγράφος τὰ οἰκεῖα
κερασάμενος χρώματα ἐπὶ τοῦ πίνακος διαγράφῃ
τοὺς τύπους ὧν ἂν διανοῆται, ὁ δ' αὖ γεωργὸς
ἀνατέμνων γῆς αὔλακας καταβάλλῃ τὰ σπέρματα,
κληματίδας δὲ καὶ μοσχεύματα δένδρων ἐμφυτεύῃ,
ἅμα δὲ τροφὴν ἀναγκαιοτάτην ἄρδῃ καὶ ἐποχετεύῃ
τοῖς φυτευθεῖσι καὶ τοῖς ἄλλοις ὅσα γεωργικὰ
πᾶσιν ἐγχειρῇ, ὁ δ' αὖ μουσικὸς αὐλοῖς καὶ
κιθάραις καὶ τοῖς ἄλλοις ὀργάνοις μέτρα καὶ
ῥυθμοὺς καὶ πάσας μέλους ἰδέας ἁρμόττῃ—δύναται[1]
δὲ καὶ δίχα τῶν χειροκμήτων τῷ τῆς φύσεως
ὀργάνῳ χρῆσθαι διὰ φωνῆς ἡρμοσμένης πᾶσι τοῖς
φθόγγοις—καὶ τῶν ἄλλων ἕκαστος τεχνιτῶν εἴπερ
ἐγχειρεῖ, τοῖς κατὰ τὰς ἐπιστήμας ἕτερα ἐξ
ἀνάγκης οἰκεῖα τοῖς προτέροις ὀνόματα προσ-
γίνεται, τῷ μὲν τέκτονι τὸ τεκτονεῖν, τῷ δὲ ζωγράφῳ
τὸ ζωγραφεῖν ἤδη, καὶ τὸ γεωργεῖν μέντοι τῷ
γεωργῷ, καὶ τὸ αὐλεῖν ἢ κιθαρίζειν ἢ ᾄδειν ἤ τι
τῶν παραπλησίων ποιεῖν τῷ μουσικῷ.
37 τίσιν οὖν οἱ ψόγοι καὶ οἱ ἔπαινοι παρακολουθοῦσιν;
ἆρ' οὐχὶ τοῖς ἐνεργοῦσι καὶ δρῶσιν; κατορθοῦντες
μὲν γὰρ ἔπαινον, ψόγον δ' ἔμπαλιν καρποῦνται

---

[1] MSS. δύνηται.

penter, the painter, the husbandman, the musician and those who practise the other arts may be unoccupied and not employing any of the activities which belong to their arts, yet none the less we are accustomed to call them by the aforesaid names, because they have the knowledge and experience which they have acquired in their respective professions. But there are times when the carpenter 36 takes and carves a piece of timber, or the painter after mixing the proper colours delineates on the canvas the forms which he has in mind, or the husbandman ploughs furrows in the land and drops the seed into them, and plants sprigs and suckers from the trees, and also supplies by watering and irrigation the nourishment so necessary to his plants, and sets his hand to all the other works of husbandry. Again there are times when the musician adjusts his metre and rhythm and any form of melody to his flute or harp or any other instrument, or he may perhaps use the natural without the handmade instrument and adapt his voice to all the notes of the gamut. At such times or when each of the other kinds of craftsmen takes his work in hand, we necessarily supplement the first set of names, which are based on the several kinds of knowledge, by others corresponding to them. We speak not only of carpenters, but of practising carpentry, not only of painters but of painting, not only of husbandmen, but of farming, not only of musicians, but of flute-playing, harp-playing, singing or some similar performance. Now which of the two 37 categories is the subject of praise or blame? Surely those who are actually engaged in doing something. They it is whose success or failure entail respectively

διαμαρτάνοντες. οἱ δ' ἄνευ τοῦ τι ποιεῖν ἐπιστήμονες αὐτὸ μόνον, ἀκίνδυνον γέρας εἰληφότες
38 ἡσυχίαν ἠρεμοῦσιν.   IX. ὁ αὐτὸς τοίνυν
λόγος ἐφαρμόττει καὶ τοῖς κατ' ἀφροσύνην[1] καὶ
συνόλως τοῖς κατ' ἀρετήν τε καὶ κακίαν· οἱ
φρόνιμοί τε καὶ σώφρονες καὶ ἀνδρεῖοι καὶ δίκαιοι
τὰς ψυχὰς μυρίοι γεγόνασι φύσεως μὲν εὐμοιρίᾳ,
νομίμοις δ' ὑφηγήσεσι, πόνοις δ' ἀηττήτοις καὶ
ἀοκνοτάτοις χρησάμενοι, τὸ δὲ κάλλος τῶν ἐν ταῖς
διανοίαις ἀγαλμάτων οὐκ ἴσχυσαν ἐπιδείξασθαι
διὰ πενίαν ἢ ἀδοξίαν ἢ νόσον σώματος ἢ τὰς ἄλλας
κῆρας ὅσαι τὸν ἀνθρώπινον περιπολοῦσι βίον.
39   οὐκοῦν οὗτοι μὲν ὥσπερ δεδεμένα καὶ
καθειργμένα ἐκτήσαντο ἀγαθά, ἕτεροι δ' εἰσὶν οἳ
λελυμένοις καὶ ἀφέτοις καὶ ἐλευθέροις ἐχρήσαντο
πᾶσι τὰς εἰς ἐπίδειξιν ὕλας ἀφθονωτάτας προσ-
40 λαβόντες· ὁ μὲν φρόνιμος ἰδίων τε καὶ κοινῶν προστασίαν[2] πραγμάτων, οἷς σύνεσιν καὶ εὐβουλίαν
ἐνεπιδείξεται· ὁ δὲ σώφρων τὸν εἰς ἀσωτίαν δεινὸν
ἐπᾶραι καὶ παρακαλέσαι τυφλὸν πλοῦτον, ἵνα
βλέποντα ἀποδείξῃ· ὁ δὲ δίκαιος ἀρχήν, δι' ἧς τὸ
κατ' ἀξίαν ἀπονέμειν ἑκάστῳ τῶν ‹ὑπ›όντων[3]
ἀκωλύτως δυνατὸς ἔσται· ὁ δ' ἀσκητὴς εὐσεβείας
[399] ἱερωσύνην καὶ χωρίων | ἱερῶν καὶ τῆς ἐν τούτοις
41 ἁγιστείας ἐπιμέλειαν. ἄνευ δὲ τούτων ἀρεταὶ μέν
εἰσιν, ἀκίνητοι δὲ ἀρεταὶ καὶ ἡσυχίαν ἄγουσαι,

---

[1] Conj. Tr. κατ' ἀφροσύνην ‹καὶ σύνεσιν›. The last two words, which are needed for antithesis, may easily have fallen out before καὶ συνόλως.

[2] So Wendland for ms. περιουσίαν, which perhaps in the sense of "abundance" is not quite impossible: Cohen παρουσίαν.

[3] Conj. Tr.: Wendland ὑπηκόων: Adler πολίτων.

[a] Here we have Philo's favourite idea of the three elements

praise or blame. Those who possess the knowledge
and nothing more, and are not actually doing anything remain in peace and find in their inactivity the
privilege of security.   IX. The same prin- 38
ciple then holds when the quality predicated is folly
or virtue and vice in general. Those whose souls are
prudent, or temperate, or courageous or just, have
become so in numberless cases partly by happy
natural gifts, partly by the directing influence of
custom, partly by their own persistent and unsparing
efforts,*a* but poverty or obscurity or bodily disease,
or the other mischiefs which beset human life, have
made it impossible for them to manifest the beauty
of the qualities *b* which adorn their minds.
These, then, possess their good qualities, as it were, in 39
chains and durance. But there are others who find
them entirely free, unconfined, unshackled in their
hands, because in their case these gifts have been
supplemented by rich and abundant material for
their display. The man of prudence may have the 40
charge of public or private business, in which he can
shew his shrewdness and good judgement. The
temperate man may have wealth, and while blind
wealth is strong to incite and urge its possessors to
licence, he may turn that blindness into eyesight.
The just man may hold office, which will enable him
to render without hindrance their several dues to
all who are under his authority. The practiser of
religion may have priesthood and the charge of holy
places and the rites there performed. Virtues they 41
still are apart from these opportunities, but they are

of education, φύσις, διδασκαλία, ἄσκησις, usually typified by
Isaac, Abraham and Jacob. *Cf.* note on *De Sac.* 5-7
(Vol. I. App. p. 488).
   b Or possibly ἀγαλμάτων may mean the " ideas," *cf.* § 3.

καθάπερ ὁ τεθησαυρισμένος ἐν ἀφανέσι γῆς μυχοῖς ἄργυρός τε καὶ χρυσὸς οὐδὲν χρήσιμος.

42 πάλιν τοίνυν κατὰ τὰ ἐναντία μυρίους ἔστιν ἰδεῖν ἀνάνδρους, ἀκολάστους, ἄφρονας, ἀδίκους, ἀσεβεῖς ἐν ταῖς διανοίαις ὑπάρχοντας, τὸ δὲ κακίας ἑκάστης αἶσχος ἀδυνατοῦντας ἐπιδείκνυσθαι δι' ἀκαιρίαν τῶν εἰς τὸ ἁμαρτάνειν καιρῶν, ἐπειδὰν δὲ τοῦ δύνασθαι πολλὴ καὶ μεγάλη κατασκήψῃ φορά, γῆν καὶ θάλατταν ἄχρι τερμάτων ἀμυθήτων ἀναπιμ-πλάντας κακῶν καὶ μηδέν, μὴ μικρὸν μὴ μέγα, ἀζήμιον ἐῶντας, ἀλλὰ ῥύμῃ μιᾷ ἀνατρέποντάς τε

43 καὶ φθείροντας· ὥσπερ γὰρ τοῦ πυρὸς ἡ δύναμις ἀπουσίᾳ μὲν ὕλης ἡσυχάζει, παρουσίᾳ δὲ ἀνακαίεται, οὕτως καὶ ὅσαι πρὸς ἀρετὴν ἢ κακίαν ψυχῆς δυνάμεις ἀφορῶσι, σβέννυνται μὲν ἀκαιρίαις, καθάπερ ἔφην, καιρῶν, τυχηραῖς δ' εὐπορίαις ἀνα-φλέγονται.

44 Χ. Τίνος δὴ ταῦθ' εἵνεκα εἶπον ἢ τοῦ διδάξαι χάριν, ὅτι ὁ μὲν υἱὸς τοῦ Νῶε Χὰμ ἠρεμούσης κακίας ἐστὶν ὄνομα, ὁ δὲ υἱωνὸς ἤδη καὶ κινου-μένης; ἑρμηνεύεται γὰρ θέρμη μὲν Χάμ, σάλος

45 δὲ Χαναάν. θέρμη δὲ ἐν μὲν σώματι πυρετὸν ἐμφαίνει, κακίαν δὲ ἐν ψυχαῖς· ὡς γάρ, οἶμαι, καταβολὴ πυρετοῦ νόσος ἐστὶν οὐ μέρους ἀλλ' ὅλου σώματος, οὕτως ὅλης τῆς ψυχῆς ἀρρώστημά ἐστι κακία. ἀλλ' ὁτὲ μὲν ἠρεμεῖ, ὁτὲ δὲ κινεῖται· τὴν δὲ κίνησιν αὐτῆς ὀνομάζει σάλον, ὃς Ἑβραίων

46 γλώττῃ Χαναὰν καλεῖται. νομοθετῶν δὲ οὐδεὶς ἐπιτίμιον ὁρίζει κατὰ ἀδίκων ἠρεμούντων, ἀλλὰ δὴ[1] κινουμένων καὶ τοῖς κατὰ ἀδικίαν ἔργοις χρω-μένων, καθάπερ οὐδὲ τῶν δακετῶν οὐδὲν ἀνὴρ

[1] Wendland conj. ἀλλ' ἤδη.

static and inactive virtues, like gold and silver laid up in hidden recesses of the earth where none can use them.   Conversely we may see 42 thousands who are cowardly, intemperate, foolish, unjust and irreligious at heart, but unable to display the ugliness of each vice, because of the inconvenience of their opportunities for sin. But when such possibility suddenly descends upon them in all its impetuous force, they fill land and sea to their utmost bounds with an untold host of evil deeds. They leave nothing great or small unharmed but work wrack and ruin in one concentrated outburst. For 43 just as the capacity of fire is dormant or kindled into activity according as fuel is absent or present, so the powers of the soul which have vice or virtue in view are quenched by inconvenience of opportunities (to repeat the phrase), but burst into flame when chance throws facilities in their way.

X. These remarks have been made solely for the 44 purpose of shewing that Ham the son of Noah is a name for vice in the quiescent state and the grandson Canaan for the same when it passes into active movement. For Ham is by interpretation " heat," and Canaan " tossing." Now heat is a sign of fever 45 in the body and of vice in the soul. For just as an attack of fever is a disease not of a part but of the whole body, so vice is a malady of the whole soul. Sometimes it is in a state of quiescence, sometimes of motion, and its motion is called by Moses " tossing," which in the Hebrew tongue is Canaan. Now 46 no legislator fixes a penalty against the unjust when in the quiescent state, but only when they are moved to action and commit the deeds to which injustice prompts them, just as in the case of animals

PHILO

μέτριος κτείνειν ἂν ἐθελήσαι μὴ μέλλον δάκνειν·
λόγου[1] γὰρ ὑπεξαιρετέον ψυχῆς ὠμότητα φύσει
47 [καὶ] κατὰ πάντων φονῶσαν.   εἰκότως
οὖν ὁ δίκαιος τὰς ἀρὰς τῷ υἱωνῷ Χαναὰν δόξει
τίθεσθαι· δόξει δὲ εἶπον, ὅτι δυνάμει τῷ υἱῷ Χὰμ
δι' ἐκείνου καταρᾶται· κινηθεὶς γὰρ πρὸς τὸ ἁμαρτάνειν Χὰμ αὐτὸς γίνεται Χαναάν. ἐν γὰρ τὸ
ὑποκείμενον κακία, ἧς τὸ μὲν ἐν σχέσει, τὸ δὲ ἐν
κινήσει θεωρεῖται· πρεσβύτερον δὲ κινήσεως σχέσις,
ὡς ἐγγόνου λόγον ἔχειν τὸ κινούμενον πρὸς τὸ
48 ἰσχόμενον· παρὸ καὶ τοῦ Χὰμ υἱὸς ὁ Χαναὰν
[400] φυσικῶς ἀναγράφεται, σάλος ἠρεμίας, ἵνα καὶ | τὸ
ἑτέρωθι λεχθὲν ἐπαληθεύῃ τὸ " ἀποδιδοὺς ἀνομίας
πατέρων ἐπὶ υἱούς, ἐπὶ τρίτους καὶ ἐπὶ τετάρτους"·
ἐπὶ γὰρ τὰ ἀποτελέσματα καὶ ὡς ἂν ἔγγονα τῶν
λογισμῶν στείχουσιν αἱ τιμωρίαι, καθ' αὑτοὺς[2]
ἐκείνων, εἰ μηδεμία προσγένοιτο πρᾶξις ἐπίληπτος,
49 ἀποδιδρασκόντων τὰ ἐγκλήματα.   διὰ
τοῦτο μέντοι κἂν τῷ νόμῳ τῆς λέπρας ὁ μέγας
πάντα Μωυσῆς τὴν μὲν κίνησιν καὶ ἐπὶ πλέον
αὐτῆς φορὰν καὶ χύσιν ἀκάθαρτον, τὴν δ' ἠρεμίαν
καθαρὰν ἀναγράφει· λέγει γὰρ ὅτι " ἐὰν διαχέηται
ἐν τῷ δέρματι, μιανεῖ ὁ ἱερεύς. ἐὰν δὲ κατὰ
χώραν μείνῃ τὸ τηλαύγημα καὶ μὴ διαχέηται,
καθαριεῖ." ὥστε τὴν μὲν ἡσυχίαν, ἐκ τοῦ[3] εἶναι
μονὴν κακιῶν καὶ παθῶν τῶν κατὰ ψυχήν,—

---

[1] So mss. Wendland needlessly changed to λόγῳ, *i.e.*
savagery must be eliminated by reason, but see *De Ebr.* 33.
[2] So Wendland conjectures, though he prints the ms. κατ'
αὐτούς. Grammatical usage seems to demand the change.
[3] Conj. Tr.: mss. ἐκτὸς : Wendland from Nicetes Serranus
(see App. p. 511) ἡσυχίαν καὶ μονήν.

that bite, unless they are going to bite, no wish to kill them would be felt by any right-minded person; for we must leave out of consideration the savagery which has a natural craving for indiscriminate slaughter. It is natural enough, then, 47 that the just man should appear to lay his curses on the grandson Canaan. I say "appear," because virtually he does curse his son Ham in cursing Canaan, since when Ham has been moved to sin, he himself becomes Canaan, for it is a single subject, wickedness, which is presented in two different aspects, rest and motion. But rest takes precedence in point of age to motion, and thus the moving stands to the stationary in the relation of child to parent. Thus it agrees 48 with the verities of nature when Canaan or tossing is described as the son of Ham or quiescence, and this serves to shew the truth of what is said elsewhere, "visiting the iniquities of the fathers upon the children unto the third and fourth generation" (Exod. xx. 5). For it is upon the effects of our reasonings, what we may call their descendants, that punishments fall, while those reasonings taken by themselves go scot-free from arraignment, if no culpable action supervene. And there- 49 fore, too, in the law of leprosy Moses with his never-failing greatness lays down that the movement and wider extension and diffusion of the disease is unclean, but the quiescence is clean. For he says, "if it spread abroad in the skin, the priest shall pronounce him unclean. But if the bright spot stay in one place and be not spread abroad, he shall pronounce him clean" (Lev. xiii. 22, 23). Thus the state of repose, because it is a standing-still of the vices and passions in the soul (and it is these which

469

ταῦτα γὰρ αἰνίττεται διὰ τῆς λέπρας—οὐχ ὑπαίτιον
εἶναι, τὴν δὲ κίνησιν καὶ φορὰν ὕποχον δεόντως.
50   τὸ παραπλήσιον καὶ ἐν τοῖς περὶ τῆς
τοῦ παντὸς γενέσεως¹ χρησθεῖσι λογίοις περιέχεται
σημειωδέστερον· λέγεται γὰρ πρὸς τὸν φαῦλον¹
ὦ οὗτος, " ἥμαρτες, ἡσύχασον," τοῦ μὲν ἁμαρτάνειν, ὅτι κινεῖσθαι καὶ ἐνεργεῖν κατὰ τὴν κακίαν
ἦν, ὄντος ἐνόχου, τοῦ δ' ἡσυχάζειν, ὅτι ἴσχεσθαι
καὶ ἠρεμεῖν, ἀνυπαιτίου καὶ σωτηρίου.
51 XI. Ταῦτα μὲν οὖν ἱκανῶς γε, οἶμαι, προείρηται.
τὰς δ' ἀρὰς [ἔχοντα]², ὃν ἔχουσι λόγον, ἴδωμεν·
" ἐπικατάρατος " φησί " Χαναάν· παῖς οἰκέτης
ἔσται τοῖς ἀδελφοῖς αὐτοῦ" καὶ " εὐλογητὸς
κύριος ὁ θεὸς Σήμ, καὶ ἔσται Χαναὰν δοῦλος
52 αὐτοῖς." ἔφαμεν πάλαι, ὅτι Σὴμ ἐπώνυμός ἐστιν
ἀγαθοῦ, καλούμενος οὐκ ὀνόματος εἴδει, ἀλλ' ὅλον
τὸ γένος αὐτοῦ ὄνομα, παρόσον τὸ ἀγαθὸν ὀνομα-
στὸν μόνον καὶ εὐφημίας καὶ εὐκλείας ἄξιον, ὡς
ἔμπαλιν ἀνώνυμον καὶ δυσώνυμον τὸ κακόν.
53 τίνος οὖν τὸν τῆς φύσεως τἀγαθοῦ μεμοιραμένον
εὐχῆς ἀξιοῖ; τίνος; καινοτάτης καὶ παρηλλαγ-

---

¹ Wendland πρὸς τὸν Κάιν, and αὐτὸν for τὸν φαῦλον. See
App. p. 511.
² For the meaningless ἔχοντα, ἑξῆς or ἐχομένως or εὐχάς τε
have been suggested. The last suits the sense well, as the
sequel deals with the blessing more than the curses. The
Translator suggests as better accounting for the corruption
τὰς δ' ἀρὰς ⟨καὶ τὰ μὴ ἀρὰς⟩ ἔχοντα.

ᵃ See App. p. 511.
ᵇ In the lxx, as usually and rightly printed, ἥμαρτες is
the apodosis of οὐκ ἐὰν ὀρθῶς προσενέγκῃς, ὀρθῶς δὲ μὴ διέλῃς.
Philo here and in De Mut. 195, takes it as beginning a
fresh sentence. Cf. De Agr. 127. So in Quaest. Gen. i.
64, 65 " Quid est, non quod non recte offeras, sed quod recte
non dividas ? . . . Quid est ' peccasti, quiesce ' ? "

are figured by leprosy), is exempt from indictment, while the state of motion and progression is rightly held liable to arraignment. And a 50 similar lesson is contained in a more striking form in the oracles in Genesis.[a] For God says to the wicked one, "man, thou hast sinned, be still "[b] (Gen. iv. 7). This implies that while sin, inasmuch as it is movement and activity with vice as its motive, is liable to punishment, stillness, because it is stationary and quiescent, is exempt from arraignment and a means of safety.

XI. This is enough, I think, by way of preface. 51 Let us now observe the form which the curses take. "Cursed," he says, " is Canaan ; a servant, a bondman, shall he be to his brethren," and " blessed is the Lord, the God of Shem,[a] and Canaan shall be their slave." We have said before [c] that Shem bears 52 a name which means " good," that is to say, the name which he bears is not any specific name or noun, but is just " name," the whole genus, thus representing good, because good alone is a thing of name and is worthy of fair speech and fair report, just as bad on the other hand is nameless and of evil name.[d] What, then, is the prayer 53 which Moses deems worthy of this participant in the nature of the good ? What indeed ? Surely a prayer unparalleled and unprecedented, to which

[c] Probably, as Adler suggests, in the lost discourse on Noah's " nakedness." See Introduction to *De Ebr.* p. 309.

[d] *i.e.* Shem is by interpretation ὄνομα, which may mean either " name " or " noun." In either case as representing the generic as opposed to the specific names or nouns, it is equivalent to the best of the genus. *Cf.* a similar argument, *Leg. All.* iii. 175. See App. p. 512.

471

μένης, ᾗ θνητὸς οὐδεὶς ὑπηρετῆσαι δυνατός, ἀφ'
ἧς σχεδὸν ὥσπερ ἀπ' ὠκεανοῦ ῥέουσιν αἱ ἄφθονοι
καὶ ἀέναοι πλημμυροῦσαι καὶ ἀναχεόμεναι τῶν
καλῶν πηγαί. τὸν γὰρ κύριον καὶ θεὸν τοῦ τε
κόσμου καὶ τῶν ἐν αὐτῷ πάντων ἰδίᾳ θεὸν κατ'
54 ἐξαίρετον χάριν τοῦ Σὴμ ἀνακαλεῖ. καὶ ὅρα·
τίνας ὑπερβολὰς τοῦτο οὐχ ὑπερβάλλει; σχεδὸν
γὰρ ἰσότιμος ὁ τούτου λαχὼν γίνεται κόσμῳ· ὅτε
γὰρ τὸ ἐπιστατοῦν καὶ κηδόμενον ἀμφοῖν ταὐτόν,
καὶ τὰ ἐπιτροπευόμενα κατ' ἀναγκαῖον εὐθύς ἐστιν
55 ἰσότιμα.   μήποτε δὲ καὶ ἐπιδαψιλεύεται
τὰ τῶν δωρεῶν· τοῦ μὲν γὰρ | αἰσθητοῦ κόσμου
[401] δεσπότης καὶ εὐεργέτης ἀνείρηται διὰ τοῦ κύριος
καὶ θεός, τοῦ δὲ νοητοῦ ἀγαθοῦ σωτὴρ καὶ εὐεργέτης αὐτὸ μόνον, οὐχὶ δεσπότης ἢ κύριος· φίλον
γὰρ τὸ σοφὸν θεῷ μᾶλλον ἢ δοῦλον. παρὸ καὶ
56 σαφῶς ἐπὶ Ἀβραὰμ φάσκει· '' μὴ ἐπικαλύψω ἐγὼ
ἀπὸ Ἀβραὰμ τοῦ φίλου μου;'' ὁ δὲ ἔχων τὸν
κλῆρον τοῦτον πέραν ὅρων ἀνθρωπίνης εὐδαιμονίας
προελήλυθε· μόνος γὰρ εὐγενὴς ἅτε θεὸν ἐπιγεγραμ-
μένος πατέρα καὶ γεγονὼς εἰσποιητὸς αὐτῷ μόνος
υἱός· οὐ πλούσιος, ἀλλὰ πάμπλουτος, ἐν ἀφθόνοις
καὶ γνησίοις, οὐ χρόνῳ παλαιουμένοις, καινουμέ-
57 νοις δὲ καὶ ἡβῶσιν ἀεὶ τρυφῶν ἀγαθοῖς μόνοις· οὐκ
ἔνδοξος, ἀλλ' εὐκλεής, τὸν μὴ κολακείᾳ νοθούμενον,
ἀλλὰ βεβαιούμενον ἀληθείᾳ καρπούμενος ἔπαινον·
μόνος βασιλεύς, παρὰ τοῦ πανηγεμόνος λαβὼν τῆς
ἐφ' ἅπασιν ἀρχῆς τὸ κράτος ἀνανταγώνιστον· μόνος

ᵃ The lxx has " My servant " (τοῦ παιδός μου), which
Philo uses in *Leg. All.* iii. 27. The Hebrew has no equivalent. See App. p. 512.
ᵇ See App. p. 512.

no mortal can act as ministrant, a prayer from which, almost as though it were from the very ocean, there pour forth fountains of things excellent, welling up and running over, unmeasured and inexhaustible. It is the Lord and God of the world and all that is therein, whom he declares to be peculiarly the God of Shem by special grace. And 54 consider! What transcendency is not here transcended? For we may well say that he to whom this belongs is put on a level of value with the world ; since when the same power rules and cares for both, the objects of this guardianship must needs by that very fact be of equal value.   Surely, too, 55 His gifts are such as shew a lavish hand. For while the words " Lord and God " proclaim Him master and benefactor of the world which is open to our senses, to that goodness which our minds perceive He is saviour and benefactor only, not master or lord. For wisdom is rather God's friend than His servant. And therefore He says plainly of Abraham, " shall I hide anything from Abraham My friend ? " [a] 56 (Gen. xviii. 17). But he who has this portion has passed beyond the bounds of human happiness. He alone is nobly born,[b] for he has registered God as his father and become by adoption His only son, the possessor not of riches, but of all riches, faring sumptuously where there is nought but good things, unstinted in number and sterling in worth, which alone wax not old through time, but ever renew their youth ; not merely of high repute, but glorious, for 57 he reaps the praise which is never debased by flattery, but ratified by truth ; sole king, for he has received from the All-ruler the sceptre of universal sovereignty, which none can dispute ; sole freeman,

ἐλεύθερος, ἀφειμένος ἀργαλεωτάτης δεσποίνης,
κενῆς δόξης, ἣν ὑπέραυχον οὖσαν ἀπὸ τῆς ἀκρο-
πόλεως ἄνωθεν ὁ ἐλευθεροποιὸς καθεῖλε θεός.

58   τούτῳ δὴ τῷ τοσούτων καὶ οὕτως
ὑπερβαλλόντων καὶ ἀθρόων ἀξιωθέντι ἀγαθῶν τί
προσήκει ποιεῖν ἢ λόγοις καὶ ᾠδαῖς καὶ ὕμνοις τὸν
εὐεργέτην ἀμείβεσθαι; τοῦτ' ἔσθ', ὡς ἔοικεν, ὃ
αἰνίττεται διὰ τοῦ[1] " εὐλογημένος κύριος ὁ θεὸς
Σήμ," ἐπειδὴ τῷ τὸν θεὸν ἔχοντι κλῆρον εὐλογεῖν
καὶ ἐπαινεῖν αὐτὸν ἁρμόττει μόνον τοῦτ' ἀντιπαρασχεῖν δυναμένῳ, τὰ δ' ἄλλα ἀνὰ κράτος πάνθ'
ἁπλῶς ἀδυνατοῦντι.

59   XII. Τῷ μὲν δὴ Σὴμ εὔχεται ταῦτα· τῷ δ'
Ἰάφεθ ὁποῖα, θεασώμεθα· " πλατύναι " φησίν
" ὁ θεὸς τῷ Ἰάφεθ, καὶ κατοικησάτω ἐν τοῖς
οἴκοις τοῦ Σήμ, καὶ γενέσθω Χαναὰν δοῦλος
60 αὐτοῖς." τοῦ ἀγαθὸν ἡγουμένου τὸ καλὸν μόνον
ἔσταλται καὶ συνῆκται τὸ τέλος—ἑνὶ γὰρ μυρίων
ὄντων τῶν περὶ ἡμᾶς τῷ ἡγεμόνι νῷ συνέζευκ-
ται—, τοῦ δὲ τρισὶν ἐφαρμόζοντος αὐτὸ γένεσιν, τῷ
περὶ ψυχήν, τῷ περὶ σῶμα, τῷ περὶ τὰ ἐκτός,
ἅτ' εἰς πολλὰ καὶ ἀνόμοια κατακερματιζόμενον
61 εὐρύνεται. διόπερ οἰκείως εὔχεται τούτῳ προσ-
γενέσθαι πλάτος, ὅπως καὶ ταῖς περὶ ψυχὴν
ἀρεταῖς, φρονήσει καὶ σωφροσύνῃ καὶ ἑκάστῃ τῶν
ἄλλων, χρῆσθαι δύναιτο καὶ ταῖς σώματος, ὑγείᾳ
καὶ εὐαισθησίᾳ δυνάμει τε καὶ ῥώμῃ καὶ ταῖς
τούτων συγγενέσιν, ἔτι μέντοι καὶ τοῖς ἐκτὸς πλεον-

_____
[1] διὰ τοῦ] mss. αὐτοῦ or αὐτῷ : Mang. ἐν τῷ.

for he is released from the most tyrannous of mistresses, vain opinion, whom God the liberator has cast down from her citadel on the hill and humbled all her pride. What, then, of him who has 58 been deemed worthy of blessings so great, so transcendent, so multitudinous? What should he do but requite his Benefactor with the words of his lips with song and with hymn? That is, it seems, the inner meaning of the saying, " blessed be the Lord, the God of Shem."[a] For it is meet that he who has God for his heritage should bless and praise Him, since this is the only return that he can offer, and all else, strive as he will, is quite beyond his power.

XII. This then is Noah's prayer for Shem. Let 59 us now consider the nature of his prayer for Japhet. " May God widen for Japhet," he says, " and let him dwell in the houses of Shem, and let Canaan become their servant " (Gen. ix. 27). [a] If we hold 60 that moral beauty is the only good, the end we seek is contracted and narrowed, for it is bound up with only one of our myriad environments, namely, with the dominant principle, the mind. But if we connect that end with three different kinds of interests, the concerns of the soul, those of the body and those of the external world, the end is split up into many dissimilar parts and thus broadened. And therefore 61 there is a fitness in the prayer that breadth should be added to Japhet, that he may be able to use not only the virtues of the soul, prudence, temperance, and each of the others, but also those of the body, health, efficiency of the senses, dexterity of limb and strength of muscle, and such as are akin to these ; and once again that he may have all the external

[a] See App. p. 512.

PHILO

ἐκτήμασιν, ὅσα εἰς πλοῦτον καὶ δόξαν ἀπόλαυσίν
τε καὶ χρῆσιν τῶν ἀναγκαίων ἡδονῶν ἄγεται.[1] |

[402] XIII. Περὶ μὲν τοῦ πλάτους ταῦτα. τίνα δὲ ἐν
62 τοῖς οἴκοις εὔχεται τοῦ Σὴμ κατοικῆσαι, σκεπτέον·
σαφῶς γὰρ οὐ μεμήνυκεν. ἔνεστι μὲν δὴ φάναι,
ὅτι τὸν ἡγεμόνα τοῦ παντός. τίς γὰρ οἶκος παρὰ
γενέσει δύναιτ' ἂν ἀξιοπρεπέστερος εὑρεθῆναι
θεῷ πλὴν ψυχῆς τελείως κεκαθαρμένης καὶ μόνον
τὸ καλὸν ἡγουμένης ἀγαθόν, τὰ δὲ ἄλλα ὅσα
νενόμισται ἐν δορυφόρων καὶ ὑπηκόων λόγῳ
63 ταττούσης; κατοικεῖν δὲ ἐν οἴκῳ λέγεται ὁ θεὸς
οὐχ ὡς ἐν τόπῳ—περιέχει γὰρ τὰ πάντα πρὸς
μηδενὸς περιεχόμενος—, ἀλλ' ὡς πρόνοιαν καὶ
ἐπιμέλειαν ἐκείνου τοῦ χωρίου διαφερόντως ποιού-
μενος· παντὶ γὰρ τῷ δεσπόζοντι οἰκίας ἡ ταύτης
64 κατὰ τὸ ἀναγκαῖον ἀνῆπται φροντίς. εὐχέσθω δὴ
πᾶς θεῷ, ὅτῳ τὸ θεοφιλὲς ὤμβρησεν ἀγαθόν,
οἰκήτορος λαχεῖν τοῦ πανηγεμόνος, ὃς τὸ βραχὺ
τοῦτο οἰκοδόμημα, τὸν νοῦν, ἐξαίρων εἰς ὕψος ἀπὸ
65 γῆς τοῖς οὐρανοῦ συνάψει πέρασι.   καὶ
τὸ ῥητὸν μέντοι συνᾴδειν ἔοικεν· ὁ γὰρ Σὴμ ὡσανεὶ
ῥίζα καλοκἀγαθίας ὑποβέβληται, δένδρον δ' ἡμερο-
τοκοῦν ἐκ ταύτης ὁ σοφὸς Ἀβραὰμ ἀνέδραμεν,
οὗ τὸ αὐτήκοον καὶ αὐτομαθὲς γένος, Ἰσαάκ, ὁ
καρπὸς ἦν, ἀφ' οὗ πάλιν αἱ διὰ πόνων ἀρεταὶ
κατασπείρονται, ὧν ἀθλητής ἐστιν ὁ τὴν πρὸς
πάθη πάλην γεγυμνασμένος Ἰακώβ, ἀγγέλοις

---

[1] Wendland suggests ἀναφέρεται.

476

advantages which have their source in wealth and reputation and the means of enjoying and using such pleasures as are necessary.

XIII. So much for the " widening." But we must 62 also consider who is meant, when he prays that " he " should dwell in the houses of Shem. For this is not clearly shewn. On the one hand, we may suggest that " he " is the Ruler of the universe. For what more worthy house could be found for God throughout the whole world of creation, than a soul that is perfectly purified, which holds moral beauty to be the only good and ranks all others which are so accounted, as but satellites and subjects? But God 63 is said to inhabit a house not in the sense of dwelling in a particular place, for He contains all things and is contained by none, but in the sense that His special providence watches over and cares for that spot. For every master of a house must needs have the care of that house laid on him as a charge. Verily let 64 everyone on whom the goodness of God's love has fallen as rain, pray that he may have for his tenant the All-ruler who shall exalt this petty edifice, the mind, high above the earth and join it to the ends of heaven. And indeed the literal story 65 seems to agree with this interpretation. For in Shem we have the foundation, the root, as it were, of noble qualities and from that root sprung up wise Abraham, a tree yielding sweet nutriment, and his fruit was Isaac, the nature that needs no voice to teach him but his own, and from Isaac's seed again come the virtues of the laborious life in which Jacob exercised himself to mastery, Jacob trained in the wrestling-bout with the passions, with the angels of

66 ἀλείπταις, λόγοις, χρώμενος. οὗτος τῶν δώδεκα κατάρχει φυλῶν, ἃς οἱ χρησμοὶ " βασίλειον καὶ ἱεράτευμα θεοῦ " φασιν εἶναι κατὰ τὴν πρὸς τὸν πρῶτον Σὴμ ἀκολουθίαν[1] οὗ τοῖς οἴκοις ἦν εὐχὴ τὸν θεὸν ⟨ἐν⟩οικῆσαι· βασίλειον γὰρ ὁ βασιλέως δήπουθεν οἶκος, ἱερὸς ὄντως καὶ μόνος ἄσυλος.

67 Ἴσως μέντοι τὰ τῆς εὐχῆς καὶ ἐπὶ τὸν Ἰάφεθ ἀναφέρεται, ὅπως ἐν τοῖς οἴκοις τοῦ Σὴμ ποιῆται τὰς διατριβάς· τῷ γὰρ καὶ τὰ σώματος καὶ τὰ ἐκτὸς πλεονεκτήματα ἀγαθὰ ἡγουμένῳ καλὸν εὔξασθαι πρὸς μόνον τὸ ψυχῆς ἀναδραμεῖν καὶ μὴ μέχρι τοῦ παντὸς αἰῶνος ἀληθοῦς δόξης διαμαρτεῖν, ἃ κοινὰ καὶ τῶν ἐπαρατοτάτων καὶ κακίστων ἐστίν, ὑγίειαν ἢ πολυχρηματίαν ἢ ὅσα ὁμοιότροπα, νομίσαντα εἶναι ἀγαθά, τῆς ἀψευδοῦς τῶν ἀγαθῶν μερίδος οὐδενὶ φαύλῳ συντατομένης· ἀκοινώνητον

68 γὰρ φύσει κακῷ τὸ ἀγαθόν. διὰ τοῦτ' ἐν ψυχῇ μόνῃ τεθησαύρισται, ἧς τοῦ κάλλους οὐδενὶ μέτεστι τῶν ἀφρόνων.   τοῦτο ὅ γε προ⟨φητικὸς⟩ λόγος[2] τὸν σπουδαῖον ἔγραψεν[3] εὔχεσθαί τινι τῶν ἑαυτοῦ γνωρίμων λέγοντα " πρὸς μὲ ἀνάστρεψον,"

[403] ἵνα ἐπὶ τὴν αὐτοῦ γνώμην ἐπανελθών, | τὸ καλὸν ὡς ἀγαθὸν μόνον δεξιωσάμενος, τὰς τῶν ἑτερο-

---

[1] Wendland changed this to εὐλογίαν, but the ms. reading makes quite fair sense.

[2] So Cohn and Wendland. The πρόλογος of the mss. does not make sense. For the correction cf. De Plant. 117.

[3] mss. ἔγραψε μὲν: Wendland suggests τῶν σπουδαίων ἔγραψεν ἕνα.

---

[a] Or "God's thought," the Divine Logos being here regarded as plural. The allusion is to Gen. xxxii. 1, "The angels of God met him," which comes shortly before the story of the wrestling in verses 24 f.

478

reason [a] to prepare him for the conflict. Once more 66
Jacob is the source of the twelve tribes, of whom
the oracles say that they are " the palace and priesthood of God " (Exod. xix. 6),[b] thus following in due
sequence the thought originated in Shem, in whose
houses it was prayed that God might dwell. For
surely by " palace " is meant the King's house,
which is holy indeed and the only inviolable sanctuary.

Perhaps, however, the words of the prayer refer 67
to Japhet also, that he may make the houses of Shem
his resort. For it is well to pray on behalf of him
who holds bodily and external advantages to be
forms of the good, that he should return to one only,
even that which belongs to the soul, and not throughout his whole life fail to gain the true conception,
nor think that health or wealth or the like, which
are shared by the most wicked and abominable of
men, are true goods. No, such participation in the
good as is real and true is never found in association
with what is worthless, for good by its very nature
can have no partnership with evil. And that is why 68
this treasure is laid up in one place only—the soul—
for in beauty of soul none of the foolish has part or
lot.   This is the prayer which the prophetic scripture declares should be the prayer of
the man of worth for anyone [c] of those who are his
familiars—even " return to me " (Gen. xlix. 22)—
the prayer that he may return to the mind of him
who prays, and, welcoming moral beauty as the only
good, leave behind him in the race those conceptions

[b] In the LXX βασιλεῖον ἱεράτευμα, where βασιλεῖον no doubt
means " royal." Philo's interpretation is, however, gram-
matically possible.
[c] Or " describes the man of worth as praying for one "
etc.

δόξων παραδράμῃ περὶ τἀγαθοῦ φήμας. ἐν οὖν
τοῖς οἴκοις τῆς ψυχῆς τοῦ λέγοντος μόνον εἶναι τὸ
καλὸν ἀγαθὸν κατοικησάτω, παροικήσας ἐν τοῖς
τῶν ἑτέρων, οἷς καὶ τὰ σωματικὰ καὶ τὰ ἐκτὸς
τετίμηται.

69 Εἰκότως μέντοι καὶ δοῦλον τὸν ἄφρονα τῶν
ἀρετῆς μεταποιουμένων ἀνέγραψεν, ἵν' ἢ κρείττονος ἐπιστασίας ἀξιωθεὶς ἀμείνονι βίῳ χρήσηται
ἢ ἐπιμένων τῷ ἀδικεῖν μετ' εὐμαρείας αὐτο-
κράτορι ἡγεμόνων ἀρχῇ τῶν δεσποτῶν κολάζηται.

of the good which are voiced by the perversely minded. Let him then dwell in the houses of the soul of him who holds that moral beauty is the only good, and merely sojourn in the houses of the others, who value also bodily and external things.

One point further. It is with good reason that 69 Moses writes down the fool as the slave of them who lay claim to virtue, either that promoted to serve under a higher control he may lead a better life, or that, if he cling to his iniquity, his masters may chastise him at their pleasure with the absolute authority which they wield as rulers.

APPENDIX TO
QUOD DEUS SIT IMMUTABILIS

§ 3. *Bounds which the lustral water has consecrated.* For this use of περιρραντήρια see *De Cher.* 96 (and footnote). Below (8) it is used for the purification itself, as in *Quod Det.* 20.

§ 6. *I give him to thee a gift.* The stress which Philo lays on δίδωμι and δοτόν suggests that he had in mind a different version of the text from that of the LXX, where, though in v. 27 we have " the Lord *gave* me my request," v. 28 runs " I lend him (κιχρῶ) to the Lord, a loan (χρῆσιν) to the Lord."

§ 14. *Multiplied a thousand-fold.* For this way of taking μυρία (as sing. fem.) it may be argued that it follows up the thought of ἡ δὲ πολλή. On the other hand the words may be a reminiscence of *Theaetetus* 156 A, where Plato, speaking of the product of the union of τὸ ποιεῖν with τὸ πάσχειν, says γίνεται ἔκγονα πλήθει ἄπειρα, in which case it would be better to take μυρία as plur. neut.

§ 18. *Some future pleasure.* A hit at the Epicureans; see note on *Quod Det.* 157 ; *cf.* also *S. V.F.* iii. 21.

§ 22. *Indeed some maintain,* etc. Evidently this refers to the Stoic doctrine of the constancy of the Sage ; see quotation from Stobaeus in *S. V.F.* iii. 548, particularly the words οὐδὲ μεταβάλλεσθαι δὲ κατ' οὐδένα τρόπον οὐδὲ μετατίθεσθαι οὐδὲ σφάλλεσθαι.

§ 24. *Like a lyre.* For the figure *cf. De Sacr.* 37. There is a hint of this thought (which should be distinguished from that of the soul as a *harmony*) in *Rep.* 554 F and *Laws* 653 B.

Ibid. The insertion suggested by Wendland is also advocated by him in *De Ebr.* 6. But though easy enough it is not required, and would be impossible in *Quis Rer. Div. Her.*

PHILO

207 ff. where τὴν τῶν ἐναντίων ἐπιστήμην is followed by a long excursus showing the universality of opposites and noting that the doctrine was taught by Heraclitus.

§ 27. *So for example.* οὕτως, which otherwise seems rather otiose, is perhaps used in the same idiomatic way as in Plato and elsewhere = " without more ado " *i.e.* " we often *just* turn from them."

§ 31. *Time.* These two sections are reminiscent of *Timaeus* 37-38 B, though there time is represented as coming into existence *with* the universe.

§ 32. *The archetype and pattern of time.* So in *Timaeus* 37 D " so he bethought him to make a moving image of eternity (εἰκὼ κινητὸν αἰῶνος) . . . moving according to number, even that which we have called time"; 38 B time was made after the pattern of the eternal nature (κατὰ τὸ παράδειγμα τῆς διαιωνίας φύσεως).

§ 34. *Thought quiescent in the mind.* This definition of ἔννοια as ἀποκειμένη νόησις is Stoic (*S.V.F.* ii. 847). The definition of διανόησις as " thought brought to an issue " or " working out of the thought " is perhaps invented by Philo to fit the διενοήθη of his text. He means presumably that an ἔννοια becomes a διανόησις when it becomes the subject of active deliberation.

§ 43. *Like a ring . . . it stamps.* There seems some confusion here between the imprint and the power which makes it. This might perhaps be avoided by taking ἑκάστη τῶν αἰσθήσεων as subject to ἐναπεμάξατο.

§ 44. *Sometimes of an appropriate kind.* Cf. Plut. *Adv. Coloten* 1122 c τὸ δὲ ὁρμητικὸν ἐγειρόμενον ὑπὸ τοῦ φανταστικοῦ πρὸς τὰ οἰκεῖα πρακτικῶς κινεῖ τὸν ἄνθρωπον. In adding to " sometimes the reverse," " *this* condition of the soul is called ὁρμή," Philo seems to be writing rather loosely, for when the impression is contrary to the nature of the animal, the resulting impulse was called ἀφορμή (aversion); see *S.V.F.* iii. 169.

Ibid. First movement. Another name for ὁρμή is φορὰ διανοίας ἐπί τι, while an ἀφορμή is φορὰ διανοίας ἀπό τινος. In using the phrase πρώτη κίνησις, which does not seem to appear elsewhere in our sources, Philo is perhaps thinking of the πρώτη ὁρμή of animals defined as the instinct of self-preservation; see Diog. Laert. vii. 88.

§ 46. *Mind is the sight of the soul.* So Aristot. *Top.* 17,

484

APPENDICES

p. 108 a, 11 ὡς ὄψις ἐν ὀφθάλμῳ νοῦς ἐν ψυχῇ, cf. Eth. Nic. i. 6, p. 1096 b 28. The saying is, however, older than Aristotle, who quotes as example of a metaphor from some unknown writer or speaker ὁ θεὸς φῶς ἀνῆψεν ἐν τῇ ψυχῇ (Rhet. iii. 10. 7, p. 1411 b, 73).

Ibid. Something better and purer. i.e. the πέμπτη οὐσία, an idea which, originally Pythagorean, was adopted by Aristotle. Cf. Reid on Cic. Acad. i. 26. It is definitely referred to under that name by Philo, Quis Rer. Div. Her. 283.

§ 53. Laws in the proper sense of the word. Because νόμος is used in a wider sense for custom and the like. So in De Praemiis 55 νόμος δὲ οὐδέν ἐστιν ἢ λόγος προστάττων ἃ χρὴ καὶ ἀπαγορεύων ἃ μὴ χρή.

Ibid. Leading statements. Or perhaps " principles." Cf. 62. Philo can hardly have regarded Balaam's words in Num. xxiii. 19 as being part of the actual legislation. He thinks of them rather as summing up the ideas upon which the law is based. Thus, in a parallel use of the two texts in De Som. i. 237, they are called " the sole two ways of all the legislation." Every command or prohibition appeals either to love or fear.

§ 57. Out of care for health. Cf. Aristot. Phys. ii. 3, p. 194 b 32 τοῦτο δ᾿ ἐστὶ τὸ οὗ ἕνεκα, οἷον τοῦ περιπατεῖν ἡ ὑγίεια. διὰ τί γὰρ περιπατεῖ; φαμὲν ἵνα ὑγιείη.

§ 59. The reading ἀποπατεῖ might seem to be supported by De Plant. 35. But not only are the terms used for the excretory process less offensive there, but any such meaning is practically given here clearly enough by καὶ τἆλλα . . . εἴποιμι. Wendland ultimately (Rhein. Mus. 82, p. 480) proposed παύεται, ἀποπαυσάμενος δὲ, but the ms. ἀποπαύεται is quite tenable.

§ 62. As the heavens or the universe. This is partly at least aimed at the Stoics, see Diog. Laert. vii. 148 (S.V.F. i. 164) where Zeno, Chrysippus, and Posidonius are all credited with holding τὸν ὅλον κόσμον καὶ τὸν οὐρανον as being οὐσίαν θεοῦ. Cf. ib. vii. 137.

§§ 65 ff. The thought of these sections has already been brought out in De Cher. 15, but with a different purpose. There it was used to illustrate the truth that the motive of the doer determines whether his action is right or wrong, here to show that falsehood may often be salutary to the

485

PHILO

person to whom it is said. In the note on *De Cher.* 15 it was pointed out that the thought might be drawn from *Rep.* 389 B. It should be added that it was adopted by the Stoics, see *S.V.F.* iii. 554, 555, where the cases of deceiving the sick and the enemy are specially mentioned.

§ 66. *He will gladly endure.* If the MS. reading is retained and ἄσμενος is taken with ἀπερεῖ, we must understand the latter as = " declines " and might translate the former by " only too gladly." But the thought is strange. Wendland suggests removing ἄσμενος to a later place in the sentence, but the slight alteration suggested seems to the translator simpler.

§§ 70-73. The argument in these sections is very strange. The discussion in 51-69 would naturally lead up to the first explanation given in *Quaest. Gen.* i. 95 that the words " I was wroth because I made them " is a hyperbolical way of saying that the sins of men grew so great that they might be expected to anger even Him who knew no anger. But the explanation here given, which appears in an even less intelligible form in the *Quaest.*, is something different. Philo seems to take the words as meaning " it was in anger that I made them," and to explain them in the sense that since when men do evil, it is due to anger (and similar passions), and since the creation of men has actually resulted in evil, the creation may be said to be due to God's anger. But not only is the explanation exceedingly strained, it can only be got by using ὅτι in a way not known to those " who settle Hoti's business." The suggestion that by putting ἐθυμώθην before ὅτι ἐποίησα instead of after it the writer meant to indicate that the wrath was coincident with the creation, instead of after it, is still wilder. There is a strong likeness, which may only be superficial, to *Leg. All.* ii. 78.

§ 78. *A condensed mass of ether.* Cf. *De Cher.* 26, where the sun is φλογὸς πίλημα πολλῆς. That αἰθέριον means " of ether " not " in ether " is shown by Plut. *Mor.* 928 C (*S.V.F.* ii. 668). " The Stoics say that τοῦ αἰθέρος τὸ μὲν αὐγοειδὲς . . . οὐρανὸν γεγονέναι, τὸ δὲ πυκνωθὲν καὶ συνειληθὲν ἄστρα." So ps.-Justin, *Quaest. et Resp. ad Graecos* 172 C ὁ ἥλιος πίλημα αἰθεροειδὲς τῇ οὐσίᾳ.

§ 79. *Friend and kinsman.* Cf. *Timaeus*, 45 B, c, where the fire in the eyes is called ἀδελφόν to that of the daylight

APPENDICES

and forms with it ἐν σῶμα οἰκειωθέν, whence vision is produced.

§ 84. *For the breath,* etc. This is the Stoic theory of hearing, *cf.* Diog. Laert. vii. 158 (*S. V.F.* ii. 872) : " We hear when the air between the sonant body and the organ of hearing suffers concussion " (πληττόμενον) (Hicks's translation). Also the definition in *S. V.F.* ii. 836 ἀκοὴ δὲ πνεῦμα διατεῖνον ἀπὸ τοῦ ἡγεμονικοῦ μεχρὶς ὤτων. For πλήξας *cf.* the derivation commonly given by ancient philologists, " verbum ab aere verberato."

Ibid. For the consonance. One may suspect that for γάρ we should read δέ or καί, as we seem to have a second reason for the view that " we hear through a dyad," founded apparently on *Timaeus* 80 B, where the two different notes μίαν ἐξ ὀξείας καὶ βαρείας ξυνεκεράσαντο πάθην.

§ 89. Philo's interpretation of the Nazarite vow has already been partially given in *Leg. All.* i. 17. When the Nazarite lets his hair grow, it signifies the growth of virtuous thoughts. The contact with the corpse which defiles the Nazarite and interrupts his vow is that temporary contact with spiritual death which may befall even the good. The hair is cut off, that is, the good thoughts are forgotten, but they will grow again. We find again what we have lost and the days of defection are blotted out.

§ 92. *Asked him . . . of the source of his knowledge.* The genitive (of the subject of the question) after πυνθάνομαι is certainly strange. If we accept " the father of his knowledge " we must suppose that Philo thinks of a father as being the father of the son's qualities. Cohn compares " the grandfather of his education," *De Sacr.* 43, where see note, and also *De Som.* i. 47 ὁ πάππος αὐτοῦ τῆς ἐπιστήμης.

§ 97. *Miserable are those.* This thought of the fruitlessness of effort, where ability is wanting, has been worked out more fully in *De Sacr.* 113-117. There, however, one important exception is made. In 115 Philo laid down that moral effort is never wasted. He does not deny this here but confines himself to the practical and intellectual life.

§ 100. *Achieve righteousness.* A καθῆκον or common duty does not become a κατόρθωμα unless done with a right motive and perhaps not even then, unless it is part of a generally virtuous course of conduct ; see Zeller, *Stoics,* p. 265.

PHILO

§ 101. ⟨τῶν⟩. This insertion turns this difficult sentence into good sense, *i.e.* to pay a large sum duly, unless it is done willingly, shows no more real honesty than the admittedly dishonest course of paying some small deposit in the hope of inducing the depositor to entrust some large sum, which the person thus trusted will be able to embezzle. This "confidence trick" has been already mentioned in *De Cher.* 14, and appears again in *De Plant.* 101. In the absence of any complete banking-system, the depositing of property with individuals and their honesty and dishonesty in discharging the debt played a great part in commercial life.

§ 108. ἥτις . . . ἑαυτῇ. The correction suggested in the footnote has this advantage over Wendland's that the scribe is more likely to have been misled by the repeated χαρίτων than by the repeated τῶν, and that αὐτή is a less violent change from ἑαυτῇ than πηγή. For the thought that the ἀγαθότης is itself a χάρις *cf. Leg. All.* iii. 78, where the ἀγαθότης καὶ χάρις is said to be the ἀρχὴ γενέσεως. For the coupling of πρεσβυτάτη with χάρις *cf. De Cong.* 38.

§§ 111-116. This allegory is evidently founded on Gen. xxxix., where in verse 1 of the LXX Potiphar is described as a chief cook and eunuch, while in verse 21 Joseph is said to find favour with the chief gaoler. Philo, of course, takes great liberties with the story, making Joseph an eunuch himself and ignoring the statement that it was the Lord who gave him this favour with the gaoler. Presumably he is so anxious to get an antithesis to Noah's finding favour with God, that he seizes on these words in verse 21, couples them with the convenient parts of the story, viz. that the person who found favour with the gaoler was the slave of the eunuch and instrument of pleasure, and ignores all the rest. It may be said in excuse that by so ignoring them he manages to find a text for a very impressive sermon.

§ 111. [σύλλογοι καί]. σύλλογοι is coupled with ἐκκλησία in *De Som.* ii. 184 (a closely parallel passage), *cf.* also *Leg. All.* iii. 81. But "meetings" or "gatherings" does not fit in well with μελετῶνται, and Wendland (who also suggests διάλογοι) may be right in omitting the words. It should be noted, however, that the phrase σύλλογοι καὶ λόγοι ἐγίγνοντο κατὰ τὴν ἀγοράν, *i.e.* gatherings and conversations after the assembly had broken up, actually occurs in Dem. *De Falsa Leg.* 133. Philo, who often shows a close acquaintance

488

with Demosthenes, may have adopted the phrase, though somewhat straining it. If the words are retained we might translate " it is ever the practice to meet and talk of virtue."

§ 129. *Does not use it as its pilot.* Philo has evidently in his mind the similar but much more elaborate parable in *Rep.* 488 B-489 c, where the pilot is the true philosopher, and the inexperienced sailor the politicians, who obtain the mastery of the ship.

§ 135. *Defiles all these.* Philo again treats his text in a very arbitrary way. Instead of the things being cleared out, before the priest enters, to prevent their defilement, they are cleared out because they are defiled.

§§ 155 and 156. The contrast between the earthly and the heavenly goods is expressed in the allegory of the well-water and the rain. The former is earthly, scanty, obtained by labour ; the latter heavenly, abundant, and showered on us without effort of our own. To labour for the former is an ἔργον δυσελπιστίας because it shows that we lack the higher hope. For δυσελπιστία cf. *Leg. All.* iii. 164. Elsewhere, as in *De Post.* 136 ff. and *De Ebr.* 112 ff., the figure of the well calls up more favourable ideas to Philo.

§§ 162-165. Here we have, of course, Aristotle's doctrine of the Mean, cf. particularly *Eth. Nic.* ii. 6 and 7, where both Philo's first two examples are given. *Cf. De Mig.* 147, where the doctrine is ascribed to the " gentle and sociable philosophy," meaning apparently the Peripatetic.

§ 167. *Its essential nature.* Observe how closely this peculiarly Aristotelian expression (τὸ τί ἦν εἶναι) follows on the Aristotelian doctrine of the Mean.

§ 176. *The best of constitutions, democracy.* Philo several times speaks in this way of democracy (*De Agr.* 45, *De Conf.* 108, *De Abr.* 242, *De Spec. Leg.* iv. 237, *De Virt.* 180). In three of these places he contrasts it with ochlocracy, or mob-rule, while in *De Conf.* he gives as its ruling characteristic that it honours equality. He does not seem to have got this view, at any rate of the name democracy, from the schools. Neither Plato nor Aristotle speak of it with such favour, and the Stoics held that the best form of government was a mixture of democracy, aristocracy and monarchy (Diog. Laert. vii. 131). Here apparently the democracy which the world enjoys consists in each getting its turn.

489

APPENDIX TO *DE AGRICULTURA*

§ 13. *But contribute nothing to the improvement of character.* The ὅσα implies that some parts of dialectic and mathematics do contribute something. With regard to dialectic, this is explained in the sequel. With regard to " geometry," apart from its use as a προπαιδευμα, Philo would probably have held that, as it included arithmetic, the lore of sacred numbers gave it a higher and spiritual value. This appears very markedly in the disquisition on Four in this treatise.

§ 14. *With its threefold division.* This fundamental Stoic doctrine is given in Diog. Laert. vii. 40, with the same illustration as here. Another comparison given there and elsewhere is to the egg-shell, the white and the yolk. See *Leg. All.* i. 57 and note.

§ 41. *They are the only real kings.* For this well-known Stoic paradox see *S. V.F.* iii. 617 ff.; *cf. De Sobr.* 57.

§ 43. *Uneven.* This word perhaps gives the idea better than " superfluous." περισσος is the regular name for " odd " numbers, *i.e.* those which are something over and above the right or even numbers (ἄρτιος). Other passages in which Jethro is described (*De Ebr.* 37 and *De Mut.* 103) were referred to in the note on *De Sacr.* 50, where, however, the translation " worldling " was perhaps too loose.

§ 73. οἰκόσιτος. Here and in *De Plant.* 104 Philo uses this word in a disparaging way, which does not appear in the examples quoted from other authors. Usually it means " living at his own expense." There is, however, an approach to it in Lucian, *Somn.* 1, where it is applied to a youth who is not yet earning his own living.

§ 80. *Sense-perception made pure and clean.* In *Leg. All.* ii. 66 and iii. 103, Miriam stood for rebellious sense.

§ 81. *So we find.* Here γοῦν as often introduces the scriptural story on which the allegory is founded, the main point of which is the concluding words " horse and rider he threw

490

into the sea." But there is also an allusion to the opening words, " Then sang Moses and *the sons of Israel*," which, as usual, he interprets as " those who see." The contrast, however, between " all the men " or " all that are men," and " *the best* women " is curious, for in Ex. xv. 20 *all* the women sing the song. Perhaps Philo's memory of the passage misled him.

§ 94. *For these are able*, etc. There seems to be an illogicality in the sequel. The prayer which follows is not as we should expect, that the horseman should be able to control the horse, but that he should fall off. The best one can make of it is that, though it is meritorious to control passion, complete safety lies in getting rid of it.

§§ 95 ff. The parable of Dan has already been worked out in *Leg. All.* ii. 94 ff. The principal difference is that there the way (which as here is distinguished from the track) is the soul itself, instead of the road on which the soul travels.

§ 114. *An iron-bound thong*. The use in boxing of the *caestus* or leathern thong loaded with lead or iron is best known from the description in *Aen*. v. 405 ff. Mr. Whitaker's ingenious suggestion of σιδηροῦν τροπόν for σιδήρου τρόπον (" like iron ") may perhaps be questioned on the ground that τροπός is the thong used for fastening the oar to the thole. But it may have been used more generally, and if so gives an excellent sense. The construction of the ordinary reading is not quite clear.—F. H. C.

§ 119. *The Olympic contest*, etc. Perhaps rather " the only Olympic contest which can be rightly called sacred is " etc. Philo plays on Ὀλυμπιακός (derived from Olympia) and Ὀλύμπιος (from Olympus).

§§ 128, 129. The view that God causes good only is often insisted on by Philo, *e.g. De Op*. 75, and *De Plant*. 53. The thought is Platonic; see *Timaeus*, 29, 30 and 40, 41, *Rep*. 379 B, C, and elsewhere.

§ 132. ὑπαναπλέουσαν. Mangey's conjecture of ἐπαναπολή-σαν has some support from *De Post*. 149 ἐκ τῆς ἐπαναπολήσεως καὶ ὥσπερ ἐπιλεάνσεως τῆς πρώτον καταβληθείσης τροφῆς. *Cf*. also ἀναπολῶν, *Spec. Leg*. iv. 107. On the other hand we have ὑπαναπλεῖ, *De Mut*. 100.

§ 134. *For what use is there* . . . " *partless* " ? The translation assumes that διαίρεσις is futile, because we ultimately arrive at a closed door. If we read ἀδιαίρετα, it is futile, because

PHILO

we *never* arrive at a point where division ceases. In this case Philo adopts the doctrine of the infinite divisibility of matter, which was generally held though not without controversy (see Reid on Cic. *Acad.* i. 27). The same sense might perhaps be obtained by retaining διαιρετά, and taking it as " never finding before you (as a result of your division) separate parts which are called atoms." It should be noted that this philosophical evidence of the futility of διαίρεσις is merely subsidiary. The true reason, *i.e.* its moral uselessness, if unaccompanied by meditation, is given in 135.

§§ 140, 141. The grammatical and logical terms of the Stoics, here given, are nearly all stated (generally under the same names) by Diog. Laert. vii. 64-76, with examples which explain their meaning clearly. These are here given for the cases in which explanation is needed (Hicks's translation is used throughout).

Complete (τέλεια, D.L. αὐτο-τελῆ)—	Incomplete (ἀτελῆ, D.L. ἐλλιπῆ)—
" Socrates writes."	" Writes," for we ask " who writes ? "
Questions (ἐρωτήματα)—	Inquiries (πύσματα)—
" Is it day ? "	" Where does he live ? " which cannot be answered, like the question, by a nod.
Simple propositions (ἀξιώματα ἁπλᾶ)—	Non-simple (οὐχ ἁπλᾶ)—
" It is day."	" If it is day, it is light."
Hypothetical (συνημμένα, as subdivision of the οὐχ ἁπλᾶ)—	Inferential (παρασυνημμένα)—
" If it is day, it is light."	" Since it is day, it is light."
Indicating more or less (τὰ διασαφοῦντα τὸ μᾶλλον καὶ ἧττον).	Disjunctive (διεζευγμένα)—
" It is rather daytime than night," or	" Either it is day or it is night."

Predicate (κατηγόρημα) was defined as " what is said of something " ; in other words, " a thing associated with one

492

or more subjects "; or " a defective expression which has to be joined on to a nominative case in order to yield a judgement " (ἀξίωμα).

Complements (συμβάματα). The words in D.L. which deal with this are corrupt. Apparently the term means a verb requiring a nominative subject, and therefore is identical with κατηγορήματα, according to the third definition given above. It is opposed to παρασυμβάματα, where the verb is impersonal and the real subject is in another case, as μεταμέλει μοι, " it repents me "=" I repent."

§ 142. *Smooth movement.* An Epicurean term (*cf.* note on *De Post.* 79), introduced here by Philo for a play on λειανούσῃ, and qualified by τῷ ὄντι to show that he uses it in a higher sense than the Epicureans.

§ 145. Heinemann proposed in preference to Wendland's suggestion καὶ γὰρ διαίρεσις ἄνευ μνήμης καὶ μελέτη ἄνευ διεξόδου τῶν ἀρίστων. No doubt μελέτη may be taken as the equivalent of μνήμη, but διέξοδος can hardly be equivalent to διαίρεσις. Perhaps the following adaptation of Wendland's might be read : καὶ γὰρ διαίρεσις ἄνευ μνήμης καὶ μελέτης καὶ διεξόδου τῶν ἀρίστων ἀγαθὸν ἀτελές, ⟨ὡσαύτως δὲ μνήμη ἄνευ διαιρέσεως ἀτελές⟩, in which the repetition of ἀτελές may have misled the scribe.

§ 160. *Solidity.* The term πῆξις is Stoic, see *S.V.F.* iii. 510. The life of ὁ προκόπτων only becomes really happy ὅταν αἱ μέσαι πράξεις . . . πῆξιν τινὰ λάβωσι.

§ 161. *Unconscious of their wisdom.* διαλεληθότες again is a Stoic term, though used rather of the fully wise, who do not yet realize their conversion, than, as here, of the man advancing to perfection ; see *S.V.F.* iii. 539, 540.

APPENDIX TO *DE PLANTATIONE*

§ 3. Mr. Whitaker had left " ride upon " for ὀχεῖσθαι, and this is the natural meaning of the word ; but the sequel shows that the fire rides upon the air, and the earth contains the water in its hollows (§ 10). At the same time the translation here substituted, " be held by," is not quite satisfactory. Probably ὀχεῖσθαι is corrupt. Some word indicating juxta-position (ὅμορον κεῖσθαι?) seems to be needed.—F. H. C.

§ 6. *Perfect parts.* Cf. *Quod Det.* 154 and note, in which the dependence of this thought on *Timaeus* 32 c was pointed out.

§ 10. *Masterpiece of literature.* Or perhaps " literature." It seems to the translators doubtful whether Mangey, whom Wendland followed, was justified in substituting φωνῆς. The phrase ἐγγ. φωνή, cf. *De Agr.* 136, means speech which is capable of being analysed into the sounds which are repre-sented by the γράμματα, and ἐγγ. μουσική will mean the same, except that while φωνή contemplates the letters as used for speech in general, μουσική contemplates them as used for the higher purpose of literary expression. The thought is enriched by the word ; the action of the Logos in creating out of discordant στοιχεῖα the harmony of the Cosmos is compared with the way in which the στοιχεῖα of sound combine to form the medium by which we express our highest thoughts.

§ 29. The insertion of εἰς will no doubt make the con-struction easier, if we may assume that αἰσθήσεις can mean the organs of sense. But this seems doubtful (the passages in L. & S. 1927 quoted for it seem rather to mean the senses themselves *as localized*). Without εἰς the passage can be translated " taking our body, like some deep-soiled plot, as tree-beds, he made the senses for it," though it is true that we should have expected δεξαμενήν.—F. H. C.

§ 33. *To say nothing of the fact*, etc. This sense can no

doubt be obtained by excluding τῷ. But the combination in a single sentence of two such disparate thoughts, as (1) that the cause cannot be contained in the caused, (2) that the trees do not bear fruits, is odd. As there is admittedly some corruption, perhaps we may extend that corruption a little further and suppose that a fresh sentence and subject begins after περιέχεσθαι. It has been shown that God does not dwell in gardens ; we now go on to show that He does not need the fruit. As a guess one might suggest φῶμεν δὲ for τῷ μηδὲ, *i.e.* " And are we to say forsooth that the trees (as they would if they were really trees) bear yearly fruit ? " Who then will eat them ?—F. H. C.

§ 41. *That is to say . . . irrational creatures.* The ms. text and also the suggestions of Cohn and Mangey involve making the ἀσκήσεις καὶ χρήσεις the recipients of the privilege denied to the irrational creatures. But clearly the ἀσκήσεις καὶ χρήσεις represent the tilling of the garden and themselves constitute the privilege. The reading adopted brings out this meaning with no more departure from the manuscripts than the transplacement of ἐστιν and the omission of οὖν. Wendland's proposal of αἱ γοῦν ἀρετῆς δεκτικαὶ φύσεις, for αἱ οὖν ἀσκήσεις τε καὶ χρήσεις, would give much the same sense, but with more drastic alteration, and the phrase ἀσκήσεις καὶ χρήσεις has every appearance of being genuine.

§ 61. *For separation.* Or " for dismissal " as R.V. in margin. Mr. Whitaker had intended to correct his translation in *Leg. All.* ii. 52 from " averter of evil " to this, though that is the usual meaning of the word. Whatever the lxx actually meant, the interpretation which follows here (*cf.* also *De Post.* 72) seems to show that Philo took the word in this passive sense, and to this he would be guided by the parallel phrase in Lev. xvi. 10 ὥστε ἐξαποστεῖλαι αὐτὸν εἰς ἀποπομπήν.—F. H. C.

§ 73 ff. The curious distortion of the story of Genesis which follows has this much excuse, that the accusative after φυτεύω would naturally mean the thing planted, whereas the lxx uses it for the soil, which again would naturally be expressed by the dative following ἐπί. The A.V. has " grove " in place of the lxx " field " or " hide " ; the R.V. has " tamarisk tree."

§ 76. 10,000 *is the end.* Apparently because Greek has

495

PHILO

no name for higher numbers, except such as are compounded with μυρίοι or lower numbers.

Ibid. If we adhere to the line of progress, etc. Literally " according to the first arrangement (or " series ")." The word " first " is obscure. Possibly it may mean the series 1, 2, 3, etc., other secondary series being 1, 3, 5, etc., and 2, 4, 6, etc. The former would not reach 10,000, and the latter does not start from 1.

§ 93. *Though by special grace*, etc. An afterthought; no such reservation is made in 79-84.

§ 94. *Natural duties.* Or, as it has been rendered in earlier passages, " simple " or " common " or " daily " duties.

§ 95. *Its crop.* In 137, however, Philo seems to take αὐτοῦ as referring to the Lord, *i.e.* " what He has produced." But it would be quite in his manner to regard it as having both meanings.

§ 100. *Indifferent.* Or " belonging to the lower or pre-liminary stage," as in 94. For the phrase *cf. De Sacr.* 43.

§ 101. *Debtors or slaves. I.e.* if anyone, slave or freeman, has entrusted a friend with some piece of property, he should retain it, if otherwise it will be seized by the master of the former, or the creditor of the latter. Heinemann would read χρεώστας ἢ δούλους, but it is improbable that slaves were entrusted in this way and surely impossible that debtors should be. For the remarks that follow *cf.* note on *Quod Deus* 101.

§ 106. *A desire that good*, etc. A verbatim quotation of the Stoic definition of εὔνοια, see *S.V.F.* iii. 432.

§ 110. Philo oddly perverts the story of Jacob and the rods. It looks as if he took the words which follow the text which he quotes καὶ ἐφαίνετο τὸ λευκὸν ποικίλον to mean " the spotted appeared white " instead of the opposite.

§ 111. *By way of leaving behind us bodily concerns.* The case of κατά is strange, and the thought, though in itself quite Philonic, seems alien to the context. Perhaps read κατὰ τὴν ἀπὸ τοῦ σώματος μετάβασιν ⟨τοῦ ποικίλου⟩ τὸ ποικίλον, κτλ., *i.e.* " Just as the variegatedness leaves the body of the leper, so we," etc.

§ 118. *The soul's chiefest good*, etc. This passage, like *De Op.* 53, is evidently dependent on the eulogy of light in *Timaeus* 47 A, see particularly, " Day and night . . . and months and years and the revolution of the years have

496

APPENDICES

created number . . . and from these we have derived philosophy, than which no greater good has come . . . to mortal men " (Archer-Hind's translation).

The correction ἀγαθόν for the senseless ἀπάτη has been universally accepted. But such a foolish corruption is strange. Is it possible that ἄκος ἀπάτης or some such phrase may have stood originally ?

§ 123. "*All*" or "*totality.*" A Pythagorean idea, *cf.* Aristot. *Met.* i. 5, 968 a, " ten is thought to be perfect and to embrace the whole nature of number " ; see Zeller, *Pre-socratic Philosophy,* vol. ii. p. 428. What applies to 10 applies to 4 also, since $1 + 2 + 3 + 4 = 10$. Philo is also probably thinking of the words πᾶς ὁ καρπός in his text from Leviticus.

§ 129. *The family of the Muses,* etc. Philo seems to be giving a spiritualized form of the legend in Hesiod, *Theog* 50 f., where Zeus lay for nine nights with Mnemosyne, who after a year bore the Nine Muses at a birth. πάμμουσον frequently means " very musical " but one can hardly help supposing that here there is an allusion to " all the Muses."

§ 137. *His products.* See note on "its crop," § 95.

§ 139. *And concerning the number* 4. The sense given in the translation can no doubt be obtained by merely omitting the καὶ before ἅ, and taking συνεκροτεῖτο in a rather unusual sense. But the phrasing is odd. The genitive τῶν ἄθλων cannot be governed by φερομένης, and must be taken as partitive, " those of the prizes which." If we retain καὶ, we might perhaps translate " and about the things which were enjoined," but the genitive τῶν ἄθλων then is unintelligible, as Wendland felt, who suggested for it ⟨τὰ πρεσβεῖα⟩ τῶν ἀριθμῶν.

But there is another possibility. The treatise up to now has consisted of three parts ; the husbandry of God (1-73), the husbandry of the wise man (74-92), and the husbandry of the ordinary (progressing) man (93-138). In this last the number four was merely incidental. It seems possible that φερομένης like ἐπομένης agrees with γεωργίας, and that the meaning is the " husbandry which wins the prize assigned to four." No doubt some corruption must be assumed to get such a meaning, but the following might be tentatively suggested : τῆς φερομένης τετράδος τὸ ἄθλον, ἢ κατά, κτλ. The last words will then mean " the husbandry which was trained (or " worked ") according to the injunc-

497

tions and directions of the law." This would give quite a usual sense to συνεκροτεῖτο. The "working" or "training" has been described in 100 ff.—F. H. C.

§ 142. *Cf.* Plutarch, *De Garrulitate* 4 (=503) F. καὶ μήποτε τὸ ζητούμενον παρὰ τοὺς φιλοσόφους λύων ὁ ποιητὴς οἰνώσεως καὶ μέθης διαφορὰν εἴρηκεν, οἰνώσεως μὲν ἄνεσιν μέθης δὲ φλυαρίαν . . οἱ δὲ φιλόσοφοι καὶ ὁριζόμενοι τὴν μέθην λέγουσιν εἶναι λήρησιν πάροινον· οὕτως οὐ ψέγεται τὸ πίνειν, εἰ προσείη τῷ πίνειν τὸ σιωπᾶν· ἀλλ' ἡ μωρολογία μέθην ποιεῖ τὴν οἴνωσιν. (*Ibid.* 504 B.)

"We may, indeed, believe that these lines of the poet[a] give the solution of the question discussed in the philosophic schools as to the distinction between mellowness and intoxication : mellowness produces unbending, but drunkenness foolish twaddling.

"In fact the philosophic definition of intoxication calls it ' *silly talk in one's cups.*' The blame, therefore, is not for drinking, if one can drink and yet at the same time hold his tongue. It is the foolish talk that converts mellowness into drunkenness " (Tucker's translation).

§ 145. "*The others.*" *I.e.* those described in 143. Arnim would render " others," making a third class who are distinguished from the first, in that they regard drunkenness as venial in the exceptional circumstances described in 146. But all that is stated there is that the wise man may be occasionally forced to relax his general rule of avoiding all occasions of heavy drinking, and this is not incompatible with the view stated in § 143.

§ 163. "*After sacrificing.*" This derivation is ascribed to Aristotle by Athenaeus, *Epit.* ii. p. 40 c.

§ 165. *Etymology.* Arguments like this and the preceding one were a recognized method of proof both in philosophy and rhetoric. *Cf.* Cicero, *Topica* 35 and *Academica* i. 32 (with Reid's note). The first proof, though of a very similar kind, would perhaps have been classed rather as an argument " from definition."

§ 171. *Right feelings.* Arnim takes this Stoic term (εὐπάθειαι) as supporting his contention that the disputant is a Stoic. But apart from the fact that the word is a favourite with Philo, Arnim himself notes that much of the Stoic " jargon " had become common property.

---

[a] Homer, *Odyssey*, xiv. 463 ff.

APPENDICES

§ 172. Arnim connects this argument with the strict Stoic view (a) that every good thing has its opposite evil; (b) that all good things belong solely to the wise man, and all bad things to the fool; (c) that what is neither good nor bad (ἀδιάφορον) is shared by both, and therefore its opposite must be shared by both. From this he argues that the ascription of this statement to οἱ πρότεροι shows that the disputant is a Stoic, since a member of an opposite school would not use such a form of words ("our predecessors"). If, however, it is assumed that the writer is a free lance, the argument seems doubtful. Moreover, the phrase ὡς ὁ τῶν προτέρων λόγος only applies to the statement that good and bad share soberness, and Arnim adduces no proof that this is Stoic.

§ 173. *Inartistic. Cf.* Aristot. *Rhetoric* i. 15. So called because "they are not due to the artist's inventive skill, but are supplied to him from the outside, as it were, of his art" (Cope). The other four are laws, documents, questions by torture, oaths.

§§ 176 ff. This argument is stated by Seneca in *Ep.* 83 as having been put forward by Zeno, and Seneca refutes it in exactly the same way as it is refuted here. He proceeds to deal in the same way with another defence of Zeno's argument, propounded by Posidonius, and then lays it down that the true way of proving the folly of drunkenness is to show its evil consequences—the loss of mental and bodily control, and the grave mischief which history shows that it has so often caused. If the suggestion made in Note (p. 211) to the Introduction is right, viz. that another speech followed, putting the case from the point of view of one who held that " the wise man will not get drunk," it may very possibly have followed these lines.

APPENDIX TO *DE EBRIETATE*

§ 2. *Sometimes he gives opposite orders.* In Numb. vi. 3 the Nazarite during the period of his vow is forbidden wine. In v. 20 the ᴌxx has " he shall drink it," which Philo takes for a command.

§ 4. The ᴍs. text, as Adler points out, gives better sense than Wendland's correction (following Mangey). It is difficult to give any meaning to " the gladness which embraces the rest," and below ἐπιθυμία is the cause of ἀπληστία, not, as Wendland would make it, a synonym.

§ 12. For the reading ἐκδιδοῦσαι see Adler, *Wiener Studien* 44, p. 220. Apart from its superior ᴍs. authority, it makes better sense; ἀπαιδευσία is not the source of all actions, as the other reading implies.

§ 14. *Riotous liver.* The odd word συμβολοκοπῶ, which is apparently only found in the ᴌxx and Apocrypha, is rightly enough traced by Philo to the συμβολαί or contributions which the feaster paid. The origin of the depreciatory suffix -κοπ . . is obscure. Philo attempts to account for it after his usual manner in 23. Other similar formations are φαντασιοκοπεῖν, δωροκοπεῖν, πορνοκοπεῖν.

§ 21. *Complete irregularity of life.* Philo several times uses ἐκδιαίτησις and its verb for the rejecting of what is required by the moral sense of the community. Thus the setting up of the golden calf is felt by the tribe of Levi to be an ἐκδιαίτησις, *De Spec. Leg.* iii. 126, and violation of the Sabbath may become ἀρχὴ τῆς περὶ τὰ ἄλλα ἐκδιαιτήσεως, *De Som.* ii. 123. The verb has occurred in *De Gig.* 21.

§ 30. " *Father and mother,*" etc. *I.e.* the terms may be used in the figurative sense given in this section, or in the other figurative sense given in 33, as well as literally. Or possibly the meaning of the sentence may be that, while in the text from

APPENDICES

Deuteronomy the father and mother are grouped together, as acting in concert, their functions are really different.

§ 31. *Obtained.* The LXX has ἔκτισε instead of ἐκτήσατο. Ryle (*Philo and Holy Scripture*, p. 296) points out that Philo's word is a more accurate translation of the Hebrew and is actually used by Aquila, Symmachus, and Theodotion. He suggests that ἔκτισε may have resulted from a corrupt ἐκτίσατο.

§ 33. *The disciples, who have followed in their company.* The parable implied is that God and His wisdom are in the truest sense the parents of mankind (as included in the All). Reason and convention have been trained by the divine Pair to be the educators of mankind and thus stand to them in a sense as parents also.

§§ 36-64. The depreciation of the " feminine " element of convention in these sections cannot altogether be reconciled with the high estimate of it in 80-92. The best we can say for it is that Philo regards this " maternal " influence as good or bad, according as it is supported and regulated, or not, by the "paternal."

§ 42. *Is not the Maker,* etc. The argument is " God should be known to us from the beginning " (1) because He is the father of all, (2) because He presides at (belongs to) the beginning. It would be stated more logically if we transposed ἀρχηγέτης and ὁ κτίστης, " Is not the Maker of the Universe its ἀρχηγέτης and Father? " Indeed this meaning might be got, though somewhat unnaturally, out of the text as it stands, if we take καὶ πατὴρ αὐτοῦ with ἀρχηγέτης as predicate instead of coupling it with ὁ κτίστης.

§ 48. *The timeless also exists in nature.* Literally " there are also timeless natures." Philo is here as often (*e.g. De Plant.* 120) contrasting the " physical " (in his sense) with the ethical. But the thought is obscure. Perhaps it is something as follows. The dealings of God (here identified with nature) are timeless and therefore the " Practiser " will neglect time-order and look to order in value and thus desire to pass from the lower to the higher (νεώτερος and πρεσβύτερος passing as often from the sense of precedence in time to that of precedence in value).

Ibid. The laws of human character. Or the department of thought which deals with human conduct; ἠθοποιός, literally "forming conduct" seems here to be used for ἠθικός. *Cf.*

PHILO

ἠθοποιίαν 92. Wendland wished to read ἠθικός, but the usage, though perhaps rare, is natural enough, as Greek philosophy holds that right conduct must be based on ethics, and conversely that a knowledge of ethics will produce right conduct.

§ 51. This section seems to mean that Philo was familiar with cases where those whose education in the Encyclia had been neglected were at pains to repair the loss in later life. This is perhaps not surprising. The Encyclia, or at least its most important elements γραμματική and rhetoric, were more studied by adults and entered more into the life of the upper classes than our school subjects do with us, and a man might well feel at a loss in good society without them. That Philo regards such a return to the Encyclia as a retrograde step follows from his peculiar view of them. Taken at the proper time, *i.e.* in boyhood, they are almost indispensable as an introduction to philosophy. Taken later, they are mere vanity and thus at the end of 52 they are equated with "external goods."

Ibid. Left the right path. Or "missed their way," "gone where no road is." The phrase ἀνοδίᾳ χρῆσθαι has occurred in *De Agr.* 101.

§ 56. *Discoursing with herself.* Rachel's answer to Laban is regarded as symbolizing the admission which every reflecting soul must make to itself of its inability to rise up against the "outward goods" which Laban represents. In using διαλόγοις thus, Philo may have been influenced by Plato, *Soph.* 263 ϝ ὁ μὲν ἐντὸς τῆς ψυχῆς πρὸς αὑτὸν διάλογος ἄνευ φωνῆς γιγνόμενος τοῦτ᾽ αὐτὸ ἡμῖν ἐπωνομάσθη διάνοια.

§ 70. *The uttered word.* For the Stoic distinction between λόγος προφορικός (speech) and λόγος ἐνδιάθετος (thought) see note on *De Gig.* 52. The latter, not the former, distinguishes men from animals, for ravens and parrots speak (*S.V.F.* ii. 135); still speech is nearer to the mind than the senses are.

§ 73. The treatment of the story differs considerably from that in *Leg. All.* iii. 242, *De Post.* 183, *De Mut.* 108. There the woman is pleasure or passion and the man is ignored; and the piercing through the "mother-part" is to prevent her engendering further evil. Here the woman is the belief which ascribes causation to creation itself, the man the ideas or reasonings based on this belief, and the piercing through the womb is to show that no real power of bearing belongs to creation. Philo is of course assisted by δόξα being feminine, and λογισμός masculine.

§ 74. Adler aptly supports the MS. reading by τοῖς κοίνοις ἀνθρώπων ἔθεσιν ἁλίσκονται 68. But it must be admitted that this use of πρός for " belonging to " " like " is strange, if not, as Wendland says, impossible. Such phrases as πρὸς γυναικός ἐστι (regularly followed by the verb " to be," expressed or understood) are hardly parallel.

§ 84. *For if you have learnt . . . mother.* Adler points out that these words also as well as the quotation which follows are reminiscent of Proverbs. *Cf.* i. 8, " My son, hear the instructions of thy father and forsake not the laws (LXX μὴ ἀπώσῃ θεσμούς) of thy mother."

§ 88. *Art of arts.* So ἀρετή is a τέχνη περὶ ὅλου τοῦ βίου (*S.V.F.* iii. 560, where we have the Stoic doctrine that the wise man does all things which he undertakes well).

§ 95. *Aggressor in wickedness.* The exact meaning of προσεπιβαίνειν is doubtful : clearly it is an antithesis to imitating their virtue. Perhaps " to go further and trample on them." Mangey translated it by " praevaricari."

Ibid. Vanity most honoured among the Egyptians. I.e. Apis, which Philo identifies with the Calf of Ex. xxxii. He is also thinking of Aaron's words in v. 4. The phrase " vanity of the Egyptians " recurs several times in Philo, generally with allusion to this incident.

§ 96. *And he said. I.e.* Moses, as the interpretation shows ; see next note.

§ 98. *Personal experience . . . the one who watches the course of events.* In this interpretation Joshua and Moses apparently represent two aspects of the man's self. He *feels* the inward tumult, and then the reasoning side of his nature (the Moses in us) interprets the true cause. This reasoning side is identified with the Holy Word in 104.

§ 113. The full text of Numb. xxi. 17-18 should be compared with Philo's interpretation. ἐξάρχετε αὐτῷ φρέαρ· ὤρυξαν αὐτὸ ἄρχοντες, ἐξελατόμησαν αὐτὸ βασιλεῖς ἐθνῶν ἐν τῇ βασιλείᾳ αὐτῶν, ἐν τῷ κυριεῦσαι αὐτῶν. The ἐξάρχετε of this is reproduced by ἐξάρχει in the previous section, and a comparison with *De Vita Mosis* i. 256 suggests that he interprets ὤρυξαν by searching for or finding wisdom (ἀναζητῆσαι, in

PHILO

V.M. εὕρεσις) and ἐλατόμησαν by building it up (κατεργά-
σασθαι, in V.M. κατασκευή), while "conquered" represents
ἐν τῷ κυριεῦσαι αὐτῶν.

§§ 114-118. In the original the captains have made the
roll-call of their men and no one has failed to answer
(διαπεφώνηκεν). In the allegory the aspirants to spiritual
power (this is based on the description of them as καθεσταμένοι
εἰς τὰς χιλιαρχίας τῆς δυνάμεως, v. 48) make themselves masters
(εἰλήφασι) of the opposing forces of false courage. These,
under the influence of the higher nature, are reduced to
the mean, i.e. true courage, and thus none "is at discord."
This, which, though not the meaning of the lxx, is the
natural meaning of the word, serves to connect the passage
with the other songs of victory. Cf. De Conf. 55.

This rendering assumes the "captains" to be the antecedent of οὕς. It would make better sense to make λόγους
the antecedent, for then πολεμικούς would be equated with
the πολεμιστῶν of Numbers. We should have, however, then
to take δυσὶν ἀντιτεταγμένους τέλεσιν as "arranged in two
battalions"—an unnatural use of the dative.

§ 115. Two battalions. Combined with this military sense
of τέλος there is perhaps the thought of the philosophical
sense "purposes," "motives."

§ 132. Copies. It will be observed that εἰκόνες is used in
a different sense to that of 134. The literal tabernacle and
altar are both εἰκόνες (or symbols) of their spiritual counter-
parts. The spiritual altar is an εἰκών of the spiritual temple
in the philosophical sense of the theory of ideas. But perhaps ταῦτα stands for the phenomenal world in general, in
which case we have the philosophical use or something like it.

§ 134. This section seems to the translator to raise difficult
questions which he is unable to answer with any confidence,
and leaves to some more accomplished Platonist. The
tabernacle is generic virtue, the altar is the particular virtues,
which one would naturally suppose to be the ordinary four,
justice, temperance, etc. In what sense are these (a) perceptible by the senses yet (b) never actually perceived by them?
The answer to (a) may perhaps be that by the particular
virtues he does not mean the specific virtues in the abstract,
but the manifestations of them in particular persons. This
will agree with De Cher. 5, where the particular and specific
virtues (ἐν μέρει καὶ κατ᾽ εἶδος) are contrasted with generic

virtue, and then these particular virtues are defined as
" virtues in the I," and therefore perishable, because the
" I " is perishable ! If this is so, what is the answer to (b) ?
Is it that while these virtues are conceivable in the individual,
they are never realized ? This hardly seems satisfactory.

The question between ἰδέας acc. plur. (Wendland and
Cohn) and ἰδέας gen. sing. (Adler) may be argued as
follows. For the acc. it may be said that Philo uses the
word in a loose sense for the νοητὰ θεωρήματα of 132.
Both generic and specific virtues belong to a different order
of things from the material altar and tabernacle. Or again,
if Philo means the specific virtues in the abstract, are not
these also ἴδεαι, as well as the generic, which is their ἰδέα ?
On the other hand, the genitive is strongly suggested by the
antithesis to αἰσθητὴ εἰκών and the similar antithesis in 137.

§ 142. *Right reason which is identical with law.* This
glorification of νόμος is definitely Stoic ; see *S.V.F.* iii. 613.

§ 146. παρακινεῖν. As Adler points out, Philo is thinking
of *Phaedrus* 249 D, where the truly inspired (ἐνθουσιάζων) is
reproved by the many as παρακινῶν.

§ 150. *Hard day.* Adler's suggestion that ἡμέρα means
" (and at the same time) easy " finds some support in the
quotation from Hesiod. But there is no such suggestion in
the varlet's words. It must be remembered that Philo found
the phrase in the LXX and did not invent it. We need not
suppose that he gave ἡμέρα any definite meaning, or again
he may have interpreted it as " a day's journey." And if
he really found in it any such edifying suggestion, as Adler
supposes, he would surely have enlarged upon it.

§ 157. *Reason . . . unreason.* The translator is baffled,
as often, by the way in which Philo combines and intertwines
λόγος as " reason " or " thought " with λόγος as " speech."
He is working out the idea of soul-sight (intuition) and soul-
hearing (learning by instruction). The latter may be equated
with λόγος " reason," but as we learn through words it
may also be equated with λόγος " word " and this is indicated by the antithesis of τοῖς λεγομένοις and τὰ ὄντα in § 158.

§ 158. *Mis-seeing or mis-hearing.* Cf. *S.V.F.* iii. 548
ἀλλ' οὐδὲ παρορᾶν οὐδὲ παρακούειν νομίζουσι τὸν σοφόν.

§ 170. *There are many reasons for this.* Here begins
Philo's version of the " tropes of Aenesidemus," see *Anal.
Intr.* pp. 314 f. It should be noted that Philo omits two of the

ten tropes, as they are stated by Sextus Empiricus (*Pyrrh. Hyp.* i. 36 f.) and Diogenes Laertius ix. 79-88. These two are (a) the differences in the sensations produced by different senses in the same individual, *e.g.* honey is pleasant to the taste, but unpleasant to the eye, (b) the different feelings produced by the same recurrence according to its rarity or frequency, *e.g.* when earthquakes are common they do not cause any excitement.

Ibid. In the first place. The first trope is called by Sextus (*Pyrrh. Hyp.* i. 36) " that of the variety in animals " (ὁ παρὰ τὴν τῶν ζῴων ἐξαλλαγήν), the argument being that, as animals are constructed so differently, we must suppose that the impressions which the same object gives them are different.

§ 172. *Those who form judgements.* The tropes were classified according as the difference of impressions arises from something in the subject who forms the impression (τὸ κρῖνον) or from the object which creates the impression (τὸ κρινόμενον), or from both combined (Sextus, *ibid.* 38). The first, second, and third as given by Philo belong to the first class, the fifth to the second, and the other four to the third.

§§ 172-174. The introduction of these examples, which have no parallel in Sextus or Diogenes, is quite illogical. Clearly there is no suggestion that the polypus, chameleon, and elk receive different impressions. If germane at all they should come under the trope of " position " etc. (181) But with the exception of the dove's neck, the examples have no bearing on the argument, since these changes of " camouflage " are supposed to be actual changes. Philo, or the source from which he drew, was attracted by the interest of these supposed changes in the animal world and could not refrain from noticing them in a passage which deals with animals. That the illogicality did not altogether escape him is shown by his remarking that they belong to the κρινόμενα, not to the κρίνοντα.

§ 173. *The dove's neck.* A common example with the " bent oar " of an illusion (see Reid on *Acad.* ii. 79). Sextus (*ibid.* 120) and Diogenes ix. 86 rightly give it under " position," but ascribe the change to the way the neck is turned (Lucr. ii. 801, like Philo, to the sun's ray).

§ 175. *Impossibility of apprehension.* This leading term of the Sceptics, properly speaking, applies to the object

APPENDICES

which cannot be apprehended, but came to signify their general doctrine. Hicks (Diog. Laert. ix. 61) translates it "agnosticism."

Ibid. Secondly. The second trope, called by Sextus ὁ παρὰ τὴν τῶν ἀνθρώπων διαφοράν (*ibid.* 79). While the variety in animals was a *prima facie* ground for thinking that the animal man was liable to a similar instability of impressions, this is supposed to need special proof, which this trope gives.

Ibid. Not only do their judgements. I.e. of the same people. Wendland's proposed insertion of οἱ αὐτοί in contrast to ἕτεροι is unnecessary, though "the same" is implied. The changes in animals just mentioned being all in the same animal, suggest that there are analogous mental changes in individual men. This, however, belongs to the third trope and is only mentioned in passing, before we pass to the subject of the second trope.

§ 176. ἐπισπασάμενοι seems elsewhere, as in *De Gig.* 44, to suggest using influence or force to attract. Adler's ἀσπασάμενοι would be more natural ; but there is hardly sufficient reason for the change. Perhaps ἐπασπασάμενοι. The word is only quoted from the 6th century A.D., but there are such things as ἅπαξ εἰρημένα in Philo.

§ 178. The third trope (Sextus's fourth), called by him ὁ παρὰ τὰς περιστάσεις, *ibid.* 100.

§ 181. The fourth trope (fifth in Sextus, who uses the same phrase as here, ὁ παρὰ τὰς θέσεις καὶ τὰ διαστήματα καὶ τοὺς τόπους), *ibid.* 119. For positions or attitudes (θέσεις), *i.e.* of the object itself, Sextus gives the dove's bent neck, and Philo's swimming fish perhaps come under this head. For surroundings (τόποι), Sextus gives the bent oar and also the faintness of candle-light in the sun. For distances from the observer (διαστήματα), Sextus gives the varying appearance of a ship at sea.

§ 184. The fifth trope (Sextus's seventh, *ibid.* 129, his sixth being taken by Philo in 190). Sextus calls it ὁ παρὰ τὰς ποσότητας καὶ σκευασίας τῶν ὑποκειμένων. It would perhaps be better to translate ἐν τοῖς σκευαζομένοις by "preparations" simply and to omit "relative" and "in the various ingredients" in what follows ; also to render συνθέσεσι by "aggregations" rather than "compounds." Sextus explains that by σκευασίας he means συνθέσεις in general and the examples show that these need not be of more than one substance.

507

PHILO

§ 186. The sixth trope (Sextus's eighth, ὁ ἀπὸ τοῦ πρός τι), *ibid.* 135.

§ 190. The seventh trope (Sextus's sixth, ὁ παρὰ τὰς ἐπιμιξίας), *ibid.* 124.

Ibid. Those which are in accord with nature, etc. *I.e.* apparently, pleasant or unpleasant. *Cf.* the definition of pleasure and pain in *Timaeus* 64 D. But the epithet would naturally be applied to the χυλοί in the sense of flavours, as in 191, rather than to the " juices of the mouth." The following point may perhaps be worth consideration. In the parallel in Sextus these mouth-juices are ὕλαι ἐν τοῖς γεύσεως τόποις ὑποκείμεναι. If we read here ἐνστομίων ⟨ὑλῶν⟩ χυλῶν ὅσοι κτλ., *i.e.* " can we, without the substances in the mouth, tell what flavours are natural and what unnatural? " we should have a text which would easily lend itself to corruption.

§ 193. The eighth and last trope (Sextus's tenth, stated by him as ὁ παρὰ τὰς ἀγωγὰς καὶ τὰ ἔθη καὶ τοὺς νόμους καὶ τὰς μυθικὰς πίστεις καὶ τὰς δογματικὰς ὑπολήψεις), *ibid.* 145. The first two of them are repeated by Philo in the same words, and the δογματικαὶ ὑπολήψεις appear in 198 ff. But there is nothing corresponding to the μυθικαὶ πίστεις, *i.e.* the popular superstitions which with the scientific theories of the philosophers are represented by the Sceptics as having such a total want of agreement as to put the coping-stone on the accumulation of evidence for human ἀκαταληψία.

Ibid. Ways of life. We might take ἀγωγαὶ αἱ ἐκ παίδων to mean "systems of education," but Sextus explains it as αἱρέσεις βίου ἢ πραγμάτων περὶ ἕνα ἢ πολλούς, illustrating it by Diogenes' asceticism and Spartan discipline.

§ 198. Here begin the δογματικαὶ ὑπολήψεις. The first part of the section bears a considerable resemblance to "Longinus," *De Sublimitate* xliv. 3, 4, describing the tyranny of custom, from the cradle (ἐνεσπαργανωμένοι) and the buffeted (κεκονδυλισμένον) condition of the multitude.

§ 199. The opinions here mentioned may be roughly classified as following :

Infinite (Epicurean)—Finite (Stoic).
Created (Stoics and Epicureans)—Uncreated (Peripatetic).
No providence (Epicurean)—Providence (Stoic).
One " good " (Stoic)—Three " goods " (Peripatetic).

§ 206. *Gluttony.* This represents the ἀπληστία of 4 and 6.

§ 208. *Cup of reconciliation.* The phrase ἐπὶ σπονδαῖς

combines the idea of pouring wine as cup-bearer (Gen. xl. 21) and the common meaning of " on the conditions of a truce."

§ 213. *Lost the organs of generation.* For the literal meaning see A.V. ἐκτετμημένῳ πίστιν interprets ἀποκεκομμένος, and παρακαταθήκην etc. interprets θλαδίας.

§ 218. *Fine bouquet.* The adj. ἄνθιμος or ἄνθινος is explained by Hesychius and the Scholiast as meaning (*a*) flavoured with herbs or flowers, (*b*) smelling like flowers. The latter is more suitable here.

§ 221. *Cavities,* or " stomachs," a use of ὄγκος not given in the dictionaries, but found in Plutarch, *Mor.* 652 E and elsewhere (see Wyttenbach's index).

APPENDIX TO *DE SOBRIETATE*

§ 12. *Comeliness of the body . . . beauty of the soul.* Philo
is thinking of *Symposium* 218 E, where Socrates says to
Alcibiades, "You must see in me that κάλλος, greatly
different from the εὐμορφία which I see in you."

Ibid. Bastard brothers. This distinction between the sons
of the concubines and those of the legitimate wives has
already been made, though in a somewhat different way, in
Quod Deus 119 ff.; see also *De Mig.* 95, where Asher in
particular is the symbol αἰσθητοῦ καὶ νόθου πλούτου. Below
(66) and elsewhere all twelve are put on a level.

§ 18. *The phrase thus set before us,* etc. The thought of
this section seems to be this ; the phrase " God blessed him "
explains in what sense Abraham was an elder, because the
εὐλογία of God necessarily produces εὐλογιστία in man and
this εὐλογιστία is moral seniority. According to the Stoics
τὸ εὐλογιστεῖν in the selection of what is according to
nature is the " end " of the individual man and brings him
into agreement with the law of the universe, which is identical
with Zeus (Diog. Laert. vii. 88). Philo, in his desire to
equate the Stoic ideal with the divine blessing, more than
once, *e.g. Leg. All.* iii. 191, 192, brings εὐλογία into close
connexion with εὐλογιστία. The mere fact that they both
contain εὖ and λόγος would be enough for him. But in *De
Mig.* 70 he strengthens the connexion by explaining εὐλογήσω
as ἐπαινετὸν λόγον δωρήσομαι.

§ 32. [δοῦλος δούλων]. This is given instead of the παῖς
οἰκέτης of the LXX in Aquila's version, whence Wendland
supposes that it was interpolated into Philo's text. Ryle on
the other hand (*Philo and Holy Scripture*, p. 44), points
out that Philo in quoting Gen. ix. 26 and 27 (in sections 51
and 59) uses δοῦλος where the LXX has παῖς, and infers that it
is more likely that he had δοῦλος δούλων here. But in 51,
where he quotes this verse 25 again, we have παῖς οἰκέτης
without any variant or addition.

APPENDICES

§ 34. *The state of rest.* Philo seems always to use σχέσις in contrast to κίνησις (see Index). In calling it " akin " to ἕξις he is in general agreement with Stobaeus (*S.F.V.* iii. 111), where, after opposing τὰ ἐν κινήσει ἀγαθά to τὰ ἐν σχέσει ἀγαθά, he adds that some of the latter are also ἐν ἕξει, others ἐν σχέσει μόνον. He gives as examples of τὰ ἐν κινήσει joy and the like, of τὰ ἐν ἕξει the virtues and the arts when transformed by virtue and permanently established, of τὰ ἐν σχέσει μόνον " orderly quietude " (εὔτακτος ἡσυχία). From this use of ἐν σχέσει μόνον in contrast to ἐν σχέσει καὶ ἕξει comes the contrast between σχέσις itself and ἕξις as something transitory opposed to the less transitory, just as ἕξις in its turn is often opposed to διάθεσις, as something less permanent, or perhaps less essential and engrained (*cf.* *De Cher.* 62). This use of σχέσις does not appear in Philo, though he uses the adverb so in *Leg. All.* iii. 210, where σχετικῶς καὶ εὐαλώτως ὡς ἂν ἐκ τύχης is contrasted with ἀπὸ ἕξεως καὶ διαθέσεως. The distinction between ἕξις and διάθεσις is ignored in *De Sobrietate* as in Stobaeus, thus bringing ἕξις into agreement with the Aristotelian use of the word.

§ 50. *The oracles in Genesis.* Wendland, in adopting the reading mentioned in the footnote (as well as in 49), is following the version of 49 and 50, quoted in Nicetes Serranus's commentary on St. Luke. The MS. of this commentary is of the 12th century, but the date of the author is not stated. If Nicetes gives the true reading here, how are we to account for the wanton alteration from πρὸς τὸν Καῖν to περὶ τῆς τοῦ παντὸς γενέσεως? The translators incline to think that the reading of the MSS. is right. It is natural enough that, as the preceding quotations come from Exodus and Leviticus, Philo should want to indicate that this comes from Genesis and since, as he says (*De Abr.* 1), this book takes its name ἀπὸ τῆς τοῦ κόσμου γενέσεως, the expression here used is not impossible. That Nicetes should have corrected a reference so vague and apt to mislead to something more definite is equally natural. Wendland's statement about the general superiority of this excerpt to the MSS. of Philo is hardly borne out by his practice. He follows them as often as he follows Nicetes.

§ 51. *Blessed be the Lord, the God of Shem.* When Philo wrote the *Quaestiones* (*Quaest. in Gen.* ii. 15), he clearly

511

PHILO

read Κύριος ὁ θεός, ὁ θεὸς Σήμ, for not only is the text quoted as " benedictus est dominus deus, deus Sem," but the comment demands this, *e.g.* " *bis* nominatur benefica virtus dei." Should we read the same here? It is against it that when the verse is cited in 58 (but see note) the MSS. again have only one ὁ θεός. On the other hand, the argument of 55 will become clearer. God is Lord God of the world, but God only of Shem.

§ 52. The interpretation of " Shem " as = " name " and thence, as the best of names, " the good," does not appear elsewhere in what we have of Philo. But the idea was taken up by the Latin Fathers, though they characteristically substituted Christ for the good. So Ambrose, *Ep.* 7. 46 " Sem dicitur Latine nomen," Augustine, *De Civitate Dei* xvi. 2 " Sem quippe, de cuius semine in carne natus est Christus, interpretatur nominatus. Quid autem nominatius Christo ? "

§ 56. *My friend.* This variant, which, as the argument shews, is deliberate, is especially noticeable in view of James ii. 23 φίλος ἐκλήθη θεοῦ. Ryle, *l.c.* p. 75, suggests that it was an earlier rendering, subsequently altered as too familiar, yet retaining its influence after the LXX became the standard version.

Ibid. He alone is nobly born. For this and the other " paradoxes " which follow see *S.V.F.* iii. 589 ff.

§ 58. *Blessed be the Lord, the God of Shem.* Observe that Philo here substitutes εὐλογημένος for the εὐλογητός of the LXX which he followed in 51, though in *De Mig.* 107 he carefully distinguishes between the two as meaning respectively " the subject of blessing (by others)," and " worthy of blessing." It is quite possible, as Heinemann suggests, that he means us here to take Σήμ as dative. Compare his treatment of Δάν in *De Agr.* 99. In this case we should translate " let the Lord God be blessed by Shem." This rendering suits the argument which follows, and it is quite in Philo's manner to suggest such a double rendering, and further to imagine or accept a variant εὐλογημένος to fit it.

§§ 60 ff. For the three kinds of goods *cf. De Ebr.* 200 ff. and note on *Quod Det.* 7. Here Philo comes nearer to the Peripatetic view than in *De Gig.* 38. He is still nearer to it in *Quis Rer. Div. Her.* 285 ff.

THE LOEB CLASSICAL LIBRARY

VOLUMES ALREADY PUBLISHED

Latin Authors

AMMIANUS MARCELLINUS. J. C. Rolfe. 3 Vols.

APULEIUS: THE GOLDEN ASS (METAMORPHOSES). W. Adlington (1566). Revised by S. Gaselee.

ST. AUGUSTINE: CITY OF GOD. 7 Vols. Vol. I. G. E. McCracken. Vols. II and VII. W. M. Green. Vol. III. D. Wiesen. Vol. IV. P. Levine. Vol. V. E. M. Sanford and W. M. Green. Vol. VI. W. C. Greene.

ST. AUGUSTINE, CONFESSIONS. W. Watts (1631). 2 Vols.

ST. AUGUSTINE, SELECT LETTERS. J. H. Baxter.

AUSONIUS. H. G. Evelyn White. 2 Vols.

BEDE. J. E. King. 2 Vols.

BOETHIUS: TRACTS and DE CONSOLATIONE PHILOSOPHIAE. Rev. H. F. Stewart and E. K. Rand. Revised by S. J. Tester.

CEASAR: ALEXANDRIAN, AFRICAN and SPANISH WARS. A. G. Way.

CEASAR: CIVIL WARS. A. G. Peskett.

CEASAR: GALLIC WAR. H. J. Edwards.

CATO: DE RE RUSTICA. VARRO: DE RE RUSTICA. H. B. Ash and W. D. Hooper.

CATULLUS. F. W. Cornish. TIBULLUS. J. B. Postgate. PERVIGILIUM VENERIS. J. W. Mackail. Revised by G. P. Goold.

CELSUS: DE MEDICINA. W. G. Spencer. 3 Vols.

CICERO: BRUTUS and ORATOR. G. L. Hendrickson and H. M. Hubbell.

[CICERO]: AD HERENNIUM. H. Caplan.

CICERO: DE ORATORE, etc. 2 Vols. Vol. I. DE ORATORE, Books I and II. E. W. Sutton and H. Rackham. Vol. II. DE ORATORE, Book III. DE FATO; PARADOXA STOICORUM; DE PARTITIONE ORATORIA. H. Rackham.

CICERO: DE FINIBUS. H. Rackham.

CICERO: DE INVENTIONE, etc. H. M. Hubbell.

CICERO: DE NATURA DEORUM and ACADEMICA. H. Rackham.

CICERO: DE OFFICIIS. Walter Miller.

CICERO: DE REPUBLICA and DE LEGIBUS. Clinton W. Keyes.

1

CICERO: DE SENECTUTE, DE AMICITIA, DE DIVINATIONE. W. A. Falconer.
CICERO: IN CATILINAM, PRO FLACCO, PRO MURENA, PRO SULLA. New version by C. Macdonald.
CICERO: LETTERS TO ATTICUS. E. O. Winstedt. 3 Vols.
CICERO: LETTERS TO HIS FRIENDS. W. Glynn Williams, M. Cary, M. Henderson. 4 Vols.
CICERO: PHILIPPICS. W. C. A. Ker.
CICERO: PRO ARCHIA, POST REDITUM, DE DOMO, DE HARUSPICUM RESPONSIS, PRO PLANCIO. N. H. Watts.
CICERO: PRO CAECINA, PRO LEGE MANILIA, PRO CLUENTIO, PRO RABIRIO. H. Grose Hodge.
CICERO: PRO CAELIO, DE PROVINCIIS CONSULARIBUS, PRO BALBO. R. Gardner.
CICERO: PRO MILONE, IN PISONEM, PRO SCAURO, PRO FONTEIO, PRO RABIRIO POSTUMO, PRO MARCELLO, PRO LIGARIO, PRO REGE DEIOTARO. N. H. Watts.
CICERO: PRO QUINCTIO, PRO ROSCIO AMERINO, PRO ROSCIO COMOEDO, CONTRA RULLUM. J. H. Freese.
CICERO: PRO SESTIO, IN VATINIUM. R. Gardner.
CICERO: TUSCULAN DISPUTATIONS. J. E. King.
CICERO: VERRINE ORATIONS. L. H. G. Greenwood. 2 Vols.
CLAUDIAN. M. Platnauer. 2 Vols..
COLUMELLA: DE RE RUSTICA. DE ARBORIBUS. H. B. Ash, E. S. Forster and E. Heffner. 3 Vols.
CURTIUS, Q.: HISTORY OF ALEXANDER. J. C. Rolfe. 2 Vols.
FLORUS. E. S. Forster.
FRONTINUS: STRATAGEMS and AQUEDUCTS. C. E. Bennett and M. B. McElwain.
FRONTO: CORRESPONDENCE. C. R. Haines. 2 Vols.
GELLIUS. J. C. Rolfe. 3 Vols.
HORACE: ODES and EPODES. C. E. Bennett.
HORACE: SATIRES, EPISTLES, ARS POETICA. H. R. Fairclough.
JEROME: SELECTED LETTERS. F. A. Wright.
JUVENAL and PERSIUS. G. G. Ramsay.
LIVY. B. O. Foster, F. G. Moore, Evan T. Sage, and A. C. Schlesinger and R. M. Geer (General Index). 14 Vols.
LUCAN. J. D. Duff.
LUCRETIUS. W. H. D. Rouse. Revised by M. F. Smith.
MANILIUS. G. P. Goold.
MARTIAL. W. C. A. Ker. 2 Vols. Revised by E. H. Warmington
MINOR LATIN POETS: from PUBLILIUS SYRUS to RUTILIUS NAMATIANUS, including GRATTIUS, CALPURNIUS SICULUS, NEMESIANUS, AVIANUS and others, with "Aetna" and the "Phoenix." J. Wight Duff and Arnold M. Duff. 2 Vols.
MINUCIUS FELIX. Cf. TERTULLIAN.

2

NEPOS CORNELIUS. J. C. Rolfe.

OVID: THE ART OF LOVE and OTHER POEMS. J. H. Mozley. Revised by G. P. Goold.

OVID: FASTI. Sir James G. Frazer. Revised by G. P. Goold.

OVID: HEROIDES and AMORES. Grant Showerman. Revised by G. P. Goold.

OVID: METAMORPHOSES. F. J. Miller. 2 Vols. Revised by G. P. Goold.

OVID: TRISTIA and EX PONTO. A. L. Wheeler. Revised by G. P. Goold.

PERSIUS. Cf. JUVENAL.

PERVIGILIUM VENERIS. Cf. CATULLUS.

PETRONIUS. M. Heseltine. SENECA: APOCOLOCYNTOSIS. W. H. D. Rouse. Revised by E. H. Warmington.

PHAEDRUS and BABRIUS (Greek). B. E. Perry.

PLAUTUS. Paul Nixon. 5 Vols.

PLINY: LETTERS, PANEGYRICUS. Betty Radice. 2 Vols.

PLINY: NATURAL HISTORY. 10 Vols. Vols. I.–V. and IX. H. Rackham. VI.–VIII. W. H. S. Jones. X. D. E. Eichholz.

PROPERTIUS. H. E. Butler.

PRUDENTIUS. H. J. Thomson. 2 Vols.

QUINTILIAN. H. E. Butler. 4 Vols.

REMAINS OF OLD LATIN. E. H. Warmington. 4 Vols. Vol. I. (ENNIUS AND CAECILIUS) Vol. II. (LIVIUS, NAEVIUS PACUVIUS, ACCIUS) Vol. III. (LUCILIUS and LAWS OF XII TABLES) Vol. IV. (ARCHAIC INSCRIPTIONS).

RES GESTAE DIVI AUGUSTI. Cf. VELLEIUS PATERCULUS.

SALLUST. J. C. Rolfe.

SCRIPTORES HISTORIAE AUGUSTAE. D. Magie. 3 Vols.

SENECA, THE ELDER: CONTROVERSIAE, SUASORIAE. M. Winterbottom. 2 Vols.

SENECA: APOCOLOCYNTOSIS. Cf. PETRONIUS.

SENECA: EPISTULAE MORALES. R. M. Gummere. 3 Vols.

SENECA: MORAL ESSAYS. J. W. Basore. 3 Vols.

SENECA: TRAGEDIES. F. J. Miller. 2 Vols.

SENECA: NATURALES QUAESTIONES. T. H. Corcoran. 2 Vols.

SIDONIUS: POEMS and LETTERS. W. B. Anderson. 2 Vols.

SILIUS ITALICUS. J. D. Duff. 2 Vols.

STATIUS. J. H. Mozley. 2 Vols.

SUETONIUS. J. C. Rolfe. 2 Vols.

TACITUS: DIALOGUS. Sir Wm. Peterson. AGRICOLA and GERMANIA. Maurice Hutton. Revised by M. Winterbottom, R. M. Ogilvie, E. H. Warmington.

TACITUS: HISTORIES and ANNALS. C. H. Moore and J. Jackson. 4 Vols.

TERENCE. John Sargeaunt. 2 Vols.

TERTULLIAN: APOLOGIA and DE SPECTACULIS. T. R. Glover. MINUCIUS FELIX. G. H. Rendall.

TIBULLUS. Cf. CATULLUS.
VALERIUS FLACCUS. J. H. Mozley.
VARRO: DE LINGUA LATINA. R. G. Kent. 2 Vols.
VELLEIUS PATERCULUS and RES GESTAE DIVI AUGUSTI. F. W. SHIPLEY.
VIRGIL. H. R. Fairclough. 2 Vols.
VITRUVIUS: DE ARCHITECTURA. F. Granger. 2 Vols.

Greek Authors

ACHILLES TATIUS. S. Gaselee.
AELIAN: ON THE NATURE OF ANIMALS. A. F. Scholfield. 3 Vols.
AENEAS TACTICUS. ASCLEPIODOTUS and ONASANDER. The Illinois Greek
    Club.
AESCHINES. C. D. Adams.
AESCHYLUS. H. Weir Smyth. 2 Vols.
ALCIPHRON, AELIAN, PHILOSTRATUS: LETTERS. A. R. Benner and F. H.
    Fobes.
ANDOCIDES, ANTIPHON. Cf. MINOR ATTIC ORATORS Vol. I.
Apollodorus. Sir James G. Frazer. 2 Vols.
APOLLONIUS RHODIUS. R. C. Seaton.
APOSTOLIC FATHERS. Kirsopp Lake. 2 Vols.
APPIAN: ROMAN HISTORY. Horace White. 4 Vols.
ARATUS. Cf. CALLIMACHUS.
ARISTIDES: ORATIONS. C. A. Behr. Vol. 1.
ARISTOPHANES. Benjamin Bickley Rogers. 3 Vols. Verse trans.
ARISTOTLE: ART OF RHETORIC. J. H. Freese.
ARISTOTLE: ATHENIAN CONSTITUTION, EUDEMIAN ETHICS, VICES AND
    VIRTUES. H. Rackham.
ARISTOTLE: GENERATION OF ANIMALS. A. L. Peck.
ARISTOTLE: HISTORIA ANIMALIUM. A. L. Peck. Vols. I.–II.
ARISTOTLE: METAPHYSICS. H. Tredennick. 2 Vols.
ARISTOTLE: METEOROLOGICA. H. D. P. Lee.
ARISTOTLE: MINOR WORKS. W. S. Hett. On Colours, On Things
    Heard, On Physiognomies, On Plants, On Marvellous Things
    Heard, Mechanical Problems, On Indivisible Lines, On Situations
    and Names of Winds, On Melissus, Xenophanes, and Gorgias.
ARISTOTLE: NICOMACHEAN ETHICS. H. Rackham.
ARISTOTLE: OECONOMICA and MAGNA MORALIA. G. C. Armstrong (with
    METAPHYSICS, Vol. II).
ARISTOTLE: ON THE HEAVENS. W. K. C. Guthrie.
ARISTOTLE: ON THE SOUL, PARVA NATURALIA, ON BREATH. W. S. Hett.
ARISTOTLE: CATEGORIES, ON INTERPRETATION, PRIOR ANALYTICS. H. P.
    Cooke and H. Tredennick.

4

Aristotle: Posterior Analytics, Topics. H. Tredennick and E. S. Forster.

Aristotle: On Sophistical Refutations.
On Coming-to-be and Passing-Away, On the Cosmos. E. S. Forster and D. J. Furley.

Aristotle: Parts of Animals. A. L. Peck; Motion and Progression of Animals. E. S. Forster.

Aristotle: Physics. Rev. P. Wicksteed and F. M. Cornford. 2 Vols.

Aristotle: Poetics and Longinus. W. Hamilton Fyfe; Demetrius on Style. W. Rhys Roberts.

Aristotle: Politics. H. Rackham.

Aristotle: Problems. W. S. Hett. 2 Vols.

Aristotle: Rhetorica Ad Alexandrum (with Problems. Vol. II). H. Rackham.

Arrian: History of Alexander and Indica. Rev. E. Iliffe Robson. 2 Vols. New version P. Brunt.

Athenaeus: Deipnosophistae. C. B. Gulick. 7 Vols.

Babrius and Phaedrus (Latin). B. E. Perry.

St. Basil: Letters. R. J. Deferrari. 4 Vols.

Callimachus: Fragments. C. A. Trypanis. Musaeus: Hero and Leander. T. Gelzer and C. Whitman.

Callimachus, Hymns and Epigrams and Lycophron. A. W. Mair; Aratus. G. R. Mair.

Clement of Alexandria. Rev. G. W. Butterworth.

Colluthus. Cf. Oppian.

Daphnis and Chloe. Thornley's translation revised by J. M. Edmonds: and Parthenius. S. Gaselee.

Demosthenes I.: Olynthiacs, Philippics and Minor Orations I.–XVII. and XX. J. H. Vince.

Demosthenes II.: De Corona and De Falsa Legatione. C. A. Vince and J. H. Vince.

Demosthenes III.: Meidias, Androtion, Aristocrates, Timocrates and Aristogeiton I. and II. J. H. Vince.

Demosthenes IV.–VI.: Private Orations and In Neaeram. A. T. Murray.

Demosthenes VII.: Funeral Speech, Erotic Essay, Exordia and Letters. N. W. and N. J. DeWitt.

Dio Cassius: Roman History. E. Cary. 9 Vols.

Dio Chrysostom. J. W. Cohoon and H. Lamar Crosby. 5 Vols.

Diodorus Siculus. 12 Vols. Vols. I.–VI. C. H. Oldfather. Vol. VII. C. L. Sherman. Vol. VIII. C. B. Welles. Vols. IX. and X. R. M. Geer. Vol. XI. F. Walton. Vol. XII. F. Walton. General Index. R. M. Geer.

Diogenes Laertius. R. D. Hicks. 2 Vols. New Introduction by H. S. Long.

Dionysius of Halicarnassus: Roman Antiquities. Spelman's translation revised by E. Cary. 7 Vols.

DIONYSIUS OF HALICARNASSUS: CRITICAL ESSAYS. S. Usher. 2 Vols.
EPICTETUS. W. A. Oldfather. 2 Vols.
EURIPIDES. A. S. Way. 4 Vols. Verse trans.
EUSEBIUS: ECCLESIASTICAL HISTORY. Kirsopp Lake and J. E. L. Oulton. 2 Vols.
GALEN: ON THE NATURAL FACULTIES. A. J. Brock.
GREEK ANTHOLOGY. W. R. Paton. 5 Vols.
GREEK BUCOLIC POETS (THEOCRITUS, BION, MOSCHUS). J. M. Edmonds.
GREEK ELEGY AND IAMBUS with the ANACREONTEA. J. M. Edmonds. 2 Vols.
GREEK LYRIC. D. A. Campbell. 4 Vols. Vols. I. and II.
GREEK MATHEMATICAL WORKS. Ivor Thomas. 2 Vols.
HERODES. Cf. THEOPHRASTUS: CHARACTERS.
HERODIAN. C. R. Whittaker. 2 Vols.
HERODOTUS. A. D. Godley. 4 Vols.
HESIOD AND THE HOMERIC HYMNS. H. G. Evelyn White.
HIPPOCRATES and the FRAGMENTS OF HERACLEITUS. W. H. S. Jones and E. T. Withington. 5 Vols. Vols. I.–IV.
HOMER: ILIAD. A. T. Murray. 2 Vols.
HOMER: ODYSSEY. A. T. Murray. 2 Vols.
ISAEUS. E. W. Forster.
ISOCRATES. George Norlin and LaRue Van Hook. 3 Vols.
[ST. JOHN DAMASCENE]: BARLAAM AND IOASAPH. Rev. G. R. Woodward, Harold Mattingly and D. M. Lang.
JOSEPHUS. 10 Vols. Vols. I.–IV. H. Thackeray. Vol. V. H. Thackeray and R. Marcus. Vols. VI.–VII. R. Marcus. Vol. VIII. R. Marcus and Allen Wikgren. Vols. IX.–X. L. H. Feldman.
JULIAN. Wilmer Cave Wright. 3 Vols.
LIBANIUS. A. F. Norman. 2 Vols..
LUCIAN. 8 Vols. Vols. I.–V. A. M. Harmon. Vol. VI. K. Kilburn. Vols. VII.–VIII. M. D. Macleod.
LYCOPHRON. Cf. CALLIMACHUS.
LYRA GRAECA, III. J. M. Edmonds. (Vols. I.and II. have been replaced by GREEK LYRIC I. and II.)
LYSIAS. W. R. M. Lamb.
MANETHO. W. G. Waddell.
MARCUS AURELIUS. C. R. Haines.
MENANDER. W. G. Arnott. 3 Vols. Vol. I.
MINOR ATTIC ORATORS (ANTIPHON, ANDOCIDES, LYCURGUS, DEMADES, DINARCHUS, HYPERIDES). K. J. Maidment and J. O. Burtt. 2 Vols.
MUSAEUS: HERO AND LEANDER. Cf. CALLIMACHUS.
NONNOS: DIONYSIACA. W. H. D. Rouse. 3 Vols.
OPPIAN, COLLUTHUS, TRYPHIODORUS. A. W. Mair.
PAPYRI. NON-LITERARY SELECTIONS. A. S. Hunt and C. C. Edgar. 2 Vols. LITERARY SELECTIONS (Poetry). D. L. Page.

PARTHENIUS. Cf. DAPHNIS and CHLOE.

PAUSANIAS: DESCRIPTION OF GREECE. W. H. S. Jones. 4 Vols. and Companion Vol. arranged by R. E. Wycherley.

PHILO. 10 Vols. Vols. I.–V. F. H. Colson and Rev. G. H. Whitaker. Vols. VI.–IX. F. H. Colson. Vol. X. F. H. Colson and the Rev. J. W. Earp.

PHILO: two supplementary Vols. (*Translation only.*) Ralph Marcus.

PHILOSTRATUS: THE LIFE OF APOLLONIUS OF TYANA. F. C. Conybeare. 2 Vols.

PHILOSTRATUS: IMAGINES; CALLISTRATUS: DESCRIPTIONS. A. Fairbanks.

PHILOSTRATUS and EUNAPIUS: LIVES OF THE SOPHISTS. Wilmer Cave Wright.

PINDAR. Sir J. E. Sandys.

PLATO: CHARMIDES, ALCIBIADES, HIPPARCHUS, THE LOVERS, THEAGES, MINOS and EPINOMIS. W. R. M. Lamb.

PLATO: CRATYLUS, PARMENIDES, GREATER HIPPIAS, LESSER HIPPIAS. H. N. Fowler.

PLATO: EUTHYPHRO, APOLOGY, CRITO, PHAEDO, PHAEDRUS. H. N. Fowler.

PLATO: LACHES, PROTAGORAS, MENO, EUTHYDEMUS. W. R. M. Lamb.

PLATO: LAWS. Rev. R. G. Bury. 2 Vols.

PLATO: LYSIS, SYMPOSIUM, GORGIAS. W. R. M. Lamb.

PLATO: Republic. Paul Shorey. 2 Vols.

PLATO: STATESMAN, PHILEBUS. H. N. Fowler; ION. W. R. M. Lamb.

PLATO: THEAETETUS and SOPHIST. H. N. Fowler.

PLATO: TIMAEUS, CRITIAS, CLITOPHO, MENEXENUS, EPISTULAE. Rev. R. G. Bury.

PLOTINUS: A. H. Armstrong. 7 Vols.

PLUTARCH: MORALIA. 16 Vols. Vols. I.–V. F. C. Babbitt. Vol. VI. W. C. Helmbold. Vols. VII. and XIV. P. H. De Lacy and B. Einarson. Vol. VIII. P. A. Clement and H. B. Hoffleit. Vol. IX. E. L. Minar, Jr., F. H. Sandbach, W. C. Helmbold. Vol. X. H. N. Fowler. Vol. XI. L. Pearson and F. H. Sandbach. Vol. XII. H. Cherniss and W. C. Helmbold. Vol. XIII. 1–2. H. Cherniss. Vol. XV. F. H. Sandbach.

PLUTARCH: THE PARALLEL LIVES. B. Perrin. 11 Vols.

POLYBIUS. W. R. Paton. 6 Vols.

PROCOPIUS. H. B. Dewing. 7 Vols.

PTOLEMY: TETRABIBLOS. F. E. Robbins.

QUINTUS SMYRNAEUS. A. S. Way. Verse trans.

SEXTUS EMPIRICUS. Rev. R. G. Bury. 4 Vols.

SOPHOCLES. F. Storr. 2 Vols. Verse trans.

STRABO: GEOGRAPHY. Horace L. Jones. 8 Vols.

THEOCRITUS. Cf. GREEK BUCOLIC POETS.

THEOPHRASTUS: CHARACTERS. J. M. Edmonds. HERODES, etc. A. D. Knox.

7

THEOPHRASTUS: ENQUIRY INTO PLANTS. Sir Arthur Hort, Bart. 2 Vols.
THEOPHRASTUS: DE CAUSIS PLANTARUM. G. K. K. Link and B. Einarson. 3 Vols. Vol. I.
THUCYDIDES. C. F. Smith. 4 Vols.
TRYPHIODORUS. Cf. OPPIAN.
XENOPHON: CYROPAEDIA. Walter Miller. 2 Vols.
XENOPHON: HELLENICA. C. L. Brownson. 2 Vols.
XENOPHON: ANABASIS. C. L. Brownson.
XENOPHON: MEMORABILIA AND OECONOMICUS. E. C. Marchant. SYMPOSIUM AND APOLOGY. O. J. Todd.
XENOPHON: SCRIPTA MINORA. E. C. Marchant. CONSTITUTION OF THE ATHENIANS. G. W. Bowersock.